Windows XP

Under the Hood

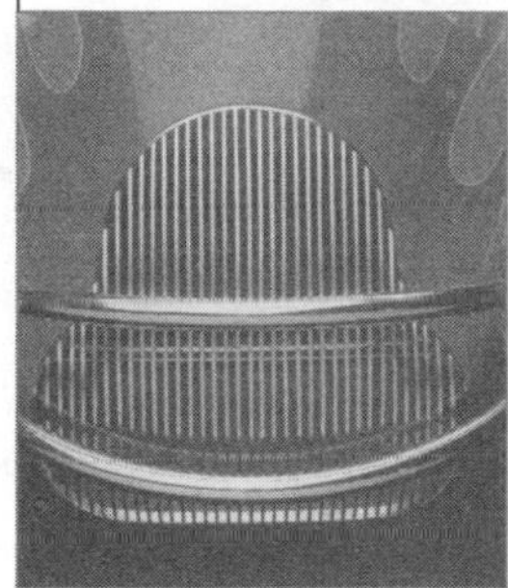

Brian Knittel

201 W. 103rd Streeet
Indianapolis, IN 46290

Windows XP Under the Hood

International Standard Book Number: 0-7897-2733-1

Library of Congress Catalog Card Number: 2001099513

Printed in the United States of America

First Printing: September 2002

05 04 03 02 4 3 2

Trademarks

Warning and Disclaimer

Associate Publisher
Greg Wiegand

Executive Editor
Rick Kughen

Acquisitions Editor
Rick Kughen

Development Editor
Todd Brakke

Managing Editor
Thomas F. Hayes

Project Editor
Sheila Schroeder

Production Editor
Maribeth Echard

Copy Editor
Bart Reed

Indexer
Ken Johnson

Proofreader
Plan-it Publishing

Technical Editor
Brian Fulk

Team Coordinator
Sharry Lee Gregory

Multimedia Developer
Michael Hunter

Interior Designer
Anne Jones

Cover Designer
Alan Clements

Contents

About the Author

Brian Knittel has been a software developer for more than 20 years. After doing graduate work in Electrical Engineering applied to nuclear medicine and magnetic resonance imaging technologies, he began a career as an independent consultant. An eclectic mix of clients has led to long-term projects in medical documentation, work-flow management, real-time industrial system control, and most importantly, over 15 years of real-world experience with MS-DOS, Windows, and computer networking in the business world. Brian has coauthored *Special Edition Using Microsoft Windows 2000 Professional*, *Special Edition Using Microsoft Windows XP Professional*, and *Special Edition Using Microsoft Windows XP Home Edition* and has contributed to several other Windows books.

Brian lives in Albany, California, halfway between the tidal wave zone and the earth-quake fault. He spends his free time restoring antique computers (for example, see `www.ibm1130.org`) and trying to perfect his wood-fired pizza recipes.

Dedication

To the teachers and staff of San Rafael High School, who gave me an education for which I am still grateful every day, 25 years later.

—Brian

Acknowledgments

I had a conversation with Que Executive Editor Rick Kughen a couple of years ago about the nifty but unglamorous tools and programs that are provided with Windows, the tools we somehow don't have room to write about in those thick *Special Edition Using* tomes. Perhaps I caught him at a weak and confused moment, but he suggested that I ought to write a book about them, and that Que ought to publish it. I bring this up because this was and is quite an honor. It's not every day that a publisher says, in essence, "If you're excited about this, we are too." So, to start with, I thank Rick Kughen for his confidence in me and in this project, and for his unflagging support, patience, encouragement, guidance, and more patience. All that and the guy is kind, funny, and one heck of a fisherman to boot.

It's an honor to work with a highly respected publisher like Que. Thanks to Associate Publisher Greg Wiegand for his faith in me and in the rest of his outstanding team during this arduous project. This book would not have made any sense at all, or at least, it would not make whatever sense it does make without Todd Brakke's hand in developing and editing it. I am grateful for his organizational guidance and enthusiasm for the material. Also, many, many thanks to Bart Reed for not only his amazing attention to detail in copy editing, but for very helpful technical questions and answers.

Don't let those job descriptions fool you—at Que at least, titles such as "development editor" and "copy editor" don't begin to describe the breadth of the contributions that each team member makes to each book.

I'd also like to acknowledge the support of our technical editor Brian Fulk, who meticulously tried every sample program and example, and who went over every syntax statement with a fine-tooth comb. Then, there is an entire army of people who labor largely unseen and unthanked—the people who do the real work. I'd like to thank the editorial, indexing, layout, art, proofing, and other production staff at Que. And finally, thanks to Sheila Schroeder and Tonya Simpson for managing the whole project through its erratic course.

I would not be writing at all if it were not for Bob Cowart who brought me into this arena to begin with. Thank you, Bob, for your confidence, partnership, and your example. I also thank Chris Van Buren for his hand in making this project come about and for taking care of the business end of all this.

Then, there are the people who have made it possible for me to get through these months of writing: Frank and Pete who made me leave the office at least a few times to go snowboarding, the crew at Peet's Coffee & Tea who kept me well-decaffeinated every afternoon, my business partner Eric who has let me turn our office into a paper- and book-strewn horror house for the last six months, Mike Holloway who helped collate, research, and test the object and command-line references, and Bryce Carter who has provided guidance and encouragement of the deepest sort.

Finally, love and gratitude to Norm, my anesthesiologist, whom I promised after the *last* round of book writing that life would soon get back to normal. Well, I may have missed by six or eight months, but it's going to happen.

Tell Us What You Think

As the reader of this book, *you* are our most important critic and commentator. We value your opinion and want to know what we're doing right, what we could do better, what areas you'd like to see us publish in, and any other words of wisdom you're willing to pass our way.

As an associate publisher for Que, I welcome your comments. You can e-mail or write me directly to let me know what you did or didn't like about this book—as well as what we can do to make our books better.

Please note that I cannot help you with technical problems related to the *topic* of this book. We do have a User Services group, however, where I will forward specific technical questions related to the book.

When you write, please be sure to include this book's title and author as well as your name, e-mail address, and phone number. I will carefully review your comments and share them with the author and editors who worked on the book.

E-mail: `feedback@quepublishing.com`

Mail: Greg Wiegand
Que
201 West 103rd Street
Indianapolis, IN 46290 USA

For more information about this book or another Que title, visit our Web site at `www.quepublishing.com`. Type the ISBN (excluding hyphens) or the title of a book in the Search field to find the page you're looking for.

Introduction

Do you long for the good-old days when you could pop the hood of your car and recognize what was underneath? When you could take a wrench and fix just about anything yourself? Cars aren't like that anymore—they've gotten so complex and intimidating that it's hard to imagine digging into one now.

You might feel the same way about Windows. Windows has grown into a huge operating system with thousands of complex parts masked behind a slick but seemingly impenetrable graphical user interface.

This book is an attempt to reclaim those days when we could dig into our machines with confidence and satisfaction. Windows XP comes with powerful tools and interfaces that let you take control of every detail, if you're willing to roll up your sleeves and dig in.

Whether you're a Windows system administrator or a "power user" who's always on the lookout for more effective ways to use your computer, you're probably familiar with batch files, scripts, and command-line programs. Although they might seem unglamorous, they've been around longer than the PC itself, and sooner or later everyone who uses a computer for serious work runs into them. They may seem like something out of the past, but they've continued to evolve along with Windows. The automation tools provided with Windows XP and 2000 are incredibly powerful and useful.

For most people, though, they remain mysterious and are seldom used. I wrote this book to help dispel the mystery. I had three aims in mind:

- To teach how to use the batch file and scripting languages provided with Windows XP and Windows 2000
- To show how to use command-line utilities and scripting objects as everyday tools
- To provide an introduction to and reference for the hundreds of command-line programs and scripting objects provided with Windows

While several books on the market are devoted to Windows Script Host, Windows automation tools, and Windows utilities, this is the only book I know of to combine all three in one volume.

By the way, if you use Windows 2000, most of the material in this book will work for you as well. I'll point out differences between Windows 2000 and Windows XP when I can.

Why Learn About This Stuff?

In the age of the graphical user interface, you might wonder why you should spend time learning about scripts, batch files, and command-line programs at all. Aren't they part of the past, something we can leave behind with a big sigh of relief?

Well, obviously, I don't think so, or I wouldn't have spent months and months slaving away over a hot keyboard, in the dark, just for you. And in case guilt alone isn't enough to make you buy this book, I have some actual good reasons for you.

To begin, here are some important points about scripts and batch files:

- They let you make quick work of repetitive tasks. When you have a large number of files or items to process, or when you perform the same tasks day after day, automation can save you an amazing amount of time. Sure, you can point-and-click your way through running a file through several different programs or adding a user to your network, but when you have to do this job a few hundred times, the graphical approach is a nightmare.
- They serve as a form of documentation. They record in very precise terms how to perform a job. If you write a script or batch file to perform some management function, years from now it can remind you or your successors what the job entails. This makes good business sense.

- They let you use the "insides" of application programs such as Word and Access as tools to write your own programs.
- They let you write procedures that can manipulate files and settings not only on your own computer, but on others in your organization, over your network. Whether you have dozens or thousands of computers to manage, scripting functions can "push" changes to computers without requiring you to physically visit each one.
- They let you write procedures to "reset" a computer's environment to a standard, known configuration. Logon scripts, especially, can set up printers, mapped network drives, and Control Panel settings the same way every time a user logs on, thus eliminating support headaches and user confusion.

So if that's the case for learning about scripting and batch files, then how about command-line utilities? Hear ye:

- Many Windows administration, maintenance, and repair functions don't appear anywhere in the Windows GUI. They're found in command-line programs only.
- Sometimes it's faster to type a few letters than to poke around the screen with a mouse!
- Because most command-line utilities are designed to act on data or text files in some particular useful way, you can often use command-line programs as building blocks to perform complex tasks such as sorting, extracting, and formatting information. Instead of writing a custom program, you sometimes use a series of command-line programs to get the job done with little effort. Think of command-line programs as the scissors and staplers on your computer desktop.

So, although the Windows GUI has all the flash and gets all the attention, you can see that these behind-the-scenes tools are the real "meat" of the Windows operating system.

How This Book Is Organized

Although this book advances logically from beginning to end, it's written so that you can jump in at any location, get the information you need quickly, and get out. You don't have to read it from start to finish, nor do you need to work through complex tutorials. (Even if you're familiar with the material, though, you should at least skim through the references, because the batch file language and Windows Script Host program have evolved considerably over the years.)

This book is broken into three major parts. Here's the skinny on each one:

- Part I, "Scripting," covers the Windows Script Host tool, introduces the VBScript programming language, discusses the use of Objects, and describes the process of writing and debugging scripts. It also provides a detailed reference for many of the scripting objects provided with Windows XP.
- Part II, "The Command-Line Environment," describes the Windows XP command language used to write batch files. The Batch language has been enhanced considerably since its origin in MS-DOS, and it has become a much more useful way to automate the manipulation of files and directories. Part II also discusses the command-line environment, MS-DOS emulation, and the ways to alter the command environment through Windows XP administrative tools. Finally, there is a guided tour of the 20 or so most important command-line programs provided with Windows XP, covering text file management, networking utilities, GUI shortcuts, and more.
- Finally, the appendixes give you concise references and indexes to the scripting and command-line tools. Where appropriate, items include page references to the sections of the book where you can find more detailed discussions. There is also an index of sample scripts and batch files that you can use as a starting point for your own projects. You can download these scripts and files from `www.helpwinxp.com/hood`.

Within these sections, each chapter follows the same common pattern. An introduction explains a particular type of tool or programming scheme, a reference section describes the tool in exhausting detail, and finally a discussion shows how to use the tool to apply to real-world programs. I chose this structure because I want this book to serve both as a tutorial for readers who are new to these "Under the Hood" techniques and as a reference for readers who are familiar with the techniques, but just need a quick refresher.

I also want the material to be somewhat challenging. The early chapters on Windows Script Host and objects take more of a "tutorial" approach, but then the pace picks up. I hope that I leave you with some questions unanswered and a few puzzles unsolved, because in your own pursuit of answers, you'll learn more than you could from reading any book.

Conventions Used in This Book

To help you get the most from this book, special conventions and elements are used throughout.

Text Conventions

Various text conventions in this book identify terms and other special objects. These special conventions include the following:

Convention	Meaning
Italic	New terms or phrases when initially defined.
`Monospace`	Information that appears in code or onscreen, or information you type.
Command sequences	All Windows book publishers struggle with how to represent command sequences when menus and dialog boxes are involved. In this book, we separate commands using a comma. Yeah, we know it's confusing, but this is traditionally how Que does it, and traditions die hard. So, for example, the instruction "choose Edit, Cut" means that you should open the Edit menu and choose Cut.
Key combinations	Key combinations are represented with a plus sign. For example, if the text calls for you to press Ctrl+Alt+Delete, you would press the Ctrl, Alt, and Delete keys at the same time.

In this book's reference lists, which describe the syntax and use of programming statements and objects, the following conventions are used:

Convention	Meaning
`boldface()`	Text and symbols in boldface are to be typed literally.
`italic`	Italics indicate names and values to be replaced by your own data.
`[options]`	Square brackets indicate optional items that are not required. The brackets are not to be typed in.
`{choice A | choice B}`	Parentheses and the vertical bar (|) indicate items from which you make a choice of one alternative.
`item [, item...]`	Ellipses (...) indicate items that may be repeated as many times as desired.

Special Elements

Throughout this book, you'll find reference lists, patterns, tips, notes, cautions, sidebars, and cross-references. These items stand out from the rest of the text so that you know they're of special interest.

REFERENCE LISTS

Describe the syntax and usage of programming statements, object properties and methods, and command-line programs.

Pattern

Patterns show how to solve a particular programming problem in a way that you can use in many situations. They provide a general-purpose way of going about some computing task.

Tip

Tips give you down-and-dirty advice on getting things done the quickest, safest, or most reliable way. Tips give you the expert's advantage.

Note

Notes are visual "heads-up!" elements. Sometimes they just give you background information on a topic, but more often they point out special circumstances and potential pitfalls in some Windows features.

Caution

Pay attention to cautions! They could save you precious hours in lost work.

Cross-References

Cross-references are designed to point you to other locations in this book (or other books in the Que family) that provide supplemental or supporting information. Cross-references appear as follows:

→ For more information on Hollerith cards, see "Learning to Love the Keypunch," p. 47.

Sidebars

Sidebars are designed to provide information that is ancillary to the topic being discussed. Read this information if you want to learn more details about an application or task.

I

Scripting

1
Introduction to Windows Script Host

ROAD MAP

- Start here to learn the mechanics of writing and running script files.
- This chapter is an overview of scripting, scripting languages, and the commands used to run scripts.
- Once you've started writing scripts, return to this chapter for a refresher on the Script Debugger.
- The last section tells where to go on the Internet to get scripting questions answered and to get more information.

What Is a Windows Script?

THE SHORT ANSWER TO THIS QUESTION might be, a Windows script is a program written in an interpreted language with access to OS components through the COM object model. Although accurate, it's not a very useful answer to anyone but a computer scientist. I think scripting is important for everyone to know about, so let's try again, in English this time.

To explain what a script is and why you should know how to write one, let's spend a moment thinking about the word *script* in its original, literary sense. A theatrical script is actually a *plan*, a series of instructions for presenting a play. All the necessary words are there along with directions that tell the actors where to move and what to do along the way. The script presents the plan but relies on capable actors to do the actual work.

In the software sense, *script* has a similar meaning. You can probably guess that scripts could be called *computer programs*, but the word *script* emphasizes the points I noted earlier:

- They're written in more or less plain English.
- They're pretty "high level."
- They take advantage of capable actors to do the hard work. Scripts just tell the actors what do to.
- They give you access to powerful tools to do your job.

This isn't really a new concept. Programs and operating systems, from AutoCAD to z/OS, have included scripting features for years. Windows Script Host (WSH), though, is a fairly recent addition in the Windows world—it appeared first in Windows 95 Service Release 2. And, as you'll see in the upcoming chapters, it gives you access to a wide variety of actors (software components and programs) to process data, manage your computer, and otherwise get your job done more efficiently.

The "Windows Script" Part

Windows Script Host let you write scripts that manipulate files, process data, change operating system settings, install and uninstall software, send e-mail, and so on. It does this by giving you access to other programs—many of which are provided with Windows, and others that you can add on later—that do the actual work. These are the actors in our theatrical model. It's a very powerful concept, because the scripting software itself only needs to be able tell other programs what it wants done and doesn't have to know the details of doing the job. This means the range of things your scripts can do isn't limited by what the scripting language has built in—Windows scripting is *extensible*.

In Microsoft's jargon, these outside software components are packaged up as *objects*. Objects are self-contained program modules that perform tasks for other programs through a set of well-defined programming links. Objects are usually meant to represent some real-world object or concept, such as a file or a computer user's account, and the programming links provide a way for other programs—scripts, for instance—to get information about and to manipulate the thing the object represents.

It's a concept that takes a little getting used to, and Chapter 3, "Scripting and Objects," is devoted to the topic. For now, I'll just say Windows Script Host comes with object components that give you access to files and folders, the e-mail system, the networking system, Active Directory, and many other parts of Windows.

Here's a concrete example: Suppose as part of my job people send me Word documents that have to be distributed to several people in the organization—vacation requests, let's say. The documents come in by e-mail at various times all day, and I save the attached documents in a folder. Every afternoon at five, I have to send an e-mail to the company supervisors containing all that day's requests as attachments.

I could do this job by hand every day, but I could also write a script to do it. With a single click, a script can take advantage of Windows objects to perform the following tasks:

- Get a list of all the files in the "to be sent" folder
- Construct an e-mail message and address it to the list of supervisors
- Attach each of the files to the e-mail and then send it
- Move the request files to a "taken care of" folder

You're not limited to the object components provided with Windows. Many software companies sell add-on components to provide services to scripts and Windows programs—from networking to graphics display to database access.

In addition, many application programs such as Microsoft Word and Excel can be used by scripts. In the jargon, they *expose* objects that represent their documents, worksheets, and so on. If you've written Word or Excel macros, you've taken advantage of this capability already. Windows scripts can manipulate these objects too. For example, a script could do all the following tasks:

- Use Word to format a report listing all the files on a computer
- Create an Excel chart showing how much disk space each network user has used
- Create and maintain an Access database listing all computers and their network settings

These are just a few examples. Finally, you can create your own add-on objects if you can write programs in C, C++, Visual Basic, or any number of other programming languages.

The "Host" Part

The "Host" part of Windows Script Host refers to the fact that Microsoft has split its scripting system into two parts: one (the script *host*) takes care of managing the script's component objects, and the another (the script *engine*) interprets the actual script language itself. This division of labor makes it possible to use any of several different programming languages to write a script. There are several to choose from, based on your personal preferences.

In other words, Windows Script Host does even less of the actual work than I let on earlier. It just serves as an intermediary between a language engine (a software component that interprets the language you've chosen for your script) and the components or objects that do the actual work, as shown in Figure 1.1.

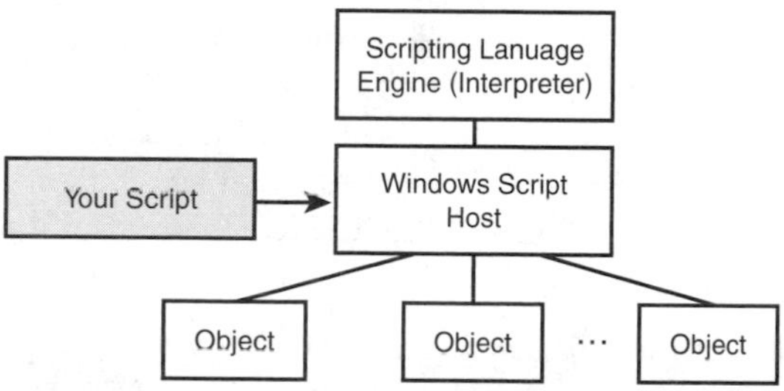

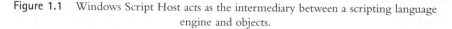

Figure 1.1 Windows Script Host acts as the intermediary between a scripting language engine and objects.

For example, the following sample VBScript script obtains the computer user's logon name and displays it:

```
set wnet = CreateObject("WScript.Network")
uname = wnet.UserName
MsgBox "Your user name is " & uname
```

In this example, VBScript and WSH don't actually do the job of finding the logon name. Instead, they use the `WScript.Network` object, which can provide information about and make changes to the Windows Networking environment. This is illustrated graphically in Figure 1.2.

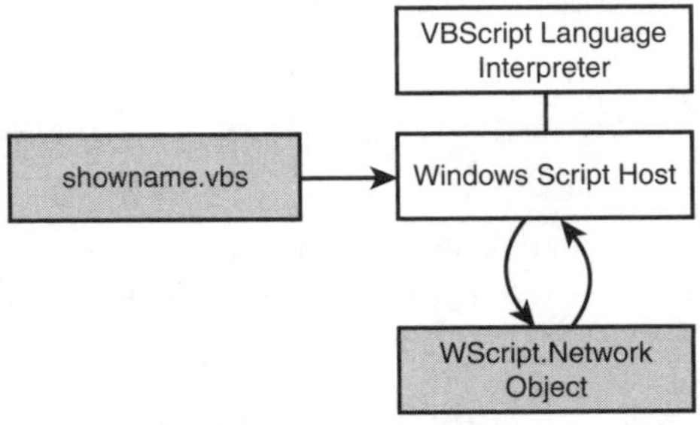

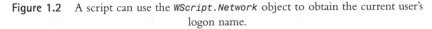

Figure 1.2 A script can use the *`WScript.Network`* object to obtain the current user's logon name.

The point of this is that Windows Script Host provides a simple, efficient way for you to take advantage of the object software modules provided with Windows. Also, you can purchase or download others, if you want to add to your collection.

And just as you can add to the collection of component objects provided with Windows, you can add interpreters for other programming languages beyond the two provided by Microsoft. I'll discuss this later in the chapter.

How Is This Different from Writing Batch Files?

If you've been working with PCs since the nearly prehistoric, pre-Windows days, you may be familiar with batch files. Batch files are scripts, too: They let you script a series of programs to run, let you scan and process files, and serve as a sort of primitive programming language. Batch files are still useful today. In fact, I'll discuss them in detail in Chapter 12, "Batch Files for Fun and Profit." Here, however, I want to make the case for scripting.

The major limitation of batch files is that they only let you start up programs and don't give you a way of interacting with them. Batch files work at the level of whole programs and files. This may be fine for some tasks, but in general, batch files *don't* give you the ability to use objects and to manipulate text and numbers, nor do they give you as powerful a programming language as VBScript or JScript. In short, scripting is a more modern and powerful approach to Windows automation.

Scripting Languages

Scripts themselves are text files that you can edit with a simple text editor such as Notepad. In the text files are instructions written in a scripting language. There are several languages you can choose from, depending on your preferences. I'll describe the options in this section.

Windows XP and Windows 2000 come with two script language interpreters: VBScript and JScript. You can do pretty much anything you'd want to do with either one of these. There are other powerful scripting languages, though, and you are free to add them to Windows Script Host. In this section, I'll list the most common scripting languages currently available.

Note

You could write a program to do the same job as any script with a standard compiled programming language such as C++. What's the difference between an interpreted language such as VBScript and a compiled language?

Interpreted languages are stored on the computer in plain-text form and have to be examined line by line every time they're run in order for the computer to determine what it is being told to do. Compiled programs are analyzed just once and are converted into hardware "machine instructions" that the processor can digest directly. As a result, compiled programs run faster. However, interpreted languages don't require the conversion step, and this saves some time when you're in the process of writing and refining them. Interpreted languages also tend to be easier to learn and use, and they can be modified as your needs change.

For the important but relatively small types of processing jobs that we discuss in this book, the complications of using a compiled language outweigh any speed benefit.

VBScript

The "VB" in VBScript stands for Visual Basic, a programming language that has evolved far from its origins at Dartmouth University in 1964. Nearly 40 years later, Basic is still a good "beginners" programming language, and in Microsoft's hands it has become a capable, though strange, modern language.

VBScript is one of several versions of Visual Basic Microsoft has developed. VBScript is the dialect used in Windows Script Host, and it can also be used in Web browsers and servers. Visual Basic for Applications (VBA) is used as the scripting or macro language for Microsoft desktop products such as Word and Excel. Programmers use the Visual Basic development product to build standalone Windows programs.

VBScript is probably the easiest scripting language to learn, and it's probably the best first language to learn if you use Microsoft desktop products. Any experience you may have writing either macros or scripts will translate easily to the other.

JScript

JScript is a programming language modeled after Netscape's JavaScript language. (Microsoft made its own variant to match its archrival's capabilities but made it slightly different, just to keep things interesting and incompatible.) The language was designed as a way of building programming capabilities into Web pages. Have you ever seen Web pages whose menus or pictures change when you move your mouse around? That's most likely done through the use of JScript or JavaScript, because it's the scripting language that most Web browsers support.

Note

JavaScript and JScript are not Java. JavaScript is a completely separate language that bears some superficial similarities to Java, but it's not the whole proverbial ball of wax. As mentioned, JScript is a variety of JavaScript, so it's not Java either.

JScript can be used for Windows scripting, and it may be the language of choice for people who are already comfortable using it due to their experience in programming scripted Web pages and server-side scripts.

Interpreters for both VBScript and JScript are provided as part of the Windows Script Host package provided with Windows XP and Windows 2000. However, other languages can be obtained from third parties or from Microsoft's Windows Resource Kits. I'll list some of these in the next sections.

Perl

Perl was developed in 1987 by developers in the Unix community. From the very start, Perl was an "open" language—its writing, debugging, and subsequent development were carried out by the public, for free. It's a wildly popular, very powerful language that's especially well suited for manipulating text. It has extensive string-handling and pattern-matching capabilities as well as all the other features of a major programming language.

The Linux community has embraced and advanced Perl, and huge repositories of free Perl scripts are available on the Internet. Chances are, whatever you want to do, there's a Perl script already out there that will do it.

ActiveState Corporation, which bills itself as "the leading provider of Open Source–based programming products and services for cross-platform development," has packaged Perl as a "Windows Script Host-able" language, and it's available for free download at `www.activestate.com`. The ActiveState product is a fully capable, Windows-integrated version of Perl, and it's a must-have for any Perl enthusiast.

Python

Python is a very popular scripting/programming language that originated at the National Research Institute for Mathematics and Computer Science (CWI) in Amsterdam. It's a portable object-oriented language, much less cryptic than Perl, and has made big inroads in the Linux community.

A free Windows Script Host plug-in is available at `www.activestate.com`.

Object REXX

REXX originated in 1979 as a scripting language for IBM mainframes. Since then, IBM has made it available for IBM Linux, AIX, OS/2, and Windows as well as its mainframe operating systems. Object REXX is its latest Windows incarnation. A developer's version is available from IBM for about $275 (U.S.) at `www.ibm.com/software/ad/obj-rexx`. You only need the developer's version to create and debug scripts. You can then install a free runtime version of Object REXX on each computer that needs to run your REXX script.

Other commercial and public domain "clones" of REXX are available for Windows, but to my knowledge none of these are compatible with Windows Script Host. You can use them as standalone script interpreters, but they don't integrate with Windows Script Host, and few of them provide access to the Windows objects that are the focus of much of this book.

Ruby

Ruby is a fairly new language that originated in Japan. It's currently more popular in Europe and Japan than in the U.S., but it's picking up steam. A port of Ruby to the Windows Script Host environment is available at `http://isweb27.infoseek.co.jp/computer/arton/index.html`. You might also search the Web for "ActiveScriptRuby."

Note

If you have a preferred scripting language that's not listed here, check to see whether a WSH-enabled version is available. If you find one, please let me know. Just visit `www.helpwinxp.com` and leave me a message.

Choosing a Language

In this book, I'll focus on VBScript because it's the most common and the most "vanilla" of the scripting languages.

If you use many Microsoft products, VBScript is definitely the most important language to learn because it's used inside Word, Excel, Access—in fact, *most* Microsoft products—as the built-in macro language. Unix and Linux enthusiasts rightly sing the praises of Perl and Python, but if you're going to learn just one language, and you work with Microsoft applications, I'd recommend learning VBScript.

To that end, the next chapter covers VBScript and provides a brief tutorial. Unfortunately, it would take many more pages than we can spare for this book to teach any of the other languages. If you know and love any of the other available scripting languages, I encourage you to use them. In Chapter 3, I'll show you how to access Windows objects in several alternative languages. You should then be able to translate the examples I'll give in the remainder of the book to your language of choice.

Note

I will use VBScript exclusively in the sample scripts in Chapters 4 through 10.

I considered teaching both VBScript and JScript and providing sample scripts in multiple languages. However, I decided on the one-language approach. With the VBScript-only approach, I can provide a greater variety of sample scripts than I could if I had to repeat each one in several languages. I also think that VBScript is the better choice for inexperienced users due to its applicability in many other Microsoft applications.

For readers who already know another scripting language, I realize I'll be making your job a little more difficult. If you already have enough experience to have a preferred language, however, I think the greater variety and depth of the VBScript examples in this book will make the translation work worthwhile.

A Simple Script

So, enough with the philosophy and overview! It's time to show you a practical example of what I've been talking about. Here is a script that examines all the files in a given directory (folder) and displays the total size of all the files, in bytes:

```
            ' script0101.vbs
            ' total up space used in a given directory
dir = "C:\"

set Fsys = CreateObject("Scripting.FileSystemObject")
totsize = 0
for each file in Fsys.GetFolder(dir).Files
```

```
8         totsize = totsize + file.size
9     next
10    wscript.echo "The total size of the files in" , dir, "is" , totsize
```

In this example, the script is set up to tally all the files in the root directory of the hard drive (`c:\`). What I've shown here is the contents of a file named `script0101.vbs`.

Note

You may want to try this script out yourself. You probably don't want to type it in though. I've made all the named and numbered sample scripts shown in this book available for download from `www.helpwinxp.com/hood`. Follow the link there to download the sample script ZIP file. The download page has instructions and tips on installing and running the sample scripts.

I should point out that the preceding printed listing contains a number in front of each of the 10 lines of code so that I can refer to them in the discussion that follows. If you look at the file, though, you'll see that the numbers aren't really part of the script file itself. If you type the script in, omit these numbers.

Now, if I double-click this file in Windows Explorer on my computer, the dialog box shown in Figure 1.3 appears. You might want to try it on your computer as well.

Figure 1.3 Result displayed when the sample script file is double-clicked.

Note

Double-clicking the file on your computer may not work. For security reasons, some people or companies configure their Windows computers not to run VBS scripts with just a double-click. If this happens to you, don't worry, just read on.

To see how this dialog box appeared, let's take a look at the contents of the script file, line by line. If you're not familiar with Visual Basic or programming in general, don't worry (yet). We'll cover the programming details in Chapter 2, "VBScript Tutorial."

Lines 1 and 2 are comments. In VBScript, anything after a single quote character (`'`) is ignored. It's a good idea to add comments to your scripts, describing what they do and how they do it. In longer scripts, you can describe things in detail. In this script, it's enough to say briefly what the script does.

Line 3 sets the name of the folder that will be counted.

Line 4 is blank. It's good programming style to use blank lines to give visual separation between parts of a program or script. Although the Windows Script Host doesn't care either way, it's easier to read and understand when separate steps in the program are broken apart by whitespace (that is, blank space).

Line 5 lets us use a programming component (object) called `Scripting.FileSystemObject` that enables the script to poke into the contents of drives and folders and lets us get information about the files inside. VBScript doesn't have this capability built in to the language, but the `FileSystemObject` object does, and we can use it in our program.

Line 6 sets up the counter (a *variable*, as it's known by programmers) we'll use to collect the total size of all the files. It starts at zero, and we'll add the size of each file to this.

Lines 7 and 9 form a *loop* that processes any program lines inside it once for each file in the chosen directory. Notice that I've indented the text inside the loop. VBScript doesn't care whether these extra indenting spaces are there—it's just a way of making the beginning and ending of the loop easier for a human reader to see, and this helps us to understand the program.

Line 8 does the real work: It adds the size of each file in the Windows directory to a variable called `totsize`. When the loop has done this for each file, we have the total size of all the files in the directory.

Line 10 displays the results in plain English. By default, the `echo` command displays text in a pop-up box.

This is a pretty simple script. It's not too useful, and I've left some details out. However, it does illustrate several important points about Windows scripting:

- Script languages have advanced programming features that the batch file language lacks, such as variables and loops.
- Scripts can take advantage of objects to extend the language with additional capabilities.
- Scripts can interact with the operating system (for example, by examining information about the files in a folder) and can interact with humans (for example, by displaying results in formatted text).
- Scripts can be made more understandable by using whitespace to make the structure of the program easy to discern.
- Script files can and should contain comments that describe and document what the scripts do and how they work. Comments help make script files an important form of documentation, by recording in writing how particular jobs get done.

Script Files

Script files are plain, basic text files, the kind you can edit with Notepad. Inside are program statements, written out in the syntax that the scripting language you're using can understand.

To let Windows know which language your script uses, it's best to use a consistent file-naming scheme when naming your script files. The most important part is the *extension* or *file type*. For example, in `myscript.vbs` the extension is `.vbs`. By default, Windows Explorer doesn't display the extension when it lists filenames—it might just list `myscript` as a VBScript Script File. The extension is a required part of a script file's name, however.

In the course of working with scripts, you may run into files with various extensions. The most common ones are listed in Table 1.1. The table also shows the icons that Windows assigns to each file type.

Table 1.1 **Script File Extensions**

Icon	Extension	File Type
	`.js`	JScript script
	`.jse`	JScript Encoded script
	`.pls`	Perl script
	`.vbe`	VBScript Encoded script
	`.vbs`	VBScript script
	`.wsc`	Windows Script Component
	`.wsf`	Windows Script File (XML format)
	`.wsh`	Windows Script Host settings

Note

If you used an earlier version of Windows Script Host and created files with the `.ws` extension, you'll need to rename them to `.wsf` in Windows Script Host version 5 and higher.

If you use PerlScript, be careful if you install RealAudio's Real Player. It will try to hijack the `.pls` file extension away from PerlScript. If this happens, first disable the Audio Playlist media type in Real Player. Then, in Windows Explorer, click Tools, Folder Options, File Types. Find PLS File in the list, and be sure the dialog box shows "Opens with: Microsoft (r) Console Based Script Host." If it doesn't, click Change and fix it.

Other scripting languages use specific extensions as well; the document for each language indicates which is conventionally used.

Some of the file types listed in Table 1.1 may be unfamiliar, so I'll discuss them in more detail in the following subsections. Feel free to skim or skip over this information if you're just getting started with scripting; not all these details will be of immediate use to you.

JSE and VBE: Encoded Scripts

Some scripts are written by commercial software developers and licensed for a fee. These developers have an interest in protecting their efforts from casual copying and piracy. Other scripts are written by system administrators who'd rather keep the details of the corporate operations away from prying eyes and tinkerers. To help these authors, some scripting languages provide encoding tools that compress and encrypt the script files so that they're no longer easily readable.

Microsoft provides a downloadable tool to encode VBScript and JScript files. It converts VBScript `.vb` files into encoded `.vbe` files, and JScript `.js` files into encoded `.jse` files. You can download the utility at `msdn.microsoft.com/scripting`. Select Downloads and look for Script Encoder.

Caution

The Script Encoder makes it difficult, but not impossible, for others to read the contents of a script. The determined hacker could still decode the file. Do not put passwords or other confidential information in a script, even if it's encoded.

WSF: Windows Script Files

To help maintain and write complex sets of scripts, Microsoft developed a file format that allows several separate scripts to be stored in one text file, and even lets you use several languages in one script. The new file format is called a Windows Script File, and the extension used is `.wsf`.

It's easier to show than explain, so I'll show it first:

```
<package>
   <job id="script1">
      <script language="VBScript">
         WScript.Echo "This is script 1!"
      </script>
   </job>

   <job id="script2">
      <script language="JScript">
```

```
        WScript.Echo("This is script 2!");
      </script>
   </job>

   <job id="script3">
      <script language="VBScript" src="c:\scriptlib\anotherfile.vbs" />
   </job>
</package>
```

Windows Script files are still plain-text files, but they're structured with text markup called *tags*. This may look familiar to you if you've ever done Web design because these files look a lot like HTML Web page files. However, this markup is called Extensible Markup Language (XML), and its required structure is very strict. XML is used to indicate where the beginning and end of the pieces of a script go—XML isn't another script programming language.

In this example, you can see that there are three separate script fragments in this file, delimited by `<package>`, `<job>`, and `<script>` tags.

Each separate script, which would otherwise have to be in a separate `.vbs` or `.js` file, is placed between `<job>` and `</job>` tags. The ID attribute gives a name to each. This may seem confusing, but the purpose is to let you put many scripts in one file, so you only have one file to copy and keep up-to-date. You can choose the desired script by its job name when you run the script file—I'll describe this later in the chapter under "Wscript and Cscript Command Options."

What makes WSF files especially useful is that you can combine different language script components in the same file, and even in the same job, by surrounding the bits of program with `<script>` and `</script>` tags. These tags specify which language the bit of program is written in. Notice in the example that the first job is written in VBScript, whereas the second is written in JScript. You can use other languages as well, if you have them installed.

The third job demonstrates another special feature of WSF files: the ability to pull in parts of the script from other files. In the example, `script3`'s program is pulled in from the file `c:\scriptlib\anotherfile.vbs`. Notice that this `<script>` tag ends with `/>` instead of the usual `>`. This is a special indicator, required by the XML language, and indicates that there is no matching `</script>` end tag. The `<script>` tag comes in two forms. It can surround some program text, as shown here:

```
<script language="VBscript">
      VBScript programming goes here
      There might be lots of it
</script>
```

It can also indicate that the script program is to be pulled in from somewhere else:

```
<script language="Vbscript" src="path or URL" />
```

In the second form of the `<script>` tag, the `src` entry tells WSH where to find the material to read in. This can be in the form of a full file and path, or even a URL, in which case the material is obtained from an Internet location. This feature makes it possible to store commonly used bits of script programming once, where it can be used by many different scripts. In Chapter 2, where we'll discuss VBScript programming with subroutines and functions, I'll have more to say on this topic.

Finally, the `<package>` tag surrounds the entire file. If there is more than one separate job in the file, the file must start with `<package>` and end with `</package>`, as shown in the example. If there's just one job, `<package>` and `</package>` may be omitted.

Note

There's quite a bit more to the WSF file format. I'll discuss it in more detail in Chapter 10, "Deploying Scripts for Computer and Network Management."

WSC: Windows Script Components

A Windows Script Component file is another type of script file with XML structure markup added to it. Component files let you develop your own programming "objects" to be used by scripts and other programs. I'll discuss components in Chapter 9, "Creating Your Own Scriptable Objects."

WSH: Windows Script Host Settings

If you right-click the icon for a script file, or a shortcut to a script file, and then choose Properties, Windows displays a special Script tab on the Properties page that's unique to that script, as shown in Figure 1.4.

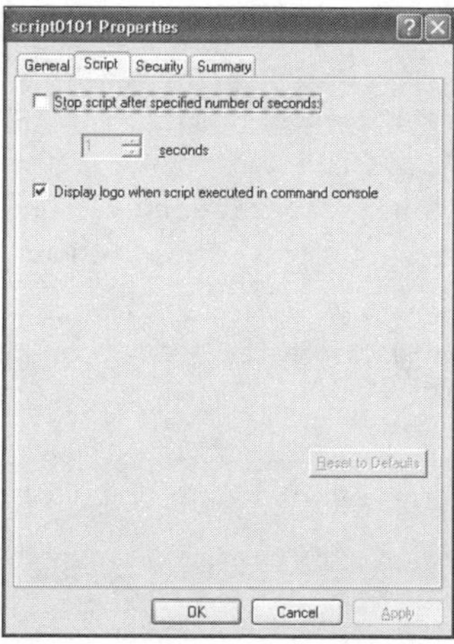

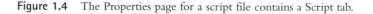

Figure 1.4 The Properties page for a script file contains a Script tab.

Here, you can specify how long the script is allowed to run before the system considers it "dead," and you can inhibit the Microsoft copyright notice that's usually printed when scripts are run in command-line mode. If you change the default settings on this Properties page, Windows stores the information in a file with the same root name as the script file, but with the extension `.wsh`. WSH files have no other content or function than to hold these settings.

These options can also be set on the command line when you run the script, but I'm getting ahead of myself. That's the topic of the next section.

Running Scripts

In the example in the previous section, I mentioned that you can usually run a script by double-clicking its file in Windows Explorer. That's one way of doing it, but there are several other ways to start scripts. In this section, I'll go over each of them. First, though, we need to discuss the two environments available in which to run scripts.

Wscript and Cscript

Windows Script Host comes in two flavors: a windowed version named Wscript, and a command-line version named Cscript. Either version can run any script. The difference between the two is that the windowed version (Wscript) displays text output messages with a pop-up dialog box like the one shown in Figure 1.3, whereas the command-line version (Cscript) displays text through the normal "standard output" mechanism common to command-line programs. Cscript is best suited for scripts that produce lots of output, such as directory listings, and for scripts whose output you'd like to capture into a file.

Wscript is best suited for scripts that do their work quietly and display very little information to the user—scripts that, for example, just display error messages and maybe an "I'm finished" message, like our scripting example did earlier in this chapter. The advantage of using a pop-up message is that the script processing stops while the message is displayed, and it waits until you've read the message and closed the dialog box.

Cscript is the command-line (or character or console mode) version of Windows Script Host. Cscript displays results in a Command Prompt window, which mimics the old DOS command-line environment. Contrast the output of our sample script when it's run by Cscript, as shown in Figure 1.5, to the Wscript version in Figure 1.2.

The advantage of using Cscript for scripts that display lots of output—or whose output you want to process with other programs—is that you can redirect the output to a file using the standard command-line technique. The following command runs the sample script file `script0101.vbs` and saves the output in a file named `results`:

```
cscript script0101.vbs >results
```

Figure 1.5 Output of the sample script when run by Cscript.

You can use either script processor according to your preferences. In the next section, I'll show you the various ways to run scripts.

Ways to Run a Script

As you know, Windows usually offers several ways to accomplish the same thing through clicking, double-clicking, right-clicking, or dragging things around. This is certainly true for running scripts. There are, in fact, six different ways to start up the processing of a script file, as listed in Table 1.2.

Table 1.2 **Ways of Running a Script File**

Action	Runs
Double-click the file in Explorer, a Find Files window, or the Desktop.	Default host
Right-click the file and select Open.	Wscript
Right-click the file and select Open with Command Prompt.	Cscript
Enter the script filename at a command prompt, in the Start, Run dialog box, or in a shortcut.*	Default host
Enter **`cscript`** or **`wscript`** followed by the script filename at a command prompt, in the Start, Run dialog box, or in a shortcut.**	Specified host
Drag one or more files and drop them onto the script file or icon in Explorer or on the Desktop.	Default host

**In Windows XP, NT, and 2000, you don't need to type the script file's extension (`.vbs`, `.pl`, or whatever). You can simply type the file's base name. With Windows 95, 98, and Me, you must include the extension with the filename.*

***You must always include the script's extension when you're explicitly running Wscript or Cscript by name.*

Three of the methods choose a specific host—either Wscript or Cscript. The other three methods use the *default host*, which is a setting you can alter. Initially, Windows uses wscript as the default host. If you wish, you can change the default host by issuing one of these commands at the command prompt:

- `wscript //H:wscript` ← Sets the default host to Wscript
- `wscript //H:cscript` ← Sets the default host to Cscript

In general, during the development of new scripts, the command-line version (cscript) is probably the most useful, because you'll probably want to have your script output debugging remarks to help you understand what it's doing. Remember that even after setting Cscript as the default, you can always force the issue with individual scripts by running the script with one of the methods that uses a specific host: use the right-click method or use the `CSCRIPT` or `WSCRIPT` command explicitly.

Note

In the remainder of this chapter, I'll describe the more arcane details of how Windows Script Host is started and how to communicate with it. If you're new to scripting and programming, you may want to just skim the remainder of this chapter now, so you know what's covered, and continue with the tutorial in Chapter 2. The following material is fairly advanced and might make more sense after you've gotten some more experience with VBScript.

Passing Information to Scripts

The command line used to start up Wscript or Cscript can come from a shortcut, from the Start, Run dialog box, or from your own fingers typing away at the command prompt. If the script is self-contained (that is, has all the information it needs to perform its job), you can simply enter the script's filename.

However, it's often useful to write a script in a more generic way and to specify some information only at the time you run the script. Our sample script earlier in the chapter provides a good example: The name of the folder whose files are to be sized is built into the script. It would be much more useful if we could tell it what folder to examine when we ran it; this way, we could use the same script to count any folder's files.

One way to do this is to have the script prompt (or *ask*) the user to type in any desired information. We'll discuss how this is done in Chapter 2.

Another technique is to specify such information on the command line when the script is run. In computer jargon, bits of information passed to a procedure such as a script file are called *arguments*. In the following command line, `myscript.vbs` and `c:\windows` are two arguments being given to the program wscript:

```
wscript myscript.vbs c:\windows
```

In a Wscript command line, arguments starting with two slashes (`//`) control the action of Wscript itself, and the first filename argument is the name of the script to run. Any *other* arguments are passed along to the script file for *it* to interpret as it sees fit. In one script, the extra command-line arguments might be used to indicate the names of folders to delete. In another, they might enable or disable functions that the script performs. There is no predetermined meaning to arguments; it's up to the script's programmer to determine whether they are to be used and how they affect the script.

Each scripting language has its own way of getting argument information passed through its command line. If you're familiar with writing DOS batch files, you may remember that when "`%1`" was used in a batch file, it was replaced with the first command-line argument. Windows Script Host makes the command-line arguments available through the use of a feature called the `WScript` object, which I'll discuss in Chapter 3. In VBScript, the first argument typed on the command line after the script's name is `WScript.Arguments(0)`. The second is `WScript.Arguments(1)`, and so on. For example, the statement

```
filename = WScript.Arguments(0)
```

assigns the first argument to the variable `filename`.

Note

This use of "`WScript`" in `WScript.Arguments`, by the way, is always `WScript`, regardless of whether you're running the script with wscript or cscript. Here, `WScript` refers to the name of an object provided by the script host, and it is named `WScript`, regardless of which version is running. Yes, it's confusing.

We could rewrite the original sample script to take advantage of this, as follows:

```
    ' script0102.vbs
    ' total up space used in the directory named on the command line

dir = WScript.Arguments(0)
set Fsys = CreateObject("Scripting.FileSystemObject")
totsize = 0
for each file in Fsys.GetFolder(dir).Files
    totsize = totsize + file.size
next
wscript.echo "The total size of the files in" , dir, "is" , totsize
```

Now, we can type these commands at the command prompt to count the files in the `Temp` and `Windows` directories:

```
Script0102 c:\temp
```

```
Script0102 c:\windows
```

Trouble arises when we try to count my `My Documents` folder, however:

```
Script0102 c:\Documents and Settings\brian\My Documents
```

Windows considers the spaces in this long pathname to indicate that we're specifying four separate arguments:

- WScript.Arguments(0) = c:\Documents
- WScript.Arguments(1) = and
- WScript.Arguments(2) = Settings\brian\My
- WScript.Arguments(3) = Documents

The solution is to put quotes ("") around the misbehaving text, so Windows knows to treat it as one long item:

```
Script0102 "c:\Documents and Settings\brian\My Documents"
```

Using command-line arguments in your own scripts will help you create more general-purpose, useful tools. In the examples later in this book, I'll show you several examples of this.

Saving the Results from Scripts

If you want a script to record information, rather than just have it appear on your screen, you have two choices.

First, you can use Cscript and have your script program write its results to the standard output—the console screen. You saw how this looks earlier in the chapter in Figure 1.5

You can save this output to a file with *output redirection*. If you add `>somefile` to any command-line program, its output will be saved in the file named `somefile`. You can then print this file, process it with some other program, view it with Notepad, and so on. Here's an example:

```
D:\scripts\01\script0102.vbs c:\windows >wincount.txt
```

This runs one of our sample scripts and saves the results in the file named `wincount.txt`.

If you only wish to view the output on the screen but too much output goes by to read at once, you can use the `more` command, using the *pipe* (|) mechanism:

```
D:\scripts\01\script0102.vbs c:\windows | more
```

In this case, | tells Windows to send the output of your script to the program `more`, which is a program built into Windows that displays output one full screen at a time. Pressing the spacebar advances you from one screen to the next.

The second way of saving information that a script has produced is to have the script program create a file directly using program commands in the script. We'll discuss this in Chapter 4, "File and Registry Access."

Wscript and Cscript Command Options

After the earlier discussion about command-line arguments, it shouldn't be a surprise that you can control the behavior of Cscript and Wscript through arguments on the command line. Indeed, you can add several special arguments to the Wscript or Cscript command line to change its behavior.

Cscript usually prints a message every time it starts up, before printing any output from your script. For example, if I type

```
cscript script0102.vbs c:\windows
```

the result looks something like this:

```
Microsoft (R) Windows Script Host Version 5.6
Copyright (C) Microsoft Corporation 1996-2001. All rights reserved.
The total size of the files in c:\windows is 10512614
```

One change I can make is to add `//Nologo` to the command line, being careful to use forward slashes rather than backslashes, like this:

```
cscript //Nologo script0102.vbs c:\windows
```

This causes the output to display as follows:

```
The total size of the files in c:\windows is 10512614
```

This is much nicer. Windows Script Host recognizes several special optional arguments, each preceded by `//` to notify the host that the argument is for its use rather than something to be given to the script. The complete list of command-line options is shown in Table 1.3.

Table 1.3 **Command-Line Options for *wscript* and *cscript***

Option	Effect
`//H:`*`host`*	Sets *`host`* to be the default script from now on. Enter `wscript` or `cscript` in place of *`host`*.
`//S`	Saves the current settings as the default settings for this user. Any of the other options listed in this table used along with `//S` will "stick" for all future runs of WSH, until you change the default settings again.
`//B`	Uses "batch" mode and suppresses any script errors and input prompts from displaying. Normally, errors in your script program cause the script to stop with an error message. `//B` makes it try to carry on regardless.
`//D`	Enables Active Debugging. When this option is used, if the script encounters an error and you've installed Windows Script Debugger (or another Microsoft visual debugging tool, such as Visual InterDev or .NET Studio), the debugger will take over and indicate the source of the error.

Option	Effect
`//E:engine`	Uses the named language *engine* to process the script. Normally, WSH guesses the correct engine from the script filename: VBScript for `.vbs` files, JScript for `.js` files, and so on. Use this option only if you're using unusual filename extensions or an unusual language that WSH can't guess.
`//I`	Uses "Interactive" mode, which is the opposite of the "batch" mode discussed earlier. Because `//I` is the default setting, you'd only need to use this option if you previously changed the default using `//S //B`.
`//Job:jobname`	Runs the script job named *jobname* from within a `.WSF` file. WSF files were discussed earlier in the chapter.
`//Logo`	Displays the Windows Script Host copyright and version information. (This is the default unless you use `//Nologo` or change the setting permanently with `//S //Nologo`.)
`//Nologo`	Suppresses the copyright and version printout.
`//T:nn`	Sets the maximum time the script is permitted to run to *nn* seconds. For example, `//T:5` means that the script will be stopped if it takes more than 5 seconds to run. This is useful if your script might "stick" or try to run forever when something goes wrong.
`//X`	Executes the script in the debugger. I'll discuss this option later in the section "Debugging Scripts."
`//U`	Used with cscript only. Tells cscript to write Unicode data instead of ASCII data to the output. You'll probably never need to use this option.

Tip

There's no need to memorize this list. At the command prompt, you can type **`cscript /?`** or **`wscript /?`** and the program displays the list of valid options. Most Windows programs do this if run with `/?` on the command line.

Note

If you're a Windows Registry guru, you may want to know where WSH setup information is stored. The `//S` switch saves preference values in the Registry under `HKEY_CURRENT_USER\Software\Microsoft\Windows Script Host\Settings`.

The `//E` switch sets the engine associations by changing the `Command` key under `HKEY_CLASSES_ROOT\xxx\Shell\Open` for each registered script file type *xxx* (`VBSFile`, `JSFile`, `PerlScriptFile`, and so on); the list of registered script file types is under `HKEY_LOCAL_MACHINE\Software\Microsoft\Windows Scripting Host\Script Extensions`.

The actual script interpreters (engines) are DLLs registered under `HKEY_CLASSES_ROOT\CLSID` under the `CLSID` associated with the script engine entries (for example, `HKEY_CLASSES_ROOT\VBScript`). The script engine file type and engine `CLSID` keys are marked with a subkey named `OLEScript`.

Let's look at some examples of using these options. I mentioned the `//H` option earlier; it sets the default host program to cscript or wscript, and the setting "sticks" until it's changed with another `//H` command. The other options usually change WSH's behavior only when they're given. Here's an example:

```
cscript somescript.vbs //T:5 //B some arguments for the script
```

This tells cscript to run script `somescript.vbs` for a maximum of five seconds and not to stop even if there are errors. The other arguments are passed along to the script.

The `//S` option, though, makes the other options stick permanently, just as the `//H` is permanent. If I want to turn off the copyright and version printout that appears every time on a permanent basis, this command does the trick:

```
cscript //Nologo //S
```

The `//S` argument makes the `//Nologo` option stick.

Note

Capitalization doesn't matter when using these options. For example, `//T:5` and `//t:5` have the same effect.

Using Scripts

Once you've written a script that you intend to use on a regular basis, I suggest you make a shortcut to the script file. This is usually only useful with scripts run with wscript or scripts that produce no output, however. If you use a shortcut with cscript (command-line version), as soon as the script finishes, its window will close and you won't have a chance to read the results.

Making a Script Shortcut

To make a shortcut to a script file, just follow these steps:

1. Right-click the Desktop and select New, Shortcut.
2. Click Browse and locate your script file. Click OK.
3. Move the cursor to the beginning of the Location box and add `wscript` before the path and filename. Be sure to add a space after `wscript`. Click Next.
4. Change the description from `wscript.exe` to something reasonable that describes the script's function, such as Count File Sizes. Click Finish.

You can then drag this shortcut anywhere you wish, including into your Start menu. Double-clicking the shortcut will run the script with a minimum of fuss.

Tip

If you use your scripts on a local area network, I recommend that you store your commonly used scripts in a shared network folder. This way, you can create shortcuts on any networked computer. When you create the shortcut, enter the script's Universal Naming Convention (UNC) pathname, for example, `\\bali\scripts\myscript.vbs`; or use Browse to locate the shared file under My Network Places. It's also handy to copy the shortcuts themselves to a shared folder. Then you can just drag these shortcuts to any networked computer without having to re-create them.

Scheduling Scripts

If you have scripts that you want to run on a regular basis, without any manual input, you can use the Windows Command Scheduler to run them automatically.

Note

The Command Scheduler is available in Windows XP, 2000, 98, and Me. On Windows NT, you can use the `at` command to schedule scripts.

To schedule a script file, follow these steps:

1. Click Start, All Programs, Accessories, System Tools, Scheduled Tasks.
2. Double-click Add Scheduled Task; then click Next to start the Scheduled Task Wizard.
3. Click Browse and locate the script file. Click Open when you've selected it.
4. Give a name to the task, such as "Send Email Reports," and select its frequency. If you need more detailed scheduling (for example, Mon-Fri only), choose the closest approximation and we'll change it later.
5. Select a start time and date.
6. Enter the username and password for the account under which this script should run. It might be your account, but whatever account you choose needs to have the necessary permissions to read the script file and any input files it needs as well as permission to write output files, if any, where they need to go.
7. Check the Open Advanced Properties for This Task When I Click Finish check box and then select Finish.
8. On the Task tab, change the Run command line to start with `wscript //B` or `cscript //B` and add any command-line arguments your script needs, as shown in Figure 1.6. `//B` ensures that your script won't get stuck waiting for the user to click any OK buttons. Set the appropriate working directory here as well.

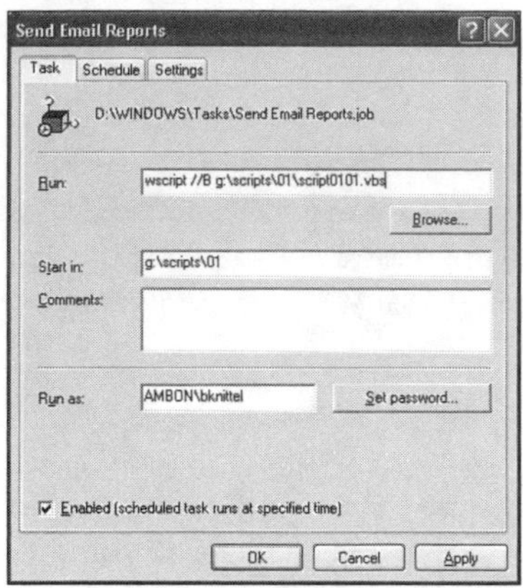

Figure 1.6 Set the command line for a scheduled script using the task's Properties page.

9. If you need a more complex schedule than just "daily" or "weekly," view the Schedule tab and check Show Multiple Schedules. For a Monday-to-Friday schedule, you can, for example, enter five separate start dates: Monday, Tuesday, and so on, up to Friday, each repeating weekly.
10. Click OK to save the scheduled task.

Now your script file will run unattended. You can alter or delete the scheduled task at any later time.

Scripts Run from Batch Files

Finally, you can also run scripts from batch files. This sounds strange, but it can be convenient. Batch files are very useful when you need to string several programs together in succession, and there's no reason that a script file can't be one of those programs. Systems administrators on Windows NT networks may also wish to run scripts from batch files as part of a logon script, which I'll discuss in the next section.

You can use either wscript or cscript to run a script in a batch file. Both versions can communicate success/failure information back to the batch file through the `errorlevel` environment variable, as shown in the following example:

```
badscript.vbs:
    Wscript.echo "Oops, I've run into a problem."
    WScript.Quit(1)

runbad.bat:
    @echo off
    wscript badscript.vbs
    echo Wscript returned %errorlevel%
    if errorlevel 1 echo The script reported an error!
```

Note

You may run into articles on the Web claiming that Wscript doesn't set `errorlevel`, but this information is obsolete. In the current version of WSH (found in both Windows 2000 and XP), both Wscript and Cscript properly set the `errorlevel` value.

Logon and Logoff Scripts

You may also wish to run a script automatically every time you log on to your computer. Scripts can be used to set up your desktop, clean out folders, set up printers, or just about any other task you may have to ensure that every time you (or your network users) sign on, Windows behaves as expected. You can use logon scripts to set up shared or mapped network drivers, clean out directories, update files, or whatever else may be appropriate.

Any user can simply create a shortcut to a script in his or her Startup program folder to have a script run automatically upon logon. To do this, create a shortcut to the desired script, right-click it, drag it over the Start button, and then wait a moment without releasing the icon. When the Start menu opens, drag the icon to All Programs, Startup and then release. Choose Copy Here or Move Here to complete the operation.

System administrators who wish to set up automatic scripts will soon find out that users can remove these Startup scripts, either intentionally or accidentally. To make these startup scripts mandatory, Windows has a built-in logon script mechanism. It's available in all user profiles on Windows XP and Windows 2000 as well as for all Windows versions if the user is a member of Windows domain network with roaming profiles.

The logon script is specified in the user profile by the local or domain administrator. On a Windows domain network, the logon script may be stored on a network shared directory. Otherwise, these script files must be stored in the system logon script folder or in one of its subfolders. By default, the default system logon script folder on Windows XP/NT/2000 is `c:\windows\system32\repl\import\scripts` unless changed by the system administrator.

For users on Windows XP, 2000, and NT, the logon script can be a script file. On Windows 9*x* systems, the logon script must be a BAT file, but the BAT file can run Wscript or Cscript.

Note

I'll discuss logon scripts in more detail in Chapter 10, "Deploying Scripts for Computer and Network Management."

Logoff Scripts?

If your computer is a member of a Windows .NET/2000 Server domain, the network manager can assign logoff scripts as well as logon scripts through Group Policy. Logoff scripts aren't guaranteed to run as logon scripts are, because the user may simply shut off the computer or it may crash. Still, it's a useful tool, because logout time can be a handy time to clean up temporary files and back up important data.

If you're not…try to make one!

There are other ways to go about this, as well. Many network managers use a popular freeware add-on product called KiXtart (`www.kixtart.org`) to provide a logoff script mechanism.

What I've done, and have found handy, is to simply create an icon that runs a batch file with the desired cleanup commands. Last of all, it runs the handy `logoff.exe` program. This program forces a logoff without manual intervention. The logoff batch file can look something like this:

```
          Rem  file logoff.bat
@echo off
cscript //B c:\path\logoffscript.vbs
logoff
```

Of course, you'll have to adjust it to match the location of your logoff script and the location of `logoff.exe` on your hard drive.

Then, place a shortcut to `logoff.bat` on the desktop. Hide the logoff command on the Start menu as a reminder to use the new icon when it's time to sign out. The new logoff method can't be enforced, but if users (or you) want to use it, it's very handy.

Security Concerns

Because Windows has a default file-type association between the filename extensions used by scripts (for example, `.vbs` and `.js`) and Windows Script Host, when you ask Windows to "start" or "open" a VBS file, it knows it's a script and runs it.

This can be a security risk, though, and there are two reasons you may wish to change the default behavior:

- Because scripts can be written to erase files and perform serious operating system changes, you might consider it too dangerous to make it this easy to run scripts on your computer.
- Hackers have exploited the willingness of Windows to run scripts by writing virus and worm scripts and sending them as e-mail attachments. If a mail recipient opens the attachment and Windows is set to automatically run VBS files with Windows Script Host, the virus will start up and do its damage.

Because you can always run scripts by explicitly running the `wscript` or `cscript` command, you can disable the Windows association between scripts files and WSH, and you won't lose any significant functionality.

If you want to do this, here's how:

1. Open Windows Explorer and select Tools, Folder Options.
2. Select the File Types tab.
3. Locate VBS in the list under Extensions and select it.
4. Click the Advanced button and under Actions select Open.
5. Click Edit. Write down the existing setting (which will look like `C:\WINDOWS\System32\WScript.exe "%1" %*`) and change the entry to `notepad %1`, as shown in Figure 1.7. Click OK to close both dialog boxes.

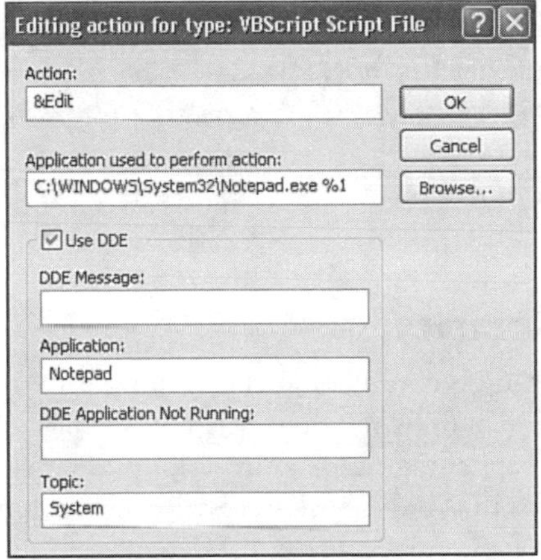

Figure 1.7 Change the "Open" program from wscript to Notepad.

6. Locate JS in the Extensions list and repeat steps 4 and 5. Afterward, you'll notice that your changes automatically apply to JSE and WSF files as well.

Now, you won't be able to right-click or double-click a script file icon to start it. Instead, you'll have to perform one of the following actions:

- Create shortcuts with `wscript` or `cscript` in the command line, as discussed earlier in the chapter.
- Run scripts from the Command Prompt or Start, Run window by typing **`wscript`** or **`cscript`**, followed by the script filename.

This isn't a strong security measure: If a malicious script manages to get started despite these changes, it can still do whatever it wants. Some people have gone so far as to delete `cscript.exe` and `wscript.exe` from their computers, or at least rename them, for this reason.

Trust Policy and Script Signing

For Windows XP users on a Windows .NET or Windows 2000 domain network (that is, a network that is controlled by Windows .NET Server or Windows 2000 Server), there is another more powerful way to prevent unauthorized scripts from running. Through the network's Group Policy feature, Windows can be instructed only to run scripts found in specified directories and/or to disallow scripts that don't contain a valid *signature*, which is an encrypted data block that guarantees the script file has come from an authorized, trusted source. A network administrator must grant this authorization, called *Trust Policy control.*

Note

If a network manager enables the Trust Policy feature, you may not even be able to write and run your own scripts! If you run into problems running scripts, contact your network administrator.

I'll discuss script security, Trust Policy, and script signing in more detail in Chapter 10.

Debugging Scripts

Just writing a program can be hard enough, but getting it to work correctly can try the patience of a saint. Thankfully, Windows scripting comes with a graphical debugger that lets you see what's happening inside your script program as it runs. If you've written and debugged macros in Word, Excel, Access, or other Microsoft applications, you've probably already encountered the visual debugger. If not, here's a short tour.

If a script encounters a glaring programming error (for example, a misplaced comma or an unrecognized word), WSH will report the error. For example, here's a script with a serious error:

```
        ' bad.vbs - a script in need of debugging
for counter = 1 to 3
    wscript.echo "Counter is now", counter
next

badcommand

wscript.echo "Got past the bad command"
```

VBScript does not recognize the word `badcommand`. Now, what happens when you try to run this script depends on which host you've used.

Cscript will print an error message describing the problem and indicating which line in the file has the error, like so:

```
Counter is now 1
Counter is now 2
Counter is now 3
D:\scripts\01\bad.vbs(7, 1) Microsoft VBScript runtime error:
   Type mismatch: 'badcommand'
```

Wscript, the graphical version, will stop and display a dialog box informing you of the error, as shown in Figure 1.8.

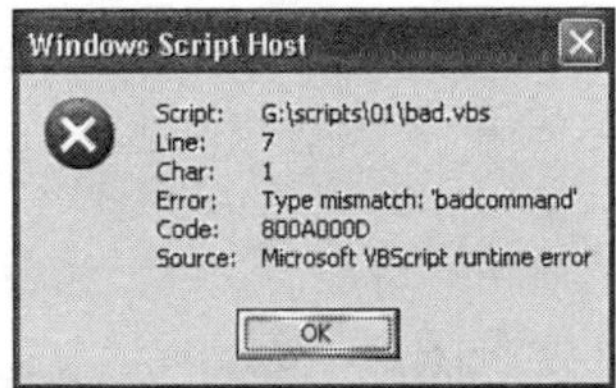

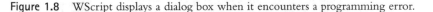

Figure 1.8 WScript displays a dialog box when it encounters a programming error.

In either case, the error message tells you that WSH is having some sort of problem with line 7 in your script file and, in many cases, this will lead you close enough to the problem that you can see and fix it.

If your script doesn't behave as you expect, and yet there aren't any glaring typographical errors—at least none that your scripting language can detect—you'll have to do a bit of detective work.

In some cases, it's helpful to insert commands to display the contents of your program's variables and intermediate results to see that they make sense. In the `bad.vbs` script we're working with in this section, for example, I've had the program display the contents of variable `counter` as the loop takes its turns. Sometimes this kind of output, called *tracing*, is helpful. You can always remove extra `echo` or other output commands when you know your script is working correctly.

This technique works, but it's so *yesterday.* We're not in the punched card era anymore, are we? If your script doesn't behave as expected or if you're in the first stages of writing it and just want to watch what is happening inside to assure yourself that it's working, there's a much more modern tool you can use to peer inside as the program runs. It's called the Script Debugger. The only catch is that you have to download it, because it's not supplied with Windows. If you're going to be developing scripts, visit `msdn.microsoft.com/scripting`, select Downloads in the index list in the left column, and select Microsoft Windows Script Debugger. You need to be logged on as a Computer Administrator to install the download.

Note

If you have installed Visual InterDev, .NET Studio, or have another "Active" debugger installed, do *not* download or install the Windows Script Debugger—you already have a more powerful debugger in place.

If you're using Windows 2000, you can either download the latest version of Script Debugger or install the copy that came on your Windows 2000 Setup CD-ROM. To do so, open the Add/Remove Programs control panel, select Windows Components, and check Script Debugger.

Once Script Debugger is installed, you can use `//X` on the command line to start up a script using the debugger. Now, the command

```
cscript //X d:\scripts\01\bad.vbs
```

causes the debugger to appear, as shown in Figure 1.9.

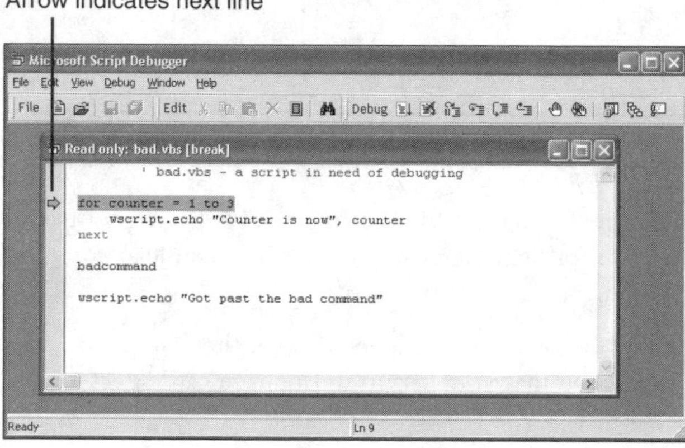

Figure 1.9 The Windows Script Debugger displays the contents of your script as it runs.

As the script runs, a yellow pointer shows the next script statement that will be processed. In Figure 1.9, because I've just started the script, the pointer is on the first actual script command after the comment and blank line.

Now, you can walk your script through its paces one step at a time, or you can let it run ahead to a desired point and make it stop. Although you can use the debugger's menus to do this, you'll find it much easier to use if you learn the keyboard shortcuts. The most important shortcut keys are shown in Table 1.4.

Table 1.4 **Windows Script Debugger Function Keys**

Key	Action
F8	Steps the script ahead one statement at a time. If the script calls a script subroutine or function, the debugger will "step into" the subprogram and stop at its first line.
Shift+F8	Similar to F8 but "steps over" any subroutines or functions.
F9	Click the cursor in any of the script's program lines and press F9 to set or clear a *breakpoint* in the line. A breakpoint stops the program in its tracks when the program reaches the marked line. This is very useful if you want to see what happens at a certain point in the program and don't want to step to that point one line at a time. Set a breakpoint and press F5.
F5	Lets the program run ahead full speed until it either ends, encounters a serious error, or encounters a breakpoint.
Ctrl+Shift+F8	If the program is inside a script subroutine or function, the script runs until the routine returns and then stops.

Viewing and Altering Variables

Besides letting you step through your script, the debugger also lets you view and modify the contents of variables inside the script. This is the debugger's most valuable feature. Click View, Command Window to display the command window, as shown in Figure 1.10.

The Command window lets you do three things to help you debug your program:

- You can display the value of any variable by typing a question mark followed by the variable name and the Enter key. In Figure 1.10, I requested the value of variable `num`, and the debugger displayed `1`.
- You can alter the value of a variable by typing an assignment statement, as shown in Figure 1.10, where I changed the value of `num` from `1` to `4`. You can use this ability when your script has made a mistake and you'd like to continue debugging. Although you can't fix the program itself while the debugger is running, you may be able to get a bit more information out of your debugging session by correcting the variables and continuing.
- You can call any subroutine, function, or object method or property by typing an appropriate program statement. Use `?` to call and display function values—for example, `? mid("ABC",2)`. To call subroutines, just type the subroutine name and any arguments, as shown in Figure 1.10. In the figure, I called subroutine `shownumber` with argument `num = 15`.

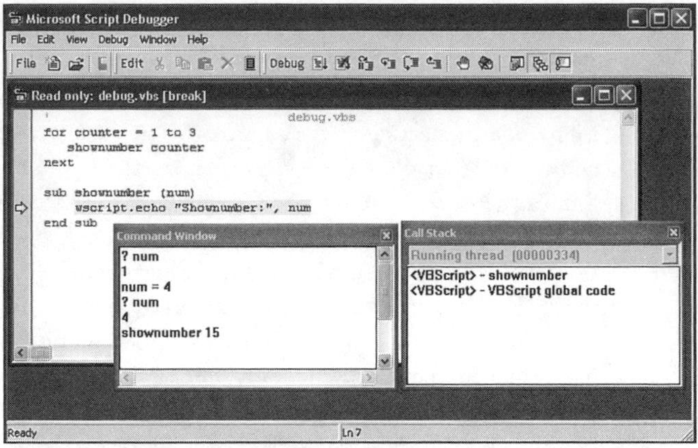

Figure 1.10 The Command window lets you view and alter variables and execute program statements manually. The Call Stack window shows the order in which subroutines and functions have been called.

Viewing the Call Stack

The Call Stack window, also shown in Figure 1.10, is another tool that helps you monitor the inner workings of a script. To display it, select View, Call Stack. This window lists the names of any subroutines or functions that are currently in use. It lists the current routine on top, followed by the name of the routine that called it, and so on down to the main script program.

Viewing the call stack is helpful when debugging scripts that call many subroutines or that use recursion, which is a programming technique I'll discuss in Chapter 4. You can double-click any of the entries in the Call Stack window and the debugger will display the location in your script where a subroutine call is in progress.

Although this is a useful tool for making sure a script runs through all the steps you think it should, if you're used to the full-featured debuggers found in other Microsoft products, you'll find this one lacks three important features:

- You can't select a "next statement to run" to change the script's order of processing statements (for example, to skip over a problem area).
- If the script encounters a serious error, it displays an error message in the usual fashion and stops. You can't work around the problem in the debugger.
- You can't edit the script and tell the debugger to restart. You must exit the debugger and start it up again.

Ah well, what do you expect for free? It's still a useful tool to have on hand when you want to know how your script is behaving inside.

Tip

If you put debugging output commands in your script to display the values of variables, when you've gotten the script working, comment these statements out rather than delete them. This way, it will be easy to restore them if you need to debug again later.

If you have a copy of Microsoft Word or Excel installed, you can develop scripts using the built-in Visual Basic for Applications environment. You can get there from the menu bar by clicking Tools, Macros, Visual Basic Editor. You won't have access to the `WScript` object here, but you can develop other aspects of your script in this more powerful debugging and testing environment.

Tip

Most scripting languages provide a special command that will activate the debugger and halt the script when it is encountered. In VBScript, this is the `stop` statement. In JScript, it's `debugger;`. These act like breakpoints, except they're built directly into your script and are especially handy when you're debugging the WSC scripts used to create objects, as I'll discuss in Chapter 9.

Where to Get More Information

The definitive source of information for Windows Script Host is the Microsoft Developers Network Web site at `msdn.microsoft.com/scripting`. Here, you'll find detailed documentation, examples, and updated versions of WSH to download.

Several other sites on the Web you might want to check out are listed in Table 1.5.

Table 1.5 **Web Resources for Windows Script Host**

Web Site or Newsgroup	Description
`msdn.microsoft.com/scripting`	The official Microsoft site.
`communities.msn.com/windowsscript`	Extensive FAQs, examples, links, and articles.
`www.serverguys.com`	Articles and examples with an emphasis on Active Directory Service Interface (ADSI) and Windows Management Instrumentation (WMI).
`www.win32scripting.com`	Archives of *Windows 2000 Magazine*'s articles on scripting. Good questions and answers in the FAQ section.
`www.winguides.com/scripting`	Online reference for VBScript and WSH.
`www.sapien.com`	Purveyors of a nifty $150 script-editing program called PrimalScript. Definitely beats using Notepad.

continues

Table 1.5 **Continued**

Web Site or Newsgroup	Description
`microsoft.public.scripting.wsh` `microsoft.public.scripting.vbscript`	Public newsgroups hosted by Microsoft. A great place to scout for scripting ideas and to post any questions you have. Although you probably won't get feedback or tech support from Microsoft employees here, the community of visitors seems to do a good job of answering questions and giving advice.

There are hundreds of others. If you find other particularly useful scripting resources, let me know by dropping me a line at `www.helpwinxp.com`.

2
VBScript Tutorial

ROAD MAP

- This chapter introduces the VBScript programming language.
- You should have some familiarity with the basics of programming. If you have previous programming experience of any sort, you'll be able to pick up VBScript.
- If you're new to programming, don't worry if you don't understand a topic. Study the examples, pick up what you can, and keep reading. In time, it will make sense.
- If you already know another scripting language, you don't have to use VBScript, but you should be familiar with it so you can follow the examples in this book.

Introduction to VBScript

VBScript is the free version of Microsoft's Visual Basic programming language provided with Windows Script Host. It's virtually identical to Visual Basic for Applications, which is built in to many Microsoft applications for use as a scripting and "macro" language. Despite being somewhat stripped down from the full-price Visual Basic language, VBScript is fully capable of performing calculations, working with filenames and dates, and manipulating external objects. Although it can't display the complex dialog boxes, windows, and menus of a full-featured Windows application, it's powerful to serve the purpose of helping you manage your computer and automate day-to-day tasks. Although you could use many other languages to write scripts, VBScript is an excellent choice because you can transfer your experience in writing macros and programs for Word and Excel to Windows scripts, and vice versa.

In this chapter, I'll introduce you to VBScript and show you its most important features. I'll assume you have at least some familiarity with computer programming.

Programming concepts change little from one language to another, so if you have experience with *any* computer language, even if it was a one-day Word macro workshop or a class on FORTRAN using punched cards back in the 1970s, I think you'll pick up VBScript pretty quickly. Pay special attention to the illustrations called *patterns*. These are programming "building blocks" you'll find yourself using over and over.

After reading this chapter, you should visit the Microsoft Developer's Network at `http://msdn.microsoft.com/scripting`. This is *the* official VBScript Web site. It has the most current VBScript language reference online, which you can browse or download. There are articles, sample scripts, and add-ons you can download. Also, when new versions of Windows Script Host and VBScript are released, the announcements and download links will appear on this site.

The program examples in this chapter are brief, because they're designed to illustrate the basic commands and functions in VBScript. Meatier examples will follow in subsequent chapters.

➔ I encourage you to test the scripts as written and also to modify them yourself, just to see what happens. For instructions on downloading and using the sample scripts, see `www.helpwinxp.com/hood`.

The first VBScript topics I'll cover are variables, and constants.

Variables

Variables hold the data you want to process. The data could be dates, times, numbers, or a series of arbitrary characters (commonly called a *string*). Strings are the most common type of data you'll work with, because your scripts will manipulate filenames, people's names, the contents of files, and other such information.

Variables are stored in the computer's memory and are accessed by a *name*. You refer to a variable by name to see or change its value. To assign a value to a variable, you use the = sign.

For example, consider the following lines of VBScript code:

```
FullName = "Sue Smith"
Age = 40
```

When VBScript encounters these statements, it stores the string value `"Sue Smith"` in a variable called `FullName`, and the integer value `40` in the variable `Age`.

Note

Though I won't really discuss this in detail until Chapter 3, "Scripting and Objects," variables can also contain *objects*, which are blocks of data managed by software add-ons to VBScript. Objects are what give VBScript its real power because they let you take advantage of the capabilities of other system programs to perform complex tasks, such as sending e-mail messages, writing files, and installing printers on the computer.

Several restrictions are placed on the names you can use for variables:

- Names must begin with an alphabetic character and can contain only letters, numbers, and the underscore (_) character.
- They cannot contain an embedded space, period, or other punctuation character. For example, `big house` and `House.Big` are invalid.
- They must not exceed 255 characters in length.

Information can be placed into variables directly by your program (as in the `Age = 40` example), it can be read in from files, or it can be derived or computed from other variables.

In most other programming languages, you have to define a variable's data type before using it—be it string, integer, object, date, or whatever. However, VBScript works the variable type out for itself, making life much simpler for the programmer as a result. In VBScript, all variables are of one fundamental data type called a *variant*. VBScript converts data from one type to another as needed. For example, if you attempt to "join" a variable containing a string to a variable containing a number, VBScript will convert the number to its text representation and then join the two strings together. If you add a number to a date, VBScript will add this number of days to the date, and so on.

Constants

In computer terminology, numbers and values that are typed into a program literally can be called, not surprisingly, *literals*, but they are most often called *constants*. The number 40 in the previous example is a constant. In fact, it's called a numeric constant because its value is...a number. VBScript lets you type in four types of constant values: Numeric, String, Date, and Boolean. Here's a rundown of all four types:

- Numeric constant values are entered using digits and, optionally, a decimal point and/or a plus (+) or minus (-) sign indicator. Examples are `40`, `-20`, and `3.14159`. Don't insert commas in large numbers: For example, `1,234` is not allowed.
- String constants are entered as text characters surrounded by quotation marks (`""`). Examples are `"ABC"` and `"Now is the time"`. If you want to put a quotation mark inside the string, double it up. For example, `"ABC""DEF"` has the value `ABC"DEF`.
- Date values are entered using the format Windows uses for your chosen locale (country), surrounded by pound signs. In the U.S., you could use `#1/3/2002#` to specify January 3, 2002. In most of the rest of the world this would be used to represent March 1, 2002. (VBScript uses the Locale setting you've made in the Windows Control Panel under Regional and Language Options to decide how to interpret this kind of date constant.)

  You can also use long date formats. For example, `#January 3, 2001#` and `#3 January, 2001#` are equally acceptable. If you don't mind typing things out like this, it's better to use a long date format because it's not subject to the regional ambiguity of the short format. Also note that if you specify a year with two digits, VBScript interprets 00 through 29 as 2000 through 2029, and 30 through 99 as 1930 through 1999. It's best to spell out years fully, though, so it's very clear to both you and VBScript what year you mean.

- Time constants should be based on a 24-hour clock or should include text to indicate whether it is A.M. or P.M., as in `#22:30:10#` or `#10:30:10 PM#`.
- You can also combine the date and time into one constant, as in `#January 3, 2001 22:30:10#`.
- Boolean values can be entered as the words `True` and `False`.

Named Constants

Sometimes you'll write scripts with literal values that play an important role. For example, in a script that deletes all temporary files more than 30 days old, the number 30 will have to appear somewhere in your script, perhaps in several places. It might look something like this:

```
for each file in folder
    if AgeOf(file) > 30 then file.Delete
next
```

Now, there's nothing magic about the number 30, and you might want to write your script in such a way that you can change this threshold later on without having to look for every occurrence of "30" in the script file. You could put the number 30 in a variable that you would use throughout the script:

```
MaximumAge = 30

...

for each file in folder
    if AgeOf(file) > MaximumAge then file.Delete
next
```

The advantage of this is that you can set `MaximumAge` once at the beginning of the script and use the variable as many places as necessary. If you want to change the value, you only need to edit the first statement. Additionally, named values make the script easier to understand; they provide context that the numeric values don't.

However, variables are designed to, well, vary, and this particular value isn't intended to change while the script runs. So, like most programming languages, VBScript lets you define *named constants* that solve the literal value versus variable dilemma.

In VBScript, the statement

```
const MaximumAge = 30
```

defines a value named `MaximumAge`, which you can use by name throughout the rest of your script, and which has the value `30`. Named constants can be defined for any of the value types we discussed earlier: dates, times, numbers, and strings.

When you use a named constant in your scripts, you signal to anyone reading the script that the value is important and that it's fixed, and you get the benefit of defining it in one place while using it in many places. It's best to define all the constants you use in your script at the beginning of the script file so that they're easy to find.

Note

The word *constant* is often used to describe both literals, such as `30`, and named constants, like `MaximumAge`. It's a bit misleading, but you'll see this in Microsoft's VBScript documentation and in the error messages that VBScript produces.

When your script starts, several constants are already defined by VBScript. For example, the constants `vbMonday`, `vbTuesday`, and so on represent the days of the week, and you may use them when working with dates and times. I'll discuss some of the predefined constants in this chapter, and there's a complete summary of them in Appendix A. Now that we've covered how to specify variables and values, we can discuss how to manipulate them with operators and expressions.

Operators and Expressions

VBScript variables can be manipulated with *operators* to perform mathematical or character-string operations. For example, the + operator adds numeric variables. To compute Sue Smith's age next year, you could use this VBScript command:

```
age = age+1
```

This means, take the variable `age`, add `1` to it, and store the result back in variable `age`.

When used with variables containing string values, the + operator *concatenates* the strings (joins them end to end). For example,

```
firstname = "Sue"
lastname = "Smith"
fullname = firstname + " " + lastname
```

concatenates `"Sue"`, a blank space (designated by the quotation marks), and `"Smith"` and then stores the result (Sue Smith) in the variable `fullname`.

In the previous example, I could also have written this:

```
fullname = firstname & " " & lastname
```

VBScript lets you use the & character as an equivalent way to join strings. With strings, & and + do the same thing, but as a matter of good programming style, & makes it clearer to someone reading your program that strings are being added rather than numbers. Also, & has the added advantage that it can be used with variables and expressions of any type.

Operators are grouped into three categories:

- **Arithmetic operators.** These include +, -, * (multiply), and / (divide).
- **Comparison operators**. For example, > (is greater than) and <= (is less than or equal to).
- **Logical operators**. For example, AND, OR, and NOT.

The comparison and logical operators produce neither a numeric nor string result, but rather a *Boolean* value (either True or False). These operators are used to direct the flow of control in a program, as in this example:

```
if Age > 40 then
    write "You're not getting older, you're getting wiser"
end if
```

A combination of values and operators is called an *expression*. Here are some examples of expressions:

Expression	Value of Expression
3+3	The number 6
2 < 20	The Boolean value True
"A" & "B"	The string "AB"
Date() + 1	Tomorrow's date

Each of the operators in each category has a *precedence*, or priority, that determines the order in which the parts of the expression are calculated. The order of precedence within calculations *does* matter. For example, the value of the expression 1+3*3 is 10, not 12. Following the conventions used by mathematicians, multiplication has a higher precedence than addition. VBScript computes 3*3 first and then adds the result to 1. (Remember this discussion from high school algebra class?) You can use parentheses to force VBScript to evaluate expressions differently. For example, (1+3)*3 produces 12. Expressions in parentheses are computed first.

Sometimes expressions contain operators from more than one category. For example, the following comparison contains both an arithmetic and a comparison operator:

```
if A+B > C then ...
```

In these situations, arithmetic operators are evaluated first, comparison operators are evaluated next, and logical operators are evaluated last. Comparison operators all have equal precedence; that is, they are evaluated in the left-to-right order in which they appear.

Tables 2.1 through 2.3 list all of the VBScript operators.

Table 2.1 **Arithmetic Operators, from Highest to Lowest Precedence**

Operator	Meaning	Example	Result
-	Unary negation	-5	-5
^	Exponentiation	2^5	32
*	Multiplication	2*3	6
/	Division	9/2	4.5
\	Integer division	9\2	4
mod	Modulus (integer remainder)	9 mod 2	1
+	Addition	3+5	8
-	Subtraction	8-5	3
&	String concatenation	"abc" & "de"	"abcde"

The + operator also concatenates strings, but as I mentioned, it's best to get in the habit of using + for numbers and & for strings. Using & makes it more clear to someone reading your program that strings rather than numbers are being manipulated.

Table 2.2 **Comparison Operators**

Operator	Meaning	Example	Result
=	Equal to	3 = 4	False
<>	Not equal to	3 <> 4	True
<	Less than	3 < 4	True
>	Greater than	3 > 4	False
<=	Less than or equal to	3 <= 4	True
>=	Greater than or equal to	3 >= 4	False
is	Object equivalence	obj1 is obj2	False

The comparison operators are used mostly to let a script choose different actions, depending on the circumstances the script encounters. For example, a script can choose to delete a file if it's more than 24 hours old:

```
file_hours = DateDiff('h', file.DateLastModified, Now())
if file_hours > 24 then
    file.Delete
end if
```

The first line determines how many hours have elapsed since the file in question was created or modified. Then, the comparison `file_hours > 24` is `True` if `file_hours` is more than 24.

Table 2.3 **Logical Operators, From Highest to Lowest Precedence**

Operator	Meaning	Example	Result
`not`	Negation	`not (3 = 4)`	`True`
`and`	Conjunction	`(3 = 4) and (3 < 4)`	`False`
`or`	Disjunction	`(3 = 4) or (3 < 4)`	`True`
`xor`	Exclusion (different)	`true xor true`	`False`
`eqv`	Equivalence (same)	`false eqv false`	`True`
`imp`	Implication (same or second value `True`)	`false imp true`	`True`

The logical operators are used to combine individual comparisons in order to address more complex situations, such as "If the file is more than 3 days old *or* the file is named `anything.TMP`, then delete the file."

Note

Advanced programmers: The logical operators can be used with both Boolean and numeric values. They perform bitwise operations on numeric values and logical operations on Boolean values.

If this is new territory, don't worry about all these operators right now. I'll use the more important ones in the examples throughout this chapter. For now, just remember that operators exist for every basic mathematical function, and you can refer back to these tables when you find the need.

Automatic Conversion

As mentioned earlier, when you combine variables or constant values of different types in one expression, VBScript tries to convert the values to appropriate types. Although it doesn't make sense to multiply a date by a number (what's two times August 4?), the addition and subtraction operators work in a surprisingly sensible way, as shown in Table 2.4.

Table 2.4 **Automatic Conversions for Add and Subtract**

Operation	Result
Number + or - String	If the string represents a number, it is converted to a number and the result is a number. Otherwise, the program stops with an error message
Date/time + or - Number	Date. The whole (integer) part of the number is added to the date as a number of days. Any fractional part of the number is added as a time offset, as a fraction of a day (1 second = 0.0000115741; 12 hours = 0.5).

Operation	Result
Date + or - String	If the string represents a number, it is converted to a number and the result is a date. Otherwise, an error occurs.
Anything & Anything	Values of any type are converted to strings and the strings are concatenated.

Flow Control

It's all well and good that you can assign values to variables and perform calculations, but the real power of programming is in the ability to perform operations over and over, and to take different actions when conditions require. That's where flow control comes in. Instead of just executing each and every line of a program in order from top to bottom, *conditional statements* let you specify how the program is to respond to various situations it may encounter. With *looping statements*, you can execute certain statements repeatedly. Looping statements record not only how to handle a repetitive task but how to know when to start and stop the task.

Note

In this chapter and in Microsoft's documentation, you'll see VBScript commands capitalized some times but not others. The case doesn't matter; VBScript is not case sensitive. For example, the commands

```
IF A = 3 THEN

if A = 3 Then

If a = 3 then
```

are all the same to VBScript. Microsoft's convention is to capitalize the words of VBScript statements, but I think this looks strange and it's too much of a bother, so I'm not going to capitalize most VBScript words in this chapter.

It is helpful to capitalize certain letters in long names, such as `CreateTextFile`, just to make them easier to read, so I do tend to capitalize the names of functions, objects, methods, and properties, as you'll see in this chapter. Remember, the case doesn't matter one bit to VBScript. It just makes the scripts easier for humans to read.

The `If...Then` Statement

The `If...Then` statement examines what is called a *condition*, and if the condition is true, it executes one or more VBScript statements.

Consider this example:

```
        ' Example File script0201.vbs
if Hour(Time()) < 12 then
    MsgBox "It's morning, rise and shine!"
end if
```

A condition is an expression that can be examined and found to be either true or false. In the preceding example, the condition is `Hour(Time()) < 12`. Now, in VBScript, `Time()` represents the current time of day, and `Hour(Time())` represents the current hour of the day—a number from 0 to 23. From midnight until just before noon, this number is indeed less than 12, so the condition `Hour(Time()) < 12` will be true, and the script will display the "It's morning" message. From noon on, the hour is 12 or greater, so the message will not be displayed. Figure 2.1 shows what I saw when I ran this script one morning.

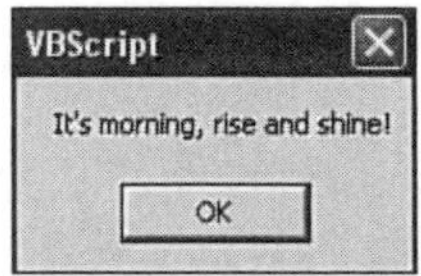

Figure 2.1 The Good Morning message is displayed when the hour of the day is less than 12.

`If...Then` statements can control your script's behavior based on any kind of condition that can be written with a combination of VBScript variables, operators, and functions and that ends up as a Boolean (true/false) value.

The `If...Then` statement has several variations that help you manage more complex situations. First of all, when there is only one command you want to use if the condition is true, you can put the entire statement on one line:

```
if Hour(Time()) < 12 then MsgBox "It's morning, rise and shine!"
```

If you need to use more than one statement when the expression is true, you must use the `If...End If` version; `Then` followed by a line break starts a block of commands, and `End If` marks the end of the statements that are executed when the condition is true. Here's an example:

```
if Hour(Time()) < 12 then
    MsgBox "Good Morning!"
    runreport "Today's Activities"
    DeleteTemporaryFiles
end if
```

In this example, if the script is run before noon, the `if` statement runs the three statements between `if` and `end if`.

If you want to perform some commands if the condition is true, but other commands if the condition is false, you can use the `If...Then...Else` version of the command:

```
if condition then
    vbscript commands to perform
    when condition is true
else
    vbscript commands to perform
    when condition is false
end if
```

Only one set of commands or the other will be performed when the script is run. Here's an example:

```
        ' example file script0202.vbs
if Hour(Time()) < 12 then
    MsgBox "Good morning"
else
    MsgBox "Good day"
end if
```

If there is just one command in the `Else` section, you can put the command on the same line as `else` and omit the `end if`. Here are the four possible arrangements:

```
if condition then
    statements
    . . .
else
    statements
    . . .
end if

if condition then
    statements
    . . .
else statement

if condition then statement else    ' note that else must go here
    statements
    . . .
end if

if condition then statement else statement
```

Finally, sometimes you'll find that one `Else` isn't enough. Another variation of the `If` command uses an `ElseIf` statement. With `ElseIf`, you test multiple conditions with one long statement:

```
if condition then
    vbscript commands go here
elseif othercondition then
    other vbscript commands here
elseif yetanothercondition
    yet more commands
else
     last set of commands
end if
```

Again, only one of the sets of VBScript commands will be performed—the commands belonging to the first *condition* that is true. If none of the conditions turn out to be true, the optional `Else` statement will be used.

If you use `ElseIf`, you cannot use the all-in-one-line format.

Note that `If` statements can also be nested one inside the other for more complex situations, as shown here:

```
if filetype = ".EXE " then
    if filename = "WINWORD" then
        MsgBox "The file is the WINWORD.EXE program"
    else
        MsgBox "The file is some other program"
    end if
else
    MsgBox "This is some other type of file"
end if
```

Here, the "inner" `If` statement is executed only if the variable `filetype` is set to `".EXE"`.

Tip

When you use nested `If` statements, you'll find it much easier to debug and understand the script if you indent the contents of each successive `If` statement as I did in the preceding example. VBScript doesn't care, but it will help you and other people read the script.

The `Select Case` Statement

Suppose I have different commands I want to run depending on the day of the week. You know from the preceding section that I could use a series of `If` and `ElseIf` statements to run one section of VBScript code depending on the day of the week. For example, I can assign to variable `DayNumber` a numeric value (using the constants `vbMonday`, `vbTuesday`, and so on) corresponding to the day of the week. Then, I can use a long `If` statement to handle each possibility:

```
DayNumber = Weekday(Date())
if DayNumber = vbMonday then
    MsgBox "It's Monday, Football Night on TV "
elseif DayNumber = vbTuesday then
    MsgBox "Tuesday, Music lessons"
elseif DayNumber = vbWednesday then
    MsgBox "Wednesday, Go see a movie"
elseif DayNumber = vbThursday then
    ... (and so on)
end if
```

However, there's an easier way. When you find that you need to perform a set of commands based on which one of several specific values a single variable can have, the `Select Case` statement is more appropriate. Here's an example:

```
        ' example file script0203.vbs
DayNumber = Weekday(Date())
select case DayNumber
```

```
    case vbMonday:    MsgBox "It's Monday, Football Night on TV"
    case vbTuesday:   MsgBox "Tuesday, Music lessons"
    case vbWednesday: MsgBox "Wednesday, Go see a movie"
    case vbThursday:  MsgBox "Thursday, fishing!"
    case vbFriday:    MsgBox "Friday, Party Time!"
    case else:        MsgBox "Relax, it's the weekend!"
end select
```

When the `Select Case` statement is run, VBScript looks at the value of `DayNumber` and runs just those commands after the one matching `Case` entry. You can put more than one command line after `Case` entries if you want, and even complex statements including `If...Then` and other flow-of-control constructions. You can also specify a `Case Else` entry to serve as a catchall, which is used when the value of the `Select Case` expression doesn't match any of the listed values. In the example, `Case Else` takes care of Sunday and Saturday.

Tip

The `Weekday` function actually returns numbers from 1 through 7 to indicate the days Sunday through Saturday. I can never remember whether 1 means Sunday or Monday or what. Luckily, VBScript includes predefined constants named `vbSunday`, `vbMonday`, `vbTuesday`, and so on, which you can use instead of the numbers. I discussed constants at the beginning of this chapter.

Although it's powerful and elegant, `Select Case` can't handle every multiple-choice situation. It's limited to problems where the decision that controls the choice depends on matching a specific value, such as `Daynumber = vbWednesday` or `Username = "Administrator"`.

If your decision depends on a range of values, if you can't easily list all the values that have to be matched, or if more than one variable is involved in making the decision, you'll have to use the `If...Then` technique.

Here are some other points about the `Select Case` statement:

- Statements can follow `case` *`value`*`:` on the same line or on a separate line. VBScript permits you to write

  ```
  case somevalue: statement
  ```

  or

  ```
  case somevalue:
     statement
  ```

  I usually use the all-on-one-line format when all or most of the cases are followed by just one statement, as in the days of the week example I gave earlier. When the statements after the cases are more complex, I start the statements on a new line and indent them past the word `case`.

- If one set of statements can handle several values, you can specify these values after the word `case`. For example, you can type `case 1, 2, 3:` followed by VBScript statements.
- If more than one `case` statement lists the same value, VBScript does *not* generate an error message. The statements after the first matching `case` are executed, and any other matches are ignored.
- You can use a variable or expression as the `case` value. Here's an example:

```
somevalue = 3
select case variable
    case somevalue:
        statements
    case 1, 2:
        statements
    case else
        statements
end select
```

If the value of `variable` is `3`, the first `case` statements will be executed. If the variable can take on values that are listed as other cases, remember that only the first match will be used.

The `Do While` Loop

Many times you'll want to write a script where you don't know in advance how many items you'll have to process or how many times some action will need to be repeated. Looping statements let you handle these sorts of tasks. As a trivial example, the task of folding socks might be described in English this way:

```
as long as there are still socks in the laundry basket,
   remove a pair of socks from the basket
   fold them up
   place them in the sock drawer
repeat the steps
```

In VBScript, we have the `Do While` statement to repeat a block of code over and over. In VBScript, the laundry-folding task might look like this:

```
do while NumberOfSocksLeft >= 2
   MatchUpSocks
   FoldSocks
   PutSocksAway
   NumberOfSocksLeft = NumberOfSocksLeft - 2
loop
```

Here, the `Do While` part tells VBScript whether it's appropriate to run the statements following it, and `Loop` sends VBScript back to test the condition and try again. `Do While` statements can be nested inside each other, if necessary. Each `Loop` applies to the nearest `Do While` before it:

```
do while somecondition
    ... statements
    do while SomeOtherCondition
       ... more statements
    loop
    ... still more stuff perhaps
loop
```

As you can see, indenting the program statements inside each `Do While` statement helps make this easy to read and follow.

There are actually five versions of the `Do While` loop, each subtly different:

```
do while condition
    statements
loop

do until condition
    statements
loop

do
    statements
loop while condition

do
    statements
loop until condition

do
   statements
   if condition then exit do
   statements
loop
```

With the first version, VBScript evaluates the Boolean *`condition`*. If its value is `True`, VBScript executes the *`statement`* or *`statements`* inside the loop and goes back to repeat the test. It executes the set of statements repeatedly, every time it finds that *`condition`* is still `True`.

The second version loops again each time it finds that *`condition`* is `False`—that is, until *`condition`* becomes `True`. You could also write

```
do while not (condition)
    statements
loop
```

and get the exact same result. Why have both versions? Sometimes you'll want to write "while there are more socks in the laundry basket" and sometimes you'll want to write "until the laundry basket is empty." The `While` and `Until` versions are provided so that you can use whichever one makes more intuitive sense to you.

Notice, though, that in these first two versions, if the `While` or `Until` condition fails before the first go-round, the statements inside will never be executed at all. In the second two versions, notice that the test is at the end of the loop, so the statements inside are always executed *at least* once.

The last version shows how you can end the loop from the *inside*. The `exit do` statement tells VBScript to stop running through the loop immediately; the script picks up with the next statement after the end of the loop. In this fifth version, the loop always executes at least once, and the only test for when to stop is somewhere in the middle. You can actually use `exit do` in any of the five variations of `Do While`. I'll discuss `exit do` more in the next section.

Every time you write a script using a `Do While`, you should stop for a moment and think which is the most appropriate version. How do you know which to use? You'll have to think it through for each particular script you write, but in general, here's the pattern to use:

Pattern

When you want to perform a task as many times as necessary, as long as there is more work to be done, put the test at the beginning, as shown here:

```
do while (condition that tells if there is work to do)
    ...statements
loop
```

When you want to perform a task at least once and stop only when something happens *during* the task, put the test at the end, as shown here:

```
do
    ...statements
while (condition that tells if there is still work to do)
```

Choose between the `While` and `Until` versions by trying both and seeing which seems to make more intuitive sense when you say the statement out loud.

Terminating a Loop with `Exit Do`

Sometimes it's desirable to get out of a `Do While` or other such loop based on results found in the middle of the statements inside, rather than at the beginning or end. In this case, the `Exit Do` statement can be used to immediately jump out of a loop, to the next command after the `loop` line.

For example, suppose you expect to be able to process five files, named `FILE1.DAT`, `FILE2.DAT`, and so on. However, if you find that a given file doesn't exist, you might want to stop processing altogether and not continue looking for higher numbered files. The following shows how you might write this up in a script:

```
set fso = CreateObject("Scripting.FileSystemObject")
num = 1
do while num <= 5                                ' process files 1 to 5:
    filename = "C:\TEMP\FILE" & num & ".DAT"     ' construct filename
    if not fso.FileExists(filename) then         ' see file exists
        exit do                                  ' it doesn't, so terminate early
    end if
    Process filename                             ' call subroutine "process"
    num = num + 1                                ' go on to next file
loop
```

In this example, the first time through the loop, we set variable `filename` to `FILE1.DAT`. Each turn through increments variable `num` by one. We test to be sure the file whose name is stored in variable `filename` really exists. If the file does not exist, `Exit Do` takes the program out of the loop before it attempts to process a missing file.

There's no reason we have to limit the `Do While` loop to a fixed number of turns. If we omit the "do" test entirely, it will run forever. The constant `True` is just what it sounds like, so we could rewrite the previous script to process as many files as can be found, from 1 to whatever:

```
          ' example file script0204.vbs
set fso = CreateObject("Scripting.FileSystemObject")
num = 1
do                                          ' process as many files as found
   filename = "C:\TEMP\FILE" & num & ".DAT"     ' construct filename
   if not fso.FileExists(filename) then         ' see file exists
      exit do                                   ' no, terminate early
   end if
   Process filename                             ' call subroutine "process"
   num = num + 1                                ' go on to next file
loop
```

Here, without a `While` or `Until` clause, the loop runs indefinitely (it's what programmers call an *infinite loop*), until `Exit Do` ends it. This means that you have to be careful that `Exit Do` eventually does get executed; otherwise, your script will churn through the loop forever (or until your patience runs out and you cancel it by typing Ctrl+C).

The `Exit Do` statement works in any of the four variations of `Do While` and `Do Until` statements.

Counting with the `For...Next` Statement

When a loop needs to run through a set number of iterations, the `For...Next` statement is usually a better choice than the `Do While` statement. The first example I used for `Exit Do` can be rewritten as a `For` loop like this:

```
          ' example file script0205.vbs
set fso = CreateObject("Scripting.FileSystemObject")
for num = 1 to 5                                ' process files 1 to 5:
```

```
        filename = "C:\TEMP\FILE" & num & ".DAT"      ' construct filename
        if not fso.FileExists(filename) then          ' see file exists
            exit for                                  ' no, terminate early
        end if
        Process filename                              ' call subroutine "process"
    next
```

The `For` loop sets a variable (`num`, in this example) to the first value (here, `1`) and processes the statements inside. It then increments the variable and repeats the statements until the variable is larger than the number after `To` (here, `5`). This loop thus processes the statements with `num = 1, 2, 3, 4` and `5`.

In the example, I also used the `Exit For` statement, which works exactly like `Exit Do`, except that it breaks out of a `For` loop rather than a `Do` loop. (Makes sense, doesn't it?!) The `Exit For` statement makes VBScript continue processing the script with the line after `Next`.

The `For` statement can be written in either of two ways:

```
for counter = startvalue to endvalue
```

or

```
for counter = startvalue to endvalue step stepvalue
```

Here, ***`counter`*** is the variable to be used; ***`startvalue`*** is the value that the variable is to take the first time through the loop; ***`endvalue`*** is the largest value the variable is to take; and ***`stepvalue`***, if specified, is the value by which to increment ***`counter`*** each time through. The ***`stepvalue`*** can be negative if you want your loop to count backward, as in this rendition of a well-known, irritating song:

```
        ' example file script0206.vbs
for number_of_bottles = 100 to 0 step -1
    wscript.echo number_of_bottles & " bottles of beer on the wall!"
next
```

Note

This example demonstrates the power of looping commands. Without the `For` loop, you would have to type out each verse

```
wscript.echo "100 bottles of beer on the wall!"
wscript.echo "99 bottles of beer on the wall!"
wscript.echo "98 bottles of beer on the wall!"
```

and on and on. If you use the `For` loop, you can take care of the whole thing with just three lines.

If the `Step` clause is left out, the ***`counter`*** variable is incremented by one each time.

Note

There's no reason why the *step* value has to be an integer. You can step by fractional values as well, if for some reason you need to do such a thing. When the variable surpasses the upper limit, by any amount, the loop will stop.

Processing Collections and Arrays with For...Each

Some special-purpose VBScript functions can return a variable type called a *collection*. A collection is a list of filenames, usernames, or other data contained in a single variable. For example, a directory-searching function might return a collection of filenames when you ask for all files named `*.DOC`. Because you'll probably want to print, view, or manipulate these files, you need a way of accessing the individual items in the collection.

The `For...Each` loop runs through the loop once for each item in a collection. Here's an example:

```
        ' example file script0207.vbs
set fso = CreateObject("Scripting.FileSystemObject")
set tempfiles = fso.GetFolder("C:\TEMP").Files

filelist = ""
for each file in tempfiles
    filelist = filelist & ", " & file.name
next

MsgBox "The temp files are:" & filelist
```

In this example, the variable `tempfiles` is set to a collection of all the files found in folder `C:\TEMP`. The `For...Each` loop creates a variable named `file`, and each time through the loop it makes variable `file` refer the next object in the collection. The loop runs once for each file. If the collection is empty—that is, if no files are included in folder `C:\TEMP`—then the loop doesn't run at all. You also can use the `For...Each` statement with array variables, executing the contents of the loop once for each element of an array, as shown in this example:

```
dim names[10]
...
for each nm in names
    ...
next
```

The VBScript statements inside this loop will be executed 10 times, with variable `nm` taking one each of the 10 values stored in `names` in turn.

➔ To learn more about arrays, see "Arrays," p. 79.

You can use any variable name you want after `for each`; I chose names `file` and `nm` in the examples because they seemed appropriate. You can use any valid variable name you wish.

VBScript Functions

Functions are special blocks of VBScript's program code that can be activated (or *called*) by name. A function can be given data to operate on, and it always returns a value to the part of the script that called it. The technical term for a value passed to a function is an *argument*.

For example, the built-in `UCase` function takes a string variable, constant, or expression as its argument and returns a string with all the letters set to uppercase. Now, check out this example:

```
str1 = "my file.dat"
str2 = Ucase(str1)
```

In this script, the variable `str2` calls the `UCase` function, which converts the value of `str1` to all uppercase and then assigns that value, `"MY FILE.DAT"`, into variable `str2`. The original variable, `str1`, is left untouched.

We'll cover many examples of functions in the coming chapters. If this doesn't make sense now, the examples will make it clearer as we go.

Calling Functions and Subroutines

In the example I gave earlier, I showed how functions are called by specifying their arguments in parentheses. For example, I might call the `MsgBox` function this way:

```
selectedbutton = MsgBox("Do you want to continue?", vbYesNo)
```

The function `MsgBox` displays a text message in a pop-up dialog box and returns a value indicating which button the script's user clicked.

In VBScript, if you don't care about and don't intend to use the value returned by a function, you can omit the parentheses. In this case, you're treating the function as a *subroutine*, which is a fancy name for a function that does something useful but doesn't need to return an answer to the program that called it.

The following example illustrates this idea with the function `MsgBox`. I might use `MsgBox` to display a useful message, but I don't care which button the user clicked. Because I am not going to use the value `MsgBox` returns, I can call it using the subroutine form, without parentheses:

```
MsgBox "The script has finished", vbOK
```

In the rest of this chapter, I'll show functions used both ways. Just remember that parentheses are used when you're using the value returned by the function, and they are omitted when you're not.

By the way, in VBScript, parentheses can also be omitted when a function doesn't take any arguments. You may see functions called this way in Microsoft's VBScript documentation. The built-in function `Now()`, which returns the current date and time, is an example. Both lines in this script do the same thing:

```
wscript.echo "The date and time are:", Now()

wscript.echo "The date and time are:", Now
```

The second line is actually calling function `Now` and printing the returned value. I find this confusing: Is `Now` a variable or a function?

Tip

To help avoid confusing variables with functions, I recommend that you always use parentheses when calling functions.

Documentation and Syntax

About 100 predefined functions are available in VBScript, provided for your convenience as a programmer. These functions manipulate strings, perform complex math functions (such as square roots), and calculate dates and times.

All these functions are listed in the summary at the end of this chapter, and they are completely explained in the VBScript documentation at Microsoft's Web site (`http://msdn.microcoft.com/Scripting`). To give you an introduction to the type of functions and their applications, I'll go through some of them in this chapter. But first, I should explain what you'll see in the online documentation.

The VBScript documentation shows the *syntax* (that is, the required formatting and wording) for each function and statement in the language. For example, the syntax for the `MsgBox` function looks like this:

```
MsgBox(prompt[, buttons][, title][, helpfile, context])
```

The parentheses tell you that `MsgBox` is a function. The list inside the parentheses shows that `MsgBox` can take five arguments. The square brackets (`[` and `]`) around some of the arguments aren't meant to be taken literally; that is, you don't type them. Instead, they indicate that the arguments are optional. Anything shown inside `[` and `]` can be omitted.

The documentation's explanation of each argument tells you what the argument signifies, what values are permitted, and what value is assumed if you don't supply one. The assumed-if-missing value is called the *default value*.

In the case of `MsgBox`, you can see that *`prompt`* is the only required argument. All the other arguments are shown surrounded by left and right brackets, so the rest are optional. The simplest use of `MsgBox` would look like this:

```
x = MsgBox("This is a message to display on the screen")
```

However, you could also use `MsgBox` with three arguments, like this:

```
x = MsgBox("This is a message to display", vbOK, "This is the title")
```

If you want to specify some of the arguments without specifying the ones in between, you can use commas with nothing between them. For example, you could write

```
x = MsgBox("This is a message to display", , "This is the title")
```

to specify the *`prompt`* and *`title`* arguments without specifying *`buttons`*. In this case, the `MsgBox` program would use the default value for *`buttons`*.

Finally, notice that the *`helpfile`* and *`context`* arguments are surrounded by a single set of brackets, which indicates that you can use both or neither.

Don't worry too much about these details right now. This example is just to show how the documentation works.

String-Manipulation Functions

Most of the work you'll probably want to do with VBScript will involve manipulating strings such as filenames and usernames, so it's helpful that VBScript has a rich complement of built-in functions to work with strings.

Searching for Strings with `InStr()` and `InStrRev()`

I've found that the most common task I perform when working with strings is to determine whether a string contains some other string. For example, if your script is to scan through the contents of a directory looking for DAT files, it needs a way of finding out whether the string `".DAT"` occurs in any given filename.

The `InStr` function does this job. The expression

```
InStr(filename, ".DAT")
```

has the value `0` if `.DAT` can't be found in the string `filename`. The value will be equivalent to the character position where `.DAT` starts, if it does occur. Here's an example:

```
filename = "TEST.DAT"
pos = InStr(filename, ".DAT")
```

In this case, `pos` will be set to `5`, because `.DAT` occurs starting at the fifth character in `filename`. If `.DAT` didn't occur in `filename`, `pos` would be set to `0`. Here's how a program might take advantage of this:

```
if InStr(filename, ".DAT") > 0 then
    msgbox filename & " is a .DAT file!"
end if
```

Keep in mind that `InStr` is case sensitive. For example, it would say that `".DAT"` can't be found in the string `"somefile.dat"`. So, when `filename` might contain both upper- and lowercase characters, the correct way to write the test would be as follows:

```
if InStr(Ucase(filename), ".DAT") > 0 then
    ...we know it's a .DAT file
end if
```

The `UCase` function returns a string identical to the string it's passed, except that lowercase characters are turned to uppercase. Then, `InStr` looks for the uppercase `.DAT`.

Tip

Case is a constant concern when dealing with strings. Always think through the consequences of having upper- and lowercase characters. To a computer, *a* and *A* are different letters. You should usually convert all user input and filenames to uppercase or lowercase before performing tests on them—or be careful to account for case when testing.

If the first argument to `InStr` is a numeric value, it's interpreted as the starting character for the search. In this case, you have to pass three arguments to `InStr`. The following expression returns the value `4`:

```
InStr(2, "ABCABC", "AB")
```

`AB` occurs at positions 1 and 4 in the string `"ABCABC"`, but you told `InStr` to start looking at position 2. Therefore, the first occurrence was skipped.

Function `InStrRev()` is similar to `InStr()`, except that it searches starting from the right end of the string. The following line returns `4` because it finds the rightmost `"AB"`:

```
InStrRev("ABCABC", "AB")
```

Extracting Parts of Strings with `Left()`, `Right()`, and `Mid()`

VBScript has several functions to pull pieces out of strings based on the starting position and length of the desired piece, as shown here:

Function	Returns
`Left(`*`string, length`*`)`	The leftmost *`length`* characters from *`string`*
`Right(`*`string, length`*`)`	The rightmost *`length`* characters from *`string`*
`Mid(`*`string,start`*`)`	That part of *`string`* from character position *`start`* onward
`Mid(`*`string,start,length`*`)`	*`length`* characters of *`string`* from position *`start`*

The following are a few examples:

Expression	Returns
`Left("ABCDEF", 3)`	`"ABC"`
`Right("ABCDEF", 3)`	`"DEF"`
`Mid("ABCDEF", 3)`	`"CDEF"`
`Mid("ABCDEF", 3, 2)`	`"CD"`

In real life, you will use these functions with variables, not fixed strings such as `"ABC"`. For example, to find the base name of a filename without its file type or extension, you could use this VBScript code:

```
filename = "My file.DAT"
dot = InStr(filename, ".")
basename = Left(filename, dot-1)
```

This code sets `dot` to the position of the period in the filename, and `basename` to that part of the filename up to, but not including, the period. In this case, `basename` would be set to `My file`. (If you find this at all confusing, you might want to work this out with paper and pencil to see that it's true).

But what happens if `filename` doesn't have a period in its name? We have a problem: `dot` would be set to zero, and VBScript would stop with an error message when you tried to set `basename` to the leftmost –1 characters! Good programming practice requires that you handle this situation as follows:

Pattern

To extract the base name from a filename with an extension, use a series of VBScript commands, like this:

```
        ' example file script0208.vbs
filename = "test.file"

dot = InStr(filename, ".")
if dot = 0 then
    basename = filename
else
    basename = Left(filename, dot-1)
end if

MsgBox "The base name is " & basename
```

In the better version of this script, we use the entire filename if it doesn't contain a period; otherwise, we extract just the base name. If you're curious, try this yourself with files named `"test.file"`, `"test."`, and `"test"`.

Other String Operations

The following are some more string manipulation functions you'll find handy:

Function	Returns
`Len(`*`string`*`)`	The length of *`string`* in characters
`Lcase(`*`string`*`)`	The same *`string`* but with all alphabetic characters in lowercase
`Ucase(`*`string`*`)`	*`string`*, with all alphabetic characters in uppercase
`Trim(`*`string`*`)`	*`string`*, with leading and trailing spaces removed
`Ltrim(`*`string`*`)`	*`string`*, with leading spaces removed
`Rtrim(`*`string`*`)`	*`string`*, with trailing spaces removed

Here are a few examples:

Expression	Returns
`Len("ABC")`	`3`
`Lcase("My Documents")`	`"my documents"`
`Ucase("My Documents")`	`"MY DOCUMENTS"`
`Trim("   ABC   ")`	`"ABC"`
`Ltrim("   ABC   ")`	`"ABC   "`
`Rtrim("   ABC   ")`	`"   ABC"`

Date and Time Functions

As you would expect, because computers frequently refer to the date and time, VBScript has a number of built-in functions to make it easy to work with dates and times.

Reading the Clock with `Date()`, `Time()`, and `Now()`

The `Date()` and `Time()` functions return the current calendar date and local clock time, respectively, as determined by the operating system. For example, to display the current date and time in a message box, you can use the following code:

```
        ' example file script0209.vbs
MsgBox "The current date is " & Date() & " and the time is " & Time()
```

The `Now()` function returns the current time and date combined.

Note

Using & to join strings with functions that return dates might seem strange, but this is a neat feature of VBScript. Because it knows that the & symbol always operates on strings, it knows to convert the date and time values to their string representations.

Dates and times are actually stored as numbers. The date is stored as an integer number of days since January 1, 0099, and times are stored as decimal fractions of a day (1 second equals 0.0000115741). You don't need to worry about *how* this is done, but it's helpful to know because you can manipulate dates using the arithmetic + operator. For example, the following line assigns today's date plus one day to the variable *tomorrow*:

```
tomorrow = date()+1
```

It's better, though, to use special built-in date and time calculation functions provided in VBScript, which I'll discuss next.

Computing a Future Date with DateAdd

Using the DateAdd function, you can add a specified interval to a given date, time, or combined date/time. The syntax of the function is as follows:

```
DateAdd(interval, number, date)
```

You use the *date* argument to set the initial date. The *interval* argument is the interval type, such as month, day, or year, and the *number* argument is the number of intervals to add. Table 2.5 shows a list of interval types. They must be passed to the DateAdd function as a string in quotation marks.

Table 2.5 **Interval Types for the *DateAdd()* Function**

Interval	Description
YYYY	Years
Q	Quarters
M	Months
W	Weeks
D	Days
H	Hours
N	Minutes
S	Seconds

The following are some examples:

Expression	Returns
DateAdd("M", 2, Date())	Today's date plus two months
DateAdd("H", -1, Time())	The current time minus one hour

The DateDiff() Function

The DateDiff() function calculates the interval between two dates. The syntax is as follows:

```
DateDif(interval, date1, date2)
```

The *interval* argument describes the format of the result you want returned. Refer to Table 2.5 for these values.

For example, `DateDiff("D", "9/9/1999", "1/2/2001")` returns the number of days between September 9, 1999 and January 2, 2001.

This function is especially useful in scripts involving the age of files. For example, you might want to delete a given file if it's older than three hours. If variable `timestamp` holds the last-modified date and time of a file, the following test determines whether the file should be deleted:

```
if DateDiff("H", timestamp, time()) > 3 then
```

Other Date Functions

The following are a few more date and time functions you should be aware of:

Function	Returns
`Day(date)`	The day of the month of the given *date*, from 1 to 31
`Weekday(date)`	The day of the week of the given *date* as a number from 1 to 7, where 1 equals Sunday, 2 equals Monday, and so on
`Month(date)`	The month of the given *date*, where 1 equals January and so on
`WeekdayName(date)`	The day of the week of *date* as a string
`MonthName(date)`	The name of the month in which *date* falls
`Hour(time)`	The hour (0 to 23) of the given *time*
`Minute(time)`	The minute (0 to 59) of the given *time*
`Second(time)`	The second (0 to 59) of the given *time*

VBScript has the predefined constants `vbSunday`, `vbMonday`, and so on that you can use to test the values returned by `Weekday` in `If` statements and others. `vbMonday` makes more sense than the number `2` to someone unfamiliar with this function.

The following are some examples of what VBScript returns when the expression is run at 3:10:37 P.M. on Tuesday, January 11, 2000:

Expression	Returns
`Day(now())`	`11`
`Weekday(now())`	`3` (for Tuesday)
`Month(now())`	`1` (for January)
`WeekdayName(Weekday(now()))`	`"Tuesday"`
`MonthName(Month(now()))`	`"January"`

Expression	Returns
`Hour(now())`	15
`Minute(now())`	10
`Second(now())`	37

Interacting with the User

VBScript is not designed for writing programs with complex user interfaces, but it can display simple messages and receive simple input strings from the user with its `MsgBox` and `InputBox` functions.

Note

Scripts can also read and write files and interact through the Command Prompt window using the `TextFile` object, which I'll discuss in Chapter 4. In this chapter, I'll only discuss the basic VBScript input and output methods.

The `MsgBox()` Function

In its most basic form, `MsgBox` displays a text message to the user. For example, the following code produces the output shown in Figure 2.2:

```
        ' example file script0210.vbs
MsgBox "This message was displayed by VBScript at " & time()
```

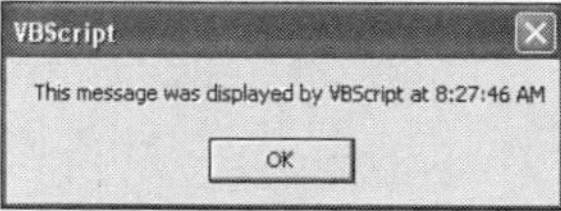

Figure 2.2 A basic message box displaying a string to the script user.

You can also use `MsgBox` to ask simple yes/no questions of the script's user. To do so, you use the advanced form of the `MsgBox` function, with the following syntax:

```
MsgBox(prompt [, buttons] [, title])
```

The three arguments are as follows:

- *`prompt`* specifies the text to display.
- *`buttons`* specifies which buttons to offer to the user.
- *`title`* is a text title displayed at the top of the resulting dialog box.

You can omit the *buttons* and *title* arguments; in their absence, VBScript displays just an OK button and the title "VBScript." The values for *buttons* needs to be one of those listed in Table 2.6. You can use the constant name or the numeric value.

Table 2.6 ***Buttons* Options for the *MsgBox()* Function**

Constant Name	Value	Displays
`VbOKOnly`	0	The OK button
`VbOKCancel`	1	The OK and Cancel buttons
`VbAbortRetryIgnore`	2	The Abort, Retry, and Ignore buttons
`VbYesNoCancel`	3	The Yes, No, and Cancel buttons
`VbYesNo`	4	The Yes and No buttons
`VbRetryCancel`	5	The Retry and Cancel buttons

For example, you can tell the user that a required file wasn't found and ask whether to proceed by using this code:

```
choice = MsgBox("The preferences file is missing, should I proceed?", vbYesNo)
```

`MsgBox` returns either the value `vbYes` or `vbNo`, depending on the button clicked. The possible return values for `MsgBox` are listed in Table 2.7. The value indicates which of the buttons the user has selected.

Table 2.7 **Return Values from the *MsgBox()* Function**

Constant Name	Value
`VbOK`	1
`VbCancel`	2
`VbAbort`	3
`vbRetry`	4
`vbIgnore`	5
`VbYes`	6
`VbNo`	7

You can ask VBScript to display an icon along with the message by adding an additional value to the *buttons* argument, using one of the values listed in Table 2.8.

Table 2.8 **Icon Values to Use with the *MsgBox()* Function**

Constant Name	Value	Displays
`VBCritical`	16	Critical Message icon
`VBQuestion`	32	Question icon
`VbExclamation`	48	Exclamation icon
`VBInformation`	64	Information icon

The following code displays a message with an Information icon:

```
        ' example file script0211.vbs
x = 33
MsgBox "The value of variable x is " & x, vbOKOnly + vbInformation,_
    "Debugging Info"
```

The results are shown in Figure 2.3. The `vbInformation` option also causes Windows to play a special Information sound, which, alas, you'll have to run the sample script yourself to hear.

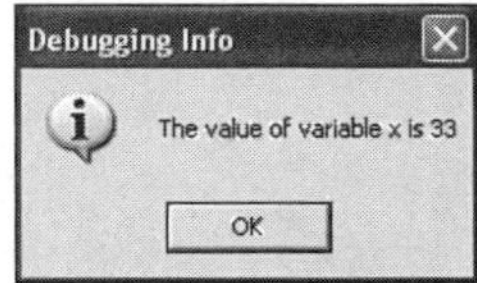

Figure 2.3 A `MsgBox` with a title and an icon.

Sometimes you'll want `MsgBox` to display some interesting message but won't care which button the user clicks. In this case, omit the parentheses from the `MsgBox` call. I discussed this point earlier in the chapter in the section "Calling Functions and Subroutines."

Tip

You can use `MsgBox` to display the contents of variables and values inside your program to help debug it. For example, if you assign the variable

```
debug = True
```

at the top of your program, you can add debugging aids like this throughout the program:

```
if debug then
   MsgBox "The value of variable x is " & x
end if
```

When you get your program working correctly, you can disable all the debugging messages by changing the first line of the program to the following:

```
debug = False
```

These are especially helpful when you use the Windows Script Host debugger, as described at the end of Chapter 1, "Introduction to Windows Script Host." The debugger will show you which statements of your script are being run, and the `MsgBox` statements can show you the contents of important variables.

The `MsgBox` function displays a dialog box that stays up until the user clicks a button. Don't use it in a script that needs to run unattended! Your script will never finish because it will be waiting for a user who isn't watching.

If you want to display information without stopping the script, you can use the `Wscript.Echo` statement, as I'll discuss in the next section.

The `InputBox()` Function

VBScript lets you ask your users for a simple text string by using the `InputBox` function, as in this example:

```
        ' example file script0212.vbs
UserName = InputBox("Please enter your first name")
MsgBox "Hello, " & UserName
```

This script displays the input-type dialog box shown in Figure 2.4.

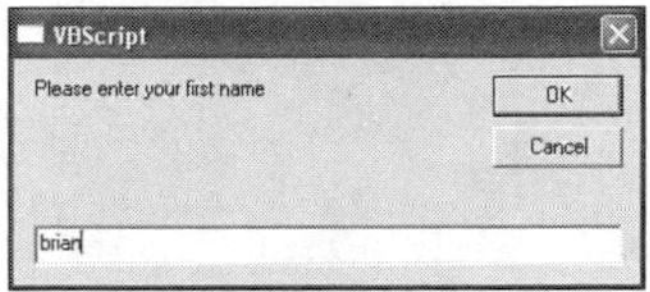

Figure 2.4 The `InputBox()` function as seen by the user.

The function returns whatever the user types. In the preceding example, this is stored in the variable `UserName`.

As with `MsgBox`, you can add additional arguments to the `InputBox` function to get better control of its appearance. You can use several options, only three of which are really interesting:

```
InputBox(prompt, title, default)
```

Here, *`prompt`* is the message to display above the input field, *`title`* is the title to display at the top of the dialog box, and *`default`* places a specific character string into the editing field when it first appears; the user can then accept or change this value.

A practical use of `InputBox` is to select a folder for the script to process, as in this example:

```
fldr = InputBox("Enter folder to be cleaned up", "Cleanup Script", "C:\TEMP")
```

Because VBScript is so flexible about the types of data stored in its variables, if your user types `23`, the value returned by `InputBox` can be treated as a number or as a string. Here's a handy script to calculate square roots (something I'm sure you need to do several times a day):

```
do
    num = InputBox("Enter a number", "Square Root Calculator", "0")
    if num < 0 then
        MsgBox "You can't take the square root of a negative number like " &_
            num, VbOKOnly+VbExclamation
    elseif num = 0 then
        exit do         ' entering 0 ends the program
    else
        MsgBox "The square root of " & num & " is " & sqr(num), VbOKOnly
    end if
loop
```

This script will fail with an error message if the user types something nonnumeric, such as "XYZ." It's always best to check a user's input for correctness so that the program will either tell the user when something is wrong or at least behave sensibly if it is. Here's how:

Pattern

When prompting a user for numeric or date input, use the `IsNumeric()` or `IsDate()` function to confirm that the value entered is legitimate, as shown here:

```
        ' example file script0213.vbs
do
    num = InputBox("Enter a number", "Square Root Calculator", "0")
    if not IsNumeric(num) then
        MsgBox "You call that a number?"
    elseif num < 0 then
        MsgBox "You can't take the square root of a negative number like " & num,_
VbOKOnly+VbExclamation
    elseif num = 0 then
        exit do         ' entering 0 ends the program
    else
        MsgBox "The square root of " & num & " is " & sqr(num), VbOKOnly
    end if
loop
```

`InputBox` displays a Cancel button. If the user clicks the Cancel button instead of OK, `InputBox` returns the empty string (`""`). You can detect this with a statement such as the following:

```
str = InputBox("Please enter your name:")
if len(str) = 0 then ...
```

Then you can respond appropriately by exiting the script, ending a loop, and so on. In the square root calculator, it turns out that the empty string satisfies the `IsNumeric` test and evaluates as `0`, so the calculator responds correctly to Cancel without this test.

Printing Simple Text Messages with `Wscript.Echo`

When you're debugging a particularly obstinate script, at some point you'll probably want to see what's held in your script's variables while the program runs. However, if you need to print debugging output inside a loop, or if you have dozens of variables to display, and you try to use `MsgBox` for this job, you'll quickly get tired of clicking OK over and over. There's a better way: The `Wscript.Echo` command can display text *without* stopping your program.

The `Wscript.Echo` command is useful in scripts even when you're not debugging—sometimes you'd like a script to display text information on your screen. Later in the book, I'll show you scripts that display lists of folder contents, user accounts, network shares, and other information in Chapters 4 and beyond.

The command is simple:

```
wscript.echo expression
```

This prints the value of any expression, of any type: Date, Numeric, Text, or Boolean. You can list any number of expressions, separated by commas, as in

```
wscript.echo expression, expression , expression
```

and VBScript will display each of them, separated by a single blank space.

Note

`Wscript.Echo` is only really helpful when you run your script with the `cscript` command. If you run your script with Wscript, WSH will display all of the `Wscript.Echo` text with pop-up dialog boxes, just like `MsgBox`.

For example, the script

```
username="Mary Smith"
lastlogondate=#03/04/2002#
wscript.echo username & "'s last logon was", lastlogondate
```

will display the text

```
Mary Smith's last logon was 3/4/2002
```

Note that I added "`'s`" to the username string using the string concatenation operator `&`. (I'm picky about this sort of thing. I like computer output to use proper English.)

As you saw earlier, VBScript is very flexible joining strings with `&` and will actually let you join any variable type with a string—it will convert a Boolean, Date, or Numeric variable or expression to a string and then join the resulting strings. You can use this to add a period to the date at the end of the sentence, like so:

```
username="Mary Smith"
lastlogondate=#03/04/2002#
wscript.echo username & "'s last logon was", lastlogondate & "."
```

This prints, properly punctuated, as follows:

```
Mary Smith's last logon was 3/4/2002.
```

A Touchy Subject

Because I've taken a bit of a diversion into the topic of formatting messages, I'll add one more thing. How often do you see a computer print a sloppy message like this?

```
1 files deleted.
```

This drives me *crazy*. There's no reason for it, because it's simple to format this type of message correctly.

Pattern

When counting in English, use the singular if the count is 1; otherwise, use the plural. This rule works for any number from 0 on up. Here's an example:

```
        ' example file script0214.vbs
for nfiles = 0 to 3
    if nfiles = 1 then plural = "" else plural = "s"
    wscript.echo nfiles, "file" & plural, "processed"
next
```

As an exercise, I'll leave it to you, the reader, to modify the sample script `script0206.vbs` so that it prints "1 bottle" rather than "1 bottles" at the end of the song.

You don't have to go to this trouble for a one-time, quick-and-dirty program, but if your program is going to be used by others, it's worth paying attention to language in this way.

Advanced VBScript Topics

I want to cover some important topics here for more advanced programmers, to help you get going in the right direction. Don't worry if these topics don't make sense now; they're applicable only to the most complex VBScript programs.

Procedures: Functions and Subroutines

Procedures are the building blocks of large VBScript programs. A procedure is a separate section of code in your program that performs a particular task. The two types of procedures are functions and subroutines.

You have already learned about many of the built-in functions in VBScript, but you can create your own, too. You can also create subroutines, which are like functions but don't return a value.

The great power in procedures is that after you have written them once in your code, you can call them as often as you want. You can concentrate on *how* to perform a particular task just once when you write a function so that later you can simply *use* the function without worrying about the details.

Functions

To create a function, use the `Function...End Function` statements. Put any functions and subroutines *after* the main body of your script. (While VBScript will run any statements in between or after your functions and subroutines as part of the "main program," scattering the code around the file this way can be extrememly confusing for anyone reading your script.)

As an example, the following simple function accepts one argument and returns the value of the argument plus 2:

```
function addtwo (value)
    addtwo = value+2
end function
```

The `(value)` part tells VBScript that the function expects one argument and is to hold the value in a variable named `value`. This variable is *local* to the function: if your script also uses a variable named `value`, it is *not* altered when function `addtwo` is called. Instead, `addtwo` has its own, temporary variable named `value` that exists only while `addtwo` is working.

The following is an example of how this function might be used elsewhere in the script:

```
a = addtwo(3)
```

When VBScript encounters the expression `addtwo(3)`, it begins to run through the statements of the function, and the variable `value` holds the argument `3`. The value to be returned by the function is set when the program assigns a value to `addtwo` (that is, to the variable with the name of the function itself). As you might guess, the end result is that ultimately the script assigns the value `5` to variable `a`.

In this way, you can extend the built-in functions of VBScript with your own. When you choose names for the argument variables, such as `value` in the example, you should choose meaningful names that explain what type of information is expected. For example, when a function is to be given a filename, I often name the argument `fname`, just out of habit. In my scripts, a variable or argument named `fname` always holds a filename.

The following function takes a filename, removes its extension (its file type), and adds the extension `.OLD`. You might use this function in a program that is going to update a file. If you want to create a backup copy of the file before changing the original, you can use this function to determine the desired name for the backup file, given the original file's name:

```
        ' example file script0215.vbs
function backup_file_name (fname)
idot = instr(fname, ".")
if idot > 0 then
    backup_file_name = left(fname, idot-1)+".OLD"
else
    backup_file_name = fname+".OLD"
end if
end function
```

Here's how the function works: The `Instr` function searches its first argument (`fname`, in this case) for the first occurrence of the second argument (in this case, just a period character). It returns the value `0` if the second string is not found; otherwise, it returns the position within the first string at which it was found—`1`, `2`, and so on. So, here, `idot` is set to `0` if no period appears in the filename argument `fname`, or it is set to a number greater than zero if a period does appear.

The remainder of the function computes the backup filename. If the period is found, the function constructs the new filename from the first characters of the old name, up to but not including the period, and adds `.OLD`. If no period is found in the old name, the function tacks on `.OLD` anyway. Put into use, the following statements would set variable `file1` to `MY.OLD`, and `file2` to `SOMEFILE.OLD`:

```
file1 = backup_file_name("MY.DATA")
file2 = backup_file_name("SOMEFILE")
```

Subroutines

Subroutines are like functions, except they don't return values. They're used to do some specific job that the remainder of your script can then take advantage of. For example, the following subroutine takes as its argument the name of a file. It prompts the user to specify whether the file can be deleted; if the user clicks OK, it deletes the file:

```
sub maybe_delete (fname)
    if msgbox("Should I delete file " & fname & "?", vbYesNo) = vbYes then
        fso = CreateObject("Scripting.FileSystemObject")
        fso.DeleteFile(fname)
    end if
end sub
```

This subroutine uses the built-in function `MsgBox` to ask the script's user whether the file can be deleted. It displays a dialog box with two buttons: Yes and No. If the user clicks Yes, the program uses a `FileSystemObject` to actually delete the file (I'll cover `FileSystemObject` in Chapter 4.)

With this subroutine at the end of your script file, you could use statements like this in your program:

```
maybe_delete filename
maybe_delete "OLD.DATA"
```

You can see how this lets you concentrate on the task at hand (deleting certain files) as you write the script, knowing that the details of *how* to delete files are taken care of in the subroutine.

Arrays

VBScript supports array variables. Arrays are variables that hold more than one distinct value. An array is a bit like an apartment building, where each apartment has a separate occupant. Just as the units in an apartment building are numbered, the individual values in an array are identified by a number called an *index*. Arrays are used when a script has to manage a varying number of items (say, usernames or filenames).

Whereas you can create an ordinary variable in VBScript simply by assigning a value to it, you must tell VBScript that a variable is to be an array before you first use it. Arrays are declared using a `dim` (or *dimension*) statement, which tells VBScript the largest index value you intend to use. Array indexes start at zero, so the statement

```
dim var(10)
```

actually creates an 11-element array, with values `var(0)`, `var(1)`, ... and `var(10)`. Once it's declared, you can assign values to the elements of the array like this:

```
var(0) = "First value"
var(1) = "Second value"
var(2) = "Third value"
```

The big advantage of using arrays is that they let you write programs that are independent of the number of items you need to process. Using the looping statements that we discussed earlier in the chapter, you can run through the items in an array and process each one in turn. Here's an example:

```
' set up an array with three items
dim var(3)
var(0) = "First value"
var(1) = "Second value"
var(2) = "Third value"
nitems = 3

' run through all items in the array using For Each

for each value in var
   wscript.echo value
next

' run through the items using indexing
```

```
for i = 0 to nitems-1
    wscript.echo var(i)
loop
```

In this example, I first created an array with three elements and stored information into each one. It's not necessary to use all the elements; you can make arrays larger than you need if you don't know in advance how many items you'll put into them.

The example prints out the contents of the array twice. The first time, it uses the `For Each` loop, which assigns the values in the array to a variable, each in turn. The `For Each` loop is the easiest to write, but it's not useful unless you want to process every one of the array's elements.

The second loop runs through the array by indexing each value in turn. This loop is a bit more complex to write, because array indexes start with 0 and you have to take this into account when deciding where to stop. To visit every element, the indexes must run from 0 to the number of items minus 1. In this example, there are three items, so we need the `For` loop to run through values 0, 1 and 2. Yes, this is awkward, but it's just the way arrays work in languages such as C and VBScript, and it's the basis of a common pattern.

Pattern

To visit the elements of a VBScript array where the number of actually used elements may be less than the dimension of the array, use a `For` loop. If the number of items used is *`nitems`*, use this loop statement:

```
for i = 0 to (nitems-1)
   ...work with array element(i)...
loop
```

This is a trivial example, but it shows how arrays can make short work of dealing with a large number of items. In this example, I'm only printing the array values out, but the script could do much more. When you use arrays, you only need to write instructions to handle the general case for one item (for example, `var(i)`), and the loop takes care of repeating the work with every item you need to process.

If necessary, arrays can be set up so that their size can be changed as the program runs. The array must first be declared without any dimensions, like this:

```
dim varname()
```

Then, before its first use and anytime thereafter, the array's dimensions can be set or reset with the `ReDim` statement, like this:

```
ReDim [preserve] varname(subscripts) [, ...]
```

The `preserve` keyword causes VBScript to preserve the existing data in arrays being resized; without `preserve`, the variables are cleared, and all elements are set to `Nothing`. (Of course, even with the `preserve` keyword, if you make an array shorter than it was before, you will lose any information stored in the elements that are dropped from the end.)

Variable Scope

By default, when a variable is declared or created in the main body of a script file, it has *global scope*; that is, it's also accessible to every procedure called in the script. Variables defined within functions or subroutines, however, have *private scope* by default. They're accessible only within the procedure in which they're declared. If a procedure containing a variable called `var` calls another procedure, that procedure can't access this variable. This protects variables in your procedures from being inadvertently altered by other procedures. When a procedure that defines the variable terminates, the variable is destroyed.

If you want to explicitly create variables with a global scope, you can do so by using the `public` statement. The same goes for private variables by using the `private` statement. Public variables are accessible to any procedure and are persistent until the script ends. For example, a procedure can use the following statement to declare a variable, `Fsh`, and an array, `MyArray`, that are available to all procedures in the script:

```
public Fsh, MyArray(10)
```

By default, variables can be used without being declared (or *dimensioned*) in advance. Seasoned programmers know that this can lead to hard-to-find bugs, because it's difficult to detect typos; you could simply create a new misspelled variable where you had intended to change the value of a preexisting one. The `Option Explicit` statement fixes that by *requiring* you to declare all variables before using them, using a `dim`, `public`, or `private` statement. I recommend this in complex scripts. It takes a little extra work when you first write the program, but it helps eliminate a whole category of bugs.

To take advantage of this feature, put the statement `option explicit` as the first line of your script file. Then, follow this with `dim` statements listing each variable you'll use in the script. Yes, `Dim` is used to declare array variables, but it can also be used to define normal variables as well.

Here's an example of a script with a typo:

```
option explicit
dim myname
myname = "Brian"
wscript.echo "Hello", mynam
```

This script will generate an error message when it runs into the undefined, misspelled variable `mynam`. Without `option explicit`, this script will simply print "Hello" and there will be no other indication of the mistake.

Where to Go from Here

There's quite a bit more to VBScript than what I've shown you. In fact, there's probably a whole shelf of books devoted solely to VBScript at your local bookstore.

For a quick reference to all VBScript statements, functions, objects, and constants, see Appendix A, "VBScript Reference." For detailed information, use the online or downloaded VBScript Language Reference, which you can get at `msdn.microsoft.com/scripting`.

Finally, I've found that some of the Microsoft public newsgroups can be a great source of information for everyone from beginners to old hands. The newsgroups `microsoft.public.scripting.vbscript` and `microsoft.public.scripting.wsh` are particularly valuable. You can learn a lot by watching the discussions, and unlike most newsgroups I've tried, in these you have a reasonably good chance of getting a useful answer if you post a question. Although some of the conversations concern the use of VBScript in Web server and Web browser applications, most of the discussions are applicable to scripting as well.

3

Scripting and Objects

ROAD MAP

- This chapter introduces the concepts of objects, methods, and properties. It provides the background you'll need for the following seven chapters.
- Read this chapter to see how to use the objects provided with Windows Script Host with different scripting languages.
- To get the most out of this chapter, you should be familiar with at least one script programming language.
- The last section of the chapter shows how you can learn about the many undocumented objects provided with Windows.

Introduction to Objects

All the Windows scripting languages that I discussed in Chapter 1, "Introduction to Windows Script Host," provide the basic tools to control a script's execution and to manipulate strings, numbers, dates, and so on, but they don't necessarily provide a way of interacting with Windows, files, or application software. These functions are provided by *objects*—add-on components that extend a language's intrinsic capabilities. In this section, I'll discuss what objects are and will introduce the terms you'll run into as you work with them. In the following sections, I'll discuss how objects are actually used in several different programming languages.

In the most general sense, *objects* are little program packages that manipulate and communicate information. They're a software representation of something tangible, such as a file, a folder, a network connection, an e-mail message, or an Excel document. Objects have properties and methods. *Properties* are data values that describe the attributes of the thing the object represents. *Methods* are actions—program subroutines—you can use to alter or manipulate whatever the object represents.

For example, a file on your hard disk has a size, a creation date, and a name. So, these are some of the properties you would expect a `File` object to have. You can rename, delete, read, and write a file, so a `File` object should provide methods to perform these tasks. An important aspect of objects is that they are self-contained and separate from the program that uses them. How the object stores and manipulates its data internally is its own business. The object's author chooses what data and procedures to make accessible to the outside world. In programming jargon, we say that an object *exposes* properties and methods; these items compose its *interface.* Figure 3.1 shows the interface of a hypothetical `File` object.

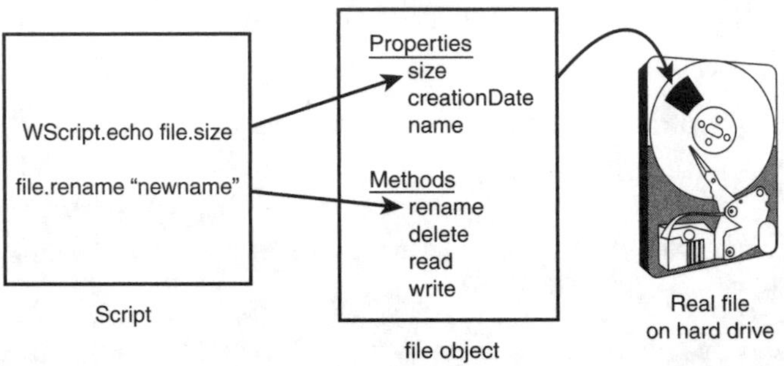

Figure 3.1 This hypothetical `File` object has an interface that can be used by other programs. How the `File` object actually stores its information and does its job are hidden.

Objects need a mechanism through which they can exchange property and method information with a program or a script. Because each programming language has a unique way of storing and transferring data, objects and programs must use some agreed-upon, common way of exchanging data. Microsoft uses what it calls the *Common Object Model* (COM). COM objects can be used by any compatible language, including VBScript, JScript, C, C++, C#, Visual Basic, Perl, Object REXX, and so on. COM objects may also be called *ActiveX Objects, Automation Objects* or *OLE* objects, but regardless what they're called, the technology is based on COM.

Note

There are object models other than COM, which operating systems other than Windows use, but in this book I'll discuss only COM.

In the next several chapters, we'll see objects that represent files, folders, network connections, user accounts, printers, Registry entries, Windows applications, e-mail messages, and many more aspects of your computer and network. Windows XP comes with software to provide you with a wealth of different objects. You can also download, buy, or create additional objects of your own devising.

Classes and Instances

Two other terms you're likely to run into while working with objects are *class* and *instance*. The distinction is the same as that between a blueprint for a house and the house itself.

The word *class* refers to the object's definition: Its interface (the properties and methods it provides) and its implementation (the hidden programming inside that does the actual work). Many object classes are provided with Windows, and you can add or create more, as discussed in Chapter 9, "Creating Your Own Scriptable Objects."

When you actually use an object in a program, the class program creates an *instance* of the object; this is a parcel of computer memory set aside to hold the object's data. The class program then gives your program a *reference* to use when manipulating the object—some identifying value that the class program can use to determine which particular instance of the object your script or program is using. Figure 3.2 illustrates this point: Variables `obj1` and `obj2` are variables that reference instances of a `File` object.

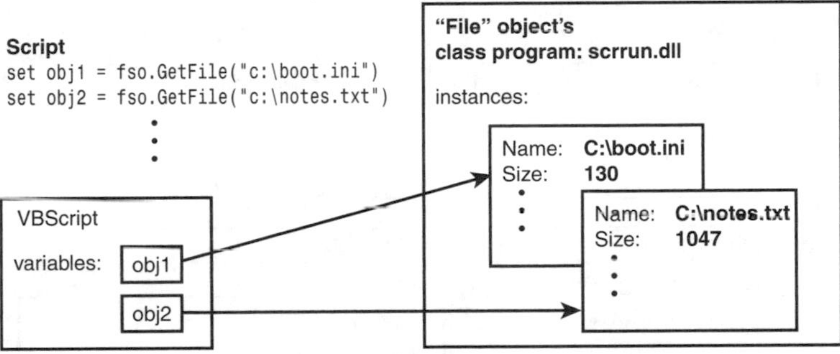

Figure 3.2 `obj1` and `obj2` refer to objects of the `File` class. This illustration shows two instances of the `File` object.

A reference is treated like any other variable in your program. Just as you can use functions such as `sqrt()` and `left()` to manipulate numeric and string values, you can use the object's methods and properties to manipulate an object reference.

Containers and Collections

As mentioned earlier, an *object* represents some real-world, tangible thing, such as a document or a hard drive, and it has properties that represent the tangible thing's attributes. For example, an `apple` object might have attributes such as `color` and `tartness`. The actual data stored for the color might be a character string such as `"red"` or `"green"`. Tartness might be represented as number from `0` (sugary sweet) to `10` (brings tears to your eyes).

An object describing a file on a hard drive might have properties such as `filename` (a character string) and `size` (a number). An object representing a hard drive might have properties describing the hard drive's size, volume name, and also the drive's contents.

Now, the contents of a hard drive could be represented as a list of filenames or an array of string values. However, it might be more useful if the hard drive could yield a list of file objects that you could then use to work with the files themselves. This is actually how many objects work. When appropriate, objects can return references to other objects. When an object needs to give you several other objects, it will give you a special object called a *collection*, which holds within it an arbitrary number of other objects. For example, a `Folder` object might represent a folder on your hard drive, and its `Files` property might yield a collection of `File` objects, which represent the files in the folder, as illustrated in Figure 3.3.

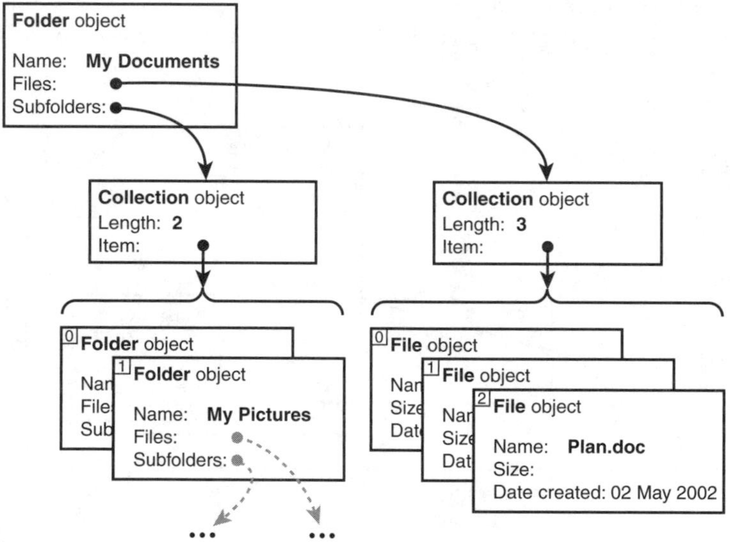

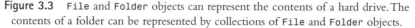

Figure 3.3 `File` and `Folder` objects can represent the contents of a hard drive. The contents of a folder can be represented by collections of `File` and `Folder` objects.

A collection object can actually hold *any* type of object inside it, and the collection object itself has properties and methods that let you extract and work with these objects. This is a common thing to see in object programming: "container" objects that contain other objects, of any arbitrary type. You'll see many examples of collections in later chapters.

Windows ActiveX objects use container objects that have two properties: `Item` and `Length`. The `Length` property indicates how many items are in the collection. The `Item` property retrieves one of the individual items. For some collections, you can extract individual objects from the `Item` collection using `Item(0)`, `Item(1)`, and so on, but for many collections, the `Item` property requires a name or other arcane bit of identifying information. Therefore, each scripting language provides a more general way of letting you examine all the objects in a collection. I'll discuss this in more detail later in the chapter.

Collections are pervasive in Windows script programming, and some languages have special means of working with them. I'll give examples of using collections in each of the scripting languages discussed later in the chapter.

Object Naming

Because objects are separate program components, scripts and other programs that use them need a way to locate them and tell Windows to activate them. In this section, I'll describe how this is done.

Each programmer who creates an object class gives it a name that, with any luck, is fairly self-explanatory. For example, `Scripting.FileSystemObject` is designed to be used by Windows Script Host (WSH) programs to view and manage hard drives, files, and folders. Each of the programming languages you can use with WSH has a way of creating an object instance given just this name. For example, in VBScript, the statement

```
set fsobj = CreateObject("Scripting.FileSystemObject")
```

does the job, whereas in Object REXX, the comparable statement is

```
fsobj  = .OLEObject~New("Scripting.FileSystemObject")
```

In either case, the statement causes the Windows Script Host interpreter to ask Windows to create an instance of the specified object. Windows looks up the object name in the Registry, finds the name of the program file that manages this object class (usually a file whose name ends in `.dll` or `.ocx`), and fires up the add-on program. The class program creates an instance of the object and gives your script a reference with which it can use and manipulate the object.

I'll show you how to do this in each WSH-compatible language later in this chapter. For almost all cases, this is all you need.

In the remainder of this chapter, I'll tell you how to use objects in VBScript and other languages. The next section on VBScript will follow the tutorial style of Chapter 2, "VBScript Tutorial," whereas the descriptions for other languages will assume more experience with programming.

Finally, at the end of the chapter, I'll tell you how to find useful objects not discussed in the later chapters of this book.

Using Objects with VBScript

To use objects in VBScript, you first need to create an instance of an object and store its reference in a VBScript variable. Then, the methods and properties of the object can be accessed using *variable.propertyname* or *variable.methodname*. This is easier to demonstrate than explain, so here's an example (this is a short script that tells whether your C: drive has a folder named \windows):

```
set fso = CreateObject("Scripting.FileSystemObject")
if fso.FolderExists("c:\windows") then
    WScript.echo "There is a folder named \Windows"
end if
```

In the first line of the script, we create an instance of a Scripting.FileSystemObject. This is an object class provided with WSH that has handy properties and methods you can use when examining and manipulating disks and files.

Except for the word set, this looks just like a typical call to a function with the returned value being assigned to a variable. That's just what it is. CreateObject is a function that creates a new object instance. What's new is the word set, which VBScript requires you to use to indicate that an object reference is being stored rather than a regular value.

In general, the syntax to create an object instance in VBScript is

```
set variablename = CreateObject("objectname")
```

where *variablename* is the variable you want to use to hold the object reference, and *objectname* is the type of object you want to create.

In the second line of the example, we use the FolderExists method to find out whether a specified folder exists. Remember that methods and properties are just like regular functions and subroutines; they just happen to "live" in a separate program that provides the object class. The presence of fso. before FolderExists tells VBScript that the FolderExists function is part of the object class to which fso refers, which in this example is Scripting.FileSystemObject.

Some properties and methods take arguments, as you saw with FolderExists. When they do, you have to use parentheses in the same way you would with any other VBScript function or subroutine call. If the method or property returns a function value, you must use parentheses:

```
variable = object.property("arguments", "in", "parens")
```

If a method doesn't return a value, you can omit the parentheses:

```
object.method "arguments", "without", "parens"
```

Does this look familiar? We used objects all through the VBScript tutorial in Chapter 2, in statements such as this:

```
WScript.echo "Today's date is", date
```

Now, you should be able to recognize that `WScript` is an object variable and that `echo` is one of its methods. We never needed to use `CreateObject` to get `WScript` set up, though, because VBScript provides it automatically. The WScript object has several other handy methods and properties that we'll discuss later in this chapter.

As mentioned earlier, some properties and methods return another object as their value. For example, `Scripting.FileSystemObject` has a `GetFile` method that returns a `File` object. The `File` object can then be used to examine and manipulate the file. Here's a sample script that gives the size and creation date of the program file `\windows\notepad.exe`:

```
set fso = CreateObject("Scripting.FileSystemObject")
set file = fso.GetFile("c:\windows\notepad.exe ")
WScript.echo "Notepad.exe was created on", file.DateCreated
WScript.echo "and is", file.Size, "bytes long"
```

The first line is the same as in the previous script, and it creates an instance of the helpful `Scripting.FileSystemObject`.

The second line asks the `FileSystemObject` to return a `File` object representing the file `c:\windows\notepad.exe`. Because I want to use this object several times, I saved it in the variable `file`, using the `set` keyword. (Although `file` is a reserved word in Visual Basic, it's not in VBScript, so it's available for use as a variable name.)

The next two lines use the `File` object's `DateCreated` and `Size` properties. Because these functions don't need arguments, there are no parentheses. The returned date/time and numeric values are printed by the `WScript.echo` method. On my computer, this prints the following:

```
Notepad.exe was created on 4/1/2001 7:27:08 AM
and is 50960 bytes long
```

Automation and Document Files

The `GetObject` function may be used to obtain an object that represents some already existing document file, through a process called *Automation*. `GetObject` uses the name of the document file to find the appropriate object class server, through the Windows standard file type association mechanism (the list of file types and applications you see in Windows Explorer when you click Tools, Folder Options, File Types).

For example, you can create a Word document object representing an existing file and print it:

```
set obj = GetObject("C:\docs\userlist.doc")   ' get object for existing document
obj.Printout                                  ' print the document
set obj = Nothing                             ' release the object
```

`GetObject` can also obtain a reference to an already existing object that was created by some other program, through a name called a *moniker*. Several preexisting objects can be used to manage networking, Windows, and Active Directory user accounts. We'll cover these in Chapter 7, "Windows Management Instrumentation (WMI)," and Chapter 8, "Active Directory Scripting Interface (ADSI)."

The Difference Between Properties and Methods

I don't know about you, but for a long time I found the distinction between properties and methods to be confusing. Now, it's not crucially important to understand the difference, but if you're curious, I'll tell you how I finally came to an understanding of sorts.

If you look back in the preceding section, you'll see I mentioned the `FolderExists` method that is part of the object `FileSystemObject`. Why is `FolderExists` a method and not a property? It comes down to these main points:

- Properties relate directly to aspects of the object, or rather, of the thing the object represents.
- Properties act like variables: You just refer to them by their name.
- Every property returns a value of some sort. Retrieving a property's value doesn't change anything about the object or whatever it represents.
- Some properties let you assign new values to them. This changes the attribute of the object and the underlying thing it represents.
- Methods are the things the object's program can do for you.
- Methods act like functions and subroutines: They can have arguments passed to them.
- Methods don't have to return a value, but some do.
- Invoking a method can change something about the object or the real-world thing it represents.

Therefore, `FolderExists` is a method because it takes an argument (the name of the file it is to look up). Properties don't need arguments because they are intrinsic attributes of the object itself. As such, they don't need any additional information in order to return a value.

There is something else I should mention about properties: In many cases you can both evaluate them (examine their values) and assign new values to them. They work just like variables in this regard. The difference is that when you assign a new value to a property, the object software makes a corresponding change in the actual thing that the object represents. For example, assigning a new value to a `File` object's `Name` property changes the actual file's name, as shown here:

```
WScript.echo file.Name           ' evaluate the property
file.Name = "newname"            ' assign a new value to the property
```

Keep in mind, however, that some objects don't let you change a property's value. In this case, the object's documentation will call it a *read-only* property.

Nested Objects

One other thing I want to point out is that you don't necessarily need to save every object reference in a variable. In the previous example that displayed information about `Notepad.exe`, if I only wanted to see the creation date, I could have skipped the step of storing the `File` object in variable `file` and could have used these statements:

```
set fso = CreateObject("Scripting.FileSystemObject")
WScript.echo "Notepad.exe was created on",_
    fso.GetFile("c:\windows\notepad.exe ").DateCreated
```

In this case, VBScript refers to `fso` to call the `GetFile` method, and the returned object is used to call the `DateCreated` property. It's not unusual to see several levels of objects this way; this is called a *nested object reference.*

When you're working with Microsoft Word objects, this is very common. In scripts or Word macros, you may often see statements like these:

```
ActiveDocument.PageSetup.Orientation = wdOrientLandscape
ActiveDocument.PageSetup.TopMargin = InchesToPoints(0.5)
ActiveDocument.PageSetup.BottomMargin = InchesToPoints(0.5)
ActiveDocument.PageSetup.PageWidth = InchesToPoints(11)
```

In this example, the `ActiveDocument` object returns a `PageSetup` object, which has orientation and margin properties you can set. You could save yourself some extra keystrokes in creating this script by saving a reference to the `PageSetup` object, as follows:

```
set ps = ActiveDocument.PageSetup
ps.Orientation = wdOrientLandscape
ps.TopMargin = InchesToPoints(0.5)
ps.BottomMargin = InchesToPoints(0.5)
ps.PageWidth = InchesToPoints(11)
```

However, VBScript has a special program construction called the `With` statement that makes this even easier. The previous example could be rewritten this way:

```
with ActiveDocument.PageSetup
    .Orientation = wdOrientLandscape
    .TopMargin = InchesToPoints(0.5)
    .BottomMargin = InchesToPoints(0.5)
    .PageWidth = InchesToPoints(11)
end with
```

The `With` statement lets you specify an object reference that is taken as the "default" object between `With` and `End With`. Inside the `With` statement, you can refer to the default object's methods and properties by preceding them with a period but no variable name. Not only can this save you a lot of typing, but it's easier to read, and it lessens the workload on VBScript, thus speeding up your script.

Note

If you need to, you can refer to other objects inside the `With` statement by using the fully spelled-out *`object.method.etc`* syntax.

Releasing Objects

When you create an object, Windows activates the object's class server program to manage the object for you. In the case of `Scripting.FileSystemObject`, you will usually create one of these objects at the beginning of your script and use it throughout. When your script completes, Windows releases the object you've created. The class server program takes care of freeing up its memory and other housekeeping chores. You really don't have to worry about it at all.

However, if you use a script to create multiple objects, you may find that it's appropriate to explicitly release them when you are through using them. For instance, a script that creates multiple Word documents should tell Word to close each document when you're finished with it, lest you end up with hundreds of documents open at once.

You can explicitly tell an object that you're finished with it by assigning the value `Nothing` to the variable that holds the object reference. Later in this book, you will see examples of this in some of the sample scripts.

Working with Collections

If you ask `Scripting.FileSystemObject` for the files or subfolders contained in a folder or drive, it may need to return multiple `File` or `Folder` objects. In order to manage this, it actually returns a single *collection* object that contains all the `File` or `Folder` objects inside it. You can then examine the contents of the collection to look at the individual items.

A collection object has a `Count` property that tells how many items are inside and an `Item` method that returns a specific item from the collection. This would lead you to expect that you could write a script like this to print the names of the files of the root folder on your hard drive:

```
set fso = CreateObject("Scripting.FileSystemObject")
set files = fso.GetFolder("c:\").Files
for i = 1 to files.Count
    WScript.echo files.Item(i).Name
next
```

However, this script doesn't work. With a folder colection, `Item` doesn't allow you to retrieve items by number. It requires you to specify the *name* of the particular object you want, and if you don't yet know the names, this isn't much very useful.

So, to scan through collection objects, each scripting language provides a way to scan through collections without knowing what they contain. VBScript, for example, provides a special version of the `For` loop called `For Each`.

Pattern

To scan through a collection object named `collection` in `VBScript`, use the `For Each` loop as follows:

```
for each objectvar in collection
   ...statements using objectvar
next
```

The `For Each` loop runs through the statements once for each object in the *collection*, and the variable `objectvar` will be made to refer to each of the individual objects in turn. Using `For Each`, and using a variable named `file` to hold the individual file objects, our folder-listing script will now work:

```
set fso = CreateObject("Scripting.FileSystemObject")
set files = fso.GetFolder("c:\").Files
for each file in files
    WScript.echo file.Name
next
```

You could even use the following:

```
set fso = CreateObject("Scripting.FileSystemObject")
for each file in fso.GetFolder("c:\").Files
    WScript.echo file.Name
next
```

Now, if you don't plan on writing scripts in any other languages, skip ahead to the section titled "Using the `WScript` Object" on p. 103 of this chapter for more information about the built-in `WScript` object.

Using Objects with JScript

JScript, like VBScript, is a strongly object-oriented language—it's expected that programmers will use objects to extend its power. JScript supplies 11 built-in object types, and programmers can create generic and structured object types in scripts. I won't discuss the intrinsic object types here because this book focuses on external scripting and Windows management objects.

External COM/ActiveX objects are created using the `new` statement, as follows:

```
variablename = new ActiveXObject("objectname");
```

Here, *`variablename`* is the declared variable that is to receive the new object reference.

Once you have an object variable in hand, its methods and properties are accessed using *`variable.propertyname`* or *`variable.methodname`*. For example, this is a short script that tells whether your C: drive has a folder named `\windows`:

```
var fso;
fso = new ActiveXObject("Scripting.FileSystemObject");
if fso.FolderExists("c:\\windows")
    WScript.echo("There is a folder named \\Windows");
```

Parentheses must be used on all method calls, even if the return value is not used. Whereas VBScript tolerates a statement such as

```
WScript.echo "There is a folder named \Windows"
```

JScript does not.

Case Sensitivity

In the Windows Script Host environment, JScript programs have access to a predefined object named `WScript`, which provides several useful methods and properties pertaining to the script's environment, execution, and debugging. Because JScript is a case-sensitive language, to use this object you must type `WScript` exactly as written here.

However, the method and property names of ActiveX and COM objects are *not* case sensitive. For example, JScript permits you to type `WScript.echo` or `WScript.Echo`.

Working with Collections

If you are used to using JScript with Internet Explorer in browser or server-side ASP scripts, you may be familiar with objects that return collections of objects. Many IE objects let you scan through the object collection using JScript's `for...in` statement.

However, most other objects' collections do not work with `for...in` and you must use an `Enumerator` object to work with them. This is true of most objects you'll encounter in the Windows Script Host environment. JScript's `Enumerator` object gives you a way of accessing a collection by stepping forward or backward through the collection's list of objects.

To use a collection provided by a scripting or other ActiveX object, you must first convert it to an enumerator:

```
enumObject = new Enumerator(collectionObject);
```

The `Enumerator` object has no properties (in particular, no `Length` property). It has an internal concept of its "position" in the collection and has methods that let you move the current position forward or back to the beginning. Its four methods are listed in Reference List 3.1.

REFERENCE LIST 3.1 Methods of the JScript Enumerator Object.

Item

Returns the current item from the collection. The return value will be an object of whatever type the collection holds. If the collection is empty or the current position is undefined, it returns `undefined`.

AtEnd

Returns a Boolean value: `True` if the current item is the last in the collection, if the current position is undefined, or if the collection is empty. Otherwise, `False` is returned.

moveFirst

Makes the first item in the collection the current item. If the collection is empty, `atEnd` will immediately be `True`.

moveNext

Makes the next item in the collection the current item. If the collection is empty or the current item is already the last in the collection, the current item will be `undefined`.

Although a newly created enumerator should be positioned on the first item automatically, it's better style to use `moveFirst` before examining `atEnd` or `item`.

Pattern

To scan through a collection object named `obj`, use an enumerator in this way:

```
e = new Enumerator(obj);
for (e.moveFirst(); ! e.atEnd(); e.moveNext()) {
    x = e.item();
    ...statements using x
}
```

Here's an example. This script lists the names of all the files in the root folder on the C: drive:

```
var fso, e, file;

fso = new ActiveXObject("Scripting.FileSystemObject");

e = new Enumerator(fso.GetFolder("c:\\").files);
for (e.moveFirst(); ! e.atEnd(); e.moveNext()) {
    file = e.item();
    WScript.echo(file.name);
}
```

Now, if you plan on writing scripts only in JScript, you can skip ahead to the section titled "Using the `WScript` Object" for more information about the built-in `WScript` object.

Using Objects with ActivePerl

ActiveState's ActivePerl lets you run Perl scripts in the Windows Script Host environment. Perl's environment is already rich with file-management and network-communication tools, and if you're already a skilled Perl programmer you may wonder what WSH can add. In other words, why use cscript or wscript to run Perl, when you could just run `perl.exe` directly?

The answer is that in the WSH environment, it's a simple matter to access COM, OLE (Automation), and ActiveX objects. The helpful `$WScript` object is predefined in the WSH environment. COM objects are the key to accessing network configuration, Active Directory, and Windows Management Instrumentation (WMI). Although you probably won't want to bother with the Windows script objects for file and directory management, the system-management tools make WSH worthwhile.

Running Perl Scripts in WSH

The ActivePerl installer creates two file associations for Perl files: `.pl` (Perl) is associated with `Perl.exe`, and `.pls` (`PerlScriptFile`) is associated with Windows Script Host.

If you use the familiar `.pl` filename extension for Perl programs that you want to run in the Windows Script Host environment, you'd have to use the command

```
cscript /engine:Perlscript myscript.pl
```

to fire them up. Because you may want to start scripts with the command line or from Explorer, your life will be much easier if you use the extension `.pls` for programs meant to be used with WSH. This way, you can just double-click files in Explorer or you can use commands such as

```
start myscript.pls
myscript
cscript myscript.pls
```

to start script files, and WSH will know what to do. You can also use PerlScript inside the structured WSF files I'll discuss in Chapter 9.

Here are some important things to remember when writing Perl scripts for use with WSH:

- You will not be able to use familiar Perl command-line switches such as `-w`. You will need to directly set option values in the script.
- Any command-line arguments specified to cscript or wscript will not be placed in the `ARGV` array. Instead, you must fetch command-line arguments from the `$WScript->Arguments` collection.

The Perl Object Interface

ActivePerl can interact with COM, ActiveX, and OLE (Automation) objects. The extended syntax for accessing methods is

```
$objectname->Method[(arguments[, ...])];
```

Here's an example:

```
$myobject->SomeMethod
$myobject->Anothermethod("argument", 47);
```

The syntax for accessing property values is

```
$objectname->{Propertyname}
```

Here's an example:

```
value = $myobject->{Length};
$myobject->{color} = "Red";
```

Because the syntax for accessing methods and properties is different, you must take care to check the COM object's documentation carefully to determine whether a value you want to use is a property or a method.

Caution

If you attempt to access an object property or method that does not exist or if you have misspelled the name, by default Perl will *not* generate an error. The result will simply be undefined (`undef`). This will make it very difficult for you to debug your script.

To avoid this pitfall, put

```
$^W = 1;
```

at the beginning of every script file. This will cause Perl to print an error message if you attempt to reference an undefined method or property. I have found that the error message may not tell you clearly that the problem is an unrecognized property or method, but at least you'll get *some* warning.

To set a read/write property, you can simply write the following:

```
$file->{name} = "newname";
```

The standard `WScript` object, which I'll discuss in more detail later in the chapter, is predefined by the Windows Script Host environment and is available to a Perl script. The current version of WSH can be printed with this script:

```
$WScript->Echo("The version is", $WScript->Version);
```

You could use conventional Perl I/O and write

```
print "The version is ", $WScript->Version;
```

instead. However, `print` writes to `stdout`, which is undefined when the script is run by WScript (the windowed version of WSH). A script using `print` will work under

Cscript, but not WScript. It's up to you, of course, but if you want your script to work equally well within either environment, use the `$WScript.Echo` method for output.

Note

Perl is a case-sensitive language, and object variable names such as `$WScript` must be typed exactly as shown here. However, an object's method and property names are *not* case sensitive.

To create an instance of an Automation, OLE, or ActiveX object, you can use either of two methods. The simplest is to use the `CreateObject` method provided with the built-in `$WScript` object, as in

```
$myobj = $WScript->CreateObject("Scripting.FileSystemObject");
```

You can also use the ActivePerl `Win32::OLE` extensions provided with ActivePerl:

```
use Win32::OLE;
$excel = Win32::OLE->new('Excel.Application')
    or die "OLE new failed";
```

For information on the OLE extensions, see the ActivePerl help file.

Working with Collections

Some of the COM objects you'll encounter in this book and elsewhere return *collection* objects, which are containers for a list of other objects. For example, the `Drive` property of `Scripting.FileSystemObject` returns a collection of `Drive` objects, and the `WScript.Arguments` property returns a collection of `Argument` objects. I discussed the methods and properties of the collection object earlier in the chapter.

Because the items of a collection object can't be obtained by an index value (at least, not directly), they must be "scanned" using an enumerator object. An enumerator gives you access to a collection object by maintaining the concept of a current location in the list, which you can then step through. To scan the list a second time, you must reset the current location to the beginning of the list and then step through the list again.

There are three ways to enumerate a collection. First, you can explicitly create an enumerator object, as in the following example:

```
$^W = 1;

$fso  = $WScript->CreateObject("Scripting.FileSystemObject");
$fls  = $fso->GetFolder("C:\\")->Files; # get collection of files in c:\
$n    = $fls->{Count};                  # just for kicks say how many there are
print $n, " files\n";

$enum = Win32::OLE::Enum->new($fls);    # create enumerator object
while (defined($file = $enum->Next)) {  # assign $file to each item in turn
    print $file->{Name}, "\n";          # print the file names
}
```

A second way uses the `in` function to hide the enumerator: the `in` operator returns `Win32::OLE::Enum->All(obj)`, which in turn returns a Perl array given a collection object. Instead of creating `$enum` and using a `while` loop in the previous example, I could have written the following:

```
foreach $file (in $fls) {
    print $file->{Name}, "\n";
}
```

Seeing this, you may guess that the third way is to use `in` to create an array of the sub-objects, which you can then access explicitly:

```
@file = in($fls);
for ($i = 0; $i < $fls->{Count}; $i++) {
    print $file[i]->{Name}, "\n";
}
```

Of the three methods, the `foreach` method is the most straightforward, and it's the easiest on the eyes and fingers. Unless you really want to use an array, I recommend `foreach` as the way to go.

Now, you may want to skip ahead to the section titled "Using the `WScript` Object" for more information about WSH built-in objects.

Using Objects with ActivePython

Many powerful CGI (Web-based) applications are written in Python, and ActiveState's ActivePython does a great job of integrating Python into the ASP scripting environment. This means it may also be used with Windows Script Host. Python, like Perl, has a rich set of built-in and add-on functions that give you complete access to the Windows API, so the scripting utility objects described in this book aren't going to be terribly interesting to the Python programmer. Still, you may want to use the scripting objects in the interest of increasing your scripts' language portability, and because COM/ActiveX objects are the only way to get programmatic access to Automation servers such as Microsoft Word.

Unlike Perl, Python was designed from the ground up as an object-oriented language. Objects, properties, and methods are its bread and butter, so to speak. If you're coming to Python from a background in other languages, there are a few points you should be aware of:

- The `WScript` object discussed throughout this chapter is predefined. Python is case sensitive, so the object must be referred to as `WScript`, exactly.
- Although Python is generally case sensitive, the names of COM object methods and properties are not.

- Perhaps the easiest way to create ActiveX/COM objects is with the `CreateObject` method provided by WScript. Here's an example:

  ```
  fso = WScript.CreateObject("Scripting.FileSystemObject")
  files = fso.GetFolder("C:\\").Files
  ```

- You cannot directly assign a value to a COM object property. You must use

  ```
  object.SetValue("propertyname", newvalue)
  ```

  instead.
- Python automatically imports all predefined constants associated with an OLE object when you create an instance of the object. The constant values are created as properties of `win32com.client.constants`. For example, if you create a Microsoft Word document, the value `win32com.client.constants.wdWindowStateMinimize` will be defined.

For more information about COM integration with Python, see the ActiveState documentation for the `win32com` package.

Working with Collections

Python automatically treats COM collection objects as enumerations. The easiest way to scan through the contents of an enumeration is with the `for...in` statement, as in this example:

```
fso = WScript.CreateObject("Scripting.FileSystemObject")
files = fso.GetFolder("c:\\").Files

for file in files:
    print file.name
```

Now, you may want to skip ahead to the section titled "Using the `WScript` Object" for more information about the built-in `WScript` object.

Using Objects with Object REXX

Object REXX is the only scripting language I discuss in this book that isn't free. However, this is more than made up for by the sophistication of the Object REXX full development edition and its powerful debugger. Because you can install the free runtime version of Object REXX on all your organization's computers and only need to buy the full REXX program for a limited number of development computers, if you're familiar with REXX already and you factor in the time you can save in debugging, it's actually a very cost-effective scripting solution.

Object REXX supports its own brand of built-in objects and lets you create objects within REXX for use by scripts. It uses the same syntax for COM/OLE/ActiveX objects. The syntax for REXX object references is

```
objectname~method
```

An instance of a standard built-in or user-defined REXX object is created with a statement like this:

```
rexxobject = .objectname~new
```

However, you must create instances of Windows COM/ActiveX objects using a special COM object "factory" class named `OLEObject`. Because `OLEObject` is not a built-in class, to use it in your REXX script you must add the following `requires` statement at the end of your script file:

```
::requires "OREXXOLE.CLS"
```

There are three ways to create OLE objects. The most common way is with the statement

```
rexxobject = .OLEObject~new("Server.Object")
```

This creates an instance of a Windows object of type *`Server.Object`*, and it returns the new object.

To create an ActiveX object given a moniker—the "nickname" of the object or the name of a document file whose file type is associated with the application server—use the `GETOBJECT` method:

```
Rexxobject = .OLEObject~GETOBJECT(moniker [, subclass])
```

Finally, to let the object create REXX events, you can use this version of the `New` method:

```
rexxobject = .OLEObject~new("Server.Object", "WITHEVENTS")
```

You should note, however, that the use of events is beyond the scope of this book.

In addition to any methods or properties defined by the ActiveX object itself, REXX adds several additional methods. These extra methods help integrate the Windows and REXX universes. The extra methods are listed in Reference List 3.2.

REFERENCE LIST 3.2 Extra Methods added to COM Objects by Object REXX.

`GETCONSTANT (name)`

Lets you access any predefined constant values that are associated with the object. Whereas VBScript simply makes an object's defined constants available automatically once an object is created, in Object REXX you must explicitly look them up. For example, the Windows `Speech` object uses a constant value named `ttxtst_READING`. To get the value of this constant in REXX, you can use the statement `flagval = talk.GetConstant("vtxtst_READING")`.

`GETKNOWNEVENTS`

Returns a stem (a REXX collection object) describing the events that the OLE object can create. See the Object REXX documentation for details.

continues

REFERENCE LIST 3.2 Continued

GETKNOWNMETHODS

Returns a stem with information on all the methods provided by the OLE object.

GETOUTPARAMETERS

Returns a REXX array consisting of any "output" parameters set by the OLE object during the last reference to one of its methods.

Here is an Object REXX script that demonstrates the use of `GetConstant`. It uses the Windows `Speech` object to greet you:

```
talk = .OLEObject~new("Speech.VoiceText")
flags = talk~GetConstant("vtxtst_READING") -- define type of speech
talk~register('',"Object REXX Test App")
talk~enabled = .true
talk~speed = 280
talk~speak("Hello, this is REXX speaking.", flags)

do while talk~isspeaking
    call SysSleep 1
end
exit

::requires "orexxole.cls"
```

Note

Object REXX does not support DCOM and does not support the creation of server objects that can be called from other languages and environments.

Creating Object REXX Files

The Object REXX installer sets up two file associations: `.rex` (REXXScript) for files meant be run by REXX directly, and `.rxs` (ObjectRexxScriptFile) for files meant to be run with cscript or wscript.

Which file extension should you use? If you want to use the REXX development environment and debugger, you should create `.rex` files. This is probably the most efficient way to go. If you want to use the `WScript` built-in object that I discuss in this chapter and elsewhere, you'll need to run your scripts with wscript/cscript, because only the WSH environment creates this predefined object and it can't be created with the `OLEObject` method. In this case, you must forgo the debugger. To be honest, I think the debugger is more valuable than the `WScript` object.

Working with Collections

Many Windows Scripting objects return groups of information called *collections*, as I discussed earlier in the chapter. Object REXX has the `do...over` statement to loop through the items of a collection.

Pattern

The structure

```
do obj over collectionobject
    statements using object obj
    ...
end
```

executes the enclosed statements once for each object in the collection. Variable `obj` refers to each one of the objects in turn; you can use any variable name in place of `obj`.

For example, the following script lists the files in the root folder of your `C:` drive:

```
fso = .OLEObject~new("Scripting.FileSystemObject")
files = fso~GetFolder("C:\")~Files

Say "There are" files~count "files"

do file over files
    say file~name
end

::requires "orexxole.cls"
```

Now that we've discussed the specifics of each WSH-compatible language, let's look at the `WScript` object that is provided to all Windows Script Host programs.

Using the `WScript` Object

Windows Script Host provides a built-in object named `WScript` for all scripts in all languages. We've used its `Echo` method in many of the examples in this book. `WScript` has several other methods and properties, as listed in Reference List 3.3, that you may find useful in writing scripts.

REFERENCE LIST 3.3 Properties and Methods of the `WScript` Object.

Properties:

`Arguments`

Returns a collection of `WshArguments` objects, representing the strings on the command line used to start WScript or Cscript. For example, if a script is started with the command

continues

REFERENCE LIST 3.3 Continued

WScript myscript.vbs aaa bbb

then `WScript.arguments.item(0)` would yield "aaa" and `WScript.arguments.item(1)` would yield "bbb". `WScript.arguments.length` gives the number of arguments.

I'll discuss arguments in more detail in Chapter 10, "Deploying Scripts for Network Management."

FullName

Returns the full path and filename of the Windows Script Host program that is running your script (for example, `"c:\Windows\System32\cscript.exe"`).

Interactive

A Boolean value: `True` if the script is running in Interactive mode and `False` if in Batch mode. You may set this property using the `//I` or `//B` switch on the command line, or you may directly set the value in a script (for example, `WScript.Interactive = False`). In Batch mode, message and input boxes will not appear.

Name

Returns the name of the script host program (for example, `"Windows Script Host"`).

Path

Returns the name of the directory containing the script host program (for example, `"c:\Windows\System32"`).

ScriptFullName

Returns the full path and name of your script file (for example, `"c:\test\myscript.vbs"`).

ScriptName

Returns the name of your script file (for example, `myscript.vbs`).

StdErr, StdIn, and StdOut

These are file streams that can be used to read from the standard input or write to the standard output and error files. I'll discuss these in Chapter 4. Available with Cscript only.

Version

Returns the version of Windows Script Host (for example, `"Version 5.1"`).

Methods:

CreateObject(*progid* [, *prefix*])

Similar to the built-in `CreateObject` function. With a *`prefix`* argument, it creates connected objects that can communicate events to the script. (Events are beyond the scope of this book.)

ConnectObject(*object*, *prefix***)**
Connects an existing ***object*** to the script using event handler functions whose names begin with the string ***prefix***.

DisconnectObject(*object***)**
Disconnects the script from an object's events.

Echo *arg* [, *arg*]...
Displays any number of arguments of any type, formatted as strings and separated by spaces. Cscript writes them to the standard output, whereas WScript displays them in a pop-up message box.

GetObject(*filename* [, *progid*][, *prefix*]**)**
Creates an object based on information stored in a file (for example, a document). If ***progid*** is not specified, it is determined from the file type. ***prefix*** may be specified to connect object events to the script.

`GetObject` can also obtain a reference to a preexisting object by specifying a special name called a *moniker*. This will be illustrated extensively in Chapters 7 and 8.

Quit [*errorcode*]
Terminates the script. If a numeric value is specified, it is returned as the process's exit code—this can be useful when running scripts from batch files.

Sleep *msec*
Causes the script to pause for ***msec*** milliseconds. For example, `WScript.sleep(1000)` pauses for one second.

Of the properties and methods listed, the most useful is the `Arguments` property.

Retrieving Command-Line Arguments

The use of command-line arguments is a common way of specifying information to a script at the moment it's run. The most common use for this is to write scripts that manipulate files, user accounts, or computers. The script can be written in a generic way, and you can specify the particular files, people, or what-have-you at the time you run the script. For example, a script to process a file could be written like this:

```
filename = "specialdocument.doc"
'statements to operate on the file named filename
...
```

However, if you wanted to use this script to work with a different file, you'd have to edit the script. If you want a more general-purpose script, you can write the script to get the filenames from its command line, so you can simply type something like this:

```
C:\> cscript myscript.vbs some.doc another.doc
```

Usually, each programming language has its own way of providing command-line arguments to a program, but in the Windows Script Host environment, there is only one way they are obtained: Through the `WScript` object's `Arguments` property.

The WScript.Arguments property returns a collection of objects, one for each item listed on the script's command line. You can write a script to use these arguments this way, more or less:

```
for each filename in WScript.arguments
    ' statements to operate on the file named filename
    ...
next
```

Of course, you'll have to use whatever method of manipulating objects and collections is appropriate to the script language you're using (this example is in VBScript). With the command line

```
C:\> cscript myscript.vbs some.doc another.doc
```

the WScript.Arguments collection will have two items: some.doc and another.doc. In VBScript, the for each statement will let your script process them in turn.

If you don't specify any command-line arguments, though, this script will do nothing at all. It's best to have a script tell the user how to use it properly in this case. Here's a scheme for writing command-line scripts that you'll find to be very handy.

Pattern

When a script uses command-line arguments to specify what files (or users, computers, or whatever) to work with, it should at the very least explain how to use the script if no arguments are specified:

```
if WScript.arguments.length = 0
    WScript.echo "This script processes the named files"
    WScript.echo "by doing etc etc etc to them".
    WScript.echo "Usage: myscript file [file ...]"
    WScript.quit
end if
for each filename in WScript.arguments
    'process filename
    ...
next
```

Alternatively, you might want your script to operate on a default file if no files are named on the command line. Such a script should use a subroutine to do the actual processing of the files so that the subroutine can be called with the default file or with specified files. In VBScript, it would look like this:

```
if WScript.arguments.length = 0
    process "default.file"
else
    for each filename in WScript.arguments
        process filename
    next
end if
```

```
sub process (filename)
    ' statements to process filename
    ...
end sub
```

In Chapter 10 I'll show how to use more powerful types of command-line processing.

Locating and Using Unusual Objects

Several powerful, commonly used objects provided with Windows are documented by Microsoft in the Windows Scripting reference documents, and I'll discuss most of these in Chapters 4 through 10 and in Appendix C, "WSF and WSC File Format Reference." If you're new to scripting, these will be enough to get you started, so you may just want to skip ahead to Chapter 4.

In addition to these standard objects, many developers and companies provide add-in objects for free or for sale. You can find many of these listed at `http://www.microsoft.com/com/tech/activex.asp` and on the many Web sites devoted to ActiveX and to scripting. Some of these sites are listed on pages 41-42.

There is, however, a wealth of objects already on your computer: Hundreds of COM objects are supplied with Windows, and hundreds more are added if you install applications such as Word, Excel, and Visio. Many were designed just for the use of specific application programs and are of no use to script authors. Others are general-purpose objects for use by scripts and by compiled programs. How can you tell what objects are installed on your computer and of those, which are useful for scripting? To be honest, identifying useful objects is tricky business. But if you enjoy detective work, read on.

To get an idea of what I mean by "hundreds of objects," take a look at the Windows Registry.

Caution

Improper changes to the Windows Registry can make your computer nonfunctional. There is no undo command in the Registry Editor, so be very careful not to make *any* changes while examining the Registry.

To view the Registry, click Start, Run, type **`regedit`**, and press Enter. Expand the entry for `HKEY_CLASSES_ROOT` and scroll down past the `.xxx`-format entries into the entries that spell out names like "something dot something," as shown in Figure 3.4. Most of the entries from here down represent object classes; you can tell which ones do by the presence of a `CLSID` or `CurrVer` key under the object name.

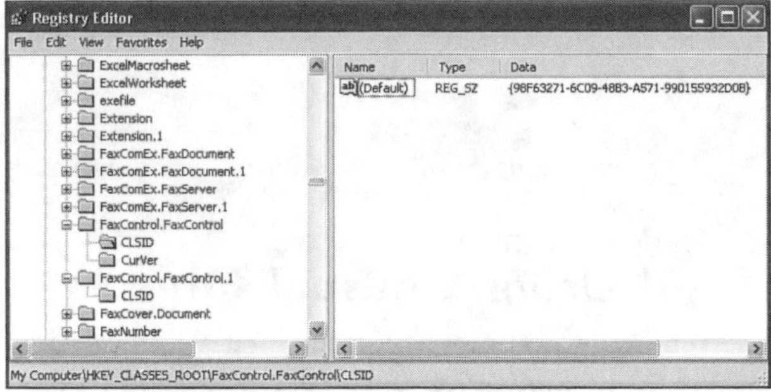

Figure 3.4 COM object classes are listed in the Registry under `HKEY_CLASSES_ROOT`, after the `.xxx` entries. Objects have an associated `CLSID` entry.

In Figure 3.4, the `FaxControl.FaxControl.1` entry has a `CLSID` entry, so it is an object. A `CLSID` (or *class ID*) is a very long, essentially random number that object authors use to give their object a unique "fingerprint." A `CurrVer` entry, such as the one found under `FaxControl.FaxControl` is used when there's a chance more than one version of the class program might be installed on your computer. The `CurrVer` value tells Windows where to look to find the class information for the most recent version of the object. Find that entry, and you'll find the object's `CLSID`.

The first step in scouting out new and interesting objects is to peruse the Registry for names that sound interesting. For this example, I'll follow up the `FaxControl.FaxControl.1` object from Figure 3.4.

When you've found a `CLSID` value for a potentially interesting object, locate the matching value under `My Computer\HKEY_CLASSES_ROOT\Clsid`, where you'll find the information Windows uses to locate and run the program file that actually manages the object.

Figure 3.5 shows the class information for `FaxControl.FaxControl.1`. The `InprocServer32` entry shows the actual program module (usually a DLL or OCX file) that manages the object. In this case, the program is `\WINDOWS\system32\Setup\fxsocm.dll`. The name of this object and the location of its DLL make it sound like it might be used for setting up the Fax service. But how?

The first thing that you have to check is whether the object is even suitable for use in script programs; some aren't. The first test, then, is to see whether you can create an object in your chosen scripting language. Use the ***`server.object`*** name that you found under `HKEY_CLASSES_ROOT`. In VBScript, it would look like this:

```
set obj = CreateObject("FaxControl.FaxControl.1")
WScript.echo "CreateObject worked!"
```

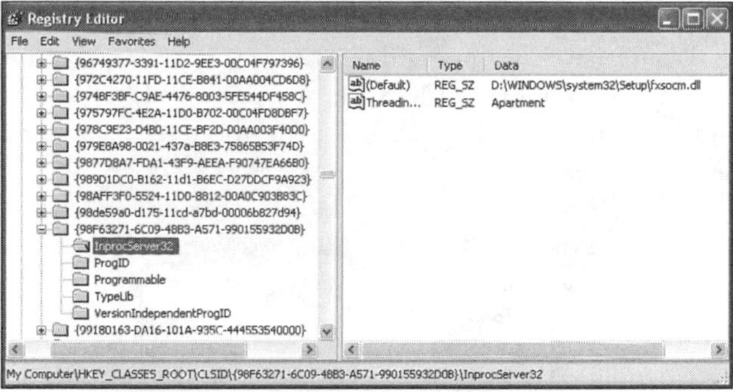

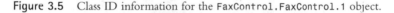

Figure 3.5 Class ID information for the `FaxControl.FaxControl.1` object.

If this script produces an error message, the object can't be used in scripts. If it runs without an error message, as it did when I tested `FaxControl.FaxControl.1`, the object has passed the first hurdle.

Tip

On `www.helpwinxp.com/hood`, I've listed all the undocumented objects provided with Windows XP that pass this test—to scout for interesting objects, start with that listing.

Now comes the hard part: extracting information about the object's methods and properties. In some cases, Microsoft or the object's creator will have supplied a help file describing the object. See if the `Clsid` registry values list has a help file ending in `.hlp` or `.chm`. If it does, at a command prompt type

```
start pathname\helpfile.xxx
```

where *`pathname\helpfile.xxx`* is the full path to the help file listed in the Registry. This may show you how the object works. In the case of `FaxControl.FaxControl.1`, there is no help file.

If no help file is named, don't give up. Because COM objects are designed to be used by many different programming languages, they have to record the types of values their properties and methods use—numeric, string, date, and so on—and they have to make this information available to any program that asks. You may be able to burrow into the object's program file to find this information.

The easiest way to do this is with an *object browser*, a program that's designed to do just this sort of burrowing. Microsoft provides one with many of its applications. If you have Microsoft Word, Excel, or PowerPoint, the Object Browser is included as part of the Macro Editor. Start the application and click Tools, Macro, Visual Basic Editor. Then click View, Object Browser. If you have the full developer's version of Visual Basic installed, run it and click View, Object Browser.

To view information for a questionable class, you'll need to tell Word (or Visual Basic, and so on) to look into the class's program file. To do this, click Tools, References. Click Browse and locate the DLL or OCX file you found in the Registry. Click Open, and the library will appear as a checked item in the Available References list, as shown in Figure 3.6.

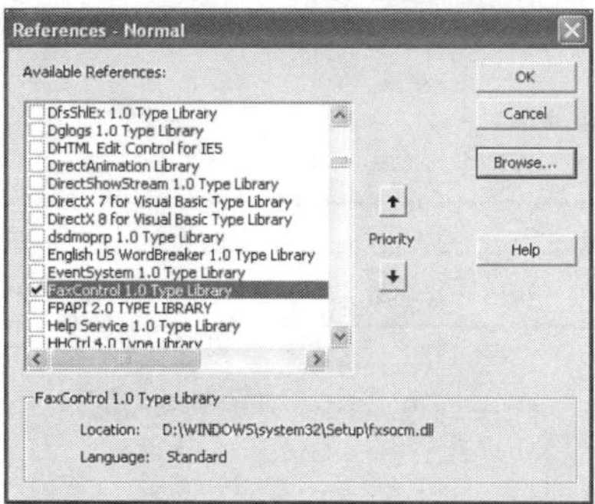

Figure 3.6 Selecting an object class type library to view in the Object Browser.

When the object type is listed and checked under Available References, click OK.

Then, select the class name from the library list in the upper-left corner of the Object Browser window, as shown in Figure 3.7. Choose object types in the left panel, and the browser will display the object's methods, procedures, and predefined constants in the right panel under "Members." You can select the objects in this list one by one, and in the bottom panel, the browser will display the method or procedure's arguments, if any, and any explanatory text it can dig up.

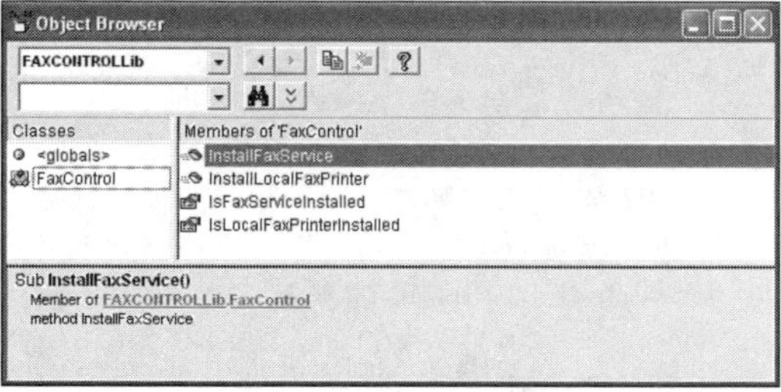

Figure 3.7 Viewing a class's type information in the Object Browser.

If you don't have any of the applications I've mentioned, another tool, called the OLE/COM Object Viewer, is provided as part of Visual C++ as well as with the Windows XP and Windows 2000 Resource Kits. You can also download it from `www.microsoft.com` by searching for "OLE/COM Object Viewer."

The OLE/COM Object Viewer is much more difficult to use than the Object Browser. Here are some tips for using this viewer:

- Try to find the object of interest under Object Classes, All Objects. I've found that not all the objects I'm interested in are listed there. For example, `Scripting.Dictionary` is present, whereas `Scripting.FileSystemObject` is missing. If you can't find it there, look under Type Libraries.
- Double-click the library or object to view its class information. This information is designed for COM object programmers, not end users, so it's going to be tough to understand.
- `Typedef` items list some predefined constant values used by all the objects provided by the server.
- `Coclass` items define the objects that the class server can create. If you view the contents of a coclass item, you'll find the class's predefined constants, properties, and methods.

You should also search the Internet for references to the object name (for example, search for `FaxControl.FaxControl.1` or `FaxControl.FaxControl`) or the program file itself. I've found that `google.com` is a great place to start. Be sure to search both the Web and Groups directories. Many programmers haunt the `comp.`*`xxx`* groups, and you may find an archived discussion about the object.

Although either object browser can show you what sorts of values the methods and properties expect and return, it can't tell you what these values mean, so you'll have to experiment to find out if and how you can use them. In the case of `FaxControl.FaxControl.1`, the Object Browser showed two properties and two methods, as listed in Reference List 3.4.

REFERENCE LIST 3.4 Properties and Methods of the `FaxControl.FaxControl` Object.

`IsFaxServiceInstalled`
Property; returns a Boolean value.

`IsLocalFaxPrinterInstalled`
Property; returns Boolean value.

`InstallFaxService`
Method; returns no value and takes no arguments.

`InstallLocalFaxPrinter`
Method; returns no value and takes no arguments.

This sounds pretty straightforward. There are no arguments to supply to these methods, so there's no detective work required there. Also, the names sound pretty self-explanatory. This object lets you know whether the Fax service and the Fax Printer are installed, and it can install them. But does it work?

Here's a sample script I wrote to check:

```
set obj = CreateObject("FaxControl.FaxControl.1")
WScript.echo "IsFaxServiceInstalled =", obj.IsFaxServiceInstalled
WScript.echo "IsLocalFaxPrinterInstalled =", obj.IsLocalFaxPrinterInstalled
```

The results when I ran it on a Windows XP computer that had a modem but did not have the fax service set up were

```
IsFaxServiceInstalled = 0
IsLocalFaxPrinterInstalled = 0
```

When I ran the script

```
set obj = CreateObject("FaxControl.FaxControl.1")
obj.InstallFaxService
```

Windows Setup asked for my Windows XP CD disk and installed the Fax service and printer. The first script's output became this:

```
IsFaxServiceInstalled = -1
IsLocalFaxPrinterInstalled = -1
```

Here, `-1` means `True`, (any nonzero value means True) so the object really does the job you'd expect it to. Here's a script that can automatically be sure a user's Windows XP system has the Fax service as well as a fax and printer installed:

```
set obj = CreateObject("FaxControl.FaxControl.1")

if not obj.IsFaxServiceInstalled then
    WScript.echo "Installing Fax Service..."
    obj.InstallFaxService
elseif not obj.IsLocalFaxPrinterInstalled then
    WScript.echo "Reinstalling Fax Printer..."
    obj.InstallLocalFaxPrinter
else
    WScript.echo "Fax printer is ready to go."
end if
```

This works like a charm. Of course, it's easier to do this same thing from the Windows XP user interface in the Printers and Faxes folder. Nevertheless, this is a good example of the functionality you can find by digging into the many objects that come with Windows, and it shows the kinds of scripts you can write to manage Windows computers so that other users don't have to poke around with the Control Panel themselves.

4
File and Registry Access

ROAD MAP

- This chapter shows how to use "stock" objects provided with Windows Script Host to manipulate and read files, folders, and the Registry.
- You should be comfortable with the material in Chapter 3, "Scripting and Objects," before reading this chapter.
- Each object can do more than I have room to describe. I'll give examples of the most important functions, and you can use the reference information to see what other functions are available.
- The first time through each section, I suggest that you skim the lists of methods and properties, study the examples, and then go back through the reference tables.

Getting Real Work Done

THE FIRST THREE CHAPTERS OF THIS BOOK covered Windows Script Host, gave an overview of VBScript programming, and showed how to use Windows COM/ActiveX objects. Now, we get to start applying all that background information toward useful ends.

In this and the following chapters, I'll discuss several powerful COM objects provided with Windows that you can use when writing scripts. These objects can manipulate files, run programs, reconfigure Windows, and help with network administration. As I introduce these objects, I'll give real-world examples of script programs that you can use in their entirety or as the basis for writing scripts of your own.

In the rest of the chapters on scripting, I'll use VBScript almost exclusively. If you use a different language, just remember that regardless of what programming language you use, the concepts remain the same, and the objects work in *exactly* the same way. You'll have to account for the peculiarities of your language's syntax and its way of handling collection objects, but the tips in Chapter 3 should make that job fairly straightforward.

Note

For beginning programmers, I'll start this chapter with a more tutorial approach to the `Scripting.FileSystemObject` object. Later in the chapter and in subsequent chapters, I'll adopt a more to-the-point style. Although I'll still use some short program fragments to illustrate points, I'll start presenting longer scripts in order to show how all the concepts fit together to make a useful program.

Manipulating Files and Folders

One of the principal reasons people write scripts is to work with files and folders. Although Windows Explorer makes it very easy to use the mouse to copy and move files, when you have a large number of files and folders to work with, the GUI can quickly become very tedious. Here are some tasks that would be a nightmare with Explorer but are a snap with scripting:

- Renaming several files
- Changing the attributes of all the files in a folder and in all levels of subfolders underneath it
- Printing all DOC files under 1MB in size from a Zip disk with Word and all of the BMP image files with the Paint program
- Periodically scanning a folder for files with a certain name or file type and automatically printing or processing them in some way

Most scripting tasks involving files and folders use the object `FileSystemObject`, so we'll start there.

Scripting.FileSystemObject

The `Scripting.FileSystemObject` object is provided with Windows Scripting Host as a "helper" object. Its methods, properties, and subobjects give you most of the tools you'll need to work with files. Many VBScript scripts start with the statement

```
set fso = CreateObject("Scripting.FileSystemObject")
```

which creates an instance of `FileSystemObject` and stores it in the variable `fso`. It's only necessary to create one instance per script program—if you create it as a global variable, it will be available to all parts of your script and any of its subroutines or functions.

Note

In some of the script fragment examples that follow in this chapter, I'll use an object named `fso` but won't explicitly show the `CreateObject` call. You can assume that in any example, `fso` is a `FileSystemObject` object that was created at the beginning of the script.

Reference List 4.1 lists the `FileSystemObject` methods and properties. We'll use many of them in the examples to follow throughout this chapter. Arguments to `Scripting.FileSystemObject` methods are strings, unless described otherwise.

Note

In these properties and methods, where a filename or folder name is called for, you can specify a full path starting with a drive letter, or you can enter a relative path. If the path you use doesn't start with a drive letter, the path is assumed to belong on the current drive. If the path doesn't start with a backslash, the path is assumed to be relative to the current working directory on the current or specified drive. For example, if the current directory is `c:\text` when you run your script, Windows will interpret the path `\temp` as `c:\temp`, and will interpret the filename `subfolder\something.doc` as `c:\text\subfolder\something.doc`.

REFERENCE LIST 4.1 Property and Methods of `Scripting.FileSystemObject`

Property:

`Drives`

Returns a collection of `Drive` objects, one for each physical or mapped network drive on the local machine.

Methods:

`BuildPath(`*`path, name`*`)`

Appends a file name to a pathname and returns the combined string. Takes care of adding any necessary : or \ characters. For example, `fso.BuildPath("C:\temp", "file.dat")` returns `"C:\temp\file.dat"`.

`CopyFile` *`source, destination`* [*`,overwrite`*]

Copies one or more files from one location to another. The `source` argument can contain wildcards in the filename, if desired. The `destination` argument can be a filename or a folder name. If the Boolean argument `overwrite` is specified and is `False`, and if the destination folder already contains a file with the same name as the source file, the script will terminate with an error; otherwise, existing files will be overwritten. The default value for `overwrite` is `True`. There is no return value, so you do not need to use parentheses when calling this method.

continues

REFERENCE LIST 4.1 Continued

`CopyFolder` *`source, destination`* [, *`overwrite`*]

Copies a folder named by the `source` argument from one location to another. Any files and subfolders are copied as well. If the destination folder already exists, the contents of the source folder are added to it, and for the contents, the `overwrite` flag works the same as it does with `CopyFile`. You can copy multiple folders by specifying a wildcard in the `source` name. A wildcard can only be used in the last name in the path, however.

`CreateFolder(`*`foldername`***`)`**

Creates a folder. The method will generate an error if the folder already exists, so you should use `FolderExists` to check before calling `CreateFolder`. `CreateFolder` will only create the lowest level folder in the specified path. The call

```
fso.CreateFolder("C:\a\b\c")
```

only works if `C:\a\b` already exists. Later in the chapter, I'll show you how to write a subroutine that can create a subfolder even when the upper-level folders don't yet exist. The method returns a `Folder` object representing the new folder.

`CreateTextFile(`*`filename`*[, *`overwrite`*[, *`unicode`*]]**`)`**

Creates a file with the specified name and returns a `TextStream` object that can be used to read from or write to the file. Text streams are discussed later in the chapter. The optional arguments are as follows:

- *`overwrite`*. If this argument is omitted or is `True`, and the specified file already exists, the original file will be deleted and a new one created. If this argument is specified as `False`, an error will occur if the file already exists. The default value is `True`.
- *`unicode`*. If this argument is specified and `True`, the file will be created using Unicode encoding. If this argument is omitted or `False`, the file will be created using ASCII.

`DeleteFile` *`filespec`* [, *`force`*]

Deletes a specified file. The deleted file is *not* placed in the Recycle Bin—it's *gone*. Read-only files will not be deleted unless the Boolean parameter `force` is specified and is `True`. You can delete multiple files by using a wildcard in the filename part of *`filespec`*.

`DeleteFolder` *`folderspec`* [, *`force`*]

Deletes a specified folder and its entire contents. The deleted files and folders are *not* saved in the Recycle Bin. Read-only folders and files will not be deleted unless the Boolean parameter `force` is specified and is `True`. If *`force`* is omitted or is `False`, `DeleteFolder` will stop with an error partway through the task if it encounters a read-only file. You can delete multiple folders by specifying a wildcard in the source name. A wildcard can only be used in the last name in the path, however.

DriveExists(*drive*)
Returns True if the specified drive (for example, "B:") exists; otherwise, it returns False.

FileExists(*filename*)
Returns True if the specified file exists; otherwise, it returns False.

FolderExists(*folder*)
Returns True if the specified folder exists; otherwise, it returns False.

GetAbsolutePathName(*pathspec*)
Returns a complete, fully qualified filename or pathname from any filename or pathname. If the specified path is relative, the current directory is used to construct the absolute path. For example, if the current directory is c:\text when you run your script, GetAbsolutePathName("some.doc") will return "c:\text\some.doc".

GetBaseName(*filepath*)
Returns the base name of the specified file, less any path or file extension. If filepath names a path and not a filename, it returns the last folder name in the path. Be warned, though: In this case, if the last folder has something that looks like a file extension in its name(.xxx), GetBaseName will remove it. Use GetFileName if you want the final folder name in a path.

GetDrive(*drivespec*)
Returns a Drive object corresponding to the specified drive. Although it would make sense that GetDrive would just look at the drive letter specified in drivespec, you cannot pass GetDrive a full pathname or the script will generate an error. You can use GetDriveName to extract just the drive.

GetDriveName(*path*)
Returns the name of the drive used in the specified path.

GetExtensionName(*path*)
Returns the extension name for the last file or folder in a path, that is, any characters after the last period in the name. (This can be handy to get the extension of a file, but it isn't very useful with folder names, because the extension of a folder name is rarely given any meaning.)

GetFile(*filespec*)
Returns a Scripting.File object corresponding to the specified file. You can use this object to change the file's name and attributes, as discussed later in this chapter.

GetFileName(*pathspec*)
Returns the name of the file or the last folder name in the specified path. GetFileName is like GetBaseName and GetExtensionName, but it returns the combined name and extension.

continues

REFERENCE LIST 4.1 Continued

`GetFolder(`*`folderspec`*`)`

Returns a `Folder` object corresponding to the specified folder pathname (for example, `"C:\temp"`). You can use this object to change the folder's name and attributes as well as to examine its contents, as discussed later in this chapter.

`GetParentFolderName(`*`path`*`)`

Returns everything up to the last item in `path`. This must be used with a path specification that does not contain a filename.

`GetSpecialFolder(`*`folderspec`*`)`

Returns the actual path of the specified special folder, as actually installed on the local computer. `Folderspec` is one of the following values:

Constant	Value	Description
`WindowsFolder`	0	The actual name of your Windows folder
`SystemFolder`	1	The actual name of the `Windows\System32` folder
`TemporaryFolder`	2	The folder used for temporary and scratch files

`GetTempName()`

Returns a randomly generated name that can be used as a scratch file. No folder name is provided. To make a temporary file in a designated temporary folder, use the name returned by

```
fso.BuildPath(fso.GetSpecialFolder(TemporaryFolder),    fso.GetTempName())
```

`GetTempName` doesn't create a file; it just gives you a name that's very unlikely to be used by an already existing file.

`MoveFile` *`source, destination`*

Moves one or more files from one location to another. `Source` can be a filename or a filename containing wildcards. *`Destination`* can be a folder name or a filename. If *`destination`* is a folder, be sure that the name you specify ends with a backslash (\) so that it's clear to Windows that you're specifying a folder rather than a filename. On Windows XP, if the destination is on the same volume (drive and partition), it is simply renamed; otherwise, it is copied and the original is deleted. The destination folder must already exist.

If a destination file already exists or the source name contains wildcards and no files match, an error occurs. If an error occurs partway through moving files, any already moved files will remain moved.

`MoveFolder` *`source, destination`*

Moves one or more folders from one location to another. Any subfolders are moved too. If the last folder in the destination path does not already exist, it is created.

`OpenTextFile(filename [,iomode [,create [,format]]])`

Opens the specified file and returns a `TextStream` object that can be used to read from, write to, or append to the file. The optional arguments are as follows:

- *`iomode`*. Determines the way the file is to be used. Here's a list of the allowed values:

Constant	Value	Description
`ForReading`	1	Opens the file for reading. This is the default value.
`ForWriting`	2	Opens the file for writing. Any existing content in a preexisting file of the same name is erased.
`ForAppending`	8	Opens the file for writing and adds whatever is written to the end of any preexisting contents.

- *`create`*. Determines whether a new file is to be created if the specified file doesn't already exist. If this argument is specified and `True`, the file will be created. If this argument is `False`, the file must already exist. The default value is `False`.
- *`format`*. Specifies the file encoding to use. Here's a list of the allowed values:

Constant	Description
`TristateTrue`	Opens or creates the file using Unicode.
`TristateFalse`	Uses ASCII.
`TristateUseDefault`	Uses the system default. This is the default value.

As you can see, the methods that `FileSystemObject` provides fall into two main categories: utility functions that help you manipulate filenames and test for file and folder existence, and methods that return objects corresponding to drives, files, and folders. We'll discuss the utility functions first and then go over the drive, file, and folder objects.

Working with File and Path Names

In scripts that manipulate files and folders you'll often want to construct full pathnames to files by combining a filename with a pathname. You'll run into this when copying and renaming files, creating temporary files, and so on. Fully qualified pathnames look something like this:

```
c:\documents and settings\bknittel\my documents\chapter.doc
```

When you're creating a fully qualified name by joining a pathname (drive and/or folder) with a filename, it's not always as simple as sticking the two parts together with a backslash in between, as in this example:

```
filename = "chapter.doc"
path     = "c:\documents and settings\bknittel\my documents"
fullpath = path & "\" & filename
```

The problem is that someone might specify the path as "a":, intending to copy a file to the *current* folder of drive A. However, this sample program would produce the name `a:\chapter.doc`, which places the file in the *root* folder of drive A. Furthermore, if someone enters a path such as "`c:\temp\`", the program will produce `c:\temp\\chapter.doc`, which is technically an improper filename. (Such a name works, but it's not good practice to count on it working in the future.)

The solution to this problem is to use the `BuildPath` method provided with `FileSystemObject`. Its job is to join paths with filenames, and it takes these details into account. The preceding sample program can be rewritten this way:

```
filename = "chapter.doc"
path     = "c:\documents and settings\bknittel\my documents"
fullpath = fso.BuildPath(path, filename)
```

`FileSystemObject` comes with several additional methods to help you manipulate paths' filenames: `GetAbsolutePathName`, `GetBaseName`, `GetDrive`, `GetDriveName`, `GetExtensionName`, `GetFileName`, and `GetParentFolderName`. You can use these methods in scripts to tear apart filenames into their component pieces.

As an example, if you were writing a script to convert a folder full of GIF files to JPG files, you'd need a way to come up with the desired output filenames given the input names. The easiest way to do this is to use the `GetBaseName` method, which removes both a filename's path and its extension. Given the base name, we can stick on a new extension and folder name to get the desired output filename.

Here's a script fragment that processes all GIF files in a given input folder and from them creates JPG files in an output folder:

```
set fso = CreateObject("Scripting.FileSystemObject")
infolder  = "C:\pictures\received"
outfolder = "C:\pictures\converted"

for each file in fso.GetFolder(infolder).Files
    if ucase(fso.GetExtensionName(file.name)) = "GIF" then
        basename = fso.GetBaseName(file.name)
        giffile  = fso.BuildPath(infolder, basename & ".GIF")
        jpgfile  = fso.BuildPath(outfolder, basename & ".JPG")
        convertGIFtoJPG giffile, jpgfile

        ' if the conversion succeeded, delete the original file
        if fso.FileExists(jpgfile) then file.Delete
```

```
    end if
loop

sub convertGIFtoJPG (giffile, jpgfile)
    . . .
    (conversion routine to create JPG from GIF would go here.
     such a routine would probably use an image processing object of some sort)
    . . .
end sub
```

Here are several points to take note of:

- The `for each` loop runs through once for each of the files in `infolder`. `GetFolder` returns a `Folder` object; `.Files` returns a collection of all the files in that folder; `for each` iterates through all the items in the collection. On each turn, `file` is a `Scripting.File` object representing one file.
- `fso.GetFileExtension(file.name)` returns just the extension part of the file's name, which it obtains from the file object's `name` property (we'll cover the file object shortly). `Ucase` turns it to uppercase before comparing it to "GIF"; otherwise, if the file's extension happened to be "gif" (in lowercase), it would not be matched.
- The statements inside the `if` statement process each of the GIF files in folder `infolder`. If `infolder` holds files other than GIF files, they won't be bothered by this script.
- The script uses `GetBasename` to extract just the part of the filename after the path and before ".gif", joins the extension ".jpg" to this, and uses `BuildPath` to join this with the output folder name. The result is that for each GIF file in `inpath`, the subroutine `convertGIFtoJPG` will be called once with the input GIF filename and the desired output JPG filename.

Deleting and Renaming Files

The `DeleteFile` method is a straightforward counterpart to the command-line `del` command. For example, the statement

```
fso.Deletefile("c:\temp\somefile.tmp")
```

deletes file `c:\temp\somefile.tmp`. You should specify a full path to the file you want to delete unless you are very sure that you know what the script's current working directory is.

To rename a file, the best approach is to obtain its `Scripting.File` object and change the object's `Name` property. I'll discuss the `File` object later in this chapter, but as a sneak preview, you might use a statement like this:

```
fso.GetFile("c:\temp\newfile.tmp").Name = "newfile.doc"
```

You can also rename a file using the `MoveFile` method. However, `MoveFile` treats the *`destination`* name as a pathname, so the statement

```
fso.MoveFile("c:\temp\newfile.tmp", "newfile.doc")
```

will not only rename the file `newfile.tmp` but will also move it from the folder `c:\temp` to the script's current working directory. If this is not what you wanted, you would have to use the full pathname for the destination name:

```
fso.MoveFile("c:\temp\newfile.tmp", "c:\temp\newfile.doc")
```

Creating a Folder

If your task requires you to create or move files into a particular folder, it might be a nice idea to have the script ensure that the destination folder exists, especially if the script is meant to run on computers other than your own.

The `Scripting.FileSystemObject` object's `CreateFolder` method can do this for you. If you are planning on using a folder named `C:\myscript\output`, you might be tempted to put a statement like the following at the top of your script so that the folder will always be there if you need it:

```
fso.CreateFolder("C:\myscript\output")
```

However, there are two problems with this:

- If the folder already exists, Windows Script Host will stop with an error message.
- `CreateFolder` can only create the lowest-level folder in a path. In the example, if `C:\myscript` doesn't already exist, `CreateFolder` can't create both `myscript` and `output` at once. Again, WSH stops with an error.

The way to solve a problem such as this is to *extend* the functionality of a built-in function. This can be done by writing a subroutine that your script can use to do a more thorough job. Here's a script containing such a subroutine to create folders—an extended version of `CreateFolder` called `CreateFullPath`. The first two lines of this script comprise a simple "main program"—they are the main body of the script. The rest of the script is the subroutine `CreateFullPath`. Here's the script:

```
                                        ' Example file script0401.vbs
set fso = CreateObject("Scripting.FileSystemObject")
CreateFullPath "c:\myscript\output"

' ------------------------------------------------------------------
' Subroutine CreateFullPath creates the folder specified by 'path,'
' creating any intermediate folders as necessary. (Note: parameter 'path'
' is specified as 'byval' because we modify it inside the subroutine).
' ------------------------------------------------------------------
sub CreateFullPath (byval path)
    dim parent                          ' temporary variable
```

```
    path   = fso.GetAbsolutePathname(path) ' be sure path is fully qualified
    parent = fso.GetParentFolderName(path) ' get name of parent folder

    if not fso.FolderExists(parent) then   ' if parent(s) does not exist...
         CreateFullPath parent             ' ...create it
    end if

    if not fso.FolderExists(path) then     ' if subfolder does not exist...
        fso.CreateFolder(path)             ' ...create it.
    end if
end sub
```

Protecting Parameters

In the example used here, `Path` isn't an ordinary variable; it's a parameter passed to `CreateFullPath` by the caller. What happens when you modify the value of a parameter to a function or subroutine?

There are two ways parameters can be passed: by *value* and by *reference*. When a parameter is passed by value, the subroutine gets a "copy" of the parameter value, so there is no problem if the subroutine modifies it. When a parameter is passed by reference, changes *can* make their way back to the calling procedure, if the value is a variable and not an expression.

In VBScript, you can explicitly declare parameters as `byval` or `byref`; the default in VBScript is `byref`, so without adding `byval` in `CreateFullPath` modifications to `path` would be reflected back to the caller's variable. In this subroutine, it's best to specify `byval` so the change can't propagate back. In this example it doesn't matter, but if used in other circumstances, it could.

Note that in JScript, this doesn't come up—all parameters are always passed by value.

You can use this subroutine in any script that needs to create a folder. This way, your script will never be tripped up because the desired folder already exists or because a parent folder doesn't exist.

How does it work? The `CreateFullPath` subroutine uses the `GetParentFolderName` method to get the name of the folder *above* the lowest one specified in `path`—its parent—and if it does not exist, creates it first. Only then, and only if necessary, does it create the final folder in `path`.

The trick in this subroutine is in the way it creates the parent folder: It calls *itself* to do the job. That way, `CreateFullPath` applies the same technique to ensure that the folder *above* the parent folder exists, and so on, up to the root folder.

This programming technique is called *recursion*, and it's quite powerful. It's used most effectively when you can divide a job up into smaller pieces and use the same procedure to handle each piece. I'll show other examples of recursion later in this chapter. It's an especially common technique when working with folders, because folders themselves are inherently recursive: Folders contain folders which contain folders.

If you want to write your own scripts or programs that use recursion, here are three tips:

- Initially, use debugging printout statements to have the script tell you what it's doing while it runs. For example, when I wrote `CreateFullPath`, I used `wscript.echo` to print out `path` at the beginning of `CreateFullPath`; this let me see if, when, and how it was called each time.
- Be sure that any variables you use to compute items inside the subroutine are local variables, which are created for each instance of the subroutine. Because several copies of `CreateFullPath` may be working at the same time, you have to be sure they don't attempt to use the same variables to store information. In `CreateFullPath`, this is done with the statement `dim parent`. If you use VBScript and want to modify the value of a subprogram's parameters, as I did with `path` in `CreateFullPath`, you will probably want to use the keyword `byval` so that any changes don't affect the subroutine's caller.
- The tricky part with recursion is getting it to stop! `CreateFullPath` will keep moving up directories as long as the parent folder doesn't exist. It could work its way up to the root folder but will stop there because the root folder will always exist as long as the specified drive exists.

Copying a Folder

Copying the contents of folders is also a recursive process because the folder being copied could contain subfolders that also need to be copied. The CopyFolder method does this automatically. You can easily copy a folder from one location to another, as shown here:

```
fso.CopyFolder "C:\book\04", "D:\bookbackup\04"
```

This would copy the contents of `C:\book\04` to a folder on the D drive, and all files and subfolders would be copied too. (I used a script like this while writing this book to keep backup copies of each chapter on a Zip disk and on a networked computer.)

Note that, by default, `CopyFolder` will overwrite preexisting files. If you want to ensure that existing files not get overwritten, specify `False` as the third argument to `CopyFolder`.

The `Scripting.Drive` Object

The `Drive` object is returned by `FileSystemObject` and lets you find out how the drive is organized, how much free space it has, its online/ready status, and other useful information.

There are two ways to obtain a `Drive` object:

- You can get an object representing a specific drive using the `FileSystemObject` method `GetDrive`. Here's an example in VBScript:

```
set drv = fso.GetDrive("C:")
WScript.Echo "Drive C has", drv.FreeSpace, "bytes free"
```

- You can get a collection of all the drives in the computer using the `FileSystemObject` property `Drives`. You can then scan through the collection using the method appropriate to your scripting language. In VBScript, this might be as follows:

```
for each drv in fso.Drives
    if drv.IsReady then
        WScript.Echo "Drive", drv.DriveLetter, "has",_
            drv.FreeSpace, "bytes free"
    else
        WScript.Echo "Drive", drv.DriveLetter, "is not ready"
    end if
next
```

  Then, if you want, you can use `if` statements inside the `for` loop to select certain drives or types of drives.

The `Drive` object has a passel of properties that can tell you about the drive's free/used space, its online status, and its drive type. Reference List 4.2 lists the `Drive` object's properties.

REFERENCE LIST 4.2 Properties of the Drive Object

`AvailableSpace`

Returns the number of bytes on the drive available to the script's user. May be lower than `FreeSpace` if disk quotas are in effect. Works on both network and local drives. This property is read-only, which means you can use the property's value but you can't assign it a new value.

`DriveLetter`

Returns the drive letter of the `Drive` object as a string (for example, `"A"`). This property is read-only.

`DriveType`

Returns a value indicating the type of a specified drive. This property is read-only. Here are the possible values:

continues

REFERENCE LIST 4.2 Continued

Value	Meaning
0	Unknown drive type
1	Removable disk (floppy, Zip, etc.)
2	Fixed disk
3	Network (mapped) drive
4	CD-ROM or DVD
5	RAM disk

`FileSystem`

Returns the type of file system in use for the specified drive. Possible return values include `"FAT"`, `"NTFS"`, and `"CDFS"`. This property is read-only.

`FreeSpace`

Returns the number of free bytes on the disk. May be greater than `AvailableSpace` if disk quotas are in use. Read-only.

`IsReady`

Returns the Boolean value `True` if the specified drive is online and ready; otherwise, it returns `False`. This property tells you if a floppy or other removable disk drive has a disk inserted. Read-only.

`Path`

Returns the path for the drive (for example, `"C:"`). This property is read-only.

`RootFolder`

Returns a `Folder` object representing the root folder of the specified drive. (This property is read-only, although you can use the returned `Folder` object to do things to the root folder, as you'll see later.)

`SerialNumber`

Returns the unique decimal serial number that identifies all FAT and NTFS fixed and removable formatted disk volumes. Read-only.

`ShareName`

Returns the network share name for the specified drive, if the drive is a mapped network drive. Returns the empty string (`""`) if it's not a mapped drive. Read-only.

`TotalSize`

Returns the total space, in bytes, of the drive. Read-only.

`VolumeName`

Returns the volume name of the drive. This property is read/write, which means you can change a drive's volume name by assigning a new value to this property.

There are no methods for the `Drive` object. You can use the `Drive` object to collect and display information about drives, to check for sufficient free space, and to check whether drives actually exist and are ready before copying files to them.

Confirming That a Drive Exists

When you're copying or creating files, it's always a good idea to have a script ensure that the target drive letter exists and is ready to use—and to gracefully quit or offer a chance to amend the problem if it isn't.

Here's a script designed to copy files from one location to another. It first ensures that the destination drive exists and quits if the drive does not exist:

```
                                         ' Example file script0402.vbs
set fso = CreateObject("Scripting.FileSystemObject")

inpath  = "C:\book\04"
outpath = "G:\bookbackup\04"

set drv = fso.GetDrive(fso.GetDriveName(outpath))
if not drv.IsReady then
    msgbox "ZIP Drive is not ready"
    WScript.quit 1
end if

CreateFullPath outpath
fso.CopyFolder inpath, outpath
msgbox "Backup of " & inpath & " complete."

' -------------------------------------------------------------------
sub CreateFullPath (path)
   dim parent                            ' temporary variable

   path   = fso.GetAbsolutePathname(path) ' be sure path is fully qualified
   parent = fso.GetParentFolderName(path) ' get name of parent folder

   if not fso.FolderExists(parent) then   ' if necessary create parent(s)
        CreateFullPath parent
   end if

   if not fso.FolderExists(path) then     ' if necessary create subfolder
       fso.CreateFolder(path)
   end if
end sub
```

The `if not drv.IsReady` statement is the important part of this example. `fso.GetDrive` returns a `Drive` object corresponding to drive G:, and `IsReady` tests to see whether the drive is turned on, has a disk, and is ready to go. If the drive is not ready, the script displays a pop-up message and exits.

If the drive is ready, the script uses the CreateFullPath subroutine we discussed earlier to ensure that the output folder exists and then copies the folder's contents.

Finding a Drive with the Most Free Space

This sample script shows how to locate which drive has the most free space of all drives on the computer. Note that it uses IsReady to be sure that the drive is online before attempting to check the free space; otherwise, an offline disk drive will make the script stop with an error message:

```
                             ' Example file script0403.vbs
freedrv   = "?"              ' holds the best drive we've seen
freespace = 0                ' the amount of space free on freedrv
for each drv in fso.Drives
    if drv.IsReady then
        if drv.AvailableSpace > freespace then
            freespace = drv.AvailableSpace  ' this drive is better
            freedrv   = drv.DriveLetter     ' so remember its details
        end if
    end if
next
                                            ' report the results
Wscript.echo "Drive", freedrv, "has the most space:", freespace, "bytes."
```

At the end of the script, freespace is the amount of space on the drive with most space, and freedrv is the drive.

The Scripting.Folder Object

The Folder object returns information about the properties and contents of folders. Similar to the Drive object, you can obtain a Folder object to work with a specific, known folder, or you can get a collection of all the folders within a specific drive or folder.

To get information for a specific folder, use the GetFolder method. Here's an example:

```
set fso  = CreateObject("Scripting.FileSystemObject")
set fldr = fso.GetFolder("C:\temp")
```

To get a collection of all folders in a Folder object, use the SubFolders property with a Folder object:

```
fldrs = fldr.SubFolders
```

or

```
fldrs = fso.GetFolder("C:\temp").SubFolders
```

To get a Folder object for a special folder such as the Desktop or the Windows directory, you can use the FileSystemObject object's GetSpecialFolder method or the

`WScript.Shell.SpecialFolders` method to get the special folder's path and then use `GetFolder` to obtain the object. Here's an example that gets the `Folder` object for the `Temporary` file folder:

```
fldr = fso.GetFolder(fso.GetSpecialFolder(2))
```

Reference List 4.3 lists the `Folder` object's properties and methods.

REFERENCE LIST 4.3 Properties and Methods of the `Folder` Object

Properties:

`Attributes`

The file system attributes of the folder.

Folder attributes include read-only, system, hidden, compressed, and so on. Each possible attribute is represented by a numeric value, and the `Attributes` property is the sum of the values of the folder's actual attributes. (I'll demonstrate how this works in a sample program later in this section.) The `Attributes` property is basically read/write, although some attributes can't be changed by a script.

Table 4.1 lists the values of the `Attributes` property.

`DateCreated`

A date/time value indicating the date and time the folder was created. Read-only.

`DateLastAccessed`

The date and time the folder was last accessed. Read-only.

`DateLastModified`

The date and time the folder was last modified. Read-only.

`Drive`

The drive letter of the drive on which the folder resides. Read-only.

`Files`

A collection of `Scripting.File` objects representing all the files contained in the folder, including those with the hidden and system file attributes set. Read-only.

`IsRootFolder`

`True` if the folder is its drive's root folder; otherwise, `False`. Read-only.

`Name`

The name of the folder. Assigning a new value to the `Name` property renames the folder. Read/write.

`ParentFolder`

A `Folder` object representing the folder's parent (containing) folder. For a root folder, this should be `null`, but it returns an object that causes an error if used. Read-only.

continues

REFERENCE LIST 4.3 Continued

`Path`

The fully qualified path of the folder.

`ShortName`

The name of the folder as seen by old DOS and Windows 3.1 programs that require the earlier 8.3 naming convention.

`ShortPath`

The full path of the folder as seen by old programs that require the earlier 8.3 file-naming convention. Read-only.

`Size`

The size, in bytes, of all files and subfolders contained in the folder. Read-only.

`SubFolders`

A collection of `Folder` objects representing all the folder's subfolders, including those with the hidden and system file attributes set.

`Type`

Not too useful. For folders that have an extension in their name, `Type` is the descriptive name associated with files having that extension. For example, if a folder is named `folder.txt`, `Type` would be "Text File." Read-only.

Methods:

`Copy` *`destination`* [*`,overwrite`*]

Copies the folder from one location to another.

`Delete` *`force`*

Deletes a specified file or folder.

`Move` *`destination`*

Moves a specified file or folder from one location to another.

File and Folder Attribute Values

File and folder attributes, such as system and read-only, are stored as a number. Each possible attribute has a numeric value associated with it, and the number stored in the `File` or `Folder` object is the sum of the values for whichever attributes apply. These values correspond to individual bits of a binary number. Table 4.1 lists the values.

Table 4.1 **Folder and File Attribute Values**

Attribute Name	Value	Attribute Protection	Description
`Normal`	`0`		If no attributes are set, the value is 0, and the file is called a "normal" file.
`ReadOnly`	`1`	R/W	The file is read-only.
`Hidden`	`2`	R/W	The file or folder is hidden.

Attribute Name	Value	Attribute Protection	Description
`System`	4	R/W	The file is an operating system file.
`Volume`	8	R/O	This is a disk volume label.
`Directory`	16	R/O	This is a folder (directory).
`Archive`	32	R/W	The file has changed since the last backup.
`Alias`	64	R/O	This is a link or shortcut.
`Compressed`	128	R/O	The file or folder is compressed.

A file with just the `ReadOnly` bit set would have an `Attributes` value of 1. A file with the `Hidden` and `System` attributes set would have a value of 6 (2 + 4).

Testing File and Folder Attribute Values

Because the `Attributes` value can be the sum of several different individual attributes, you can't just compare its value to a specific number. For example, the test

```
if file.Attributes = 1
```

won't work if the file also has the `Archive` attribute set, because the value would be 33, not 1. The best way to work around this is to use *bitwise* testing of the attribute values. Each scriptable programming language has a way of performing bitwise testing. Here's an example in VBScript:

```
if file.Attributes and 1 then ...
```

The value of the expression `File.Attributes and 1` is 0 if the 1 bit is not set, and 1 if it is set; `If` considers 0 to be `False` and any nonzero value to be `True`. Therefore, the test is `True` if the `Attributes` value has the 1 bit set.

Tip

If you use file or folder attributes, your script will be easier to understand if you define named constants for the attribute values rather than use the numeric values. Put lines such as

```
const ReadOnly = 1
const Hidden = 2
```

and so on at the very top of your script and then use these more meaningful names in attribute tests.

Using constants, we'd write this:

```
const ReadOnly = 1

if file.Attributes and ReadOnly then ...
```

Testing Multiple Attributes

If you need to test multiple attributes, you must be very careful. For example, the test

```
if file.Attributes and Hidden and Readonly then ...
```

doesn't work. In fact, this test will *never* be true. File attribute values are numeric quantities, and with numbers, the operators `and` and `or` don't work in the intuitive way that you'd expect. With numbers, they perform *bitwise boolean* mathematics. Understanding bitwise math can take a bit of doing and is not something I'll be getting into here. However, you can use the following pattern and just modify the examples given there to fit your application.

Pattern

To select files that have *any one or more* of several file attributes, use the statement

```
if File.Attributes and (attribute or attribute or attribute...) then
```

For example, to list all files that are marked as either hidden or read-only or both hidden and read-only, you could use these statements:

```
const Readonly = 1
const Hidden   = 2

for each file in fso.GetFolder("c:\windows\system32").Files
    if file.attributes and (Hidden or Readonly) then
       WScript.echo file.name
    end if
next
```

However, to select files that have *all* of several file attributes, use the statement

```
if (File.Attributes and (attribute or attribute or attribute...)) =_
   (attribute or attribute or attribute...) then
```

For example, these statements list all files that are marked as both hidden *and* read-only:

```
for each file in fso.GetFolder("c:\windows\system32").Files
    if (file.attributes and (Hidden or Readonly)) = (Hidden or Readonly) then
       WScript.echo file.name
    end if
next
```

Changing File and Folder Attributes

You can change some of the attributes of a file or folder by assigning a new value to the `Attributes` property. However, only the attributes noted as R/W under "Attribute Protection" in Table 4.1 can be changed from a script. You can't, for instance, set the `Directory` attribute; this would correspond to an attempt to turn a file into a folder.

To turn on and off individual attributes, you must use bitwise math. Bitwise math uses the `or` operator to add bit values together.

To turn on a bit, use the `or` operator:

```
file.Attributes = file.Attributes or (bit(s) to turn on)
```

Here's an example that gives a file `ReadOnly` and `Hidden` attributes:

```
file.Attributes = file.Attributes or (ReadOnly or Hidden)
```

The advantage of this expression versus the following one is that the bitwise `or` expression works whether or not the attributes were set before you started:

```
file.Attributes = file.Attributes + ReadOnly + Hidden
```

The numeric `+` expression will give incorrect results if the `ReadOnly` or `Hidden` bits are already set—you'll end up adding in the `Attributes` value twice!

To turn off an attribute, use `and not`:

```
file.Attributes = file.Attributes and not (bit(s) to turn off)
```

This has the effect of leaving set all bits that were originally set, *except* the ones listed. For example, the statement

```
file.Attributes = file.Attributes and not (Hidden or ReadOnly)
```

removes the `Hidden` and `ReadOnly` attributes from a file.

Note

Files with the `Hidden`, `System`, and `ReadOnly` bits set are called *super hidden*. They usually don't show up in Explorer windows unless you've enabled displaying both hidden and system files.

Additionally, the `Scripting.File` object lets you manipulate simple attributes such as Hidden, but it does not provide a way to manipulate user-level permissions for files and folders stored on an NTFS disk partition. For that, you can use the `cacls` command-line program, which is discussed in Chapter 14, "Command-Line Programs," or the Windows Management Instrumentation's `Security` provider. WMI is discussed in Chapter 7, "Windows Management Instrumentation (WMI)."

The `Scripting.File` Object

The `Scripting.File` object lets you see and alter information about individual files: names, attributes, sizes, and dates. As with the `Drive` and `Folder` objects, you can get the `Folder` object for a specific named file, or you can get a collection of all files in a given folder. If you wish, you can run through all the members of a collection and select files based on name, extension, size, date, and so on.

Reference List 4.4 lists the properties and methods of the `File` object.

REFERENCE LIST 4.4 Properties and Methods of the `File` Object

Properties:

`Attributes`
Sets or returns the attributes of the files. Attribute values are listed in Table 4.1. This property is read/write or read-only, depending on the attribute.

`DateCreated`
Returns the date and time the specified file was created. Read-only.

`DateLastAccessed`
Returns the date and time the specified file was last accessed. Read-only.

`DateLastModified`
Returns the date and time the specified file was last modified. Read-only.

`Drive`
Returns the drive letter of the drive on which the specified file resides. Read-only.

`Name`
Sets or returns the name of a specified file. You can rename a file by assigning a new value to its `Name` property. Read/write.

`ParentFolder`
Returns the folder object for the folder in which this file lives. Read-only.

`Path`
Returns the fully qualified path to the file, including the filename. Read-only.

`ShortName`
Returns the short name used by programs that require the earlier 8.3 naming convention. Read-only.

`ShortPath`
Returns the short path used by programs that require the earlier 8.3 file naming convention. Read-only.

`Size`
Returns the size, in bytes, of the specified file. For folders, returns the size, in bytes, of all files and subfolders contained in the folder. Read-only.

`Type`
Returns information about the type of a file or folder. For example, for files ending in `.txt`, "Text Document" is returned. Read-only.

Methods:

`Copy` *`destination`* [, *`overwrite`*]
Copies the file to a new location, which can be a folder name or filename. By default, if the destination file already exists, it is overwritten. If the Boolean parameter `overwrite` is specified and is `False`, the script will instead stop with an error message.

`Delete` *`force`*
Deletes the file. If the Boolean parameter `force` is specified and is `True`, a read-only file will be deleted; otherwise, the script generates an error.

`Move` *`destination`*
Moves the file to a new location, specified as the path `destination`. If a file of the destination name already exists, the script generates an error.

`OpenAsTextStream(`[*`iomode`*`,` [*`format`*]]**`)`**
Opens a specified file and returns a `TextStream` object that can be used to read from, write to, or append to the file. (We'll discuss this later in the chapter.)

Renaming a File

A script can rename a file by obtaining a `File` object for the file and changing its `Name` property, as in this example:

```
fso.GetFile("C:\folder\somefile.txt").Name = "somefile.bak"
```

Note that you can only change the name, not the folder, during this operation. To actually move the file, you must use the `Move` or `Copy` method. The `Name` property includes the file's extension, so if you change the name of a file from `"test.doc"` to `"newname"`, the extension `.doc` will be lost.

Scanning for Files Based on Name, Type, Size, and So On

If you want to process, delete, rename, or copy files based on some properties of the file, you'll need to scan through a collection of all files in a folder. Here's a script that deletes all BAK and TMP files in a folder:

```
                                  ' Example file script0404.vbs
set fso = CreateObject("Scripting.FileSystemObject")
cleanpath = "C:\TEMP"

for each file in fso.GetFolder(cleanpath).Files
    upext = ucase(fso.GetExtensionName(file.Name))
    if upext = "TMP" or upext = "BAK" then
        wscript.echo "deleting", file.path
        file.Delete
    end if
next
```

In this example, we use `GetFolder` and its `Files` property to get the collection of all files in `C:\TEMP`. Inside the `for` loop, we use the `FileSystemObject` object's `GetExtensionName` method to get just the file extension from each file's name and convert it to uppercase. Then, we match the extension against "TMP" and "BAK". If it matches, we delete the file.

Now, how would we clean up these files from `\TEMP` *and* from any folders within `TEMP`? We'd use the recursion technique we discussed earlier. What's needed is a subroutine to delete all junk files in a given folder as well as from any folders within the folder. Here's what such a program might look like:

```
                                        ' Example file script0405.vbs
set fso = CreateObject("Scripting.FileSystemObject")
cleanpath = "C:\TEMP"

cleanup fso.GetFolder(cleanpath)

' ------------------------------------------------------------------
sub cleanup (folder)
    dim file, subfolder                 ' declare local variables

    for each file in folder.Files       ' clean up files
        upext = ucase(fso.GetExtensionName(file.Name))
        if upext = "TMP" or upext = "BAK" then
            wscript.echo "deleting", file.path
            file.Delete
        end if
    next
                                        ' clean up any subfolders
    for each subfolder in folder.SubFolders
        cleanup subfolder
    next
end sub
```

This script contains a subroutine to clean up temporary and backup files given a `Folder` object. The script starts out by calling `cleanup` with the `Folder` object for `C:\TEMP`.

`Cleanup` uses the same technique used in the previous example to remove all of this folder's BAK and TMP files.

The fun part comes next: `Cleanup` then scans through any subfolders within `\TEMP`. A folder's `Folders` property returns a collection of any folders within. `Cleanup` then calls *itself* with each of the subfolders, in turn.

As `cleanup` is invoked each time, it does what we want: It scans through files and deletes the BAK and TMP files, and it scans through and calls itself to remove these files from any deeper subfolders.

You can use this same technique to work on files based on size, attributes, modification or creation dates, and so on, based on your own needs. It's common enough that it should be noted as a pattern.

Pattern

To process all files in a folder and all subfolders, use a recursive subroutine that works with a `Folder` object:

```
                                       ' Example file script0406.vbs
set fso = CreateObject("Scripting.FileSystemObject")
startfolder = "c:\xxx"                 ' identify starting folder name

dofolder fso.GetFolder(startfolder)
. . .

' --------------------------------------------------------------------
sub dofolder (folder)
    dim file, subfolder                ' declare local variables

    for each file in folder.Files      ' do something with the files
        . . .
    next
                                       ' call again to process subfolders
    for each subfolder in folder.SubFolders
        dofolder subfolder
    next
end sub
```

You can use `If...Then` tests to limit the processing of files and/or folders to specific categories, if you wish.

To select files more than a certain number of days old, you can subtract the file's modification date from today's date, as in this example:

```
if (Now()-file.DateLastModified) > 3 then
    wscript.echo file.Name, "is more than 3 days old"
    ...
end if
```

You can also select files based on file attributes. While writing this very chapter, in fact, I received an e-mail from my editor, Rick Kughen, who asked if there was an easy way to remove the read-only attribute from all the MP3 files in his music folder and all subfolders. (Talk about perfect timing!) Here's a version of this pattern that solves his problem:

```
                                       ' Example file script0407.vbs
const ReadOnly = 1                     ' ReadOnly bit in file attributes
set fso = CreateObject("Scripting.FileSystemObject")

makerw fso.GetFolder("C:\music")       ' start in C:\music and work down

' --------------------------------------------------------------------
sub makerw (folder)
   dim file, subfolder
```

```
                                   ' tell user where we are
    wscript.echo "Processing", folder.Path, "..."

    for each file in folder.Files    ' fix attribute on MP3 files only
        if (instr(ucase(file.Name), ".MP3") > 0) and _
                (file.Attributes and ReadOnly) then
            file.Attributes = file.Attributes and not ReadOnly
        end if
    next

    for each subfolder in folder.Subfolders
        makerw subfolder
    next
end sub
```

Given the number of file and folder properties available, you should be able to construct `if` statements to meet just about any file selection needs you have.

Tip

When testing a file selection procedure, at first put only a `WScript.Echo` statement inside the `if` statement. When you know it's selecting the right files, only then go back and put in the statements that actually make changes, such as deleting or copying files.

I should add that after writing this script, I found that you can solve the problem by typing a single line at the command prompt. Scripting is very powerful, but as I'll show in Section II of this book, the command line has its moments of glory, too. The solution, by the way, is to type `attrib -r *.mp3 /s` from the top-level folder `\music`. More about this in Chapter 14.

Reading and Writing Files

It's often useful to be able to read and write text files in a script. Here are some ways you can use this ability:

- Scripts often need to operate on a series of users, computers, files, or other targets. Rather than putting this information in the script itself, it may be better to keep the data separate from the script program, in a text file, where it can be edited without molesting the script itself. The script can read this file to get the list of items to work with.
- Scripts can keep a log of their activities in a text file.
- Scripts can operate on externally generated data files such as comma-delimited export files from a spreadsheet program.
- Scripts can generate and place data into a text file for later printing, or they can import into a spreadsheet or database program.
- A script can act as a filter, like the `sort` and `more` commands, reading the standard input and writing to the standard output.

Text file input and output uses an object called `TextStream`. This object represents a file as a series of characters from which you can read or to which you can write new information.

The `TextStream` Object

Text files consist of characters using ASCII (American Standard Code for Information Interchange) or Unicode encoding. The encoding scheme maps letters and symbols to their numerical representation inside the file. ASCII is the default, and the usual format on the PC, so unless you use one of the Asian-language multibyte characters sets, ASCII will be the symbol set of choice. If you need to use Unicode, you can tell Windows to use it when you open the file for reading or writing.

`TextStream` objects are created using the `FileSystemObject` object's `CreateTextFile` or `OpenTextFile` method, or a `Scripting.File` object's `OpenAsTextStream` method. These methods were outlined earlier in the chapter in Reference Lists 4.1 and 4.4.

Pattern

Here are three typical ways to open a file:

- To open an existing file for reading, use `OpenTextFile`, as illustrated here:

  ```
  set stream = fso.OpenTextFile("some input file.txt")
  ```

  Alternatively, if you have a `File` object for the file, you can use the statement

  ```
  set stream = file.OpenAsTextStream(forReading)
  ```

- To create a new text file, replacing any previous version of the file, use `CreateTextFile` with the `Overwrite` parameter set to `True`:

  ```
  set stream = fso.CreateTextFile("some input file.txt", True)
  ```

  If you have a file object, you can use the statement

  ```
  set stream = file.OpenAsTextStream(forWriting)
  ```

- To create a new file or add to any previous contents if the file already exists, use `OpenTextFile` in `ForAppending` mode and with the `create` option set to `True`:

  ```
  set stream = fso.OpenTextFile("some input file.txt", ForAppending, True)
  ```

- With a `File` object, use this:

  ```
  set stream = file.OpenAsTextStream(forAppending)
  ```

The resulting object, `stream`, is a `TextStream` object that you can use to read or write the file, as described in the remainder of this section.

Note

If you need to force the use of Unicode or ASCII, you can specify an additional argument to `CreateTextFile` or `OpenTextFile`, as described in Reference List 4.1. For example, to force the use of Unicode, the three statements in the preceding pattern would be replaced with the following:

```
set stream = fso.OpenTextFile("some input file.txt", ForReading,_
    False, TriStateTrue)

set stream = fso.CreateTextFile("some input file.txt", True, True)

set stream = fso.OpenTextFile("some input file.txt", ForAppending,_
    True, TriStateTrue)
```

In between the codes for letters and numbers are special characters that indicate the end of each line of the file, tabs, and so on. On DOS- and Windows-based computers, each line is separated by the control characters carriage return (CR) and linefeed (LF; also called *newline*), which have the values `13` and `10`, respectively. On Unix, Linux, and some other operating systems, the custom is to separate lines only by the linefeed (newline) character.

If you read and write files a character at a time, you'll encounter these special codes. For most applications, though, it's easiest to read and write text a whole line at a time; in this case, there are handy methods provided as part of the `TextStream` object that let you ignore these line-delimiting control character details.

The `TextStream` object represents a text file's contents and keeps track of a "current location" in the file. As you read characters or lines from a file, the `TextStream` object remembers the next character waiting to be read. It also remembers how many lines you've read as well as how many characters you've read from the current line. As you write a file, it remembers the current line and column as well.

Reference List 4.5 lists the properties and methods of the `TextStream` object.

REFERENCE LIST 4.5 Properties and Methods of the `TextStream` Object

Properties:

`AtEndOfLine`

Boolean value. When reading from a stream, if this property is `True`, the next character to be read is a carriage return or linefeed control character.

`AtEndOfStream`

Boolean value. When reading from a stream, if this property is `True`, the entire file has been read and there is no more data left. Read-only.

`Column`

Returns the column number of the next character to be read or written. Goes back to 1 after a carriage return/linefeed has been read or written. Read-only.

`Line`

Returns the line number of the next line to be read or written. Read-only.

Methods:

`Close`

Closes the stream. After closing, the object can no longer be used. Use `Close` when you're finished reading or writing a stream to commit any changes to disk and to unlock the file so other applications can use it. If you do not explicitly close a `TextStream` object, the file will not be closed until the script ends.

`Read(`*`nread`*`)`

Reads up to `nread` characters from the stream and returns them as a string. If there aren't `nread` characters left in the file, one would think that the method would just return what's available. However, at least in WSH version 5.6, the script will hang if you try to read past the end of the file. Be careful, therefore, to get the file's length from the `File` object's `Size` property to be sure the file is as long as you expect.

`ReadAll`

Returns the entire contents of the file as a string object. This can be problematic with very large files (say, over a few megabytes), but it does let you use string-manipulation functions to easily search and modify the file.

`ReadLine`

Reads a whole line of text from the file, up to and including a CR+LF or newline character, and returns the text as a string. The carriage return and/or linefeed is *not* included as part of the returned string.

`Skip` *`nskip`*

Skips over the next `nskip` characters in the stream without reading them.

`SkipLine`

Skips the next line in the stream without reading it. That is, it skips characters up to and including a CR+LF or LF.

`Write` *`string`*

Writes a string to the file. No CR+LF or newline is written unless these characters are in the string.

`WriteBlankLines` *`nlines`*

Writes `nlines` blank lines to the file; that is, it writes `nlines` CR+LF pairs.

`WriteLine` [*`string`*]

Writes the text of the string to the file, followed by a CR+LF. If `string` is omitted, it writes just a CR+LF.

Reading Text from Files

There are several ways to read all the lines of a file. Here is one basic pattern.

Pattern

To read all the lines of a file, ignore blank lines, and process each line with a subroutine, you can use this pattern:

```
                                                ' Example file script0408.vbs
    ' set name of file to process; can also get this
    ' from a command line argument
filename = "c:\somefolder\somefile.txt"

set fso = CreateObject("Scripting.FileSystemObject")

    ' be sure the file exists and inform user if it doesn't
if not fso.FileExists(filename) then
    MsgBox "The file '" & filename & "' does not exist"
    wscript.quit 1
end if

    ' open the stream and read each line in turn
set stream = fso.OpenTextFile(filename)
do while not stream.AtEndOfStream
    str = stream.ReadLine
        ' if string is not blank, call the subroutine "process"
    if len(trim(str)) > 0 then process str
loop
stream.Close

...

' -------------------------------------------------------------------
' subroutine to process lines from the input file
sub process (str)
    Wscript.Echo "Input:", str
    ...
end sub
```

In this pattern, the name of the file is fixed in the script. You can let the user specify it on the command line by retrieving it from the command-line argument collection:

```
if Wscript.Arguments.Length <> 1 then
    MsgBox "Usage: " & Wscript.ScriptName & " filename"
    Wscript.Quit 1
end if
filename = WScript.Arguments.Item(0)
```

The subroutine `process` can do anything you want. If this script were designed to create new user accounts, for example, you might want each line in the file to specify the information for one user. The subroutine process would do the job of creating one user account.

Note

ReadLine works with either DOS-type (CR+LF-delimited) or Unix-type (LF-delimited) text files.

You can use your preferred scripting language's string-manipulation functions to work with the strings you read from an input file.

Writing Text to Files

You can easily write text files with a script. This is handy for creating log files of activity, for exporting data unearthed by the script to a spreadsheet or word processing program, or to create listings that can be printed.

As mentioned earlier in the chapter, to create a new file overwriting any previous file, use

```
set outstream = fso.CreateTextFile("\somefolder\filename.txt")
```

with whatever names you wish to use for the `TextStream` object `outstream` and the filename. You can also add to a preexisting file using

```
set outstream = fso.OpenTextFile("\somepath\filename.txt", ForAppending, True)
```

which will either append to any previous content or create the file if it doesn't already exist.

Tip

Appending is useful when you want your script to keep a log of what it does each time it runs. Keeping a log file is especially valuable when you run a script unattended using the Task Scheduler.

Tip

You can have your script send text output to a printer by using `CreateTextFile` with the name of a printer, if the printer is connected to a parallel port or is shared on the network. Use a name such as `"LPT1"` for a local printer connected to port LPT1 or `"\\sumatra\okidata"` to print to a network shared printer. (If your printer is connected via USB or a wireless connection, you'll have to share it and use its network share name, because only parallel port printers have an LPT port name that `CreateTextFile` can write to.) If you're sending output to a laser printer, be sure to finish with a form feed character (ASCII character 12) just before you close the stream so that the last page prints out. In VBScript this might look like the following:

```
outstream.Write(vbFormFeed)
outstream.Close
```

Once you have a `TextStream` object, writing files is made easy through the use of the `WriteLine` method; it writes a string and adds the appropriate carriage return/linefeed characters automatically.

For example, the following script lists the names of any MP3 or WMA files it finds in your My Music folder, or any subfolder, into a text file called `Music Listing.txt`:

```
                                                ' Example file script0409.vbs
set fso = CreateObject("Scripting.FileSystemObject")
set shl = CreateObject("WScript.Shell")

                            ' get pathname of "My Documents"
mydocs  = shl.SpecialFolders("MyDocuments")
                            ' create output file in the My Music folder
set out = fso.CreateTextFile(fso.BuildPath(mydocs, "My Music\Music Listing.txt"))

nfiles  = 0                 ' list the music files
listdir "My Music"

out.Close                   ' close the output file
                            ' tell user what we did
wscript.echo "Listed", nfiles, "files"

' ----------------------------------------------------------------------
' listdir - list the music files in subfolder 'path' under My Documents.
' We print the path relative to My Documents to make the listing more
' readable, but we must add this relative pathname to the My Documents
' path (in variable mydocs) to use GetFolder.

sub listdir (path)
    dim fldr, file, folder, extn, first

    first = True            ' we've seen no files in this folder yet
                            ' get the folder info by creating full path
    set fldr = fso.GetFolder(fso.BuildPath(mydocs, path))

                            ' scan through files for MP3's or WMA's
    for each file in fldr.Files
       extn = ucase(fso.GetExtensionName(file.name))
       if extn = "MP3" or extn = "WMA" then
            if first then    ' print the folder name before first file
                out.WriteLine path
                out.WriteLine replicate("-", len(path))
                first = False
            end if
                               ' list the music file name
            out.WriteLine "    " & file.name
            nfiles = nfiles+1
       end if
    next
                               ' if we listed any files, print blank line
    if not First then out.WriteLine

                               ' now list contents of any subfolders
    for each folder in fldr.subfolders
```

```
        listdir fso.BuildPath(path, folder.Name)
    next
end sub

' -------------------------------------------------------------------
' replicate - return the string 'str' duplicated 'n' times

function replicate (str, n)
   dim i
   replicate = ""          ' start with a blank string
   for i = 1 to n          ' append as many copies as requested
       replicate = replicate & str
   next
end function
```

This script goes through some funny contortions to make the printout look good. Here are three things to look for in the script:

- The script only prints the name of a folder it's scanning if it actually finds a music file. This way, folders for artists, which generally contain only album folders, won't be listed. The variable `first` keeps track of whether any files have been listed on a given folder. If `first` is `True`, no files have been listed.
- The script prints the name of the folder, followed by a row of dashes the same length as the name of the folder. This gives the appearance of underlining. The function `replicate` copies the dash character (-) as many times as needed. After listing the folder, if any files have been listed (that is, variable `first` is `False`), a blank line is printed to visually separate each folder.
- The subroutine `listdir` uses the pathname in string form as its argument. In previous sample scripts that dive into folders, we use the `Folder` object itself, which is easier. In this script, however, we want to be able to display just the part of the pathname *after* My Documents, so we keep track of just this part of the string and use `BuildPath` to create the actual full path only when it's needed by `GetFolder`.

The script produces a listing like this:

```
My Music\Baguette Quartet\Rendez-Vous
-------------------------------------
   Ça gaze.wma
   Si l'on ne s'était pas connu.wma
   Reine de musette.wma

My Music\Iris Dement\Infamous Angel
-----------------------------------
   Let the Mystery Be.wma
   These Hills.wma
   Hotter Than Mojave in My Heart.wma
```

Constructing More Complex Text Files

The previous example created a listing by writing whole lines at a time. You can create text files a bit at a time using the TextStream object's Write method. Write outputs any text it's given, but it doesn't add line breaks. You can generate text lines a bit at a time this way:

```
outstream.Write "The filename is: "
outstream.Write filename
outstream.WriteLine
```

This creates one line in the output file by writing two strings and adding a carriage return/linefeed afterward. You can also write a CR/LF with the Write command. In VBScript, these three variations all produce the exact same result in the output file:

```
outstream.Write "The filename is: "
outstream.Write filename
outstream.WriteLine

outstream.Write "The filename is: " & filename & vbCRLF

outstream.WriteLine "The filename is: " & filename
```

You can also insert tabs (ASCII 9) into text files; this is especially useful when you want to create a file to import into a spreadsheet, database, or word processing file. In VBScript, there's even a convenient predefined constant, vbTab, to make this easier. The following script is a variation of the MP3 listing program. Instead of making a nicely formatted text file meant to be viewed directly or printed, it creates a table with three columns (foldername, filename, and size):

```
                                          ' Example file script0410.vbs
set fso = CreateObject("Scripting.FileSystemObject")
set shl = CreateObject("WScript.Shell")

                          ' get pathname of "My Documents"
mydocs  = shl.SpecialFolders("MyDocuments")
                          ' create output file in the My Music folder
set out = fso.CreateTextFile(fso.BuildPath(mydocs, "My Music\Music Listing.dat"))

nfiles  = 0               ' list the music files
listdir "My Music"

out.Close                 ' close the output file
                          ' tell user what we did
wscript.echo "Listed", nfiles, "files"

' -------------------------------------------------------------------
' listdir - list the music files in subfolder 'path' under My Documents.
' We use the path relative to My Documents to make the listing more
```

```
' readable, but we must add this relative pathname to the My Documents
' path (in variable mydocs) to use GetFolder. This version creates a
' tab-delimited table rather than a formatted text listing.

sub listdir (path)
    dim fldr, file, folder, extn

                        ' get the folder info by creating full path
    set fldr = fso.GetFolder(fso.BuildPath(mydocs, path))

                        ' scan through files for MP3's or WMA's
    for each file in fldr.Files
       extn = ucase(fso.GetExtensionName(file.name))
       if extn = "MP3" or extn = "WMA" then
                           ' format the path, name and size
            out.WriteLine path & vbTab & file.name & vbTab & file.Size
            nfiles = nfiles+1
       end if
    next
                           ' now list contents of any subfolders
    for each folder in fldr.subfolders
        listdir fso.BuildPath(path, folder.Name)
    next
end sub
```

This creates a DAT file that looks like this:

```
My Music\Baguette Quartet\Rendez-Vous→ Ça gaze.wma→1031008

My Music\Baguette Quartet\Rendez-Vous→ Si l'on ne s'était pas connu.wma→883952

My Music\Baguette Quartet\Rendez-Vous→ Reine de musette.wma→1286196

My Music\Iris Dement\Infamous Angel→ Let the Mystery Be.wma→1349134

My Music\Iris Dement\Infamous Angel→ These Hills.wma→1784372

My Music\Iris Dement\Infamous Angel→ Hotter Than Mojave in My Heart.wma→1196018
```

This file can be imported into Excel in a snap.

Writing Unix-Compatible Text Files

`WriteLine` and `WriteBlankLines` write DOS-type files using CR+LF as the line delimiter. To write text files on a Windows system that will be usable on a Unix-based system, you'll have to write the line-ending codes yourself. Instead of using `WriteLine`, use `Write` and append a linefeed character yourself. In VBScript, at least, this is easy.

Note

VBScript has some predefined string constants that can be handy when writing text files. The value `vbCRLF` consists of a carriage return/linefeed pair, and `vbLF` is a linefeed only. `vbNewLine` is a "platform-independent" line delimiter you could use when writing a script that might run under either Unix or DOS/Windows; however, generally you'll probably want to exercise explicit control over the line delimiters by using `vbCRLF` or `vbLF` directly.

➔ To learn more about command lines and redirection **see** Chapter 11.

In VBScript, instead of using `WriteLine` you might write something like this:

```
stream.Write(str & vbLF)
```

This appends the linefeed character to the string before writing it. Instead of using `WriteBlankLines n`, you could write something like this:

```
for i = 1 to n
    stream.Write(vbLF)
next
```

Working with Stdin and Stdout

When you run a script from the command line using the `cscript` command, your script has access to the command-line environment's "standard input" and "standard output" files. These are, by default, input from your keyboard and output to the screen, but you can redirect them to files using the familiar command-line syntax

```
program arguments <infile >outfile
```

which instructs the program to read its input from file `infile` and write its output to file `outfile`.

➔ To learn how to change the default host, **see** "Ways to Run a Script," **p. 24**.

You can write scripts to take advantage of this, which can make your programs more "general purpose" in nature. For example, if we wrote a file-listing script that sends its output to the standard output, it would do the following:

- Display the listing to the screen if the script was run with a plain command line
- Display the listing a screenful at a time with `| more` added to the command line
- Store the listing in a file with `>filename` added to the command line
- Print the listing with `>prn` on the command line*
- List only entries containing "jazz" by adding `| find /i "jazz"` to the command line

**This works only if your printer is connected to parallel port LPT1, or if you've redirected LPT1 to a shared network printer using the* `net use` *command as described in Chapter 14.*

Likewise, a script that reads from the standard input takes its input from the following:

- The user's keyboard, if the script is run with a plain command line
- A file, with `<filename` added to the command line
- The output of another program, if `program |` precedes the script command

You can see that using standard input and output can give a script many runtime options, virtually for free.

All you have to do to take advantage of this is to use the predefined `TextStream` objects provided by Windows Script Host. Instead of using `fso.CreateTextFile` to create a stream for an output listing or `fso.OpenTextFile` to get a stream to read an input file, just use the predefined objects listed in Table 4.2.

Table 4.2 **Predefined *TextStream* Objects**

Object	Use
`WScript.Stdin`	Standard input. Used to read input from the user's keyboard or, if redirected, from a file or program.
`WScript.Stdout`	Standard output. Used to write to the user's window or, if redirected, to a file or another program.
`WScript.Stderr`	Standard error output. Used primarily to print error messages that you want the user to see, even if the standard output is redirected. Can be redirected with `2>filename`.

Note

In Windows Script Host versions 5.6 and earlier (that is, in the version distributed with the original release of Windows XP and all earlier versions), a bug prevents the standard input object from working if you run a script by simply typing its name and use input redirection or input from another program. For example, if you type *`scriptname <filename`* and the script attempts to read from `WScript.Stdin`, the script will terminate with an error. You must explicitly run the script with the `cscript` command (for example, `cscript` *`scriptname`*`.vbs` *`<filename`*).

If you have a later version of WSH, check to see if this bug has been fixed. When it is fixed, it will be much easier to use scripts as filters, which I'll discuss in a moment.

Here is a sample script that reads text lines from the standard input, replaces any tabs with commas, and writes the results to the standard output:

```
                                                ' Example file script0411.vbs
do while not WScript.Stdin.AtEndOfStream
    str = WScript.Stdin.ReadLine
    do
        i = instr(str, vbTab)
```

```
        if i <= 0 then exit do
        str = left(str, i-1) & "," & mid(str, i+1)
    loop
    WScript.Stdout.WriteLine str
loop
```

Programs that read from the standard input, massage the input in some way, and then write to the standard output are called *filters*. Filters can be handy tools, because you can string them together like this:

```
someprogram | onefilter | anotherfilter > outfile
```

When writing scripts that process information, if you can write them with the filter concept in mind, you may find that you get more mileage out of your efforts.

Prompting for User Input

You can use the standard input and output streams to interact directly with the user. WSH-based programs don't have much to work with in the way of user interaction, and having to use the command prompt to enter information may seem like a trip back 20 years in computer history, but it still can be useful.

One simple way a program can receive user input is to *prompt* for it and then read from the standard output. Here's a rather silly sample script to show what I mean:

```
                                        ' Example file script0412.vbs
wscript.stdout.WriteLine "Enter QUIT to stop the program"
wscript.stdout.WriteLine

do
    wscript.stdout.Write "What is your name? "
    if wscript.stdin.AtEndOfStream then exit do
    name = wscript.stdin.ReadLine
    if ucase(name) = "QUIT" then exit do

    wscript.stdout.WriteLine "Hello, " & name & "."
    wscript.stdout.WriteLine
loop
```

This script will prompt for and read names until the user types QUIT or indicates end of file by typing Ctrl+Z. The script looks for both `QUIT` and `AtEndOfStream` so that it will work when the script is run with input redirected.

Note

If you use prompting, be careful to place the test for `AtEndOfStream` *after* the prompt has been typed. `AtEndOfStream` actually stops the script until Windows can determine whether you're going to type something or you're going to type Ctrl+Z to end input. If you try to test `AtEndOfStream` before printing the prompt, the prompt will not appear.

Reading Binary Files

You can use the `TextStream` object to read binary files as well as text, if you're careful and you know the structure of the file you're reading. (This is a more advanced topic, so feel free to skip this section if you're new to programming and are still looking to build a foundation of knowledge.)

To read binary information using `TextStream`, you must use the `Read` method, not `readline`, to read in blocks of data. For example, to skip the first 10 bytes of a file and read the next 50, you could write the following:

```
stream.skip(10)
str = stream.read(50)
```

This reads 50 bytes into a string. To extract the binary information, you must then pick the string apart, character by character. In VBScript, you could display the bytes in the string just read with this:

```
for i = 1 to 50
    value = asc(substr(str, i, 1))
    wscript.echo "Byte", str(i,2) & ":", value
next
```

Here, `substr()` picks the string apart one character at a time, and `asc()` yields the byte value of the extracted character.

To interpret word values, you must pick the string apart two bytes at a time and then combine them, as in this example:

```
wordval = asc(substr(str,10,1)) + 256*asc(substr(str,11,1))
```

The preceding line extracts a 16-bit word value from bytes 10 and 11, assuming standard Intel-*x*86 byte ordering. (Although other computer architectures may use different ordering, most Microsoft-compatible file formats use the Intel ordering, so most files must be read this way.) In like fashion, you must construct a long or DWORD value by combining four bytes:

```
wordval = asc(substr(str,10,1)) + 256*asc(substr(str,11,1)) + _
    65536*asc(substr(str,12,1)) + 16777216*asc(substr(str,13,1))
```

To solve the problem in a general-purpose way, and to make the script easier to read, it's handy to use a function to extract binary values from strings. Here is a function that retrieves an *n* byte value starting at an offset position in string `str`:

```
function binaryval (byref str, offset, n)
    dim i
    binaryval = 0
    for i = offset+n-1 to offset step -1
        binaryval = binaryval*256 + asc(mid(str,i+1,1))
    next
end function
```

In this function, the offset value is zero based, because that's the way most documentation describes the position of items inside file structures. The 10th character in a string corresponds to an offset of 9, so the statement

```
wordval = binaryval(str, 9, 4)
```

is another way to get the DWORD value illustrated earlier.

Example: Reading BMP Image Data

As an illustration of reading binary information, suppose we want to have a script fetch information about the properties of a Microsoft BMP image file. By searching the Internet for "BMP File Format Specification," I found that all BMP files start with the following information:

```
Offset

 0   WORD  bfType        the characters "BM"
 2   DWORD bfSize        length of file
 6   WORD  bfReserved1   not used
 8   WORD  bfReserved2   not used
10   DWORD bfOffBits     offset in file to bitmap data
14   DWORD biSize        size of header information, usually 40
18   LONG  biWidth       width of image in pixels
22   LONG  biHeight      height of pixels
26   WORD  biPlanes      number of image planes, always 1
28   WORD  biBitCount    bits per pixel: 1, 4, 8, 16, 24, or 32
```

Therefore, if we read the first 30 bytes of a BMP file into a string named `hdr`, we can extract the width and height of the image in pixels using the `binaryval` function listed earlier. Here's an example:

```
width  = binaryval(hdr, 18, 4)
height = binaryval(hdr, 22, 4)
```

We can use this to write a script that displays the dimensions of any BMP files named on the command line:

```
                                    ' Example file bmpsize.vbs
set fso = CreateObject("Scripting.FileSystemObject")

for each filename in Wscript.Arguments
    if not fso.FileExists(filename) then
```

```
        ' the file doesn't exist
        result = "does not exist"

    elseif fso.GetFile(filename).Size < 32 then
        ' the file is not long enough to be valid
        result = "is not a BMP file"

    else
        ' open the file and read the first 32 bytes
        set stream = fso.OpenTextFile(filename)
        hdr = stream.Read(32)
        stream.Close        ' close the stream

        if left(hdr,2) <> "BM" then
            ' the file didn't start with the required marker
            result = "is not a BMP file"
        else
            ' extract the size information
            width  = binaryval(hdr, 18, 4)
            height = binaryval(hdr, 22, 4)
            result = "Width: " & width & "  Height: " & height
        end if
    end if

    ' display whatever information we got for this file
    wscript.echo filename & ":", result
next

' -------------------------------------------------------------------
function binaryval (byref str, offset, n)
    dim i
    binaryval = 0
    for i = offset+n-1 to offset step -1
        binaryval = binaryval*256 + asc(mid(str,i+1,1))
    next
end function
```

When I ran the command

```
cscript bmpsize.vbs test.txt xray.bmp "nasa sfbay.bmp"
```

the script dutifully printed the correct results:

```
test.txt: is not a BMP file

xray.bmp: Width: 980  Height: 980

nasa sfbay.bmp: Width: 1024  Height: 725
```

Example: Reading MP3 Tag Data

Another example of reading a binary file illustrates how to extract string information from a block of binary data. MP3 files contain an information block called a *tag* that describes the song's title, artist, album, and so on. Although various tag formats are being developed, the most common one puts this information in the last 128 bytes of the file and has the following format:

```
offset

   0   STRING(3)  Tag       must be the letters "TAG"

   3   STRING(30) Title     padded with spaces

  33   STRING(30) Artist

  63   STRING(30) Album

  93   STRING(4)  Year

  97   STRING(30) Comment

 127   BYTE       Genre     numeric code
```

To read this block, we can use the `TextFileObject` object's `Skip` method to skip all but the last 128 bytes of the file. Then we can use `Read` to read the 128 bytes. We can use a script similar to the preceding example to read the MP3 file information. When extracting a string, however, we have to use the string position, which starts at 1, rather than the offset, which start at 0. Here's a script to print the title information in any MP3 files named on the command line:

```
                                    ' Example file script0413.vbs
set fso = CreateObject("Scripting.FileSystemObject")

genre = array("Blues","Classic Rock","Country","Dance","Disco",_
    "Funk","Grunge","Hip-Hop","Jazz","Metal","New Age","Oldies",_
         ... (the full list is in the downloadble version of the script)
    "Punk Rock","Drum Solo","Acapella","Euro-House","Dance Hall")

for each filename in Wscript.Arguments
    if not fso.FileExists(filename) then
        ' the file doesn't exist
        result = "does not exist"

    else
        filelen = fso.GetFile(filename).Size
        if filelen < 128 then
            ' the file is not long enough to be valid
            WScript.echo filename, "is not an MP3 file"
        else
            ' open the file and get the tag information
            set stream = fso.OpenTextFile(filename)
            stream.Skip(filelen-128)
            hdr = stream.Read(128)
            stream.Close        ' close the stream
```

```
            if left(hdr,3) <> "TAG" then
                ' the block didn't start with the required marker
                WScript.echo filename, "has no title/artist info"
            else
                ' extract and print the size information
                WScript.echo filename & ":"
                WScript.echo "  Title: ", trim(mid(hdr, 4,30))
                WScript.echo "  Artist:", trim(mid(hdr,34,30))
                WScript.echo "  Album: ", trim(mid(hdr,64,30))
                WScript.echo "  Year:  ", trim(mid(hdr,94, 4))
                WScript.echo "  Genre: ", genre(binaryval(hdr,127,1)+1)
            end if
        end if
    end if
next

function binaryval (byref str, offset, n)
... (as seen before)
```

The sample output is as follows:

```
iris mojave.mp3:

  Title:  Hotter Than Mojave In My Heart
Artist: Iris DeMent
Album:  Infamous Angel
Year:   1993
Genre:  Folk
```

Of course, this works only if whomever created the MP3 file ensures that the tag information was added or downloaded correctly.

Reading and Writing XML and HTML

The Extensible Markup Language (XML) is an important new tool for storing complex information in a way that's both easy to read for humans and easy to parse by computer. XML is becoming a popular form for storing information and for interchanging information between computers. XML is used by Windows as a packaging format for scripts (which I'll discuss in Chapter 9, "Creating Your Own Scriptable Objects," and Chapter 10, "Deploying Scripts for Computer and Network Management") and is becoming very important as a tool for storing configuration information. In fact, Microsoft's latest .NET programming platform encourages programmers to start using text-based INI files again, rather than the Windows Registry, and many programmers are discovering that XML is the best format for human-readable information storage. Therefore, you may find it useful to be able to read and write data in XML format in your scripts.

Remember also that HTML can be viewed as an application of XML—the syntax is the same—so all of the following discussion on reading and writing XML applies to HTML as well.

Note

This section is pretty geeky, so if you're just beginning to work with scripting, you may want to save this section for another day. Also, as with all of this book's sections on objects, on the first pass through you may find it most helpful to skip ahead to the examples that follow each reference section.

Some XML Basics

XML files contain both text and markup "tags," as in this example:

```
<?xml version='1.0' encoding='utf-8'?>
<!-- An XML representation of a slide show -->
<slideshow title="Sample Slide Show" date="1/1/2002" author="Yours Truly">
    <slide>
        <title>Wake up to WonderWidgets!</title>
    </slide>
    <slide>
        <title>Overview</title>
        <item>Why <em>WonderWidgets</em> are great</item>
        <item/>
        <item>Who <em>buys</em> WonderWidgets</item>
    </slide>
</slideshow>
```

In this example, `<slide>` and `<title>` are tags. Tags delimit and describe the meaning or purpose of the information in the file and are enclosed in angle brackets to distinguish them from the data they describe. Tags come in pairs called a *start tag* and an *end tag* (for example, `<slide>` and `</slide>`) because their purpose is to clearly define the beginning and ending of each block of information. The end tag version always uses the name of the start tag preceded by a slash (`/`).

Together, a start tag, an end tag, and everything in between is called an *element*. The "everything in between" is the element's *content*, and it can consist of text or combinations of text and other tags. In the slideshow example, the content of each `<title>` tag is plain text, whereas the content of each `<slide>` tag is a series of subsidiary tags. For the most part, any blank spaces and carriage returns between tags are ignored, so XML files can be formatted to be easy to read by humans.

Besides marking off information, tags can carry additional information called *attributes* that describe their content. For example, `<slideshow ...>` is a tag with attributes `title`, `date`, and `author`. If you're familiar with the HTML markup system used for Web pages, this will look very familiar. Whereas HTML uses a fixed set of tags (such as `<TITLE>` and `<IMG>`), the tags in an XML file may be different—the list of allowed tags and their attributes are defined by a schema or document type definition (DTD) that varies from application to application—but the structure of XML is basically the same. HTML can be viewed as a particular application of XML; therefore, this section applies to reading and writing HTML files as well as XML.

Unlike HMTL, though, XML requires strict attention to the use of end tags; they're never optional. To save space, there is a special format that can be used to indicate an element with no content. For any given tag `<xxx>`, the format `<xxx/>` is equivalent to `<xxx></xxx>` (that is, a start tag immediately followed by its end tag). Notice that this was used in the slideshow example. The tag `<item/>` indicates a contentless item.

Clearly, XML files have a complex structure and can use several different formats to represent the same information. Such a file would be excruciatingly difficult to read, parse, and use in a script if your only tools were the text file objects discussed in the preceding sections.

Fortunately, there's an object that will do the work for you. The `MSXML2.DOMDocument` object (DOM stands for *Domain Object Model*) is not really a standard Windows Script Host object, but it's provided with all Windows XP and Windows 2000 computers, and you can get to it with Windows Script Host.

The `DOMDocument` object lets you write and read (parse) XML and HTML files as objects rather than as text files. You can read an XML file like the sample file provided earlier into a `DOMDocument` object. The `DOMDocument` object has methods and properties that let you examine and modify the XML data; for example, to scan through the slideshow data to find the `item` or `title` elements. The `DOMDocument` object also lets you create or modify XML data and then save the results to an XML text file.

There's a lot more to the `DOMDocument` object than I can present in this book—it would take several chapters to cover it thoroughly. I won't list all the object's properties and attributes here; I'll only discuss the some of the most useful ones in the examples that follow. I have also omitted all discussion of entity references (items such as HTML's `&`), which open up whole new areas of complication. You can get more information on the `DOMDocument` system by visiting `msdn.microsoft.com` and searching for "Microsoft XML Parser." Here, I'll just give you enough information to let you read and write XML files of the sort that you may encounter as a Windows system administrator working with installation scripts, setup files, and so on.

Note

Microsoft continually updates its XML software. The version included with Windows 2000 was version 2, and the initial release of Windows XP includes version 3. You can download and install updated versions of the XML parser; just be sure to read the release notes that Microsoft provides because you may need to pass a different name to `CreateObject` to activate the new version.

As mentioned earlier, XML data is inherently hierarchical: Elements of XML data can contain other elements, and these, too, can contain other elements. Microsoft calls each XML document element a *node*, and any elements inside an element are called *child nodes*. When there is a list of consecutive items, these items are called *siblings*. The structure of the XML example given earlier is shown in Figure 4.1.

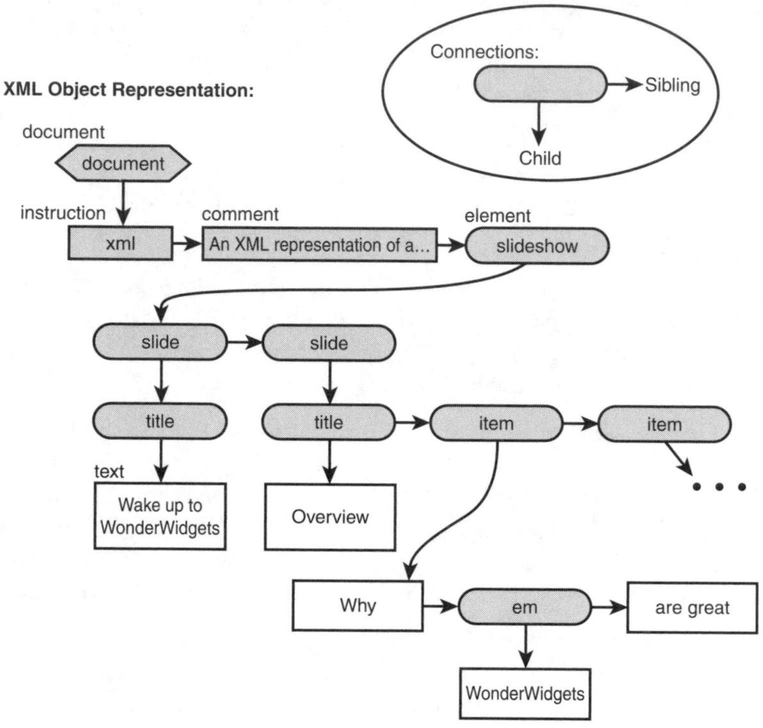

Figure 4.1 Node structure of the sample XML document.

The XML object system uses several different objects, including `DOMDocument` (the root node of the XML data structure), `IXMLDOMNode` (a single node of the document tree; nodes can contain document text or subnodes), `IXMLDOMParseError` (information about errors discovered in the XML document structure) and `IXMLDOMNamedNodeMap` (a list of attributes and their values).

Reference List 4.6 lists the most important properties and methods of the `DOMDocument` object. `DOMDocument` describes the document as a whole and is the one you create with `CreateObject` to get things going.

REFERENCE LIST 4.6 Some Properties and Methods of the `DOMDocument` Object

Properties:

`async`

Determines whether the entire XML document is immediately loaded when the `Load` method is used (`async` = `False`), or if the XML system can return from `Load` and parse the document later (`async` = `True`). Note that you should set this property to `False` in scripting applications. This property is read/write.

`childNodes`

Returns a collection of `IXMLDOMNode` objects; these are the contents of the document. You can scan this collection for contents or use `GetElements`. This property is read-only.

`documentElement`

Returns the root (highest) element of the document; it may not be the same as `firstChild` if there are processing instructions, comments, or a document type at the beginning of the file.

`parseError`

Returns an `IXMLDOMParseError` object describing the last error encountered when the document was read in. This object has four interesting properties: `errorCode` is nonzero if there was an error, `reason` describes the problem, `line` gives the line number in the file on which the error is located, and `srcText` is the text of the line containing the error. You can use this information to see whether the XML system detected a problem, such as a missing end tag, and to report it to the script user. This property is read-only.

`xml`

Returns the representation of the entire document as XML text, in Unicode encoding. This property is read-only.

Methods:

`createCDataSection(`*`data`*`)`

The `Create`... methods create new `IXMLDOMNode` node objects. To add them to an XML document, you must populate the new nodes with information and then use the `Insert`... and `Append`... methods to add the new nodes to the existing document. We'll discuss this later in this section. `createCDataSection` creates a CDATA node, which contains arbitrary uninterpreted data. The data argument is a string.

`createComment(`*`text`*`)`

Creates a Comment node containing the `text` string.

`createDocumentType(`*`name`*`, `*`publicid`*`, `*`systemid`*`, `*`internalsubset`*`)`

Creates a Document Type node, which defines the DTD in use. If used, it must be added as the first child node of the document node.

continues

REFERENCE LIST 4.6 Continued

`createElement(`*`name`*`)`

Creates a Document Element node with the given `name`. Elements correspond to tags in the XML file (for example, `<slideshow>`). Elements are generally populated with lists of other elements and text nodes.

`createProcessingInstruction(`*`target, data`*`)`

Creates a processing instruction (`<? ?>` tag). Most XML files start with a processing instruction with target `"xml"` and data something like `"version='1.0' encoding='utf-8'"`.

`createTextNode(`*`text`*`)`

Creates a Text node with the specified text. This is the actual document text.

`getElementsByTagName(`*`name`*`)`

Returns a collection of all element nodes in the document that have the specified tag name. You can then scan the collection and examine the contents and subnodes of these elements. The collection lists matching elements in preorder: A parent node is listed first, followed by all its children, in order. More complex searches can be performed by the `selectNodes` method.

`load(`*`XMLSourceFile`*`)`

Loads the named XML file. `XMLSourceFile` can be a filename or a URL. Any previous contents in the object are discarded and replaced with the contents of the file. Returns `False` if the load failed; otherwise, it returns `True`.

`loadXML(`*`XMLSourceText`*`)`

Like `Load` but loads XML source text directly. `XMLSourceText` is a complete XML document or well-formed fragment. Returns `False` if the load failed; otherwise, it returns `True`.

`Save` *`destination`*

Saves the current XML document in `destination`. For scripting purposes, this should be a filename, including the path.

`selectNodes(`*`expression`*`)`

Returns a collection of all the nodes in the document that match a specified searching expression. The search expression syntax is called *XPath* (XSL Path Language). Note that `SelectNodes` is the meatiest part of the XML object. You can use it to zero in directly on the information you want to extract from an XML or HTML file. For example, `"/book//name"` will return all `name` elements that occur anywhere inside `book` elements. For more information, visit `msdn.microsoft.com` and search for "XSLT Reference."

`selectSingleNode(`*`expression`*`)`

Like `selectNodes` but returns only the first node of any nodes identified by the search expression. This is handy when you only expect one, so you don't need to bother scanning the collection.

To read an XML file, create an instance of `MSXML2.DOMDocument`, use the `Load` method to read in the file or URL, and then use `DOMDocument`'s other methods and properties to extract information from the file. We'll discuss those later in the section.

Here is a script fragment that loads the existing XML document:

```
set xdoc = CreateObject("MSXML2.DOMDocument")
xdoc.load("c:\mydata\test.xml")
```

Once you have an XML document stored in a `DOMDocument` object, you can use the `selectNode` methods to identify certain components of the file from which you may want to extract information, or you can scan through the entire collection of objects. I'll show an example of this later in this section.

To create a new XML file, create an instance of `MSXML2.DOMDocument`, create data within the object using the `CreateNode` methods, and add these to the document structure using `IXMLNode`'s `Insert`... methods. Finally, use the `Save` method to store the document to a file.

Reference List 4.7 lists a few important properties and methods of the `IXMLDOMNode` object, instances of which describe the document's structure and content.

REFERENCE LIST 4.7 Some Properties and Methods of the MSXML2 `IXMLDOMNode` Object

Properties:

`attributes`
Returns an `IXMLDOmNamedNodeMap` list that enumerates the element's attributes. This isn't a collection that VBScript can peruse with `for each`. See the discussion of `Attributes` following this table. This property is read-only; use `setAttribute` to change or add an attribute.

`childNodes`
Returns a collection of the child nodes; these are the contents of the current element. You can scan this collection for contents, or you can use `FirstChild` and then `NextSibling` to visit the list of children. This property is read-only.

`firstChild`
Returns the first child object. This property is read-only.

`lastChild`
The last of an element's child nodes. This property is read-only.

`nextSibling`
The next node in a list of elements. This property is read-only. Unfortunately, due to a bug in the object, if you scan through the list by visiting `nextSibling` objects, you will run off the end of the list. Be sure to stop when the current object is its parent's `lastChild`. In VBScript, this is detected by the expression `node is node.parentNode.lastChild`.

continues

REFERENCE LIST 4.7 Continued

nodeName

For Element nodes, this is the tag name of the element (for example, `"Slideshow"`). For Document, Comment, and Text nodes, this is the fixed string `"#document"`, `"#comment"`, or `"#text"`. This property is read-only.

nodeType

As you might expect, this is the type of the node. Node type values are listed in Table 4.3. This property is read-Only.

nodeTypeString

The node type as a descriptive string (for example, `"element"` or `"text"`). This property is read-only.

nodeValue

The contents of a Text or Comment node. This is where you'll find the document text. This property is read/write.

ownerDocument

Yields the `DOMDocument` object that's the "parent" document of this node. This property is read-only.

previousSibling

The previous sibling in the list. If the current object is its parent's `firstChild`, there is no previous sibling. This property is read-only.

xml

Returns an XML text fragment that describes this node and its content, including any child nodes. This property is read-only.

Methods:

appendChild(*child*)

Appends a new child node `child` to the node's list of children. Returns the `child` object.

hasChildNodes

Returns `True` if the node has any children.

insertBefore(*newchild*, *child*)

Inserts a new node `newchild` before node `child` wherever it occurs in the document.

removeChild(*child*)

Removes the specified child from the node's list of children. Returns a reference to the removed child node (which should be the value of the parameter `child`.)

replaceChild(*newnode*, *oldnode*)

Requires two `IXMLDOMNode` arguments. Replaces `oldnode`, wherever it occurs in the XML document, with `newnode`. You can use this to replace part of a document. `ReplaceChild` doesn't care which `IXMLDOMNode` you apply the method to; any will do (that is, `anynode.replaceChild(...)`). The method finds `oldnode` in the document and replaces that node.

`selectNodes`
See `selectNodes` in Reference List 4.6.

`selectSingleNode`
See `selectSingleNode` in Reference List 4.6.

`setAttribute(`*`name`*`, `*`value`*`)`
Sets this node's attribute *`name`* to the string *`value`*.

Note

You can use `DOMObject`'s `xml` or `save` method to save just a fragment of the XML data.

Table 4.3 lists the various types of node types you may encounter while scanning the structure of an XML document. (Other node types are described in Microsoft's XML DOM documentation, but you're not likely to encounter them while scanning a document.)

Table 4.3 **Important *nodeType* Values for *IXMLDOMNode***

Value	Type
1	Element. Represents a `<tag>`.
3	Text. Contains document text in `NodeValue`.
4	CDATA. Contains arbitrary data.
5, 6	Entity reference and entity (not discussed here).
7	Processing instruction. Special markup that is not document text.
8	Comment. Descriptive text that again is not considered part of the document text.
10	Document type. Corresponds to a `<!DOCTYPE >` element, which specifies the document's DTD.

The `attributes` property of `IXMLDOMNode` returns an object representing all of the element's attributes. An element's `attributes` property describes the element's variable information. For example, a "font" element might have attributes to describe the typeface and the font size. In XML, this might look like `<font face="Times" size="3">`.

There are a couple of problems with the `attributes` property:

- The `attributes` property is only valid on Element, Entity, and Notation nodes. On other node types, in VBScript at least, `attributes` should return null but instead returns what looks like but isn't a valid object.

- Unfortunately, `attributes` is not a collection object that VBScript can scan with the `for each` statement. You can extract a specific attribute with `getNameItem`, or you can scan the list with a `for` loop, as shown following Reference List 4.8.

However, on the plus side, every Element, Entity and Notation node has an `attributes` list, even if it is of zero length. The `attributes` list object has a property and two methods, which are listed in Reference List 4.8.

REFERENCE LIST 4.8 Property and Methods of the `IXMLDOMNamedNodeMap` Collection

Property:

`length`
The number of attributes in the collection. This property is read-only.

Methods:

`getNamedItem(`*`name`*`)`
Finds the attribute with the specified name and returns the attribute as yet another variant of an `IXMLDOMNode` object. (Its properties are covered next.)

`item(`*`index`*`)`
Retrieves attribute objects by index number, which ranges from 0 to the collection's length minus 1.

In working with XML files, you'll usually use `getNamedItem` to extract a specific attribute node by name. If you want to scan the entire list, though, you must use a loop, as shown here:

```
set alist = node.attributes
for i = 0 to alist.length-1
    set attr = list.item(i)
    wscript.echo attr.nodeName, "=", attr.nodeValue
next
```

Attributes are stored in `IXMLDOCNode` objects, with the interesting properties listed in Table 4.4.

Table 4.4 **Useful Properties of *IXMLDOCNode* When It Contains an Attribute**

Property	**Description**
`NodeName`	The attribute's name. Read-only.
`nodeValue`	The attribute's value. Read/write.
`specified`	A Boolean value. If `True`, the attribute's value was explicitly specified in the XML file. If `False`, the value was derived from the default value defined by the document's schema. Read-only.

As an example, the following script fragment displays the `width` attribute of all `<img>` tags in an XML document:

```
for each node in xmldoc.getElementsByTagName("img")
    wscript.echo node.attributes.getNamedItem("width").nodeValue
next
```

Reading an XML or HTML File

Now, with the reference material aside, let's see how these objects are used in practice. The following script reads an XML file and lists its structure. The script first loads the document and then uses subroutine `xmldump` to list the first element; `xmldump` calls itself recursively to list any subelements, as deeply as necessary, until the bottom-level text nodes have been listed. Here's the code:

```
                            ' Example file script0414.vbs
set xdoc = CreateObject("MSXML2.DOMDocument")

xdoc.load("test.xml")       ' load the file into the object

xmldump xdoc, 0             ' dump the entire document structure

' ---------------------------------------------------------------------
' xmldump - list contents of XML object 'x'; lvl is current depth

sub xmldump (x, lvl)
    dim gap, child, i

    gap = space(lvl*3)   ' make an indenting string to show the depth
                         ' list the node type and name
    wscript.echo gap & "--------------------"
    wscript.echo gap & x.nodeTypeString, "'" & x.nodename & "'"

                         ' list any attributes
    if x.nodetype = NODE_ELEMENT then
        set alist = x.attributes
        for i = 0 to alist.length-1
            set attr = alist.item(i)
            wscript.echo gap & "Attribute", attr.nodeName, "=", attr.nodeValue
        next
    end if
                         ' if the node has any text content, list it
    if not isnull(x.nodeValue) then _
         wscript.echo gap & "nodeValue:",      "'" & x.nodeValue & "'"
```

```
                        ' now list any children, indented one level deeper
      if x.hasChildNodes then
         for each child in x.childNodes
            xmldump child, lvl+1
         next
      end if
   end sub
```

The output of this script with the XML sample file introduced earlier starts out like this:

```
   --------------------
   document '#document'
      --------------------
      processinginstruction 'xml'
      nodeValue: 'version="1.0" encoding="utf-8"'
      --------------------
      comment '#comment'
      nodeValue: ' An XML representation of a slide show '
      --------------------
      element 'slideshow'
         --------------------
         element 'slide'
            --------------------
            element 'title'
               --------------------
               text '#text'
               nodeValue: 'Wake up to WonderWidgets!'
         --------------------
         element 'slide'
            --------------------
            element 'title'
               --------------------
               text '#text'
               nodeValue: 'Overview'
            --------------------
            element 'item'
               --------------------
               text '#text'
               nodeValue: 'Why '
               --------------------
               element 'em'
                  --------------------
                  text '#text'
                  nodeValue: 'WonderWidgets'
               --------------------
               text '#text'
               nodeValue: ' are great'
```

Note

A bug exists in the current version of the XML DOM implementation: It occurs when you use `nextSibling` to scan through a list of child nodes, such as this:

```
* step through x'ls child list sibling by sibling
set child = x.firstChild
do
   process child
   if isNull(child.nextSibling) then exit do
   set child = child.nextSibling
loop
```

Your script will encounter an invalid object at the end of the list—even at the last child in the list. `nextSibling`, for all intents and purposes, looks like a valid object but will fail when you try to reference it. If you want to traverse the list without using `for each`..., use this method:

```
* step through x's child list sibling by sibling
set child = x.firstChild
do
   (process child)
   if child is x.lastChild then exit do   ' this was the last one
   set child = child.nextSibling
loop
```

If you don't explicitly know x, you can use the following:

```
if child is child.parentNode.lastChild then exit do
```

Creating an XML or HTML File

Creating XML or HTML is much harder than reading it. The difficulty is that you have to create node objects individually and then stick them into the appropriate place in the document. It's tedious, as I'll show you.

For starters, let's create a simple HTML file that contains just an unordered (bulleted point) list of three items. The script looks like this:

```
                              ' Example file script0415.vbs
set xdoc = CreateObject("MSXML2.DOMDocument")

                ' create the outer HTML element
set html = xdoc.appendChild(xdoc.CreateElement("HTML"))

                ' add the unordered list
set list = html.appendChild(xdoc.createElement("UL"))

                ' add three list (LI) items
set item = list.appendChild(xdoc.createElement("LI"))
item.appendChild xdoc.createTextNode("This is item 1")
```

```
set item = list.appendChild(xdoc.createElement("LI"))
item.appendChild xdoc.createTextNode("This is item 2")

set item = list.appendChild(xdoc.createElement("LI"))
item.appendChild xdoc.createTextNode("This is item 3")

                ' save the created structure as an HTML file
xdoc.save "test.html"
```

The resulting HTML output file looks like this:

```
<HTML>
<UL>
<LI>This is item 1</LI>
<LI>This is item 2</LI>
<LI>This is item 3</LI>
</UL>
</HTML>
```

(Although, actually, it comes out as one long string, which is fine for a Web browser but ugly in a book, I broke it into several lines.)

The script is so complex because each element in the file must be created and then placed into position. Adding text to an element, as the sample script did with the `<LI>` elements, adds an additional step.

If you want to use formatting tags such as `<I>` for italics, you must jump through some extra hoops. For example, to add an item to our HTML list with the content "This is *italicized* text," we'd need the following HTML:

```
<LI>This is <I>italicized</I> text</LI>
```

This is actually a string of three "sibling" items: a text item, an `<I>` element with text content, and a third text item. The script code to add this item would be

```
set ital = xdoc.createElement("I")
ital.appendChild xdoc.createTextNode("italicized")

set item = list.appendChild(xdoc.createElement("LI"))
item.appendChild xdoc.createTextNode("This is ")
item.appendChild ital
item.appendChild xdoc.createTextNode(" text")
```

As you can see, creating HTML or XML in a script is not for the faint of heart, and probably isn't worth the trouble for very simple output files. Still, it can be useful when the output file is complex or when its final structure can't be determined in advance but must be computed on-the-fly.

Here's an example. The following script file creates a "slideshow" XML file by reading lines from the standard input. If an input line starts with an asterisk (`*`), it's considered to be the title of a new slide. Any other lines are considered to be "item" points of the current slide. Here's the code:

```
                                            ' Example file script0416.vbs

set xdoc = CreateObject("MSXML2.DOMDocument")
                         ' add the standard XML version marker
xdoc.appendChild xdoc.CreateProcessingInstruction("xml", "version=""1.0""")
                         ' create the outer slideshow element
set slideshow = xdoc.CreateElement("slideshow")
xdoc.appendChild slideshow

curslide = null          ' there is no current slide yet
                         ' read lines from standard input
do while not WScript.Stdin.AtEndOfStream
    str = WScript.Stdin.ReadLine

    if left(str,1) = "*" then
                         ' this is a new slide. Create text node
        set text = xdoc.CreateTextNode(mid(str,2))
                         ' add text to a title element
        set title = xdoc.CreateElement("title")
        title.appendChild(text)
                         ' add title to a new slide element
        set curslide = xdoc.CreateElement("slide")
        curslide.appendChild(title)
                         ' append slide to the slideshow's list
        slideshow.appendChild(curslide)

    elseif isnull(curslide) then
                         ' can't add an item before first slide
        wscript.echo "File must start with a * slide item!"
        wscript.quit 1

    else
                         ' a new item: create text node
        set text = xdoc.CreateTextNode(str)
                         ' add text to a new item element
        set item = xdoc.CreateElement("item")
        item.appendChild(text)
                         ' add item to current slide's list
        curslide.appendChild(item)
    end if
loop
                         ' save as XML text
xdoc.save "myshow.xml"
```

With the input data

```
*first slide
an important point
another point
*second slide
final point
```

the script created the following XML file (and again, I added line breaks to make it more readable, because the `Save` method writes the entire thing out as one long string):

```
<?xml version="1.0"?>
<slideshow>
<slide>
<title>first slide</title>
<item>an important point</item>
<item>another point</item>
</slide>
<slide>
<title>second slide</title>
<item>final point</item>
</slide>
</slideshow>
```

Although it's a difficult and tedious process, using the XML DOM object to create XML does have the advantage that the software is guaranteed to write a properly structured XML file.

Manipulating Programs and Shortcuts

You will sometimes want a script to run an external program such as Notepad, the `sort` command, or some other type of utility program. You might do this when writing a script to automatically collect and process information. You may also wish to have a script create desktop and Start menu shortcuts, as part of an installation routine, during logon, or for network maintenance. All these tasks can be managed using the `WScript.Shell` object. The word *shell* is a generic term for the command interface that computer users interact with to run programs. In the case of Windows XP, the shell is the desktop, a display managed by Windows Explorer.

The `WScript.Shell` Object

Like `WScript.FileSystemObject`, `WScript.Shell` is a utility object provided with Windows Script Host. `WScript.Shell` provides a way of interacting with the Windows program execution environment and Windows Explorer. This object's properties and methods let you interact with special folders, such as Desktop and My Documents, run programs, manage shortcuts, and examine environment variables, such as `Path`. `WScript.Shell` also lets you work with the Windows Registry, which is discussed in a later section. The properties and methods of the `WScript.Shell` object are listed in Reference List 4.9.

REFERENCE LIST 4.9 Properties and Methods of the `WScript.Shell` Object

Properties:

`CurrentDirectory`

Returns the name of the "current directory" of the Windows Script Host program. The current directory is the one searched when you attempt to access files without specifying a drive and path. This property is read/write.

`Environment`[(*`location`*)]

The `Environment` property returns a collection of `WshEnvironment` objects. The optional `location` argument specifies the set of environment data to modify, which can be one of the following values:

Location	Description
`"system"`	The base set of predefined environment definitions that are provided to every user
`"user"`	User-specific environment variable definitions that may add to or replace the system-wide definitions
`"process"`	The current set of environment variables from this logon session, as provided to the script program when it started
`"volatile"`	A list of variables that are computed from dynamic data when you log on

If the Location argument is omitted, `Environment` returns the `"system"` collection when the script is running on Windows XP, NT or 2000, and the `"process"` collection when running on Windows 9x and Me. You should *always* specify the location to ensure that you get the collection you need.

Use the `"system"` or `"user"` collections to modify the system-wide or current user's settings for *future* logons. However, to look up environment variable values for use in most script applications, you must specify the `"process"` location to retrieve the most complete and up-to-date list of environment variable values.

See the section "Reading the Environment" later in this chapter for more information. This property is read-only, although the elements of the collection it returns can be modified.

`SpecialFolders`[(*`folder`*)]

Returns a collection of `SpecialFolder` objects. These objects relate special user-specific Windows folders, such as the Desktop folder, to their actual locations on the hard disk. You can ask for the location of a specific folder by naming it as an argument to `SpecialFolders`. In this case, the return value is a string naming the path of the folder, rather than a collection. Here's a list of the special folder names:

continues

REFERENCE LIST 4.9 Continued

`AllUsersDesktop`	`NetHood`
`AllUsersStartMenu`	`PrintHood`
`AllUsersPrograms`	`Programs`
`AllUsersStartup`	`Recent`
`Desktop`	`SendTo`
`Favorites`	`StartMenu`
`Fonts`	`Startup`
`MyDocuments`	`Templates`

This property is read-only.

Methods:

`AppActivate` *`title`*

Activates an application window (brings it to the top and selects it for keyboard and mouse input). The window is chosen by matching its title text. Returns `True` if it was able to find and activate the window; Otherwise, it returns `False`. If you know the process's PID number, you can also pass that as a numeric argument to `AppActivate`. You can obtain an application's PID if you start it using `Exec`, or from the WMI objects discussed in Chapter 7.

`CreateShortcut(`*`strPathname`*`)`

Creates a new shortcut or opens an existing shortcut. Returns a `WshShortcut` or `WshURLShortcut` object; you must set this new object's properties to actually create a working shortcut. See the section titled "Creating Shortcuts" for details.

`Exec(`*`strCommand`*`)`

Runs an application in a child command prompt shell. The application's standard input, standard output, and standard error streams may be read and written by the script. Returns a `WshScriptExec` object, which is discussed later in this chapter.

`ExpandEnvironmentStrings(`*`strString`*`)`

Replaces any occurrences of environment variable names marked by percent signs (for example, `%path%`) in the input string with the contents of the environment variables.

`LogEvent` *`Type`*`,` *`Message`* [`,`*`Target`*]

Adds an event entry to a log file. The `Type` value indicates the event severity level, and must be one of the following values:

Value	Event Type
`0`	Success
`1`	Error
`2`	Warning

Value	Event Type
4	Information
8	Audit success
16	Audit failure

`Message` is a string, the text of the message to be recorded. If specified, `Target` specifies the machine whose Event Log is to receive the new entry. If desired, `LogEvent` can send an event to another computer across the network. If `Machine` is omitted, the event is stored in the local computer's log.

`Popup(`*`strText`***`, [`***`nWait`***`], [`***`strTitle`***`], [`***`nType`***`])`**
Displays text in a pop-up message box. It's like the `MsgBox` function but has an optional timeout value. The arguments are:

`strText`—The text to display.

`nWait`—The number of seconds to wait before closing the box; 0 means wait until the user clicks OK.

`strTitle`—The title to display at the top of the pop-up box.

`nType`—Indicates what sorts of buttons and icons to display. See "`MsgBox` Constants" in Appendix B, "Object Reference," for a list of values.

`Popup` returns one of the following values to indicate which button the user pressed to dismiss the message box:

Constant	Value	Button Title
vbOK	1	OK
vbCancel	2	Cancel
vbAbort	3	Abort
vbRetry	4	Retry
vbYes	6	Yes
vbNo	7	No

If the box closes itself due to a timeout, `Popup` returns `-1`.

`RegDelete` *`strName`*
Deletes a key or one of its values from the Registry. `strName` is the path to the key or value. See "Working with the Registry," later in this chapter for details.

`RegRead(`*`strName`***`)`**
Returns the value of a key or value from the Registry.

`RegWrite` *`strName`*, *`value`* [,*`strType`*]
Creates a new key, adds value to an existing key, or changes the value of an existing value.

continues

REFERENCE LIST 4.9 Continued

Run(*strCommand*, [*intWindowStyle*], [*bWaitOnReturn*])

Runs a program in a separate window. Here are the three arguments:

`strCommand`—The command to run. The string should list the name of the program and any arguments it requires.

`intWindowStyle`—The size of window to create. The values you can specify are `1`, which opens the window normally, `3`, which opens the window maximized, or `7`, which opens the window minimized (as an icon).

`bWaitOnReturn`—A Boolean value. If this is specified and `True`, the script will wait until the program terminates and will return its error status as the return value from `Run`. If this is omitted or `False`, the script will continue running after the program is started, and the `Run` method will return 0.

SendKeys(*string***)**

Sends one or more keystrokes to the active window (as if typed on the keyboard).

Running Programs

`WScript.Shell` can be used to run other programs at the behest of your script. You might do this as part of a complex procedure to gather and manipulate information or as a way of automating some repetitive task. Four of `WScript.Shell`'s methods may come into play:

- `Run`. Starts a Windows program.
- `SendKeys`. Sends keystrokes to the program as if you were typing them manually.
- `AppActivate`. Selects the program that `SendKeys` works with.
- `Exec`. Starts and interacts with a command-line program.

Running Windows Programs

You can run Windows programs using the `WScript.Shell` object's `Run` method, which starts up the program in its own window.

The first argument to `Run` is a string naming the program (with a path, if the program is not in one of the standard folders found in the `PATH` environment variable) and any arguments required. For example, a script could write data to a text file and display it with the Notepad program, as in this example:

```
                                                ' Example file script0417.vbs
set shell = CreateObject("WScript.Shell")   ' create utility objects
set fso   = CreateObject("Scripting.FileSystemObject")
                                                ' get name of scratch file
tmpfile   = fso.BuildPath(fso.GetSpecialFolder(TemporaryFolder),_
    fso.GetTempName())
```

```
set file = fso.CreateTextFile(tmpfile)      ' create a text file
for i = 100 to 0 step -1
   file.WriteLine i & " bottles of beer on the wall!"
next
file.Close
set file = Nothing                          ' release the File object

' run notepad to display the file, and wait for it to terminate
shell.Run "notepad " & tmpfile, 1, True

' delete the scratch file
fso.DeleteFile(tmpfile)
```

In this example, the `Run` method starts Windows Notepad with the name of the created text file as its argument. The second argument, `1`, tells Notepad to open a standard window, and the third argument, `True`, tells the script to wait until the user closes Notepad.

You can interact with programs you've run in a limited way, by sending keystrokes to them as if the user had typed them. I don't consider this terribly useful, so I'll only outline how it's done:

- You must know the title of the window that you wish to control. For programs that change their title to the name of an open file, this can be tricky. Use `AppActivate("`*`title`*`")` to cause Windows to bring this desired program to the foreground. `AppActivate` returns `True` if successful; if it fails, there's not much you can do.
- You can send keystrokes to the application with the `SendKeys` method. `SendKeys` sends messages to the application that make it think the user has pressed keyboard keys. You can't simulate mouse movement, but you can send special keys such as END using `"{END}"` and Alt+F with `"%F"`; you can find the complete list of key symbols in the Microsoft Script Host documentation.
- It's best to have the script pause briefly between each keystroke it sends to an application to give the application time to process the request. `WScript.Sleep 100` pauses for 100 msec (one-tenth of a second), which should be adequate in most cases.

`SendKeys` lets you script interactions with Windows programs in the manner of a player piano. You can actually accomplish some sophisticated things using this method, which I call *key stuffing*, such as running a database report on a scheduled basis. However, writing this kind of script and debugging it can be nightmarish. If possible, it's usually better and easier to do "automated" processing using an application's Automation interface or command-line interface.

Running Command-Line Programs

You can run command-line programs from a script using the `WScript.Shell` object's `Run` or `Exec` methods. If you only want to start the application and let it run in its own window, `Run` is adequate. However, `Exec` has two advantages over `Run`:

- You can start a program, let the script perform other tasks, and later determine if and how the program terminated.
- When running a command-line program, `Exec` lets you send data directly to the program through its standard input file stream, and you can read data from the program's standard output and standard error output using `TextStream` objects.

Start a command-line program using the `Shell` object's `Exec` method, specifying a full command line, as shown here:

```
set shell = CreateObject("WScript.Shell")
set program = shell.Exec("ping www.someplace.com")
```

You can specify a full path to the program you're running, or, if it can be found in `PATH`, you can just specify its name, as in the preceding example.

Notice that `set` is used to get the return value of Exec. `Exec` returns a `WshScriptExec` object that gives you control over the program you just started. The properties and methods of `WshScriptExec` are listed in Reference List 4.10.

REFERENCE LIST 4.10 Properties and Method of the `WshScriptExec` Object

Properties:

`ExitCode`

Returns the application's exit status after it has terminated. If the process is still running, `ExitCode` and `Status` are 0.

`ProcessID`

Returns the process identification number (PID) for the application. You can use this number as an argument to the `AppActivate` method

`Status`

Indicates whether the program is still running: `0` means it's running, and `1` means it has terminated.

`StdErr`

A `TextStream` object that may be read to get any output the program writes to the standard error output.

`StdIn`

A `TextStream` object that may be written to; anything written to `StdIn` is sent to the standard input of the program.

`StdOut`

A `TextStream` object that may be read to get any output the program writes to the standard output.

Method:

`Terminate`
Terminates the program if it's still running. Usually this is only used in an abnormal situation (for example, when a program that was expected to have completed within a few seconds is still running after a longer time).

After starting a command with `Exec`, you'll usually interact with it by writing to its standard input or reading from its standard output or standard error. Therefore, you can use an external program to perform any sort of task to assist the script. In this example, a script uses the ping program to test a list of Internet hosts to be sure they're online. If any are offline, a message is printed. Here's the code:

```
                                     ' Example file script0418.vbs
set shell = CreateObject("WScript.Shell")
hosts     = array("www.netsol.com", "www.google.com","www.yahoo.com")

failed    = ""                       ' list of failed hosts
for each host in hosts
    if not pingtest(host) then
        failed = failed & " " & host ' if failed, add name to list
    end if
next
                                     ' if any failed, display the list
if len(failed) > 0 then MsgBox "Warning: can't reach" & failed

' ------------------------------------------------------------------------
' pingtest - try to ping the host named 'host'. If even one ping
' returns, consider the test a success.

function pingtest (host)
    pingtest = False                      ' assume failure

    wscript.echo "Pinging", host

    set ping = shell.Exec("ping " & host) ' run the command

    do while not ping.Stdout.AtEndOfStream
        str = ping.Stdout.ReadLine        ' read its results

        if instr(str, "could not find") > 0 then exit do

        if instr(str, "Reply from") > 0 then
            pingtest = True               ' a reply means success
            exit do                       ' we can stop right now
        end if
    loop
    ping.Terminate                        ' stop ping if it's still going
end function
```

With or without interaction, after the program has done its job, you may want to wait for it to terminate voluntarily. Because you don't know exactly when this will happen, your best bet is to have the script test to see whether the program is still running (`Status = 0`), and if so, wait a moment, as in this example:

```
set shell = CreateObject("WScript.Shell")

set program = shell.Run("someprogram")

... (interact with program)

do while program.status = 0   ' while program is still running
    WScript.Sleep 100          ' pause 100 msec before trying again
loop
```

The `Sleep` method is used here to pause the script while waiting for the program to terminate. If you didn't put the pause in, the `do` loop would circle at a furious pace waiting for the program to end. With the script program making this kind of demand on the processor, the external program would have a harder time getting its job done.

If you wanted to give the program, say, five seconds to terminate before forcing it to stop, you could use a `for` loop to limit the number of times the loop is executed:

```
for nwait = 1 to 50
    if program.status <> 0 then exit for
    WScript.Sleep 100
next
program.Terminate
```

Here, we will wait 100 msec up to 50 times, for a total of at most five seconds. If the program terminates earlier, `exit for` keeps us from waiting longer than necessary. After the loop, `Terminate` stops the program if it hasn't already stopped by itself.

Creating and Modifying Shortcuts

`WScript.Shell` can also be used to create and modify shortcuts on the desktop and the Start menu. You could use this feature to ensure that a necessary shortcut was always installed on every user's desktop, or as part of an installation procedure for a new program. You can create both standard program shortcuts and so-called "URL shortcuts" that link to a Web site.

Shortcuts are actually small files that contain the data Windows Explorer uses to fire up the program represented by a shortcut. Normal shortcut files use the extension `.lnk`, whereas URL shortcuts use the extension `.url`. The data inside shortcut files isn't plain, readable text, so `WScript.Shell` provides an object to represent this data and make it easy to manage.

Here's how it works: You first use `WScript.Shell`'s method `CreateShortcut` or `ModifyShortcut` to "open" a new or existing shortcut for editing. This creates an instance of a `WshShortcut` object that represents the shortcut you're working with.

Then you can change this object's properties, and Windows will update the corresponding shortcut.

Note

Windows actually has two varieties of the `WshShortcut` object: `WshShortcut`, for standard shortcuts, and `WshURLShortcut`, for links to Web pages. You create regular shortcuts with a `.lnk` extension and URL shortcuts with a `.url` extension. When you modify a shortcut, the methods and procedures are identical for both types.

The properties and the one method of `WshShortcut` and `WshUrlShortcut` are listed in Reference List 4.11.

REFERENCE LIST 4.11 Properties and Method of the `WshShortcut` and `WshUrlShortcut` Objects

Properties:

`Arguments`
Specifies any arguments to be passed to the program. This is a string value. Read/write.

`Description`
The shortcut's description text, which appears as a tooltip if you hover the mouse over the shortcut icon. Read/write.

`FullName`
The fully qualified path to the shortcut object's target program, which is set by the `TargetPath` attribute. Read-only.

`Hotkey`
Identifies the key combination to activate the shortcut. Read/write.

`IconLocation`
The icon assigned to the shortcut. Read/write.

The format of the `IconLocation` property is `"`*`filename, iconnumber`*`"` where `filename` is the name of an EXE or DLL file containing one or more icons and `iconnumber` is the zero-based index into the file's list of icons. For most applications, the first icon is the one used for shortcuts, so `"filename.exe, 0"` is the usual `IconLocation` setting.

`TargetPath`
The path to the shortcut's target program or a URL in the case of a link to a Web page. Read/write.

continues

REFERENCE LIST 4.11 Continued

WindowStyle
Assigns a window style to a shortcut or identifies the type of window style used by a shortcut. Read/write.

`WindowStyle` determines how the application will be started. The possible values are `1`, which opens the window normally, `3`, which opens the window maximized, and `7`, which opens the window minimized (as an icon).

WorkingDirectory
The working directory used by a shortcut. Read/write.

Method:

Save
Saves a new or edited shortcut object to disk. This method must be used after the shortcut object's properties are changed to commit the changes to the `.lnk` file.

Here is script to create a desktop shortcut to a text file containing a "to-do" list that you edit with Notebook:

```
                                           ' Example file script0419.vbs
set shl = CreateObject("WScript.Shell")   ' make objects
set fso = CreateObject("Scripting.FileSystemObject")
desktop = shl.SpecialFolders("Desktop")  ' get folder locations
mydocs  = shl.SpecialFolders("MyDocuments")
                                           ' create shortcut object
set sc  = shl.CreateShortcut(fso.BuildPath(desktop, "\BOOK To Do.lnk"))

sc.TargetPath       = "notepad.exe "        ' set program to run
sc.WorkingDirectory = mydocs               ' set working folder
sc.Arguments        = fso.BuildPath(mydocs, "todo.txt") ' specify file
sc.WindowStyle      = 1                    ' open as normal window
sc.Hotkey           = "Ctrl+Alt+T"         ' set hotkey
sc.IconLocation     = "notepad.exe, 0"     ' use normal notepad icon
sc.Description      = "View and Edit To Do List"
sc.Save                                    ' create the shortcut
```

The script first creates the utility objects it needs and then looks up the locations of the Desktop and My Documents folders. It creates the new shortcut, named `to do.lnk`, in the Desktop folder. The shortcut runs Notepad with a file named `todo.txt` in My Documents.

If the program or file specified by `TargetPath` can't be found in the environment variable `PATH`, you must specify the full path the program or document named in `TargetPath`. Windows will find `notepad.exe` by itself, but we could have specified its full path with

```
sc.TargetPath = shl.ExpandEnvironmentStrings("%WINDIR%\notepad.exe ")
```

or, equivalently, with

```
sc.TargetPath = fso.BuildPath(_
    fso.GetSpecialFolder(WindowsFolder), "notepad.exe ")
```

You can add items to the Start menu by adding shortcuts to the special folders used to populate the menu. You can't add icons to the large Start menu panel with a script, but you can add them to the All Programs list.

To create Start menu items, create shortcuts in a subfolder of one of these two main folders:

- To create a shortcut that will be seen by all users on the computer, create the shortcut under `SpecialFolders("AllUsersStartMenu")`.
- To create a shortcut for the current user only, create the shortcut under `SpecialFolders("StartMenu")`.

For example, to create a "Special Tools" folder and shortcut for all computer users, you could write a script based on this outline:

```
set shl    = CreateObject("WScript.Shell")' make objects
set fso    = CreateObject("Scripting.FileSystemObject")

startmenu  = shl.SpecialFolders("AllUsersStartMenu")
toolfolder = fso.BuildPath(startmenu, "Special Tools")

CreateFullPath(toolfolder)                 ' create folder if necessary

set sc = shl.CreateShortcut(fso.BuildPath(toolfolder, "first tool.lnk"))
   ... set shortcut properties
sc.Save

sub CreateFullPath (path)
   ...
   (the CreateFullPath subroutine was shown earlier in the chapter)
```

This script constructs the name of the folder under the Start menu in the variable `toolfolder`. It uses the subroutine `CreateFullPath` to be sure that the folder exists and then creates one or more shortcuts in the new folder.

Working with the Environment

Environment variables such as the program `PATH` and the temporary file folder name `TEMP` can be examined by looking through the `Environment` property of `WScript.Shell`. `Environment("process")` returns a collection of `WshEnvironment` objects that define the current set of environment variables. You can examine this collection to extract environment variable definitions. Here are some reasons you may want to do this:

- To find the name of the folder to be used for scratch files, which is named by the `TEMP` environment variable.
- To look through the program search path (variable `PATH`) to see where a program is installed.

- To look up special settings communicated in the environment, such as the location of library files (variable `LIB`), the logged-on user's name (variable `USERNAME`), or the current processor type (`PROCESSOR_ARCHITECTURE`). Although these settings may be tampered with by the computer's user, they're convenient when security is not at stake.

You may also use the `Environment` property to modify the settings that Windows uses to set up the environment each time you log on. This is somewhat complex and needs some explanation.

Every time you log on, Windows sets up a list of environment variables. It gets these from several sources. Windows keeps a list of default "systemwide" environment variable definitions that every user receives when he logs on. In addition, each user can have an additional set of personalized variables; these can add to or override the system default values. (You can see these initial settings if you right-click My Computer, select the Advanced tab, and click Environment Variables.) In addition, there is a set of dynamic or "volatile" values that are computed when you log on, such as the name of your logon server and the current computer name.

When you log on, Windows first initializes your environment with the dynamic "volatile" variables, then adds in the "system" definitions, and then adds the "user" definitions to come up with your initial environment.

You can modify these initial definitions either through the Computer Properties dialog box or through scripting. `Environment("system")` and `Environment("user")` return collections of `WshEnvironment` objects that represent the initial settings, and if you modify the values in these collections, Windows will make the changes apply for future logons. (There is another set of values in `Environment("volatile")` listing the variables that are computed "dynamically" using current logon information, but there is no need ever to modify these.)

After logging on, you may change environment variable values from the command line using the `set` command, as described in Chapter 11, "The CMD Command-Line Environment." These changes persist as long as you stay logged on. Every time you start a program, the program inherits a copy of the current settings, which is called the "process" environment. The "process" set is the sum total of all definitions and changes. However, any changes made to the process environment by a program aren't seen by other programs, and they don't persist when the program terminates.

Note

This is the reason for the important distinction between the collections returned by the `Environment` property. The `"process"` collection gives you current environment values. Use this collection to extract *current* information from the environment. The `"system"` and `"user"` collections are used only for management purposes to set the initial values for *future* logons.

The `Environment` collection's properties and methods are shown in Reference List 4.12.

REFERENCE LIST 4.12 Properties and Methods of the `Environment` Collection

Properties:

`Item(`*`name`*`)`
Returns the contents for the environment variable `name`. The value returned is the definition of the named variable. If the variable is undefined, the property returns the empty string ("").

This property is read/write: You can assign a new value to it to alter an environment variable's definition or to create a new environment variable definition. If you alter a value in `"process"` collection, the change will be visible only to the instance of the script that makes the change. If you alter a variable in the `"system"` or `"user"` collection, the definition will not take effect until the next time you log on.

`Length`
Returns the number of Windows environment variables in the collection. Read-only.

Methods:

`Count`
Returns the number of environment variables in the collection; appears to be the same as `Length`.

`Remove` *`strName`*
Removes an existing environment variable by name. If you remove a variable from the "process" collection, the change will be visible only to the instance of the script that makes the change. If you delete a variable in the "system" or "user" collection, the change will not take effect until the next time you log on.

Extracting Environment Information

The `Environment("process")` collection contains the entire current set of environment variables (those with names and those without). To retrieve individual environment variables (and their values) from this collection, use the environment variable name as the index. For example, the `TEMP` environment variable can be fetched with the following:

```
username = shl.Environment("process").Item("TEMP")
```

Caution

You must specify `"process"` as the `Environment` method's *`location`* argument if you want to view current environment settings. On Windows NT, XP, and 2000, if you omit the argument, Windows will return the system default environment, not the complete current environment.

You can list all the current environment variables with this script:

```
                                        ' Example file script0420.vbs
set shl = CreateObject("WScript.Shell")
for each env in shl.Environment("process")
    wscript.echo env
next
```

Printing the environment object itself (`env` in the sample script) prints `"name=value"`, in contrast to the `Item(name)` method, which extracts just the value.

If you only need to convert an environment variable to its value, the `ExpandEnvironmentStrings` method may be more useful. `ExpandEnvironmentStrings` scans a string for items that look like `%XXX%`, where *XXX* is the name of an environment variable. `%XXX%` is replaced with the definition of the environment variable. This method makes short work of filling out pathnames that are based on the Windows directory, as mentioned earlier in the discussion of shortcuts. This expression

```
shl.ExpandEnvironmentStrings("%WINDIR%\notepad.exe ")
```

replaces `%WINDIR%` with `C:\WINDOWS`, or whatever the Windows directory is on the current computer, and returns the proper path, `C:\WINDOWS\notepad.exe`.

Tip

Using `ExpandEnvironmentStrings` is a handy way to get environment variable values. You can simply use the expression

```
shl.ExpandEnvironmentStrings("%varname%")
```

where you need the value of variable `varname`. This is especially useful with environment variables that are defined recursively; some variables contain `%XXX%` items in their definitions. `ExpandEnvironmentStrings` takes care of expanding all the items until no more instances of `%` are left.

Managing Environment Settings

As mentioned earlier, when you log on, your environment settings are obtained from a set of calculated values, plus a list of systemwide default settings, plus user-specific settings. These initial values are stored in the Registry, and they can be edited by modifying items in the `Environment("system")` or `Environment("user")` collections. To modify the systemwide environment definitions, you must have Administrator privileges.

The following sample script shows how to add a new folder to the `PATH` list so that all users will have access to a newly installed application:

```
                     ' Example file script0421.vbs
set shl = CreateObject("WScript.Shell")
                     ' obtain system-wide default environment collection
set env=shl.Environment("system")
                     ' append semicolon plus "c:\newfolder" to the path
env.Item("PATH") = env.Item("PATH") & ";c:\newfolder"
```

Changes made to these collections only affect the users' environments at their next logon.

Working with the Registry

The Windows Registry is a repository of system and user information that is accessible to any Windows program. The Registry provides a centralized, well-managed place to store settings, preferences, and security information.

Note

If you're new to Windows XP and are used to Windows 95, 98, and Me, you may have heard horror stories about peoples' Registry databases becoming corrupted, or you may have experienced this nightmare yourself. If the Registry gets mangled, Windows can't function. The good news is that the Registry in Windows XP and Windows 2000 is well protected against *inadvertent* crashes and corruption.

However, this won't help you if your script deliberately deletes or alters important Registry information. Be very careful when modifying Registry information, especially in the `Control`, `System`, and `Classes` sections, and under any section titled `Windows`.

Now that we've gotten past the obligatory warnings, I can say that the Registry doesn't have to be all that scary, and scripts can take good advantage of the ability to read and write Registry data.

The Registry is organized much like a file system. Just as a disk drive holds folders, and folders can contain files or nested folders, the Registry holds information in *keys*, and keys can contain *values* or nested keys. The syntax for specifying the location of information in the Registry is even similar to the file path. For example, `\HKEY_CURRENT_USER\Software\Microsoft` is a typical key name.

And just as a computer can have several disk drives, the Registry has several separate branches of keys, whose names all start with `HKEY_`. When specifying the names of keys or values with the script objects we're about to discuss, you must specify the full path to any key or value in which you're interested, and each path must start with one of the five standard branches. You must use the full names or one of the abbreviations listed in Table 4.5.

Table 4.5 **Registry Key Root Names and Abbreviations**

Root Name	Abbreviation
HKEY_CLASSES_ROOT	HKCR
HKEY_CURRENT_CONFIG	—
HKEY_CURRENT_USER	HKCU
HKEY_LOCAL_MACHINE	HKLM
HKEY_USERS	—

Values are named items within keys and are specified by adding the value name to the key's pathname. For example, under Windows XP, the Registry key `HKEY_CURRENT_USER\SessionInformation` has a value named `ProgramCount` that tracks the number of programs the user is running. The pathname for this value is `HKEY_CURRENT_USER\SessionInformation\ProgramCount`.

Examining Registry Keys and Values

The `WScript.Shell` object's `RegRead` method lets you read values from Registry entries. You can get values just by specifying their pathname. (A key can also have a *default value*, which is specified by the name of the key itself with a trailing backslash but no value name.)

The `RegRead` method returns the value for a specified value, as in this example:

```
set shell = CreateObject("WScript.Shell")
wscript.echo shell.RegRead("HKCU\SessionInformation\ProgramCount")
```

`RegRead` can return one of several types of values, depending on the type of data stored in the Registry value. The Registry data types and the corresponding data types returned by `RegRead` are listed in Table 4.6. The most common two types are listed first.

Table 4.6 **Registry Value Types and *RegRead* Results**

Registry Type	RegRead return type	Purpose
REG_DWORD	Integer	Single number
REG_SZ	String	Text data
REG_EXPAND_SZ	String	Text with embedded environment variables
REG_MULTI_SZ	Array of strings	Multiple lines of text
REG_BINARY	Array of integers	Generic binary data

The requested item must exist in the Registry when you use `RegRead`; otherwise, the script generates an error.

Saving Information in the Registry

You might use a script to modify Registry settings as part of network management (for example, to enforce certain settings upon logon). Also, the Registry can be a very handy place to store information used by scripts: It's *persistent*. That is, information placed in the Registry stays there between runs of your script and between logon sessions. You can take advantage of this to store counters of the number of times a script is run, default parameter values, and so on.

Caution

Saving information in the Registry requires care—trust me, you really can mess up your computer. It's best to do a backup of the Registry and your important files before embarking on the adventure of debugging a Registry-modifying script.

The `RegWrite` method creates Registry values. You can use `RegWrite` to create a key by assigning it a default value. Here are the three arguments to `RegWrite`:

- `strName`. The path of the value or key to be created. To specify a key, the path should end with a backslash (\).
- `Value`. The data to assign to the value. Only string or integer values are accepted; arrays are not.
- `strType`. The name of a Registry data type to use, specified as a string. Allowed values are `"REG_SZ"`, `"REG_DWORD"`, `"REG_BINARY"`, and `"REG_EXPAND_SZ"`. If `strType` is omitted, the object automatically chooses between `REG_DWORD` or `REG_SZ`, depending on whether `Value` is a number or a string.

Although modifying system settings is fairly dangerous, you can safely use the Registry to store configuration information that you'd like to make available to scripts, such as default server names, important IP addresses, and usernames, or to run counts or error counts. The Registry is a good place to store information that you'd like to have persist from one run of the script to another. You can also store setup information, such as the name of a user who should be informed of problems, and so on. This way, the settings can be changed without modifying the script itself, and the same information can be used by several scripts.

You can fairly safely store information in the Registry if you adopt a standard location. Here's the method I use:

- For information that is unique to each user, store values under `HKCU\Software\`*`YourCompanyName`*`\`*`ScriptName`* but substitute your actual company name and the actual name of your script. This way, your keys won't collide with those used by manufactured software or by your other scripts.
- For information that is common for all users of a given computer, use `HKLM\Software\`*`YourCompanyName`*`\`*`ScriptName`*.

The following example shows how a script can store a number in the Registry that counts how many times the script has been run:

```
                                              ' Example file script0422.vbs
set shell = CreateObject("WScript.Shell")

nruns = shell.RegRead("HKCU\Software\Mycompany\RunCount\number of runs")
nruns = nruns+1
wscript.echo "Number of runs:", nruns

Shell.RegWrite "HKCU\Software\Mycompany\RunCount\number of runs",_
    nruns, "REG_DWORD"
```

However, the script starts by reading from the "number of runs" value, so this must exist before the script is run for the first time.

In general, you must either manually create the keys your application needs or create an "install" script that creates the keys the first time around. And just as you must create a top-level folder on the disk before creating a subfolder, you must create upper-level Registry keys before lower-level keys. An "install" script for the counting example might look like this:

```
                                              ' Example file script0423.vbs
set shell = CreateObject("WScript.Shell")

Shell.RegWrite "HKCU\Software\Mycompany\", ""
Shell.RegWrite "HKCU\Software\Mycompany\RunCount\", ""
Shell.RegWrite "HKCU\Software\Mycompany\RunCount\number of runs",_
    0, "REG_DWORD"
```

This ensures that the keys Mycompany and `RunCount` exist, and then it initializes the `number of runs` value to `0`. The `Software` key always exists; it is created when Windows is installed.

Another example shows how a maintenance script might use the Registry to store the name of a server that is to be managed. This script gives you the option of specifying the server name on the command line. If the server is specified, the script stores the name in the Registry for future use. If the server is not specified, the script uses the name previously stored in the Registry. Here's the code for this example:

```
                                                     ' Example File script0424.vbs
set shell = CreateObject("WScript.Shell")

if WScript.Arguments.Count = 0 then
    ' server was not named on command line. Get default value from Registry
    ' but don't stop on errors, in case the value is not defined.
    on error resume next
    servername = shell.RegRead("HKCU\Software\Mycompany\ServerClean\servername")
    if isempty(servername) or err.Number <> 0 then
        ' there was no default name found... display message and quit
        MsgBox("You must specify the server name on the command line "&_
```

```
            "the first time you run this script")
        WScript.Quit 1
    end if
else
    ' server was named on command line. Save in Registry. Be sure to
    ' create MyCompany and ServerClean keys if they don't already exist.
    servername = WScript.Arguments(0)
    Shell.RegWrite "HKCU\Software\Mycompany\", ""
    Shell.RegWrite "HKCU\Software\Mycompany\ServerClean\", ""
    Shell.RegWrite "HKCU\Software\Mycompany\ServerClean\servername",_
        servername, "REG_SZ"
end if

WScript.echo "Cleaning up server \\" & servername & "..."

' now manage the server: clean up temporary files, etc.
.
.
.
```

5

Network and Printer Objects

ROAD MAP

- This chapter shows how to use the `WScript.Network` object to control mapped network drives and network printer connections.
- You should be comfortable with the material in Chapter 3, "Scripting and Objects," before reading this chapter.
- You can use `WScript.Network` to control printing from DOS applications as well as Windows applications.
- The last section shows how you can send output from a script directly to a printer; this is especially useful with scripts that you run unattended from the Task Scheduler.

Managing Network and Printer Connections

WINDOWS SCRIPT HOST PROGRAMS can query and manage your computer's network and printer connections. You might want to do this for several reasons, such as the following:

- You want to collect and report network information as part of a documentation-generating script.
- You want a logon script to ensure that every time your users log on, the correct network drives and printer connections are available, regardless of how badly the users may have mangled things during their previous sessions.
- Your network environment changes frequently, so you want to use a script to record and invoke the proper settings.
- You want to standardize and simplify the setup of newly installed computers in your organization.
- You use a workstation or server on a test bench and want to be able to easily select one of several standard configurations.

Windows Script Host can help you accomplish all these tasks. Although the command line's `net` command can perform some of the same tasks, WSH scripts offer more detailed control and can work with the Registry, files, and other system components at the same time as the network.

Scriptable objects can also let you use printers to automatically generate output from your scripts. After discussing network and printer management, we'll cover the use of printers in scripts.

The first object I'll introduce is the `WSHNetwork` object, which is created with the name `"WScript.Network"`, as in the following statement:

```
set wshNetwork = CreateObject("WScript.Network")
```

This is a "utility" object. As with `Scripting.FileSystemObject`, you only need one instance of `WScript.Network` in your script to perform network tasks. Its properties and methods are shown in Reference List 5.1.

REFERENCE LIST 5.1 Properties and Methods of the `WSHNetwork` Object

Properties:

`ComputerName`

Returns the computer name set on the Computer Name tab in the System Properties dialog box. This is the computer's name for Windows Networking. (Read-only.)

`UserDomain`

Returns the Windows networking domain name of the current logged-on user's account. For non-domain or local account logons, this is the same as the computer name. (Read-only.)

`UserName`

Returns the logon name of the currently logged on user. (Read-only.)

Methods:

`AddPrinterConnection` *`LocalName`*, *`RemoteName`*[, *`UpdateProfile`* [, *`UserName`*, *`Password`*]]

Redirects one of the emulated LPT printer ports available to MS-DOS applications on the local computer to a remote networked printer.

Here are the arguments:

- `LocalName`. The name of the DOS printer port (`"LPT1"`, `"LPT2"`, or `"LPT3"`) to redirect to the network printer. You cannot redirect an LPT port that is already being used by a physical local printer.
- `RemoteName`. The share name of the network printer in UNC notation (`\\`*`machine`*`\`*`sharename`*). You can specify the printer's short share name or its "friendly" name (for example, `"\\sumatra\okidata"` or `"\\sumatra\Okidata OL 810"`).

- `UpdateProfile`. Optional Boolean value. If `True`, the network mapping is saved to the current user's profile so that it will be restored upon the next logon.
- `UserName`. Optional. The name of a user account valid on the remote computer to use for this network connection. Will not work if there is already a network drive or printer connection to the same remote computer using the default username or some other username. Only one set of credentials at a time can be used to connect to a given remote computer. Can be specified as `"`*`username`*`"` to use one of the remote machine's local accounts or as `"\\`*`domain`*`\`*`username`*`"` to use a domain account.
- `Password`. Optional. This is the logon password associated with the specified *`UserName`*.

An error is generated if the port is already redirected or is used by a locally attached printer.

`AddWindowsPrinterConnection` *`PrinterPath`* [, *`DriveName`* [, *`Port`*]]
Adds a connection to a remote network printer that will then be available to Windows applications. This adds an icon to the user's `Printers` folder.

Here are the arguments:

- `PrinterPath`. The share name of the network printer in UNC notation (for example, `"\\`*`machine`*`\`*`sharename`*`"`). You can specify the printer's short share name or its "friendly" name as displayed by the remote computer.

  This method takes one or two additional arguments if the script is running under Windows 9*X* or Me. These arguments are ignored if specified on Windows XP/2000/NT. If you need to write a script that works under any version of Windows, you can pass all the arguments, or you can examine the `OS` environment variable to identify the Windows version and then choose the appropriate way to use `AddWindowsPrinterConnection`.
- `DriverName`. The name of the printer as defined by its Windows device driver (for example, `"Lexmark Optra S 1650"`). On Windows 9*X* and Me, the driver must already be installed on the local computer; it will not automatically be downloaded even if it's available from the remote computer as it would be using the Printer control panel's Add Printer Wizard.
- `Port`. Optional. This is the emulated local MS-DOS LPT port to redirect to the network printer. See `AddPrinterConnection` for a discussion of LPT port redirection.

No error is generated if there is already a connection icon for the indicated printer.

continues

REFERENCE LIST 5.1 Continued

`EnumNetworkDrives()`

Returns a collection of objects that lists drive letters mapped to remote network drives. The objects are strings and come in pairs. The first item in each pair (`.Item(0)`, `.Item(2)`, and so on) is a mapped drive name (for example, `"F:"`). The second item in each pair (`.Item(1)`, `.Item(3)`, and so on) is the UNC share name to which the drive is redirected.

`EnumPrinterConnections()`

Returns a collection of objects that lists LPT ports that are redirected to remote network printers. These objects are simple text strings, and they come in pairs. The first item in each pair (`.Item(0)`, `.Item(2)`, and so on) is a local port name (for example, `"LPT1"`). The second item in each pair (`.Item(1)`, `.Item(3)`, and so on) is the name of the remote printer. The names returned may not be the short UNC share names but may instead be the remote machine's "friendly" printer name. For example, instead of `"\\sumatra\okidata"` the name may be listed as `"\\sumatra\Okidata OL 810"`.

`MapNetworkDrive` *`LocalName, RemoteName`* [, *`UpdateProfile`* [, *`UserName, Password`*]]

Redirects a local drive letter to a remote shared folder. Here are the arguments:

- `LocalName`. The drive letter to redirect. This may also be an empty string to establish a connection to the remote share without mapping a letter; this can increase the speed with which the remote drive can be subsequently accessed.
- `RemoteName`. The UNC share name of the remote folder (for example, `"\\`*`server`*`\`*`sharename`*`"`).
- `UpdateProfile`. Optional Boolean argument. If `True`, the drive mapping is added to the current user's profile so that the mapping will be reestablished upon the next logon.
- `UserName`. Optional. This is the name of a user account valid on the remote computer to use for this network connection. Will not work if there is already a network drive or printer connection to the same remote computer using the default username or some other username. Only one set of credentials at a time can be used to connect to a given remote computer. Can be specified as `"`*`username`*`"` to use one of the remote machine's local accounts or as `"\\`*`domain`*`\`*`username`*`"` to use a domain account.
- `Password`. Optional. This is the password to use to authenticate the specified `UserName`.

The method fails if the drive letter is already mapped, if the letter corresponds to a local physical disk drive, or if the network path does not exist.

RemoveNetworkDrive *Name* [,*Force* [, *UpdateProfile*]]
Disconnects a mapped drive letter from a remote shared folder.

Here are the arguments:

- Name. The drive letter to unmap (for example, "F:"). Note that the colon is required. If the network path was attached without a network drive, specify the remote network path instead of the drive letter.
- Force. Optional Boolean argument. If specified and True, the drive mapping will be disconnected even if the mapped drive is currently in use. Otherwise, if the drive is in use, the script will generate an error. "In use" means that a local program is using a file or viewing a folder on the remote drive or that a command-prompt window has the mapped drive as its current drive.
- UpdateProfile. Optional Boolean argument. If specified and True, the drive mapping will be deleted from the current user's profile so that the mapping will not be automatically reestablished at the next logon. If the mapping is in the user's profile and UpdateProfile is not specified, the mapping will remain in the profile.

An error is generated if the connection does not exist.

RemovePrinterConnection *Name* [, *bForce* [, *bUpdateProfile*]]
Removes redirection from a local emulated LPT port to a remote network printer.

Here are the arguments:

- Name. The name of the redirected port (for example, "LPT1") or the UNC share name to which a port is redirected; the latter can unmap multiple LPT redirections to the same printer. To cancel DOS redirection, set *Name* to the name of the local redirected DOS port (for example, "LPT2").
- Force. Optional Boolean argument. If specified and True, the redirection will be removed even if a program on the local computer is currently spooling output to the printer.
- UpdateProfile. See RemoveNetworkDrive for a description.

An error is generated if the specified connection or printer does not exist.

SetDefaultPrinter *PrinterName*
Sets a shared network printer to be the local computer's default printer. PrinterName is the UNC share name of the remote printer. This must be done after using AddWindowsPrinterConnection to make a connection to the same shared printer.

This method cannot select a local printer as the default printer, nor is there any way to determine the current default printer.

You should note that `WScript.Network` is limited in its capabilities. It can perform the following tasks:

- It can view, but not modify, the logged-on user's name, the computer name, and the current logon domain.
- It can list, add, and delete drive mappings, but it cannot create shared folders.
- It can list, add, and delete connections to shared network printers but cannot install local (directly connected) printers.
- It can set the default printer to be one of the network printers, but not a local printer.

In addition, although the `WScript.Network` object can make and break drive mappings and report user information, there are many networking functions it can't manage for you. For example, it can't change the computer's workgroup name, change or even report on user account and security information, and alter network adapter settings. For these functions, you'll have to turn to Chapter 7, "Windows Management Instrumentation (WMI)," and Chapter 8, "Active Directory Scripting Interface (ADSI)." Still, `WScript.Network` is useful for many basic network-management tasks, as you'll see in the next several sections.

Displaying Network User Information

The `WScript.Network` object's three properties display information about the current user, computer, and domain from which the user logged on, as illustrated in the following sample script:

```
set sn = CreateObject("WScript.network")
WScript.echo sn.userName
WScript.echo sn.computerName
WScript.echo sn.userDomain
```

On my computer, for example, this prints as follows:

```
bknittel
JAVA
JAVA
```

As you might guess, my login user name is `bknittel` and the computer I was using at the time is named `Java`. (I name the computers on my network after islands in Indonesia. With over 14,000 to choose from, there's little chance of running out of names very soon.) The `UserDomain` property was also `Java`, even though that's not my workgroup's name. Why? `UserDomain` tells you who authorized this account. This will be either a domain name or the name of the local computer, because user accounts come from one of two places:

- Local accounts are those set up only on the individual computer. When the current user logs on using a local account, the `UserDomain` reported is the computer's name.
- Domain accounts are those set up by an administrator on a domain network. If permitted by the network's security setup, users of one domain may log on to computers that are part of another domain. Therefore, the `UserDomain` reported may not necessarily be the domain to which the computer belongs, and in any case is not the same as the computer name.

On a computer that's a member of a workgroup rather than a domain, including all Windows XP Home Edition computers (which cannot be domain members), all accounts are local accounts, so `UserDomain` will always match the computer name.

Being able to display the user and domain information may not seem terribly useful. However, it can be handy to have access to this information in scripts that are used by more than one user or on more than one computer. Writing a script that can be run by all users on all computers can make your life as a network administrator easier, but you may still need to accommodate different setups based on the computer or username. Here are some ways this can be done:

- You can write a script to set up drive mappings, environment variables, or the program `PATH` to include folders that are based on the user's name. For example, your network may have a set of shared folders of the form `\\SERVER\homefolders\`*`username`*, one for each user, in which users can store files in a standard place that gets backed up daily. Mapping a drive to this "home" folder can be automatic on a domain network, but you're on your own on a workgroup network. It can still be done, though: In a logon script program, you can use the `UserName` property to construct the desired shared folder name and use this to map a drive.
- You can write a script that performs certain actions only for specific users or computers. For example, after setting up standard programs and mappings, you might have a logon script start up certain programs only on those computers that are known to have extra hardware, or you might make special settings for specific users.

Here's an example that shows how a general-purpose logon script might perform special operations for each user:

```
set wshNetwork = CreateObject("WScript.Network")
set wshShell   = CreateObject("WScript.Shell")

user = ucase(wshNetwork.userName)

MapDrive "H", "\\bali\home\" & user   ' map home drive

select case user
    case "BKNITTEL"           ' map drive F and G
```

```
        MapDrive    "F:", "\\sumatra\photos"
        MapDrive    "G:", "\\ambon\software"
        wshShell.run "notepad c:\todo.txt" ' display to-do list
        UsePrinter "\\bali\okidata"

    case "NALEKS"                        ' just map the simulator folder
        MapDrive    "F:", "\\bali\ibm360"

    case "ACCOUNTING"
        MapDrive    "X:", "\\sumatra\quicken"

    case else ' for any other user, just set up network printer
        UsePrinter "\\bali\hp laserjet"
end select

function MapDrive (driveletter, path)
...
```

I'll show you the functions `MapDrive` and `UsePrinter` later in the chapter. Logon scripts are discussed further in Chapter 10.

This script maps two drives, fires up Notepad and ensures that a specific printer is available if `bknittel` logs on, maps a different drive for user `naleks`, and so on. As you can see, a script like this can let you embed all logon information in one script. If you place a shortcut to this script in `\Documents and Settings\All Users\Start Menu\Programs\Startup`, it will be run when any user logs on.

Tip

This type of user-specific setup is as valuable on a small workgroup network as on a large corporate domain. However, with a large number of users, you may find it most useful to perform setup operations based on group membership rather than by individual usernames. I'll show you how to test group membership in Chapter 8.

However useful it is to know these user and computer names, `WScript.Network` doesn't let you *change* them or learn anything about the users' privileges or account settings. For that, you'll need to use the Windows Management Instrumentation (WMI) tools described in Chapter 7.

Managing Drive Mappings

One of the most common network functions needed in scripts is the mapping of drive letters to shared network folders. Usually, drive mappings are made by a user using Explorer or the command-line command `net use`. Mappings made in one logon session are usually recorded in the user's profile and are made available again the next time the user logs on. However, there are times when you may want to take more direct control of mappings, such as the following:

- In a logon script, you may wish to set up standard drive mappings that your users always need. The script should override changes made by the user in a previous logon session so that the correct mappings are guaranteed to be available.
- In utility, backup, and maintenance scripts, you may wish to create temporary drive mappings so that files may be moved to another network location.
- In a script that is run automatically by the Task Scheduler, you may want to use mapped drive letters. However, by default, the Task Scheduler runs scripts in the context of a special system user account and not your own user account. Therefore, your own personal standard drive mappings are not available. The script will need to create any drive mappings it needs to use.

The `WScript.Network` object provides methods to let you control drive mappings in these situations.

Listing Drive Mappings with `EnumNetworkDrives`

The `EnumNetworkDrives` property returns a collection of objects that describes any existing drive letter mappings. However, this collection is not like those we've seen so far, where the collection contains full-fledged objects, each with its own properties and methods. This collection is one of a very few that must be examined by looking at its `Item` properties in numerical order; the collection is simply a list of text strings, which when taken in pairs describes the current mappings.

➔ To learn more about collections and the `Item` property, see "Containers and Collections," p. 85.

The values of this collection can be extracted with the `Item` property. The first string (item 0) gives a mapped drive name (for example, `"F:"`). The second string (item 1) gives the share name to which the drive is mapped, in UNC path format. The collection continues on in this way with pairs of strings—the third string (item 2) gives another mapped drive name, and so on. For example, the script

```
set wshNetwork = CreateObject("WScript.Network")
set maps = wshNetwork.EnumNetworkDrives
```

might yield the collection similar to Listing 5.1.

Listing 5.1 **Sample *EnumNetworkDrives* Collection**

```
maps.item(0)        "F:"                        ]— first drive name and path
maps.item(1)        "\\sumatra\chapters"        ]
maps.item(2)        "H:"                        ]— second drive name and path
maps.item(3)        "\\bali\home\bknittel"      ]
```

continues

Listing 5.1 **Continued**

```
                  .
                  .
                  .
maps.item(maps.Length-2)        "X:"                        ]— last drive name and path
maps.item(maps.Length-1)        "\\bali\incoming faxes"     ]
```

A straightforward way to examine this collection is to use your preferred scripting language's version of the `for` loop. In VBScript, the following script prints the drive mappings by stepping through the list of items by twos:

```
set wshNetwork = CreateObject("WScript.Network")
set maps = wshNetwork.EnumNetworkDrives
for i = 0 to maps.Length-2 step 2
    WScript.echo "Drive", maps.item(i), "is mapped to", maps.item(i+1)
next
```

On each turn through the loop, `maps.item(i)` is a drive name, and `maps.item(i+1)` is a shared folder path. On my computer, this script produces the following output:

```
Drive F: is mapped to \\sumatra\chapters
Drive H: is mapped to \\bali\home\bknittel
Drive J: is mapped to \\bali\shared documents
Drive X: is mapped to \\bali\incoming faxes
```

Printing a list of mapped drives isn't usually a useful thing to do, because typing `net use` at the Windows command prompt will do the same thing. However, you might find it useful when debugging scripts that are run from the Task Scheduler; using the file-writing tools covered in Chapter 4, "File and Registry Access," you can create a log file and record the drive mappings, like this:

```
set fso = CreateObject("Scripting.FileSystemObject")
set wshNetwork = CreateObject("WScript.Network")

' create log file and record date and time in it
set log = fso.CreateTextFile("c:\temp\myscript.log", True)
log.writeline "The script was run at " & now()

' map drive letters needed by the script
...

' list current drive mappings to be sure they're correct
set maps = wshNetwork.EnumNetworkDrives
for i = 0 to maps.Length-2 step 2
    log.writeline "Drive " & maps.item(i) & " is mapped to " & maps.item(i+1)
next

' do things with these mapped drives
...
```

```
' close the log file
log.close
set log = Nothing
```

After the script is supposed to run, you could check `c:\temp\myscript.log` to be sure that the date and time are as expected and that the correct drives have been mapped.

More often, though, the `EnumNetworkDrives` property is needed to check to see whether existing drive mappings exist before attempting to create a new one, or before deleting a mapping. The script will terminate in an error if you attempt to map a drive letter that belongs to a local drive, is already mapped or if you try to delete a drive mapping that does not exist.

Here are two subroutines that can help in scripts that need to manipulate drive mappings. The first tests whether a given drive letter is already a mapped network drive:

Pattern

To determine whether a drive letter is mapped, use the following `IsDriveMapped` function in your scripts.

```
function IsDriveMapped (byval Drive)
    ' use only the letter, not :, and make sure it's uppercase
    drive = ucase(left(drive,1))

    ' assume it's not mapped
    IsDriveLetterMapped = False

    ' if no such drive, return False right now
    if not fso.DriveExists(drive) then exit function

    ' get Drive object and check its type: 3 = mapped
    isDriveMapped = (fso.GetDrive(drive).driveType = 3)
end function
```

The keyword `byval` ensures that changes to the parameter `drive` don't alter the actual variable passed to the subroutine by the caller.

To use this function, you will need to create the `FileSystemObject` (`fso`) just once at the beginning of your script with the statement

```
set fso = CreateObject("Scripting.FileSystemObject")
```

Then, the function can be used in this way:

```
if IsDriveMapped("G") then
   ... ' actions to take if G is already mapped
end if
```

The second handy function returns the network path to which a given drive is mapped. It returns the empty string if the drive letter is not mapped.

Pattern

To determine whether a drive letter is mapped, use this `IsDriveMapped` function in your scripts:

```
function GetDriveMapping (byval Drive)
    dim i, maps

    ' use only the letter, not :, and make sure it's upper
    drive = ucase(left(drive,1))

    ' get list of mappings
    set maps = wshNetwork.EnumNetworkDrives

    ' assume it's not mapped
    GetDriveMapping = ""

    ' scan the list of mapped drives
    for i = 0 to maps.Length-2 step 2
        if ucase(left(maps.item(i),1)) = drive then
            ' the letter was listed, we have our answer
            GetDriveMapping = ucase(maps.item(i+1))
            exit for
        end if
    next
end function
```

To use this function, you will need to create the `wshNetwork` object just once at the beginning of your script with the statement

```
set wshNetwork = CreateObject("WScript.Network")
```

Then, the function can be used in this way:

```
if GetDriveMapping("G") = "\\BALI\TEXT"
    ... 'actions to take if drive G is mapped to \\bali\text
end if
```

Adding Drive Mappings

The `WScript.Network` object provides the `MapNetworkDrive` method to create drive letter mappings. It takes between two to five arguments:

`MapNetworkDrive` *`LocalName`*, *`RemoteName`*, [*`UpdateProfile`*], [*`UserName`*], [*`Password`*]

- *`LocalName`* is the drive letter to map (for example, `"F:"`). The colon is required, although I don't see why Microsoft couldn't have written this method to work with or without it. You can pass the empty string to create a connection to the remote computer without mapping a drive letter; an open connection makes subsequent accesses to the shared folder faster when you use UNC names in file open, copy, move, and delete operations.

- `RemoteName` is the shared network folder to use, in UNC format (`"\\server\sharename"` or `"\\server\\sharename\subfolder"`); `server` is the name or IP address of one of the computers on your network, and `sharename` is the name of the shared folder. If you specify subfolder names, the mapped drive will connect to the specified folder and the user will not be able to "see" folders above this. (Novell network users will recognize this as the "map root" feature.)
- `UpdateProfile` is an optional Boolean value—either `True` or `False`. The default is `False`. If specified and `True`, the mapping is saved in the current user's profile, so the next time he or she logs on, the drive mapping is restored. This is the equivalent of checking the Reconnect at Logon box when mapping network drives with Explorer or specifying the `/persistent:yes` option when using the `net use` command-line program.

  For temporary mappings created and then deleted by a script, you can omit this value or specify `False`. For mappings that are to be reset at each logon, you can specify `True`.
- `UserName` and `Password` are optional arguments that can let you connect to a remote computer using a username and password different from the one you used to log on. This has some pitfalls that we'll discuss in a moment.

Here is an example of the `MapNetworkDrive` method's use:

```
set wshNetwork = CreateObject("WScript.Network")
wshNetwork.MapNetworkDrive "F:", "\\bali\Shared Documents"
```

As you can see, the `MapNetworkDrive` method is pretty straightforward to use. There are, however, some shortcomings you should be aware of:

- If the drive letter is already mapped or belongs to an existing physical drive, the method will cause the script to fail with an error.
- If you wish to use an alternate username and password to connect to the shared folder, you must be sure that there are no other connections (mapped drives or Explorer views) to the same computer using your own or any different username. Windows permits only one connection to each remote computer, so all drives mapped to a given computer must use the same credentials.
- If you need to connect using an alternate username that requires a password, the script will either have to prompt the script user for the password or store the password in the script. The latter can be a huge security risk: Anyone able to read your script will be able to obtain a username and password valid on the remote computer. For this reason, I suggest that you try *not* to use alternate credentials. If you must, it's best to prompt the user for a password or, if that's impossible, be sure that the remote user account has as few privileges as possible. You could set up a special account that is set not to allow local logon and has access to only a limited number of necessary files.

Even if you supply a valid shared folder name and drive letter, the mapping can still fail if there are network problems or if the remote computer is down. You can let the script fail with an error, or you can catch the error and report it gracefully. I'll show you a way of doing this at the end of the next program.

Deleting Drive Mappings

When a drive mapping is no longer needed, your script can delete it with the `RemoveNetworkDrive` method. Your script can delete a named drive mapping or a "nameless" connection made by calling `MapNetworkDrive` with an empty string as the drive name. It takes one to three parameters:

`RemoveNetworkDrive(`*`Name`***`, [`***`Force`***`], [`***`UpdateProfile`***`])`**

- *`Name`* is the name of the drive to ummap (for example, `"F:"`) or the UNC path to disconnect if there is no associated drive letter (for example, `"\\bali\sharedfolder"`).
- *`Force`* is an optional Boolean parameter. If `True`, the mapping will be undone even if some program is still using a folder or file on the shared drive. This can happen if an application has a document open on the shared folder, if you have an active Explorer view of the shared folder or any subfolder, or if you have a command-prompt window open with the shared drive as the current drive. The default is `False`. When *`Force`* is omitted or `False`, rather than sever an active connection, the `RemoveNetworkDrive` method will fail.
- *`UpdateProfile`* is another optional Boolean parameter. If `True`, the mapping will be removed from the user's profile so that it will not be reestablished the next time the user logs in. If *`UpdateProfile`* is omitted or specified as `False`, and the mapping is stored in the user's profile, it will remain there.

`RemoveNetworkDrive` will cause the script to fail if the drive or connection in question does not exist, so you should either verify that it does exist or trap the error. The following Pattern shows how this can be done.

Pattern

To delete a network drive mapping in a script, use the following function:

```
function UnMap(byval Drive)
    UnMap = True                                ' assume success

    if len(drive) = 1 then drive = drive & ":" ' ensure there's a colon

    on error resume next                        ' try to unmap, but don't halt
    wshNetwork.RemoveNetworkDrive drive, False, True ' if an error occurs
    on error goto 0
```

```
    if err > 0 then                            ' there was an error
         UnMap = False                         ' report failure
    end if
end function
```

The function returns `True` if the unmapping was successful or `False` if it failed. You can call this as a function if you care about the return value. Here's an example:

```
if not UnMap("G:") then
    WScript.echo "Drive unmap failed, can't continue"
    WScript.quit 1
end if
```

You can call it as a subroutine if you don't care whether or not the operation succeeded:

```
Unmap "G:"
```

You must create the `wshNetwork` object once at the beginning of your script with the following statement:

```
set wshNetwork = CreateObject("WScript.Network")
```

Setting Up Mappings in a Script

Because there are numerous ways a drive mapping can fail, and because the correct drive mapping may already exist when your script runs, it's best to use a function to handle the various possibilities. This way, the coding needs to happen once, and your script can take advantage of it as many times as necessary. Here is an example of such a subroutine you can use in your scripts.

Pattern

To map a network drive letter in a script, you can use the following function:

```
function MapDrive(byval drive, byval path)
    dim errnum
    MapDrive = True                            ' assume success

    if len(drive) = 1 then drive = drive & ":" ' ensure there's a colon

    if DriveIsMapped(drive) then               ' already mapped?
        if GetDriveMapping(drive) = ucase(path) then
            exit function                      ' ...as desired; quit now
        end if
        UnMap drive                            ' ...unmap before proceeding
    end if

    on error resume next                       ' try to map, but don't halt
    wshNetwork.MapNetworkDrive drive, path     ' if there is an error
    errnum = err.Number
    on error goto 0
```

```
    if errnum > 0 then                                ' there was an error
        MapDrive = False                             ' report failure
    end if
end function
```

You can add the optional `UpdateProfile` parameter to the `MapNetworkDrive` method if it's appropriate for your script.

The function returns `True` if the mapping was successful or `False` if it failed. You can call this as a function if you care about the return value. Here's an example:

```
if not MapDrive("G:", "\\myserver\someshare") then
    WScript.echo "Drive mapping failed, can't continue"
    WScript.quit 1
end if
```

You can call it as a subroutine if you don't care whether the operation succeeded:

```
MapDrive "G:", "\\myserver\someshare"
```

This function requires the `DriveIsMapped`, `GetDriveMappings`, and `UnMap` functions listed earlier in the chapter. You must create the `fso` and `wshNetwork` objects once at the beginning of your script with the following statements:

```
set fso        = CreateObject("Scripting.FileSystemObject")
set wshNetwork = CreateObject("WScript.Network")
```

Managing Network Printer Connections

The `WScript.Network` object has methods to manage network printer connections comparable to the methods for managing mapped drives, as shown in Reference List 5.1. Adding and deleting connections to networked printers adds and deletes icons from the current user's Printers folder, so you can use scripts to ensure that your computer's users have the most up-to-date and appropriate set of network printer choices. This is a good task for logon scripts.

In the next few sections, we'll cover the topics of listing, adding, and deleting printer connections. There is also a way to control the redirection of output from DOS programs to network printers—through the mapping of the DOS environment's virtual LPT devices.

Displaying Printer Information

The `EnumPrinterConnections` method returns a collection that describes the printers set up on the current computer—both locally connected and networked. Like `EnumNetworkDrives`, the collection returned by this method is not a standard list of objects but rather a set of pairs of strings, each of which describes one printer. The discussion of EnumNetworkDrives earlier in the chapter explains this type of collection, so I won't repeat that discussion here.

The pairs of strings returned by EnumPrinterConnections lists the printers' ports and names. The first string in each pair lists the port to which the printer is connected, for both local and network printers. (This information isn't terribly useful for networked printers.) The second string in each pair lists the name of the printer. For local printers, this is the printer's full name. For networked printers, it's the share name of the printer.

The following sample script lists the current printer connections:

```
set wshNetwork = CreateObject("WScript.Network")

set maps = wshNetwork.EnumPrinterConnections
for i = 0 to maps.Length-2 step 2
    WScript.echo "Port:", maps.item(i), "  Name:", maps.item(i+1)
next
```

On my computer, this produces the following odd listing:

```
Port: LPT1:   Name: HP LaserJet 4V
Port: SHRFAX:   Name: Fax
Port: LPT2   Name: \\sumatra\okidata
Port: LPT1:   Name: \\sumatra\Okidata OL810
```

The first printer listed is a local printer, directly connected to my computer. It's connected to port LPT1.

The second printer represents the standard Windows fax printer device that I use to send faxes through my modem. The port is listed as SHRFAX:, but this is not a standard Windows device and, as tantalizing as it sounds, it can't be used from DOS applications.

The third printer is the result of redirecting DOS device LPT2: to \\sumatra\okidata using the command line net use command, as shown here:

```
net use lpt2: \\sumatra\okidata
```

Note that the EnumPrinterConnections port item does not include a colon in this case.

The fourth printer is a network printer for which I've set up a printer icon. It's also listed as using port LPT1:. This is the port to which the printer is connected on the remote computer, Sumatra, and has nothing to do with my own computer's LPT1 port. In this case, it indicates the port to which this computer is connected on the remote computer.

You can use this information in the same way we used the EnumNetworkDrives information earlier in the chapter (that is, in procedures to create or delete network printer connections), although you must be careful how you interpret the values, as detailed in the following list:

- If `Name` starts with two backslashes (`\\`) *and* `Port` includes a colon (`:`), the entry describes a Windows Network printer connection and icon. `Name` is the network share name. `Port` indicates how the printer is connected on the remote networked computer, and can be ignored.
- If `Name` starts with `\\` but `Port` does *not* include a colon, the entry describes redirection for DOS applications to a network printer. `Name` is the network share name, and `Port` names the local DOS device that is redirected.
- If `Name` does not start with `\\`, the entry describes a local printer. `Name` is the printer's device drive name, and `Port` is the device to which the printer is connected.

Yes, it's strange.

Connecting to Network Printers

The `AddWindowsPrinterConnection` method lets you install a new network printer connection (and icon). Like mapped network drives, this is done on a per-user basis; unlike mapped network drives, printer connections are always permanent and persist from one logon session to another. This means you only need to set them up once, and they stick. The method's parameters are as follows:

```
AddWindowsPrinterConnection PrinterPath [, DriveName_[, Port]]
```

- *`PrinterPath`* is the server name and printer share name for the network printer in UNC format (for example, `"\\sumatra\okidata"`). You can use either the official short share name (for example, `"okidata"`) or the longer "friendly" name that Windows displays on the Printers page (for example, `"Okidata OL810"`.

  The remaining two arguments are optional under Windows 2000 and XP, and they are ignored if specified. However, they are required if the script is run on Window 9*X* or Me computers, so it's a good idea to include them if you want to be able to use the same script on multiple Windows platforms.
- *`DriverName`* is the full name of the printer model as listed in the Windows Printer driver list (for example, `"Okidata OL810"`). This will be used to select the correct printer drive.
- *`Port`* is the local DOS LPT port that will be redirected to the network printer. This corresponds to the "capture" setting on the Windows 9*X* and Me Printer control panel. On all Windows platforms, this redirection can be made by the `AddPrinterConnection` method, which we'll discuss in the next section.

The `AddWindowsPrinterConnection` method will *not* fail with an error message if you attempt to duplicate an existing printer connection, so if your script wants to ensure that a specific printer icon exists, it's fine to simply attempt to add it. The printer will be added if necessary; otherwise, nothing happens.

The following pattern shows a reliable way of adding network printer connections.

Pattern

To add a network printer connection in a script, you can use the following function:

```
function UsePrinter (path)
    dim errnum
    UsePrinter = True               ' assume success

    on error resume next            ' make connection, don't stop on error
    wshNetwork.AddWindowsPrinterConnection path
    errnum = err.Number
    on error goto 0
                                    ' if error occurred, return False
    if errnum > 0 then UsePrinter = False
end function
```

The function returns `True` if the printer was added (or already exists) and `False` if it could not add the printer. You can call this function as a subroutine if you do not care about the return value—for example, you can use the following statement:

```
UsePrinter "\\sumatra\okidata"
```

In order for you to use this function, the `wshNetwork` object must be created at the beginning of your script with this statement:

```
set wshNetwork = CreateObject("WScript.Network")
```

You will probably only use `AddWindowsPrinterConnection` or the function `UsePrinter` as part of a logon script that verifies that all necessary network printer connections are installed. It can be very handy to set up such logon scripts in advance. Then, if your network environment changes, you won't have to instruct tens to thousands of users to set up new printer icons.

Redirecting DOS Session Printers

If you (or your organization) use legacy DOS applications, you know that it can be difficult to manage printer output from these applications. Whereas Windows applications can choose from a list of installed printers that are connected locally or through the network, DOS applications can't; they only know how to use parallel ports LPT1, LPT2, and LPT3. To make it possible for DOS applications to print to network printers, Windows provides a way of *redirecting* the DOS printer devices to network printers. (On Windows 9*X* and Me, this was called *capturing*.) Whatever it's called, the effect is that DOS applications see a simulated printer port that appears to be connected to a printer; it happily accepts print output, which Windows then funnels through the network to a real printer. In the absence of printer redirection, if a DOS application attempts to direct output to an LPT port, Windows attempts to use the indicated port hardware.

The WScript.Network object's AddPrinterConnection method can be used to set up printer redirection so that DOS applications can send output to a selected network printer. Unlike AddWindowsPrinterConnection, this method does *not* create a printer icon or make the printer accessible to Windows applications. It simply makes the network printer available to DOS applications. As shown in Reference List 5.1, the method's arguments are as follows:

```
AddPrinterConnection LocalName, RemoteName [, UpdateProfile] _
    [, UserName, Password]
```

Note that this method provides for making the connection using an alternate user account, whereas AddWindowsPrinterConnection does not. Specifying an alternate username adds complications; see the discussion under "Adding Drive Mappings," earlier in this chapter, for more information.

Also, this method *will* fail with an error if the connection already exists, so you should examine EnumPrinterConnections before attempting to make the connection or else catch errors while making the attempt. I'll show you how to do this after we discuss how to delete Windows printers and cancel printer redirection.

Deleting Printer Connections

You can delete network printer connections (and the associated Printers folder icon) and cancel DOS printer direction with the RemovePrinterConnection method. It takes one to three arguments, which are described in detail in Reference List 5.1:

```
RemovePrinterConnection Name, [bForce], [bUpdateProfile]
```

The optional *Force* parameter determines what happens if some application is currently using the printer. The default is False. When *Force* is omitted or False, rather than sever an active connection, the RemovePrinterConnection method will fail.

The RemovePrinterConnection method will generate an error if the designed printer connection does not exist, so you should check to see whether it does before attempting to delete a connection. The following function shows you how.

Pattern

To delete a Windows networked printer, use the following function:

```
function DeletePrinter (path)
    dim maps, i, ismapped errnum                ' local variables

    path = ucase(path)                          ' be sure path is uppercase

    DeletePrinter = True                        ' assume success

    ismapped = False                            ' see if printer exists
    set maps = wshNetwork.EnumPrinterConnections
```

```
    for i = 0 to maps.Length-2 step 2
        if ucase(maps.item(i+1)) = path then
            ismapped = True                      ' we are using this printer
            exit for
        end if
    next

    if not ismapped then exit function         ' printer not used, just return

    on error resume next                       ' delete connection
    wshNetwork.RemovePrinterConnection path, True, True
    errnum = err.Number
    on error goto 0

    if errnum <> 0 then
       DeletePrinter = False                   ' we failed
    end if
end function
```

If you change your network configuration, you can use `UsePrinter` and `DeletePrinter` in a logon script to remove obsolete printers and add new ones so that your users will automatically see the correct printers.

Note

You could write a function to exercise more stringent control by setting the network printers to a specific list and deleting any network printers not listed.

Now that you have seen how to cancel printer redirection, we can write a function to safely set up printer redirection.

Pattern

The following function takes three arguments: `device`, `path` and `updateProfile`. `Device` is the name of a DOS printer port to redirect, `path` is a network printer name in UNC format, and `updateProfile` determines whether the assignment is made permanent. It handles the situation where the redirection may already have been done and correctly changes the mapping to the specified path. It returns `True` if the redirection was completed or `False` if it could not be performed.

```
function RedirectPrinter (byval device, byval path, byval updateProfile)
    dim maps, i, ismapped errnum               ' local variables
    dim devcolon, devnocolon

    device = ucase(device)                     ' put port name in uppercase
    i = instr(device, ":")                     ' get versions of name with
    if i > 0 then                              ' and without the colon
        devcolon   = device
        devnocolon = left(device, i-1)
    else
```

```
        devcolon   = device & ":"
        devnocolon = device
    end if

    RedirectPrinter = True                        ' assume success

    ismapped = False                              ' see if port already mapped
    set maps = wshNetwork.EnumPrinterConnections
    for i = 0 to maps.Length-2 step 2
        if maps.item(i) = devnocolon and _
                left(maps.item(i+1),2) = "\\" then ' port is already redirected
            ismapped = True
            exit for
        elseif maps.item(i) = devnocolon then ' port hooks to a local printer
            RedirectPrinter = False           ' we cannot redirect it
            exit function
        end if
    next

    if ismapped then
        on error resume next                      ' delete existing  connection
        wshNetwork.RemovePrinterConnection device, True, updateProfile
        errnum = err.Number
        on error goto 0

        if errnum <> 0 then
            RedirectPrinter = False               ' return False if error
            exit function
        end if
    end if

    on error resume next                          ' try to make the connection
    wshNetwork.AddPrinterConnection device, path, updateProfile
    errnum = err.Number
    on error goto 0

    if errnum <> 0 then RedirectPrinter = False    ' return False if error
end function
```

In order for you to use this function, the wshNetwork object must be created at the beginning of your script with the following statement:

```
set wshNetwork = CreateObject("WScript.Network")
```

Setting the Default Printer

A final issue in managing network printers is ensuring that users always have an appropriate default printer selected. Of course, users can change the default printer at any time with the Printers and Faxes control panel (or with any of several add-on utilities that let users change the default printer with a pop-up menu). Still, when you've added or deleted printers in a logon script, you should select an appropriate default printer using the `SetDefaultPrinter` method; simply pass it the network share name of the desired printer, as in this example:

```
wshNetwork.SetDefaultPrinter("\\sumatra\okidata")
```

The `SetDefaultPrinter` method can only select a network printer, not a local printer; if your script deletes all network printers, you can let the user select a local default printer.

Printing from Scripts

Thus far we've discussed how to manage printers from scripts. Now let's take a short look at *using* printers in scripts. You may wish to have your script generate printed output if it generates reports that you want to view in printed form, or if it runs automatically under the Task Scheduler.

Tip

In a business environment, for scheduled scripts that perform critical tasks such as backups, I recommend printing a report every day. This way, if the scheduled task stops working, you'll know that something is wrong by the details in the report or by the report's absence. If you're concerned about the wasted paper, you might write a script to summarize the results of all the scheduled tasks and print a single sheet, or you might use the e-mail tools discussed in the next chapter. In any case, automatic status reports can really help avoid losing track of those things that go crash in the night. I'll talk about this in more detail in Chapter 10.

You can send printed output to a network printer in one of two ways:

- You can use Word or other applications that expose themselves as an automation object. For example, you can create a `Word.Document` object, use methods such as `Selection.Type` to insert text, and then use the `.Print` method to print the document.
- You can use `AddPrinterConnection` to redirect an LPT device to a network printer. Use the `FileSystemObject`'s `CreateTextFile` method to write to the LPT device (for example, you can redirect LPT2 and use `"LPT2:"` with `CreateTextFile`). Write report output to the `TextStream` object. After the `TextStream` object is closed, the report will print.

Whereas the first method can create nicely formatted reports, the second method can be done on any Windows computer and doesn't need any additional installed applications. Here is an example that shows how you can print directly to a network printer from a script:

```
' create utility objects
set wshNetwork = CreateObject("Wscript.Network")
set fso = CreateObject("Scripting.FileSystemObject")
```

```
' use the RedirectPrinter function shown earlier in the chapter
' to set up LPT2 for remote printing
RedirectPrinter "LPT2", "\\sumatra\okidata", False

' Open a TextStream object, with output to LPT2
set pfile = fso.CreateTextFile("LPT2:")

' write the report
pfile.WriteLine "---------- " & now() & " ----------"
pfile.WriteLine "This is the report"
pfile.WriteLine "This more of the report"
pfile.WriteLine "This is end of the report"

' end the report and remove the printer redirection
pfile.Close
wshNetwork.RemovePrinterConnection "LPT2"

' (function from earlier in the chapter)
function RedirectPrinter (byval device, byval path, byval updateProfile)
...
end function
```

6

Messaging Objects

ROAD MAP

- Scripts can send e-mail to report problems and automate workflow.
- CDO messaging objects can send plain text and HTML-formatted messages with any number of attachments.
- This chapter contains a detailed reference section, followed by explanations and sample scripts.
- The CDO objects are complex, but they're easier to use than you'd first guess. Use the examples provided here as your starting point.

Sending E-mail from Scripts with CDO

As we've all found out over the last couple of decades, e-mail is a great way to deliver information to people. You can send e-mail at any time of the day or night from any location in the world to any other. It saves paper, and most importantly, although e-mail doesn't demand the recipient's immediate attention, it does sit there in the inbox until it's read.

Although we usually think of e-mail as a person-to-person medium, you can also send e-mail directly from Windows Script programs. All of e-mail's advantages apply to delivering information from scripts. Here are some examples:

- For automated, scheduled scripted operations such as backups, reports, or disk cleanups, it's important to know whether the scheduled operation completed successfully. You might want to have scripts used with the Task Scheduler send an e-mail message to a system administrator with a report of the operation's success or failure. If the daily message is missing or contains error reports, you'll know that something is amiss.
- You can write scripts to automatically send information to network users, such as reports of excessive disk usage, distribution of incoming files or faxes, and so on.

- You can create a script that will e-mail any files specified on its command line to a particular destination. If you create a shortcut to this script, Explorer will let you drag and drop files onto it. Any file(s) you drag onto the icon will be automatically mailed to the chosen destination. This might be handy in some work environments—for example, to forward purchase orders or edited files to another person in the organization.

So, how do you send e-mail messages from a script? The answer is, you use the Collaboration Data Objects (CDO) package.

Microsoft developed Collaboration Data Objects as an add-on tool for Microsoft Office and Outlook, but it has evolved into a standalone tool that can be used by WSH scripts and `.asp` Web pages as well as standard Windows applications. CDO provides a complex set of objects that can be used to send, receive, and display e-mail and newsgroup messages, handle attachments, and even perform some of the tasks of an e-mail server. Most of these topics are beyond the scope of this book. Here, I'll show how CDO can be used to send text or HTML-formatted e-mail messages. It can send anything from plain text, to complete Web pages, to complex formatted messages with multiple attachments.

Note

You can find more about CDO on the Microsoft Developers Web site at `msdn.microsoft.com`. Search for "CDO for Windows 2000" (using the quotes) or open the index listings for MSDN Library, Messaging and Collaboration, Collaboration Data Objects, CDO for Windows 2000. I have to warn you, though: If you think *my* writing is obtuse, wait till you read theirs.

The CDO version distributed with Windows XP and Windows 2000 is called CDO for Windows 2000. Although several other CDO flavors are mentioned in Microsoft's documentation, for the remainder of this chapter, *CDO* refers only to CDO for Windows 2000. It's installed on your computer in the `\windows\system32` folder as file `cdosys.dll`.

If the `cdosys.dll` file is missing from your system, your best option is to copy it from another Windows 2000 or XP system. Put it in the `system32` folder, open a command-prompt window, and type **`regsvr32 %windir%\system32\cdosys.dll`**. However, this object will only work on Windows XP and Windows 2000. If you need to send e-mail from scripts on Windows NT or Windows 9x/Me, you'll need to research the `CDONTS` object or get a third-party mail object. The discussion in this chapter won't apply to these older systems.

The CDO Object Model

CDO uses several object types to represent an e-mail message. Here are the primary objects that you'll use directly:

- `CDO.Message`. Represents a single e-mail message. It contains several other objects within it: `BodyPart`, which is the content of the message, `Attachments`, which is a collection of objects representing attached documents, and `Fields`, which describes the sender, subject, and other message attributes.
- `BodyPart`. An object that represents a message component. `BodyPart` can contain other `BodyPart` objects nested inside it, which represent subelements of the message.
- `CDO.Configuration`. A collection of `Field` objects that describe how CDO is to deliver the message.
- `Field`. An object that defines one parameter, such as the subject line or the sender of the message.

The objects and their relationships are illustrated in Figure 6.1. If this doesn't make sense right away, hang in there. The text that follows should help clear things up.

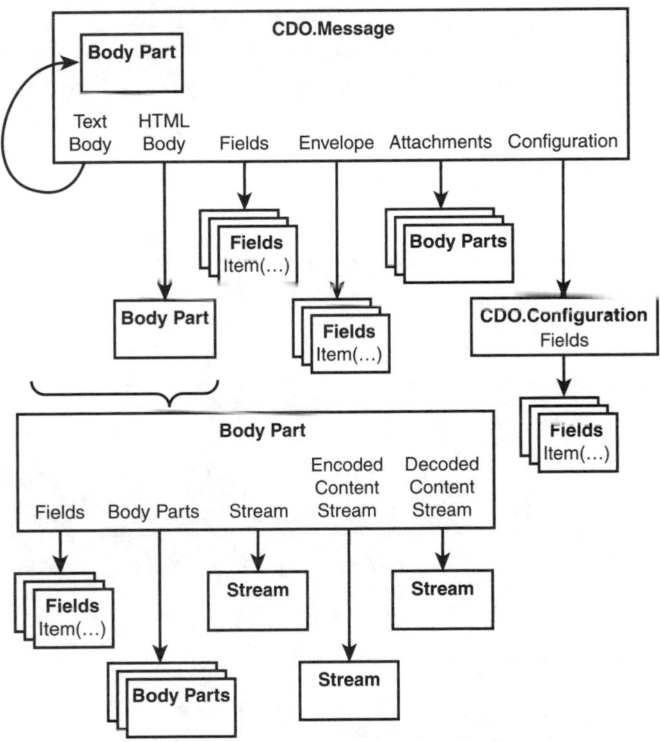

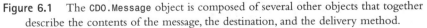

Figure 6.1 The `CDO.Message` object is composed of several other objects that together describe the contents of the message, the destination, and the delivery method.

In a simple message containing only a single text message, the message content will be stored in the `CDO.Message` object's internal `BodyPart` object, as shown in Figure 6.2.

The `TextBodyPart` property, which the `Message` object uses to provide quick access to the text version of the message, refers to this internal `BodyPart` object.

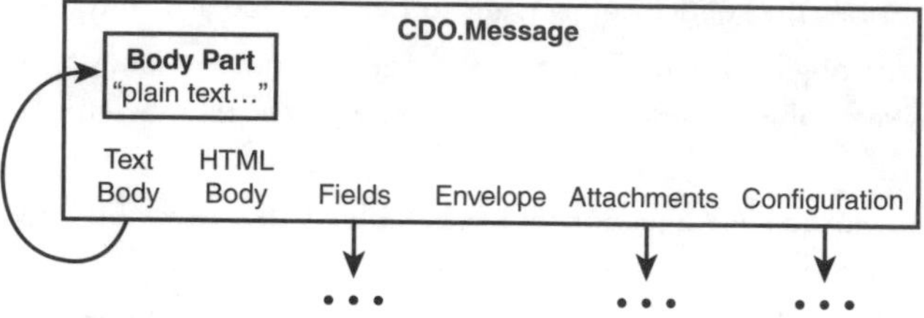

Figure 6.2 CDO objects for a simple text-only message.

CDO also lets you send a message in both HTML and plain text using the "multipart/alternative" MIME format. In this case, there are two sub-`BodyPart` objects under the main message: one containing the text version of the message and one containing the HTML version. The HTML version might contain further subparts, which contain images referenced by the formatted message. The objects and the resulting message structure are illustrated in Figure 6.3.

Note

MIME stands for Multipart Internet Mail Extensions. It's a standardized way of packaging text, images, documents, and other data into plain-text files that can be moved about through the Internet's e-mail systems. For detailed information about MIME formats, see the documents RFC 2045, RFC 2046, and RFC 2047, which you can view at www.`ietf.org/rfc`.

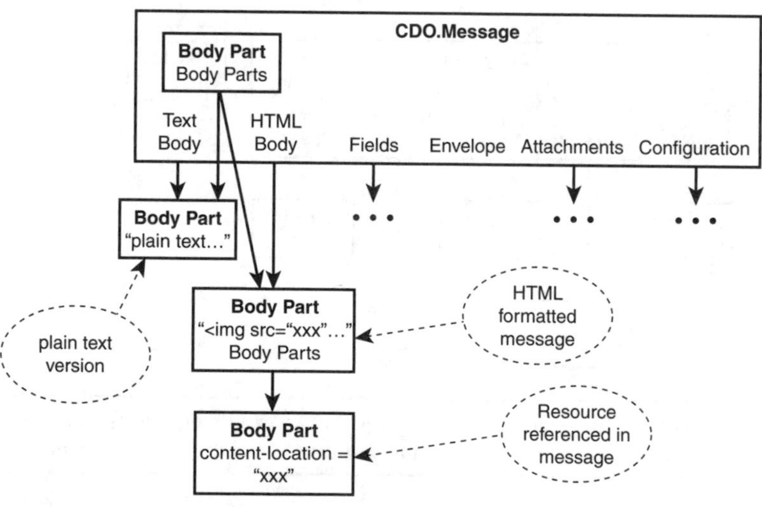

Figure 6.3 The CDO objects and MIME message structure for a multipart/alternative message with both HTML and plain-text versions.

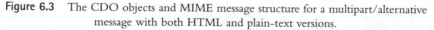

This might seem confusing at first, but it makes more sense when you look at the steps necessary to send a message:

1. Create a `CDO.Message` object.
2. Create a `CDO.Configuration` object and link it to the `CDO.Message` object.
3. Assign the subject line, the recipients, the sender's address, and so on to properties of the `CDO.Message` object. This information is stored in the `Message` object's `Fields` collection.
4. Add text content or formatted HTML content to the message's `BodyPart` object.
5. Optionally, add additional `BodyPart` objects to the `Attachments` collection and attach files to them. This can be done with one line of code.
6. Add `Field` values to the `CDO.Configuration` object to describe how the message is to be delivered (for example, give the name of your network's SMTP mail server).
7. Finally, use the `CDO.Message` object's `Send` method to deliver the message.

This procedure sounds complex, but it's easy to use and extend once you have a working script in hand. It was no piece of cake getting my first message script to work, but all the subsequent examples were easy to create. You can download these sample scripts from `www.helpwinxp.com/hood` and take it from there.

The next several sections provide a complete reference listing of the objects and their methods, properties, and parameters. Then we'll go through some examples of their use. You might want to take a look at the examples, which start with "Sending a Message with CDO" on page 243, just to see how this stuff looks in actual use, before looking through the reference material.

The `CDO.Message` Object

The `CDO.Message` object is the primary object used to send e-mail or newsgroup messages. The properties and methods of the `CDO.Message` object are described in Reference List 6.1. Some are used only when processing *received* messages, a topic not covered in this book. These items are included for reference only.

Properties that involve e-mail addresses use standard e-mail format. Multiple addresses may be entered, separated by commas. Each address can take any one of the following forms:

- `"Full name" <emailaddress@domain>`
- `"Full name" emailaddress@domain`
- `Full name <emailaddress@domain>`
- `emailaddress@domain`

If you put e-mail addresses inside your scripts and you use a format with quotes, remember that you may need to escape the quotes to enter them in your scripting language. For example, in VBScript, I would have to type

```
msg.from = """Brian Knittel"" <brian@helpwinxp.com>"
```

to use the first format.

REFERENCE LIST 6.1 Properties and Methods of the `CDO.Message` Object

Properties:

`Attachments`

Read-only. Returns a `BodyParts` collection that holds the message's attachments. Attachments can be added with the `AddAttachment` method.

`AutoGenerateTextBody`

A Boolean value. If this property is set to `True`, a `TextBodyPart` will automatically be generated for this message from the `HTMLBodyPart`. You should only set the `HTMLBodyPart` in this case. The examples show how this is done.

`BCC`

A text string listing the Blind Carbon Copy recipients for this message. The BCC addresses are not shown in copies of the message sent to others.

`BCC` and several other properties are actually stored in the `Fields` collection but are made available through properties to make viewing and setting them more convenient.

`BodyPart`

Read-only. Returns a reference to the main message `BodyPart` object contained in the `CDO.Message` object. This is the primary message part, the root of the hierarchy of elements in the message. You work with this object to set the message content.

`CC`

A text string listing Carbon Copy recipients for this message.

`Configuration`

Returns or sets the `CDO.Configuration` object associated with this message.

`DataSource`

Read-only. The `DataSource` property gives access to a data-management object that can be used to manipulate the content of the message or of its `BodyPart` objects. The `DataSource` object is not necessary for sending or receiving messages, so it's not described in this book.

`DSNOptions`

An integer value that instructs downstream mail servers to send your e-mail messages (*delivery status notifications*, or *DSNs*), indicating success or failure in transferring or delivering your message. The permitted values for `DSNOptions` are listed in

Table 6.1. Multiple options may be selected by adding the numeric values together. For a convoluted explanation of DSNs, see www.faqs.org/rfcs/rfc1894.html.

EnvelopeFields
Read-only. A collection of Field objects that describe Simple Mail Transport Protocol (SMTP) transport information. This property is available on received messages only, a topic beyond the scope of this book.

Fields
Read-only. The collection of Field objects for this message. The fields describe the sender, recipient, and other message information. You can alter the collection by changing individual Field items and then using the collection's Update method. For convenience, some of the fields can be set using properties such as From and Subject. The object automatically puts values assigned to these properties into the Fields collection.

FollowUpTo
For newsgroup messages, this is a list of any newsgroups to which any responses to this message should be posted.

From
The e-mail address of the message's author. This is one of the most common fields to set. It corresponds to the "From:" line in the message.

HTMLBody
The main body of the message in HTML format, as a text string. You can set the HTML content of the message in several ways; one is by assigning a string value to this property.

HTMLBodyPart
Read-only. Returns a reference to the BodyPart object holding the main body of the message in HTML format. This refers to a subobject of the BodyPart.BodyParts collection, if the message is being sent in multipart/alternative format, or the main BodyPart itself, if the message is being sent as HTML only.

The HTMLBody property reflects the content of this object. If no HTML content has been defined, attempting to read this property will cause an error.

Keywords
Any keywords to be associated with the message (relevant only for newsgroup messages).

MDNRequested
A Boolean value. If this property is True, the message is sent with a header that requests delivery notification. More detailed control of delivery notifications is available by setting the To Disposition-Notification-To and Disposition-Notification-Options fields. Values of these fields are inserted as header lines of the same name. These options are discussed in RFC 2298, available at www.ietf.org/rfc.

continues

REFERENCE LIST 6.1 Continued

`MIMEFormatted`

A Boolean value. If this property is `True`, the message is formatted as multipart/alternative, and you should ensure that both the `TextBodyPart` and the `HTMLBodyPart` versions are set up. If this property is `False`, only one of `TextBodyPart` and `HTMLBodyPart` should be set up.

`Newsgroups`

The newsgroups to which this message should be sent (not used with standard e-mail messages).

`Organization`

The organization (company) name of the message sender.

`ReceivedTime`

Read-only. The date/time that the message was received. Not applicable when sending messages.

`ReplyTo`

The preferred address for replies to this message. Usually the same as the From address.

`Sender`

The e-mail address of the message sender, if different from the author (`From`). This field corresponds to the rarely used "Sender:" line in an e-mail message.

`SentOn`

Read-only. The date/time that the message was sent. This field is valid on received messages or in outgoing messages *after* they have been sent. The field is filled in automatically.

`Subject`

The subject line of the message. Although supplying a subject line is always a good idea, it is required only for newsgroup messages.

`TextBody`

The main body of the message in plain-text format, as a string. This is the content of the `TextBodyPart` object. Multiple lines are delimited with carriage return/linefeed characters. You can set the text body in several ways, as discussed later in the chapter.

`TextBodyPart`

Read-only. A `BodyPart` object that represents the text version of the message. Like `HTMLBodyPart`, this refers to a subelement of the main `BodyPart` if the message is being sent in multipart/alternative format, or to the main `BodyPart` itself if the message is being sent as text only. The `TextBody` property reflects the content of this object.

To

The principal recipient(s) of the message, as a text string. The message is also sent to CC and BCC addresses. Each e-mail address should be separated by a comma and a space.

Methods:

AddAttachment(*path* [, *username*, *password*])

Creates an attachment to the message and returns a reference to the new `BodyPart` object. The object is added to the message's `Attachments` collection. ***Path*** can refer to a filename or it can be a URL pointing to a Web page. In the case of a URL, `AddAttachment` will fetch the Web page and store the contents in the message. If you specify a Web page that is password protected, you can specify the optional parameters ***username*** and ***password*** as the credentials to use when picking up the page.

Attachments are transmitted as MIME-encoded parts, and you should be sure that the attachment is assigned the correct MIME *content type*, which describes how to interpret the attachment data; examples of content types include "text/plain," "text/html," and "application/MS-Word." Windows will attempt to determine the correct content type for you using information in the Registry. If you find that your attachments are not given the correct content type, you can use the object reference returned by `AddAttachment` to make adjustments to its `ContentMediaType` property. The properties and methods of the `BodyPart` object are discussed shortly.

Note

Because `AddAttachment` expects a URL-formatted name, if you are sending a file, you must specify the path using the `file://` prefix in the name, or you must specify a drive and path to the file. If you are sending a Web page, you must use the `http://` prefix. You can also use the `ftp://` and `https://` prefixes to obtain a file using FTP or Secure HTTP, respectively.

AddRelatedBodyPart(*path*, *reference*, *referencetype* [, *username*, *password*])

Used with HTML-formatted messages to embed subsidiary items (*resources*), such as graphics and frame contents, that are referenced by the main message body. Returns an object reference to the added `BodyPart`. Using this method automatically sets the `MIMEFormatted` property and sets up a multipart-MIME message. ***Path***, ***username***, and ***password*** work as with `AddAttachment` and specify the filename or URL of the content to add. ***Reference*** specifies the name to give the embedded component. This is the name that the main body document will use to reference the items. ***Referencetype*** is a value that indicates how the main document references the attached resources. The allowed values for ***referencetype*** are listed in Table 6.2. `AddRelatedBodyPart` returns a reference to the added body part.

continues

REFERENCE LIST 6.1 Continued

You do not need to use this method if you use `CreateMHTMLMessage` to construct an HTML-formatted message; `CreateMHTMLMessage` automatically adds any related elements to which the message refers.

The usual method is to use `cdoRefTypeLocation` for *`referencetype`* and to specify a simple name for the *`reference`* value. For example, if the main document had an embedded image that was tagged with `<IMG SRC="aname">`, the image could be attached with

```
msg.AddRelatedBodyPart "c:\images\some.gif", "aname", cdoRefTypeLocation
```

As with `AddAttachment`, `AddRelatedBodyPart` requires a prefix that indicates how to pick up the file. *`Path`* must start with a drive and folder name, or `file://`, `http://`, and so on.

`CreateMHTMLBody(`*`path`* [, *`flags`* [, *`username, password`*]]**`)`**
This method converts the HTML document specified by the filename or URL indicated in *`path`* to a multipart HTML message and saves it as the message's `HTMLBodyPart`. The method should not be used with a message object that already contains HTML content.

As with `AddAttachment`, *`path`* must start with a drive and folder name, or `file://`, `http://`, and so on.

Subsidiary components of the Web page, such as graphics and frame contents, are automatically attached, unless you indicate otherwise with the *`flags`* value. If *`path`* is a URL that refers to a password-protected Web page, the optional parameters *`username`* and *`password`* specify the credentials to use. The optional *`flags`* value indicates which, if any, subparts of the document should be omitted; the default value is `CdoSuppressNone`. The possible values for *`flags`* are listed in Table 6.3.

Multiple flags can be specified by adding their numeric values.

`Forward()`
Returns a `CDO.Message` object based on a received message, which can be addressed and forwarded to other recipients. Used only with incoming messages.

`GetInterface(`*`objecttype`***`)`**
The `CDO.Message` object actually has several interfaces; that is, it can be treated as any of several different object types. `GetInterface` returns an object reference of the specified type to give you access to these alternate objects. The possible values for *`objecttype`* are `"IDataSource"` and `"IBodyPart"`. The returned objects give you access to the main (root) message `BodyPart` or the primary data source, respectively. The `BodyPart` and `DataSource` properties do the exact same thing, so this method is not of much importance.

GetStream()
Returns a `Stream` object representing the entire message, including header lines and content formatted with any required MIME markup. This method is only of use when processing received messages. The `Stream` object is discussed later in the chapter.

Post
Sends a newsgroup message to the specified newsgroups using the method that was set in the `CDO.Configuration` object. Used only with newsgroup messages. (For e-mail messages, use `Send`.) After calling `Post`, you can release the message object from memory, as in this example:

```
msg.post
set msg = Nothing
```

PostReply()
Returns a new `CDO.Message` object based on a received newsgroup message, which is addressed back to the newsgroup. The attachments are omitted, and a new message body should be constructed. Used only with incoming messages.

Reply()
Returns a contentless `CDO.Message` object addressed to the original sender, based on the original `ReplyTo` or `To` property. Used only with incoming messages.

ReplyAll()
Returns a contentless `CDO.Message` object addressed to the original sender plus all CC (Carbon Copy) recipients and any visible BCC recipients, based on the original `ReplyTo` or `To` property. Used only with incoming messages.

Send
Sends the e-mail message to the specified recipient(s) using the method that was set in the `CDO.Configuration` object. This method is used only to send e-mail messages. (To send a newsgroup message, use `Post`.) After calling `Send`, you can release the message object from memory, as in this example:

```
msg.send
set msg = Nothing
```

Table 6.1 lists the constant values used by the `DSNOptions` property.

Table 6.1 ***cdoDSNOptions* Constants**

Name	Value	Description
`cdoDSNDefault`	0	Issue no status notifications
`cdoDSNNever`	1	Issue no status notifications
`cdoDSNFailure`	2	Issue a notification if the delivery fails
`cdoDSNSuccess`	4	Issue a notification if the delivery succeeds
`cdoDSNDelay`	8	Issue a notification if the delivery is delayed
`cdoDSNSuccessFailOrDelay`	14	Issue a notification if the delivery succeeds, fails, or is delayed

Note

If you enclose your script in a WSH format file, as discussed in Chapter 10, "Deploying Scripts for Computer and Network Management," you can use a `<reference>` tag to have Windows Script Host define these constants automatically.

Otherwise, if you write a `.vbs` or `.js` file, you'll either have to put definitions for the constants you need in your script program or use the numeric values directly. To make it easier to add constant definitions, you can download a file containing VBScript constant definitions for all the CDO constants listed in this chapter from `www.helpwinxp.com/hood`.

Table 6.2 lists the constant values used by the ***`referencetype`*** parameter of the `AddRelatedBodyPart` method.

Table 6.2 ***cdoReferenceType*** **Constants**

Name	Value	Description
`cdoRefTypeId`	0	The ***`reference`*** parameter contains a value for the "Content-ID" MIME header. The HTML message refers to this resource using this Content-ID header.
`cdoRefTypeLocation`	1	The ***`reference`*** parameter contains a value for the "Content-Location" MIME header. The HTML message refers to this resource using this message-relative Uniform Resource Locator (URL). This is the usual method.

Table 6.3 lists the constant values used by the `flags` parameter of the `CreateMHTMLBody` method. Multiple flags can be specified by adding their values together.

Table 6.3 ***cdoMHTMLFlags*** **Constants**

Name	Value	Description
`CdoSuppressNone`	0	Omit nothing; download all the items referred to in the HTML document (default).
`CdoSuppressImages`	1	Don't include images referenced in `<IMG>` elements.
`CdoSuppressBGSounds`	2	Don't include sound resources specified by `<BGSOUND>` elements.
`CdoSuppressFrames`	4	Don't include frame contents specified in `<FRAME>` elements.

Name	Value	Description
CdoSuppressObjects	8	Don't include object resources specified by `<OBJECT>` elements.
CdoSuppressStyleSheets	16	Don't include style sheets referenced by `<LINK>` elements.
CdoSuppressAll	31	Omit all referenced objects.

Working with Fields

Several CDO messaging objects use a collection of named values called `Fields`. A `Fields` collection operates a bit like an array, except it is indexed by a text name rather than by a number.

Some `Field` values can be viewed or set through properties on the object that contains the `Fields` collection; these properties are provided as a convenience so that you don't have to fool around with the collection. If you need to examine or alter a `Field` value for which no helpful property was provided, you must manipulate the `Fields` collection directly.

Note

The `Fields` collection is borrowed from another Microsoft object toolkit called ActiveX Data Objects (ADO). There is quite a bit more to it than we'll need for its use with CDO, so I'll only present the most important details. You can find out more about the `Field` object and `Fields` collection at `msdn.microsoft.com`. Search for "ADO API Reference" (using the quotes).

For our purposes, a `Field` object contains three important properties:

Property	Description
Name	The name of the field
Value	The associated value
Type	The value type

`Type` indicates the type of the value (integer, string, and so on), but, because most scripting languages convert all values to type `Variant`, this is not relevant. However, if a `Field` object's `Type` is `0`, the value is undefined and an error may occur if you attempt to display it.

A `Fields` collection contains one or more `Field` objects. The properties and the one method of the `Fields` collection are listed in Reference List 6.2.

REFERENCE LIST 6.2 The Properties and Method of the `Fields` Collection

Properties:

`Count`

Returns the number of items in the collection.

`Item(`*`index`*`)`

Returns an individual item from the collection. *`Index`* can be a string—the `Name` of the desired `Field` item—or a number, the ordinal index of the desired item in the range `0` to `Count-1`.

Method:

`Update`

`Update` sends any changes made to the `Fields` collection back to the parent object that contains the collection. If you fail to invoke `.Update`, any changes you make to the collection will have no effect and the mail message will not be delivered correctly.

The following example sets a `Field` for a `CDO.Message` object named `msg`:

```
set fields = msg.Fields       ' get copy of Fields from object msg'
                              ' make alterations
fields.Item("http://schemas.microsoft.com/cdo/configuration/name") = value
fields.Update                 ' store changed values
```

As an alternative, you could use the VBScript `with` statement:

```
with msg.Fields
    .Item("http://schemas.microsoft.com/cdo/configuration/name") = value
    .Update                   ' store changed values
end with
```

In actual use, *`name`* would be replaced with one of the names listed in the tables that follow. The field names are quite long and consist of a long prefix plus a parameter name. Here's an example:

```
"http://schemas.microsoft.com/cdo/configuration/name"
```

There tends to be several `Field` objects in each collection with the same prefix, and only the *`name`* part varies from item to item. The fields in the upcoming tables are grouped by prefix to make the lists easier to read.

You may examine a `Fields` collection using your scripting language's normal method for examining collections. In VBScript you can use a `For Each` loop or a `For` loop, as shown in the following example:

```
set msg = CreateObject("CDO.Message")

for each fld in msg.Fields       ' use a "for each" loop
    if fld.type = 0 then
        wscript.echo fld.name, "is undefined"
    else
        wscript.echo fld.name, "=", fld.value
    end if
next
                          ' -- OR --
set flds = msg.Fields            ' use a for loop and numeric indexing
for i = 0 to flds.Count-1
    if flds.item(i).type = 0 then
        wscript.echo flds.item(i).name, "is undefined"
    else
        wscript.echo flds.item(i).name, "=", flds.item(i).value
    end if
next
```

Several fields use integer values to choose one of several options. The discussion that follows refers to tables that list the acceptable values.

Fields for the CDO.Message Object

The Field values for the CDO.Message object contain the message's sender and recipient names, the message's subject, and other "overall" message settings. The list of possible values is shown in Table 6.4. Note that the fields in the httpmail category contain the most important message header information and can use the full local character set.

Note

Many fields can be viewed or set through CDO.Message properties. For brevity's sake, those fields are omitted from this listing.

Table 6.4 **Values in the *CDO.Message* Object's *Fields* Collection**

Name	Description
PREFIX "URN:SCHEMAS:HTTPMAIL:"	
content-disposition	Corresponds to the "Content-Disposition" MIME header for a BodyPart.
content-media-type	Corresponds to the "Content-Type" in the MIME message header. Usually something such as "image/gif", "text/html", and so on.
Date	The date on which the message was sent. This will automatically be set by the Send or Post method.

continues

Table 6.4 **Continued**

Name	Description
Prefix "urn:schemas:httpmail:"	
`Datereceived`	For incoming messages, the date/time that the message was received by the mail server.
`Fromemail`	The e-mail address part of the `From` string.
`Fromname`	The name part of the `From` string.
`Hasattachment`	A Boolean value that indicates whether the message has attachments.
`Htmldescription`	The HTML version of the message (the `HTMLBodyPart` content) as a text string.
`Importance`	The message's importance. Must be one of the `cdoImportanceValue` constants specified in Table 6.5.
`Normalizedsubject`	The `Subject` string with prefixes such as "Re:" or "Fwd:" removed.
`Priority`	The message's priority. Must be one of the `cdoPriorityValue` constants specified in Table 6.6.
`Senderemail`	The e-mail address; part of the sender string.
`Sendername`	The name part of the sender string.
`Textdescription`	The plain-text content of the message body. This is the content of the `TextBodyPart` as a text string.
`thread-topic`	The topic identifier used for message threading.
Prefix "urn:schemas:mailheader:"	
`approved`	For newsgroup messages only. The address of the moderator that approved and posted the message.
`comment`	A comment for the message. Rarely used.
`content-base`	The base URI (URL) to use for relative URIs in the other header fields, and for any HTML message parts that do not contain a `<BASE>` tag.
`control`	A Boolean value for newsgroup messages only. Indicates that this is a server control message, not a standard user message.
`summary`	A summary header describing the message. Rarely used.
`thread-index`	An identifier for a threaded message.
`thread-topic`	The topic (subject) of a threaded message. Corresponds to the "Thread-topic:" message header.

In addition, the `mailheader` category contains ASCII text RFC 1522–encoded versions of the fields in the `httpmail` category. It's not necessary to view or alter the fields that are duplicated; the `CDO.Message` object sets them automatically from the `httpmail` versions.

Tables 6.5 and 6.6 list constants used by the Importance and Priority fields, respectively.

Table 6.5 ***cdoImportanceValues* Constants**

Name	Value	Description
`cdoLow`	0	Low importance
`cdoNormal`	1	Normal importance
`cdoHigh`	2	High importance

Table 6.6 ***cdoPriorityValues* Constants**

Name	Value	Description
`cdoPriorityNonUrgent`	-1	Not urgent
`cdoPriorityNormal`	0	Normal priority
`cdoPriorityUrgent`	1	Urgent

The CDO `BodyParts` Collection

E-mail messages may contain multiple parts: a text version, an HTML version, attached documents, attached Web pages with resources such as images and frames, and so on. Also, messages that are forwarded can contain a hierarchy of messages. (Have you ever gotten one of those e-mail jokes that's been forwarded from person to person to person?) These are known as Multipart-MIME messages, and the text file that carries such messages contains markers that show where one piece ends and another begins.

The `CDO.Message` object represents these compound messages using an object structure called a `BodyPart` and a collection called `BodyParts`. A `BodyPart` object contains one piece of a multipart message (for example, a message or an image). The message subelements contained within a `BodyPart` are represented by a `BodyParts` collection.

Reference List 6.3 lists the properties and methods of the `BodyParts` collection. If you're only interested in sending simple text messages, you don't need to bother with `BodyParts`, and you can skip ahead to the section "The `CDO.Configuration` Object."

The `BodyParts` collections can be examined using a `for each` loop or a `for` loop, as with the `Fields` collection described earlier in the chapter.

REFERENCE LIST 6.3 Properties and Methods of the CDO `BodyParts` Collection

Properties:

`Count`
Returns the number of items in the collection. Read-only.

`Item(`*n*`)`
Returns the specified `BodyPart` object from the collection, where *n* can range from `0` to `.Count-1`.

Methods:

`Add(`[*n*]`)`
Adds a new, empty `BodyPart` to the collection and returns an object reference to the new object. If a numeric argument is given, the new object is inserted as the *n*th item in the list (for example, `1` to `.Count+1`). If *n* is `-1` or is omitted, the new `BodyPart` is added to the end of the collection. If *n* is `1`, the new `BodyPart` is added to the beginning of the list. Note that *n* cannot be `0`.

`Delete` *x*
Deletes the specified object from the collection, where *x* can either be an ordinal number from `1` to `.Count` or an object reference to the `BodyPart` to be deleted.

`DeleteAll`
Removes all `BodyPart` objects from the collection.

Just to emphasize the point, `Item()` uses index numbers from `0` to `.Count-1`, while `Add` and `Delete` use numbers from `1` to `.Count` to represent the existing objects. Although inconsistent, this is the way Microsoft designed it.

The CDO `BodyPart` Object

An individual component of the message is represented by a `BodyPart` object. Every `CDO.Message` contains a `BodyPart` object that represents the message to be sent, which in turn may contain nested `BodyPart` objects. The properties and methods of the `BodyPart` object are described in Reference List 6.4.

REFERENCE LIST 6.4 Properties and Methods of the CDO `BodyPart` Object

Properties:

`BodyParts`
Returns a reference to the `BodyParts` collection that represents all subparts of this message element. The easiest way to add a new item to this collection is with the `AddBodyPart` method.

`Charset`
The standard descriptor for the character set used in the message (for example, "us-ascii", "shift-jis"). Corresponds to the `charset` parameter of the Content-Type field in the message header.

`ContentMediaType`

Describes the MIME type of a subdocument (for example, "text/plain", "image/gif"). This is used along with the `Charset` value to construct the message's Content-Type header line.

`ContentTransferEncoding`

Describes the method to be used to encode the content of the message. The default type is "7bit". Text should usually be encoded as "7bit" or "quoted-printable". Image and binary data are usually encoded using "base64". The permitted encoding types are listed in Table 6.8.

`Fields`

Returns the `Fields` collection attached to this `BodyPart`. Many of the object's properties are actually stored in `Fields`; the properties simply provide a more convenient way to get to them. See the section "Working with Fields" earlier in the chapter for more information. This property is read-only; you can alter it by changing individual `Field` items and then using the collection's `Update` method.

`Filename`

Corresponds to the filename specified by the MIME header's Content-Disposition line. (Read-only.)

`Parent`

Returns a reference to the object that contains this message element (that is, the `BodyPart`'s parent `BodyPart` or the primary `BodyPart` in the `Message` object).

Methods:

`AddBodyPart(`*`n`*`)`

Adds a new, empty `BodyPart` to the list of message subelements contained within this `BodyPart` as well as returns an object reference to the new object. Using this method is the same as using the `Add` method of the object's `BodyParts` property; that is, the statements

```
set newpart = bp.AddBodyPart(n)
```

and

```
set newpart = bp.BodyParts.Add(n)
```

are equivalent. See the discussion for the `Add` property under "The CDO `BodyParts` Collection," earlier in the chapter.

`GetDecodedContentStream()`

Returns an ADO `Stream` object, which can be read to extract the decoded contents of the message part; it can also be used to save the contents to a file. This method is used with received messages, rather than when sending. (I expect that with some effort, you could also use this method to decode an encoded file by using these objects without actually sending a message.)

continues

REFERENCE LIST 6.4 Continued

`GetEncodedContentStream()`

Returns an ADO `Stream` object, which can be read to view the encoded contents of the message part. This method is not very useful when sending or receiving messages, but again, I think it could come in handy if you needed a way to just encode a file.

`GetFieldParameter(`*`fieldname, parameter`*`)`

Extracts a field from a MIME header string; this is most often used with received messages. *`Fieldname`* is a fully qualified field name (for example, "urn:schemas:mailheader:content-type"), and *parameter* is a component of the field (for example, "boundary"). This is used with received messages only.

`GetInterface(`*`interfacename`*`)`

Returns an alternate object type for objects with multiple personalities. Not needed by scripting applications.

`GetStream()`

Returns an ADO `Stream` object containing both the header lines and content for this message component, encoded as it was received. This is the "raw view" of the message. Used with received messages only.

`SaveToFile` *`filename`*

Writes the contents of the `BodyPart` object to a file. The filename can be specified in normal format (for example, `"C:\message.doc"`) or URI format (for example, `"file://c:\message.doc"`).

The values in the `BodyPart` object's `Fields` collection are listed in Table 6.7. Fields that are accessible as properties are not listed. Because the `CDO.Message` object contains a `BodyPart` object, all the fields listed under `CDO.Message` appear as fields of the primary `BodyPart` object, as well as the ones listed below.

Table 6.7 **Values in the *BodyPart* Object's *Fields* Collection**

Name	Description
PREFIX "URN:SCHEMAS:HTTPMAIL:"	
`attachmentfilename`	Corresponds to the "filename:" parameter of the Content-Disposition mail header in an attachment `BodyPart` object. (Read-only.)
`content-disposition-type`	The type part of a content-disposition header. Can be one of the values "unspecified", "other", "attachment", or "inline".

Name	Description
PREFIX "URN:SCHEMAS:MAILHEADER:"	
`content-description`	A comment describing a part of a multipart message.
`content-disposition`	The Content-Disposition MIME header for this part of a multipart message.
`content-id`	A unique identifier for the resource.
`content-language`	The two-letter code describing the language used in the resource (for example, "en" or "de").
`content-location`	The URI that corresponds to the resource (for example, where the embedded part came from).
`content-type`	The Content-Type MIME header for this `BodyPart` object, containing a content-media-type and optionally a character set identifier.
PREFIX "HTTP://SCHEMAS.MICROSOFT.COM/"	
`sensitivity`	Defines the sensitivity level of the message and corresponds to the "Sensitivity:" mail header. Set to one of the integer values listed in Table 6.9.

Tables 6.8 and 6.9 list constants used by the `ContentTransferEncoding` property and the `sensitivity` field, respectively.

Table 6.8 ***cdoEncodingType* Constants**

Name	Value	Description
`cdo7bit`	"7bit"	Simple 7-bit ASCII.
`cdo8bit`	"8bit"	8-bit coding with line-termination characters.
`cdoBase64`	"base64"	Three octets encoded into four sextets with offset.
`cdoBinary`	"binary"	Arbitrary binary stream.
`cdoMacBinHex40`	"mac-binhex40"	Macintosh binary-to-hex encoding. CDO can decode but not encode binhex.
`cdoQuotedPrintable`	"quoted-printable"	Mostly 7-bit, with 8-bit characters encoded as "=HH".
`cdoUuencode`	"uuencode"	Unix Uuencode encoding.

Table 6.9 ***cdoSensitivityValues* Constants**

Name	Value	Description
`cdoSensitivityNone`	0	Not specified (default)
`cdoPersonal`	1	Personal
`cdoPrivate`	2	Private
`cdoCompanyConfidential`	3	Confidential

The ADO `Stream` Object

The contents of a `CDO.Message` or `BodyPart` object are exposed (made available) as a `Stream` object that can be saved to a file. `Stream` is another object borrowed from the ActiveX Data Objects system, and there isn't enough room to cover it completely here. `Stream` objects aren't important for sending messages, but if you're working with CDO to manipulate received messages or to encode or decode data files, some of `Stream`'s methods and properties may be helpful.

The one property and the methods of the `Stream` object that you can use for message processing are described in Reference List 6.5.

REFERENCE LIST 6.5 The Property and Methods of the `Stream` Object

Property:

`EOS`
Boolean value for "end of stream." The value is `True` when there is no more data to read from the stream (that is, when it is at end-of-file).

Methods:

`ReadText(`[*`nbytes`*]**`)`**
Reads the specified number of characters of text data (*`nbytes`*) from the stream and returns a character string; fewer bytes may be returned if there are no *`nbytes`* left. Returns `Null` if the stream is at end-of-stream. If *`nbytes`* is omitted, all remaining data is read.

`SaveToFile` *`filename`*, *`saveoption`*
Writes the stream data to a file named *`filename`*. *`Saveoption`* specifies how the object should treat an existing file. It can take one of three values:

Value	Description
1	Creates the file if it does not exist but will not overwrite an existing file.
2	Overwrites an existing file, but the file must already exist.
3	Creates the file if it does not exist or overwrites an existing file.

After writing the file, the stream pointer is repositioned to the beginning of the stream data.

The `CDO.Configuration` Object

The `CDO.Configuration` object contains `Field` values that instruct the `Message` object on how to deliver the e-mail message. There are two ways the message can be delivered:

- By sending the message to an SMTP or NNTP mail or news server, either on your own network or at your ISP. This is the most direct way of delivering the message.
- By dropping the message into a folder that your mail server periodically scans for outgoing messages. This technique can be used if you are using the Microsoft SMTP or NNTP server that is part of Internet Information Services (IIS) on a Professional or Server version of Windows XP, 2000, or NT. If the "drop directory" for the SMTP server is on the computer that is running the script or is reachable through the network, you can use this method.

The `CDO.Configuration` object contains just one property: `Fields`. The `Fields` collection contains a list of values that describe the method to be used to deliver the message. The field values are set using the methods described earlier, under "Working with Fields." There is one method—`Load`—that lets you pull in default server delivery information from other applications.

Reference List 6.6 describes the property and method. The values of the configuration object's `Fields` collection are listed in Table 6.10.

REFERENCE LIST 6.6 The Property and Method of the `CDO.Configuration` Object

Property:

`Fields`

Returns a `Fields` collection object containing the `Field` values that determine how the message is to be sent. The `Field` values are listed in Table 6.10.

Method:

`Load` *`loadFrom`*

Sets `Fields` with default settings made for the Outlook Express and/or Internet Information Services SMTP and NNTP server connections. If your script will always be run on a computer that has IIS installed and is configured for outbound mail, or if you will always run the script from a user account that has a default identity set up for Outlook Express, you can use this method to avoid having to "hard-wire" the outgoing delivery method and server information. The *`loadFrom`* value must be one of the `cdoConfigSource` constants listed in Table 6.11.

For most scripting applications, it's probably best to ignore the `Load` method, assume that all values need to be set, and set them in your script.

The full list of all `Fields` values for the `CDO.Configuration Fields` collection is shown in Table 6.10. In a scripting application that only sends e-mail messages, you do not need to set any of the "post" or "nntp" parameters, which are used to send newsgroup messages.

Table 6.10 **Values in the *Fields* Collection of *CDO.Configuration***

Name	Description
PREFIX: "HTTP://SCHEMAS.MICROSOFT.COM/CDO/CONFIGURATION/"	
`Autopromotebodyparts`	Boolean value. If this value is `True`, any `BodyPart` objects containing only one embedded `BodyPart` are sent as a single part.
`Flushbuffersonwrite`	Boolean value. If this value is `True`, when sending via pickup directories, message files are committed to disk immediately, bypassing normal file caching. This slows performance but can protect against loss due to crashes.
`Httpcookies`	List of cookies (separated by semicolons) to send to HTTP servers when fetching pages using `CreateMHTMLBody` or `AddAttachment`.
`Languagecode`	RFC 1766 Language Code (for example, "en" or "de") to use when generating response text for reply or forwarded messages.
`nntpaccountname`	The NNTP account name as displayed by Outlook Express; not actually used for anything.
`nntpauthenticate`	Authentication method to use when sending messages to a news server. The value must be one of the `cdoProtocolsAuthentication` constants listed in Table 6.12.
`nntpconnectiontimeout`	Number of seconds to wait before timing out an NNTP connection. The default is 30 seconds or, if loaded, the setting used in Outlook Express.
`nntpserver`	Name of the server to use when posting news messages via NNTP. Loaded from Outlook Express.
`nntpserverpickupdirectory`	Path to the pickup directory to use when posting news messages to a server using a pickup directory.
`nntpserverport`	TCP port to use when posting news messages with NNTP. The default is 119 or, if loaded, the Outlook Express entry.
`nntpusessl`	Boolean value that indicates whether to use Secure Sockets Layer (SSL) when posting via NNTP.
`postemailaddress`	The sender's return e-mail address to use in news messages.
`postpassword`	The password to use when connecting to the NNTP server, if `nntpauthenticate` is set to `cdoBasic`.
`postusername`	The user name to use when connecting to the NNTP server, if `nntpauthenticate` is set to `cdoBasic`.
`postuserreplyemailaddress`	The reply-to e-mail address for the message.

Name	Description
PREFIX: "HTTP://SCHEMAS.MICROSOFT.COM/CDO/CONFIGURATION/"	
`postusing`	Method to use when sending news messages. Must be one of the `cdoPostUsing` constants defined in Table 6.13.
`sendemailaddress`	The sender's default e-mail address. This is used as the "from" address with the SMTP server.
`sendpassword`	The password to use when connecting to the SMTP server, if `smtpauthenticate` is set to `cdoBasic`.
`sendusername`	The username to use when connecting to the SMTP server, if `smtpauthenticate` is set to `cdoBasic`.
`senduserreplymailaddress`	The sender's "reply-to" e-mail address to use in e-mail messages. If this is not specified, the message's "From" address is used.
`sendusing`	Method to use when sending e-mail messages. Must be one of the `cdoSendUsing` constants defined in Table 6.14.
`smtpaccountname`	The SMTP account name as displayed by Outlook Express; not actually used for anything.
`smtpauthenticate`	Authentication method to use when sending messages to a mail server. The value must be one of the `cdoProtocolsAuthentication` constants listed in Table 6.12.
`smtpconnectiontimeout`	Number of seconds to wait before timing out an SMTP connection. The default is 30 seconds or, if loaded, the Outlook Express setting.
`smtpserver`	Name of server to use when posting e-mail messages via SMTP. This can be a DNS name or an IP address in dotted decimal format and can be loaded from Outlook Express setup.
`smtpserverpickupdirectory`	Path to the pickup directory to use when posting e-mail messages via a pickup directory.
`smtpserverport`	TCP port to use when posting mail messages with SMTP. The default is 25 or, if loaded, the setting used in Outlook.
`smtpusessl`	Boolean value that indicates whether to use Secure Sockets Layer (SSL) when posting via SMTP.
`urlgetlatestversion`	Boolean value. If this value is `True`, `AddAttachment` and `CreateMHTMLBody` will always go fetch a specified page rather than use a cached local copy.

continues

Table 6.10 **Continued**

Name	Description
PREFIX: "HTTP://SCHEMAS.MICROSOFT.COM/CDO/CONFIGURATION/"	
`urlproxyserver`	The proxy server to use when fetching HTTP resources. Must be specified as an IP address or server name plus port (for example, `"1.2.3.4:80"` or `"proxy.somewhere.com:80"`).
`urlproxybypass`	String value. If set to `"<local>"`, local addresses do not use the proxy server.
`usemessageresponsetext`	Boolean value that indicates whether to automatically generate response text when using the `Reply`, `PostReply` or `Forward` method. The default is `True`.
PREFIX: "URN:SCHEMAS:CALENDAR:"	
`timezoneid`	Time zone identifier to use when adding timestamps to outgoing messages and when reading incoming messages. Defaults to the local computer's setting. Must be one of the `cdoTimeZoneId` constants listed in Table 6.15.

Table 6.11 lists the constants used in the `LoadFrom` method.

Table 6.11 ***cdoConfigSource*** **Constants**

Name	Value	Description
`CdoSourceDefaults`	-1	Loads default values from both Internet Information Services and Outlook Express
`CdoSourceIIS`	1	Obtains server settings from the SMTP configuration values for IIS on this computer
`cdoSourceOutlookExpress`	2	Obtains server settings from the default identity in the current user's Outlook Express configuration

Table 6.12 lists the constants used by the `nntpauthenticate` and `smtpauthenticate` fields.

Table 6.12 ***cdoProtocolsAuthentication*** **Constants**

Name	Value	Description
`cdoAnonymous`	0	Do not authenticate.
`cdoBasic`	1	Use basic (clear-text) authentication. The specified username and password are sent.
`cdoNTLM`	2	Use NTLM authentication. The current process's credentials are used (for example, the current user's credentials).

Table 6.13 lists the constants used by the `postusing` field.

Table 6.13 ***cdoPostUsing* Constants**

Name	Value	Description
cdoPostUsingPickup	1	Post the message by dropping into the IIS NNTP service pickup directory
cdoPostUsingPort	2	Post the message directly using NNTP

Table 6.14 lists the constants used by the `sendusing` field.

Table 6.14 ***cdoSendUsing* Constants**

Name	Value	Description
cdoSendUsingPickup	1	Send the message by dropping into the IIS SMTP service pickup directory
cdoSendUsingPort	2	Send the message directly using SMTP

Table 6.15 lists the constants used by the `timezoneid` field.

Table 6.15 ***cdoTimeZoneId* Constants**

Name	Value	GMT Offset	Locations
cdoUTC	0	0:00	Universal Coordinated Time
cdoGMT	1	0:00	Greenwich Mean Time; Dublin, Edinburgh, and London
cdoLisbon	2	+1:00	Lisbon and Warsaw
cdoParis	3	+1:00	Paris and Madrid
cdoBerlin	4	+1:00	Berlin, Stockholm, Rome, Bern, Brussels, and Vienna
cdoEasternEurope	5	+2:00	Eastern Europe
cdoPrague	6	+1:00	Prague
cdoAthens	7	+2:00	Athens, Helsinki, Istanbul
cdoBrasilia	8	-3:00	Brasilia
cdoAtlanticCanada	9	-4:00	Atlantic Time (Canada)
cdoEastern	10	-5:00	Eastern Time (U.S. and Canada)
cdoCentral	11	-6:00	Central Time (U.S. and Canada)
cdoMountain	12	-7:00	Mountain Time (U.S. and Canada)
cdoPacific	13	-8:00	Pacific Time (U.S. and Canada); Tijuana
cdoAlaska	14	-9:00	Alaska

continues

Table 6.15 **Continued**

Name	Value	GMT Offset	Locations
cdoHawaii	15	-10:00	Hawaii
cdoMidwayIsland	16	-11:00	Midway Island and Samoa
cdoWellington	17	+12:00	Wellington and Auckland
cdoBrisbane	18	+10:00	Brisbane, Melbourne, and Sydney
cdoAdelaide	19	+9:30	Adelaide
cdoTokyo	20	+9:00	Tokyo, Osaka, Sapporo, Seoul, and Yakutsk
cdoHongKong	21	+8:00	Hong Kong SAR, Perth, Singapore, and Taipei
cdoBangkok	22	+7:00	Bangkok, Jakarta, and Hanoi
cdoBombay	23	+5:30	Bombay, Calcutta, Madras, New Delhi, and Colombo
cdoAbuDhabi	24	+4:00	Abu Dhabi, Muscat, Tbilisi, Kazan, and Volgograd
cdoTehran	25	+3:30	Tehran
cdoBaghdad	26	+3:00	Baghdad, Kuwait, Nairobi, and Riyadh
cdoIsrael	27	+2:00	Israel
cdoNewfoundland	28	-3:30	Newfoundland
cdoAzores	29	-1:00	Azores and Cape Verde Island
cdoMidAtlantic	30	-2:00	Mid-Atlantic
cdoMonrovia	31	0:00	Monrovia and Casablanca
cdoBuenosAires	32	-3:00	Buenos Aires and Georgetown
cdoCaracas	33	-4:00	Caracas and La Paz
cdoIndiana	34	-5:00	Indiana (East)
cdoBogota	35	-5:00	Bogota and Lima
cdoSaskatchewan	36	-6:00	Saskatchewan
cdoMexicoCity	37	-6:00	Mexico City and Tegucigalpa
cdoArizona	38	-7:00	Arizona
cdoEniwetok	39	-12:00	Eniwetok and Kwajalein
cdoFiji	40	+12:00	Fiji Islands, Kamchatka, and Marshall Islands
cdoMagadan	41	+11:00	Magadan, Solomon Islands, and New Caledonia
cdoHobart	42	+10:00	Hobart
cdoGuam	43	+10:00	Guam, Port Moresby, and Vladivostok
cdoDarwin	44	+9:30	Darwin

Name	Value	GMT Offset	Locations
`cdoBeijing`	45	+8:00	Beijing, Chongqing, and Urumqi
`cdoAlmaty`	46	+6:00	Almaty and Dhaka
`cdoIslamabad`	47	+5:00	Islamabad, Karachi, Sverdlovsk, and Tashkent
`cdoKabul`	48	+4:30	Kabul
`cdoCairo`	49	+2:00	Cairo
`cdoHarare`	50	+2:00	Harare and Pretoria
`cdoMoscow`	51	+3:00	Moscow and St. Petersburg
`cdoInvalidTimZone`	52		Invalid time zone identifier

OK, enough with the reference information. Let's see how you can make use of all of this information.

Sending a Message with CDO

The reference material in the previous section describes a complex set of objects for sending messages. All that complexity is there to make it possible to construct and manipulate multipart, multiformat messages. It turns out that in real-life applications, you'll likely use only a few of all those methods and properties.

The basic steps involved in sending a message are as follows:

1. Create one `CDO.Message` and one `CDO.Configuration` object.
2. Add message content to the `CDO.Message` object.
3. Add delivery method information to the `CDO.Configuration` object.
4. Send the message.

The first step is to create objects, using standard object calls. For example, in VBScript, the following statements create and link `Message` and `Configuration` objects named `msg` and `config`, respectively:

```
set msg = CreateObject("CDO.Message")          ' create objects
set config = CreateObject("CDO.Configuration")
set msg.Configuration = config                 ' link msg to config
```

The third statement tells `msg` that its associated `Configuration` object is `config`. In the remaining examples, if these `CreateObject` calls aren't shown, you can assume that they're part of the script.

In the next few sections, I'll show you how to go through the remaining steps, with several variations.

Constructing the Message

In most cases, you will just want to send a simple text or HTML-formatted message. The content of the message can come from a text string, a file, or, if you want to send a Web page as a message, a URL.

The `CDO.Message` object contains one `BodyPart` object that can be used in one of two ways: If you are sending a simple text or HTML message, it holds the message content. If you are sending a multipart message, with alternative and/or subsidiary parts, this `BodyPart` object holds the component parts of the message in its `BodyParts` collection, as illustrated earlier in Figures 6.2 and 6.3.

Therefore, to construct a simple message, you must assign content to the main `BodyPart` object. To construct a multipart message, you'll add components to the `BodyPart`.

Sending a Text String

If you are sending a simple text message, you only need to put the message text into the CDO message's `BodyPart` object. It's easiest to use the `TextBody` property to do this. If no other message content has been added to the object, the `TextBodyPart` property refers to the main `BodyPart` (as illustrated earlier in Figure 6.2), and the `TextBody` property to its content. If you assign a text string to `TextBody`, that becomes the content of the message.

A text message should consist of lines of text of at most 75 characters or so, separated by carriage return/linefeed pairs. This lets the message display properly in text-based e-mail programs. For example, you could construct a message using these statements:

```
reminder = "This is a reminder message:" & vbCRLF & _
           "Go to your weekly meeting at 1:15" & vbCRLF & _
           "Bring a pencil."
```

You could construct a message that lists all the DOC files in a certain directory with statements such as:

```
                                                  ' Example File Script0601.vbs
set fso = CreateObject("Scripting.FileSystemObject")
set dir = "C:\Documents and Settings\All Users\Documents\Orders"

txt = ""
for each file in fso.GetFolder(dir).Files        ' scan for .DOC files
    if instr(".DOC", ucase(file.Name)) > 0 then
        if txt = "" then                          ' first one, start the message
            txt = "There are new documents in the Orders folder:" & _
                  vbCRLF & vbCRLF
        end if
        txt = txt & file.Name & ", " & _
              file.DateCreated & vbCRLF           ' add name to the list
```

```
    end if
next

if txt = "" then WScript.Quit(0)     ' no files to announce, just quit
set msg.TextBody = txt               ' assign the message content
```

This will create a message such as the following:

```
There are new documents in the Orders folder:

fromPTP.doc, 3/11/2002 1:13:10 PM
fromZandar.doc, 3/11/2002 2:13:15 PM
```

Sending a Message from a Text File

You can tell CDO to use the contents of a text file as the message body by reading the text into a string variable and assigning it to the TextBody property we used in the previous section. Here's an example:

```
sendfile = "C:\temp\message.txt"          ' file to send
set fso = CreateObject("Scripting.FileSystemObject")

set infile = fso.OpenTextFile(sendfile)       ' read file into a string
txt = infile.ReadAll
infile.Close
set infile = Nothing

msg.TextBody = txt                            ' set message content
```

Sending the Output of a Program

You can e-mail the output of a command-line program through the aid of the WScript.Shell object, which is covered in Chapter 4, "File and Registry Access." For example, the following statements grab the output of a ping command as a text e-mail message:

```
set shell = CreateObject("WScript.Shell")
set ping  = shell.Run("ping www.someplace.com")
txt = "The ping test results are:" & vbCRLF & ping.Stdout.ReadAll
set ping = Nothing

msg.TextBody = txt                            ' set message content
```

Sending an HTML Message

HTML messages can be created by filling in the HTMLBodyPart object or assigning a string to the HTMLBody property. This can be the sole message component or part of a multipart/alternate message that contains both text and HTML versions.

You can create HTML-based messages by inserting the appropriate HTML tags into a text string. The file listing message shown earlier could be sent in HTML using a `<UL>` unordered list, with these statements:

```
' Example File script0602.vbs
txt = ""
for each file in fso.GetFolder(dir).Files     ' scan for .DOC files
    if instr(".DOC", ucase(file.Name)) > 0 then
        if txt = "" then                      ' first one, start the message
            txt = "There are new documents in the Orders folder:" & _
                  "<P><UL>"
        end if
        txt = txt & "<LI>" & file.Name & ", " & _
              file.DateCreated                ' add name to the list
    end if
next

if txt = "" then WScript.Quit(0)    ' no files to announce, just quit
txt = txt + "</UL>"                 ' end the list
set msg.HTMLBody = txt              ' assign the message content
```

In this script, a new list item is added for each file using an HTML `<LI>` tag. The entire list is displayed as a `<UL>` (unordered, bulleted) list.

Sending a Web Page or HTML File

If you wish to send an HTML message that is already contained in a file or is available as a Web page, you can use the `CDO.Message` method `CreateMHTMLBody` to extract the file or Web page as the message body.

`CreateMHTMLBody` takes a ***flags*** argument that indicates whether CDO is to obtain and embed into the message any images or other resources referred to by the main HTML document. Table 6.3 lists these constants. In general you will want to use `cdoSuppressNone` (value 0) so that all referenced images, sounds, and other resources will be included.

Tip

You can download a VBS file with `const` definitions for all these values from `www.helpwinxp.com/hood`. You can then copy these definitions into your scripts.

The following statements show how a file named `servers.html` can be sent as a formatted message:

```
const cdoSuppressNone = 0
msg.CreateMHTMLBody("file://C:\servers.html", cdoSuppressNone)
```

This statement takes the document `"c:\servers.html"` and uses it as the e-mail message body. Any resources are fetched and included as well, as additional `BodyPart` objects.

`CreateMHTMLBody` can also obtain the message document from a Web server, if you specify a standard URL rather than a filename. For example,

```
msg.CreateMHTMLBody("http://www.somewhere.com/somepage.html", _
    cdoSuppressNone)
```

visits `www.somewhere.com`, downloads the page and any included images or other resources, and uses this as the content of the message. You could use this technique in a script that runs on a schedule to automatically mail you, say, a network status page or a stock portfolio valuation.

If the Web page requires a username and password, you can specify these after the *`flags`* argument. You should be careful about storing passwords in scripts, however, because anyone who obtains access to your script file will have the password to the remote Web site.

Note

If the script is run more than once with the same URL, CDO may find that the page you are requesting is in the Temporary Internet Files cache of recently viewed pages, and it may send that copy. Although this speeds things up when you're sending a fixed page, if the page changes or is generated on-the-fly by a CGI program, CDO may send a stale copy. You can tell CDO never to look in the cache for pages by setting the `urlgetlatestversion` field in the `Configuration` object to `True`. The `Configuration` object is discussed later in the chapter.

Sending a Multiformat Message

If you want to send HTML-based messages, it's good to include the text version for people who don't like HTML or whose e-mail programs can't read it. When you assign values to both `HTMLBody` and `TextBody`, CDO automatically creates the subsidiary `BodyPart` objects.

You can manually construct both text and HTML versions and assign them using the statements used in the previous sections, or you can create just the HTML version and let CDO derive the text version automatically. This technique is the easiest way to produce a text version when you use `CreateMTHMLBody` to include a file or Web page. Simply set the property `AutoGenerateTextBody` to `True`. Here's an example:

```
msg.CreateMHTMLBody("http://www.somewhere.com/somepage.html, _
    cdoSuppressNone)
msg.AutoGenerateTextBody = True
```

Adding Attachments

E-mail attachments are sent by adding `BodyPart` objects to the main message object's `Attachments` collection. Most of the work can done using the message's

AddAttachment method. This adds the new BodyPart object, loads the contents of a specified file into the BodyPart, and returns a reference to the new object. Here is an example:

```
set attach = msg.AddAttachment("C:\text\proposal.doc")
```

This is 99% of the job. The only other thing to worry about is that the attachment should be labeled with the correct content-type string (in property ContentMediaType), which describes the type of data inside the attachment. This information tells the message recipient's e-mail program what application to use to open the attachment. A few common content types are listed here:

Content Type	Description
Text/plain	Plain ASCII text
Text/html	HTML formatted text
Image/jpg	A JPG image
Application/postscript	A PostScript document file
Application/octet-stream	Unspecified, binary data

Windows can often determine the proper content type from the attachment's file extension. If you wish, however, you can set the content type explicitly and override what Windows guesses by using statements like these:

```
set attach = msg.AddAttachment("C:\text\proposal.doc")
attach.ContentMediaType = "application/msword"
```

If you don't need to worry about setting the content type, you don't need to store the object reference returned by AddAttachment, and you can simply use the method to attach files to your message with statements like these:

```
msg.AddAttachment "C:\text\proposal.doc"
msg.AddAttachment "C:\text\response.doc"
```

Finally, as with CreateMHTMLBody, you can give AddAttachment a URL instead of a filename, and it will retrieve the specified document from a Web server and add it as an attachment. In this case, the content type will be set to the value that the Web server provides. If the URL is password protected, you can pass a username and password as additional arguments to AddAttachment.

Specifying the Recipients and Subject

The CDO.Message object has several properties that echo the familiar fields you fill in whenever sending an e-mail message:

Property	Description
`To`	Primary recipient(s)
`CC`	Secondary recipient(s)
`BCC`	Private recipient(s) whose existence is invisible to the other recipients
`From`	The e-mail address of the message author
`ReplyTo`	The address to which responses should be sent, if not the From address
`Subject`	A short description of the message

All but the Subject entry are e-mail address that can be formatted as described earlier in the chapter under the section "The `CDO.Message` Object." If you enter multiple addresses, simply separate them with commas.

As an example, to send a message from `"sales@mycompany.com"` to `"orders@mycompany.com"`, with a carbon copy going back to `"sales@mycompany.com"`, you could use these statements:

```
msg.To      = "orders@mycompany.com"
msg.From    = "sales@mycompany.com"
msg.CC      = "sales@mycompany.com"
msg.Subject = "Orders received " & date()
```

Specifying the Delivery Server

The preceding sections described how to construct a message in the `CDO.Message` object. The next step is to set the `CDO.Configuration` object with the information needed to actually deliver the message.

CDO does not attempt to deliver the message directly to its recipients. Instead, it relies on a mail server to do the necessary work of finding the recipient's own mail servers and passing the message on. The forwarding server can be one run by your organization or by your ISP; whatever setup you use for sending e-mail—with Outlook Express or some other e-mail program—can be used to send mail from a script.

All the information in the `Configuration` object is stored in its `Fields` collection using the prefix `"http://schemas.microsoft.com/cdo/configuration/"`. It's strange and cumbersome, but we have to live with it. I've found that the easiest way to set the `Field` values is to store the prefix in a variable and to use the `with` statement, when using VBScript. These minimize the amount of typing and clutter. For example, you can set configuration properties using statements of this sort:

```
const cdoSendUsingPort = 2              ' standard CDO constants
const cdoAnonymous     = 0

set msg  = CreateObject("CDO.Message")  ' create objects
set conf = CreateObject("CDO.Configuration")
```

```
set msg.configuration = conf
                                            ' set delivery options
prefix = "http://schemas.microsoft.com/cdo/configuration/"
With conf.fields
    .item(prefix & "sendusing")              = cdoSendUsingPort
    .item(prefix & "smtpserver")             = "mail.mycompany.com"
    .item(prefix & "smtpauthenticate")       = cdoAnonymous
    .item(prefix & "urlgetlatestversion")    = True
    .update                                 ' commit changes
End With
```

There are two ways to send the message, depending on whether you use the SMTP mail service provided as part of Internet Information Services (IIS) or a standard SMTP server located on your network or at your ISP.

Note

CDO must use one of the following two types of delivery agents; it won't work with Web-based e-mail services such as `hotmail.com`. Also, if you use `cdoSendUsingPort`, the SMTP server you select must be willing to accept e-mail from your computer's IP address.

Using an SMTP Server

If you route mail through an SMTP server in your organization or at your ISP, you must specify `cdoSendUsingPort` for the `sendusing` field. This instructs CDO to send the message using standard Internet methods to a specified mail server. You must also tell CDO whether it needs to sign on to the mail server and how this is done. In most cases, no sign on is necessary, and you can use an "anonymous" connection. If your mail server requires a username and password in order to *send* e-mail, you can use "basic" authentication and provide the name and password through `CDO.Configuration`.

In most cases, here are the field values you need to set:

Field	Value
`sendusing`	`cdoSendUsingPort` (2).
`smtpserver`	Name or IP address of the mail server.
`smtpauthenticate`	Refer to Table 6.12 for options.
`sendusername`	Username, if required.
`sendpassword`	Password, if required.

An example of this configuration was shown in the previous section.

In some circumstances, for example, if your mail server uses a Secure Sockets connection, you may need to specify some of the other field values listed earlier, in Table 6.10.

Using the SMTP Service Provided with IIS

If you are using the SMTP service provided with IIS on your computer or somewhere on your local network, you may be able to send messages by simply having CDO drop them into a folder that is periodically scanned for outgoing mail. Setting up the SMTP service is beyond the scope of this book, and I don't recommend using it if you have other options available.

However, if the IIS SMTP service is available, you can take advantage of it using CDO. This makes CDO's life easier, because it doesn't need to establish a connection with the mail server—it only has to write the outgoing message to a file in the "pickup" folder.

The field values you need to set are as follows:

Field	Value
`sendusing`	`cdoSendUsingPickup` (1)
`smtpserverpickupdirectory`	Pickup folder

If the script is run on the same computer on which IIS runs, the pickup folder will be on a local drive. If IIS is running on another computer, the pickup folder can be specified using a UNC-format shared-folder address (for example, `"\\ourserver\smtpoutgoing"`), assuming that you or your network administrator has set up such a share.

Sending the Message

The final step in sending an e-mail message with CDO is to use the `Send` method to deliver the message. Because any number of things can go wrong during this process—the remote SMTP server may be down, there may be a network error, or the `Configuration` object may be missing some information—you want to have your script catch and report the error rather than just failing. This is especially important with scheduled scripts that run unattended.

To send the message while detecting errors, you'll need to use your scripting language's exception handling mechanism. In VBScript, this is done with the `on error` statement. Here's how to send the constructed message safely:

```
on error resume next        ' do not stop on errors
msg.Send                    ' deliver the message
send_errno = err.Number     ' remember error number
on error goto 0             ' restore normal error handling
if send_errno <> 0  then    ' if something went wrong...
    ' report the problem somehow
end if
```

After `.Send`, if the message is not delivered, `send_errno` will be nonzero, so the `if` statement will be true, and you can take whatever action is appropriate.

Putting It All Together

Now, let's look at a few examples of sending a message, with all the steps put together.

This basic example sends a simple, no-frills text message every time the script is run:

```
' Example File script0603.vbs
const cdoSendUsingPort = 2                   ' standard CDO constants
const cdoAnonymous     = 0

set msg  = CreateObject("CDO.Message")      ' create objects
set conf = CreateObject("CDO.Configuration")
set msg.configuration = conf

With msg                                     ' build the message
    .to       = """Sue Smith"" <ssmith@somewhere.com>"
    .from     = """Mad Max"" <madmax@somewhere.com>"
    .subject  = "Message from a script"
    .textBody = "This is the message!"
End With

prefix = "http://schemas.microsoft.com/cdo/configuration/"
With conf.fields                             ' set delivery options
    .item(prefix & "sendusing")             = cdoSendUsingPort
    .item(prefix & "smtpserver")            = "smtp.mycompany.com"
    .item(prefix & "smtpauthenticate")      = cdoAnonymous
    .update                                 ' commit changes
End With

on error resume next        ' do not stop on errors
msg.send                    ' deliver the message
send_errno = err.Number     ' remember error number
on error goto 0             ' restore normal error handling

if send_errno <> 0 then     ' if something went wrong...
    wscript.echo "Error sending message"
    wscript.quit 0
else
    wscript.echo "Message sent"
end if
```

This script generates and delivers the following message to the `ssmith@somewhere.com` e-mail address:

```
Received: from java (unverified [192.168.0.8]) by smtp.mycompany.com
 (MAIL SERVER 1.0) with SMTP id <B0000292575@smtp.mycompany.com>;
 Tue, 12 Mar 2002 00:32:31 -0800
thread-index: AcHJoDuGWvnh1UafTpmXHn+9pC20RQ==
Thread-Topic: Message from a script
From: "Mad Max" <madmax@somewhere.com>
To: "Sue Smith" <ssmith@somewhere.com>
Subject: Message from a script
Date: Tue, 12 Mar 2002 00:30:57 -0800
```

```
Message-ID: <000001c1c9a0$3bab31b0$6400a8c0@smtp>
MIME-Version: 1.0
Content-Type: text/plain
Content-Transfer-Encoding: 7bit
X-Mailer: Microsoft CDO for Windows 2000
Content-Class: urn:content-classes:message
Importance: normal
Priority: normal
X-MimeOLE: Produced By Microsoft MimeOLE V6.00.2600.0000

This is the message!
```

Now, in another example, we'll write a script that takes any files specified on its command-line arguments and mails them to a specific place. As mentioned earlier in the chapter, if you create a shortcut icon for this script, you can drag files onto it, and the script will mail the file to the built-in recipient. You might use this if you have to frequently forward files to one specific person.

The `AddAttachment` method in the middle of the script does all the work:

```
                                            ' Example File mailfiles.vbs
if WScript.arguments.count <= 0 then        ' no files were specified
    MsgBox "Usage: mailfiles filename..., or drag files onto shortcut"
    WScript.quit 0
end if

const cdoSendUsingPort = 2                  ' standard CDO constants
const cdoAnonymous     = 0

sender      = "myname@mycompany.com"        ' sender of message
recipient   = "somebody@mycompany.com"      ' recipient of this message
relayserver = "mail.mycompany.com"          ' SMTP server

set msg  = CreateObject("CDO.Message")      ' create objects
set conf = CreateObject("CDO.Configuration")
set msg.configuration = conf

With msg                                    ' build the message
    .to       = recipient
    .from     = sender
    .subject  = "Files for you"
    .textBody = "Attached to this message are files for you."

    nfiles = 0                              ' count of files attached
    for each arg in WScript.arguments       ' treat each argument as a
        .AddAttachment arg                  ' file to be attached
        nfiles = nfiles+1
    next
End With

prefix = "http://schemas.microsoft.com/cdo/configuration/"
With conf.fields                            ' set delivery options
```

```
    .item(prefix & "sendusing")          = cdoSendUsingPort
    .item(prefix & "smtpserver")         = relayserver
    .item(prefix & "smtpauthenticate")   = cdoAnonymous
    .update                              ' commit changes
End With

on error resume next       ' do not stop on errors
msg.send                   ' deliver the message
send_errno = err.Number    ' remember error number
on error goto 0            ' restore normal error handling

if send_errno then         ' if something went wrong...
    MsgBox "Error sending message"
else
    if nfiles = 1 then plural = "" else plural = "s"
    MsgBox "Sent " & nfiles & " file" & plural & " to " & recipient
end if
```

Tip

If you find this kind of script useful, be sure to check out Chapter 9, "Creating Your Own Scriptable Objects," where I show you how to create your own simplified "send some e-mail" object that encapsulates all this code.

As a final example, here is a script that can be run from the Task Scheduler to periodically scan a specified folder for files. Any file found in this folder is e-mailed to a fixed address, and the files are moved to an archive folder. This creates a "dropoff" folder that can be used in several ways:

- If you have your unattended scripts create log files in this folder, the logs can be mailed to an administrator for review.
- The folder can be shared on a network so that users can drop off files for someone else to review or process.
- If the script scans your incoming fax folder, this will automatically e-mail the faxes to a specified user.

The script takes care not to move the files out of the pickup folder unless the message was successfully sent. Also, the script stores the list of files it finds in an array and works with this array when sending and later moving the files. If the program uses one `for each file in folder` statement to add the attachments and a second to move the files, there is a chance that a file might be added between mailing and moving, and it would never get mailed. Here's the code for this script:

```
                                              ' Example File scanmail.vbs
                                              ' folder to scan for files
scanfolder    = _
    "c:\Documents and Settings\All Users\Documents\MailThese"
```

```
                                        ' folder to place mailed files
archivefolder = "c:\Documents and Settings\All Userss\Documents\Mailed\"

sender        = "sales@here.com"        ' sender of message
recipient     = "fulfillment@here.com"  ' recipient of this message
relayserver   = "mail.here.com"         ' SMTP server

' --------------------------------------------------------------
' GET LIST OF FILES
' --------------------------------------------------------------

WScript.echo "Scanning " & scanfolder & "..."

set fso = CreateObject("Scripting.FileSystemObject")
set folder = fso.GetFolder(scanfolder)

maxfiles = 50                        ' largest number of files expected
dim filelist()                       ' create resizable array to hold filenames
redim filelist(maxfiles)

nfiles = 0                           ' count of files stored

for each file in folder.Files        ' scan the folder
    if nfiles >= maxfiles then       ' if array is already full,
        maxfiles = nfiles+50         ' make it larger
        redim preserve filelist(maxfiles)
    end if

    WScript.echo "  Found", file.name ' list the files we find

    filelist(nfiles) = file.path     ' save filelist(0, 1, ...)
    nfiles = nfiles+1                ' add one to count of files
next

if nfiles = 0 then
    WScript.echo "No files to send"
    WScript.quit(0)                  ' nothing to do, just quit
end if

' --------------------------------------------------------------
' COMPOSE THE MESSAGE
' --------------------------------------------------------------

set msg  = CreateObject("CDO.Message")' create objects
set conf = CreateObject("CDO.Configuration")
set msg.configuration = conf

if nfiles = 1 then plural = "" else plural = "s"

With msg                             ' build the message
    .to      = recipient
```

```
    .from      = sender
    .subject   = "Files for you"

    .textBody = "Attached to this message are " & nfiles & plural &_
        " files for your attention."

    for i = 0 to nfiles-1              ' attach all of the files
        .AddAttachment filelist(i)
    next
End With

' ------------------------------------------------------------------
' SET DELIVERY INFO
' ------------------------------------------------------------------

const cdoSendUsingPort = 2             ' standard CDO constants
const cdoAnonymous     = 0

prefix = "http://schemas.microsoft.com/cdo/configuration/"
With conf.fields                            ' set delivery options
    .item(prefix & "sendusing")             = cdoSendUsingPort
    .item(prefix & "smtpserver")            = smtpserver
    .item(prefix & "smtpauthenticate")      = cdoAnonymous
    .update                                 ' commit changes
End With

WScript.echo "Sending message..."

on error resume next        ' do not stop on errors
msg.send                    ' deliver the message
send_errno = err.Number
on error goto 0             ' restore normal error handling

if send_errno <> 0 then     ' if something went wrong...
    wscript.echo "error sending message"
    wscript.quit 1          ' just quit, as this is an unattended script
end if

wscript.echo nfiles & " file" & plural & " sent to " & recipient

' ------------------------------------------------------------------
' ARCHIVE THE FILES
' ------------------------------------------------------------------

WScript.echo "Moving files..."
for i = 0 to nfiles-1
    fso.MoveFile filelist(i), archivefolder
next

WScript.echo "Done"
```

Normally, a script like this would be used with the Task Scheduler so it could be run at appropriate intervals. If you use this technique, be sure to specify `cscript` as the command to use to run the script. The `WScript.Echo` statements, which are so useful for debugging, will have no effect if the script is run under the Task Scheduler with `cscript`, but will stop the program if run with `wscript`: Nobody will ever see the pop-up boxes or click their little OK buttons.

7

Windows Management Instrumentation (WMI)

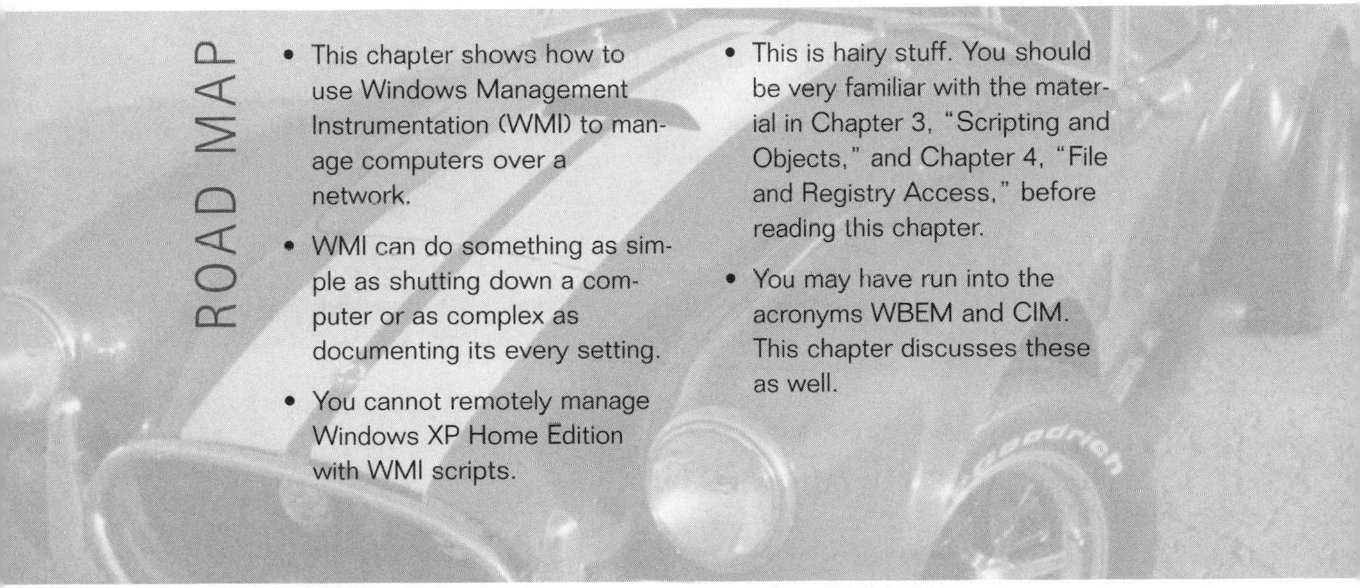

ROAD MAP

- This chapter shows how to use Windows Management Instrumentation (WMI) to manage computers over a network.
- WMI can do something as simple as shutting down a computer or as complex as documenting its every setting.
- You cannot remotely manage Windows XP Home Edition with WMI scripts.
- This is hairy stuff. You should be very familiar with the material in Chapter 3, "Scripting and Objects," and Chapter 4, "File and Registry Access," before reading this chapter.
- You may have run into the acronyms WBEM and CIM. This chapter discusses these as well.

Introduction to Windows Management Instrumentation

If you own even just one Windows computer, you know that maintenance can be a frustrating, time-consuming job. Multiply this by hundreds or thousands, and imagine what corporate IT managers face every day. Just keeping track of the computer inventory is a large-enough task; then there are the frequent network configuration changes, the addition and removal of network printers, updating applications and moving-target shared folders—not to mention crashes, hardware failures, and user-induced disasters. Keeping an organization's computers together is like trying to hold 50 Ping-Pong balls underwater with your bare hands. An IT job can be a one-way ticket to a padded cell and some very serious medication.

One way out of this mess is to eliminate, to the extent possible, the need to walk from computer to computer in order to make changes. On large networks, Active Directory helps by automating the installation of application software. Windows Management Instrumentation (WMI) can help with the rest of the maintenance burden.

WMI provides a way to peer into the inner workings of Windows, to monitor settings, and make changes. Like the Performance Monitor, WMI has its fingers in just about every aspect of the Windows operating system, including device drivers, system services, and applications. WMI works over a network, so one computer running a WMI monitoring program (or script...hint, hint) can get into any computer on the organization's network.

Needless to say, WMI is a huge topic—it could easily fill several books this size—so I can only provide a brief overview in this chapter. I present some sample scripts at the end of this chapter that perform practical tasks while demonstrating what WMI can accomplish. Also at the end of the chapter, I list some Web sites and books that can lead you to more information.

Note

If you want to work with WMI, I suggest that you download Microsoft's WMI Documentation and Software Development Kit. Visit `msdn.microsoft.com` and search for "(WMI) SDK" using the quotes and parentheses. This will locate the download page.

Functions of the WMI

One of the main goals of WMI is to standardize the way computer management information is organized. Because WMI is all about accessing a system's setup information, every piece of hardware as well as every parameter and setting in every component of Windows has to be given a fixed name, so that WMI-aware programs can refer to them. It wouldn't make sense to tell a program to "open the Control Panel, choose Networks, select the second network adapter, click TCP/IP Protocol, Properties and read me the IP address." This just isn't systematic enough. Instead, WMI uses an organized system of names that look a lot like the path names of files and folders and of Registry keys.

This naming scheme is based on CIM, which stands for *Common Interface Model*. CIM is an industry-wide standard concocted by the Distributed Management Task Force (DMTF), of which Microsoft is a member, along with 3Com, Cisco, Hewlett-Packard, IBM, Novell, Sun...in other words, everybody. (And, as you'd expect of the output of any such committee, it tries to be everything for everyone, and it's almost hopelessly complex.)

Namespaces

In the CIM scheme, the various groups of setting and parameter names are called *namespaces*. In each namespace is a set of objects that describe some aspect of the computer's hardware or software. The primary namespaces are listed in Table 7.1.

Table 7.1 **WMI Namespaces**

Namespace	Description
`\Root\CIMV2`	Objects representing Windows, hardware, and software. This namespace is the one you'll use for Windows management.
`\Root\Cli`	Holds command aliases used by WMIC; you can ignore this namespace.
`\Root\DEFAULT`	Objects representing the Registry.
`\Root\directory`	Objects related to Active Directory.
`\Root\Microsoft\Homenet`	Internet Connection Sharing and Personal Firewall configuration.
`\Root\Policy`	Access to Group Policy configuration.
`\Root\RSOP`	Access to Group Policy "Resultant Set of Policy" data for enterprise management applications.
`\Root\WMI`	Objects related to low-level networking and interface hardware performance statistics.

Other namespaces may appear as well, if you've installed WMI-integrated services and applications such as SNMP and Microsoft Office.

In each namespace are numerous objects that describe some aspect of Windows and/or the hardware. These objects can be viewed and modified to document or modify Windows settings. Although there isn't room to describe all the objects in detail, Table 7.2 gives you an idea of what is available. The table lists the objects in the major namespace `\Root\CIMV2`. Each of these objects represents some aspect of computer hardware or a component of one of the 32-bit family of Windows operating systems (Windows 95, 98, Me, NT, 2000, and XP). In the following sections, I'll show you how to use a few of them.

Note

The names of the objects in `\Root\CIMV2` all start with `Win32_`. Although WMI is based on the industry-wide CIM standard object definitions, the object definitions have been extended slightly to provide Windows-specific information, so the names all start with `Win32_` rather than `CIM_`. If you're familiar with CIM, you'll find that all the standard model components are present.

You'll also see the acronym WBEM appear all over Microsoft's WMI literature. *Web-Based Enterprise Management* is another management standardization initiative, and the acronym WBEM is applied to WMI in an apparently random fashion. In fact, the objects you'll use to work with WMI are part of the `WbemScripting` object package.

Table 7.2 **List of *Root\CIMV2* Objects**

Win32_1394Controller	Win32_OperatingSystem
Win32_1394ControllerDevice	Win32_OperatingSystemQFE
Win32_Account	Win32_OSRecoveryConfiguration
Win32_AccountSID	Win32_PageFile
Win32_ACE	Win32_PageFileElementSetting
Win32_ActionCheck	Win32_PageFileSetting
Win32_AllocatedResource	Win32_PageFileUsage
Win32_ApplicationCommandLine	Win32_ParallelPort
Win32_ApplicationService	Win32_Patch
Win32_AssociatedBattery	Win32_PatchFile
Win32_AssociatedProcessorMemory	Win32_PatchPackage
Win32_BaseBoard	Win32_PCMCIAController
Win32_BaseService	Win32_PhysicalMemory
Win32_Battery	Win32_PhysicalMemoryArray
Win32_Binary	Win32_PhysicalMemoryLocation
Win32_BindImageAction	Win32_PnPAllocatedResource
Win32_BIOS	Win32_PnPDevice
Win32_BootConfiguration	Win32_PnPEntity
Win32_Bus	Win32_PointingDevice
Win32_CacheMemory	Win32_PortableBattery
Win32_CDROMDrive	Win32_PortConnector
Win32_CheckCheck	Win32_PortResource
Win32_CIMLogicalDeviceCIMDataFile	Win32_POTSModem
Win32_ClassicCOMApplicationClasses	Win32_POTSModemToSerialPort
Win32_ClassicCOMClass	Win32_PowerManagementEvent
Win32_ClassicCOMClassSettings	Win32_Printer
Win32_ClassInfoAction	Win32_PrinterConfiguration
Win32_ClientApplicationSetting	Win32_PrinterController
Win32_CodecFile	Win32_PrinterDriverDll
Win32_COMApplication	Win32_PrinterSetting
Win32_COMApplicationClasses	Win32_PrinterShare
Win32_COMApplicationSettings	Win32_PrintJob
Win32_COMClass	Win32_PrivilegesStatus
Win32_ComClassAutoEmulator	Win32_Process
Win32_ComClassEmulator	Win32_Processor
Win32_CommandLineAccess	Win32_ProcessStartup
Win32_ComponentCategory	Win32_Product
Win32_ComputerSystem	Win32_ProductCheck
Win32_ComputerSystemProcessor	Win32_ProductResource
Win32_ComputerSystemProduct	Win32_ProductSoftwareFeatures
Win32_COMSetting	Win32_ProgIDSpecification
Win32_Condition	Win32_ProgramGroup

```
Win32_CreateFolderAction
Win32_CurrentProbe
Win32_DCOMApplication
Win32_DCOMApplicationAccessAllowedSetting
Win32_DCOMApplicationLaunchAllowedSetting
Win32_DCOMApplicationSetting
Win32_DependentService
Win32_Desktop
Win32_DesktopMonitor
Win32_DeviceBus
Win32_DeviceMemoryAddress
Win32_DeviceSettings
Win32_Directory
Win32_DirectorySpecification
Win32_DiskDrive
Win32_DiskDriveToDiskPartition
Win32_DiskPartition
Win32_DisplayConfiguration
Win32_DisplayControllerConfiguration
Win32_DMAChannel
Win32_DriverVXD
Win32_DuplicateFileAction
Win32_Environment
Win32_EnvironmentSpecification
Win32_ExtensionInfoAction
Win32_Fan
Win32_FileSpecification
Win32_FloppyController
Win32_FloppyDrive
Win32_FontInfoAction
Win32_Group
Win32_GroupUser
Win32_HeatPipe
Win32_IDEController
Win32_IDEControllerDevice
Win32_ImplementedCategory
Win32_InfraredDevice
Win32_IniFileSpecification
Win32_InstalledSoftwareElement
Win32_IRQResource
Win32_Keyboard
Win32_LaunchCondition
Win32_LoadOrderGroup
Win32_ProgramGroupContents
Win32_ProgramGroupOrItem
Win32_Property
Win32_ProtocolBinding
Win32_PublishComponentAction
Win32_QuickFixEngineering
Win32_Refrigeration
Win32_Registry
Win32_RegistryAction
Win32_RemoveFileAction
Win32_RemoveIniAction
Win32_ReserveCost
Win32_ScheduledJob
Win32_SCSIController
Win32_SCSIControllerDevice
Win32_SecurityDescriptor
Win32_SecuritySetting
Win32_SecuritySettingAccess
Win32_SecuritySettingAuditing
Win32_SecuritySettingGroup
Win32_SecuritySettingOfLogicalFile
Win32_SecuritySettingOfLogicalShare
Win32_SecuritySettingOfObject
Win32_SecuritySettingOwner
Win32_SelfRegModuleAction
Win32_SerialPort
Win32_SerialPortConfiguration
Win32_SerialPortSetting
Win32_Service
Win32_ServiceControl
Win32_ServiceSpecification
Win32_ServiceSpecificationService
Win32_SettingCheck
Win32_Share
Win32_ShareToDirectory
Win32_ShortcutAction
Win32_ShortcutFile
Win32_ShortcutSAP
Win32_SID
Win32_SMBIOSMemory
Win32_SoftwareElement
Win32_SoftwareElementAction
Win32_SoftwareElementCheck
```

continues

Table 7.2 **Continued**

Win32_LoadOrderGroupServiceDependencies	Win32_SoftwareElementCondition
Win32_LoadOrderGroupServiceMembers	Win32_SoftwareElementResource
Win32_LogicalDisk	Win32_SoftwareFeature
Win32_LogicalDiskRootDirectory	Win32_SoftwareFeatureAction
Win32_LogicalDiskToPartition	Win32_SoftwareFeatureCheck
Win32_LogicalFileAccess	Win32_SoftwareFeatureParent
Win32_LogicalFileAuditing	Win32_SoftwareFeatureSoftwareElements
Win32_LogicalFileGroup	Win32_SoundDevice
Win32_LogicalFileOwner	Win32_StartupCommand
Win32_LogicalFileSecuritySetting	Win32_SubDirectory
Win32_LogicalMemoryConfiguration	Win32_SystemAccount
Win32_LogicalProgramGroup	Win32_SystemBIOS
Win32_LogicalProgramGroupDirectory	Win32_SystemBootConfiguration
Win32_LogicalProgramGroupItem	Win32_SystemDesktop
Win32_LogicalProgramGroupItemDataFile	Win32_SystemDevices
Win32_LogicalShareAccess	Win32_SystemDriver
Win32_LogicalShareAuditing	Win32_SystemDriverPNPEntity
Win32_LogicalShareSecuritySetting	Win32_SystemEnclosure
Win32_ManagedSystemElementResource	Win32_SystemLoadOrderGroups
Win32_MemoryArray	Win32_SystemLogicalMemoryConfiguration
Win32_MemoryArrayLocation	Win32_SystemMemoryResource
Win32_MemoryDevice	Win32_SystemNetworkConnections
Win32_MemoryDeviceArray	Win32_SystemOperatingSystem
Win32_MemoryDeviceLocation	Win32_SystemPartitions
Win32_MethodParameterClass	Win32_SystemProcesses
Win32_MIMEInfoAction	Win32_SystemProgramGroups
Win32_MotherboardDevice	Win32_SystemResources
Win32_MoveFileAction	Win32_SystemServices
Win32_MSIResource	Win32_SystemSetting
Win32_NetworkAdapter	Win32_SystemSlot
Win32_NetworkAdapterConfiguration	Win32_SystemSystemDriver
Win32_NetworkAdapterSetting	Win32_SystemTimeZone
Win32_NetworkClient	Win32_SystemUsers
Win32_NetworkConnection	Win32_TapeDrive
Win32_NetworkLoginProfile	Win32_TemperatureProbe
Win32_NetworkProtocol	Win32_Thread
Win32_NTEventlogFile	Win32_TimeZone
Win32_NTLogEvent	Win32_Trustee
Win32_NTLogEventComputer	Win32_TypeLibraryAction
Win32_NTLogEventLog	Win32_UninterruptiblePowerSupply
Win32_NTLogEventUser	Win32_USBController
Win32_ODBCAttribute	Win32_USBControllerDevice

```
Win32_ODBCDataSourceAttribute            Win32_UserAccount
Win32_ODBCDataSourceSpecification        Win32_UserDesktop
Win32_ODBCDriverAttribute                Win32_VideoConfiguration
Win32_ODBCDriverSoftwareElement          Win32_VideoController
Win32_ODBCDriverSpecification            Win32_VideoSettings
Win32_ODBCSourceAttribute                Win32_VoltageProbe
Win32_ODBCTranslatorSpecification        Win32_WMIElementSetting
Win32_OnBoardDevice                      Win32_WMISetting
```

Note

You can explore WMI and the WMI namespaces using the WMIC command-line program provided with Windows XP. For information about WMIC, open the Help and Command Center and search for WMIC.

Enabling WMI on Your Network's Computers

By default, WMI may not be enabled on versions of Windows earlier than XP. You may need to enable both DCOM (for network software access to WMI) and WMI on each computer in your organization. WMI can be enabled by Group Policy on domain networks managed by Windows 2000 or .NET servers with *only* Windows 2000 and XP Professional workstations. That doesn't describe any networks I know. Therefore, if you have a workgroup network or have older versions of Windows on your network, you'll have to do some work to get every workstation ready for WMI.

Windows NT, 2000, and XP

WMI is installed by default on Windows NT, 2000, and XP. However, you'll probably want to upgrade the version found on Windows NT. WMI version 1.01 was supplied with Windows NT Service Pack 4. You can download the current version (1.5 at the time of this writing) from `www.microsoft.com/download`, file `wmint4.exe`. Windows 2000 and XP have WMI version 1.5 preinstalled, so they're ready to go out of the box.

Be sure that DCOM is enabled by typing **`dcomcnfg`** at the command line. The procedure depends on the version of Windows you're using:

- For Windows NT and 2000, `dcomcnfg` displays a dialog box. Select the General tab and be sure that Enable Distributed COM on This Computer is checked.
- On Windows XP, `dcomcnfg` displays the Component Services management console. In the left pane, expand Component Services and Computers, and then right-click My Computer. Select Properties and view the Default Properties tab. Be sure that Enable Distributed COM on This Computer is checked, as shown in Figure 7.1. On Windows XP, this is the default setting.

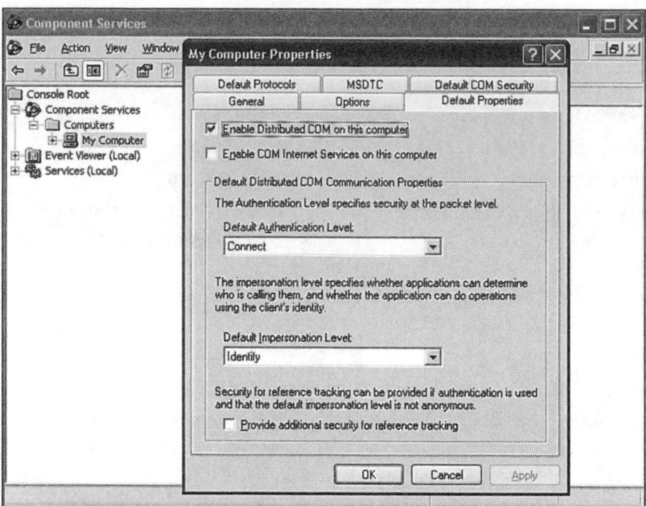

Figure 7.1 Use `dcomcnfg` to ensure that Distributed COM is enabled on all computers that are to be managed through WMI.

You can configure WMI by typing **`start wmimgmt.msc`** at the command prompt. Right-click WMI Control (Local) and select Properties. You can enable logging, backup and restore the CIM model information, and set the default namespace with the various property tabs, as illustrated in Figure 7.2. (The management tool's title bar still uses WMI's old name, *Windows Management Infrastructure*.)

Note

When you tell WMI to connect over the network to a Windows XP Professional computer that has Simple File Sharing (SFS) enabled, you will not be able to manage the computer because SFS makes all network connections use the Guest account. To use WMI to manage remote Windows XP Pro computers, they must be members of a domain network or have Simple File Sharing disabled.

Because you cannot disable Simple File Sharing on Windows XP Home Edition, you *cannot* remotely manage XP Home Edition computers with WMI.

However, you can still run WMI scripts directly on a computer, regardless of its Windows version.

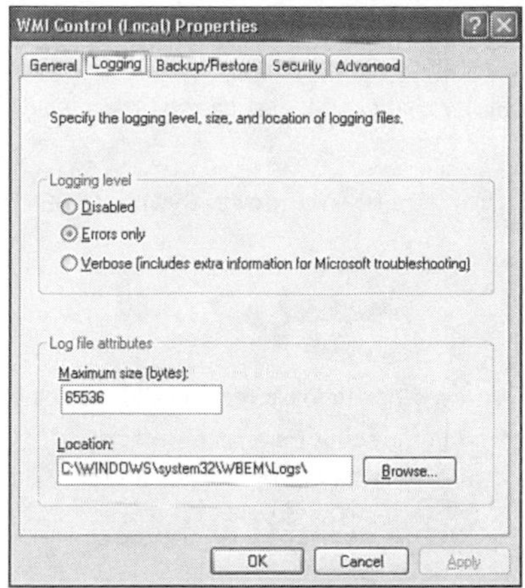

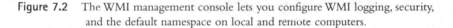

Figure 7.2 The WMI management console lets you configure WMI logging, security, and the default namespace on local and remote computers.

Windows 95, 98, and Me

These older versions of Windows are WMI capable but you'll have to make them run the WMI software automatically upon startup.

First, you need to make sure each computer has the correct version of WMI installed. The following list shows what you'll need to do:

- **Windows 95 OSR2**. Download the latest version of the WMI Core (version 1.5 at the time of this writing), file `wmi9x.exe` from `www.microsoft.com/download`. You will also need to update DCOM with version 1.3, file `dcom95.exe`. WMI is not available for versions of Windows prior to Win95 OSR2.
- **Windows 98 and 98 SE**. Download and install `wmi9x.exe` as indicated for Windows 95.
- **Windows Me**. WMI version 1.5 is preinstalled, so there's nothing to download.

To enable WMI as an automatic, always-on service, you will need to make the following Registry settings:

Key	Value
`HKLM\SOFTWARE\Microsoft\OLE`	`EnableDCOM="Y"`
`HKLM\SOFTWARE\Microsoft\OLE`	`EnableRemoteConnect="Y"`
`HKLM\SOFTWARE\Microsoft\WBEM\CIMOM`	`AutostartWin9x=2`

Caution

Editing the Registry can be hazardous to your computer's health. It would be a good idea to make a backup before making any Registry changes, at least on the first computer with which you attempt this.

Also, you'll need to put a shortcut to `\windows\System\WBEM\winmgmt.exe` in the Startup folder.

Tip

To make this easier, you can write a script to make these changes using the file and Registry objects described in Chapter 4 and then run the script from each workstation.

You can configure WMI by typing **`wbemcntl`** at the command prompt.

Making WMI Connections

WMI is one of the service processes that runs "behind the scenes" in Windows. If WMI is configured as discussed in the previous section, it's always there, waiting for a client program—that is, a script or other management program—to connect to it. WMI provides COM objects that let a script interact with the underlying Windows settings and values. Figure 7.3 illustrates how this works. Your script uses `WbemScripting` objects that communicate with the WMI service on a selected computer through Distributed COM (DCOM). WMI returns information about the computer through the `WbemScripting` object's methods and properties and then saves changes back to the remote computer. The "remote computer" can be *any* computer on the network, even the same computer that is running the script.

WMI Object Hierarchy

WMI uses several objects to represent the connection to another computer, its namespaces, the objects within the namespaces, and so on. The primary objects are listed in Table 7.3.

Table 7.3 **The Primary *WbemScripting* Objects**

Object	Purpose
`SwbemLocator`	Establishes connections to remote computers and returns one of the objects in this list.
`SwbemSecurity`	Configures security settings that WMI is to use for a connection to another computer.
`SWbemServices`	Represents a connection to a namespace on a managed computer. This is *not* a collection. It's an odd object that will be discussed later in the chapter.

Object	Purpose
SWbemObjectSet	A collection of SWbemObject objects, most commonly used to represent one of the major service categories in a namespace (for example, one of the items shown earlier in Table 7.2). The collection represents the components in the given service category.
SWbemObject	One instance of a managed item, such as a network connection, a file, a hard drive, or a user account. The methods and properties of SWbemObject are variable and depend on the type of item the object represents. This object is discussed later in the chapter.
SWbemMethodSet	A collection of SWbemMethod objects that lists the methods available for a given SWbemObject object.
SWbemMethod	Describes the purpose of and parameters used with a given method.
SWbemPropertySet	A collection of SWbemProperty objects that lists the properties available for a given SWbemObject object.
SWbemProperty	Describes the purpose and data type of a given property.

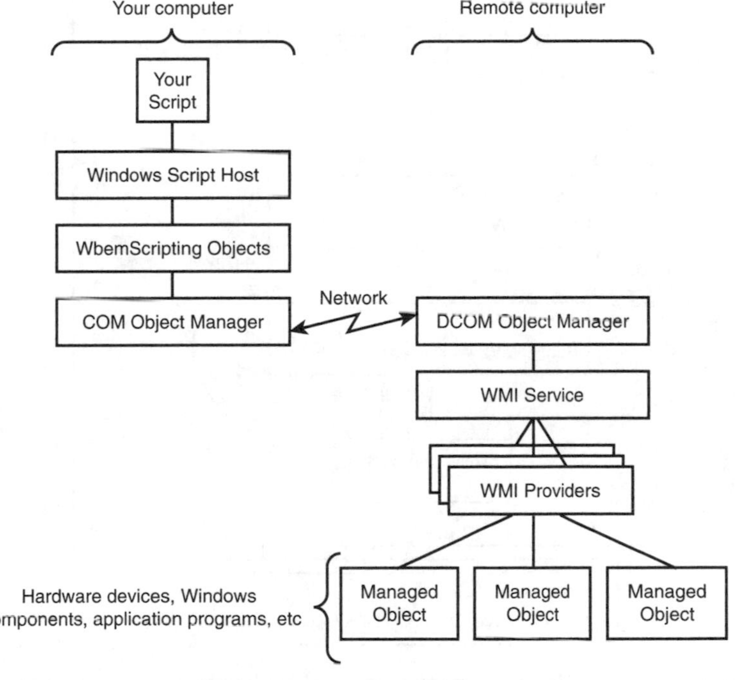

Figure 7.3 A WMI client program communicates with the WMI service on a specified computer, which dips into Windows settings through WMI provider services.

Note

For complete documentation on all the WMI objects, download and install the WMI Software Development Kit, as explained in the Note at the beginning of the chapter.

As mentioned earlier, WMI objects are nested like folders and files. For example, you might specify a file path as `c:\documents\myproject\plan.doc`. WMI objects can be specified using a comparable path naming system. Table 7.4 lists paths starting from the `CIMV2` namespace to a specific instance of a `Win32_LogicalDisk` object that manages the "C:" drive. Figure 7.4 illustrates the relationships between the various levels of objects and shows some of the methods and properties that can be used to obtain one from the other. `GetObject` can create an object at any level, given its path.

Note

If you are using a scripting language other than VBScript or JScript, the `GetObject` function may not be available. You can use the `wscript.GetObject` method instead.

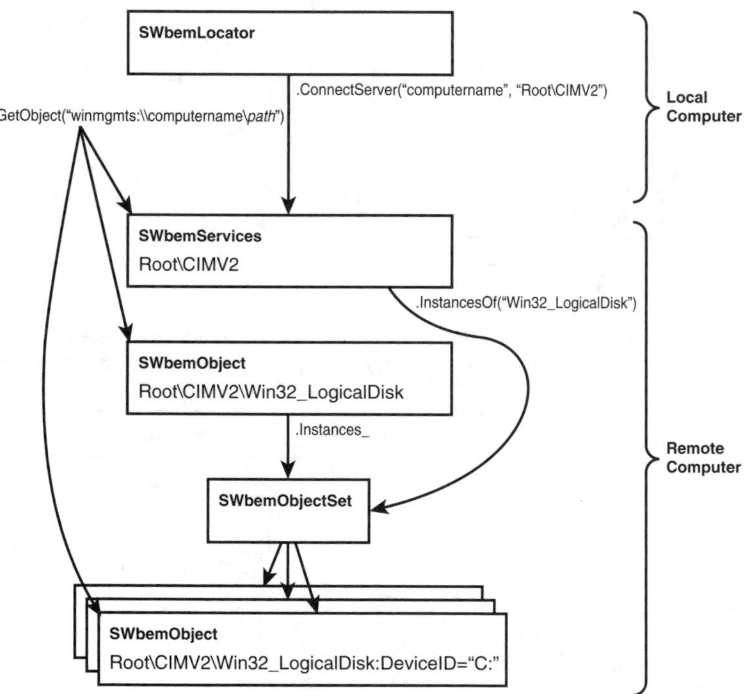

Figure 7.4 Relationship between various levels of the WMI object hierarchy.

Some objects require more than one property to be specified in order to get a single object, as illustrated in the last row of Table 7.4. In these examples, Java is the name of my computer.

Table 7.4 **Examples of WMI Path Specifications and Resulting Objects**

Path	Leads To
`\\Java\root\cimv2`	`SWbemServices`
`\\Java\root\cimv2:Win32_LogicalDisk`	`SWbemObject`
`\\Java\root\cimv2:Win32_LogicalDisk.Instances_`	`SWbemObjectSet`
`\\JAVA\root\cimv2:Win32_LogicalDisk.DeviceID="C:"`	`SWbemObject`
`\\JAVA\root\cimv2:Win32_SystemAccount.Domain= "JAVA", Name="Everyone"`	`SWbemObject`

When you create a WMI connection to a remote computer, you can specify how "deep" an object you want to extract. If you want to examine many objects, you might want to start with one of the top-level objects and then examine the objects within it. If you're only concerned with one specific item, you can specify the full path to the object and save yourself the trouble of digging for it.

Note

Because CIM is supposed to be operating system and platform independent, WMI treats / and \ identically in pathnames. You can use either. Also, the object and parameter names are case insensitive.

You can establish a connection to a remote computer in two ways: You can use an `SWbemLocator` object, or you can use object monikers to obtain objects from their pathname. Both methods are discussed in the following sections.

Connecting with the `WbemScripting.SWbemLocator` Object

You can connect to WMI on a remote computer by creating an `SWbemLocator` object and using its `ConnectServer` method to establish a connection to a desired computer. Let's suppose that we want to work with a computer named Java and that we want to examine its `CIMV2` namespace. The following statements show how to make a connection using the `Locator` object:

```
set locator = CreateObject("WbemScripting.SWbemLocator")
set svcs = locator.ConnectServer("Java", "root\CIMV2")
```

This yields object `svcs`, which is an `SWbemServices` object that represents the `root\CIMV2` namespace on the computer Java. I'll show you how to use `svcs` to manage the remote computer later in the chapter.

The `ConnectServer` method can take several optional arguments. Its syntax is

```
ConnectServer(servername, namespace [, username, password], [locale],
    [authority], [security], [namedvalueset])
```

The parameters are described in Table 7.5.

Table 7.5 **Parameters for the *ConnectServer* Method**

Parameter	Description
`Servername`	The name of the computer to which to connect. If this parameter is blank or omitted, the connection is made to the local computer (the one on which the script is running).
`Namespace`	The namespace to which to connect (for example, `"Root\CIMV2"`). If this parameter is blank or omitted, the default namespace is used (usually `CIMV2`, but this can be changed by the WMI management tool described earlier).
`Username`	Optional. The username to use when connecting to the remote computer. You cannot specify an alternate username when connecting to the local computer.
`Password`	Optional. The password to use when connecting to the remote computer.
`Locale`	Localization (language) code. For example, `"MS_409"` specifies American English. If this parameter is left blank, the Windows default locale is used.
`Authority`	The authentication method to use when connecting: `"kerberos"`, `"NTLM"`, or `"negotiated"`. If this parameter is omitted, `"negotiated"` is the default and is the best choice in almost all cases.
`Security`	This argument is not used, and it must be `0` (zero) or omitted.
`Namedvalueset`	This argument is not useful in scripts and should be omitted.

The username and password parameters may be required if you wish to connect to a computer on which you have no account, or on which you do not have Administrator privileges. Without Administrator privileges, you can usually connect to WMI and view properties, but cannot make changes. It's not a good idea to store passwords in scripts, however, so if you don't run your management script from a privileged account that has the necessary permissions by default, you should have the script prompt you for the necessary password.

The object returned by `ConnectServer` is an `SWbemServices` collection that you can examine or from which you can extract any desired `SWbemService` objects. I'll cover this in the section titled "`SWbemServices`."

Connecting with a Moniker

The second method of creating a connection uses a moniker—a pathname version of an object—and the `GetObject` function, which was discussed in Chapter 3. The moniker for a WMI object always starts with the string `"winmgmts:"`. The following statement shows how to make a connection using a moniker:

```
set svcs = GetObject("winmgmts:\\java\CIMV2")
```

This statement produces the same `SWbemServices` collection as the `ConnectServer` example in the previous section. With this method, however, you could specify a deeper pathname and get a specific management object, if that was all you needed. Table 7.4 shows how you may obtain lower-level WMI objects by specifying a longer path to `GetObject`.

Which method should you use? The moniker method is a bit easier to write, whereas the `Locator` method runs faster when your script needs to access many objects and/or computers. If you want to process a long list of computers, you might be better off using a script like this:

```
                              ' Example File script0701.vbs
set locator = CreateObject("WbemScripting.SWbemLocator")
manage "java"             ' manage each of the computers in turn
manage "bali"
manage "ambon"
manage "sumatra"
manage "kalimantan"
manage "buru"

' ---------------------------------------------------------
' subroutine 'manage' works with the specified computer

sub manage (computername)
    on error resume next ' make connection while trapping errors
    set svcs = locator.ConnectServer(computername, "root\CIMV2")
    errnum = err.number
    errmsg = err.description
    on error resume next
    if errnum <> 0 then  ' connection failed; say why and return
        wscript.echo computername, errmsg
        exit sub
    end if

    ' ... (work with object svcs to manage the computer)

    set svcs = Nothing  ' delete the object and terminate the connection
end sub              ' end of subroutine
```

Note

If the computer name you specify after \\ in the moniker string uses the dotted domain format (for example, `computer.mycompany.com`), Windows uses DNS to resolve the name. If you specify a simple name, Windows tries to find the name with DNS first, and if the name is not found there, it tries the NetBIOS resolver. As a result WMI will not work if your network's DNS system has the wrong IP addresses for your computers.

Connecting to the Local Computer

WMI lets you manage *any* networked computer, including the one on which you're running the script. You can connect to the "local" computer using either of the two connection methods described in the previous sections. Then, you can either specify the name of the computer directly, specify the name as `"."`, or *omit* the computer name entirely. For example, if the local computer is named JAVA, any of these statements return the `SWbemServices` collection of JAVA's `CIMV2` namespace:

```
set svcs = locator.ConnectServer("JAVA", "root\CIMV2")
set svcs = locator.ConnectServer(".", "root\CIMV2")
set svcs = locator.ConnectServer("", "root\CIMV2")

set svcs = GetObject("winmgmts:\\java\root\CIMV2")
set svcs = GetObject("winmgmts:\\.\root\CIMV2")
set svcs = GetObject("winmgmts:\root\CIMV2")
```

In fact, because `CIMV2` is the default namespace, the following statements also produce the same result:

```
set svcs = locator.ConnectServer("JAVA", "")
set svcs = locator.ConnectServer(".", "")
set svcs = locator.ConnectServer("", "")
set svcs = GetObject("winmgmts:\\java")
set svcs = GetObject("winmgmts:\\.")
set svcs = GetObject("winmgmts:")
```

Note

You can set the default namespace by modifying the Registry value `Default Namespace` in the key `HKLM\SOFTWARE\Microsoft\WBEM\Scripting`.

However, connections to the local machine *always* use your user account, and you cannot specify an alternate account to `ConnectServer`.

Security and Authentication

If WMI can really do all it's cracked up to do, from altering network settings to shutting down a computer to creating or modifying user accounts, then you know it must be subject to very strict security restrictions.

It is, and here's how these restrictions work: WMI security is based on the remote connection facilities that are part of Distributed COM (DCOM). There are four aspects to DCOM security:

- **Authentication**. Identifies you to the remote computer.
- **Encryption**. Protects the information transmitted between computers from eavesdropping.

- **Impersonation**. Causes the remote DCOM service (and therefore WMI) to run in the context of *your* login account instead of the high-privilege SYSTEM account that most services use.
- **Permission control**. Involves extra privileges not normally associated with your user account being granted to the DCOM process to perform its task.

I regret to say that it's going to take several pages to go through this process, but it's necessary. WMI will usually not work properly without you making special consideration of these security details.

Authentication and Encryption

By default, the connection to a remote computer uses the identity of whatever account you use to run the script. This will be *your* account when you run a script from the command line, or the specified account if you use the Task Scheduler. The DCOM service on the remote computer checks your logon credential to see whether you are permitted to use that computer and what permissions you're allowed. On a domain network, the security identifier (SID) associated with your account is recognized by all computers on the network, and you'll have the permissions appropriate to your domain account. On a workgroup network or on a foreign domain, Windows may send your username and password in encrypted form to the remote computer. If an account with this name and password exists on the remote computer, you'll be given access.

Tip

To use WMI on a workgroup (peer-to-peer) network, you'll have to make sure that each computer you want to manage has an account set up with the same username and password as the account you use to run the script.

Normally, your computer will remain connected as long as your script maintains an object that refers to the remote computer, and one user-password check is enough. You can step up the security by having DCOM verify your logon credential every time it makes a request; this may help prevent someone with hostile intent and a direct connection to your network from hijacking the DCOM connection and making management operations on your behalf. The security can be turned up even further by making Windows encrypt each data packet sent between the two computers. Table 7.6 lists the various authentication and encryption options in ascending order of paranoia.

Table 7.6 **Authentication and Encryption Modes**

Name	Value	Constant Name/Description
Default	0	`wbemAuthenticationLevelDefault` The default Windows setting. This varies between versions of WMI and Windows, so it's best to specify one of the following levels explicitly.
None	1	`wbemAuthenticationLevelNone` No authentication; the connection is made as "Guest."
Connect	2	`wbemAuthenticationLevelConnect` Authenticates during the initial connection. This is the usual value to use.
Call	3	`wbemAuthenticationLevelCall` Checks authentication at every WMI request.
Pkt	4	`wbemAuthenticationLevelPkt` Authenticates every packet of data sent to WMI.
PktIntegrity	5	`wbemAuthenticationLevelPktIntegrity` Like Pkt, but this mode additionally verifies that the data packets have not been tampered with.
PktPrivacy	6	`wbemAuthenticationLevelPktPrivacy` This mode is like Pkt, but additionally every data packet is encrypted. This is the most secure value.

In most cases, Connect mode will work and is the default. However, on some networks, the administrators may require a higher security level, or the default level will not work and attempts to use WMI will result in error messages. In this case, you may need to specify a higher level when you make a WMI connection. You'll learn how to use alternate authentication modes in the next section.

Note

You can use the numerical values for these constants or you can create named constants for these values and use them in your scripts. Alternatively, you can write your scripts using the `.WSF` file format, which is discussed in Chapter 10. In a `.WSF` file you can use a `<reference>` tag to automatically import all of WMI's named constants.

Impersonation

Normally, WMI runs as a system service, part of the Windows operating system itself, and has unlimited access to all parts of Windows. Although WMI is designed to check your logon credentials and only perform tasks that your account is authorized to perform, WMI's designers understand the likelihood that WMI contains programming bugs and that these bugs could be exploited by an unscrupulous programmer. Therefore, there's a chance that the authentication scheme might not be adequate to prevent network users from using WMI to gain access to all parts of the computer.

WMI is set up to minimize this risk by running under *your* login account when you've connected to it. This is called *impersonation*, and the result is that WMI can't do any more damage than you could if you were sitting right at the computer. When you connect with an Administrator-level account, WMI will have that account's full access, but an "average Joe" won't be able to take over the computer.

Table 7.7 lists the various impersonation options that WMI can use.

Table 7.7 **Connection Impersonation Modes**

Name	Value	Constant Name/Description
Anonymous	1	`WbemImpersonationLevelAnonymous` Prevents WMI from sending your user credentials to the remote computer. Note that most computers are configured to reject Anonymous connections.
Identify	2	`WbemImpersonationLevelIdentify` Lets the remote WMI service verify the connecting user's identity but lets the service run at its "native" privilege level. This mode also usually is not permitted.
Impersonate	3	`WbemImpersonationLevelImpersonate` The remote computer's WMI service runs as if the authenticated user were logged on. This is the most likely setting to work.
Delegate	4	`WbemImpersonationLevelDelegate` Lets the remote computer's WMI providers use the impersonated user's identity when connecting to yet another computer to gather information. This is supported only under Windows 2000 and XP Professional on a domain network with Kerberos authentication.

Normally, WMI requires that an *incoming* connection must use impersonation (options 3 or 4). However, some older versions of the WMI scripting objects don't specify impersonation mode by default when making connections *to* remote computers, so it's safest to specify that you want WMI to use impersonation in your scripts. You'll learn how to specify impersonation options in the next section.

Note

You can set the default mode used by outgoing connections on a given computer by setting the Registry value `Default Impersonation Level` in the key `HKLM\SOFTWARE\Microsoft\WBEM\Scripting` to one of the numeric values listed in Table 7.7.

Privileges

Thanks to the authentication and impersonation mechanisms, you can perform any action through WMI that the user account you're using is allowed to perform. Some of the user's standard privileges are not normally granted to WMI and have to be explicitly enabled when you make the WMI connection. If you need to perform operations governed by these privileges, you will have to inform WMI that you intend to use them by specifying privilege options when you make the WMI connection to the remote computer.

Note

You can't add any privileges that the user account WMI is using doesn't normally have. If you try to, the connection to the remote computer will fail. You can only indicate privileges the account already has but that WMI doesn't enable by default. Also, privilege attributes are not required when managing computers running Windows 95, 98, or Me.

Table 7.8 lists the specific privileges relevant to WMI and their numeric code values. The next section describes how to add them to a WMI connection.

Table 7.8 **Privileges Useful for WMI Connections**

Name	Value	Constant/Capability
SeMachineAccountPrivilege	5	`WbemPrivilegeMachineAccount` Create a machine account on a domain network
SeTcbPrivilege	6	`WbemPrivilegeTcb` Act as part of the operating system
SeSecurityPrivilege	7	`WbemPrivilegeSecurity` Manage auditing and the security log
SeTakeOwnershipPrivilege	8	`WbemPrivilegeTakeOwnership` Take ownership of files, for example
SeLoadDriverPrivilege	9	`WbemPrivilegeLoadDriver` Load and unload device drivers
SeSystemtimePrivilege	11	`WbemPrivilegeSystemtime` Change the date/clock
SeCreatePagefilePrivilege	14	`WbemPrivilegeCreatePagefile` Create or modify pagefile settings
SeCreatePermanentPrivilege	15	`wbemPrivilegeCreatePermanent` Create a permanent object such as a device
SeBackupPrivilege	16	`wbemPrivilegeBackup` Back up the system
SeRestorePrivilege	17	`wbemPrivilegeRestore` Restore the system

Name	Value	Constant/Capability
SeShutdownPrivilege	18	`wbemPrivilegeShutdown` Shut down the computer while logged on locally
SeSystemEnvironmentPrivilege	21	`wbemPrivilegeSystemEnvironment` Modify firmware settings stored in Flash/EEROM
SeChangeNotifyPrivilege	22	`wbemPrivilegeChangeNotify` Change directories to authorized subfolders, even if there is no access allowed to the parent folders (also called *bypass traverse checking*)
SeRemoteShutdownPrivilege	23	`wbemPrivilegeRemoteShutdown` Shut down the computer from a remote connection
SeUndockPrivilege	24	`wbemPrivilegeUndock` Remove the computer from its docking station
SeEnableDelegationPrivilege	26	`WbemPrivilegeEnableDelegation` Let the computer or user account be trusted for delegation

Specifying Security Options

If the default settings will not work for your network environment, you will need to specify alternate authentication, impersonation, or privilege settings for each WMI connection. Unless you are sure that all computers on your network are upgraded to WMI version 1.5 or higher, you'll at least need to specify Impersonate mode.

There are two ways to specify security options. One is used with the `SWbemServices` object that is returned by the `Locator` object, and the other method is used with the moniker system.

Specifying Security Options with the `SWbemServices` Object

If you connect to a remote computer with the `Locator` object, the result is an `SWbemServices` object. It has a property named `Security_` that returns an `SWbemSecurity` object that in turn has three properties: `AuthenticationLevel`, `ImpersonationLevel`, and `Privileges`, the last of which is a collection. After connecting to the remote computer, you can assign new values to these items, as shown in the following script sample:

```
set locator = CreateObject("WbemScripting.SWbemLocator")
set svcs = locator.ConnectServer("Java", "root\CIMV2")
```

```
svcs.Security_.AuthenticationLevel = 2 ' Connect
svcs.Security_.ImpersonationLevel  = 3 ' Impersonate
svcs.Security_.Privileges.Add 21       ' seSystemEnvironmentPrivilege
svcs.Security_.Privileges.Add 23       ' seRemoteShutdownPrivilege

... ' work with object conn to manage the remote computer.
```

Note

You can also add privileges with the `AddAsString` method. `AddAsString` takes the text name of the privilege as listed in the first column of Table 7.8. Here's an example:

```
svcs.Security_.Privileges.AddAsString "seSystemEnvironmentPrivilege"
```

At the very least, you will want to set the `ImpersonationLevel` property in every WMI script that deals with remote computers.

Specifying Security Options in Monikers

If you create WMI objects using moniker notation, you can specify alternate security and locale settings in the moniker string. The optional information goes just after `winmgmts:` inside curly brackets and is followed by an exclamation point, as in this example:

```
set svcs = _
    GetObject("winmgmts:{impersonationLevel=impersonate}!\\java\root\CIMV2")
```

One or more of the following items may be placed in the curly brackets:

- `AuthenticationLevel=`*`name`*, where *`name`* is one of the words listed in the Name column in Table 7.6, to specify an authentication and encryption scheme
- `ImpersonationLevel=`*`name`*, where *`name`* is one of the words listed in the Name column in Table 7.7, to specify an impersonation level
- `Authority=kerberos:`*`domain\server`* or `Authority=ntlmdomain:`*`domain`* to specify a specific Kerberos or Windows domain name in which to validate the user credentials
- `Privileges=(`*`name,name,...`*`)`, where the *`name`* items are one or more privilege names derived from the constants listed in Table 7.8 by stripping off the leading "`wbemPrivilege`" part, to specify additional privileges
- `Locale=`*`name`*, where *`name`* is one of the Microsoft `MS_`*`xxx`* locale identifiers, to specify an alternate language

If more than one item is used, separate the items with commas. Here is an example that obtains an `SWbemServices` object with the same settings as the earlier `Locator` example, but this time using moniker notation:

```
set svcs = GetObject("winmgmts:{authenticationLevel=Connect," &_
    "impersonationLevel=Impersonate," &_
    "privileges=(SystemEnvironment,RemoteShutdown)}!\\JAVA\root\CIMV2")
```

At the very least, you will want to set the `ImpersonationLevel` property in every WMI script that deals with remote computers, using a moniker like this:

```
set svcs = GetObject("winmgmts:{impersonationLevel=Impersonate}!" &_
    "\\JAVA\root\CIMV2")
```

WMI Collections and Queries

As discussed in the previous section, you can connect to the WMI service on the local computer or a remote computer and obtain a WMI object at any of three levels in the namespace hierarchy:

- You can connect at the level of the entire namespace with a path such as `\root\CIMV2`. The resulting object is called an `SWbemServices` object, which has methods and properties that let you obtain lower-level objects representing the parts of Windows you want to manage. One of its methods lets you extract information from WMI using a special query language called the Windows Management Instrumentation Query Language (WQL).
- You can connect to a specific management object with a path such as `\root\CIMV2:Win32_DiskDrive`. The resulting object is an `SWbemObject` object, but it represents a category, not a real manageable item. To obtain objects that represent items in the category, you can use its `Instances_` property to obtain a collection called `SWbemObjectSet`.
- You can connect to a specific instance of a management object with a path such as `\root\CIMV2:Win32_DiskDrive="C"`. This isn't always easy, because some of the qualifying parameters are very strange. I'll discuss this in a moment. These instances are represented by `SWbemObject`, whose properties and methods let you manage the part of Windows the object represents.

Once you have obtained one of these three object types, you can manage the local or remote computer by modifying the WMI object. The next few sections describe how to do this.

SWbemServices

The `SWbemServices` object is returned by the `Locator` object's `ConnectServer` method, or by `GetObject` with a moniker that includes a namespace but no object name (for example, `"winmgmts:\\JAVA\Root\CIMV2"`). The most important of the methods and properties of the `SWbemServices` object are detailed in Reference List 7.1.

REFERENCE LIST 7.1 Properties and Methods of the `SWbemServices` Object (Partial List)

Property:

`Security_`

Returns an `SWbemSecurity` object that you can use to configure the DCOM authentication, impersonation, and privilege settings for this connection to a remote computer. See "Specifying Security Options with the `SWbemServices` Object" earlier in the chapter for more information.

Methods:

`Delete(`*`path`*`)`

Deletes the `SWbemObject` instance specified by the *`path`* string. This is applicable only for certain nonphysical objects such as network drive mappings and files. The effect is to delete the Windows component represented by the object. *`Path`* must specify an object in the same namespace as the `SWbemServices` object. The syntax of object paths is discussed later in the chapter.

`ExecMethod(`*`path, methodname, inparams`*`)`

Executes one of the dynamic methods of the `SWbemObject` specified by *`path`*. The method named by the *`methodname`* parameter is called and given the parameters specified by the collection object *`inparams`*. `ExecMethod` is provided for languages that do not support output (by reference) parameters, such as JScript. For more information about `ExecMethod`, download the Microsoft WMI SDK documentation and search for "SWbemServices.ExecMethod." `ExecMethod` is not needed with VBScript scripts.

`ExecQuery(`*`query`*`)`

Processes a query (search request) written in the WQL query language and returns an `SWbemObjectSet` collection of objects representing the results. For example, the query `"select * from Win32_LogicalDisk"` returns a set of objects representing all the disk drives on the computer. WQL is discussed in more detail in the next section.

`InstancesOf(`*`class`*`)`

Returns an `SWbemObjectSet` collection of objects representing all the instances of a given WMI category (class). For example, `InstancesOf("Win32_LogicalDisk")` returns the same set of objects as the preceding `ExecQuery` example.

The two main functions of `SWbemServices` in scripting applications are to provide access to `ExecQuery` and `InstancesOf`.

`InstancesOf` is the most straightforward: You can get a collection of all objects of a given type and then scan through the collection to list or alter information. For example, you can list all the disk drives on a computer and tell Windows to run `chkdisk` on them during the next startup with this script:

```
                                        ' Example File script0702.vbs
set svcs = GetObject("winmgmts:{impersonationLevel=Impersonate}!" &_
    "\\JAVA\root\CIMV2")
set drives = svcs.InstancesOf("Win32_LogicalDisk")
for each drv in drives
    wscript.echo drv.name
    drv.ScheduleAutoChk
next
```

You don't always have to use the `SWbemServices` object and `InstancesOf` to get a list of objects. For example, you could get the `drives` collection directly by using this moniker:

```
set svcs = GetObject("winmgmts:{impersonationLevel=Impersonate}!" &_
    "\\JAVA\root\CIMV2:Win32_LogicalDisk")
```

That is, if this is all you want to do with the connection to Java.

WQL Queries

The other main reason to use the `SWbemServices` object is to gain access to its `ExecQuery` method. Through a query language that's very similar to the Structured Query Language (SQL) used by databases, WQL lets you specify what set of objects you'd like to extract from WMI. There are three forms of WQL queries:

- `select`. These queries return a set of objects based on matching the object type and/or parameter values.
- `references of`. These queries return all objects that are directly related to a specified object. This can return, for instance, all Windows services that depend on a particular service.
- `associators of`. These queries return all objects that are indirectly related to a specific object. For example, `associators of {Win32_LogicalDisk.DeviceID="C:"}` might be the objects representing the computer system itself, the C drive's root directory, and the disk partition that contains logical drive C.

There isn't enough room to describe `associators of` and `references of` in any more detail than this, but you can find more information in the WMI SDK documentation described at the beginning of the chapter.

`Select` queries can be used to extract WMI objects based on specific criteria, such as drive letters, disk types, network provider types, and so on. Although you can use a moniker or the `InstancesOf` method (discussed earlier) to get *all* objects of a given class, `select` gives you more fine control.

Here's the basic format of a `select` statement for object queries:

```
select propertylist from class [where conditions]
```

`Propertylist` can be a comma-delimited list of the object properties you're interested in or `*` to return all the object's properties. You can use `*` for most scripting applications. If you find that the `ExecQuery` method takes too long to run, you might enter a list of just the object properties you're interested in, to reduce the amount of data that has to be transmitted back from the remote computer.

`Class` is one of the object classes in the namespace—for example, one of the items in Table 7.2. However, you are not limited to the `Win32_xxx` classes and instead may choose one of the superclasses from which these are derived. For example, superclass `Device` includes all the device classes, including `Modems`, `Keyboards`, and so on.

`Where Conditions` is an optional clause with a Boolean conditional expression. `Where` limits the result set to only those objects whose properties match the conditional expression.

When you're using queries in your script, the query expression is entered as a text string, so remember that you may have to pay special attention to the quotation marks in order to enter them in your chosen scripting language. In VBScript, for example, they have to be doubled up. Alternatively, you can use single quote characters in the query. Here are some sample `select` statements.

```
set disks = svcs.ExecQuery(_
    "select * from Win32_LogicalDisk where Filesystem = ""NTFS""")

set codes = svcs.ExecQuery(_
    "select * from Win32_Codecs where Group = 'Video'")

set dirs = svcs.ExecQuery(_
    "select Name, LastModified from Win32_Directory")
```

You must also double up any backslashes (\) in your queries, because WMI treats them as special characters. This means that in JScript and other scripting languages that also treat the backslash as a special character, you'll need to enter *four* backslashes when coding a query string.

You can use WQL queries not just to list items, but to locate items to be managed. For example, you can use WMI to terminate application programs by name. To kill all copies of Notepad, for instance, you could run the following script:

```
                                    ' Example File script0703.vbs
dim processes

set processes = GetObject("winmgmts:").ExecQuery(_
    "select * from Win32_Process where Name='notepad.exe'")
for each process in processes
    process.Terminate
next
```

SWbemObjectSet

SWbemObjectSet is a collection object that holds a number of SWbemObject items. SWbemObject can be treated like any standard scripting collection object. It has Count and Item properties that you can use to select individual objects, or you can use an enumerating procedure such as VBScript's for each statement to scan through the collection.

It can be difficult to know in advance how to select a specific item from the collection. The Item property doesn't take a numeric index, so you can't view the items with collection.item(0), collection.item(1), and so on. In some cases, the indexing value is reasonable. With disk drives, for example, it's the drive letter. However, for many other object types, the indexing value is a strange internal Windows identifying code.

For objects that occur only singly, such as the Win32_ComputerSystem object that represents the computer as a whole, it's common practice to use a for each or other enumeration loop to scan through the collection object and save a copy of the first (only) object found.

This is a common pattern in fact, so let's write it up as such:

Pattern

To obtain from a collection a single WMI object whose full pathname isn't known in advance, use a for each loop to pick the object out of the collection. For example, to get the first (and only) instance of the Win32_OperatingSystem object from the Win32_OperatingSystem collection, use these statements:

```
set loc  = CreateObject("WBemScripting.Locator")
set svcs = loc.ConnectServer("JAVA", "Root\CIMV2")
set oss  = svcs.ExecQuery("select * from Win32_OperatingSystem")
```

Then, use a loop to pick the object out of the collection:

```
for each item in oss   ' examine the collection
    set os = item      ' save the first item and stop
    exit for
next
```

Now, you can use the object in the remainder of the script. Here's an example:

```
os.ShutDown()
```

If you obtain a single-instance object with a moniker, using a statement such as

```
set collection = _
    GetObject("winmgmts:\\COMPUTER\root\CIMV2:Win32_OperatingSystem")
```

WMI returns the object itself, not the expected SWbemObjectSet collection. In this case, then, you can use the object directly.

SWbemObject

Ultimately, all system information returned by WMI is represented by the SWbemObject object, either alone or in a collection.

SWbemObject has a base set of methods and properties common to all instances. These are called *static* methods and properties, because they're fixed and present on every SWbemObject. Then there are additional methods and properties that vary depending on what system component the object represents. These are called *dynamic* properties and methods, because they appear only when appropriate. For example, an SWbemObject object that is representing a Win32_CDROMDrive object has additional properties, such as Drive and VolumeName. An SWbemObject object representing a Win32_NetworkConnection object has properties relevant to network connections, such as UserName and RemotePath.

This is the meat of WMI! Each of the objects listed in Table 7.2 has a number of dynamic properties and methods to let you examine and manipulate all the internal aspects of Windows.

If the important methods and properties are dynamic, how do you know what their names are, and how do you use them in your scripts? There are so many objects, each with its attendant properties and methods, that I can't list them all here or even in the appendixes. Your best bet is to download the SDK. The objects are detailed in the WMI documentation under the following headings in the Contents pane:

- Windows Management Instrumentation
- WMI Reference
- WMI Classes
- Win32 Classes

You can also view them online at msdn.microsoft.com. You'll find the class listing under Setup and System Administration, Windows Management Instrumentation (WMI), SDK Documentation, and from there, look under the headings just listed for the downloaded version.

Reference List 7.2 provides the most useful of the static (fixed) methods and properties of SWbemObject. See the WMI SDK documentation for a complete listing.

REFERENCE LIST 7.2 Partial List of the Static Properties and Methods of SWbemObject

Properties:

Methods_

Returns a collection of SWbemMethodSet objects that describes all the dynamic methods for this object. The SWbemMethodSet object is discussed in the next section.

`Path_`
Returns a full path description of this particular object in moniker format. You can use this path to create this object directly with `GetObject()`.

`Properties_`
Returns a collection of `SWbemPropertySet` objects that describe all the dynamic properties for this object. The `SWbemPropertySet` object is discussed in the next section.

Methods:

`Delete_`
Deletes the object and deletes the Windows information that it represents, such as a Registry entry or a file. This method is only allowed on objects that represent something that can be deleted.

`Instances_`
Returns an `SWbemObjectSet` collection of *all* instances of the object class to which this object belongs.

`Put_`
Saves any changes made to the object back to the computer that the object represents. WMI objects are *copies* of information about Windows. You can modify an object through its properties and methods, but the changes don't affect Windows until you use the `Put_` method.

Note

The last method in Reference List 7.2 is very important. If you change the value of any property of a WMI object, you must use `Put_` to actually make the change take effect in whatever part of Windows the object represents.

Now, let's take a look at some concrete applications of WMI in managing computers across a network.

SWbemMethodSet and SWbemPropertySet

As mentioned in the previous section, every instance of `SWbemObject` sprouts whatever properties and methods are appropriate to the CIM model object it represents. It also has two static properties, named `Methods_` and `Properties_`, that provide descriptions of the dynamic additions. You can scan through these collections in the usual way to learn what the dynamic methods and properties are.

SWbemMethodSet is a collection of SWbemMethod objects, each of which describes one of the original object's dynamic methods. Here are the most relevant properties of SWbemMethod:

Property	Description
InParameters	An SWbemObject object whose Properties_ collection describes the method's input parameters
Name	The name of the method
OutParameters	An SWbemObject object whose Properties_ collection describes the method's output parameters

This is very tricky—InParameters and OutParameters each return another SWbemObject object whose Properties_ property you have to examine to find the list of arguments. Kind of makes your head spin, doesn't it?

SWbemPropertySet is a collection of SEbemProperty objects, each of which describes one of the original object's dynamic properties. Here are the most relevant properties of SWbemProperty:

Property	Description
IsArray	Boolean value. If True, the associated property is an array value.
Name	The name of the property.
Value	The property's current value.

These methods and properties were used to obtain the object documentation posted on www.helpwinxp.com/hood. Here is a shortened version of the script used to create that listing. This script lists the methods and properties of a single object:

```
                                    ' Example file listprops.vbs
set obj = GetObject("winmgmts:{impersonationlevel=Impersonate}!" & _
    "//JAVA/root/CIMV2:Win32_ComputerSystem")

wscript.echo obj.path_ & vbCRLF       ' List the object's full path

wscript.echo "Properties:"            ' List all property names

for each prop in obj.Properties_
    wscript.echo "    ", prop.name
next

wscript.echo                          ' List all methods
wscript.echo "Methods:"

for each meth in obj.Methods_
    arglist = ""                      ' construct list of parameters
```

```
        for each arg in meth.InParameters.Properties_
            if arglist <> "" then arglist = arglist & ", "
            arglist = arglist & arg.Name
        next

        for each arg in meth.OutParameters.Properties_
            if arg.Name <> "ReturnValue" then
                if arglist <> "" then arglist = arglist & ", "
                arglist = arglist & arg.Name
            end if
        next            ' ignore the ReturnValue item; it represents
                        ' the return value of the method itself

        wscript.echo "  ", meth.name & "(" & arglist & ")"
    next
```

The output of this script looks like this:

```
\\JAVA\ROOT\CIMV2:Win32_ComputerSystem

Properties:
    AdminPasswordStatus
    AutomaticResetBootOption
    AutomaticResetCapability
    BootOptionOnLimit
    BootOptionOnWatchDog
    BootROMSupported
    .
    .
    .
    WakeUpType
    Workgroup

Methods:
   SetPowerState(PowerState, Time)
   Rename(Name, Password, UserName)
   JoinDomainOrWorkgroup(AccountOU, FJoinOptions, Name, Password, UserName)
   UnjoinDomainOrWorkgroup(FUnjoinOptions, Password, UserName)
```

You can see from their names that the dynamic properties and methods of the `Win32_ComputerSystem` object could be very useful tools for managing a workstation over the network.

WMI Applications

WMI is much easier to use than it is to describe, as you'll see. The remainder of the chapter shows several scripts that use WMI to monitor or manage one or more computers.

The sample scripts in this section are written to use a subroutine to process each computer. The subroutine is called for each computer that the script is to work with; you can extend the list of computers to suit your network, or you can make the script operate on computers named on the command line by replacing the list of subroutine calls

```
process "JAVA"
process "BALI"
process "SUMATRA"
```

with the following statements:

```
nargs = 0
for each arg in WScript.Arguments
   process arg
   nargs = nargs+1
next
if nargs = 0 then wscript.echo "Usage: script computername..."
```

Use the actual name of the script in place of the word `script` in the last line; this statement prints the script's command-line usage information if no computers are named on the command line.

Collecting System Information

WMI scripts can extract information about your computer systems for documentation purposes. The following script collects network adapter information from each named computer:

```
                                        ' Example File script0704.vbs
process "JAVA"
process "BALI"
process "SUMATRA"

sub process (name)
    wscript.echo name & ":"

    ' get collection of network adapters
    set adapters = GetObject("winmgmts:{impersonatelevel=impersonate}!" &_
        "//" & name & "/root/CIMV2:Win32_NetworkAdapterConfiguration")

    ' list information for each
    for each card in adapters
        wscript.echo "  ",    card.Caption
        wscript.echo "    IP Addr ", card.IPAddress
        wscript.echo "    Gateway ", card.DefaultIPGateway
        wscript.echo "    MAC Addr", card.MACAddress
    next
end sub
```

Managing Printers

Interestingly enough, Windows XP comes with several VBS scripts that use WMI to manage printers. Look for the following files in your `\windows\system32` folder:

Filename	Description
prncnfg.vbs	Manages printer configuration
prndrvr.vbs	Manages printer drivers
prnjobs.vbs	Lists and manages print jobs
prnmngr.vbs	Installs and deletes local and network printers
prnport.vbs	Views and alters printer ports
prnqctl.vbs	Prints a test page

Although they're on the verbose side compared to the examples I've been giving, they demonstrate many aspects of good "utility" scripts: the use of command-line options, detailed error detection and reporting, and practical applications of WMI in managing printers.

Monitoring Windows Service Packs and Hotfixes

The `Win32_QuickFixEngineering` object provides information about hotfixes installed on the computer. Hotfixes are those "updates" provided by Windows Update. In a large organization, the Windows automatic updating feature may create a nightmare of incompatible and inconsistent updates. You can use WMI to monitor the updates installed on a given computer. Here's a list of the properties of `Win32_QuickFixEngineering`:

Caption	InstalledBy
CSName	InstalledOn
Description	Name
FixComments	ServicePackInEffect
HotFixID	Status
InstallDate	

The following script scans a list of Windows XP and 2000 computers and reports on the hotfixes installed on each. This script also shows how you might detect errors in connecting to the remote computer. This script prints an error message rather than stopping, if one of the remote computers won't cooperate:

```
                                             ' Example File script0705.vbs
set loc = CreateObject("WBemScripting.SWbemLocator")

process "BALI"
process "JAVA"
.
.
.

sub process (name)
    wscript.echo name & ":"

    on error resume next     ' don't stop on errors
```

```
    set qfe = GetObject("winmgmts:{impersonationlevel=impersonate}!" &_
        "//" & name & "/root/CIMV2:Win32_QuickFixEngineering")

    errno = err.number          ' save info in case GetObject failed
    msg   = err.description
    on error goto 0             ' back to normal error handling
    if errno <> 0 then          ' oops, report the error
        wscript.echo "Connect to", name, "failed:", msg
        exit sub
    end if

    ' list information for each installed item
    for each hotfix in qfe.Instances_
        wscript.echo "  ", qfe.hotfixid, qfe.description
    next
end sub
```

On my network, the listing looks like this:

```
BALI:
   Q147222
   Q293826 Windows 2000 Hotfix (Pre-SP3) [See Q293826 for more information]
   Q299553 Windows 2000 Hotfix (Pre-SP3) [See Q299553 for more information]
   Q300972 Windows 2000 Hotfix (Pre-SP3) [See Q300972 for more information]
JAVA:
   Q147222
   Q307869 Windows XP Hotfix (SP1) [See Q307869 for more information]
   Q308210 Windows XP Hotfix (SP1) [See Q308210 for more information]
   Q309521 Windows XP Hotfix (SP1) [See Q309521 for more information]
   .
   .
   .
```

`Win32_QuickFixEngineering` information is only available on Windows 2000 and Windows XP computers.

Managing Services and Tasks

WMI provides the `Win32_Service` class to let you manage system services on Windows NT, 2000, and XP. Each instance of a `Win32_Service` object represents one installed service and indicates its current running status and its startup mode setting. The WMI documentation lists all the object's properties and methods. Some of the more interesting ones are provided in Reference List 7.3.

REFERENCE LIST 7.3 Partial List of the Properties and Methods of the `Win32_Service` Object

Properties:

`DesktopInteract`

Boolean value. `True` if the service can interact with the desktop (read-only).

`DisplayName`

Short name for the service (read-only).

`Name`

Longer descriptive name (read-only).

`PathName`

Fully qualified path and name of the executable file that implements the service (Read-only).

`Started`

Boolean value. `True` if the service manager attempted to start the service (read-only).

`StartMode`

Startup mode for this service. Can be any one of the strings `"Boot"`, `"System"`, `"Auto"`, `"Manual"`, or `"Disabled"` (read-only).

`StartName`

The account name under which the service runs. If this value is `NULL`, the service runs under the LocalSystem account (read-only).

`State`

Current run state of the service. Can be one of the following strings: `"Stopped"`, `"Start Pending"`, `"Stop Pending"`, `"Running"`, `"Continue Pending"`, `"Pause Pending"`, `"Paused"`, or `"Unknown"` (read-only). It may be best to use the `InterrogateService` method before examining `State` or `Status`.

`Status`

The current status of the service. Can be one of the following strings: `"OK"`, `"Error"`, `"Degraded"`, `"Unknown"`, `"Starting"`, `"Stopping"`, `"Service"`, or `"Pred Fail"` (read-only).

Methods:

`StartService`

Starts the service up.

`StopService`

Shuts the service down.

`PauseService`

Pauses the service.

`ContinueService`

Resumes the service after pausing.

`InterrogateService`

Requests the service to update its state and status properties.

`ChangeStartMode(`*`newmode`*`)`

Sets the service's startup mode to a new value. *`Newmode`* must be one of the following string values: `"Boot"`, `"System"`, `"Automatic"`, `"Manual"`, or `"Disabled"`.

The `Win32_Service` object can let you write a script to monitor and manage services on remote computers; this can be especially helpful with servers running IIS, Exchange, or other critical services. Although Windows 2000 and XP Server now include setup functions that make it possible for Windows to automatically restart dead services, a script-based approach can let you combine service monitoring with reporting and recording.

The following shows how you can monitor crucial services on several computers with a script:

```
                                              ' Example File script0706.vbs
check "BALI",    "W3Svc"
check "JAVA",    "W3Svc"
check "BALI",    "DNS"
check "SUMATRA", "DNS"

sub check (server, servicename)
    set service = GetObject("winmgmts:{impersonationlevel=Impersonate}!" & _
        "//" & server & "/root/CIMV2:Win32_Service.Name='" & servicename & "'")

    wscript.echo server, servicename, service.state, service.status
end sub
```

The output of the script looks like this:

```
BALI W3Svc Running OK
JAVA W3Svc Stopped OK
BALI DNS Running OK
SUMATRA DNS Running OK
```

For More Information

As I stated earlier, this chapter just gives the barest introduction to WMI. Personally, at first I found WMI to be fairly opaque, and it took quite a while to get the feel of it. I hope that this introduction has given you enough of a start to be able to tackle the Microsoft documentation and other resources. If you like what you've seen of WMI so far, you'll definitely want to dig deeper.

For more information about WMI, visit `msdn.microsoft.com` and search for "WMI." Under Best Bets, choose "Download the Microsoft WMI Software Development Kit" and/or "Platform SDK Documentation: Windows Management Instrumentation." After you install the SDK, click Start, All Programs, WMI SDK, WMI SDK Documentation. Browse around a while, but eventually you should end up under WMI Reference, Scripting API for WMI.

Microsoft has a downloadable WMI tutorial, file `lrnwmi.exe`, that you can find on `www.microsoft.com/downloads`. Be warned, though, that it's an introduction to the concepts behind WMI, not a practical introduction to WMI scripting and programming.

I have found that the Microsoft newsgroup devoted to WMI (`microsoft.public.win32.programmer.wmi`) is a *terrific* source of information, sample scripts, and discussion. If you post a (sensible) question here, it'll probably be answered within a few hours. If your ISP doesn't offer this newsgroup, you can point your newsreader at `news.microsoft.com`. In Outlook Express, you can simply add an additional News account aimed at this server so that you'll have access to this and your regular newsgroups.

You'll find many, many useful WMI scripts—or at least usable fragments of scripts—on the Web. Google "winmgmts" and you'll see what I mean.

Actually, you'll find a few scripts on your own computer. Windows XP comes with several WMI scripts preinstalled. Look in `\windows\system32` for files ending with the extension `.vbs`. All but `pubprn.vbs` use WMI. These are very lengthy and advanced programs, but they show you some practical applications of Windows Script Host and WMI.

Finally, you should also check out the following two books:

- *Windows Management Instrumentation (WMI)*, by Ashley Meggitt and Matthew M. Lavy (New Riders)
- *WMI Essentials for Automating Windows Management*, by Marcin Policht (Sams)

8

Active Directory Scripting Interface (ADSI)

ROAD MAP

- ADSI can manage workgroups, computers, NT domains, Active Directory domains, and Novell networks, as well as IIS and Exchange.
- Although no single chapter can completely dissect the topic, this chapter will help you get your foot in the door.
- You should be very familiar with the material in Chapter 3, "Scripting and Objects," and Chapter 4, "File and Registry Access," before reading this chapter.
- If you want to write scripts to manage Active Directory, you'll need a strong background in LDAP syntax.

Managing the User Directory

One common task that network administrators face is the maintenance of user accounts. A new employee needs a computer account immediately in order to contribute, while the account of a former employee must be disabled instantly as a security measure. As employees' responsibilities change, so do their requirements for access to various secured network resources. In a large organization, with people being hired, fired, retired, released, relocated, and reassigned every day, keeping user accounts in sync is quite a task, and it simply isn't feasible to spend several minutes clicking through dialog boxes to make every change.

As you've guessed by now, the solution for this complex puzzle is scripting. Active Directory Scripting Interface (ADSI) objects give you scriptable access to almost all aspects of the Windows user account and security infrastructure. You can script additions, deletions, and changes to user accounts, passwords, logon preferences, and so on, as well as manage network resources such as shared folders and printers.

Uses of the Active Directory Scripting Interface

ADSI is especially well suited to work with Active Directory, the enterprise management system provided with Windows 2000 Server and .NET Server (the server version of XP). However, ADSI works even without Active Directory and can give you access to the user directories of non-Active Directory–based domain and workgroup networks. ADSI can manage:

- Active Directory on Windows 2000/.NET Server
- Windows NT–style domains
- Novell NetWare Directory Services (NDS)
- Novell Bindery-mode servers
- Microsoft Exchange Server
- Microsoft Internet Information Server (IIS)
- Microsoft Site Server
- Any LDAP-based directory system. (The Lightweight Directory Access Protocol is an industry standard for network access to user and network resource databases.)
- Shared printers and folders on individual computers
- Shared files in use
- Local users and groups
- Installed Service Configuration

You can see that with so many network databases covered, ADSI has the potential to "integrate" the management of a large heterogeneous network. The inclusion of Exchange, IIS, and Site Server means that you can automate the maintenance of e-mail and Web site accounts at the same time, making ADSI even more valuable for corporate and service provider administrators.

As you've probably also guessed, ADSI is based on a set of scriptable COM objects that represent the underlying user and network data. In the next few sections, I'll discuss some of the more important of these objects. I can't cover all of ADSI in this book, but as I did with WMI in Chapter 7, "Windows Management Instrumentation (WMI)," I can give you working code to get you started. At the end of the chapter, I'll list some resources you can use to get more information.

Limitations of ADSI with Windows Script Host

I'd like to comment on the practical usefulness of ADSI with Windows Script Host. *Very* large organizations will probably want to purchase or develop an enterprise management system using a higher-level language than VBScript, out of performance and user interface considerations. With directories of tens to hundreds of thousands of objects, such companies will want to use advanced programming techniques to limit the amount of data that must be transferred over the network and packaged into objects. Such a system would probably be integrated with the Active Data Objects (ADO) database toolkit. All of this is beyond the scope of this book.

Another advanced topic that I can't cover here is the use of ADSI in Internet Information Server ASP scripts. With ASP, it's possible to develop an efficient Web-based interface to manage your organization's users. But again, this is beyond the scope of the book.

So, are ADSI and WSH and *Windows XP Under the Hood* still useful? Yes. Larger organizations can develop and test concepts for large applications and for ASP scripts with command-line scripts. Also, small to mid-size organizations often can't justify the purchase or development of a six-figure-price enterprise management system, so for most of us, WSH scripting is a good middle-of-the-road solution.

Finally, writing a script to perform a management task can not only make your job easier, it serves as important documentation. For example, you might want to write a script to add a new user, with all the necessary bells and whistles of group membership, home directory sharing, and default profile configuration. When the script can do its job correctly, you've written complete and accurate documentation for the task. Scripting makes good business sense just for this reason alone.

Note

Most ADSI scripting only works when run from an account with Administrator privileges on the computer or domain to which ADSI is connecting.

ADSI Concepts

ADSI objects reflect the structure of the user directory information they represent. Microsoft's Active Directory and Novell's NDS were designed with an "object-oriented" approach in mind, so the objects have a natural, one-to-one correspondence with the structures of the directory.

For example, a network domain can "contain" many subgroups that represent corporate divisions or locations; these are further divided into subgroups or departments, possibly in many layers. Finally, there are the individual users, as shown in Figure 8.1.

There is a corresponding ADSI object type to represent a domain, which contains a collection of subobjects representing the divisions, departments, and so on, until finally a collection contains only user and/or computer objects. You can manipulate the ADSI objects to add to, rename, delete, or reconfigure the directory items they represent, using the same scripting techniques you've seen in the last several chapters.

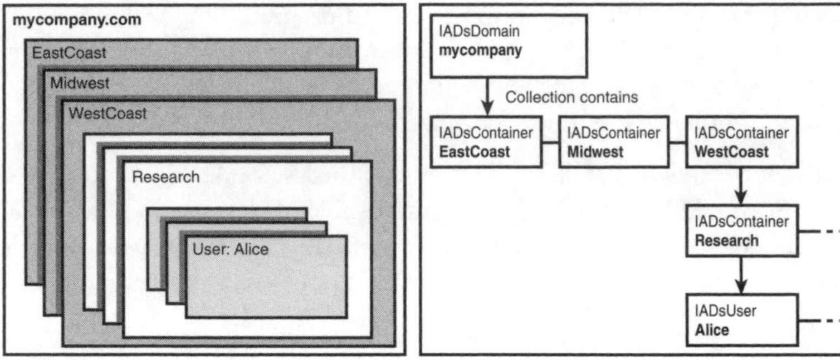

Figure 8.1 Active Directory or NDS can represent the structure of an organization, which is ultimately populated with users. ADSI objects exactly mimic the structure of the directory.

As mentioned, although ADSI provides objects to represent Active Directory, it doesn't *require* that your network use Active Directory. ADSI can still manage the other services mentioned earlier without it.

To start our introduction to ADSI, Table 8.1 lists the most significant of the ADSI objects—those that represent directory data and active network resources.

Table 8.1 **Description of ADSI Objects**

Object	Purpose
`IADs`	This is the base ADSI object. The methods and properties of `IADs` are common to all ADSI objects.
`IADsCollection`	The base object for ADSI collections. You won't actually encounter this object in its plain form; you'll see other objects *derived* from it, which means they'll have all the properties and methods of `IADsCollection`, and then some.
`IADsContainer`	Another base class; represents directory containers and file system folders. Containers can hold other containers, computers, users, and so on (refer to Figure 8.1).
`IADsComputer`	Represents a single computer (either a server or a workstation) and describes its name, location, capacity, operating system, and other information. As a container, `IADsComputer` lists the computer's users, groups, and services.
`IADsDomain`	Represents a domain or workgroup member computer. As a container, `IADsDomain` lists the domain or workstation's users, groups, and computer accounts.

Object	Purpose
`IADsFileService`	This is a variant of the `IADsService` object when it's describing a service that shares files. `IADsFileService` extends `IADsService` with additional descriptive properties. As a container, it lists active user connections, called *sessions*.
`IADsFileShare`	Represents a single shared folder.
`IADsGroup`	Represents a security group defined in the directory or on an individual computer. Oddly enough, `IADsGroup` is not a collection object itself, but its `Members` property returns a collection of `IADsUser` and `IADsGroup` objects.
`IASsNamespaces`	A collection of all available directory providers.
`IADsO`	Describes the organization to which a container or user account belongs.
`IADsOU`	A container object that represents an organizational unit and its contents. This object has all the properties of `IADsO` as well.
`IADsOpenDSObject`	Provides a way of accessing a directory using an alternate user account and password.
`IADsPrintJob`	Represents a single pending print job waiting to print on a networked printer.
`IADsPrintQueue`	Represents a networked printer. As a collection, `IADsPrintQueue` lists pending and active print jobs.
`IADsResource`	Represents a shared file currently in use.
`IADsService`	Describes a service task (for example IIS, file sharing, DNS, and so on) on a given computer.
`IADsSession`	Represents the connection between a user and a file server.
`IADsUser`	Represents a single computer user account.

You'll likely encounter other objects that are used to hold ancillary information, such as lists of what permissions are granted to which users. I'll describe some of these later in the chapter, and you can learn about the rest as you encounter them in practice. When you're beginning to tackle a particular directory or network-management task, start with Table 8.1 to see which object or objects represent the information you're interested in, and then delve into the Microsoft documentation for that object. This will lead you to any others you'll need to be aware of.

Multiple Inheritance

Multiple inheritance sounds like a great idea—I mean, who wouldn't love to have lots of very rich, very old relatives? But that's not what the phrase means here. Many ADSI objects are described in the Microsoft documentation as "implementing multiple interfaces." What this means in practical terms is that an object borrows methods and properties from other, simpler objects and then adds more of its own. It's the beautiful part of object-oriented programming systems, that objects can be based on each other. A new type of object can just take care of a few additional details and let the original object do the heavy lifting. You'll run into this more with ADSI than with other object packages described in this book, and you'll need to be on the lookout for it, because you might misinterpret the documentation otherwise.

A good example of this is in the write-up for the `IADsFileService` object. The documentation for `IADsFileService` lists only two properties: `Description` and `MaxUserCount`. However, there is a telling phrase in the object's description: "`IADsFileService` is a dual interface that inherits from `IADsService`." This means that `IADsFileService` sports all of the methods and properties of `IADsService`, as well as its own `Description` and `MaxUserCount`. You have to look at the documentation for `IADsService` to get the rest of the details. There, you'll find 12 more properties: `HostComputer`, `DisplayName`, `Version`, and so on. All these apply to an `IADsFileService` object as well.

You'll find this happening with the various `IADs`...`Operations` objects as well. ADSI has objects that represent shared folders, printers, system services, and so on. When these resources are part of an operating system for which ADSI can perform management functions, the objects present an additional `Operations` interface that adds extra management properties and methods. You'll never see an `IADsServiceOperations` object by itself, but you will find its methods and properties available on an `IADsService` object.

It starts at the top. ADSI objects are based on an object called `IADs` that provides the foundational methods and properties shared by *all* the various objects. One of these common properties is `Class`, which identifies the particular flavor of object. You can use this value to determine the type of the objects you find in a collection and to create new objects, such as user accounts and security groups. You can also use it in the `Filter` property, which I'll describe under "Working with ADSI Collections," to select objects out of a collection based on their `Class`.

Table 8.2 lists the class names of the various ADSI objects you may encounter. Each of these objects is discussed in detail later in the chapter.

Table 8.2 **Class Property Values for ADSI Objects**

Class Name	Object Type	If a Collection, Contains...
`Computer`	`IADsComputer`	`Group`, `Service`, and `User`
`Container`	`IADsContainer`	`Container`, `OrganizationalUnit`, `Group`, and `User`
`Domain`	`IADsDomain`	`Computer`, `Group`, and `User`
`FileService`	`IADsFileService`	
`FileShare`	`IADsFileShare`	
`Group`	`IADsGroup`	(Not a collection!)

Class Name	Object Type	If a Collection, Contains...
`OrganizationalUnit`	`IADsOU`	`Container`, `OrganizationalUnit`, `Group`, and `User`
`PrintJob`	`IADsPrintJob`	
`PrintQueue`	`IADsPrintQueue`	
`Resource`	`IADsResource`	
`Service`	`IADsService`	
`Session`	`IADsSession`	
`User`	`IADsUser`	

Creating ADSI Objects

ADSI objects are created with the `GetObject()` function that is provided with VBScript. If you're using another programming language, you can use `WScript.GetObject()` in the same way. Once you've used `GetObject()` to gain access to one ADSI object, you can use that object's properties and methods to extract other objects, collections, and information.

If you read Chapter 7 on Windows Management Instrumentation, you're now familiar with the *display moniker* system used to specify objects by name. `GetObject()` takes as its argument a display moniker, which is a string that names the type of object you want to create. For ADSI, this consists of the name of a network provider service to which you want to connect, a colon, and, optionally, the path to an object within the provider's namespace.

Here's a list of the primary ADSI providers:

Provider	Description
`WinNT:`	Active Directory and other Windows user directories; File and Printer Sharing services
`NDS:`	Novell NetWare Directory Services
`NWCOMPAT:`	Novell NetWare Bindery mode
`LDAP:`	Other LDAP-based directories
`IIS:`	Internet Information Server
`ADs:`	The master list of all available providers

For example, a VBScript program to manage a Windows Active Directory or Windows NT domain named "mycompany" can use this statement:

```
set obj = GetObject("WinNT://mycompany")
```

Whereas you could use

```
set obj = GetObject("NDS://mycompany")
```

to access a similarly named Novell NDS domain.

The path that follows the provider name—the part after the colon—depends on what kind of ADSI object you want. Here's where the fun starts. Table 8.3 lists the paths you'd use to directly obtain the most useful ADSI objects.

Table 8.3 **Paths Used to Obtain ADSI Objects and the Associated Object Type Created**

`GetObject()` **Path***	**Object**
`"ADs:"`	`IADsCollection`
`"IIS://`*`computer`*`/MSFTPSVC"`	`IISFTPService`
`"IIS://`*`computer`*`/MSFTPSVC/`*`n`*`"`	`IISFTPServer`
`"IIS://`*`computer`*`/MSFTPSVC/`*`n`*`/`*`folder`*`"`	`IISFTPVirtualDir`
`"IIS://computer/W3SVC"`	`IISWebService`
`"IIS://`*`computer`*`/W3SVC/`*`n`*`"`	`IISWebServer`
`"IIS://`*`computer`*`/W3SVC/`*`n`*`/`*`folder`*`"`	`IISWebVirtualDir`
`"LDAP://`*`ldapserver`*`/o=`*`orgname`* `[/ou=`*`unitname`*`]"`	`IADsContainer`
`"LDAP://RootDSE"`	`IADsContainer`
`"NDS://`*`treename`*`/O=`*`orgname`*`/OU=`*`ouname`*`"`	`IADsContainer`
`"NDS://`*`treename`*`/O=`*`orgname`*`/OU=`*`ouname`*`/` `CN=`*`groupname`*`"`	`IADsGroup`
`"NDS://`*`treename`*`/`*`orgname`*`/`*`ouname`*`"`	`IADsContainer`
`"NDS://`*`treename`*`/`*`orgname`*`/`*`ouname`*`/` *`username`*`"`	`IADsUser`
`"`*`provider`*`:"`	`IADsNamespaces`
`"`*`provider`*`://`*`computer`*`"`	`IADsComputer`
`"`*`provider`*`://`*`domain`*`"`	`IADsDomain`
`"`*`provider`*`://`*`domain`*`/`*`computer`* `[,computer]"`	`IADsComputer`
`"`*`provider`*`://`*`domain`*`/`*`computer`*`/` `LanManServer/`*`queue`*`"`	`IADsPrintQueue`
`"`*`provider`*`://`*`domain`*`/`*`computer`*`/` `LanManServer/`*`share`*`"`	`IADsFileShare`
`"`*`provider`*`://`*`domain`*`/`*`computer`*`/`*`service`*`"`	`IADsService`
`"`*`provider`*`://`*`domain`*`/`*`group`*`[,group]"`	`IADsGroup`
`"`*`provider`*`://`*`domain`*`/`*`user`*`[,user]"`	`IADsUser`
`"WinNT://domain/`*`computer`*`/` `LanManServer"`	`IADsFileService`

**Words in italics (such as* provider, domain, *and* computer*) are meant to be replaced with an actual provider name, domain name, computer name, and so on. Square brackets, [ ], indicate an optional part, and ellipses, …, indicate that the preceding part may be repeated.*

Caution

In pathnames, in ADSI paths, \ and / are *not* interchangeable. Always use the forward slash as a path separator.

Table 8.4 lists the more important ADSI objects and shows which providers support them. Only the providers with check marks may be used in `GetObject` calls to obtain the listed objects.

Table 8.4 **ADSI Objects Available from the Primary Four Providers**

Object	WinNT	NDS	NWCompat	LDAP
`IADsComputer`	✓		✓	
`IADsContainer`	✓	✓	✓	✓
`IADsDomain`	✓			
`IADsFileService`	✓		✓	
`IADsFileShare`	✓		✓	
`IADsGroup`	✓	✓	✓	✓
`IADsMembers`	✓	✓	✓	✓
`IADsNamespaces`	✓	✓	✓	✓
`IADsO`		✓		✓
`IADsOU`		✓		✓
`IADsPrintJob`	✓		✓	
`IADsPrintQueue`	✓	✓	✓	✓
`IADsService`	✓			
`IADsSession`	✓			
`IADsUser`	✓	✓	✓	✓

Note

For complete and detailed documentation on ADSI providers and the interfaces they support, go to `msdn.microsoft.com` and search for "Provider Support of ADSI Interfaces" (using the quotes).

Directory Security

Many ADSI objects cannot be used unless you are running the script under a user account that has Administrator privileges on the computer being managed.

If you find that the script will not run under an ordinary user account, your options depend on the provider you're using. `WinNT:` does not permit you to use an alternate username, so you'll have to run the script with an Administrator-level account.

For the LDAP: provider, which is used for Active Directory and LDAP management, you can use the OpenDSObject method to connect to ADSI using alternate user credentials. To use an alternate user account, create an IADsNamespaces object bound to LDAP with the statement

```
set ldap = GetObject("LDAP:")
```

and use this object's OpenDSObject method to obtain management objects, instead of GetObject. OpenDSObject's syntax is as follows:

```
ldap.OpenDSObject(adspath, username, password, flags)
```

Like GetObject(), OpenDSObject takes an ADsPath name, the desired object's moniker. If you pass the value NULL for the username and password, the current process's security context is used. You may also specify a privileged account's username and password with one or more of the flag values listed in Table 8.5 to specify the level of security desired. Multiple flags can be specified by adding their values together. However, not all flags may be honored if the target LDAP server does not support them.

Table 8.5 ***OpenDSObject* Security Option Flags**

Constant	Value	Meaning
ADS_SECURE_AUTHENTICATION	1	Requests secure authentication to avoid sending the password as clear text. The WinNT provider uses NTLM. Active Directory uses Kerberos, if possible, or NTLM.
ADS_USE_ENCRYPTION	2	Forces ADSI to encrypt data transmitted over the network. Requires that the domain have a Certificate Server installed.
ADS_USE_SSL	2	Same as ADS_USE_ENCRYPTION.
ADS_READONLY_SERVER	4	Informs ADSI that no changes will be made; this may increase performance and allow ADSI to use backup domain controllers.
ADS_PROMPT_CREDENTIALS	8	If possible, the script user will be prompted for a password. Microsoft recommends against using this flag because it may not be supported in the future.
ADS_NO_AUTHENTICATION	16	Attempts to connect as an anonymous user. The WinNT provider does not accept anonymous connections.

Constant	Value	Meaning
ADS_FAST_BIND	32	Instructs ADSI not to add the dynamic object-specific methods and properties but rather to provide the base object methods and properties only. This can speed up requests in some advanced and unusual circumstances.
ADS_USE_SIGNING	64	Adds data-verification checks to inter-computer communications. The ADS_SECURE_AUTHENTICATION flag must also be used.
ADS_USE_SEALING	128	Adds Kerberos-based encryption to intercomputer communications. Requires ADS_SECURE_AUTHENTICATION.
ADS_USE_DELEGATION	256	Permits ADSI to delegate the user credentials when communicating across domains; that is, it permits the ADSI service on a remote computer to impersonate you in conversations with other domain controllers.
ADS_SERVER_BIND	512	Reduces network traffic and speeds performance when connecting to the LDAP provider with an ADsPath that includes a server name.

You may create other objects using the same alternate credentials by calling `OpenDSObject` repeatedly with the same username and `Null` for the password value.

The `NWCOMPAT:` provider does not support `OpenDSObject`. You must connect to the NetWare server with alternate credentials using the command-line `net use` program, as follows, before running your scripts:

```
net use \\netwareserver /U:username
```

Determining the Difference Between Containers and Leaves

You've probably heard the word *tree* used to describe hierarchical structures such as the folders on a hard disk or the series of containers in a directory. Figure 8.2 shows a directory structure laid out as a tree. The end objects, those that aren't containers, are appropriately enough called *leaves* because they sit at the end of the tree's branches. In a directory, user accounts and computer accounts are considered leaf objects because they're the final objects at the end of a series of containers.

Containers can hold both leaf objects and other containers at the same time. Figure 8.2 shows an example of this, where the Administrator user account is in the main domain container, which also holds subcontainers.

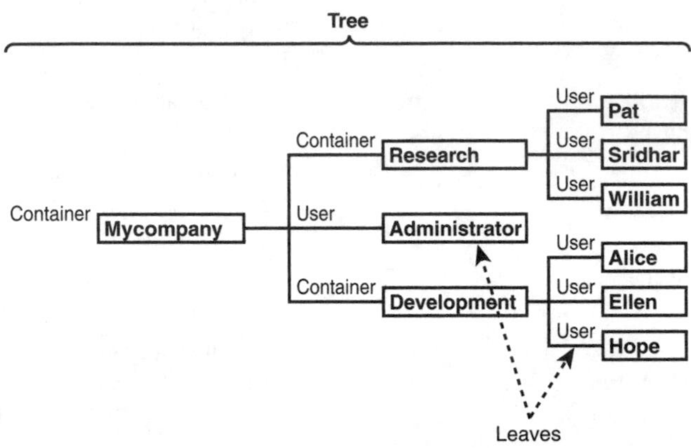

Figure 8.2 A directory structure is often called a *tree*, and the final objects—those that aren't folders or containers—can be called *leaves*. (It might help to turn the book counterclockwise 90°. Don't turn it clockwise or you'll end up with roots instead of leaves.)

When you scan the collection of objects inside a container, it's possible that the collection will hold both container and leaf objects. You'll have to determine the type of each member object as you encounter it.

The Microsoft documentation tells you to use each object's `Schema` property, which returns the display moniker name of an `IADsClass` object that describes the object's data definition and structure—that is, its type. All ADSI object varieties have a `Schema` property because they are all derived from the basic `IADs` object and inherit `Schema` from `IADs`. You can use `GetObject` to obtain the `IADsClass` object, which has a Boolean property named `Container` that is `True` if the object is a container, or `False` if it is a leaf. Got all that? The following code shows how Microsoft would have you do this:

```
set container = GetObject("WinNT://mydomain")
for each obj in container
   if GetObject(obj.Schema).Container then
       WScript.echo obj.name, "is a container"
   else
       WScript.echo obj.name, "is a leaf"
   end if
next
```

The thing is, *it doesn't work*. Sometimes ADSI returns objects that don't have all the expected properties, and the `Schema` object is particularly prone to this. The script will frequently crash because the schema's `Container` property doesn't always appear for every object type. This is apparently a bug in ADSI.

To get around this, you'll have to use the brute-force method of looking at each object's `Class` and `Name` properties and decide for yourself whether the object is a container or a leaf. Table 8.2, shown previously, lists the most common object classes and indicates whether the object is a leaf or container. If the object has items listed in its "Contains" column, it's a container.

Because containers may contain leaves, or may be nested *ad infinitum*, it's the perfect situation to use recursion to list the contents of each level of container. For example, the following script lists the contents of a computer or domain named in the `GetObject` call:

```
                                ' Example Script script0801.vbs
set comp = GetObject("WinNT://sumatra,Computer")  ' object to view

on error resume next            ' ignore inevitable errors
                                ' make services visible
comp.filter = array("Service","User","Group")

ListContainer comp, 0

sub ListContainer (obj, depth)
    dim member, cls             ' private local variables

                                ' list the object's class and name
    WScript.echo space(depth*3) & obj.class & ":", obj.name

    cls = lcase(obj.class)      ' check for container classes

    if cls = "container" or cls = "computer" or cls = "domain" then
        for each member in obj  ' list contents recursively
            ListContainer member, depth+1
        next

    elseif instr(cls, "group") then
                                ' list group members recursively
        for each member in obj.members
            ListContainer member, depth+1
        next
    end if
end sub
```

Even this script requires the `on error resume next` statement to bypass the inevitable errors in obtaining some groups' contents.

ADSI Objects for the WinNT: Provider

There are too many ADSI objects with too many methods and properties to list them all in this book. In this section, I'll give you an overview of the most important objects used to manage Windows networks and their most important properties. This reference should give you an overview of ADSI's capabilities and enough information to write useful scripts. You should, however, check the Microsoft ADSI documentation for the complete reference. Later in the chapter, I'll briefly cover the objects used for Active Directory management under the `LDAP:` provider as well as Internet Information Services management. There just isn't enough room to cover the objects and techniques used to manage Novell NetWare, Novell NDS, Microsoft Exchange, and generic LDAP servers (that, and the ends of my fingers are wearing off from typing all this stuff). At the end of the chapter, however, you'll find additional information sources listed.

Important Notes Regarding the Microsoft Documentation

The ADSI objects are written up in the Microsoft ADSI documentation that you can download from `msdn.microsoft.com`, under the heading Active Directory Service Interfaces Version 2.5, ADSI Reference, ADSI Interfaces. You'll need to use this documentation to get anywhere with ADSI, and you'll need to remember some quirky and important things when you're reading it:

- In these references, object properties are listed with names such as `Get_LastLogin` and `Get/put_Description`. When you use the objects in WSH scripts, omit the `Get_` or `Put_` part of the name. That is, you'll actually work with properties with names such as `LastLogin` and `Description`. The `Get_` and `Put_` parts of the names are used only with compiled programming languages such as C++.
- Properties whose names are listed as `Get_`*`Something`* are read-only properties. Properties listed as `Get/Put_`*`Something`* are read/write properties.
- If you get a script error message stating that a given property doesn't exist for the object you're using, try changing the reference in your code from *`object.propertyname`* to *`object`*`.Get("`*`propertyname`*`")` or *`object`*`.Put("`*`propertyname`*`", `*`newvalue`*`)`. This sometimes solves the problem.
- Remember that you must use the `.SetInfo` method to actually save any changes you make to ADSI object properties. `SetInfo` won't be listed as a method for each object. It's inherited from the core `IADs` object, and you just have to remember that it's there.
- Every object has an inherited property named `Schema` that refers to an object that describes the object type. Many objects have other properties, such as `Parent`, `AdsPath`, and `SeeAlso`, that appear to refer to other related ADSI objects. These are not actual object references that you can use to directly manipulate the related objects. They're monikers—string values—that you can print or use as arguments to the `GetObject()` function, if you want to actually work with the other objects.

The following sections list the methods and properties of the most important objects.

IADs

The `IADs` object is the base object from which all other ADSI objects are derived. That is, all the other objects described in this chapter start with the methods and properties shown in Reference List 8.1 and extend `IADs` with additional functions. To keep things brief, I've not repeated these properties in every one of the other objects, so you must remember that these are an integral part of every ADSI object.

REFERENCE LIST 8.1 Properties and Methods of the Base IADs Object (Present on All ADSI Objects)

Properties:

`ADsPath`

The moniker name of the object, of the form used by `GetObject()`; for example, `"WinNT://`*`domain`*`/`*`computer`*`"`. If you've obtained an object from a collection, `ADsPath` gives the moniker you can use to create the object directly in the future.

`Class`

The class name of the object in question. This is one of the class names listed in Table 8.2: `"User"`, `"Domain"`, and so on.

`GUID`

The Globally Unique Identifier for this object. It's a long string that identifies this object in the Active Directory (if the object is part of AD).

`Name`

The name of the object. Most object names are what you'd expect for the object type: a user name for an `IADsUser` object, and so on.

`Parent`

The `ADsPath` name of the container object that holds this object, if applicable. You can use the `Parent` property value in a `GetObject()` call to create the object representing the container, if you need it.

`Schema`

The `ADsPath` of an `IADsSchema` object that describes the properties expected on this object. For more information about `IADsSchema`, see the Microsoft documentation.

Methods:

`Get(`*`propertyname`*`)`

Returns the value of the property whose name is passed as a character string. In the WSH scripting environment, you can also manipulate properties using the usual object syntax, but in any case these two statements are equivalent:

```
wscript.echo object.someproperty
wscript.echo object.Get("someproperty")
```

continues

REFERENCE LIST 8.1 Continued

When the property has a simple value, a normal Variant value is returned. If the property has multiple values, an array is returned.

GetEx(*propertyname*)
Like `Get`, but `GetEx(propertyname)` always returns an array containing the property value, even if there is just one. You can use this method when examining properties that can have multiple values, so you don't need to check to see whether a single value or an array has been returned.

GetInfo
Forces ADSI to retrieve the property values for this object from the underlying Windows computer directory or service. This occurs automatically the first time you reference an object, but you can call `GetInfo` explicitly if you think the underlying information may have changed between the time you created an object and the time you want to view its properties.

GetInfoEx *namearray, 0*
Forces ADSI to retrieve from the provider (for example, the computer or domain server being managed) the values of only the parameters whose names are listed in the array *`namearray`*. The second argument must be zero. `GetInfoEx` is not normally needed in scripting applications.

Put *propertyname, newvalue*
Assigns the value *`newvalue`* to the property whose name is passed as the character string *`propertyname`*. In the WSH scripting environment, you will normally use the standard object property syntax, but just for the record, the following two statements are equivalent:

```
object.someproperty = newvalue
object.Put "someproperty", newvalue
```

However, modifying the value of an object's properties by either method does not automatically update the information stored in Active Directory or on the managed computer. The `SetInfo` method must be called to actually save the information.

PutEx *controlcode, propertyname, valuearray*
Updates the multiple-valued property *`propertyname`* using one or more values stored in the array *`valuearray`* according to the value of *`controlcode`*, which can be one of the following:

Constant	Value	Function
ADS_PROPERTY_CLEAR	1	Removes all values from the property
ADS_PROPERTY_UPDATE	2	Replaces the property's current values with the specified values
ADS_PROPERTY_APPEND	3	Adds the specified values to the current values
ADS_PROPERTY_DELETE	4	Deletes the listed values

`SetInfo`

Saves any changes made to the object's properties back to the underlying computer or directory that the object represents.

Note

`SetInfo` must be used after any object is modified or created in order to actually change the associated user account, system service, Active Directory entry, or other managed object. This applies to *all* the ADSI objects discussed in this chapter.

`IADsCollection` and `IADsContainer`

`IADsCollection` and `IADsContainer` are also "base" object classes (interfaces) that are used as the foundation for ADSI objects such as `IADsDomain`.

`IADsCollection` is a collection object, so you can scan its contents using the normal means of enumerating a collection in your chosen scripting language. In VBScript, this is done with the `for each` loop.

➔ To learn more about enumerating collections, see "Containers and Collections," p. 85.

The combined properties and methods of `IADsCollection` and `IADsContainer` are listed in Reference List 8.2. Because `IADsContainer` expands on `IADsCollection` and adds additional properties, and because they always appear together, I've mixed them together in this listing. In actual use, the objects that are derived from these interfaces will have additional properties and methods, as discussed in the remaining sections of this chapter.

REFERENCE LIST 8.2 Properties and Methods of the `IADsContainer` and `IADsCollection` Interfaces

Properties:

`Count`

Returns the number of items in the collection. (Read-only.)

`Filter`

Can be used to limit the apparent number of objects in the collection to only those of a selected class or classes. To do this, create an array of class names (for example, `"Group"`, `"LocalGroup"`, `"GlobalGroup"`, `"User"`, and so on) and assign it to the `Filter` property. I'll discuss the `Filter` property in more detail in the next section.

`Hints`

This property lists object properties that should be cached for faster performance; it's not relevant to VBScript programming.

continues

REFERENCE LIST 8.2 Continued

Methods:

CopyHere(*sourcepath*, *newname*)

Adds a copy of an existing object to this container. *Sourcepath* is a string, the ADsPath name of the object (for example, "//java/bknittel,User"). *Newname* is the name the copy of the object is to have in this container. It can be Null, in which case the copy has the same name as the original. This method returns a reference to the new object. After creating the copy, you should set any required properties and finish by using the SetInfo method on the new object. The new group, user, or what-have-you is not actually created in the underlying directory until you use SetInfo.

Create(*class*, *name*)

Creates a new object of the specified *class* in this container and gives it the specified *name*. *Class* is typically "OU", "Group", "User", or "FileShare". This method returns a reference to the new object. After creating the object, you should set any required properties and finish by using the SetInfo method on the new object. The object is not actually created in the underlying directory until you use SetInfo.

For example, to create a new user, obtain the domain object for a domain account or the computer object for a local account, and use this:

```
set domain = GetObject("WinNT://domainname")  ' (or //computername)
set user = domain.Create("user", "username")
' set properties:
user.property = value
.
.
.
user.SetInfo  ' actually create the user account
```

A full-fledged script to create a user account would need to set the other user properties, such as the home directory, the password, and the profile path. It would also need to actually create the home directory and assign the new user full-control privileges in it, which is beyond ADSI's ability. This last step can be done with the cacls command-line program, and cacls can be run from the script. I'll discuss cacls in Chapter 14, "Command-Line Programs."

Note

If you want to examine or alter properties of the new object, you should follow SetInfo with GetInfo. This will read back into the object all the actual properties of the newly created directory entry. Create does not fill in all the default values that a newly created physical directory entry will receive. After GetInfo you can view and alter the object's properties.

Delete *class*, *name*

Deletes an object in this container given its name and class. The action takes place immediately. There is no need to call SetInfo. Be sure to release any object references you might have stored to the deleted object. For example, this script deletes a user account:

```
                               ' Example Script script0802.vbs
set domain = GetObject("WinNT://domainname")  ' (or //computername)
domain.Delete("user", "username")
```

GetObject(*class, name*)

When you have a collection of items, you can use `GetObject` to extract a particular object of interest, given its `class` and `name`. For example, I could extract the `IADsUser` object for a particular user, say `"Norm"`, from the domain with these statements:

```
set domain = GetObject("WinNT://mydomain")
set norm = domain.GetObject("user", "Norm")
```

However, unless you need the larger collection object for other purposes, it's more efficient to get a single object directly with a more precise moniker. Here's an example:

```
set norm = GetObject("WinNT://mydomain/norm,User")
```

The first method requires Windows to fetch the entire list of domain user and group names from the domain controller; the second only requests the one object.

MoveHere(*sourcepath, newname*)

Moves an object from another container into this container, given the object's `ADsPath` name. *Newname* is the name the moved object is to have in this container. It can be `Null`, in which case the object is not renamed. This method returns an object reference to the moved object. Here's an example of its use:

```
set user = container.MoveHere("WinNT://mydomain/someuser,User", Null)
```

Note

In the discussions of the other ADSI objects that follow, when any object is said to be derived from `IADsContainer`, remember that the object will have all the properties and methods shown in Reference Lists 8.1 and 8.2, even if they're not listed again later.

Working with ADSI Collections

ADSI collections based on the `IADsContainer` object often contain a mixture of object types, reflecting the organization of real Windows objects: A domain may contain user accounts, computer accounts, and security groups. A computer contains all those plus system services. It can be difficult to sort through such a collection if you only want to examine objects of a particular type.

You can examine the `Class` property of each object to see whether it's an object of interest. For example, when printing a list of groups in a domain, you might write the following:

```
                              ' Example Script script0803.vbs
set domain = GetObject("WinNT://mydomain")
for each object in domain
    if object.class = "Group" then
        WScript.echo object.name
    end if
next
```

This gets cumbersome if you're looking for more than one group at once. The `IADsContainer` object provides a special property named `Filter` to help out. If you assign an array value to a collection's `Filter` property, where the array contains one or more `Class` names, the collection will appear to contain only objects of the named classes. The easiest way to create such an array in VBScript is with the `array()` function, which returns its arguments as an array. The previous script example can be rewritten as follows:

```
                              ' Example Script script0804.vbs
set domain = GetObject("WinNT://mydomain")

domain.Filter = array("group")    ' view Groups only

for each object in domain         ' scan the collection
    Wscript.echo object.name
next
```

If you've set a container's `Filter` property, you can later assign another array to view different objects, or you can assign it the value `Nothing` to remove filtering entirely. Also, you can create a filter that accepts more than one class type by simply creating a larger array:

```
domain.Filter = array("group", "user")
```

Oddly enough, I have found that you cannot use an array created with the standard VBScript `dim` statement; the script will generate an error when you attempt to assign the array to the `Filter` property. This appears to be a bug in either VBScript or ADSI.

IADsComputer and IADsComputerOperations

The `IADsComputer` object represents a computer account in a Windows NT, 2000, or .NET Server Domain network. There is a computer account for each member computer in the domain. The `IADsComputer` object lets you view and manage information about each member computer. Its properties are listed in Reference List 8.3.

REFERENCE LIST 8.3 Properties of the `IADsComputer` Object

`Division`

The division, organization, or company name under which this computer's operating system was registered.

`OperatingSystem`

The operating system family that this computer is running. For Windows NT, XP and 2000, this is `"Windows NT"`.

`OperatingSystemVersion`

The version of the operating system on this computer. For Windows XP and 2000, this is `"5.1"` and `"5.0"`, respectively.

`Owner`

The name of the person who registered the operating system running on this computer.

`Processor`

The brand and model of CPU running in this computer (for example, my AMD processor is reported as `"x86 Family 5 Model 8 Stepping 0"`).

`ProcessorCount`

Indicates whether Windows is configured for a single processor or multiple processors. For Windows 2000 and XP with one CPU, this might be the string `"Uniprocessor Free"`.

The Microsoft ADSI documentation describes dozens more informative properties, but they are not present in version 2.5 of ADSI, as shipped with Windows 2000 and XP. The documentation also describes the additional properties as read/write, but in actuality you cannot change them through ADSI. You may modify the object's properties, but the `SetInfo` method is not available.

The `IADsComputer` object also provides management properties and methods through its `IADsComputerOperations` interface. The items in Reference List 8.4 appear in addition to the properties listed in Reference List 8.3. Well, they only sort of appear, as you'll see.

REFERENCE LIST 8.4 Property and Method of the `IADsComputerOperations` Interface

Property:

`Status`

The status property is vaguely defined in the Microsoft documentation and appears to be unimplemented in ADSI 2.5. It might be defined in the future.

continues

REFERENCE LIST 8.4 Continued

Method:

`Shutdown` *`reboot`*

Shuts down the associated computer. If the Boolean value *`reboot`* is `True`, the computer is reset and restarted. If *`reboot`* is `False`, the computer is simply turned off, assuming that the computer has the proper power-management hardware and software, and assuming that the power-management software works. In my experience, computers are just as likely to restart as to shut off, especially if running Windows 9x or Me.

You can obtain an IADsComputer object with a `GetObject()` call in one of these formats:

```
set computer = GetObject("WinNT://computername")

set computer = GetObject("WinNT://computername,Computer")

set computer = GetObject("WinNT://domainname/computername ")
```

You can specify "`,Computer`" after the name to avoid ambiguity between computer, group, and domain names.

Finally, `IADsComputer` can be treated as a collection. The objects in its collection include `IADsService` objects representing all installed services on the computer, and `IADsUser` and `IADsGroup` objects for the computer's local users and groups.

IADsDomain

The `IADsDomain` object represents a Windows or NetWare security domain, a group of users and computers that share a common user account database. `IADsDomain` provides methods and properties to view and manage the user accounts in a domain. Individual computers, whether they are members of a domain or of a simple workgroup (peer-to-peer) network, also have local user account databases, and `IADsDomain` can manage these as well.

The properties and the one method of `IADsDomain` are discussed in Reference List 8.5. `IADsDomain` is derived from the `IADsContainer` and `IADs` objects, so it has these objects' properties and methods as well. A couple of these additional properties are listed in Reference List 8.5, but you should remember that the other inherited properties and methods are present also.

REFERENCE LIST 8.5 The Properties and Method of the `IADsDomain` Object

Properties:

`AutoUnlockInterval`

The time in seconds that an account remains disabled after a series of invalid password logon attempts.

Filter
Limits the view into the object's collection to only those object classes listed in the array assigned to the filter. See the discussion in the "Working with ADSI Collections" section for more information.

IsWorkgroup
A Boolean value that is `True` if this `IADsDomain` object represents a local computer's individual user directory, rather than a domain directory. This will be true for all members of workgroup networks as well as for the individual computers of a domain network.

LockoutObservationInterval
The maximum time, in seconds, between invalid password login attempts for the attempts to be considered part of a cluster and to be counted. That is, the count of attempts resets to zero after `LockoutObservationInterval` seconds.

MinPasswordAge
The minimum time, in seconds, before a new password can be changed. This property can prevent users from rapidly changing their password back to a previously used value.

MinPasswordLength
The minimum password length allowed.

MaxBadPasswordsAllowed
The maximum number of bad password logon attempts allowed before the account is locked out.

MaxPasswordAge
The maximum time, in seconds, that a password can be left unchanged, after which a user is forced to change his or her password.

PasswordAttributes
A value indicating the required password complexity to be enforced by the system. It can be one of the following values:

Constant	Value	Description
PASSWORD_ATTR_NONE	0	No complexity requirement.
PASSWORD_ATTR_MIXED_CASE	1	Passwords must use upper- and lowercase characters
PASSWORD_ATTR_COMPLEX	2	Passwords must use at least one punctuation or nonprinting character.

continues

REFERENCE LIST 8.5 Continued

Note

In most cases, I'd suggest that you encase your script in a `.WSF` file and use a `<reference>` tag to automatically import ADSI's predefined constants. However, for ADSI, sorry to say, this is not very helpful. There are several problems with the ADSI object library. First, not all of ADSI's constants are defined by the type library that `<reference>` pulls in; many are missing. Second, you must use the awkward tag `<reference guid="{97D25DB0-0363-11CF-ABC4-02608C9E7553}"/>` to get even the partial list. And third, in my testing, the `<reference>` operation caused a 30-second delay when a script it's in was run. For ADSI scripts, you should define the constants yourself, as in this VBScript example:

```
const PASSWORD_ATTR_MIXED_CASE =     1
```

You can download a VBS file with all the ADSI constants listed in this chapter from `http://www.helpwinxp.com/hood`.

`PasswordHistoryLength`

The number of previous passwords that the system remembers. This property is used to help prevent users forced to change their passwords from promptly switching back to their original passwords. A `PasswordHistoryLength` value of, say, 10, coupled with a large value for `MinPasswordAge` (say, 120 seconds) can make it too annoying for users to try to resist changing passwords. Instead, they'll choose a new password and attach it to their monitor with a sticky note.

Method:

`SetInfo`

As with all objects based on `IADs`, you must use the `SetInfo` method to commit any changes you make to the object's property values back to the Windows directory they represent. (`IADsDomain` sports all the other properties and methods of `IADs` and `IADsContainer` as well, which are listed in Reference Lists 8.1 and 8.2. I repeated this one here for emphasis).

To obtain an `IADsDomain` object, use `GetObject()` as follows:

```
set domain = GetObject("WinNT://domainname")
```

`IADsDomain` is also a container object. The members of its collection can be a mixture of user accounts (`IADsUser`), security groups (`IADsGroup`), computer accounts (`IADsComputer`), and possibly the Active Directory schema for the domain (`IADsSchema`).

You can scan through the entire collection using the normal method used by your scripting language, or you can use the `Filter` property to restrict the view to a limited set of object types. For example, this script lists only the users in a specified domain:

```
                                     ' Example Script script0805.vbs
set domain = GetObject("WinNT://domainname")
domain.Filter = array("User")    ' view only User-class objects
```

```
for each user in domain         ' scan collection and print each username
    wscript.echo user.name
next
```

IADsFileService and IADsFileServiceOperations

`IADsFileService` represents the File Sharing service on a given computer. It's based on the `IADsService` object, which represents any kind of system services. That is, this file service object has multiple interfaces, a feature discussed earlier in the chapter.

An `IADsFileService` object has all the properties and methods of `IADsService` and `IADsServiceOperations`, which are described later in the chapter, with additional functions specific to file sharing. On top of this, the `IADsFileServiceOperations` interface adds even more properties and methods.

The net result is that this file service management object has all the properties listed in Reference Lists 8.6 and 8.14.

REFERENCE LIST 8.6 Combined Properties of the IADsFileService and IADsFileServiceOperations Interfaces

`Description`

Describes the file service. (This is pretty much meaningless.)

`MaxUserCount`

According to the Microsoft documentation, `MaxUserCount` returns or allows you to set the maximum number of users allowed to connect to shared files on the associated computer. However, in my testing, it always returns a value of `-1`, and the script generates an error if you attempt to change the value. So, sorry to say, those of you hoping to use this to get around Windows XP Professional's 10-connection limit are out of luck.

`Resources`

Returns a collection of `IADsResource` objects listing each of the associated computer's shared resources (for example, files, named pipes, and so forth) that are actually in use. I'll describe the `IADsResource` object later in this section.

`Sessions`

Returns a collection of `IADsSession` objects that represent the connections between the associated computer and any clients (users) attached to the File Sharing service. See the section "`IADsSession`" later in the chapter for a description of this object.

You can obtain the `IADSFileService` object for a given computer by binding to the `LanManServer` service with a statement like

```
set fs = GetObject("WinNT://computername/LanManServer")
```

or

```
set fs = GetObject("WinNT://domainname/computername/LanManServer")
```

The following script lists the users connected to the computer named "sumatra":

```
                                    ' Example Script script0806.vbs
set fs = GetObject("WinNT://sumatra/LanManServer")

wscript.echo "Users connected to sumatra:"
for each session in fs.Sessions
    wscript.echo "  ", session.user, "from", session.computer
next
```

The `Resources` property returns a collection of `IADsResource` objects, whose properties are noted in Reference List 8.7.

REFERENCE LIST 8.7 Properties of the `IADsResource` Object

`Name`

Each `IADsResource` object has a name, as do all ADSI objects, but in this case it's a random string of digits assigned by the computer sharing the resource, and isn't of any use.

`User`

Returns the account name of the user who has opened this resource.

`UserPath`

Returns the `ADsPath` of the user who has opened this resource. You can use `GetObject()` with this string to obtain the `IADsUser` object representing this user.

`Path`

Returns the path and filename of the resource on its host computer.

`LockCount`

Returns the number of file locks in place on this resource. (A *file lock* is an operating system mechanism used by multiuser databases and other programs to avoid having several people attempt to modify the same information at the same time.)

The following script lists all files shared by a specified computer that are currently in use:

```
                                    ' Example Script script0807.vbs
set cname = "sumatra"
set fs = GetObject("WinNT://" & cname & "/LanManServer")
```

```
wscript.echo "Shared files in use on", cname & ":"
on error resume next

for each resource in fs.Resources
    WScript.echo resource.path, "by", resource.user
next
```

The `on error resume next` statement is necessary because when the `IADsFileService` object refers to a computer other than the one running the script, one of the objects returned in the `Resources` collection is invalid—it does not have a `Path` or `User` property and can't be listed. In all likelihood, the resource refers to the ADSI connection used to gather the remote resource information. But whatever these mystery objects are, they can't be detected in any way other than trying to view them and failing, so it's best just to have the script ignore the error that occurs.

This script doesn't display the user's computer name, though, and it's often useful to know where to go to get someone to stop using a file that you need to move, rename, or back up. This version of the script lists users by session and then lists any files they have in use:

```
                                        ' Example Script script0808.vbs
cname = "sumatra"
set fs = GetObject("WinNT://" & cname & "/LanManServer")

wscript.echo "Shared files in use on", cname & ":"
on error resume next

for each session in fs.Sessions                 ' list each session's user
    WScript.echo "*", session.user, "from", session.computer & ":"

    for each resource in fs.Resources          ' scan resources but only
        if resource.user = session.user then ' print items for this user
            WScript.echo "    ", resource.path
        end if
    next
next
```

IADsFileShare

The `IADsFileShare` object represents a single shared folder on a workstation or server. Its properties are described in Reference List 8.8.

REFERENCE LIST 8.8 Properties of the IADsFileShare Object

CurrentUserCount

Indicates the number of users currently connected to this shared folder. (Read-only.)

continues

REFERENCE LIST 8.8 Continued

Description

A description of the shared folder (perhaps its purpose).

HostComputer

The `ADsPath` name of the computer that is sharing this folder. You can use `HostComputer` with `GetObject()` if you need access to the corresponding `IADsComputer` object.

MaxUserCount

The maximum number of users that can connect to this resource at once. (Read-only.)

Name

The share name for this folder (This property is inherited from the base object `IADs` and is read-only.)

Path

The file system path of the shared file on the host computer.

You can obtain access to `IADsFileShare` objects through the collection of all shares on a specified computer:

```
                        ' Example Script script0809.vbs
set lm = GetObject("WinNT://computername/LanManServer")
for each share in lm
    wscript.echo share.name, "=", share.path
next
```

Alternatively, if you know its name, you can use a moniker, as shown below:

```
set share = GetObject("WinNT://computername/LanManServer/sharename"
```

You can share a folder on a computer by creating a new `IADsFileShare` object:

```
                        ' Example Script script0810.vbs
set lm = GetObject("WinNT://myserver/LanManServer")
set share = lm.Create("FileShare", "Sharename")
share.path = "C:\somefolder\some other folder"
share.description = "Some Descriptive Text"
share.SetInfo           ' save the altered object
```

Note

The current version of ADSI cannot set sharing restrictions (sharing permissions).

IADsGroup

The `IADsGroup` object represents a security group, which is a set of users who are all granted a given set of specific privileges and file access rights. The concept of a security group exits on Windows XP, NT, 2000, and .NET as well as on all versions of

NetWare. The properties and methods of the `IADsGroup` object are described in Reference List 8.9. Interestingly enough, `IADsGroup` is *not* itself a collection object. To find the group's members, you have to use the `Members` method to retrieve a collection that represents the members.

REFERENCE LIST 8.9 Properties and Methods of the `IADsGroup` Object

Properties:

`Description`
A string describing the purpose of the group.

`Name`
The name of the group. (This property is inherited from the base `IADs` object.)

Methods:

`Add` *`adsPath`*
Adds a member to the group. `ADsPath` describes the user or group to add—for example, `"WinNT://`*`domainname/username`*`"`.

`IsMember(`*`user`***`)`**
Tests whether the specified ***`user`*** is a member of the group and returns either `True` or `False`. ***`User`*** must be specified as an `ADsPath` representing the user account (for example, `"WinNT://`*`domain/username`*`"`).

`Members()`
Returns an `IADsMembers` collection listing all the users currently in the security group. The `IADsMembers` collection is described in the next section.

`Remove` *`user`*
Removes the specified user from the security group. ***`User`*** must be specified as an `ADsPath` representing the user account.

You can obtain an `IADsGroup` object for a specific group with `GetObject()`, as in this statement:

```
set group = GetObject("WinNT://domain/groupname,Group")
```

Alternatively, you can scan for all the groups in a given domain by examining the domain object's collection:

```
set domain = GetObject("WinNT://domain")

domain.filter = array("Group")

for each group in domain
    wscript.echo group.name, group.class
next
```

Note

In any of these examples, you can replace *domain* with a computer name to manage the local groups of a server, or the security groups in the computers on a non-domain network.

You can create a new local or global group using the `IADsContainer` method `Create` with the object representing a computer or domain. Here's an example:

```
                    ' Example Script script0811.vbs
set server = GetObject("WinNT://mycomputer")

set newgrp = server.Create("Group", "IBM 1130 Enthusiasts")
newgrp.SetInfo     ' tell ADSI to save the new group

newgrp.Add "WinNT://mycomputer/bknittel,User"
newgrp.Add "WinNT://mycomputer/norm,User"
```

IADsMembers

The `IADsMembers` object is a collection object that represents the individual user accounts belonging to a security group (an `IADsGroup`). It's the usual scripting collection object with a `Count` property indicating the number of items in the collection, plus an additional `Filter` property that can be set to a string value to limit the items seen in the collection.

The `Filter` property can be left to its default value, `Nothing`, or can be set to an array of strings naming object classes you wish to see. The following scriptlet lists just the users in a given security group and omits groups that are also members:

```
                                ' Example Script script0812.vbs
set ptu = GetObject("winnt://mydomain/PeachTree Users,Group")
set members = ptu.Members

members.filter = array("User")  ' list users in PeachTree Users
for each user in members
    wscript.echo "user:", user.name
next
```

The objects in the `IADsMembers` collection are potentially a mix of `IADsUser` and `IADsGroup` objects. You can determine the type of each object by examining its `Class` property. All objects based on `IADs` have this property, and it describes which particular flavor of ADSI object you have: `"User"`, `"Group"`, `"PrintServer"`, and so on.

IADsNamespaces

The `IADsNamespaces` object is a collection of all ADSI providers available to the computer running an ADSI script. The collection lists the names of the providers as strings that can be used to form object monikers. The object is created with GetObject("ADs:"). On my test computer, the script

```
set namespaces = GetObject("ADs:")

wscript.echo "Namespaces ------"
for each ns in namespaces
    wscript.echo ns.name
next
```

printed the following:

```
Namespaces ------
WinNT:
NWCOMPAT:
NDS:
LDAP:
IIS:
```

The object is also purported to have one property named DefaultContainer, which can be set to an ADsPath. I say "purported to have" because every attempt I have made to reference it has failed with an "Object doesn't support this property" error.

Should this property be available on your systems, it can be set to the name of the default container for the current user's account. This is a good container to start with, for example, when displaying "neighboring" user accounts. DefaultContainer is said to be a read/write property; you can store a default container path there for the current user's future ADSI queries. You do not need to call .SetInfo after changing DefaultContainer.

IADsPrintJob and IADsPrintJobOperations

The IADsPrintJob object represents a single print job in a network printer's queue. You can use this object to view the name of the user who submitted the job and other job parameters. The object's properties are described in Reference List 8.10. If the print queue is on a Windows or NetWare server that can be managed by ADSI, the object will contain the additional properties and methods defined by the IADsPrintJobOperations interface, which is described in Reference List 8.11.

REFERENCE LIST 8.10 Properties of the IADsPrintJob Object

Description

A string describing the print job. This is often the name of the document being printed, but it's sometimes blank and sometimes the cryptic "Remote Downlevel Document," which means output from a DOS application.

continues

REFERENCE LIST 8.10 Continued

HostPrintQueue

The ADsPath name of the IADsPrintQueue object representing this job's print queue. Use this string with GetObject() if you need to obtain the corresponding object. (Read-only.)

Notify

The name of the user to be notified when this print job is completed or canceled.

NotifyPath

The ADsPath name of the IADsUser object representing the user account to be notified when the print job is completed or canceled. Use NotifyPath with GetObject() if you need the user object.

Priority

The priority of this print job, a number from 1 up.

Size

The size of the print job in bytes. (Read-only.)

StartTime

A date/time value indicating the earliest time of day that this job can be considered for printing. The date part is ignored.

TimeSubmitted

A date/time value indicating the time that the job was submitted. (Read-only.)

TotalPages

The total number of pages in the print job. (Read-only.)

UntilTime

A date/time value indicating the latest time of day that the job can be considered for printing. The date part is ignored. If StartTime and UntilTime are equal, the job can print at any time.

User

The name of the user who submitted this print job.

UserPath

The ADsPath name of the IADsUser object representing the user who submitted the print job. Use UserPath with GetObject() if you need the user object.

IADsPrintJob objects are obtained as a collection from the IADsPrintQueue object's PrintJobs property. Here's an example:

```
                                   ' Example Script script0813.vbs
set server = GetObject("WinNT://servername/sharename")
for each job in server.Printjobs
    wscript.echo job.User, job.TotalPages
next
```

For jobs on Windows and NetWare servers, `IADsPrintJob` sports the additional `IADsPrintJobOperations` interface, which gives the object an additional set of properties and methods. These properties and methods are described in Reference List 8.11.

REFERENCE LIST 8.11 Properties and Methods of the `IADsPrintJobOperations` Interface

Properties:

`Status`

Returns one of the following values describing the current status of this print job (Read-only):

Constant	Value (in Hexadecimal)
ADS_JOB_PAUSED	&H001
ADS_JOB_ERROR	&H002
ADS_JOB_DELETING	&H004
ADS_JOB_PRINTING	&H010
ADS_JOB_OFFLINE	&H020
ADS_JOB_PAPEROUT	&H040
ADS_JOB_PRINTED	&H080
ADS_JOB_DELETED	&H100

`TimeElapsed`

Returns the time elapsed, in seconds, since the print job started printing, or `0` if it has not yet started printing. (Read-only.)

`PagesPrinted`

Returns the number of pages already printed. (Read-only.)

`Position`

Returns this job's position in the print queue. (Read-only.)

Methods:

`Pause`

Halts the processing of this print job. If the job has not yet started printing, other jobs ahead of and behind this one queue can continue to print.

`Resume`

Permits this print job to continue printing or to be considered for printing.

Note

You must have Administrator privileges on the server hosting the queue to view or modify print jobs.

IADsPrintQueue and IADsPrintQueueOperations

The `IADsPrintQueue` object represents a network shared printer. This object lets you view the printer's location and description information as well as obtain lists of pending print jobs. The object's properties are described in Reference List 8.12. For print queues on Windows and NetWare servers, you may use the additional methods and properties provided by the `IADsPrintQueueOperations` interface to manage the print queue. These methods and properties appear as part of the same `IADsPrintQueue` object and are discussed in Reference List 8.13.

REFERENCE LIST 8.12 Properties of the IADsPrintQueue Object

BannerPage

Returns the pathname of the separator file inserted between print jobs, or `NULL` if no separator page is configured.

Datatype

The default print data type preferred by this queue. This is a string with one of the following values: `"RAW"`, `"RAW [FF appended]"`, `"RAW [FF auto]"`, `"NT EMF 1.003"`, `"NT EMF 1.006"`, `"NT EMF 1.007"`, `"NT EMF 1.008"`, or `"TEXT"`.

DefaultJobPriority

The default priority value given to print jobs that do not specify a specific priority, an integer from 1 up.

Description

A brief descriptive name for the printer; this information displays in Active Directory and in Network Neighborhood. This information corresponds to the Description field in the Windows Printer Properties dialog box.

HostComputer

This property ostensibly names the computer that hosts the print queue. However, in my testing, a "Property does not exist" error occurred whenever I attempted to reference this property. The property is apparently not implemented in every ADSI provider.

Location

A brief description of the location of this printer. This corresponds to the Location field in the Windows Printer Properties dialog box.

Model

A text string naming the make and model of the printer. This is descriptive only. Changing this string does not change the associated printer driver.

Name

The name of the print queue. (This property is inherited from the base `IADs` object.)

PrintDevices
An array of strings that contain the names of the ports that serve this queue. If the queue uses printer pooling, more than one port may be listed.

PrinterPath
A string that gives the UNC pathname that refers to this printer (for example, `"\\servername\sharename"`).

PrintProcessor
The name of the default print processor for this queue. For Windows printers, this is almost always `"WinPrint"`.

Priority
The priority of jobs from this queue relative to any other queues that feed to the same printer ports. All jobs from the highest-priority queue will be processed before any jobs from lower-priority queues are considered.

Starttime
A date/time value indicating the time of day that the queue begins processing jobs. The date part of the date/time is ignored.

UntilTime
A date/time value indicating the time of day that the queue stops processing jobs. The date part of the date/time is ignored. If `StartTime` and `EndTime` are the same value, the queue is always operational.

You can obtain `IADsPrintQueue` objects using `GetObject`, with statements like this one:

```
set queue = GetObject("WinNT://servername/sharename")
```

In this case, *servername* is the name of the computer hosting the print queue, and *sharename* is the name of the queue. You can also scan the list of all printers shared by a particular server with a filter:

```
                                    ' Example Script script0814.vbs
servername = "servername"
set server = GetObject("WinNT://" & servername)
wscript.echo "Print queues on", servername & ":"

server.Filter = Array("PrintQueue")
for each printer in server
    wscript.echo "***", printer.name
    for each job in printer.printjobs
       if job.totalpages = "1" then plural = "" else plural = "s"
       wscript.echo "    ", job.user & ":", job.totalpages, "page" & plural
    next
next
```

Here's some sample output from this script:

```
Print queues on sumatra:
*** Okidata
    bknittel: 1 page
```

`IADsPrintQueueOperations` is an additional interface that provides management functions. If an `IADsPrinter` object refers to a Windows or NetWare print queue, the additional methods and properties described in Reference List 8.13 will be available on the same object.

REFERENCE LIST 8.13 Properties and Methods of the `IAdsPrintQueueOperations` Interface

Properties:

`PrintJobs`

Returns a collection of `IADsPrintJob` objects representing all pending and active jobs in this queue. `IADsPrintJob` was described earlier in this section.

`Status`

Returns a value indicating the current status of this print queue (read-only). `Status` will be one of the values listed in Table 8.6, or possibly the sum of several values.

Methods:

`Pause`

Halts the processing of print jobs for this queue. If other queues are directed at the same printer(s), those queues might continue sending jobs to the printer(s).

`Purge`

Removes all pending print jobs from the queue.

`Resume`

Resumes the processing of print jobs.

You can use the `IADsPrintQueue` object to view and manage print queues but not create new ones.

Table 8.6 lists the status values returned by `IADsPrintQueueOperations`. The `Status` property may be one of these values or a sum of several values.

Table 8.6 **Status Values Returned by *IAdsPrintQueueOperations***

Constant	Value (in Hexadecimal)
ADS_PRINTER_PAUSED	&H00000001
ADS_PRINTER_PENDING_DELETION	&H00000002
ADS_PRINTER_ERROR	&H00000003
ADS_PRINTER_PAPER_JAM	&H00000004
ADS_PRINTER_PAPER_OUT	&H00000005
ADS_PRINTER_MANUAL_FEED	&H00000006
ADS_PRINTER_PAPER_PROBLEM	&H00000007

Constant	Value (in Hexadecimal)
ADS_PRINTER_OFFLINE	&H00000008
ADS_PRINTER_IO_ACTIVE	&H00000100
ADS_PRINTER_BUSY	&H00000200
ADS_PRINTER_PRINTING	&H00000400
ADS_PRINTER_OUTPUT_BIN_FULL	&H00000800
ADS_PRINTER_NOT_AVAILABLE	&H00001000
ADS_PRINTER_WAITING	&H00002000
ADS_PRINTER_PROCESSING	&H00004000
ADS_PRINTER_INITIALIZING	&H00008000
ADS_PRINTER_WARMING_UP	&H00010000
ADS_PRINTER_TONER_LOW	&H00020000
ADS_PRINTER_NO_TONER	&H00040000
ADS_PRINTER_PAGE_PUNT	&H00080000
ADS_PRINTER_USER_INTERVENTION	&H00100000
ADS_PRINTER_OUT_OF_MEMORY	&H00200000
ADS_PRINTER_DOOR_OPEN	&H00400000
ADS_PRINTER_SERVER_UNKNOWN	&H00800000
ADS_PRINTER_POWER_SAVE	&H01000000

IADsService and IADsServiceOperations

The `IADsService` object represents and manages the settings for a system service installed on an individual computer. System services are the programs run "behind the scenes" by Windows to perform basic functions such as file sharing, UPS monitoring, event logging, and so on. The object's properties and one method are described in Reference List 8.14. All the `IADsService` properties are read/write, but you must use the `SetInfo` method to commit any changes you make.

`IADsServiceOperations` is an additional interface available on service objects that represent Windows computers. That is, for `IADsService` objects that represent Windows NT, XP, 2000, and .NET Server computers, and possibly NetWare servers as well, there are *additional* properties and methods that you can use to manage the service. The additional properties and methods are described in Reference List 8.15.

Note

You can also manage Windows services with the WMI objects described in Chapter 7. For service management, WMI is probably easier and faster.

REFERENCE LIST 8.14 The Properties and Method of the `IADsService` Object

Properties:

`Dependencies`

An array of strings containing the names of services upon which this service depends (that is, services that must be started first). Each entry in the array consists of "Service:", followed by a service name, or "Group:", followed by a load order group name.

`DisplayName`

The "display" name of the service.

`ErrorControl`

Indicates how Windows should respond if the service fails to start. This property takes one of the values listed in Table 8.7.

`HostComputer`

The name of the computer running this service. It appears to be a read/write property, although I can't quite see what it would mean to change it.

`LoadOrderGroup`

The name of the load order group to which this service belongs.

`Name`

The name of the service object. (This property is inherited from the base `IADs` object.)

`Path`

The path and filename of the executable program that provides this service.

`ServiceAccountName`

The name of the account that the service uses. This is usually `"LocalSystem"` or `"NT AUTHORITY\LocalService"`.

`ServiceAccountPath`

This is purportedly the `ADsPath` string of the account associated with the service that could be used with `GetObject()` to examine the account's properties. However, in ADSI version 2.5, this property appears to be absent.

`ServiceType`

The type of service this program performs. It can one of the following values:

Constant	Value (in Hexadecimal)
ADS_SERVICE_KERNEL_DRIVER	&H01
ADS_SERVICE_FILE_SYSTEM_DRIVER	&H02
ADS_SERVICE_OWN_PROCESS	&H10
ADS_SERVICE_SHARE_PROCESS	&H20

`StartType`
Indicates when, during the Windows boot-up process, the service is started. This can be one of the following values:

Constant	Value (in Hexadecimal)
ADS_SERVICE_BOOT_START	&H00
ADS_SERVICE_SYSTEM_START	&H01
ADS_SERVICE_AUTO_START	&H02
ADS_SERVICE_DEMAND_START	&H03
ADS_SERVICE_DISABLED	&H04

`StartupParameters`
An optional string that is passed as the command-line argument to the service when it is started.

`Version`
The version information for this service.

Method:

`SetInfo`
Saves any changes you have made to the object's properties back to the Windows computer that the object represents.

Table 8.7 lists the values returned by the `ErrorControl` property.

Table 8.7 **Values for the *ErrorControl* Property**

Constant	Value	Error Action
ADS_SERVICE_ERROR_IGNORE	0	Windows logs the error and continues startup.
ADS_SERVICE_ERROR_NORMAL	1	Same as for ADS_SERVICE_ERROR_IGNORE. In addition, the user is notified with a dialog box.
ADS_SERVICE_ERROR_SEVERE	2	Windows logs the error and restarts the system in Last Known Good mode. If the error occurs in Last Known Good mode, startup continues.
ADS_SERVICE_ERROR_CRITICAL	3	Same as for ADS_SERVICE_ERROR_SEVERE, but if the error occurs in Last Known Good mode, as well, startup is halted.

To obtain the list of services installed on an individual computer, you must first obtain an `IADsComputer` object for the individual computer, and then scan through its collection contents looking for `IADsService` objects. The `Filter` property makes this easy:

```
                                        ' Example Script script0815.vbs
set computer = GetObject("WinNT://computername,Computer")
computer.Filter = Array("service") ' limit view to Services only

for each service in computer
   wscript.echo service.name, service.status
next
```

You must have Administrator privileges to view or modify service information.

For objects that represent services on Windows computers, one property and extra methods are available, as part of the `IADsServiceOperations` interface. These are shown in Reference List 8.15.

REFERENCE LIST 8.15 The Property and Methods of the `IADsServiceOperations` Interface

Property:

`Status`
Returns the current status of the service. It can be one of the following values (Read-only):

Constant	Value (in Hexadecimal)
ADS_SERVICE_STOPPED	&H01
ADS_SERVICE_START_PENDING	&H02
ADS_SERVICE_STOP_PENDING	&H03
ADS_SERVICE_RUNNING	&H04
ADS_SERVICE_CONTINUE_PENDING	&H05
ADS_SERVICE_PAUSE_PENDING	&H06
ADS_SERVICE_PAUSED	&H07
ADS_SERVICE_ERROR	&H08

Methods:

`Continue`
Resumes the service after pausing.

`Pause`
Pauses the service.

`SetPassword` *`newpassword`*
Sets the password that is to be used with the service's associated user account.

Start

Starts the service. To restart a service, you need to stop it, wait for its status to equal `ADS_SERVICE_STOPPED`, and then start it again.

Stop

Stops the service.

You must have Administrator privileges to manage services.

IADsSession

The `IADsSession` object represents an active connection between a user on one computer and another computer that is sharing files. The session object describes only the connection between a user and another computer and doesn't contain detailed information (for example, which files are in use). The object's properties, which are all read-only, are shown in Reference List 8.16.

REFERENCE LIST 8.16 Properties of the IADsSession Object

Properties:

Computer

Returns the name of the user's client workstation.

ComputerPath

Returns the `ADsPath` moniker for the computer account, for members of Active Directory networks only.

ConnectTime

Returns the number of minutes since the user connected to the shared resource.

IdleTime

Returns the number of minutes since the user last accessed a shared resource.

User

Returns the name of the user account for this session.

UserPath

Returns the `ADsPath` moniker for the user account; this can be used with `GetObject()` to obtain the corresponding `IADsUser` object.

You can obtain `IADsSession` objects as a collection from the `IADsFileService` object's `Sessions` property. The statements

```
                                ' Example Script script0816.vbs
set fileserv = GetObject("WinNT://computername/Lanmanserver")
if not isempty(fileserv) then
    for each session in fileserv.sessions
        wscript.echo "User:", session.user, "Computer:", _
            session.computer, "idle:", session.idletime, "min"
    next
end if
```

list all the sessions being served by a specific computer. To find the session for a particular user, you have to scan through the collection and test the `User` property for a match to the desired name.

IADsUser

The `IADsUser` object represents a single computer user account in a domain or on an individual workstation. The `IADsUser` object has at least 47 properties and three methods that let you configure the account's username and contact information, set its password, login script, and profile, examine or alter group membership, and reset account lockout after the user has made too many attempts to log on with the wrong password. The Microsoft documentation lists all the properties, and you'll want to examine that documentation if you're going to use ADSI to manage accounts on an Active Directory network.

The most important properties are listed in Reference List 8.17, along with the three methods.

REFERENCE LIST 8.17 Properties and Methods of the `IADsUser` Object

Properties:

`AccountDisabled`
A Boolean value that is `True` if the account has been disabled. You can set this value to disable or enable the account. Remember to use `.SetInfo` after making any changes.

`Description`
The description text for this user account.

`FullName`
The user's full name.

`Groups`
This is an `IADsMembers` collection containing the security groups to which this user belongs. You can manipulate this collection to add or remove groups. See the listing for `IADsMembers` earlier in this section for more information.

`HomeDirectory`
The home directory path for this user.

`IsAccountLocked`
A Boolean value that is `True` if the account has been locked out due to too many attempts to log on with the wrong password.

`LastLogin`
Date and time of last logon to this account. (Read-only.)

LastLogoff

Date and time of the last logoff from this account. (Read-only.)

Profile

The user's profile path; on a local machine this is usually a folder named `\Documents and Settings\`*`username`*. On a domain network with roaming user profiles, this is a path to a shared profile folder.

Methods:

ChangePassword *oldpassword*, *newpassword*

Changes the user's password from *oldpassword* to *newpassword*. You must use `ChangePassword` rather than `SetPassword` and must know the account's old password, if you do not have Administrator privileges.

SetInfo

Saves any changes you've made to the object's properties to the actual Windows user directory. This method is inherited from object `IADs`.

SetPassword *newpassword*

Sets the user account's password to the new string value. The change takes place immediately; you do not have to use `.SetInfo` to make the change permanent. You must have Administrator privileges to use `SetPassword`.

You can obtain a specific user object with the statement

```
set user = GetObject("WinNT://domain/username,user")
```

where *domain* is the account's domain name for a global domain account or the name of an individual workstation for a local or workgroup account, and *username* is the name of the account. You can also create a new domain user account with the following statements:

```
set domain = GetObject("WinNT://domainname")
set user = domain.Create("user", "newusername")
```

You can create a new local workstation account with this:

```
set computer = GetObject("WinNT://computername,Computer")
set user = computer.Create("user", "newusername")
```

You should set all the relevant properties and finalize the account with

```
user.SetInfo
```

and then add the user to any necessary groups and directory containers. Because the `IADsGroup` and `IADsContainer` objects' `Add` method takes a pathname argument, rather than a direct object reference, you'll need to use statements like these:

```
set group = GetObject("WinNT://domainname,groupname,Group")
group.Add user.AdsPath
```

IIS and Exchange

Some of the most powerful applications for ADSI scripting are in the management of Internet Information Services and Microsoft Exchange. For managers of small to mid-size networks, maintaining the comings and goings of multiple Web sites and users can be a tedious job. ADSI scripting can give you a way of adding users or sites by typing one line at the command prompt; if you've ever spent 20 minutes poking at the IIS Manager, the Users and Groups Manager, and Windows Explorer to add one new server, you know what an improvement this would be.

However, it would take several chapters this size or larger just to delve into IIS management, and there simply isn't room to do that in this book. If you become familiar with the material in this chapter and gain experience writing scripts to manage user accounts and services, you'll find that extending your skills to manage IIS and Exchange will be a snap. The ADSI learning curve is steep, but it levels out fairly quickly. I'll show you where to get more information at the end of the chapter.

Managing Active Directory

Managing Active Directory shouldn't be a huge conceptual leap ahead of anything we've discussed so far in this chapter. It's all about containers, about moving little people around in tidy little boxes—a simulacrum of life in the business world—and it's all represented by tidy little objects. What could be so difficult about it? Ah! If the mention of X.500 doesn't strike fear into your heart now, it will within a few minutes.

Because Active Directory is designed to work alongside other manufacturers' operating systems and network services, it was designed to conform to industry-wide standards for networkable directories. This is both a blessing and a curse. In the interest of interoperability, its syntax for specifying users, groups, containers, organizational units, and so forth is based on the X.500 standard, which was designed by a committee—a huge committee. That should give you a big clue right there!

So, before we go into the objects and techniques involved in managing Active Directory, you'll need a quick introduction to X.500 and LDAP terminology.

X.500 and LDAP Terminology

Every item in an X.500 or LDAP-compatible directory has a unique name, just as every file on your hard drive has a unique pathname, and every ADSI object has its `ADsPath`. In LDAP, this is called a *distinguished name*, or DN. A directory object's DN is a full specification, naming this one person, group, computer, or whatever, out of the directory's entire universe of objects. If an Active Directory is organized as shown earlier in Figure 8.1, the user Alice has the following distinguished name:

```
o=mycompany.com/ou=WestCoast/ou=Research/cn=Alice
```

This looks a lot like a file's pathname, except that in a distinguished name, the name at each level of the hierarchy has to be marked with its structural significance: `o` = organization, `ou` = organizational unit, `cn` = common name, and so on. Because containers could conceivably hold different types of objects with the same name, these qualifiers make the path unambiguous.

The name shown above is specified in what's called *Big-Endian form*, because the name starts with the "big" end of the name—the organization. In Little-Endian form, Alice's DN is as follows:

```
cn=Alice, ou=Research, ou=WestCoast, o=mycompany.com
```

You can see that this starts with the little end, the lowest level of the directory organization, and works up toward the top. Active Directory will accept DNs in either format, but always returns them to you in Little Endian form. Because a name could conceivably contain a comma, DNs use a backslash (\) to escape commas in the name. If a username is "Knittel, Alice", for example, the DN might look like this:

```
cn=Knittel\, Alice, ou=Research, ou=WestCoast, o=mycompany.com
```

The parts of a distinguished name are called *relative distinguished names*, or RDNs, because they specify an object relative to the container in which they're held. "Alice" is an RDN because it uniquely specifies a user only within the West Coast Research division; there might be other Alices in other divisions.

The identifiers `cn`, `ou` and `o` are called *attribute names*. Here are the most commonly used attributes in Active Directory distinguished names:

Attribute	Meaning
`dc`	Naming context
`o`	Organization
`ou`	Organizational unit
`l`	Locality
`cn`	Common name (applies to containers, users groups, computers, and so on)

Note

Most of this discussion about the `LDAP:` provider applies to the Novell NetWare Directory Services `NDS:` provider as well, because it is also based on LDAP. Some of the `NDS:` naming attributes differ, however.

Now, hopefully, with this background, it won't be too distressing to see how this works in practice. Given an Active Directory network user's distinguished name, you can obtain an `IADsUser` object using an LDAP moniker like this:

```
set user = GetObject(_
    "LDAP://CN=Alice,OU=Research,OU=WestCoast,O=mycompany.com")
```

This returns the same `IADsUser` object that you would get if you specified this user with her down-level Windows NT domain name, as in

```
set user = GetObject("WinNT://mycompany/alice,User")
```

You can obtain the object representing an organization unit given its DN. Here's an example:

```
set user = GetObject("LDAP://OU=WestCoast,O=mycompany.com")
```

This returns an enhanced version of `IADsContainer` called `IADsOU`, which will be discussed in the next section.

One last bit about constructing distinguished names: In most Active Directory networks, the top-level structure is specified not as `O=mycompany.com` but rather with "naming context" attributes specified in this way:

```
DC=mycompany,DC=com
```

That's the LDAP version of "mycompany.com" in Little-Endian form.

Rather than trying to guess the name of the top level of your organization's network, ADSI provides a way of giving you the top-level distinguished name, called the *Default Naming Context.* The information is obtained from a property of a special object, called the *Root DS Entry*, with this script code:

```
set rootDSE = GetObject("LDAP://RootDSE")
context = rootDSE.Get("DefaultNamingContext")
```

`RootDSE` is discussed in more detail in the next section.

Note

If you want to connect to a specific LDAP server, you can speed up the servicing of ADSI requests by connecting with the `OpenDSObject` method and specifying `ADS_SERVER_BIND` in the flag's argument. See the "Directory Security" section earlier in the chapter for more information.

You must use the `Get` method of the `IADs` object to obtain most special Active Directory object properties, because they are not part of the various `IADs` objects discussed earlier in the chapter. You can use this default context name to construct DNs in organization-independent scripts, as in this example:

```
set rootDSE = GetObject("LDAP://RootDSE")    ' get default naming context
context = rootDSE.Get("DefaultNamingContext")

set westcoast = GetObject("LDAP://OU=WestCoast" & context)
```

This fetches the `WestCoast` container from the top level of the organization, no matter how its top level is named.

Note

Because the Default Naming Context is returned in Little-Endian order, stick it onto the *end* of any DN you're constructing.

The collection of objects in this container can be scanned like any other ADSI enumeration. In fact, you can list the entire contents of Active Directory with a recursive program like this:

```
                                            ' Example Script script0817.vbs
set rootDSE = GetObject("LDAP://RootDSE")   ' get default naming context
context = rootDSE.Get("DefaultNamingContext")

set top = GetObject("LDAP://" & context)    ' get top level container
ListContainer top, 0                        ' start listing at the top

sub ListContainer (obj, depth)              ' subroutine to list a container
    dim member                              ' private local variable

    WScript.echo space(depth*3) & obj.name ' list the container's name

    on error resume next                    ' ignore error if no collection
    for each member in obj                  ' display anything inside
        ListContainer member, depth+1
    next
end sub
```

I have to tell you, though, that if you run this script in a Fortune 500 company, it may take a *long* time to run itself out.

Tip

To get acquainted with the structure of Active Directory, I suggest that you actually do run this script and redirect its output to a file so that you can examine it.

You can also browse through Active Directory with the Microsoft Management Console ADSI Edit plug-in. To use it, click Start, Run and then enter **`mmc`**. Click Console, Add/Remove Snap-In. Add the ADSI Edit snap-in. Click Action, Connect To and select the default LDAP server. You can then browse through Active Directory in its raw form.

For more information about Active Directory, LDAP, and X.500, you may want to visit `msdn.microsoft.com/activedirectory`, `www.kingsmountain.com/ldapRoadmap.shtml`, and probably `www.priloseconline.com/facts` as well.

Active Directory Objects

A few special ADSI objects appear when you work with Active Directory and other LDAP directories. When you try to work with the added Active Directory properties, you may need to use the `Get` and `Put` methods, as shown here, rather than the standard `object.`*`property`* syntax:

```
WScript.echo object.Get("propertyname")
object.Put("propertyname", newvalue)
```

In many cases, the normal syntax you would expect to use does not work and generates a script error. Here's an example:

```
WScript.echo object.propertyname
object.propertyname = newvalue
```

This is a bug in either WSH or ADSI.

RootDSE

The `RootDSE` object describes the properties of the local LDAP server. There is no custom `IADsRootDSE` interface for this object, so you cannot access its properties using the standard `object.`*`property`* syntax. It's based on plain-old `IADs`, so you must use the `Get()` method to retrieve the properties listed in Reference List 8.18.

REFERENCE LIST 8.18 Partial List of the Properties of the `RootDSE` Object

`currentTime`
Current date and time reported by the LDAP server.

`defaultNamingContext`
The default name context ("big end") of all DNs in the local domain.

`dnsHostName`
The current LDAP server's DNS hostname.

`namingContexts`
An array of string values listing the top-level sections of the directory. For Active Directory, these include the following:

- The Default Naming Context
- The DN of the Configuration section, which contains AD's internal configuration information
- The DN of the Schema section, which contains lists of the structure, properties, and allowed values for all directory objects

`rootDomainNamingContext`
The name context ("big end") of all DNs in this directory.

`serverName`
The current LDAP server's DN.

`supportedLDAPVersion`
An array of LDAP version numbers supported by the current server.

You can obtain the RootDSE object with this moniker:

```
set rootDSE = GetObject("LDAP://RootDSE")
```

IADsO and IADsOU

IADsO and IADsOU are objects that represent an entire organization and a subunit of the organization, respectively. They are based on the IADsContainer object, so all of IADsContainer's methods and properties appear as part of IADsO and IADsOU as well. In particular, they both act like collection objects and can contain computers, users, or other container objects. In addition, IADsO and IADsOU inherit the properties of IADsLocality, which describes such items as the local fax and telephone numbers.

For simplicity's sake, I've listed all the combined methods and properties available for these objects.

The properties and methods of IADsO and IADsOU are described in Reference List 8.19. The IADsOU object represents a subpart of an organization and has the same set of properties as IADsO, with the addition of BusinessCategory.

REFERENCE LIST 8.19 Properties and Methods of the IADsO and IADsOU Objects

Properties:

BusinessCategory
Describes the business function performed by this organizational unit. (IADsOU only.)

Count
The number of subobjects in the container (from IADsContainer; read-only).

Description
A string describing the organization or unit (for example, the company name).

FaxNumber
A string describing the primary fax number.

Filter
See IADsContainer.

LocalityName
A string describing the physical location of the organization or unit.

Name
The name of the container. (This property is inherited from the base IADs object.)

Parent
The ADsPath name of the container that holds this object (also inherited from IADs).

continues

REFERENCE LIST 8.19 Continued

PostalAddress

A string giving the primary mailing address.

SeeAlso

Any additional pertinent information.

TelephoneNumber

The organization or unit's primary telephone number.

Methods:

See `IADsContainer`

You can obtain `IADsO` and `IADsOU` objects using their distinguished names or by scanning other containers, as described earlier in this section.

Developing ADSI Scripts

Throughout this chapter, I've provided scriptlets that you can modify and test to get acquainted with ADSI. These short scripts list the members of groups and individual properties. You can write more useful scripts by extending these beginnings with additional functions.

It's especially useful to write scripts that take arguments from the command line. You can use this technique to write scripts in a general-purpose fashion, and you'll only need to specify the particulars on the command line when you run the script.

For example, on a small peer-to-peer workgroup network that doesn't use Simple File Sharing, it's useful for every user to have an account on each computer, with the same password on each. When a user changes his or her password, the password has to be changed on every computer—a real hassle. The following script can make this an easy job:

```
' allpass.vbs - change a password on all computers in the group

if WScript.Arguments.count <> 3 then  ' explain the command syntax
    WScript.echo "Usage: allpass username oldpassword newpassword"
    WScript.quit 0
end if
username = WScript.Arguments(0)        ' store the values
oldpass  = WScript.Arguments(1)
newpass  = WScript.Arguments(2)

Wscript.echo "Working..."              ' it may take a while, show we're alive

fix "bali"                             ' call fix once for each of the
fix "java"                             ' workgroup's computers.
fix "sumatra"
```

```
fix "ambon"
fix "kalimantan"

wscript.echo "Done."

sub fix (compname)                      ' subroutine to update one computer
    on error resume next                ' get user object
    set user = GetObject("WinNT://" & compname & "/" & username & ",User")
    if err then                         ' failed; tell them
        wscript.echo "Unable to change password on", compname
        exit sub
    end if
    user.changePassword oldpass, newpass
    if err then
        wscript.echo "Unable to change password on", compname
        exit sub
    end if
    user.setinfo   ' changePassword is immediate but best be sure
    wscript.echo compname & ": OK"
end sub
```

For example, when I typed the command

```
allpass bknittel myoldpassword anewpassword
```

this is what printed:

```
Working...
bali: OK
java: OK
sumatra: OK
ambon: OK
Unable to change password on kalimantan
Done.
```

This is reasonable, because the computer named kalimantan was not turned on. That computer will have to be updated manually.

Caution

I suggest that when you start using ADSI to create and modify directory information, you develop your scripts on an isolated test computer and not your company's network. You'll need to be logged on with Administrator privileges, and if things go wrong, the damage could be catastrophic.

For More Information

This chapter has just touched on ADSI's capabilities. If you've found this interesting so far, I definitely encourage you to get more information. As with the previous chapter on Windows Management Instrumentation, the material in this chapter should be enough to show you how this stuff actually works and to give you enough background to make effective use of the Microsoft documentation that covers ADSI in its entirety.

On the Web, you can find Microsoft's online documentation at `msdn.microsoft.com`. Search for "Platform SDK: Active Directory Service Interfaces SDK" (without the quotes). From there you can view tutorials, information about the ADSI internals, and the ADSI Reference, which lists all the `WinNT:` provider's ADSI objects, properties, and methods. For Active Directory information, visit `msdn.microsoft.com/activedirectory`.

The current version of ADSI is 2.5, and you can download the most current ADSI program code and documentation from Microsoft's Web site. Search `msdn.microsoft.com` for "Download ADSI 2.5" to find it. Having the documentation on your own computer, rather than browsing it over the Net, will speed things up considerably. You probably don't need to download or update the ADSI software, however.

Note

Be sure to read the section "Important Notes Regarding the Microsoft Documentation" earlier in the chapter.

You can also find many Web sites that discuss ADSI scripting. A Google.com search for "getobject winnt" will give you enough to keep you busy for several days!

Microsoft's public newsgroup for ADSI programming support is `microsoft.public.adsi.general`. I found that, like the comparable groups for Windows Management Instrumentation support, a high proportion of user questions get answered promptly here, but the topics discussed on this newsgroup tend toward the esoteric. Most of the discussion centers on the `LDAP:` provider, because most visitors are working with or trying to work with Active Directory. So, you may not find this newsgroup to be as rich a source of useful information as the WMI group, unless you want to (or have to) commit yourself to getting into the most arcane parts of ADSI.

For a printed reference, I recommend *Windows NT/200 ADSI Scripting for System Administration* by Thomas Eck, published by New Riders Publishing. It's well written and is full of useful sample scripts, presented cookbook style. Some of the examples are a bit too trivial, but it does do a good job of showing each ADSI object in action.

For more information about using ADSI for IIS management, visit `msdn.microsoft.com` and search for "IIS Admin Objects Reference." You can find tutorials and sample scripts on the Web by searching for the IIS object names listed earlier in Table 8.3.

9

Creating Your Own Scriptable Objects

ROAD MAP

- Creating your own objects makes it easier to reuse already-debugged code later.
- You can also create objects to present your own simplified interfaces to complex Windows management tools.
- You can easily create your objects using VBScript or JScript in Windows Script Component (WSC) files.
- WSC files use XML formatting to define both the object's interface and its script implementation.

Why Create Your Own Objects?

WE'VE SPENT THE LAST SIX CHAPTERS discussing just a few of the scriptable objects provided with Windows XP. Now, in this chapter, I'll show you how to create objects of your own.

Why would you want to do this? Well, remember what objects are about: They do a particular job while hiding the details of how the job is actually accomplished. It turns out that using this "divide and conquer" approach has three advantages:

- Faster development and debugging
- Simplification of the scripts and programs that use objects
- Code reusability

Let's look at these advantages one by one. First, when you're creating a new object, your immediate task is simply to make sure that the object does what it is supposed to do and that its methods and properties do the right thing. Your coding and debugging job is to write a small program to perform a particular, discrete task, which is easier than writing and debugging a huge script with all the steps necessary to attack some larger job.

Second, after your new object has been added to the Windows repertoire and you are writing a script to do some larger maintenance task, you can focus on this larger task without worrying about the details that are embedded in the object. Because objects are off "somewhere else," your WSH scripts are smaller and easier to write and debug.

Third, you can use a new object's capabilities in many different scripts without repeating the object's code in each of them. When you find a bug or need to change the way things work, you only have to modify one program, not several.

Why do objects make it easier to write more reliable programs? Objects can protect the data they hold. An object lets you change its data only on the *object's* terms. For example, whereas you can change a script variable's value willy-nilly, an object can intercept attempts to change a property and can determine whether the value you want to assign is legitimate. The variables that actually hold the property's value can only be changed from inside the object's program. It's easier to write correct programs when you can limit what parts of the program have access to your data.

Another good reason to write an object is to provide a new data type for your scripts to use. VBScript provides numbers and text strings and has tools to manipulate them, but when you work with more concrete information such as people's names, computers' IP addresses, and soon you'll find yourself doing the same things over and over: combining first and last names into proper names, validating that an entered IP address is correctly formatted, and so on. Objects let you write one program to do these things that you can take advantage of in scripts, Word macros, C programs—in other words, in any language that can use COM objects.

Finally, you can create a new object that either extends or simplifies the capabilities of an existing object. This is called *subclassing*, and you can use this to add new properties or methods to an object like the built-in `WScript.Network`. The new object can simply pass on most properties and methods to an instance of the original object and only needs to handle the ones it has added.

Programming Language Options

The technical term for an object that is usable in Windows Script Host programs is *Automation object*. An Automation object has several required attributes:

- It's based on the Common Object Model (COM). This means it has a standard interface that lets other Windows programs gain access to its properties and methods.
- Other programs can "query" the object about its methods and properties. The software has a built-in mechanism for describing its interfaces so that any external program can find out what properties and methods are available, what arguments they take, and what sorts of data values are returned.

- An object is implemented as a program that represents the object's class; that is, one program takes care of all instances of a given object type.
- The class program has functions to return each of the object's property values, and it has subroutines that accept new values to assign to the object's properties.
- A class program has subroutines or functions to implement each of the object's methods. These may take arguments and may return values.

Several languages can be used to create Automation objects. The most common are C++, Visual Basic, VBScript, and JScript.

VBScript and JScript

Windows Script Host lets you write object programs in VBScript or JScript. This is the easiest way to create new objects. Of course, there are some limitations:

- The objects can't do anything that you can't do with Windows Script Host. For example, the nitty-gritty power of the core Windows Application Program Interface (API) routines is not available.
- The objects run in an interpreted language, so they're somewhat slower than objects created with a compiled language.
- The objects don't stand by themselves; they require that Windows Script Host be installed on any computer where they're to be used.

Still, you can use WSH to create useful objects. I'll spend most of this chapter showing you how.

Visual Basic

Visual Basic is a popular language for COM/Automation object programming. Visual Basic is a superset of the VBScript language: It's largely the same but has additional powerful features. It has access to the entire Windows API, which means Visual Basic programs can take advantage of any facility Windows offers, from networking and cryptographic encoding to graphical display and database access. Because Visual Basic is a compiled language, object programs are fast. It is designed with COM in mind, so as with VBScript, creating and using objects is very easy. These are significant advantages over VBScript and other programming languages, but there are some downsides as well. First, whereas VBScript is free, you have to buy Visual Basic, and it can cost $250 or more, depending on what other software you purchase with it. (Academic versions are less expensive.) It's also more complex than VBScript, and this makes the learning curve steeper.

Visual Basic is the language of choice for entry-level programmers who need the simplicity of the Visual Basic language but require access to Windows API functions or the higher speed of a compiled language.

C and C++

C and C++ are the old standby programming languages of systems programmers. They produce fast, efficient programs, they have very low-level access to all parts of Windows, and they are considered somewhat more "highbrow" than Visual Basic. However, Microsoft's C/C++ programming environment for Windows is also not free, it's not easy to learn, and working with COM objects in C and C++ can be a huge pain.

If you want to create low-level objects, or fast, compiled objects, I suggest that you visit your local bookstore and look through the two or three shelves of books devoted to COM programming before deciding which language to use.

If you want to see how to create simpler, yet still useful objects with Windows Script host, read on.

Creating Objects with WSC Files

We've been working with objects from the scripting side for the last six chapters. Now, we'll change our viewpoint to the other side—the implementation of the object itself. In the remainder of this chapter, I'll show you how to create objects using Windows Script Host. Here, I'll focus on the basics of object programs using the Windows Script Component technology provided with Windows Script Host, and again, with advance apologies to JScript programmers, the examples will be written in VBScript.

Note

If you've downloaded Windows Script Host version 5.6 and its documentation from `msdn.microsoft.com`, you can find more information on WSC files in the downloaded documentation in the section "How Script Components Work."

An object based on Windows Script Host uses a script program with the usual parts: variables, functions, and subroutines. The script's global variables hold the object's data (its property values), and the script's functions and subroutines serve as the interface between outside programs and the object. They implement the object's methods and properties.

When a client program (that is, a script or other program that wants to use your object) asks Windows to create an instance of your object, Windows locates your Windows Script Component file and runs the script inside. The script's variables hold the data for each instance of the object. If client programs create more than one instance, you don't have to worry about keeping track of what data goes with which instance—Windows Script Host takes care of this for you. Each time an object is created, Windows Script Host sets aside memory to hold all the script's variables. Figure 9.1 shows how this works.

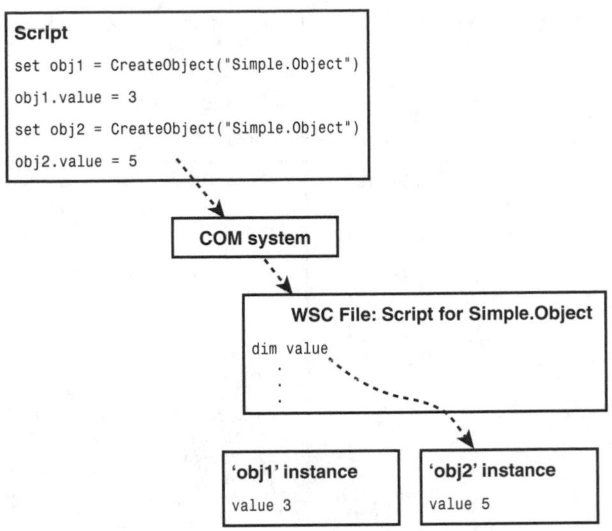
Script
set obj1 = CreateObject("Simple.Object")
obj1.value = 3
set obj2 = CreateObject("Simple.Object")
obj2.value = 5
COM system
WSC File: Script for Simple.Object
dim value
'obj1' instance
value 3
'obj2' instance
value 5

Figure 9.1 WSC objects use a script to implement methods and properties, and they use global variables to hold the data for each object instance.

Each object gets its own separate copy of all the variables, so the script doesn't have to worry about keeping track of what data goes with which object instance.

WSC File Format

Objects based on scripts have to be packaged up in a file with the extension `.wsc`, which stands for Windows Script Component. So, for the rest of this chapter, I'll refer to script-based objects as "WSC objects" and the script files as "WSC files."

A WSC file contains the script that manages your object and additional information that Windows uses to tell client programs or scripts just how your object works: what properties it has, what methods are available, and what arguments they take. The file is structured as an Extensible Markup Language (XML) file. The various parts of the file are marked with *tags* that make XML files look a lot like the HTML files used to create Web pages.

Let's start this discussion by looking at a simple object that has one property named `value`, which can contain any number, and one method named `multiply`, which multiplies the property by some factor. Here's how a client script might *use* such an object:

```
set obj = CreateObject("Simple.Object")  ' create the object

obj.value = 3                            ' set the property to 3
obj.multiply 4                           ' use the method to multiply by 4
wscript.echo "Result:", obj.value        ' print the property's value
```

This should be familiar and sensible, after all the objects we've worked with in the last six chapters.

Now, for the other side: Figure 9.2 shows a WSC file that implements this object.

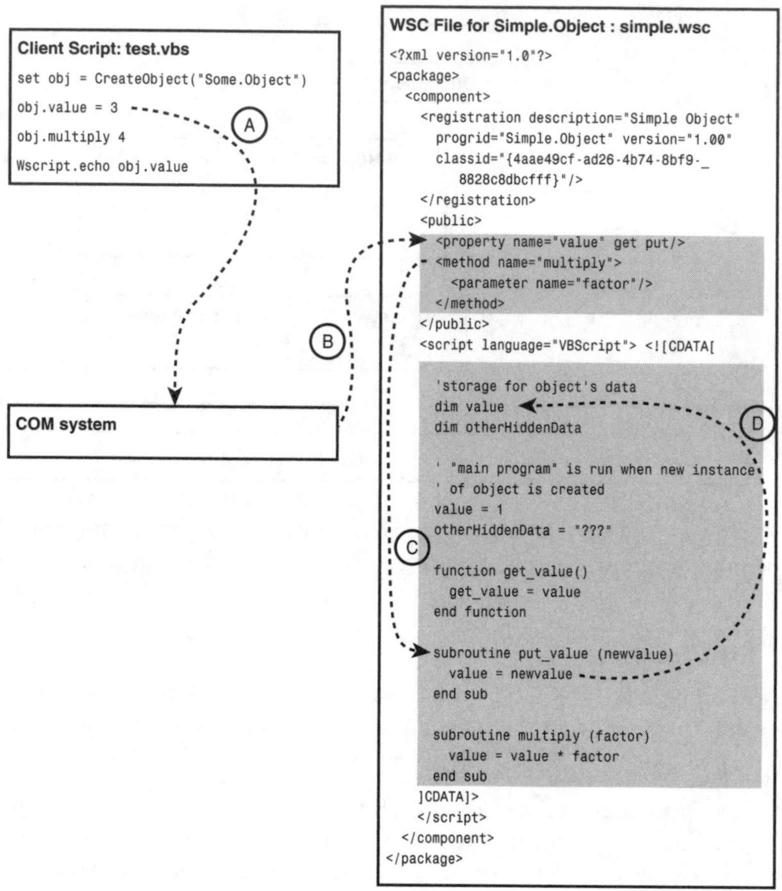

Figure 9.2 A WSC file defines an object's properties and methods, and it contains a script to implement them.

Let's take a look at this file, bit by bit, to see how it works. Two parts of the file are shaded in gray. The first is the descriptive part that tells Windows what properties and methods the object has. The second is the script itself—the program that makes the object work. Let's follow what happens when the client script sets the object's `value` property to `3`, as illustrated in Figure 9.2:

A. The client script tells the object to set its `value` property to `3`. This request is passed to the Windows COM system.

B. COM identifies the WSC file that is associated with this object and passes along the request. Windows Script Host examines the script's property definitions and finds that there is indeed a property named `value`, that writing to it is acceptable, and that because no alternate subroutine name is specified, the new property value is to be passed to a subroutine named `put_value`.

C. Subroutine `put_value` is called with the value `3` as its argument. The script assigns this new property value to the global variable `value`.

D. The number `3` is stored in `value`, which is located in the memory set aside for just this object instance.

Reading properties or calling methods follows a similar sequence. Note that in this scheme, the object's program maintains its data, and the calling script or program cannot access the object's variables directly. All the work is done by the object's methods and procedures. The object therefore has complete control over its little universe.

XML Basics

If you look again at the WSC file contents in Figure 9.2, besides the VBScript program you'll see other text surrounding it. If you've ever created Web pages or looked at the Hypertext Markup Language (HTML) files that describe them, you may notice that the contents of a WSC file are similar. The format is called *XML*. Before we go into the details of this example, we need a crash course in XML terminology. You'll run into several of XML's specialized terms if you read the Microsoft documentation for WSC files.

Items such as `<public>` are called *tags*. Tags are enclosed in angle brackets (`< >`) and can contain descriptive values within them called *attributes* (such as `name="value"`). Tags can enclose text or other information—a tag such as `<public>` has a corresponding *end tag*, which is written `</public>`. Anything between a tag and its end tag is the tag's *content*. For example, the content between `<public>` and its end tag `</public>` describes what must be made available to programs that want to use the object. In XML lingo, a tag and its content together are called an *element*.

Not every element has to have content. XML requires you to use special markup for a tag with no content and no end tag (in this case, the tag has to end with `/>`). You can see this in the `<property/>` and `<parameter/>` tags. The `/>` at the end means there is no corresponding end tag, and no content.

Caution

If you're accustomed to working with HTML, beware. HTML allows much flexibility on this point, but in XML every tag *must* either have a matching end tag, or end with `/>` to indicate that there is no end tag.

Now look at the <registration> tag. It has a several attributes, but no content. There's just the tag followed immediately by its end tag. Could I have written <registration description=.../> and omitted </registration>? Yes, but this version is also correct. In this case, it appears this way because the Windows Script Component Wizard, which is discussed in the next section, wrote the bulk of this particular script, and it used the lengthier version.

The strange tag that starts with <?xml is called a *directive*. Directives don't have end tags because they're technically not really tags, and they never enclose content. They provide special information about how the XML is to be interpreted.

In general, XML doesn't care about extra blank lines, spaces inside tags, or the capitalization of tag and attribute names. To an XML application, <tag>something</tag> and

```
<tag>
something
</tag>
```

are equivalent, as are <tag> and <TAG> as well as <tag> and < tag >. Usually, attribute values are enclosed in quotation marks (' or "), but if an attribute value has no embedded spaces, XML will tolerate <tag attribute=something> as well as <tag attribute="something">. For the value "something else" you'd need the quotes.

However, if you put the <?xml?> directive in the first line of an XML file, this tells the XML application that it is to use *strict compliance* rules, thus making formatting requirements much stricter. This is a good thing, because it's easier for Windows and XML editing programs to detect errors. This topic is discussed later in the chapter under "WSC File Format Reference."

Understanding the Example

Now, let's look back at the sample object script. The <package> element encloses the whole file. Everything inside the <component> element describes a single object. A WSC file can have several <component> elements, each of which manages a separate object type.

The <registration> element gives the object its name, its progid (which other programs must use in calls to CreateObject), its version number, and its classid. A classid consists of long, essentially random numbers that distinguish one object from all others in the world. You don't need to make these numbers up: The Component Wizard we'll discuss shortly will provide one for you. All this information is ultimately stored in the Windows Registry so that a program can say CreateObject("Simple.Object") and Windows will know to run your script.

The <public> element lists all the object's properties and methods, which are described by the <property> and <method> elements it contains.

Note

An object can also define *events*, which provide a way for the object to trigger subroutines in the calling program when the object deems it necessary. Events are often used in Web server and Web browser scripts. However, they're not as useful in WSH scripts and therefore are not covered in this book.

The markup for the `value` property has the attributes `get` and `put`, which indicate that the value can be read and written, respectively. That is, it's a read/write property. The markup for the `multiply` method lists one parameter: `factor`. Notice that the data types are not specified as Integer, String, or other types. For WSC objects, all parameters and return values are type Variant.

The `<public>` information is made available to any program that wants to use `Simple.Object`.

Finally, there is the script itself—the program that actually implements the object. The strange `<![CDATA[` tag and its end tag, `]]>`, tell XML that what's inside is not XML but rather "private" data for Windows Script Host. Otherwise, XML might interpret the < and > symbols in the program as XML tag markers.

The program itself is fairly straightforward. The script's "main program" is run when an object of this type is created. Here, the script declares a global variable `value` and initializes it to `1`. This variable holds the object's one property.

The script has the functions `get_value` and `put_value`, which return and set the property, respectively. These are called *accessor* functions, and they're invoked by WSH when a client program using this object uses or assigns to the property. In this script, the "get" subroutine return's the property's value from the variable it's kept in, and the "put" subroutine only has to store a new value in the variable.

Finally, the subroutine `multiply` takes care of the multiply method.

Once the script component has been registered by typing

```
regsvr32 file://c:\path\simple.wsc
```

at the command prompt (I'll discuss this later, just accept it as a magical incantation for now), it even works. Here's the sample client script shown earlier:

```
                                      ' Example script script0901.vbs
set obj = CreateObject("Simple.Object")   ' create the object

obj.value = 3                         ' set the property to 3
obj.multiply 4                        ' use the method to multiply by 4
wscript.echo "Result:", obj.value     ' print the property's value
```

It prints out the value `12`, just as it should. Here's a more complex client script:

```
                                        ' Example script script0902.vbs
set obj1 = CreateObject("Simple.Object")  ' create an object
set obj2 = CreateObject("Simple.Object")  ' create another instance
```

```
obj1.value = 3                          ' set the properties to different
obj2.value = 5                          ' values

wscript.echo "value 1:", obj1.value
wscript.echo "value 2:", obj2.value
```

It prints `3` and `5`, proving that there really are two separate instances of the object and of the script's variable `value`.

WSC File Format Reference

The overall structure of a WSC file is shown here. Not every one of these directives and elements must be used in every case; this listing just shows the ordering that is usually used:

```
<?xml?>              <!-- optional                                              -->
<package>            <!-- required only if there is more than one component    -->
  <comment>          <!-- can appear anywhere in the file                      -->
  <component>        <!-- there can be more than one component element         -->
    <?component?>    <!-- optional                                              -->
    <public>         <!-- there can be any number of property, method, element -->
      <property><get/><put/></property>...
      <method><parameter/>...</method>...
      <event>...
    </public>
    <registration>
    <object/>...       <!-- zero or more                                        -->
    <reference/>...    <!-- zero or more                                        -->
    <resource>...      <!-- zero or more                                        -->
    <script>
  </component>...      <!-- can be followed by another component               -->
</package>
```

Reference List 9.1 describes all these tags and their attributes.

First, however, here are some notes on the syntax descriptions in Reference List 9.1:

- Text in `this typeface` is typed literally; text in *`italics`* is replaced with an appropriate name or value.
- Square brackets, [ ], enclose optional items; curly brackets, { }, indicate a set of alternate choices that are separated by vertical bars, |, and ellipses, …, indicate that the previous item may be repeated any number of times.
- XML ignores extra whitespace or line breaks between tags, attributes, or elements. However, text inside `<description>`, `<resource>`, `<helptext>`, and other display elements is displayed literally, so you may want to type such text in a concise format. For example, you would type

```
<description>text goes here</description>
```

rather than

```
<description>
    text goes here
</description>
```

In the latter case, the carriage returns and indenting spaces would be printed when the script prints its usage information.

- This reference only lists WSC elements appropriate for scripting of objects for use with Windows Script Host. Elements used only when creating objects for ASP scripting and DHTML Web pages are not listed.

REFERENCE LIST 9.1 WSC Tag Listing

`<?XML Version="1.0"` `[standalone="yes"]>`

The `<?XML?>` element requests that the WSH interpreter perform strict XML validation. With validation enabled, XML's stringent formatting and interpretation rules are applied. "Strict" mode is usually required when you will be editing the WSC or WSF file with an XML editor.

Strict mode affects the interpretation of the file in the following ways:

- **Case sensitivity**. In strict mode, element names and attribute names are case sensitive. In the default mode, case is ignored.
- **Attribute quotation**. In strict mode, all attribute values must be enclosed in single (`'`) or double (`"`) quotes. In the default mode, quotes are required only when the attribute value has embedded spaces.
- **Opacity**. In strict mode, the XML parser can "see" into the `<script>` element. Therefore, the content of each `<script>` element (script program code in VBScript, JScript, or another scripting language) must be enclosed in a `<![CDATA[ ... ]]>` section to prevent its being interpreted as XML. In the default mode, `<script>` elements are opaque: The parser does not look into them, and the `<![CDATA [ ... ]]>` tag must not be used inside them.

If present, the `<?XML?>` element must be the first line in the file and must not be preceded by blank lines. The `version` number should be specified as `1.0`. The optional `standalone` attribute indicates that the XML file does not reference an external Document Type Definition (DTD) and can be omitted or specified as `"yes"`.

`<?component error="`*`value`*`" debug="`*`value`*`" ?>`

Enables the reporting of error messages from and the debugging of the component's script. By default, errors are *not* reported and debugging of component scripts is *not* enabled. The `<?Component?>` element lets you alter this default behavior by specifying `True` or `False` to enable or disable error message reporting and debugging with the Windows Script Debugger or an equivalent script debugger.

continues

REFERENCE LIST 9.1 Continued

Place this directive as the first item inside the <component> element.

```
<! [CDATA[
    protected text
    .
    .
    .
]]>
```

The CDATA section encapsulates script code inside a <script> element and indicates that it is not to be treated as XML markup. The CDATA section is used only in conjunction with the <?XML?> directive; without <?XML?>, the presence of CDATA markup will generate a syntax error.

```
<!-- any text
    .
    .
    .
-->
```

Anything inside <!-- ... --> is treated as comment text, including any XML markup. This can be used to comment out blocks of code during testing or to enter comments or descriptive information. The <comment> element can also be used to enclose comments, but <comment> cannot contain any XML tags or other markup.

```
<comment>
    any text
    .
    .
    .
</comment>
```

Indicates comment text that is to be ignored by the parser. You can embed multiple lines in a comment, but not XML tags.

```
<component [id="componentID"]>
    component definition: <registration>, <public>,
    and <script> elements
    .
    .
    .
</component>
```

Encapsulates the definition of a Windows Script Component (object). If an id is specified, this is the name that will appear as the class name in object browsers. The default value for id is "ComponentCoClass". If multiple components are defined in one WSC file, the <component> elements must be enclosed in a <package> element, and each component must have a distinct id property.

```
<event name="name" [dispid="id"]/>
```

Defines an event that the object can generate. Events are beyond the scope of this book.

```
<get [internalName="functionname"]/>
```

Used inside of a property element and indicates that the property is readable and that a function supplies the value. When the object client's program requests the value of the property, WSH calls the function `get_propertyname()`, which must be defined in the script. An alternate function can be specified with the `internalName` attribute.

```
<method name="methodname" [internalName="functionname"]
 [dispid="dispID"]>
    [<parameter name="paramname"/>...]
</method>
```

Declares a method that the object provides. This tag is placed inside `<public>`. The associated script must implement a function or subroutine of the same name as the method, or you may specify an alternate name with the `internalName` attribute. In either case, the procedure must exist; otherwise, WSH generates an error. The method's arguments are specified by `<parameter/>` tags placed between `<method>` and `</method>`.

One method may be designated the default method by specifying attribute `dispid="0"`. For more information about declaring methods, see "Defining Properties and Methods" later in the chapter.

```
<object id="name" (classid="clsid:GUID" | progid="progid")
   events="boolval"/>
```

Creates an instance of a specified object, in a global variable of the indicated *name*, as if you had used the statement `set name=createObject (progid)`. You must specify either the object's `progid` name (for example, `"Scripting.FileSystemObject"`) or its `classid`. Be sure to close the object tag with `/>`.

The `events` attribute specifies whether the script is prepared to handle events fired by the object. Events are beyond the scope of this book.

```
<package>
    one or more <component> elements
    .
    .
    .
</package>
```

Encloses one or more separate components in a WSC file. The `<package>` element is optional when the file contains only one component.

```
<property name="propertyname" [internalName="varname"]/>
              or
<property name="propertyname" [get] [put]/>
              or
<property name="propertyname">
    [<get [internalName="functionname"]/>]
    [<put [internalName="subroutinename"]/>]
</property>
```

Declares a property provided by the object. This tag is used inside `<public>`.

continues

REFERENCE LIST 9.1 Continued

If neither `get` nor `put` are specified as attributes or as tags, the property is bound to a variable of the same name as the property and is read/write. This is the first syntax form shown. You can specify a different variable with the `internalName` attribute.

If you wish to use accessor functions, the property must be designated as readable and/or writable with `get` and/or `put` either as attribute names or as `<get/>` and/or `<put/>` tags, using one of the other two forms shown.

By default, the property is read by function `get_propertyname()` and written by subroutine `put_propertyname(newvalue)`, but alternate names can be specified with the `<get/>` and/or `<put/>` tags.

For more information about specifying properties, see "Defining Properties and Methods" later in the chapter.

```
<public>
    Interface definition: <property>, <method>, <event> tags
</public>
```

The public element contains `<property>`, `<method>`, and/or `<event>` tags to define the public interface of your object.

Every property and method listed in the interface definition *must* correspond to an actual variable or function in the script code, even if the methods or properties are never actually used, as mentioned under `<method>` and `<property>`.

```
<put [internalName="subroutinename"]/>
```

Used inside of a property element and indicates that the property is writable by a function or subroutine. When the object client's program assigns a new value to the property, WSH will call `put_propertyname(newvalue)` with the new value as its argument. An alternate procedure name can be specified with the `internalName` attribute.

```
<reference (object="progid" | guid="GUID")
    [version="version"]/>
```

Instructs WSH to load the type library for a specified object. In effect, this loads all the predefined constants associated with an object type. The object can be specified by its `progid` name (for example, to load the WMI constants, `object="WbemScripting.SWbemLocator"`) or its GUID number. By default, WSH will load the most recent version of the object class, but if necessary, you can specify an older version with the `version` attribute. Be sure to close the tag with `/>`.

```
<registration progid="progid" [classid="GUID"]
    [description="text"] [version="number"]
    [remotable="value"]>
  [<script>
      <! [CDATA[
      registration and unregistration script
      ]]>
   </script>]
</registration>
```

Defines the attributes necessary to register the object with Windows. This information is used by the `regsvr32` command, which is described later in the chapter. Here are the attributes:

- `progid`. The text name for this object. It is used, for example, by client programs in calls to `CreateObject()`. The usual form for a `progid` is `"category.objectType"`, where `category` is a name that describes an entire category of object type (for instance, `"MyObjects"`) and `objecttype` specifies a particular object. This is entirely up to you, but you must be sure that the name you choose doesn't conflict with an existing object. To check, run `regedit` and look under `HKEY_CLASSES` to be sure that you don't see the name you want to use.
- `classid`. The class ID number for this object (a string with lots of numbers inside curly braces). If you omit this, the script registration program that I'll describe later will create one when it installs the script component. However, it's best to specify one so that the `classid` is the same on every computer on which your object is installed. The easiest way to get a valid GUID is to use the Windows Script Component Wizard to create a skeleton WSC file. If you have Microsoft Visual Studio, you can also use the GUIDGEN program—if you do, select Registry Form. But do not attempt to make up a GUID!
- `description`. A brief description of the purpose of the object. This information is displayed in object browsers.
- `version`. The version number for this object ("1"). If you make changes to an object that are not backward-compatible and have programs or scripts that depend on the old object's behavior, you can create different versions of the same object in different WSC files or different `<component>` elements, and have them all available. If you specify a version number, use only digits (no decimal points or other characters).
- `remotable`. Can be specified with the value `"True"` if you wish to allow this object to be created by remote scripts using the remote server version of the `CreateObject` function. When the WSC script is installed on a given computer, `remotable="True"` makes it possible for the WSC script to be activated by scripts or programs running on *other* computers.

Normally, the attributes of the `<registration>` tag are enough to let Windows register and use the object. When this is the case, you can use the `<registration` *`attributes`* `/>` form of the tag and omit the `</registration>` end tag.

If you need to perform additional actions when the object is installed—for example, if the object depends on finding certain Registry entries—you can specify a script to be run when the object is registered and unregistered. The registration script should be placed inside a `<script>` element between `<registration>` and `</registration>`. If the registration script defines a function named `register()`, it will be run when the object is registered. The function can install Registry keys, check for the existence of required files, and so on. If the script defines a function

continues

REFERENCE LIST 9.1 Continued

named `unregister()`, it will be run when the object is unregistered. This function can remove Registry information, although doing so is probably unnecessary.

WSC objects can be registered with Windows with the following command at the Windows command prompt:

```
regsvr32 file://drive:path/filename.wsc
```

```
<resource id="resourceid"><![CDATA[text or number]]>
</resource>
```

or

```
<resource id="resourceid">text or number</resource>
```

Creates a named value that can be retrieved in the script using the `GetResource()` function. `<resource>` tags provide a way to concentrate all language-specific text in one place in the file so that alternate language versions can be created at a later date. A `<resource>` tag assigns a name ***resourceid*** to some text or numeric data. The ***resourceid*** string is passed to `GetResource()` to retrieve the data into the script. The content should be encased in `<![CDATA[ ... ]]>` if the WSC file uses strict XML compliance. For more information about `<resource>`, see "Defining Resources" later in the chapter.

```
<script [language="name"]>
<![CDATA[
    script code
    .
    .
    .
]]>
</script>
```

This element contains the actual script program that includes the object's initialization procedure, methods, properties, and any additional subroutines and functions necessary. You may specify the script language; the default is `"VBScript"`.

If you used the `<?xml?>` strict-compliance directive at the top of your script, you should enclose the script inside `<![CDATA[` and `]]>` to prevent any `<` or `>` characters in your script from being interpreted as tags. If you did not use the `<?xml?>` directive, do not use `<![CDATA[` and `]]>`.

Creating a WSC Component

The first step in creating a WSC component is, of course, deciding what you want your object to do. You should spend some time thinking about what its properties should be and what its methods should do. You may even have some script programs already written that do most of the work that the object will be doing. Once you've made your design, the next step is to create the WSC file that will contain your object's property and method definitions, and the script program itself.

Setting up even a simple WSC object is pretty tricky; there's a lot to type, every tag has to have its proper end mark or end tag, and every *i* has to be dotted and *t* crossed. Thankfully, Microsoft has a wizard program that gives you correctly formatted WSC files for your objects; all you have to do is fill in the program steps for the methods and procedures.

Using the Windows Script Component Wizard

You can download the wizard from `msdn.microsoft.com`. Search for "Windows Script Component Wizard" (with the quotes). Follow the download and installation instructions you'll find there. When you install the wizard, it appears on your Start menu under All Programs, Microsoft Windows Script, Windows Script Component Wizard.

The wizard displays six screens, requesting the following information:

- The name to give the object and the WSC file, the object's desired `progid` (the name you want to use in `CreateObject` calls), and the version number, as shown in Figure 9.3.
- The language to use (VBScript or JScript), whether to enable the "implements" feature for DHTML and ASP scripting (this is not applicable to WSC objects), and whether to enable error checking and debugging. Be sure to check both Error Checking and Debugging when you are creating a new object.
- Properties to define, their read/write attributes, and their default values, as shown in Figure 9.4.
- Methods to define and their argument names, if any.
- Events to define, which are not discussed in this book.

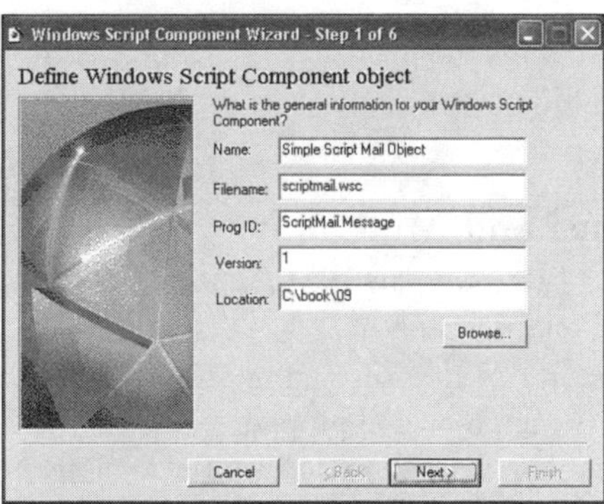

Figure 9.3 The general information page lets you assign the name and `progid` for the object.

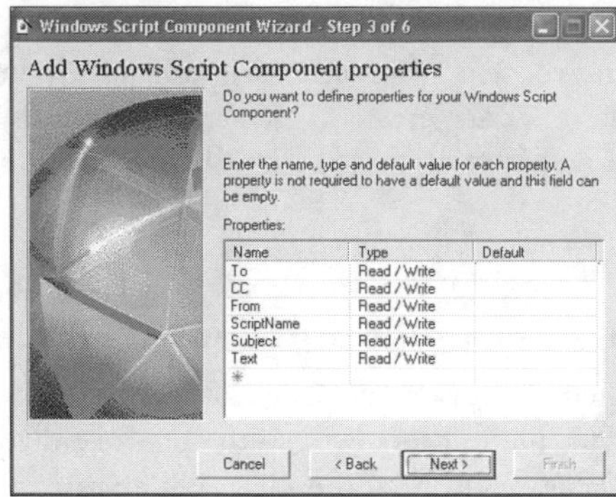

Figure 9.4 The properties form lets you define properties and set initial (default) values.

The last screen lets you confirm the information entered. When you click Finish, the wizard writes a `.WSC` file with proper XML tags to define the properties and methods you defined. The script section contains definitions of variables to hold the properties and basic `get_`, `put_`, and methods functions, followed by any additional helper functions and subroutines you want to use. All you have to do is flesh out these functions to get a working object.

Tip

When you're first writing and debugging a script, the `<?component error="yes" debug="yes"?>` element enables script debugging. If you're using VBScript, you can use the `stop` statement in your procedures, which will stop the script program and activate the script debugger. You can then trace through the script and use breakpoints to help debug it.

In the next sections, I'll discuss the formatted XML needed to describe an object. Whether or not you use the wizard, you'll need to know how the file is organized.

Defining Properties and Methods

The `<public>` section of the WSC file lists the object's properties and methods, and it describes how they're linked to your script. As shown earlier in the chapter, the object's properties and methods are managed by functions and subroutines in the associated script program. The names of the properties and methods and their associated program parts are defined by `<property>` and `<method>` elements.

Each of your object's properties must be defined by a `<property>` element.

If you take a look at the `<property>` syntax in Reference List 9.1, you'll see that there are several different allowed formats for this element. You can write it as a single, contentless tag using `<property` ...*`attributes`*`/>`, or you can use the end-tag version: `<property` *`attributes`*`>`...`</property>`.

Binding a Property to a Variable

Properties can be implemented in one of two ways. They can be directly *bound* (linked) to a global variable in the script, or they can be implemented by functions that return and set the property's value. The first method can be used when the property is a simple value that can be stored in a variable and whose value doesn't need to be validated by the object or determined from other variables or objects. The client's program will be able to assign any value to the property; WSH will simply stick the value into the associated variable. This method is simpler than providing `get_` and `put_` functions, but you do lose the ability to validate the values being stored in the property. Properties bound to variables are always read/write.

To specify that a property should be stored directly in a variable, omit `get` and `put` as attributes and as tags. By default, the property will be stored in a global variable of the same name as the property; you can specify a different variable name with the `internalName` attribute in the `<property>` tag. You may need to do this if the property has a name that is not a legal variable name in your scripting language (for example, "to" in VBScript).

Your script should initialize the property variable to a sensible default value in the script's "main body" (that is, before any of its functions or subroutines). Here are some examples that show how this works:

- A read/write property named `color` stored in the variable `color`:

```
<property name="color"/>
```

- A read/write property named `To` stored in the variable `msgTo`:

```
<property name="To" internalName="msgTo"/>
```

Implementing a Property with Functions

The second method for managing properties is to bind them to functions that set and return the property value. These are called *accessor functions*. This technique lets you inspect and validate values that the user is trying to assign to the property, and it must be used when the property is obtained from another object (as is the case when you are subclassing another object) or is calculated from other values.

If you specify `get` and/or `put` as attributes of the `<property/>` tag, or as `<get/>` or `<put/>` tags inside the `<property>` element, WSH assumes that the property is read and written with functions that you have supplied. By default, WSH calls a function named `get_`*`propertyname`*`()` when the client wants to read the property's value, and it calls a subroutine named `put_`*`propertyname`*`(`*`newvalue`*`)` when the client wants to write a new value to the property with the new value passed as an argument.

As before, you must specify whether reading and/or writing is allowed using the `put` and `get` attributes or tags. If you want to specify a different name for the `get` or `put` functions, you must use the long form and supply the new function name as the `internalName` attribute of the `<get/>` or `<put/>` tag. Here are some examples showing the alternatives:

- A read-write property named age whose value is returned by a function named get_age() and set by a function named put_age(*newvalue*):

  ```
  <property name="age" get put/>
  ```

  or

  ```
  <property name="age"><get/><put/></property>
  ```

- A read-only property named age whose value is returned by function calculate_age():

  ```
  <property name="age">
      <get internalname="calculate_age"/>
  </property>
  ```

Note

Whether you use a variable or functions to implement a property, the variable or functions *must* be defined in your script, even if they are never used; otherwise, WSH generates an error. If you don't use the <?component?> directive with attribute error="True", you get an "unspecified error." If you do use the directive, you get the message "The property accessor is not defined: *MissingItemName*."

Defining Methods

Methods are subroutines or functions provided as part of the object. Like any other subroutine or function, methods can take arguments, and they can return a value to the client.

By default, when the client invokes your object's method, Windows Script Host calls a function or subroutine of the same name as the method. An alternate procedure name can be specified with the internalName property. If the method does not return a value, the associated procedure can be a function or a subroutine. If the method is to return a value, the associated procedure must be a function.

The dispid attribute can be used to specify the COM dispatch ID for the method. This has uses beyond the scope of this book, but for our purposes it's handy to know that you can specify dispid=0 for *one* of the object's methods, making this the object's *default* method. The default method should return a value such as a name or other identifier, because this is the value that Windows Script Host uses when you attempt to print the value of the object itself. That is,

```
set obj = CreateObject("Some.WSCObject")
WScript.echo obj
```

will print the value returned by the default method.

If the method takes arguments, they must be listed, in order, by one or more <parameter/> tags placed between <method> and </method>. If the method takes no arguments, the method tag can be closed with /> and, if so, the </method> end tag is omitted.

If you declare a method with a <method> tag, the associated function or subroutine *must* exist in your script, even if it is never used; otherwise, WSH will generate an error. If you don't use the <?component?> directive with the attribute error="True", you will get an "unspecified error." If you do use the directive, you will get the message "The method is not defined: *methodname*."

Using Other Objects and Type Libraries

If your object script uses other helper objects, such as Scripting.FileSystemObject, instead of creating them with a CreateObject() call, you can declare them with the <object> tag. The <object> tag creates an object reference in a global variable that you can use in your script. For example, using

```
<object id="msg" progid="CDO.Message">
```

accomplishes the same thing as beginning your script with something like this:

```
dim msg
set fso = CreateObject("CDO.Message")
```

Strangely, although you would expect the <object/> tag to automatically import the object's predefined constants while it's creating the object, it doesn't. You have to use the <reference/> tag to get those.

If you want to use the predefined constants associated with an object, you can pull in the definitions with a <reference/> tag. For instance, in the previous example, if I wanted to create a CDO.Message and use its predefined constants, I could use

```
<component>
   <registration>...
   <public>...
   <object id="msg" progid="CDO.Message"/>
   <reference object="CDO.Message"/>
   <script>
   .
   .
   .
</component>
```

This will connect the script to the CDO *type library*, which WSH uses to import all the CDO constants. You can use <reference/> whether or not you use <object/> to create objects.

Note

In rare cases, <reference/> doesn't work due to problems with COM, WSH, or the referenced object itself. If you find that your script or your new object stalls out for 30 seconds or so when you try to run it, or you get an error saying that the <reference/> tag cannot load the required type information, you may be better off removing the <reference/> tag and entering the constant definitions into your program by hand. This is unfortunately the case with the Active Directory ADSI objects; <reference object="ADs"/> does not work.

Defining Resources

If you plan to make versions of your script in several languages, the `<resource>` tag lets you put all language-specific text in one place in your script file. This makes it easier to edit and maintain the script. Here's how it works: Create `<resource>` elements for each of the text strings or numbers that you want to maintain in separate localized versions. Give each a distinct name in the `id` attribute. Place the text or numbers between `<resource>` and `</resource>`, being careful not to add any extra carriage returns or spaces. If you used the `<?xml?>` strict-compliance directive at the top of your script, you should enclose the text with `<![CDATA[` and `]]>` to prevent any < or > characters in your text from being interpreted as tags.

Resource elements *cannot* be enclosed in the `<public>` or `<script>` elements of your WSC file. They must be placed inside the `<component>` element at the same level as `<public>` and `<script>`.

Then, in the body of your script, use the function `GetResource("`*`idvalue`*`")` to retrieve the text or number. Here's an example:

```
<? xml version="1.0">
<component id="MyObjects.Multilingual">
    <public>
        <property name="value"/>
        .
        .
        .
    </public>

    <resource id="uninit"><![CDATA[Value has not been set!]]></resource>
    <resource id="msg"><![CDATA[Here is the message:]]></resource>
    .
    .
    .

    <script language="VBScript"><![CDATA[
        dim value
        value = GetResource("uninit")
        .
        .
        .

        wscript.echo GetResource("msg")
    ]]></script>
</component>
```

With all the language-specific information in one place, it's easier to create different versions later.

Registering the Component

When you have created a WSC object file, you need to register the script with Windows in order to begin testing and using it. This is done at the Windows command prompt with the command

```
regsvr32 scrobj.dll /n /i:drive:\path\filename.wsc
```

where `drive:\path\filename.wsc` is the full pathname of the WSC file. `Regsvr32` is used to register objects. `Scrobj.dll` is recorded as the "server" program that the COM system runs to create the object; this in turn activates Windows Script Host to actually run the script file.

`Regsvr32` stores the object's `classid`, `progid`, and location information in the Windows Registry, where it's available to any Windows program that wants to create your new object type.

If you need to relocate the WSC file, you will need to reregister the object using its new pathname. If you want to remove the object script entirely, unregister the object with the following command line:

```
regsvr32 scrobj.dll /u /i:drive:\path\filename.wsc
```

Tip

You can also quickly register and unregister WSC files by locating them in Windows Explorer. Then right-click and select Register or Unregister.

Testing

When you are debugging and testing a new WSC object for the first time, be sure to place

```
<?component error="True" debug="True"?>
```

on the line just after each `<component>` tag. This lets Windows Script Host display error messages when there are syntax or other programming errors in the script. It also lets you trace into the object's script with the Windows Script Debugger.

You should write small test scripts to exercise all aspects of your object. Besides testing each of the properties and methods to be sure that they work correctly, be sure to see whether the object behaves gracefully when it's given invalid data. Give it invalid parameter values and data types, try methods out of order, and be sure that if you fail to initialize properties, the object still behaves well.

However, debugging WSC scripts isn't a simple matter of running the script with the following command line:

```
cscript //D myobject.wsc
```

Remember, object scripts are run at the behest of some other client program when that program creates an object defined by your script file. If you use a script program to create your object and debug that, you'll find that the debugger doesn't step through the `CreateObject` call into the WSC file. How do you debug a WSC file, then?

The solution is to use your scripting language's breakpoint statement to cause the debugger to turn its attention to the object script. In VBScript, use the `stop` statement. In Jscript, use `debugger;`. Place the appropriate statement somewhere in your script program. You can place it in the main body of the script to cause a breakpoint when the object is first created, or you can place it in a method or procedure function. If you include the `<?component debug="true"?>` directive, when the breakpoint statement is encountered, you'll be able to set other breakpoints in the script file, as needed, and to debug it in the usual way.

Note

You can't use `WScript.echo` to print values and debugging information from a WSC component script. The only way to see inside the object is to use the Script Debugger or an alternate debugger such as Visual Studio.

After the object has been thoroughly tested and debugged, you may wish to remove the `<?component?>` directive or change the attribute values to `False`. This disables any `stop` or `debugger;` statements and prevents the object from generating error messages of its own.

COM objects generally don't generate error message by themselves. Your object's script program should do all it can to avoid errors and to handle bad situations gracefully. If it would be helpful, you could communicate error information back to client programs with an "error" property on your object that indicates when an error has occurred by returning a number, a descriptive message, or the value `True`.

Using Scripted Objects from Other Programs

Once your WSC file is registered and working, you can create the object it represents just as you would any other object—built in or otherwise—in any program that supports Automation objects. Of course, you can use `CreateObject("yourobjectname")` in Windows Script Host programs, but also in C++, Visual Basic programs, and scripts written in Visual Basic for Applications (VBA).

Deploying the Object to Other Computers

To use the object on other computers in your organization, you must either copy the WSC file to a specific location on each of your organization's computers or make the WSC file available on a shared folder or Web server that is accessible by each computer.

Then, you have to register the object on each computer. There are two ways of doing this. You can run the `regsvr32` program on each computer, using one of these versions of the command:

- `regsvr32 scrobj.dll /i:`*`drive:\path\filename.wsc`*. Use this version if the file is copied to a specific place on each computer.
- `regsvr32 scrobj.dll /i:\\`*`server\sharename\path\filename.wsc`*. Use this version if the file is located on a network share.
- `regsvr32 scrobj.dll /i:http://`*`servername/path/filename.wsc`*. Use this version if the file is placed on a Web server.

This can be done in a logon script, if necessary.

You can also manually create the necessary Registry entries. Register the object script on a sample computer; then look in the Windows Registry under `HKEY_CLASSES_ROOT` under the following keys:

- *`Object.Name`* (that is, the object's `progid`)
- *`Object.Name.versionnumber`*
- `CLSID\{`*`object's classid`*`}`

You can record all the information in the subkeys and values under these keys and write a script to re-create them on other computers, using the objects described in Chapter 4, "File and Registry Access," in the section "Working with the Registry."

Creating a Practical Object

I've found that Microsoft throws out and replaces its messaging objects about as often as it does with its top management. Right now, Collaboration Data Objects (CDO) is in vogue, but next year, who knows? CDO and my Chapter 6, "Messaging Objects," could disappear as quickly as Rick Belluzzo. (What do you mean, "who?") This means that scripts that use CDO to send messages might work on today's Windows XP but might not work with future releases of Windows.

Because I don't want to have to update dozens of scripts when this happens, I've decided to create a simplified object that I'll use to send e-mail from all my scripts. That way, when the procedure for sending messages changes, I only have to update one WSC file. I'll call this object `ScriptMail.Message`.

Wrapping up management e-mails in an object has other benefits. For example, I could make the default destination for all messages the system administrator; if scripts don't need to change it, they don't have to. Automatically addressing e-mail to my sysadmin is something that CDO can't do!

Finally, at a later date I could extend this object to add paging, pop-up messages, or other forms of delivery that might be useful. With your own objects, you can add whatever features you want. What's more, adding a feature to the definition of an object in the WSC file makes the feature available to every script or program that uses the object.

The first step in designing a useful object is to decide how it should appear to the client. What are the properties and methods? How do they work? As a first step, we'll write the object's documentation as if it already existed. This will guide us later as we implement the object. I've decided I want a very simple e-mail object whose properties and methods are listed in Reference List 9.2.

REFERENCE LIST 9.2 Properties and Methods of the Not-Yet-Written `ScriptMail.Message` Object

Properties:

`To`
The recipient of the message. By default, the message is addressed to `Administrator@mycompany.com`.

`CC`
The recipient for a copy of the message. By default, the recipient is the user who is running the script, with the e-mail address *`username`*`@mycompany.com`. If the administrator is running the script, however, the default CC recipient is left blank because he or she is already the primary recipient.

`From`
The e-mail address of the person sending the message. By default, this is set to the user who is running the script, with the e-mail address *`username`*`@mycompany.com`.

`ScriptName`
The name of the script file or program from which I'm sending a message (the client script, not the object script). If no subject line is specified, this will be used to create a default subject line.

`Subject`
The subject of the message. If this property is not set, the message will be sent with the default subject line "Script *scriptname* on *computername*," where *computername* is the name of the computer on which the script is running and *scriptname* is the name set by the `ScriptName` property, if any.

`Text`
The message to send.

Methods:

`Send`
Sends the message.

Because this object sets sensible defaults for each of its properties, I could send a message from a script with just a few lines, as illustrated here:

```
set msg = CreateObject("ScriptMail.Message")
msg.ScriptName = "diskclean.vbs"
msg.text = "The disk cleanup script was run"
msg.send
```

This sure beats using CDO directly!

Now, it's time to build the object. To start with, I ran the Windows Script Component Wizard and entered the information shown earlier in Figure 9.3.

I told the wizard to use VBScript, unchecked Special Implements Support, and checked Error Checking and Debugging. I entered the properties and methods listed earlier but entered no default values, because the default values will have to be calculated.

After I edited the wizard's basic script, this was the result. Take a look at the following script, and afterwards I'll point out what I did to the wizard's original version. Here's the finished product, file `scriptmail.wsc`:

```
'                                ' Example script scriptmail.wsc
<?xml version="1.0"?>
<component>
    <?component error="true" debug="true"?>

    <!-- the registration information was created by the Wizard -->
    <registration
        description="Simple Script Mail Object"
        progid="ScriptMail.Message"
        version="1"
        classid="{3b977054-5cb4-4d7a-98b8-d3bed070f3ce}">
    </registration>

    <public>
        <!-- The properties are bound to variables of the same name
             except "To" which makes VBScript barf, so we use msgTo -->
        <property name="To" internalName="msgTo"/>
        <property name="CC"         />
        <property name="From"       />
        <property name="ScriptName"/>
        <property name="Subject"    />
        <property name="Text"       />
        <method   name="Send"       />
    </public>

    <!-- objects we need: -->
    <object id="netobj" progid="WScript.Network"/>
    <object id="msg"    progid="CDO.Message"/>
    <object id="conf"   progid="CDO.Configuration"/>

    <!-- get the CDO constants like cdoSendUsingPort -->
    <reference object="CDO.Message"/>
```

```
<script language="VBScript">
<![CDATA[
    ' the object's properties
    dim msgTo, CC, From, Subject, Text,  ScriptName
    ' extra variables
    dim SMTPServer, maildomain, admin

    ' set company-specific stuff not changeable by object user
    SMTPServer = "mail.mycompany.com"
    admin      = "Administrator"
    maildomain = "mycompany.com"

   ' set default property values
    msgTo      = admin & "@" & maildomain
    From       = netobj.UserName & "@" & maildomain
    Subject    = ""
    Text       = ""

    ' address a copy to the script user, if it's not the administrator
    if lcase(netobj.username) = lcase(admin) then
        CC = ""
    else
        CC = netobj.username & "@" & maildomain
    end if

    ' end of main body & object initialization
    '-----------------------------------------------------

    ' Send method - send the message using CDO or whatever
    function Send()
        dim prefix

        ' if no subject was specified, make up a reasonable one
        if Subject = "" then
           if ScriptName = "" then
               Subject = "Script on " & netobj.ComputerName
           else
               Subject = "Script '" & ScriptName & "' on " &_
                   netobj.ComputerName
           end if
        end if

        With msg                              ' build the message
            .to       = msgTo
            .cc       = CC
            .from     = From
            .subject  = Subject
            .textBody = Text
        End With

        ' set delivery information. Predefined constants are available
```

```
            prefix = "http://schemas.microsoft.com/cdo/configuration/"
            With conf.fields                        ' set delivery options
                .item(prefix & "sendusing")            = cdoSendUsingPort
                .item(prefix & "smtpserver")           = smtpserver
                .item(prefix & "smtpauthenticate")     = cdoAnonymous
                .update
            End With

            set msg.configuration = conf        ' deliver the message
            on error resume next
            msg.Send

            Send = err.number = 0               ' return True if it went OK
        end function

        ]]>
    </script>
</component>
```

Now let's look at what I changed. The wizard wrote a script that stores its properties in variables, and it used `get` and `put` functions to set them. This is overkill for this object; here, I'll do all the hard work during initialization and in the `Send` method. The users can set the properties to anything they want, and I don't need to do any processing when the properties are set, so I took the simple approach and decided to just bind the properties to variables.

To do this, I had to remove the `get` and `put` tags and the `get` and `put` accessor functions that the wizard created. They were fine for illustrating a point back in Figure 9.2, but we don't need them here. Unfortunately, I can't have a VBScript variable named "`to`" because this is a reserved word. So, I'll store the `To` property in a variable named `MsgTo`, which is named with an `internalName` attribute. All the `<property/>` tags use the short form ending with `/>`.

Because the `Send` method has no parameters, I used the short form for the `<method>` tag as well.

Now, on to the real work: In the script's main body, I created default values for each of the properties. The `WScript.Network` object from Chapter 5, "Network and Printer Objects," helps with this job by providing the `UserName` and `ComputerName`. I only needed one network object, so I used an `<object>` tag to create it.

From Chapter 6, I used one each of `CDO.Message` and `CDO.Configuration`, which I made the same way. Now, I could have created these objects at the moment they were needed with `CreateObject()` and released them right afterward, which would keep memory usage to a minimum. But, that's not as much fun as using `<object>`.

When the script's main body finishes, the object is ready to go and is given to the client program. It can change the properties as it pleases, and it finally calls the `Send` method. Back in the object script, `Send` constructs the subject line and sends the message using CDO. It returns the value `True` or `False`, indicating whether it was able to send the message.

To install and use the object, I just located it in Explorer, right-clicked, and chose Register. The first few times I tried this I was treated with messages informing me of the syntax errors in the script file. Only when the blatant syntax errors were fixed did the registration procedure work.

Once the object was registered, I ran the sample script, and to my utter amazement, it worked:

```
                                    ' Example script script0903.vbs
set msg = CreateObject("ScriptMail.Message")
msg.ScriptName = "diskclean.vbs"
msg.text = "The disk cleanup script was run"
if msg.send then wscript.echo "Message sent"
```

This is just one example of a useful WSC-based script. If you find others, let me know—visit `www.helpwinxp.com/hood` and tell me what you've done.

10

Deploying Scripts for Computer and Network Management

ROAD MAP

- This chapter shows you how to write and distribute scripts for end users.
- You'll learn how to configure logon scripts on standalone, workgroup, and domain computers.
- You'll learn how to write scripts for unattended, scheduled processing.
- You should be very comfortable with Windows Script Host before digging into this chapter's material.

Using Scripts in the Real World

THE PREVIOUS NINE CHAPTERS COVERED the basics of Windows Script Host and the powerful data processing, management, and maintenance objects and functions it provides. If you've been experimenting with these tools along the way, you've probably already started using WSH to solve day-to-day problems.

It's one thing to write a quick-and-dirty script to address some immediate need—for instance, to fix a directory full of misnamed files. I find myself doing this all the time. For such one-time-use scripts, you don't have to worry about proper formatting, documentation, generality, reliability, portability, or any of the other hallmarks of good programming style.

However, in what's called a "production environment"—that is, in situations where your scripts may be used by other people, on other computers, on a repeated basis—good programming style *is* a concern. In this chapter, I'll cover some of the tools that WSH provides to make it easier to write good, solid scripts that will stand up to day-to-day use. Later, I'll give you some tips for deploying them in a real-world networked environment.

Designing Scripts for Other Users

It's one thing to write a script for your own use. You wrote it, and you know how it works, so you probably won't care to invest much effort in making it "user friendly." However, when you're writing a script for others, you'll have to take into account that others haven't gone through the process of writing the script, so they won't understand its nuances. They'll need some hand-holding. Even for your own scripts, chances are, six months after you write one, you'll have forgotten how it works yourself, and on inspection, the program will be about as comprehensible as a cuneiform tablet. So, for scripts that you intend to share or just keep around a while, it's worth investing some time to make them self-documenting and forgiving to the novice user.

Here are some of the attributes of a well-written, user-friendly script:

- The script should be written in as general a way as possible. For example, instead of writing a script to clean temporary files out of a particular named folder, you might write a script to clean any folder or folders named on the command line. If no folder is named on the command line, then it might go ahead and clean a default folder. Making the script more general increases the likelihood that it will be able to serve more than one purpose.
- As a programmer, you should use every tool at your disposal to help you write correct code. This means, for example, that if you're writing VBScript, you should use the `option explicit` statement, which requires you to declare *every* variable in a `dim` statement. This makes it possible for VBScript to detect any misspelled variable names. It won't catch other sorts of bugs, but this does take care of one category, for free. (Option Explicit is discussed in Chapter 2, "VBScript Tutorial," under the heading "Variable Scope," page 81.)
- The script should not make assumptions about its operating environment. For example, the Windows folder isn't always `C:\WINDOWS`. It could be `D:\WINDOWS`, `C:\WINNT`, or...who knows? Instead of writing a script that uses fixed paths to system folders, use environment variables and the `WScript.Shell` object to get the real scoop. For details, see the entries for `GetSpecialFolder` in Reference List 4.1 (page 118) and `SpecialFolders` in Reference List 4.9 (page 171).
- The script should validate the existence of all files and folders named on the command line using the `FileExists` method discussed in Reference List 4.1 (page 118). If any specified files do not exist, have the script acknowledge that and quit before attempting to actually use the files. It's better to display a message such as "File input.dat does not exist" than to have the script user encounter a cryptic message such as the following:

```
C:\scripts\process.vbs(33, 1)
➥Microsoft VBScript runtime error: File not found
```

- The script should carefully check any command-line arguments for proper syntax. If errors are found, it should tell exactly what is wrong *and* display a concise, but helpful, description of what command-line arguments are allowed.

- The script should be written to assume sensible default values for optional command-line arguments. For example, if your script has an option to display lots of debugging information with `WScript.echo` statements, you might use the command-line argument `/verbose` to enable it, but have the verbose option default to "off" if it's not requested. We'll discuss these last two points in this chapter.

Writing a script with these properties takes time and makes the script larger and, ironically, increases the likelihood that there will be bugs lurking in the script due to the added code. Therefore, when you're making a script for public consumption, you'll have to carefully test every possible variation and outcome. Still, in the long run, this is all worthwhile because it makes your programs much more reliable and user friendly.

One way to make it easier to write more user-friendly scripts is to package them as WSF files.

Using WSF Files

In Chapter 9, "Creating Your Own Scriptable Objects," I showed you how to create Automation objects by wrapping a script up in a Windows Script Component file. The XML (Extensible Markup Language) formatting that defines a WSC object can also be used to package regular scripts. In this case, the files are given the extension `.wsf`, so for the remainder of this chapter, I'll call them WSF files. There are several good reasons to put your scripts into WSF files instead of plain-old VBScript, JavaScript, Perlscript, or other plain script files:

- You can package several distinct but related script programs into one WSF file and then choose which program(s) to run when you launch the script.
- WSF files help you to process command-line arguments in a consistent way and to provide online help to script users.
- WSF files can give you automatic access to the symbolic constants associated with external objects so that you don't need to manually define these constant values in your scripts.
- WSF scripts can refer to subroutines and functions stored in other WSF files. This lets you maintain just one copy of a WSF file that contains all the handy procedures you develop, and you can refer to this library from any number of WSF programs. If you need to change or fix one of the functions, you won't have to edit every file in which it's used.

If you're not familiar with XML file formatting, I suggest that you read "XML Basics" in Chapter 9 (page 355). That section gives background on the format and structure of XML files.

The overall structure of a WSF file is shown next. Note that end tags are not shown, and not every one of the directives and elements listed must be used in every script. This just shows the ordering that is usually used in a WSF file.

```
<?XML?>             <!-- optional                                           -->
<package>           <!-- required only if there is more than one job       -->
  <comment>         <!-- can appear anywhere in the package                -->
  <job>
    <?job?>         <!-- optional                                           -->
    <runtime>       <!-- definition of parameters & online help            -->
       <named/>     <!-- optional definitions                              -->
       <unnamed/>
       <description>
       <example>
       <usage>
    </runtime>
    <object/>       <!-- zero or more -->
    <reference/>    <!-- zero or more -->
    <resource>      <!-- zero or more -->
    <script>        <!-- one or more script elements contain the program  -->
  </job>...         <!-- can be followed by another job                    -->
</package>
```

Here are the main sections of a WSF file:

- `<package>` encloses all the scripts in the file.
- `<job>` encloses a single, independent script program. There may be more than one `<job>` in the file; you can specify which one or more WSH is to run when you type in the script's command line. Likewise, a `<job>` can contain more than one `<script>` element containing script program code, subroutines, and functions.
- `<runtime>` encloses the description of the job's command-line arguments. The information in `<runtime>` lets WSH print a nicely formatted command-line description and syntax help if the user types `/?` on the script's command line, or if the user specifies command-line arguments incorrectly. This lets WSF scripts behave like all standard Windows command-line programs.
- `<object/>`, `<reference/>`, and `<resource>` set up references to objects and predefined data that the script program can use.
- `<script>` elements contain script program code for the job.

The next section describes all the valid WSF file tags in detail. After that, we'll go through their actual application.

WSF File Format Reference

Reference List 10.1 lists all the tags and attributes allowed in a WSF file. This reference only lists elements appropriate for enclosing script programs. Elements that are used only when creating WSC objects were covered in Chapter 9 and are not discussed here.

Note

XML ignores extra whitespace or line breaks between tags, attributes, or elements. However, text inside `<description>`, `<resource>`, `<helptext>`, and other display elements is displayed literally, so inside these tags you should only add whitespace and line breaks that you want to appear in the script's output.

REFERENCE LIST 10.1 WSF Tag Listing

```
<?XML version="1.0" [standalone="yes"]?>
```

The `<?XML?>` element requests that the WSH interpreter perform strict XML validation. With validation enabled, XML's stringent formatting and interpretation rules are applied. "Strict" mode is usually required when you will be editing the WSF file with an XML editor. For more information on strict XML validation, see the entry for `<?XML?>` in Chapter 9 (page 359).

If present, the `<?XML?>` element must be the first line in the file and must not be preceded by blank lines. The `version` number should be specified as `1.0`. The optional `standalone` attribute indicates that the XML file does not reference an external Document Type Declaration (DTD) and can be omitted or specified as `"yes"`.

```
<?job error="value" debug="value" ?>
```

enables the reporting of error messages from and the debugging of the job's script. By default, errors are *not* reported and debugging of scripts is *not* enabled. The `<?job?>` element lets you alter this default behavior by specifying `True` or `False` to enable or disable error message reporting, as well as debugging with the Windows Script Debugger or an equivalent script debugger.

Place this directive as the first item inside of a `<job>` element.

```
<! [CDATA[
   protected text
   .
   .
   .
]]>
```

The `CDATA` section encapsulates script code inside a `<script>` element and indicates that it is not to be treated as XML markup; otherwise, the presence of characters such as <, >, and `&` in the script will generate errors. The `CDATA` section must be used only in conjunction with the `<?XML?>` directive; without `<?XML?>`, the presence of `CDATA` markup itself will generate a syntax error.

```
<!-- any text
     .
     .
     .
-->
```

continues

REFERENCE LIST 10.1 Continued

Anything inside `<!-- ... -->` is treated as comment text, including any XML markup. This can be used to comment out blocks of code during testing or to enter comments or descriptive information. The `<comment>` element can also be used to enclose comments, but `<comment>` cannot contain any XML tags or other markup.

```
<comment>
    any text
    .
    .
    .
</comment>
```

indicates comment text that is to be ignored by the parser. You can embed multiple lines in a comment, but not XML tags.

```
<description>any text
</description>
```

describes the purpose of the script. Any text inside the `<description>` element is displayed when the `WScript.Arguments.ShowUsage` method is executed or when the script is run with the `/?` command-line argument. The text can span multiple input lines if necessary. This element is an optional part of the `<runtime>` element.

Whitespace (line breaks, spaces, and tabs) between the start and end tags are significant. Output will look best if you begin the descriptive text immediately after the start tag, put any subsequent lines at the left margin, and put the end tag on a line by itself.

```
<example>Example: example usage text
</example>
```

is used to give an example of proper usage of the script's command line. This is printed when the `WScript.Arguments.ShowUsage` method is executed or when the script is run with the `/?` command-line argument. Start the text with "`Example:`". Whitespace is significant; see the comments under `<description>`. This element is an optional part of the `<runtime>` element.

```
<job [id="jobid"]>
    job content: <?job?>, <runtime>, <script>, etc.
    .
    .
    .
</job>
```

encloses a self-contained script program. More than one `<job>` can be placed in a single WSF file. If this is done, you should name each job with a distinct name in the `id` attribute. These job names are used on the command line to select which job or jobs to run. If there are multiple jobs in the file and you don't specify which to run, WSH runs each of them in turn, in the order in which they appear in the file.

<named name="*argname*" helpstring="*description*" type="*argtype*" required="*boolean*"/> defines an option (switch) argument that is permitted on the command line that runs the script. Named command arguments begin with a slash. Here's an example:

```
scriptname /someoption /otheroption=3
```

Here's a list of the attributes of <named/>:

- name—Name of the command-line option.
- helpstring—A brief description of the option's meaning or purpose.
- type—The type of data expected. This must be one of the following values: "string", "boolean", or "simple". The default value is "simple".
- required—"True" if the argument is always required or "False" if the argument is optional. The default value is "False".

The type attribute specifies how you want the user to enter the command-line option. If you want the argument to have the form /someoption=*textvalue*, specify type="string". If just the presence of the argument is all that matters (for example, /verbose), specify type="simple". If the option is an on/off switch of the form /someoption+ or /someoption-, specify type="boolean". This latter format is pretty strange, and as far as I'm concerned, a bad idea. No Windows command-line program has ever used this form of argument, and I see no good reason to start using it now.

The information in <named> is used only when WSH is asked to display the script's usage information, by calling the WScript.Arguments.ShowUsage method or by running the script with /? on the command line. Unfortunately, WSH does *not* use this information to automatically validate command-line arguments.

<object id="*name*" {classid="clsid:*GUID*" | progid="*progid*"}
[events="*boolval*"]/>
creates an instance of a specified object, in a global variable of the indicated *name*. You must specify either the object's progid name (for example, "Scripting.FileSystemObject") or its classid. Be sure to close the object tag with />.

The events attribute specifies whether the script is prepared to handle events fired by the object. Events are beyond the scope of this book.

```
<package>
    one or more <job> elements
    .
    .
    .
</package>
```

encloses one or more separate script programs in a WSF file. The <package> element is optional when the file contains only one job.

continues

REFERENCE LIST 10.1 Continued

```
<reference {object="progid" | guid="GUID"}
    [version="version"]/>
```

instructs WSH to load the type library for a specified object type. In effect, this loads all the predefined constants associated with the object. The object can be specified by its progid name (for example, to load the WMI constants, use `object="WbemScripting.SWbemLocator"`) or its GUID number. By default, WSH will load the most recent version of the object class, but if necessary, you can specify an older version with the `version` attribute. Be sure to close the tag with `/>`.

```
<resource id="resourceid"><![CDATA[text or number]]>
</resource>
```

or

```
<resource id="resourceid">text or number</resource>
```

creates a named value that can be retrieved in the script using the `GetResource()` function. Note that `<resource>` tags provide a way to concentrate all language-specific text in one place in the file so that alternate language versions can be created at a later date. A `<resource>` tag assigns a name ***resourceid*** to some text or numeric data. The ***resourceid*** string is passed to `GetResource()` to retrieve the data into the script. The content should be encased in `<![CDATA[ ... ]]>` if the WSC file uses strict XML compliance. For more information about `<resource>`, see "Defining Resources" in Chapter 9 (page 370).

```
<runtime>
    argument definitions: <named>, <unnamed>, <usage>,
    <description>, <example> tags
    .
    .
    .
</runtime>
```

The `<runtime>` element contains tags that define the command-line syntax for a script job. The tags are described elsewhere in this reference list.

```
<script [language="name"]>
<![CDATA[
    script code
    .
    .
    .
]]>
</script>

<script language="name" src="location"/>
```

The first form of the `<script>` element encloses the actual script program code and/or subroutines and functions. You may specify the script language; the default is `"VBScript"`.

The second form of the script element indicates that WSH is to incorporate the script program stored at the location indicated by the `src` attribute. The location can be a filename (including the path), a UNC-formatted share name, or a URL, which must begin with `http://`. In this form, the script tag ends with `/>`, and there is no content or end tag. The file referenced by this "import" version of the script tag should be a plain script program file with no XML formatting.

If you use multiple `<script>` elements of either form, if more than one contains a program "body," the scripts are executed in sequence. For subroutine and function procedures to be shared across `<script>` elements, procedures must be defined in the same script element or in an *earlier* script element than the one in which it is used. In particular, if you want to use `<script src=.../>` to import a library of subroutines and functions, the importing tag must occur before the `<script>` in which you use the procedures.

If you used the `<?XML?>` strict-compliance directive at the top of your script, you should enclose the script code itself inside `<![CDATA[` and `]]>` to prevent any `<` or `>` characters in your script from being interpreted as tags. If you did not use the `<?XML?>` directive, do not use `<![CDATA[` and `]]>`. And in either case, do not use the `CDATA` markup in any of the import files referenced by `<script src=.../>` elements.

`<unnamed name="`*`argname`*`" helpstring="`*`description`*`" many="`*`boolean`*`" required="`*`value`*`"/>`
In the `<runtime>` element, the `unnamed` element indicates a command-line argument that is unnamed (that is, does not start with the `/` character). These are typically filenames or items whose meaning is conveyed by their placement (order) on the command line.

Here's a list of the attributes of `<unnamed/>`:

- `name`—The name of the command-line option. At first it seems peculiar to give a name to an "unnamed" argument. There is a reason: This name is used if WSH has to print out the script's command-line syntax. This is the name it uses as a placeholder in the sample syntax line. Pick a name that represents the purpose of the argument: "filename", "username", or something along these lines.
- `helpstring`—A brief description of the option's meaning or purpose.
- `many`—A boolean value: `"True"` if the user can enter a variable number of these arguments; `"False"` if the user must enter a fixed number.
- `required`—The number of occurrences of this item that are *required* to be entered.

As with `<named>`, the information in `<unnamed>` is used only when WSH is asked to display the script's usage information.

continues

REFERENCE LIST 10.1 Continued

<usage>*descriptive text*
</usage>

This element can be used in the `<runtime>` element. If present and if the script executes the `WScript.Arguments.ShowUsage` method or the user types `/?` on the command line, the text inside `<usage>` will be printed instead of the automatically generated text that WSH normally produces from the `<named>`, `<unnamed>`, `<description>`, and `<example>` tags. If you use `<usage>`, there is no reason to specify the other tags.

Whitespace in `<usage>` is significant. For best formatting, start the text immediately after `<usage>`, begin any extra text lines at the left margin, and place the `</usage>` tag on a line by itself.

Now, let's go over ways to use the features of a WSF file.

Enclosing More Than One Script

In a WSF file, there may be one or more `<job>` elements, each of which contains a complete script program. If there is more than one `<job>` in a WSF file, you can specify which job to run on the command line that you use to run the script. For example,

```
cscript somefile.wsf //job:cleanup
```

tells WSH to find the job section that is marked with the attribute `id="cleanup"`, and run the script inside. You can name more than one job. The command line

```
cscript somefile.wsf //job:report //job:cleanup
```

runs the script job named "report" and then "cleanup." If you have multiple jobs in a file and don't put any `//job` parameters on the command line, WSH runs *all* the jobs in the order in which they appear in the file.

Providing Online Help with WSF Files

As mentioned in Reference List 10.1, the WSF file format uses the `<runtime>` element to describe the command-line arguments that your script expects. This lets WSH automatically print help information for the user. This happens in two circumstances:

- If the user puts `/?` on the command line when he or she runs the script, WSH will display the script's usage information and quit. This is standard behavior for most Windows command-line programs, and it's very nice that WSF script programs behave the same way.
- If you execute the method `WScript.Arguments.ShowUsage` using the built-in object `WScript`, WSH will display the usage information and continue.

The first circumstance happens all by itself. The second is under your control. What I suggest is that anytime you detect that the user has entered command-line arguments incorrectly, use `WScript.echo` to type a message explaining exactly what is wrong and then issue these statements:

```
WScript.Arguments.ShowUsage
WScript.Quit 1
```

This will display the correct usage information and stop the script with the exit status 1. A nonzero exit status indicates that something went wrong, and this can be detected if, for example, the script was run from a batch file.

What does `ShowUsage` print? If you specified a `<usage>` element, it prints the contents of `<usage>`. Otherwise, it extracts the information from the other tags in `<runtime>` and prints it in the format

```
text from <description>
Usage: scriptname /named_arguments unnamed_arguments

Options:

name: description
text from <example>
```

with the named and unnamed arguments formatted with the usual syntax notation: square brackets around optional arguments, ellipses after repeatable arguments, and so on.

Here's an example. For a script that we want to take the optional arguments `/copies` (which takes a numeric argument) and `/verbose` (which is just a switch whose presence turns on debugging) as well as one or more filenames, the `<runtime>` markup might look like this:

```
<runtime>
    <named name="copies"  type="string" required="False"
           helpstring="Specifies number of copies to burn, default=1"/>
    <named name="verbose" type="simple" required="False"
           helpstring="Enables output of debugging messages"/>
    <unnamed name="filename" many="True" required="1"
           helpstring="Name(s) of files to process"/>
    <description>Sends the named music/sound files to the CD burner.
</description>
    <example>Example: cdburn /copies:2 /verbose somefile.wav otherfile.mp3
</example>
</runtime>
```

When a WSF file containing this information is run with the argument `/?`, this is the result:

```
C:\scripts>cdburn /?

Sends the named music/sound files to the CD burner.
Usage: cdburn.wsf [/copies:value] [/verbose] filename1 [filename2...]

Options:

copies   : Specifies number of copies to burn, default=1
verbose  : Enables output of debugging messages
filename : Name(s) of files to process

Example: cdburn /copies:2 /verbose somefile.wav otherfile.mp3
```

Note that the `/copies` and `/verbose` options were automatically displayed in square brackets, because they both were marked `required="False"`. The unnamed argument was listed as `filename1` because one is required, and the option for entering more was shown because of `many="True"`.

Although you could probably format this stuff yourself and enter it in a `<usage>` tag faster than you can enter all the other `<runtime>` tags, this method has the advantage that WSH always formats the information in a consistent way.

Processing Command-Line Arguments

The script's command-line arguments are made available through the built-in collection object `WScript.Arguments`. I discussed this collection in Chapter 3, "Scripting and Objects." In WSF files, it is a useful tool, because it will automatically sort out the named and unnamed command-line arguments.

`WScript.Arguments` has two properties that return collections that are a subset of the contents of `WScript.Arguments` itself:

- `WScript.Arguments.Named` is a collection of the named (/*xxx*) command-line arguments passed to the script.
- `WScript.Arguments.Unnamed` is a collection of all the other command-line arguments (that is, filenames and the like).

I'll describe and discuss how to use both collection objects in turn.

Processing Named Arguments (Switches)

Reference List 10.2 lists the methods and properties of the `Named` collection.

REFERENCE LIST 10.2 Properties and Methods of the `Named` Collection

Properties:

`Item(`*`name`*`)`
returns the *`value`* part of the command-line argument `/`*`name`*`:`*`value`*, as a string. If no argument with the given name is specified on the command line, it returns the value `Empty`. If the argument value has been enclosed in quotes, as in the following command line:

```
somescript /title:"This is the title I want to use"
```

then `WScript.Named.Item("title")` returns the string value `This is the title I want to use` without the quotation marks.

For simple arguments such as `/`*`name`*, the return value is always `Empty`; you must use the `Exists` method to determine whether the argument was specified.

For those weird boolean switches specified as `/`*`name`*`+` or `/`*`name`*`-`, the return value is `True` (`-1`) if the argument ended with `+`, or `False (0)` if the argument ended with `-`.

`Length`
returns the number of items in the collection. For named items, this isn't very interesting because you'll usually examine the contents of the collection with `Item()` or `Exists()`.

Methods:

`Count`
also returns the number of items in the collection.

`Exists(`*`name`*`)`
returns `True` if the named argument was specified on the command line and returns `False` otherwise. Use this method to detect the presence of "simple" arguments such as `/verbose`.

Note

If you scan through the `Named` collection, the values you'll see are the names of the arguments. To get their values, you have to use the `Item()` property. For example, this code lists all the arguments' names and values:

```
for each arg in WScript.Arguments.Named
   WScript.echo arg, "=", WScript.Arguments.Named.Item(arg)
next
```

The `Named` collection makes it easy to extract information about "switch" command-line arguments. It would be wonderful if WSH provided a way to automatically validate the user's command line against the items listed in the `<runtime>` section and then print the usage information and stop if there is a mismatch, but unfortunately, WSH doesn't do that. So, you'll have to handle this manually.

First, you'll have to decide what you want to do if the user types a named argument that you didn't expect. It's easiest to ignore such arguments—they'll sit in the `Named` collection, but if you don't look for them, you'll never know they're there. This is not the best policy perhaps; the user will never know about the mistake until the script does something other than what he or she intended. Still, if the consequences of this are not serious, this is the easiest way to handle named arguments in a script. The following pattern shows how to do this.

Pattern

To extract named command-line arguments (switches), perform the following steps:

1. In the `<runtime>` section, define each of the desired arguments. Forget about the "boolean" type, and use "simple" instead. These will always default to off (`False`) if absent and will be on (`True`) if present.
2. If you need a feature to be on by default, change the corresponding switch name to "no*xxx*" so that its presence means "turn the feature off."
3. In the script, declare variables for each of the arguments.
4. Initialize the variables for numeric or string options to a sensible default value. You don't need to initialize the boolean values.
5. Check for each of the named arguments with `Exists()`. For simple (boolean) arguments, `Exists()` returns the variable's value. For string arguments, set the variable to the `Item()` value if `Exists` is `True`.

Here is an example. This script accepts a switch named `/verbose`, a negative switch named `/nolisting`, and a value switch named `/copies`:

```
dim verbose, nolisting, copies    ' declare variables

copies = 1                        ' initialize values

with WScript.Arguments.Named      ' fetch argument values
    verbose   = .Exists("verbose")
    nolisting = .Exists("nolisting")
    if .Exists("copies") then copies = .Item("copies")
end with
```

If you do care about catching mistyped switch values, you'll have to inspect the collection manually to look for improper values. Perhaps the easiest way to do this is with a subroutine that inspects all the arguments for you. The subroutine is listed in the following pattern.

Pattern

To validate all the named arguments (switches) on a script's command line, call a validation subroutine with a list of all valid switch names, as illustrated here:

```
<script><![CDATA[
   dim verbose, nolisting, copies

   validate_args "verbose,nolisting,copies"

   ' remainder of script as in previous Pattern

   sub validate_args (goodlist)
        dim pattern, arg

        pattern = "," & lcase(goodlist) & ","

        for each arg in WScript.Arguments.Named
            if instr(pattern, "," & lcase(arg) & ",") = 0 then
               WScript.echo "Argument", arg, "is not recognized"
               WScript.Arguments.ShowUsage
               WScript.Quit 1
            end if
        next
    end sub
   .
   .
   .
]]></script>
```

The variable `pattern` holds the value `",verbose,nolisting,copies,"`. The subroutine checks whether each of the argument names can be found in `pattern`. If so, it's a valid argument; otherwise, the script prints an error message, the proper syntax information, and quits.

The commas surrounding the strings make sure that the entire argument string has to match. Without the commas, a mistyped option name such as "ver" would appear to be a legal name.

Whether you validate argument names or not, be sure to check that all arguments with values have been assigned appropriate values.

Note

You can use these techniques in normal `.vbs` or `.js` script files, too; the `WScript.Named` and `WScript.Unnamed` collections are available even when you're not using a WSF file.

Processing Unnamed Arguments

The `WScript.Arguments.Unnamed` collection provides a list of all command-line arguments that don't start with `/`. Unnamed arguments, in most cases, specify a list of files, users, or other items to process.

The properties and methods of the `Unnamed` collection are shown in Reference List 10.3.

REFERENCE LIST 10.3 Properties and Method of the Unnamed Collection

Properties:

`Item(`*`n`*`)`
returns one of the arguments in the collection, where *n* is a number from `0` to `Length-1`.

`Length`
returns the number of arguments in the collection.

Method:

`Count`
also returns the number of arguments in the collection.

In most cases, you can write your script to process each of the items in turn, as indicated in the following pattern. If you want to ensure that a certain number of items were specified, you can check the value of `Length` or `Count`.

Then you can simply use the usual collection iterator to handle each of the items. When all the arguments represent the same sort of items, such as filenames or usernames, it's often best to write a subroutine to process each item in turn. The following pattern illustrates this:

Pattern

When processing an arbitrary number of arguments that are identical in meaning, such as a list of filenames to be processed, it's best to use a subroutine to process each file. This makes it easier to see how the program works when you're reading the script. The following code illustrates a good way to do this:

```
' ensure there is at least one file
if WScript.Arguments.Unnamed.Length < 1 then
    WScript.echo "You must specify at least one filename"
    WScript.Arguments.ShowUsage
    WScript.Quit 1
end if

' process each file in turn
for each arg in WScript.Arguments.Unnamed
    process arg
next

' process one file
sub process (filename)
.
.
.
end sub
```

Putting It All Together

The following sample script uses a hypothetical library of CD-burning subroutines, which are contained in another file, to let a user type a list of files to burn onto a CD. The script ties together all the concepts in this section:

- It has built-in online help.
- It uses sensible default values.
- It validates all of its arguments before doing anything.

Here is the script:

```
                                                    ' Example File cdburn.wsf
<?XML version="1.0"?>
<comment>
CDBURN - sends files named on the command line to the CD burner
</comment>
<package>
   <job>
      <runtime>
         <named name="copies"  type="string" required="False"
                helpstring="Specifies number of copies to burn, default=1"/>
         <named name="verbose" type="simple" required="False"
                helpstring="Enables output of debugging messages"/>
         <unnamed name="filename" many="True" required="1"
                helpstring="Name(s) of files to process"/>
         <description>
Sends the named music/sound files to the CD burner.</description>
         <example>
Example: cdburn /copies:2 /verbose somefile.wav otherfile.mp3</example>
     </runtime>

     <!-- create a FileSystemObject in variable 'fso' -->
     <object id="fso" progid="Scripting.FileSystemObject"/>

     <!-- include the Perl-language CD burning functions -->
     <script language="PerlScript" src="\\java\lib\cdlib.pls"/>

     <script language="VBScript">
     <![CDATA[
         ' require all variables to be declared to help detect typos
         option explicit
         dim verbose, copies, filename, failed

         ' set default value
         copies = 1

         ' process named arguments (options)
         validate_args "copies,verbose"
```

```
        with WScript.Arguments.Named
            verbose = .Exists("verbose")

            if .Exists("copies") then
                if isNumeric(.Item("copies")) then
                    ' convert string to a numeric value
                    copies = cint(.Item("copies"))
                else
                    ' exists but is not numeric? That's an error
                    Wscript.Echo "You must specify a number with /copies"
                    WScript.Arguments.ShowUsage
                    WScript.Quit 1
                end if
            end if
        end with

       ' be sure there is at least one filename, quit if not
        if WScript.Arguments.Unnamed.Count = 0 then
           WScript.Arguments.ShowUsage
           WScript.Quit 1
        end if

        ' verify that each file exists before starting the process
        failed = False
        for each filename in WScript.Arguments.Unnamed
           if not fso.FileExists(filename) then
              WScript.echo "No such file:", filename
              failed = True
           end if
        next

        ' if we saw one or more missing files, exit with error status
        if failed then WScript.Quit 1

        ' start the burning process
        cdburn_start copies

        ' process each named file
        for each filename in WScript.Arguments.Unnamed
           if verbose then WScript.echo "Processing", filename & "..."
           if not cdburn_add(filename) then
              WScript.echo "Error recording file", filename
           end if
        next

        ' make the CD's
        cdburn_go
        cdburn_close
        if verbose then WScript.echo "Finished"
    ]]>
    </script>
  </job>
</package>
```

You might look at this and say, "There are about five lines of useful code in there," and you'd be right. However, this script is nearly bulletproof, and the support it gives novice (or forgetful) users makes the extra effort worthwhile.

Deploying Scripts on a Network

The tools presented so far in this book give you the ability to manage a Windows XP, 2000, NT, or 9*x* computer. However, we've only discussed scripts from the standpoint of managing an individual computer. When you're managing a whole network of computers, you'll want to use scripts in several ways:

- On a single computer, to remotely manage many others. In this case, a script needs to manipulate a computer other than the one on which it's running.
- On multiple computers, with scripts stored in a common location. In this case, the goal is to have a repository of script programs and script components available for use wherever they're needed, with only a single copy extant in order to reduce maintenance time and cost.
- On multiple computers, with scripts available on each computer. When a computer might not always be connected to a centralized network, but you still want to have scripts available for use by administrators or end users, you'll need a mechanism to distribute scripts and keep them up-to-date. Of course, this entails more work than keeping all scripts in one place.
- On multiple computers, during user logon. Windows NT, 2000, and XP provide for "logon scripts" that can reconfigure a user's computer every time he or she logs on. This lets you ensure a consistent work environment and provide automatic updating of required software tools.

Together, Windows Script Host and Windows 2000/.NET Server provide you with the tools to use scripts in all these scenarios. We'll discuss how in the next few sections.

Note

Remember that besides managing the deployment of scripts, you need to ensure that Windows Script Host and any required objects are also properly installed on every managed computer. If your script uses nonstandard objects built into DLL or WSC files, you may need to copy the object files to the remote computers and run `regsvr32` on the remote computers to register the objects. You might be able to do this using the remote scripting tools discussed later in this chapter.

Creating Simple Installation Programs with IExpress

Windows XP comes with a program called `Iexpress` that creates simple "setup"-type installation programs that you can use to distribute programs and scripts to other users.

`Iexpress` is part of every Windows XP installation, yet it appears nowhere in the Windows Help and Support center. It was created as a tool to help network administrators maintain Microsoft Outlook. You can read a bit about it by visiting `support.microsoft.com` and searching for article `q237803`.

`Iexpress` provides a great way to disseminate the scripts, WSC components, and batch files that you might create using the tools described in this book, as well as regular Windows and command-line applications you've developed using other software development tools. The `Iexpress` wizard creates an executable program (sadly, not a Windows Installer .MSI file) that walks an end-user through the installation process and extracts files onto the hard disk. The installer can create Registry entries, and can even run an installation program or script to register WSC objects, modify the path, or perform other initial housekeeping actions.

The installation package created by `iexpress` will copy your applications' files into a temporary folder on an end-user's system. You'll need to supply a script that will ask the user for a permanent location for the files, and will copy them from the temporary folder to the chosen location. You can write your own script to do this, or you can use an .INF file. I'll discuss .INF files shortly.

To use `Iexpress`, prepare the files you want to distribute as well as any of the following items:

- A license agreement explaining your terms for releasing the software, copyright notices, and so on.
- An installation program or script that will copy the files to their permanent location. The installation program can be an EXE file, a WSH script, or an .INF file.
- A post-installation program that is to be run after the installation is finished. This program might perform housekeeping duties like registering .WSC or ActiveX components, creating folders, adjusting the PATH or initializing Registry entries. It too can be an EXE file, WSH script, or an .INF file.

When your materials are ready, type `iexplore` at the command prompt and step through the Wizard's screens as follows:

1. Welcome dialog—Choose Create New Self Extraction Directive File to create a new installer, or Open Existing Self Extraction Directive File to edit a package you've created previously.
2. Package Purpose—Select what kind of installation file `iexpress` should make. It can create a program that extracts files and runs an installation command, a program that only extracts files, or it can create a .CAB file with no self-extraction functionality. In most cases, you'll want to automatically install the files in a target directory, so you should choose the first option.
3. Package Title—Enter a name to describe your software.

4. Confirmation Prompt—Choose whether you want the installer to confirm that the user really wants to run the installer. You can type in the question that the user will be asked, something like, "Do you really want to install this program?" If the installation will delete or alter files, you should explain this in the confirmation question.
5. License Agreement—If you wish, you can specify a text file that contains a license agreement the user will be shown and will be asked to agree with as a condition of continuing the installation.
6. Packaged Files—Select all of the files that comprise the programs or scripts that you're distributing. You must include the .INF files and/or setup programs that you'll specify in the next step.
7. Install Program to Launch—Under Install Program, specify the program or script that will copy the files from the temporary folder to their permanent location. It must be one of the files you selected in step 6. You can use the drop-down list to select an .INF file from the packaged file set, or you can type in a command line to be run. If you want to use a WSH script as the installation program, you must enter a command line starting with `cscript` or `wscript`, for example, `cscript install.vbs`.

   Under Post Install Command, you can enter a command line to be run after the Install Program has completed, or you can select another .INF file. Again, if you want to run a WSH script, you must explicitly specify `cscript` or `wscript` in the command line.
8. Show Window—Choose the type of window that the installer should display: Default, Hidden, Minimized or Maximized. To create a silent, hidden installation procedure, choose Hidden. (In this case you should have entered no prompt in step 4 and no license agreement in step 5.) Otherwise, for a normal installer experience, choose Default.
9. Finished Message—Enter a short text string that will be displayed when the installation is complete. This might tell how to run the program or whom to call if problems are encountered.
10. Package Name and Options—Enter the path and filename for the installer program that `iexpress` is to create. Don't add the extension .EXE; the wizard will do that.
11. Configure Restart—Specify whether or not the user's system should be restarted after the installation. The default is Always Restart, but in most cases this is unnecessary, so you should select No Restart.
12. Save Self Extraction Directive—Use this page to save the entries you've made in this wizard as a .SED file. This will let you rerun the wizard later to re-create the installation package or to change some of your choices without having to retype everything.
13. Create Package—Click Next, and then Finish to complete the installer creation process.

You should find a new .EXE file in the path you specified in step 10. If you run this program, you will be walked through the installation of your application.

Tip

After you've run the wizard once, you can recreate the installation program by typing the command

`iexpress /n filename.sed`

where *`filename.sed`* is the name of the .SED file that you created in step 12. You can use this command to quickly update the installation package after changing the files that you're distributing.

Creating INF files

`IExpress` creates a program that will copy your application's files into a temporary folder on the end user's system. You're responsible for moving the files from the temporary folder to a permanent location.

You can write a script or program to do this, if you wish. You can also create what's called a .INF file, which uses an installer script language created by Microsoft. .INF files can prompt the user to choose an installation location, copy files to various locations on the user's hard disk, install registry keys and values, and more.

Unfortunately, the .INF file format is very strange and I don't have room to describe it all here. You can find fairly detailed—and cryptic—information at `msdn.microsoft.com`; examine the MSDN Library and open the following items in turn: Setup and System Administration, Setup, Setup API, SDK Documentation, Overview, Setup Applications, Using INF files.

To give you an example of how IEXPRESS can be used to deploy applications and scripts, here is an .INF file that installs a pair of .VBS scripts into folder \program files\scripts, and creates value in the registry:

```
;                                                   Example file test.inf
; This .INF file copies the test scripts test1.vbs and test2.vbs
; to \program files\scripts and installs a sample registry value

    ; This is the required version identifier
[Version]
Signature="$Chicago$"
AdvancedINF=2.5

    ; This lists the tasks that the installer is to perform
[DefaultInstall]
AddReg=AddRegSection
CopyFiles=install.files

    ; This tells where to store the installed files. The magic number
    ; 16422 tells the installer to use the system's "\program files" folder
```

```
[DestinationDirs]
install.files=16422,"scripts"

; This lists the files that are to be installed in \program files\scripts
[install.files]
test1.vbs
test2.vbs

 ; This creates a DWORD registry value named "NumberofRuns" and sets it to zero
[AddRegSection]
HKCU,"Software\MyCompany\Scripts\Test","NumberofRuns",0x00010001,"0x00000000"
```

Here is a .VBS script that makes sure that \program files\scripts is in the system PATH so that the installed scripts can be run from the command line:

```
'                                                Example File instpath.vbs
' This script is run at the end of the installation process
' to ensure that \program files\scripts is in the path.

set wshl = CreateObject("WScript.Shell")
set fso  = CreateObject("Scripting.FileSystemObject")

    ' Get the system default environment
set sysenv = wshl.Environment("system")

    ' Get the system default path
path = sysenv.Item("path")

    ' if \program files\scripts is already in the default
    ' path, we can just exit without doing anything
if instr(lcase(path), "\program files\scripts") > 0 wscript.quit 0

    ' Add "x:\program files\scripts"; (enclosed in quotes) to the beginning of
    ' the PATH environment. Use the same drive as the Windows folder.

newpath = """" & fso.GetDriveName(fso.GetSpecialFolder(0)) &_
          "\program files\scripts"";" & path

on error resume next
sysenv.Item("path") = newpath

if err.Number > 0 then
    ' We were unable to set the system-wide environment. Tell them why
    MsgBox "You must log on as a Computer Administrator " &_
           "to install these scripts, or use the RUNAS command"

else
    ' Don't restart Windows. Just tell them they have to log off and back on
    ' to get the new path setting.
    MsgBox "You should log off and back on to make the new " &_
           "PATH setting take effect."
end if
```

The script files that we're installing—`test1.vbs` and `test2.vbs`—as well as `test.inf` and `instpath.vbs` must be listed as the Packaged Files in the Iexpress wizard step 6. In step 7, the file `test.inf` is selected from the drop-down list as the Install Program, and `cscript instpath.vbs` is typed in as the Post-Installation Program.

The program file that `iexpress` creates from these files can be distributed to end-users over your network or through a Web page, added to logon scripts, or delivered by any other means that you desire.

Writing Scripts to Manage Other Computers

One way to manage multiple remote computers is to sit at one computer and reach through the network to manage others. This is a big win in large organizations, because the cost of sending administrative staff from desktop to desktop can be enormous.

I should point out that even without scripting, there are several ways to accomplish this with Windows XP and its predecessors. Windows XP Professional includes the Remote Desktop feature, and Windows 2000/.NET Server provides Terminal Services for Administration. Third-party applications such as Symantec's PCAnywhere, AT&T's VNC (which is free, by the way, and supports many operating systems), and Altiris's Carbon Copy provide the same functionality. With these technologies, you can "visit" another computer and manage it through remote control. As far as I'm concerned, these are essential management tools.

Yet, these powerful tools can't chug through a list of hundreds of computers and tweak a few settings on each in turn, as a WMI or ADSI script can. In Chapter 7, "Windows Management Instrumentation (WMI)," and Chapter 8, "Active Directory Scripting Interface (ADSI)," we covered objects that can manage computers by name, through your network.

One difficulty in using a script-based technique to deploy some sort of change through all of an organization's workstations is (a) obtaining and managing the list of all computers, and (b) dealing with computers that are unavailable at the time you run the script. There are at least two ways to get the list of all workstations:

- If your organization uses only Windows NT, 2000, and XP for end-user workstations, and it uses Windows 2000 or .NET Server with Active Directory, you can use the directory to scan for all computer accounts, using the techniques discussed in Chapter 8. You'll just have to obtain the necessary containers and examine their collections and subcollections for computer accounts.
- If you don't have Active Directory available, or if your organization uses Windows 9*x*/Me, you will have to maintain a list of workstations by name and/or IP address by hand. You might be able to use network scanning to find all the names, but this is probably not as reliable as maintaining an inventory manually. You'll have to exercise lots of control of the network and over procedures, to be sure that new computers don't get added without updating the list.

Regardless of the means you use to get the list of computers, when you need to deploy a change through the entire organization, I suggest that you create a text file listing all the computer names, as a copy that is used *only* for this specific project. Then, write a script that can scan this list, perform the required changes using WMI or ASDI, and remove the computer name from the list if the operation is successful. This way, you'll be able to rerun the script periodically until all the computers have been updated. Here is a sample script that does this sort of list editing:

```
                                  ' Example File deploy.vbs
option explicit
dim complist, maxcomputers, compname(), fso, s, nleft, str, i

complist = "update_printers.dat"  ' file containing names of computers to fix
maxcomputers = 100                ' size of array, grows automatically
redim compname(maxcomputers)      ' list of computers still to be updated
nleft = 0                         ' number of computers in list

' read list of computers
set fso = CreateObject("Scripting.FileSystemObject")
set s = fso.OpenTextFile(complist)
do while not s.AtEndOfStream          ' read file line-by-line
    str = trim(s.ReadLine)
    if len(str) > 0 then              ' for each name
        if nleft >= maxcomputers then ' grow the array if necessary
            maxcomputers = nleft+100
            redim preserve compname(maxcomputers)
        end if
        compname(nleft) = str         ' save name
        nleft = nleft+1
    end if
loop
s.close
set s = Nothing

' process each of the computers
i = 0
do while i < nleft
    WScript.echo "Updating", compname(i) & "..."
    if process(compname(i)) then      ' if successfully updated
        nleft = nleft-1               ' remove the name from the array and
        compname(i) = compname(nleft) ' fill the hole with the last name
    else
        WScript.echo "... FAILED"
        i = i+1                       ' skip this computer, get it next time
    end if
loop

' write list back, without fixed computers
set s = fso.CreateTextFile(complist, True)
for i = 0 to nleft-1
    s.WriteLine compname(i)
```

```
next
s.Close
set s = Nothing

' final report
WScript.echo
select case nleft
    case 0    WScript.echo "ALL COMPUTERS HAVE BEEN UPDATED"
    case 1    WScript.echo "There is 1 computer left to update"
    case else WScript.echo "There are", nleft, "computers left to update"
end select

' function process - update whatever needs updating
function process (computername)
    process = False               ' assume failure
    on error resume next          ' don't halt script on error

    '... update the named computer. Be very careful to check for
    '... errors. Set return value to True only if sure of success

    if (the update was successful) then
        process = True
    end if
end function
```

In the script, the function `update` performs the actual work on a specific computer, and it must return `True` only if the update succeeds. In this case, it's important not to let script or network errors halt the script; otherwise, the final update to the list of computers will not be made. You might consider updating the list after each computer is processed, if this is a concern. When all computers have been updated, the project-specific computer list file will be empty.

Remote Scripting

While WMI and ADSI are great for reaching into the insides of Windows on remote computers, there is another way to manage remote workstations called *remote scripting*. Remote scripting actually runs a script on another computer, as illustrated in Figure 10.1.

Here's how it works. On the master or originating computer, the master script creates an object called `WSHController`. This object copies a second script file to a remote computer and starts up Windows Script Host on that computer to run the copied script. Because this remote script runs on the remote computer, it can use any of the techniques you'd use for managing a local computer—you can use `Scripting.FileSystemObject` to examine the computer's hard drives, and so on. In the remote script, references to drive "C:" refer to drive C on the remote computer.

You can apply the remote scripting with the multiple-computer management technique I discussed in the previous section to run a remote management script on a whole network's worth of computers.

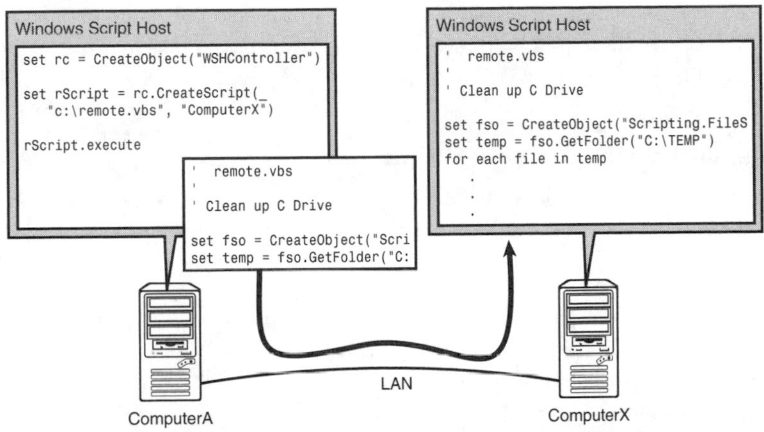

Figure 10.1 The `WSHController` object copies a script file to a remote computer and has Windows Script Host on that computer run the script.

> **Note**
>
> The remote script service is managed by DCOM (Distributed COM). There is no way to specify alternate authentication information with remote scripting. The remote script will run with *your* logon name and password. You must either be a member of the same domain as the remote computer or have an account on the remote computer.

Enabling Remote Scripting

Each computer that is to run a remote script (that is, each computer that is to play the role of ComputerX in Figure 10.1) must have Windows Script Host version 5.6 or later installed. You may need to update WSH on computers running Windows 2000, 98, NT 4, or Me.

DCOM must be enabled on each remote computer. It is usually enabled by default. You can check by running DCOMCNFG as an administrator. On the Default Properties tab, the Enable Distributed COM on This Computer box should be checked.

Additionally, remote scripting must be enabled separately, and it is *not* enabled by default. It must be enabled by setting a Registry entry on each computer in a workgroup network or through a policy setting on a domain network.

To enable remote scripting through the Registry, create a new string value named `Remote` under `HKEY_LOCAL_MACHINE\SOFTWARE\Microsoft\Windows Script Host\Settings` and give it the value `1`.

For more information about enabling remote scripting, see the downloaded WSH documentation or view the library at `msdn.microsoft.com` and search for "Setting Up Remote WSH."

Writing and Running Remote Scripts

To run a remote script, have your local script create a `WSHController` object. `WSHController` has one method: `Createscript(`*`scriptfile`*`, `*`computername`*`)`. Here are the arguments:

- `scriptfile`—The path and name of the script file to copy to the remote computer. The file can be a `.vbs`, `.wsh`, `.wsf`, or other file type registered as a Windows Script file. You must specify a path that is valid on *your* computer—it can be a file on your hard drive or on a network share that you can reach. This file will be copied by `WSHController` to the remote computer and run there.
- `computername`—The name of the computer on which you want to run the script. This can be a simple NetBIOS computer name or a fully qualified domain name.

`Createscript` returns a `WSHRemote` object that represents the remote connection. The properties and methods of `WSHRemote` are listed in Reference List 10.4.

REFERENCE LIST 10.4 Properties and Methods of the `WSHRemote` Object

Properties:

`Status`

Returns a value that indicates the status of the script running on the remote computer. Check this value only after starting the script with the `Execute` method. The value returned is `0` if the script has not yet been executed, `1` if the script is still running, or `2` if it has completed.

`Error`

Returns a `WSHRemoteError` object that tells whether the remote script encountered an error and describes the problem.

Methods:

`Execute`

Starts the script on the remote computer. You will need to make your script wait until the remote script finishes its job. See the discussion after this reference list for details.

`Terminate`

Halts the script running on the remote computer. This is considered a last resort, to be used only when the remote script doesn't finish on its own after a reasonable length of time, because the script could be in the middle of updating a file or running an application on the remote computer.

When the script has finished running, the `Status` property will equal `2`. You can then check the `Error` property to see whether the script encountered any problems. The `Error` property returns a `WSHRemoteError` object, which has the following properties:

Property	Description
`Description`	Explanation of the error
`Line`	The line number in the script file on which the error occurred
`Character`	The column number in the error line on which the error occurred
`SourceText`	The script program line that contains the error
`Source`	The name of the COM object in which the error occurred, if appropriate
`Number`	The error number (`0` if this was no error)

If the `Error` property is `0`, there was no error. A nonzero value indicates the problem. The sample script at the end of this section shows how to use this information.

Note

At the time of this writing, Microsoft's online and downloaded documentation for the `WSHRemote` object has a bug. If you follow the link from the `WSHRemote` object's page to the `Status` property's page, it leads you to the write-up for the `Status` property of the wrong object. To see the correct write-up, view the `Execute` method's page. At the bottom of this page, click on Status Property.

To run a script on a remote computer, first prepare the script file and store it in a convenient location—for example, `c:\scripts\remote\cleantemp.vbs`. The remote script might look like this:

```
                                    ' Example File cleantemp.vbs
set fso = CreateObject("Scripting.FileSystemObject")
cleanpath = "C:\TEMP"

cleanup fso.GetFolder(cleanpath)

' ------------------------------------------------------------------

sub cleanup (folder)
    dim file, subfolder              ' declare local variables

    for each file in folder.Files   ' clean up files
        upext = ucase(fso.GetExtensionName(file.Name))
        if upext = "TMP" or upext = "BAK" then
            wscript.echo "deleting", file.path
            file.Delete
        end if
    next
```

```
                                        ' clean up any subfolders
    for each subfolder in folder.SubFolders
        cleanup subfolder
    next
end sub
```

Use a script like this one to run the remote script on another computer:

```
                                        ' Example File script1001.vbs
set rc = CreateObject("WSHController")  ' create remote controller object
                                        ' run script on ComputerX
runremote "c:\scripts\remote\cleantemp.vbs", "ComputerX"

' -------------------------------------------------------------
' runremote - subroutine to run a script on a remote computer

sub runremote (scriptfile, computername)
    dim rScript, runtime

    WScript.echo "Running script", scriptfile, "on", computername & "..."
                                        ' create remote script object
    set rScript = rc.CreateScript(scriptfile, computername)

    rScript.execute                     ' start the remote script

    runtime = 0                         ' wait up to 30 seconds for it to finish
    do while rScript.Status <> 2
        if runtime >= 30000 then        ' it's taken too long
           rScript.Terminate
           WScript.echo "...Script did not finish, terminated it"
           exit sub
        end if
        WScript.Sleep 500               ' wait 500 msec (1/2 second) more
        runtime = runtime+500
    loop

    with rScript.Error    ' it terminated by itself, check for errors
        if .number = 0 then
            WScript.echo "...ok"
        else
            WScript.echo "...Script terminated due to error #", .number
            WScript.echo .description
            WScript.echo "Line", .line & ":", .sourceText
        end if
    end with
end sub
```

The following common conditions can make the `CreateScript` method fail:

- If you get the error message "The remote server machine does not exist or is unavailable," it's likely that the target computer name is spelled incorrectly or the machine is not running.

- If you get the error "ActiveX component can't create object," it's likely that the remote computer doesn't have Windows Script Host 5.6 or better installed. You'll need to update WSH before you can run a remote script on it.
- If you get the message "Call was rejected by callee," it is likely that DCOM is disabled on the remote computer. See the section "Enabling Remote Scripting" to see how to enable it.
- If you get the error "ActiveX component can't create object" after a long delay, it's likely that remote scripting is not enabled in the Registry of the remote computer. See the section "Enabling Remote Scripting" to see how to enable it.

In any case, if you have trouble getting remote scripting to work, check the System Log with the Event Viewer on the remote computer; there may be an explanation there.

By the way, if the script file itself does not exist, the script will not generate an error until you use the `Execute` method.

Tip

You can use remote scripting's error-reporting mechanism to communicate a small amount of information from the remote computer back to the originating computer. To do this, have the remote script generate an error with a specific, nonstandard error number and then put the information in the error's `Description` property. If the originating script sees that the remote script terminated with the magic error number, it can read the information out of the `Error.Description` property.

There's a trick to making this tip work, however. For the prearranged error number, you must use the sum of the predefined constant `vbObjectError` (-2147221504) with some number of your choosing. If you don't, WSH modifies the error number before it is returned to the local computer.

Although this technique sounds complex, it's easy to use. Here's a bit of VBScript code that you could use in a remote script to send information back to the originating computer:

```
                                      ' Example File checkfree.vbs
set fso = CreateObject("Scripting.FileSystemObject")
nfree = fso.GetDrive("C:").FreeSpace

Err.Raise vbObjectError+47, "", "My C drive has " & nfree & " bytes free"
```

This causes the script to terminate. The originating computer can receive the information this way:

```
                                      ' Example File script1002.vbs
' ... run the remote script, then, when it's finished:

with rScript.Error
   select case .Number
```

```
        case (vbObjectError+47)     ' this is the magic number
            WScript.echo "The remote script said:", .Description

        case 0                      ' exited without throwing an error?
            WScript.echo "Remote script exited with no message"

        case else                   ' it encountered a real error
            WScript.echo "Remote script encountered error #", .Number
            WScript.echo .Description
    end select
end with
```

Replicating Scripts to Multiple Computers

For scripts that you'll need to use on several computers on your network, you can put the script files in a shared network folder, where they'll be available from any computer.

When you have to maintain computers that are *not* on your primary network—for example, workstations for home workers, field personnel, or computers on remote networks that may not be permanently connected—you'll need some means of distributing the script files in advance of needing them. It would be most helpful if the distribution was automatic and kept the files up-to-date.

Between sites of a large corporate network, part of the job *can* be automated using the File Replication Service that is provided with Windows 2000, .NET and NT 4.0 Server. The File Replication Service makes sure all server computers in a large internetwork have up-to-date copies of a set of shared, common files. On Windows NT 4.0 Server, files placed in `\winnt\system32\repl\export` or one of its subdirectories on the primary domain controller are copied to `\winnt\system32\repl\import` on all domain controllers. On Windows 2000/.NET Server, files and subdirectories under `\winnt\sysvol\sysvol\`*`domainname`* on *any* domain server are copied to all other domain servers. There is no "master" copy in this case; if a file is created or edited on any server, it's copied to all the others. You can share a script's folder in one of the replicated directories and have the same set of scripts available on every local network in your organization. Scripts are also stored under the policy subdirectories.

Getting scripts copied to individual workstations, with or without a domain-based network, is another matter. For this, you'll have to be innovative. Here are some suggestions:

- On a domain network, you can have every user's logon script call a batch file or script subroutine that will copy scripts from the replication folder on the domain server to a folder on each workstation. This way, whenever someone logs on, the workstations' cache of scripts will be updated. The updating procedure should be "smart" and only copy new or changed files. Script files can do this by applying the `FileSystemObject` methods of Chapter 3; I'll give you a sample script to do this. A batch file will have to call a file-updating program such as the Resource Kit's `robocopy` to do this sort of job.

- If you are not on a domain network, you can put an icon in a shared network folder to run a similar replication batch file or script. You'll just have to ask your users to click the update icon periodically. On small networks, this works quite well. It also works on domain networks when users work remotely (for example, over a VPN). I like to put a shortcut to a server shared folder on each remote user's desktop. Once they connect through dial-up networking or the VPN, they can open this shortcut to see a folder full of relevant network-related tasks.

The following script shows how you might replicate a folder full of script files from a server (or other central location) onto the local computer. This script can be run from a logon script or manually:

```
                                                            ' script REPL.VBS
' replicate a directory of files from the domain server onto a workstation

set fso      = CreateObject("Scripting.FileSystemObject")
set wshShell = CreateObject("WScript.Shell")
set environ  = wshShell.Environment("Process")

' assume master copies are kept in a shared replicated folder on the domain
' logon server.  You can replace this with a fixed path name if your
' network does not have a domain controller or if you do not use replication.
' Here, we use the environment variable LOGONSERVER, since any DC could have
' logged the user on. This should work anywhere in the enterprise.
srcpath  = environ("LOGONSERVER") & "\scripts\path"

' specify location to keep copies on all workstations
destpath = environ("WINDIR") & "\scripts"

wscript.echo srcpath
wscript.echo destpath

if fso.FolderExists(srcpath) then
    checkfolder fso.GetFolder(srcpath), destpath
end if

' checkfolder - replicate the contents of a master folder to a destination
' path. Folder is a Folder object, destpath is the name of the target
' directory.

sub checkfolder (folder, destpath)
    dim file, subfolder

    if not fso.FolderExists(destpath) then fso.CreateFolder(destpath)

    for each file in folder.Files    ' replicate each file
        checkfile file, destpath & "\" & file.Name
    next
                                     ' call again to process subfolders
    for each subfolder in folder.SubFolders
        checkfolder subfolder, destpath & "\" & subfolder.Name
```

```
    next
end sub

' checkfile - check one file and copy to destination if necessary.
' srcfile is a File object representing the master copy, destname is full
' pathname of the target copy.

sub checkfile (srcfile, destname)
    dim copyit, destfile

    if fso.FileExists(destname) then         ' file exists already?
        set destfile = fso.GetFile(destname) ' see if it needs to be replaced
        copyit = (srcfile.DateLastModified > destfile.DateLastModified) or _
                 (srcfile.size <> destfile.size)
    else
        copyit = True                        ' file does not yet exist
    end if

    if copyit then                           ' copy the file
        on error resume next                 ' don't stop if an error occurs
        fso.CopyFile srcfile.Path, destname, True
        if err.number then                   ' report error
           MsgBox "Unable to update " & srcfile.Name & ": " & err.description
        end if
        on error goto 0
    end if
end sub
```

Scripting Security Issues

As you've seen in the last few hundred pages, scripts are powerful tools and can get their fingers into every nook and cranny of Windows. It's bad enough that anyone can write and run a script on their own computer, but in this chapter, you've seen that they can be invisibly sent to and run on other computers. It's enough to keep a network security manager up nights with bad dreams and indigestion. (I have mentioned Prilosec® already, haven't I?)

The good news is that most of the serious management functions require Administrator privileges. All scripts, including remote scripts, execute in the security context of the users who run them. Therefore, the damage they can do is limited to whatever damage the user can do sitting at the computer directly. This isn't much help if a user gets duped into running a malicious script contained in a Web page, sent in an e-mail attachment, or just found lying around.

One way to protect your organization's computers from unwanted WSH experimentation is to instruct WSH to run only *signed* scripts. Signing is the process of marking a script with a cryptographic signature that guarantees that the script was written by a known, trusted user. Windows Script Host versions 5.6 and later let you specify a Registry value that will prevent unsigned scripts from running. The Registry value

HKEY_CURRENT_USER\Software\Microsoft\Windows Script Host\Settings\TrustPolicy can be set to any of three DWORD values to determine how WSH will treat unsigned scripts:

Value	Restriction Level
0	Run any script, signed or not.
1	Prompt the user if a script is unsigned.
2	Never run unsigned scripts.

Note

Word on the Windows support newsgroups is that the signed-scripts-only restriction may cause problems with the ability of Windows to run remote scripts. If you use remote scripts and then restrict scripting to permit signed scripts only, check to be sure that your remote scripts still work.

You can set this Registry value on all your organization's computers to whatever level you deem necessary. On a domain network, you can enforce this restriction through a policy. You can also make the setting manually by editing the Registry or by distributing a .reg Registry file.

Another area of concern is that end users might learn a bit too much by snooping around in the scripts on their computers and on the network. Scripts can contain a lot of fairly high-level information—the names of servers and possibly hidden shares, the location of important files, and even the techniques used by scripts to manipulate Windows. In a security-conscious environment, you should think twice about making this information easy to come by. I won't go so far as to suggest that you ban this book, but you can take the step of encrypting scripts so that they're not easily readable.

In this section, I'll show you how to sign your own scripts so that they'll be trusted on your network, and how to encrypt scripts for increased privacy.

Script Signing

Code signing is the process of attaching to a program file a cryptographically generated message that could only have been generated by a known, trusted person or organization. As it applies to scripts, signing marks a script as authentically produced by the trusted source and guarantees that the script has not been modified by others between signing and delivery. Signing can increase security if you take three steps:

- You or your organization must acquire a certificate, a special file that is issued by a Certification Authority (CA) that can vouch for your identity. A *certificate* is a special data file that contains information and encryption keys and makes it possible to encode a file so that anyone who receives the file can be sure that you sent it, insofar as they trust the certification authority. Certification Authorities include companies such as VeriSign, Certisign, Thawte, and others.

Certificates of this sort usually cost $200–400. Windows 2000 and .NET Server can generate certificates on their own for free for use within an organization, but without the "stamp of approval" of a Certification Authority, there is no way for these certificates to be verified outside the organization's domain network.

- Each script that you want your users to be able to run must be digitally "signed" with this certificate. I'll show you how to do this in a moment.
- Each of your organization's computers should be set through Local Security Policy or through Registry settings not to run unsigned scripts, or to at least warn users if they attempt to run an unsigned script.

To sign scripts, you'll need to choose a Certification Authority (CA). You can use a public, fee-based CA, or you can use your organization's own CA, if your scripts are for internal use only and you have Windows 2000/.NET Server available.

Then, you must request and install a code-signing certificate. For a public CA, you'll do this by e-mail, following the procedure specified by the CA. For an organizational CA, follow the instructions specified by your network administrator. When you have the certificate installed, you should be able to see it in the Certificates MMC snap-in; an example is shown in Figure 10.2.

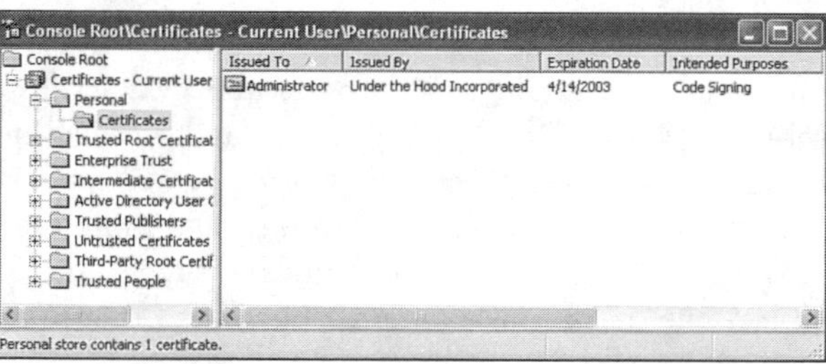

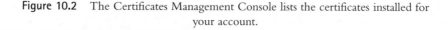

Figure 10.2 The Certificates Management Console lists the certificates installed for your account.

WSH comes with an object that can sign script files using only a few statements. Here is a script named `signfile.vbs` that can be used to sign script files:

```
                                              ' signfile.vbs - sign script files
set signer = CreateObject("Scripting.Signer") ' create signing object

for each arg in WScript.Arguments             ' sign any file(s) named
    sign arg                                  ' on the command line
next

' sign - sign the specified file with the specified certificate. The second
' argument to SignFile is the name to whom the certificate is assigned.

sub sign (filename)
    signer.SignFile filename, "Administrator"
end sub
```

You may find it necessary to set up a special account used just for script signing (I have found that the `Signer` object has difficulty locating the correct certificate if the account has more than one certificate installed). The account name used for this could be something like "My Company, Inc." so that this name will appear as the signer name.

You sign script files with the following command line:

```
signfile scriptname...
```

Here's an example:

```
signfile test.vbs
```

This places comments at the end of the script. The resulting file might look like this:

```
MsgBox "This is a signed script"
'' SIG '' Begin signature block
'' SIG '' MIIIMAYJKoZIhvcNAQcCoIIIITCCCB0CAQExDjAMBggq
'' SIG '' hkiG9w0CBQUAMGYGCisGAQQBgjcCAQSgWDBWMDIGCisG
.
.
.
'' SIG '' Hn7AhAQwZGWgpTbAYPWh0AT5Wz6rQdSpnuAj6w9zviVP
'' SIG '' qvCa6VFH9/0iE9VqBc+zuwIGYn11
'' SIG '' End signature block
```

The signature data occupies about 200 lines! If a script has been signed, when you view its Properties page in Explorer, an additional tab labeled Digital Signatures appears, as shown in Figure 10.3. Clicking Details and then View Certificate lets you check the identity of the signer and of the Certification Authority.

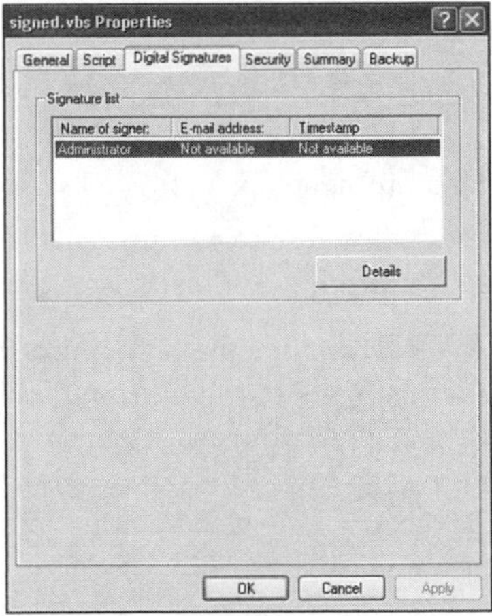

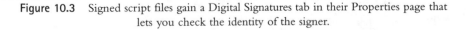

Figure 10.3 Signed script files gain a Digital Signatures tab in their Properties page that lets you check the identity of the signer.

To secure a standalone or workgroup Windows 2000 Professional workstation so that it requires WSH to check the authenticity of scripts, you must apply a security policy. On a domain network, this can be applied through Group Policy. On a standalone workstation, it can be applied through Local Policy, which is administered by the Group Policy MMC snap-in.

The settings are made through the policy entries under Computer Configuration, Windows Settings, Security Settings, Software Restriction Policies, Additional Rules. The administrator can add a "path rule" to block access to specific file types. For example, entering a "disallowed" rule for `*.vbs` without a pathname prevents the user from running any VBS file, from any location. Similar rules can block `.js` and `.wsf` files. The rules could also be written to block execution of scripts only in the temporary folders used by Internet Explorer and Outlook Express for downloaded files.

In addition, the administrator must add "certificate rules" that specify trusted certificates—in particular, the certificate used to sign your scripts. Scripts signed by the listed certificates are allowed to run even if blocked by other policy rules.

If a user under this policy regime attempts to run a script that is unsigned or has been altered since the signing, this message is displayed:

```
CScript Error: Execution of the Windows Script Host failed. (Windows cannot open
this program because it has been prevented by a software restriction policy. For
more information, open Event Viewer or contact your system administrator.)
```

A simpler Registry-based mechanism is available that is backward compatible with older versions of Windows. Windows Script Host version 5.6 checks the Registry entry `HKEY_CURRENT_USER\SOFTWARE\Microsoft\Windows Script Host\Settings\TrustPolicy`, which may be set to one of the following `DWORD` values:

Value	**Result**
`0`	Windows runs any script regardless of signing.
`1`	Windows prompts the user with a warning dialog box before running an unsigned or untrusted script.
`2`	Windows will refuse to run unsigned scripts and signed scripts whose Certification Authority is not known and trusted.

This Registry key can be set for a specific user, or it can be set for all users by making the same Registry entry under `HKEY_LOCAL_MACHINE` and additionally setting the `DWORD` value of `HKEY_LOCAL_MACHINE\SOFTWARE\Microsoft\Windows Script Host\Settings\IgnoreUserSettings` to `1`. To maintain security, you should change the security settings on the `Settings` key so that the end users cannot change the value; this should be changeable by administrators only.

Caution

Microsoft's documentation describes the Registry key technique as "backward" compatible. However, in my testing, it did not restrict scripts in Windows XP, only older versions of Windows. Whether this is a bug or due to something I did wrong, who knows? Therefore, you should carefully test any restriction settings you make to be sure they work in your environment. You may need to use both methods to ensure that all users are restricted regardless of operating system.

The Script Encoder

The Script Encoder is a downloadable command-line utility available at `msdn.microsoft.com`. Its job is to scramble the contents of `.vbs` or `.js` script files into a binary mishmash not easily read by humans, but which WSH can decipher as easily as the original script. This can give your scripts some measure of protection from snooping and theft. I say not *easily* read by humans because, unlike the strong encryption that the Windows Encrypted File System uses, the Script Encoder is fairly simple-minded. It's possible for a determined person to reverse the process and read the encrypted file. Consider script encoding a *mild* deterrent from casual snooping.

To use the Script Encoder, first make a backup copy of all the scripts you plan to encode and distribute, preferably on a different computer than the one you'll use to encode. This is to avoid the chance that you'll encode your only copy and lose the human-readable copy.

Encoded scripts use a different file extension than plain-text scripts. Table 10.1 lists the normal and encoded extensions.

Table 10.1 **File Extensions for Regular and Encoded Scripts**

Type	Regular File Extension	Encoded File Extension
VBScript	`.vbs`	`.vbe`
JScript	`.js`	`.jse`

The syntax for the renaming conversion is

```
screnc originalname newname
```

Here's an example:

```
screnc myscript.vbs myscript.vbe
```

Although the Script Encoder permits the use of wildcards and has some other options, these are not applicable for encoding VBS and JS script files.

Setting Up Logon Scripts

One important use of scripts is to set up user accounts in a consistent way at every logon. This is important in business environments, where network resources may be moved from time to time, or when users may inadvertently alter mapped network drives or other network settings. A script that runs whenever the user logs on can ensure that the user will always have access to correct network resources. Logon scripts can also perform checks for software updates, clean up temporary folders, and otherwise perform maintenance tasks on a routine basis, automatically.

Windows NT 4, 2000, and XP all let you assign scripts on a per-user basis. A login script can be a WSH file or an old-style `.bat` or `.cmd` batch file; you can use whatever format you wish. A batch file can even launch Windows Script Host, if you need to use both environments.

In addition, Windows 2000 and XP support Group Policy–based script assignments that let you run a script upon user logon/logoff and computer startup/shutdown.

In this section, I'll show you how to assign logon scripts to users and groups.

User Profile Logon Scripts

The oldest and most common way to assign logon scripts is through the user profile mechanism. Windows NT 4, 2000, and XP all let you assign a script to a user account. This can be done both for domain accounts and for local computer accounts. Here's how to do this:

- On a Windows 2000 or .NET Server machine, run User Manager for Domains or Active Directory Users and Groups, whichever is appropriate.
- On Windows XP Professional (for example, for a standalone or workgroup computer or for local accounts on a domain member), right-click My Computer, select Manage, and then select Local Users and Groups.

For local accounts and for standalone or workgroup computers, Windows looks for logon scripts on the local computer in a peculiar, fixed location: under the Windows directory in `\windows\system32\repl\import\scripts`. This folder is used because, historically, it was a folder that was automatically copied to all domain servers in an organization, as mentioned earlier in the chapter.

For domain user accounts, Windows retrieves scripts from the NETLOGON shared folder on the domain controller (server). On a Windows .NET/2000 domain server, they are stored in `\winnt\sysvol\sysvol\`*`domainname`*`\scripts`, which is shared as NETLOGON.

View the properties for a user and select the Profile tab, as illustrated in Figure 10.4. Enter the name of the logon script file, which can be of any registered script or batch file type. The filename you enter here is relative to `\windows\system32\repl\import\scripts`, and although you can enter either a plain filename (for example, `logon.vbs`) or a ***`subfolder\filename`***, you cannot enter an absolute path (that is, one starting with `\`). Nor can you use `..` to attempt to climb to a higher folder. In most cases, logon scripts are stored in the top-level scripts folder, and you can enter their names without any path information.

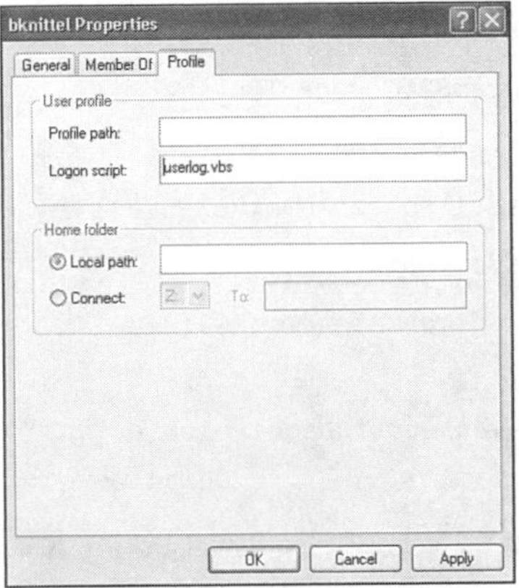

Figure 10.4 Enter the location of the logon script in the Profile tab of a user's Properties page.

Caution

Because logon scripts can do anything the user can do, you *must* be sure no one can maliciously edit a logon script that belongs to another user.

Be very careful to set proper access-control permissions on logon script files and on the scripts folder itself. Script files should only be stored on an NTFS-formatted partition; they should be readable by Everyone but writeable and modifiable only by Administrator.

The script is executed each time the user logs on, just after Windows restores any persistent network settings (that is, after network drives mapped with the Reconnect at Logon are box checked). The script can then rearrange network settings, Windows printers, software and Registry settings, and desktop icons, or do whatever else is needed.

Group Policy Logon, Logoff, Startup, and Shutdown Scripts

On Windows XP Professional and on Windows 2000 Professional, you can specify login scripts though Group Policy. Policy-based scripts are separate from the user profile script discussed in the previous section. Policy-assigned scripts run in addition to any script defined in the user profile. This feature is available even without Active Directory, through each computer's Local Policy settings, so it's available on standalone and workgroup computers as well as domain members.

To assign logon, logoff, startup, or shutdown scripts, first create and test the scripts. Then, store them in the correct location, which will be one of the following folders:

Policy	**Locations**
Local	`\WINDOWS\system32\GroupPolicy\User\Scripts\Logon`
	`\WINDOWS\system32\GroupPolicy\User\Scripts\Logoff`
	`\WINDOWS\system32\GroupPolicy\Machine\Scripts\Startup`
	`\WINDOWS\system32\GroupPolicy\Machine\Scripts\Shutdown`
Group	`\\server\sysvol\`*`domainname`*`\Policies\{...}\User\Scripts\Logon`
	`\\server\sysvol\`*`domainname`*`\Policies\{...}\User\Scripts\Logoff`
	`\\server\sysvol\`*`domainname`*`\Policies\{...}\Machine\Scripts\Startup`
	`\\server\sysvol\`*`domainname`*`\Policies\{...}\Machine\Scripts\Shutdown`

For standalone and workgroup computers, Local Policy is the only option available.

Next, assign the scripts in the Group Policy MMC snap-in using these steps:

1. As Administrator, click Start, Run and then type **MMC** and press Enter.
2. Click Console, Add/Remove Snap-In, and Add. Select Group Policy and click Add.
3. Select the desired policy. The default is Local Computer, which is the only option on a standalone or workgroup computer. On a domain network, you can click Browse and select another policy object.
4. Click Finish, Close, and then OK to start the policy console, which is shown in Figure 10.5.

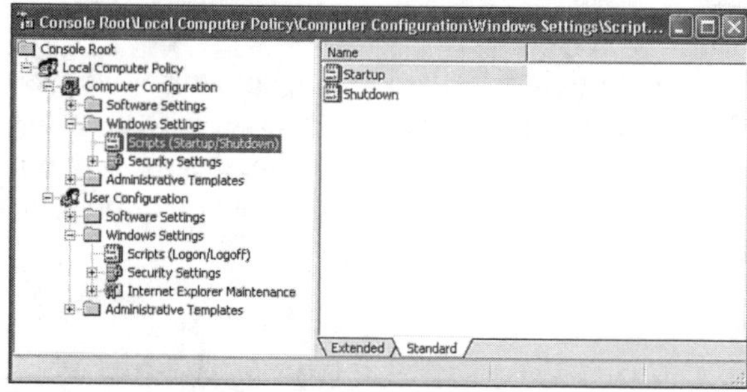

Figure 10.5 The Group Policy Editor lets you assign startup, shutdown, logon, and logoff scripts.

5. To add startup or shutdown scripts, open Computer Configuration, Windows Settings, Scripts. To add logon or logoff scripts, open User Configuration, Windows Settings, Scripts. In the right pane, double-click the appropriate script category.
6. In the script's Properties dialog box, click Add. Enter a script name and any desired script parameters. You can also click Browse to locate a script file manually. Click OK to confirm, and the script will be added to the list of designated scripts, as shown in Figure 10.6.

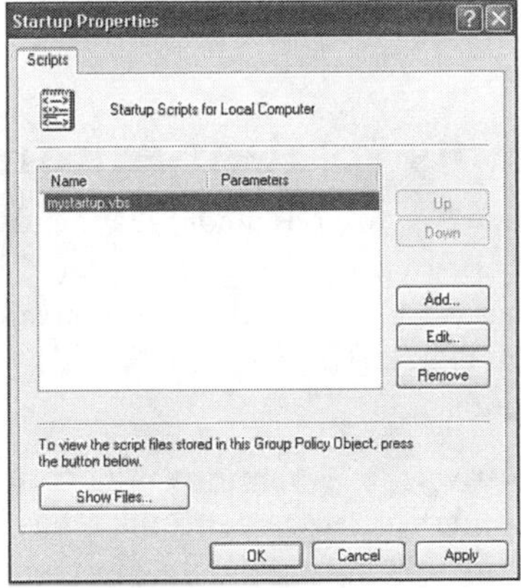

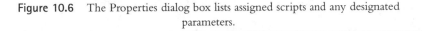

Figure 10.6 The Properties dialog box lists assigned scripts and any designated parameters.

7. You can add multiple scripts and use the Up and Down buttons to order them. These scripts are executed in turn, with one starting after the previous has exited. Click the Remove button to delete a script assignment. Click OK to save the script settings.

Here are some observations I've made about policy-based scripts:

- Policy-based logon scripts run after Windows establishes any memorized network connections, and they are *started* before the user profile login script, but the logon process does not wait until either of these scripts completes. The user profile logon script can't be sure when it starts up that the policy-based script has finished, or even that it has begun to do its work. Meanwhile, once any startup scripts have been initiated, Windows proceeds to run any programs listed in `WIN.INI` and in the All Users and personal Startup folders.
- Logoff scripts are run before Windows shuts down network connections, and the logoff process waits until the logoff script has exited before proceeding.
- The Local Machine Policy user logon script is *not* run for the Administrator account, but the logoff script is run for every account.

- Logon and logoff scripts are not run if the user signs off using Fast User switching. Even though the desktop is not visible, the user remains logged on.

Note

Using logoff and shutdown scripts is a neat idea, but there's no guarantee that either will run every time they should—sometimes Windows crashes, sometimes the power goes out, sometimes users log off with the reset button. Therefore, although you can use these scripts for cleanup and maintenance work, they're not reliable for billing, time tracking, or other applications where missing runs could make a significant difference.

Scheduling Scripts to Run Automatically

Besides writing Windows books, I work as a consultant and develop software for several companies. For large-scale database projects, I've found it useful to set up scheduled programs—scripts—that run on a nightly basis to create reports, archive old data, perform backups, and so on. This isn't a new idea: Nightly "batch" processing has been around as long as the computer itself.

Automatic scripting is a great way to be sure that important operations take place even if you forget to start them, and they can be performed during off hours so there is minimal disruption to your work. Often, the only convenient time to perform procedures such as backups and database cleanups is at night when most users are gone, because these tasks usually require all applications to be shut down and all data files to be closed.

Windows XP has the Task Scheduler, which makes it easy to schedule scripts for automatic startup. The Task Scheduler appears in Windows 2000 as well, and in a different form in Windows NT, where it was called the `at` command. In this section, I'll talk a bit about some extra considerations to make when writing scheduled scripts, and then I'll show how to use the Task Scheduler to set them up.

Writing Unattended Scripts

You'll usually write scheduled scripts for either or both of these reasons: to process information when nobody is around, and to ensure that necessary processing isn't forgotten. In either case, this processing is usually very important, and it's crucial that you know whether some problem is preventing it from occurring. Although automated processing is a great idea, it's very easy and dangerous to succumb to an "out of sight, out of mind" obliviousness; there is no more horrifying experience in the computing realm than to find after a disk crash that the last month's worth of automatic backups never took place.

So, at the risk of laboring a point, I want to discuss some ways you can make scheduled scripts accountable for their proper operation. The key concepts here are logging and notification.

The problem with scheduled programs is that they don't interact with the user's desktop, so if they stop working, it could be some time before anyone notices.

As a sort of failsafe mechanism, I've found it useful to have every automatic process produce some sort of annoying reminder of its presence so that a missed run will be noticed. This can take the form of a log file, a printed report, or an e-mail message.

As a matter of policy, every automated script should keep a log file record of its operation, indicating the date and time when key steps in the script have completed their task, and certainly recording any errors or anomalous conditions that the script encounters, such as empty input files.

The following sample script has a procedure named `loggit` that can be used to record text messages in a log file. The procedure opens and closes the log file every time it records a message so that the information is sure to be written out. If the script crashes, you'll know that the problem occurred after the point in the script where the last message was written. Here's the script:

```
                                        ' Example File sched.vbs
dim logfilename, fso
logfilename = "C:\scripts\logs\sched.log"
set fso = CreateObject("Scripting.FileSystemObject")

const ForAppending = 8

loggit "* Sched started"

' ... gather input

if input_file_was_empty then            ' (these are fictitious statements)
    loggit "Error: input file was empty"
    wscript.quit 0
end if

for each item in list_of_things_to_do
    loggit "starting to process item " & item
next

loggit "* Sched finished successfully"

' ----------------------------------------------
' loggit - write a message to the script log file

sub loggit (msg)
    set stream = fso.OpenTextFile(logfilename, ForAppending, True)
    stream.writeline date & " " & time & ": " & msg
    stream.close
    WScript.echo msg ' show on console window too in case someone is watching
end sub
```

Logged messages should always use a consistent format. For example, error messages might always start with the string "Error:". This will help you to automatically identify problems with a summarizing script, as we'll discuss shortly.

Controlling the Amount of Information Logged

When you're first debugging a script, you'll often add many logging and debugging `wscript.echo` statements. I suggest that you keep all these statements even after the script is working and change them all to logging procedure calls. To keep the log file from becoming bloated, control the amount of detail recorded with a "log-level" variable defined at the beginning of the script. For example, you could define three information levels: 0 = normal, 1 = moderate, 2 = maximum. Then, you can use `if` statements to control each log entry, as shown here:

```
dim loglevel
loglevel = 0    ' enable minimal logging
.
.
.
if loglevel >= 0 then loggit "* this is always logged"
.
.
.
if loglevel >= 1 then loggit "* this is logged at level 1+"
.
.
.
if loglevel >= 2 then loggit "* this is only logged at level 2+"
```

If trouble occurs, all the debugging statements will still be there. You can set the `loglevel` variable to its maximum value and run the script again to get more detailed information.

Sending Messages to the Event Log

You can also record logging information to the Windows Event Log. This should probably be reserved for errors, because the Event Log tends to lose its usefulness if it's filled with "chatter" (that is, success and informational messages).

I covered event logging briefly in Chapter 4, "File and Registry Access," but here are the basics again: The `WScript.Shell` object has a `LogEvent` method that lets you store a message in the Event Log. The method call is

```
LogEvent(intType, strMessage [,strTarget])
```

where ***`strTarget`*** is an optional argument giving the name of the computer whose Event Log the message should be sent to, ***`strMessage`*** is the text of the message to record, and ***`intType`*** is a number indicating the severity of the incident. Here are the values for ***`intType`***:

Value	Meaning
0	Success
1	Error
2	Warning
4	Informational
8	Audit success
16	Audit failure

For script logging, only the first four values are appropriate. An Event Log entry can be recorded with the following statements:

```
                                             ' Example File script1003.vbs
set fso   = CreateObject("Scripting.FileSystemObject")
set shell = CreateObject("WScript.Shell")
.
.
.
' script program goes here

filename = "c:\scripts\data\input.dat"

if not fso.FileExists(filename) then
    shell.LogEvent 1, "SCHED.VBS - unable to find input file " & filename
    wscript.quit 1
end if
.
.
.
```

The information that is recorded in the Event Log is shown in Figure 10.7.

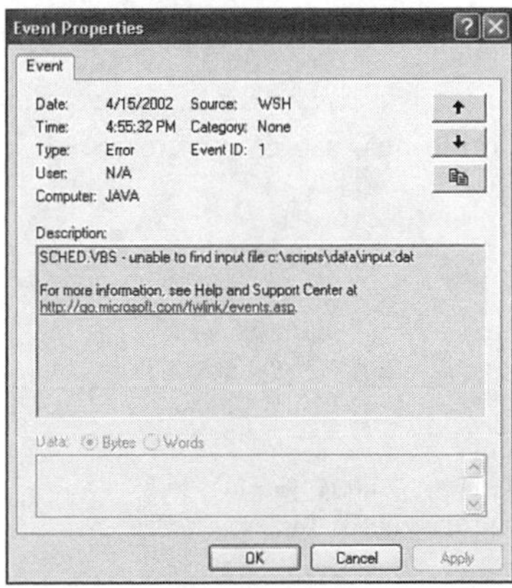

Figure 10.7 The `WshShell.LogEvent` method writes an arbitrary string to the Application Log in the Windows Event Log.

If you prefer to collect all event information on a particular computer, perhaps one whose Event Log is monitored more carefully than the one on which the scheduled script runs, you can add the computer name as a third argument to `LogEvent`.

Printing and Messaging

Although it's not the "green" thing to do, you can write logging information to a printer where the physical presence of a report page will call attention to any problems the script may have reported.

Another, more environmentally correct way to make sure that information about a scheduled job gets the proper attention is to send log file results and error messages via e-mail. I covered the CDO Messaging objects in Chapter 6, "Messaging Objects," so I won't go through all that again here. I'll just suggest that after running a scheduled script, you can send the output or a log file to an administrator or other responsible party.

You could mail the log file at the end of the script. However, if the script doesn't run to completion, the mail won't be sent, and the recipient will have to notice the absence of the daily (or weekly or monthly) announcement to realize that something went wrong. It's better when using printing or e-mail to report on batch file results to schedule a separate script job to mail or print the results from the previous script(s). This way, the news goes out whether or not the processing scripts finish.

Summarizing Results

When several scheduled tasks are to be performed each night, or if scripts are to be run on several different servers, it's useful to run one final scheduled task after all the others have finished to summarize the night's processing. It need only extract a simple success/failure note for each process. This way, if the nightly summary is missing or contains error messages, the administrative staff will know to look for a problem.

Sending such a report by e-mail is a nifty way to go, because it saves paper and is unlikely to get lost in the shuffle near a busy printer. Such a script might look like this:

```
                                                ' Example File summary.vbs
option explicit
dim fso, summaryfile, recipient, summary, sum, msg
set fso = CreateObject("Scripting.FileSystemObject")
const ForAppending = 8

summaryfile = "c:\scripts\logs\summary.log"
recipient   = "Administrator@quarterbyte.com"

summary     = ""    ' summary text is accumulated in this string
```

```
' summarize all of the nightly scheduled scripts
summarize "c:\scripts\logs\sched.log"
summarize "c:\scripts\logs\cleanup.log"
summarize "c:\scripts\logs\backup.log"

' add a final line
summary = summary & string(64, "-") & vbCRLF

' create a new summary file
set sum = fso.CreateTextFile(summaryfile, True)
sum.Write summary
sum.Close

' then mail the summary using the object developed in Chapter 9
set msg = CreateObject("ScriptMail.Message")
msg.To = recipient
msg.ScriptName = "summarize"
msg.Text = summary
msg.Send

' ---------------------------------------------------
' summarize - record the last line and any errors from 'filename'

sub summarize (filename)
    dim stream, outstream, line, lastline

    ' first time through, note the date and time
    if summary = "" then
        summary = "Batch summary, " & date & " " & time & vbCRLF & vbCRLF
    end if

    ' note the file we're examining
    summary = summary & filename & ":" & vbCRLF

    ' if file doesn't exist, that's all we can say
    if not fso.FileExists(filename) then
        summary = summary & "    FILE NOT FOUND!" & vbCRLF & vbCRLF
        exit sub
    end if

    set stream = fso.OpenTextFile(filename)

    ' we don't want to summarize the same log info every night, so
    ' tack the log file contents onto the end of the same filename + ".old", and
    ' delete the original log when we're done.

    set outstream = fso.OpenTextFile(filename & ".old", ForAppending, True)

    ' run through the log file, picking up errors and saving the last line
    lastline = "(empty file)"
```

```
        do while not stream.AtEndOfStream
            line = stream.ReadLine                  ' get line from log file
            outstream.WriteLine line                ' append to .OLD copy

            if instr(ucase(line), "ERROR") > 0 then
                summary = summary & "    " & line & vbCRLF
            elseif len(line) > 0 then
                lastline = line
            end if
        loop
        stream.close
        outstream.close

        ' note the last line; it should be the "completed successfully" line
        summary = summary & "    " & lastline & vbCRLF & vbCRLF

        ' we've copied the log to .OLD, so delete the original log file now
        fso.DeleteFile(filename)
    end sub
```

This script sends the last line from each listed log file on the assumption that the last line is something like "script completed successfully." If this line appears in the e-mail, then we know the script didn't crash before finishing. The message will also include any log entries with the word "error." Also, this script saves the logged data and deletes each log file so that it can detect whether the associated script has run. A missing log file indicates a big problem.

The e-mail message generated by this script might look like this:

```
Batch summary, 4/15/2002 5:45:04 AM

c:\scripts\logs\sched.log:
    4/15/2002 2:12:02 AM: * Sched finished successfully

c:\scripts\logs\cleanup.log:
    4/15/2002 3:45:02 AM: ERROR: can't find folder \temp\database
    4/15/2002 3:47:35 AM: * Cleanup finished successfully

c:\scripts\logs\backup.log:
    FILE NOT FOUND!
---------------------------------------------------------------
```

This summarizing script should be scheduled to run long after any other scheduled scripts should have completed, but before the administrator arrives at work, if possible. It's nice to see a comforting "everything worked" message first thing every morning.

Such a system of daily or weekly reporting can go a long way to ensure that automated batch processing is functioning correctly, even if invisibly.

Scheduling Scripts with the Task Scheduler

Now, let's see how to schedule scripts for automatic processing. I'll describe the process of using the Windows XP Task Scheduler. The older Windows NT `at` command is still available, but it's not as flexible as the Task Scheduler.

To start the Task Scheduler, click Start, All Programs, System Tools, Scheduled Tasks. The Scheduled Tasks window displays any previously scheduled programs, the time each is next scheduled to run, the time each last ran, and the last run's status (this indicates whether the program quit with a normal "0" exit status or returned a nonzero error status).

To schedule a script for automatic execution, follow these steps:

1. Double-click Add Scheduled Task. Then click Next to start the Scheduled Task Wizard.
2. Click Browse and locate the script file. Select the file and click Open.
3. Select an interval at which the script should be run. Choose Daily, Weekly, or Monthly. If you want a more complicated schedule, you can adjust it later. After selecting an interval, click Next.
4. Select a start time for the script, as illustrated in Figure 10.8. You can also pick a starting date as well as choose the repeat frequency—either Every Day, Weekdays, or Every ### Days. Click Next.

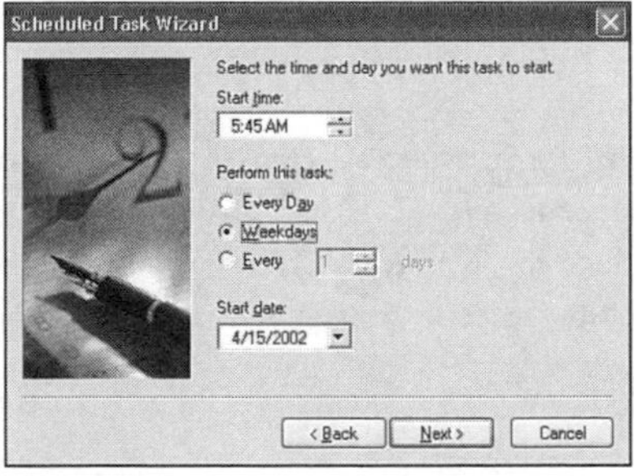

Figure 10.8 The Scheduled Task Wizard lets you choose the start time and days to run the script.

5. Enter the username and password under which the script should run. Think carefully about this; use an account with sufficient privileges to read and write any necessary files, and to perform whatever system operations are necessary, but no more. Don't use the Administrator account unless you really need its power. When you've entered an account and password, click Next.
6. Click Finish.

7. The script will appear in the list of scheduled tasks. Double-click the entry to display its property pages. Select the Task page and edit the Run command line. It will initially contain the full pathname to your script. Before this filename, insert **`cscript //B`**, as illustrated in Figure 10.9. Be sure to use forward slashes (`//`) instead of backslashes (`\\`), and be sure there is a space after `B`.
8. Click OK to complete the scheduling process.

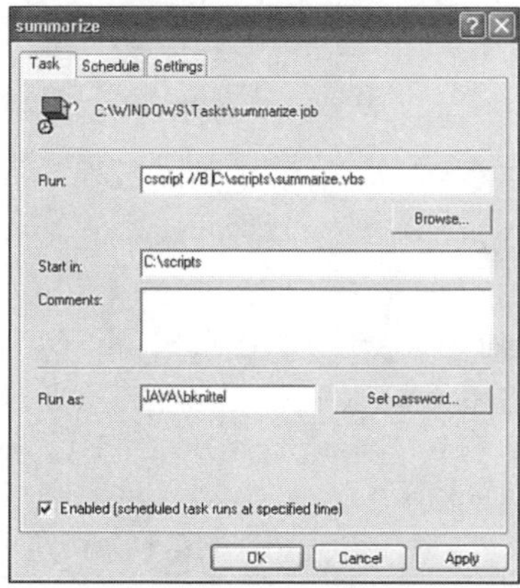

Figure 10.9 Be sure to use `cscript //B` to run every scheduled script.

Tip

When entering scripts into the Task Scheduler, always use the full command line `cscript //B` *`drive:\path\scriptfile arguments...`*. `Cscript` forces the use of the command line rather than the Windowed version of WSH, and `//B` prevents cscript from displaying a message box or other dialog box that would otherwise halt the script. If the script is run by the scheduler without `//B`, nobody will be there to click the OK button.

To test the scheduled item, you don't have to wait until its next scheduled run time—just click the item name under the Name column in the Task Scheduler and choose Run. If the status entry changes to "Could not start," you have probably entered the incorrect password or the incorrect path to the script file. If there are spaces in the pathname, the path must be enclosed in quotes.

If necessary, you can go back into the Properties dialog box to make changes:

- On the Task tab, you can change the script filename and the user account and password under which the script runs. You can also uncheck the Enabled box to temporarily stop future runs without deleting the scheduled entry.

- On the Settings tab, you can select how much time the script is given to run, after which it will be terminated. The default setting is 72 hours, but most scripts will need much less time than this.
- On the Schedule tab, you can alter the run times and days or select Show Multiple Schedules, which lets you enter complex schedules with multiple periodic intervals.

However, after making any changes, you will have to reenter the password used to run this script.

Caution

Be sure that script files you've set up to run under the scheduler can only be edited by the user whose account is used to run the script. This can be a *terrible* security hole. If a script runs with the Administrator privilege, but the file is editable by other users, then someone could modify the script to do whatever he or she wanted.

Be sure that scheduled scripts are stored only on an NTFS-formatted disk drive. Also, view the files' security permissions periodically to be sure that only appropriate users are listed as having write or modify rights to the file.

II

The Command-Line Environment

11

The CMD Command-Line Environment

ROAD MAP

- This chapter introduces the command-line environment.
- Command-line programs can be powerful and useful. Honest.
- The CMD shell has many improvements over `COMMAND.COM`.
- The built-in commands provided by CMD perform many file and management functions.

The Command Prompt

I spent the first 10 chapters of this book extolling the virtues of Windows Script Host programming and proclaiming it to be the right tool for all Windows automation tasks. Now it's time to confess that "all" may not be the right word, and in the remainder of the book, I'll show you why.

While most of the fanfare over programming advances in the last decade has been over windowed applications with pull-down menus, dialog boxes, and all that jazz, the old-fashioned command line has been quietly becoming more sophisticated and capable as well. If you click Start, All Programs, Accessories, Command Prompt, a window will appear that looks a lot like what you would have seen back in the days of the original Microsoft MS-DOS. You can type the old commands such as `dir` and `cls` and Windows XP will dutifully print out a directory listing and clear the screen

However, as much as this looks like the MS-DOS prompt, under the hood, it's a completely different animal. New commands, some spiffy new user interface tricks, and access to some of the most powerful maintenance and configuration tools in Windows make the command-prompt environment a very effective place to work with programs and files.

For example, there's a large number of utilities for network and Internet file copying, troubleshooting, configuration, and management. Many Windows maintenance tasks can be performed from the command line, and many file- and graphics-conversions tools have command-line access. The batch file scripting language lets you write command-line tools of your own. I'll cover these topics in the next few chapters. This chapter covers the command-prompt environment itself.

CMD Versus COMMAND

One tip-off that the command prompt is new is that it's managed by a program called `CMD.EXE`. CMD was introduced in Windows NT and is the new command shell. If you were poking around with MS-DOS back in the prehistoric days, you may remember that the original MS-DOS command program was called `COMMAND.COM`. Most people became aware of it thanks to DOS's propensity to print "Cannot load COMMAND.COM" and then come to a screeching halt. Thankfully, that doesn't happen with Windows XP.

Programs such as CMD and COMMAND are called *shells* because they encase an operating system. Their purpose is to mediate between the user and the programs he or she wants to run. Shells were the only user interfaces available in early mini- and microcomputer operating systems such as Unix, Multics, RSX-11M, and CP/M. In fact, the phrase "graphical user interface" came about as a way to distinguish the new generation of graphical interfaces from the old command-line shells.

The earliest shells could do little more than prompt for the name of a program to run and then locate and run the program. People got tired of typing the same commands over and over, so operating system developers provided ways to let the shell read a list of commands from a file and then run each in turn. Eventually, shells grew into little programming languages of their own, and the *shell script* or *batch file* was born. This concept blossomed on the Unix operating system back in the 1970s and ultimately made its way to MS-DOS, although in a much degraded form. The MS-DOS command prompt and its batch language were limited, peculiar, and inflexible.

Although `CMD.EXE` and its batch file language are still burdened with the legacy of `COMMAND.COM`, some significant new features make the command line a more friendly place to work. Personally, I use it on a daily basis, and I think that you'll find it to be just as useful as I do.

In this chapter, I'll focus on aspects of CMD that apply to direct use in the Command Prompt window. Everything in this chapter applies to batch files as well, which I'll discuss in more detail in the next chapter.

Tip

Microsoft's TechNet Web site has a good article about the command-prompt environment. It was originally published in *Windows NT Shell Scripting*. Although it's missing a few of the enhancements added between NT 4 and Windows XP, it's still a detailed and lucid paper. To find it, search `www.microsoft.com` for "The Windows NT Command Shell", using the quotes.

Command-Line Processing

The Command Prompt window prompts for commands one line at a time. In this section, I'll describe how CMD interprets commands. Even if you are familiar with these concepts from MS-DOS, and even if you already know what > and < do, you should read through this section, because there are several very handy new features you might not yet know about.

CMD's most basic job is to read command lines that have this form:

```
programname arguments
```

Given this command, CMD tries to find an executable program file named *`programname`*. If it does find such a file, it instructs Windows to start the program. Any additional text typed on the command line—the command's *arguments*—are passed to that program to interpret. Of course, in practice things aren't quite this simple:

- CMD recognizes some built-in commands such as `set` and `cls`. For these, CMD doesn't search for a file but rather handles the command itself.
- If the command isn't built in, CMD looks for a file named *`programname`* first in the current working directory and then in a list of directories called the *search path*, which you can adjust. The default search path includes several of the subfolders under `\WINDOWS`. (Later in the chapter, I'll show you how to modify the path to include your own folders.)
- If you explicitly add a filename extension such as `.EXE` (or even `.DOC`) when you type the command, CMD will look through the search path only for this type of file. If you don't specify the file type, CMD will look for certain known file types. The list of file types is called the `PATHEXT` list, and you can modify the listed file types and their precedence if necessary.
- When CMD has located a file matching the name of the command you typed, CMD looks at the file's extension to determine what to do with it. If the file has the extension `.EXE` or `.COM`, it's an executable program and is run directly. Files with the extensions `.BAT` and `.CMD` are taken to be batch files, and CMD interprets them itself.

  For any other file type, CMD uses the file association information from the Windows Registry to determine what to do. If the file type is associated with an application program, CMD starts the associated application to open the file. For example, Windows Script Host runs files with the extensions `.VBS`, `.WSF`, and `.JS`, as we discussed in the first part of this book. If you type the name of a Word document file as a command, CMD automatically runs WordPad or Microsoft Word.
- Many characters—including `< > ( ) ; , | ^ & %` and `!`—have special meaning to CMD and alter the interpretation of the command. We'll cover this topic shortly.

Once CMD has identified the program to run, it starts up that program. If you've run a Windows program, it will pop up onto the screen and leave the Command Prompt window free to do other things. If you've run a command-line program, it will occupy the Command Prompt window until it completes or until you terminate it.

Stopping Runaway Programs

Occasionally you'll type a command that starts spewing page after page of text to the screen, or one that displays some sort of ominous warning about making a change to Windows that can't be undone, and you'll want to stop it—pronto.

Most command-line programs will quit if you type Ctrl+C. If that doesn't work, Ctrl+Break often works. As a last resort, you can simply close the Command Prompt window by clicking its close box in the upper-right corner. This will kill the program in at most a few seconds.

You may also find the `tasklist` and `taskkill` command-line programs useful. I'll discuss them in detail in Chapter 14, "Command-Line Programs."

Console Program Input and Output

Unlike Windows programs that display a window panel with menus and buttons, most programs designed to be run from a command prompt simply type out information line by line into the Command Prompt window. These programs are called *console programs* because they interact through plain-text input and output like old-fashioned programs that ran on a computer's main terminal, and back then the main terminal was often called a *console*.

The `tasklist` command is a good example of a console program. If you type **`tasklist`** in the Command Prompt window and press Enter, this program displays a list of all programs and services that are currently running on your computer, as shown in Figure 11.1.

Each Command Prompt window has the concept of a *current directory*, its default folder, which is its starting place when looking for files. Although Windows Explorer displays its current directory in its status and address bars, it's most common for the Command Prompt window to show the current directory name in its *prompt*, the indicator it prints to tell you it's ready to accept another command. In Figure 11.1, the prompt is

```
C:\Documents and Settings\bknittel>
```

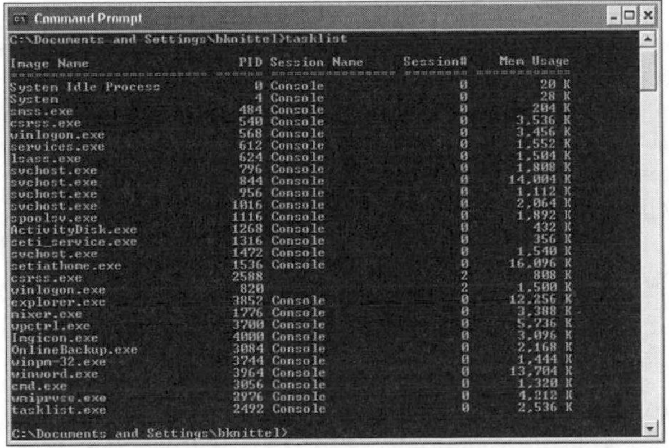

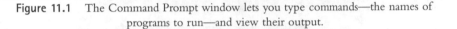

Figure 11.1 The Command Prompt window lets you type commands—the names of programs to run—and view their output.

Note

Because the prompt varies depending on the directory you are currently using, in this book I won't show the prompt when I give examples of commands to type.

Whereas you use dialog boxes and menus to tell Windows programs how to modify their behavior, you have to type this information into console programs. The `tasklist` command is another good example of this. The printout from the `tasklist` command in Figure 11.1 shows all the system's programs and services. If I want to see the tasks and programs running on the computer named bali, which is connected to my network, I can type the following command:

```
tasklist /s bali /u Administrator
```

In this command, `/s` tells `tasklist` that I want to query the networked computer named bali, and `/u` indicates that I want to use the Administrator logon to get this information. `/S` and `/u` are called *switches* or *options*. Most console programs will display the list of options they accept if you put `/?` on their command line.

Those are the basics. Now, let's look at some of CMD's more involved features.

Using the Console Window

Normally, command-prompt programs run in a normal window that has a title bar, resize points, a close button, and scrollbars.

Unlike a true DOS screen, you can peer back in time to previously typed output using the scrollbars. This is particularly handy for programs that print more output than can fit on the screen at once. You can also halt a program's output momentarily by typing Ctrl+S. When you've caught up with your reading, type Ctrl+S to let the program resume typing.

For better visibility, or to make a program look more like it's running with DOS, you can press Alt+Enter to run the program in *full-screen* mode. If you run a DOS graphics program, this will happen automatically. In this mode, the program takes over the whole screen and all other Windows features disappear. You can press Alt+Enter to bring back the Windows desktop.

You can set the screen mode and the number of lines that the window can scroll using the window's Properties dialog box, as shown in Figure 11.2. You can also set the window's colors and font. Usually, you won't need to adjust the font. It's best to simply resize the window in the normal way and Windows will size the characters accordingly.

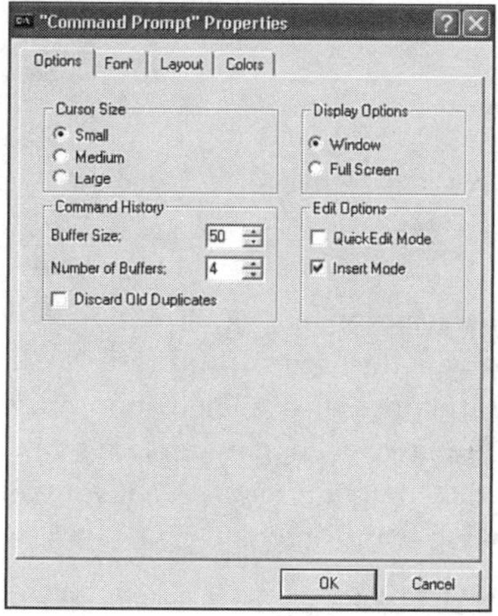

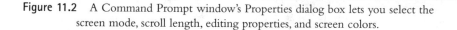

Figure 11.2 A Command Prompt window's Properties dialog box lets you select the screen mode, scroll length, editing properties, and screen colors.

I/O Redirection and Pipes

Normally, any output from a console program appears in the Command Prompt window, but you can *redirect* it into a file using the > character. For example, the command

```
tasklist >tasks.txt
```

generates the same listing as the previous example, but stores it into a file named `tasks.txt`. Command-line programs send their output to what is called the *standard output stream*. By default, anything the program sends to the standard output is printed in the Command Prompt window. Figure 11.3 shows how this looks. The first `tasklist` command in the Figure sends its output to the Command Prompt window. The second `tasklist` command has its output redirected into a file.

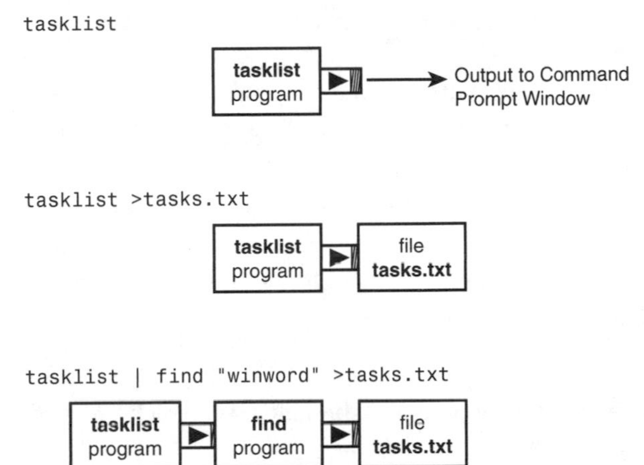

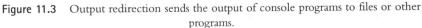

Figure 11.3 Output redirection sends the output of console programs to files or other programs.

Some programs read input through a *standard input* stream. By default, this is connected to your keyboard, and whatever you type is read by the program. For example, the `sort` command reads lines of text from the standard input, sorts them alphabetically, and writes the results to the standard output. If you type the following lines at the command prompt

```
sort
c
b
a
Ctrl+Z
```

`sort` will spit out the lines in order: `a`, `b`, `c`. (Note that Ctrl+Z on a line by itself indicates the end of input.) You can redirect the standard input with the `<` character. For example, the command

```
sort <somefile.txt
```

tells `sort` to read input from the file `somefile.txt`. You can use both input and output redirection at the same time. The command

```
sort <somefile.txt >sortedfile.txt
```

rearranges the contents of `somefile.txt` and creates a new file named `sortedfile.txt`.

You can also specify that the output isn't to replace an existing file but rather should simply be stuck onto the end (that is, *appended*) with the characters >>, as in this example:

```
dir /b c:\ >listing.txt
dir /b d:\ >>listing.txt
```

The first command creates the file `listing.txt`, and the second appends its output onto the end of `listing.txt`. (If the file `listing.txt` doesn't already exist, don't worry: >> will create it).

Finally, you can hook the output of one program directly to the input of another by using the vertical bar symbol (|), usually found above the backslash (\) on a keyboard. For example, the `find` command reads lines from the input and passes out only lines containing a designated string. The command

```
tasklist | find "winword"
```

has `tasklist` send its list of all programs through `find`, which types out only the line or lines containing "winword". Finally,

```
tasklist | find "windword" >tasks.txt
```

connects `tasklist` to `find`, and `find` to a file, as illustrated in the third part of Figure 11.4.

Input and output redirection let you connect programs and files as if you were making plumbing connections. In fact, the | symbol is often called a *pipe* for this reason, and programs such as `find` are often called *filters*.

Note

One very handy filter to know about is `more`, a program that simply passes whatever it's given as input to its output. What makes `more` useful is that it pauses after printing a screen full of text. `More` lets you view long listings that would otherwise just scroll off the screen too quickly to read. For example, the command

```
tasklist | more
```

will help you see the entire list of programs. When you see the prompt `-- More --` at the bottom of the screen, press the spacebar to view the next screen full.

The *standard error* is another output stream available to console programs. By default, if a program writes information to the standard error stream, the text appears in the Command Prompt window. Programs usually use this to display important error messages that they want you to see, even if the standard output is redirected to a file or pipe. You can redirect standard error too, though, if you want to capture the error messages in a file.

If you've worked with DOS, Linux, or Unix, this is probably already familiar to you. However, there are several input redirection variations you may not be familiar with. Table 11.1 lists all the redirection instructions that CMD recognizes.

Table 11.1 **Input and Output Redirection**

<table>
<tr><th>Redirection Option</th><th>Action</th></tr>
<tr><td><<i>file</i></td><td>Reads standard input from <i>file</i>.</td></tr>
<tr><td>>file</td><td>Writes standard output to file.</td></tr>
<tr><td>>>file</td><td>Appends standard output to file.</td></tr>
<tr><td>1>file</td><td>Writes standard output to file.*</td></tr>
<tr><td>1>>file</td><td>Appends standard output to file.</td></tr>
<tr><td>2>file</td><td>Writes standard error to file.</td></tr>
<tr><td>2>>file</td><td>Appends standard error to file.</td></tr>
<tr><td>2>&1</td><td>Directs standard error through the same stream as standard output. Both may then be redirected to a file or piped to another program.</td></tr>
<tr><td>| nextcommand</td><td>Sends output to the input of nextcommand.</td></tr>
</table>

* *The number 1 refers to the standard output stream and the number 2 to the standard error stream.*

Two special forms of output redirection are output to the `NUL` device and output to a printer. Windows recognizes the special filename `nul` in any folder, on any drive, and treats it as a "black hole" file. If you issue a command and redirect its output to `nul`, the output is discarded. This type of direction is useful in batch files when you want a command to do something, but don't want or need the user to see any error messages it might print. For example,

```
net use f: /del >nul 2>nul
```

runs the `net use` command and makes sure that no output appears to the user.

Special filenames `LPT1`, `LPT2` and so on, represent your default printer and your local printer connected to ports LPT1, LPT2, and so on. You can direct the output of a command to the printer using redirection to these names. You can also direct output to network-connected printers by mapping these devices to network printers using the `net use` command, which I'll discuss in Chapter 14. Special name `PRN` is the same as `LPT1`.

In practical day-to-day use, standard output redirection lets you capture the output of a console program into a file, where you can edit it or incorporate it into your documents. Standard error redirection is handy when you need to gather hardcopy evidence from a program that is printing error messages. Input redirection is used most often in a batch file setting, where you want to have a command run automatically from input prepared ahead of time.

Here are some examples:

```
cmd /? | more
```

This has the CMD command-line shell print its built-in help information, and it passes the text through `more` so it can be read a page at a time.

```
cmd /? > cmd.info
notepad cmd.info
```

This has CMD print its help information again, but this time, the text is stored in a file, and you view the file with Notepad. (Window-based programs can be useful on occasion.)

```
tasklist | sort /+60 | more
```

This has `tasklist` list all running programs, and it pipes the listing through `sort`, which sorts the lines starting with column 60. This produces a listing ordered by the amount of memory used by each running program. The sorted output is piped through `more` so it can be viewed a page at a time.

```
date /f >ping.txt
ping www.mycompany.com 2>&1 >>ping.txt
```

This checks whether the site `www.mycompany.com` can be reached through the Internet. The results, including any errors, are stored in a file named `ping.txt`. You could then view this file or analyze it with a program.

Copy and Paste in Command Prompt Windows

Although console programs don't have the display windows and menus of ordinary Windows programs, you can still use the mouse to copy and paste text to and from Command Prompt windows.

To copy text to the Clipboard, you have to extract a rectangular block of text—you can't select text line by line as you're used to. Position the mouse at the upper-left corner of the block of text you want, drag it down to the bottom-right corner, and then press Enter. While you're selecting text, the word *Select* appears in the window's title. Figure 11.4 shows how a Command Prompt window looks when selecting text.

You can also select text using the window's System menu. Click the upper-left corner of the window or press Alt+space and then select Edit, Mark. Use the arrow keys to move the cursor to the upper-left corner of the desired area; then hold the Shift key down while moving the cursor to the lower-right corner. Press Enter to copy the selected text.

You can paste text into a Command Prompt window using the same menu, except to paste, select Edit, Paste. To paste to a Command Prompt window, however, the program running in the window has to be expecting input.

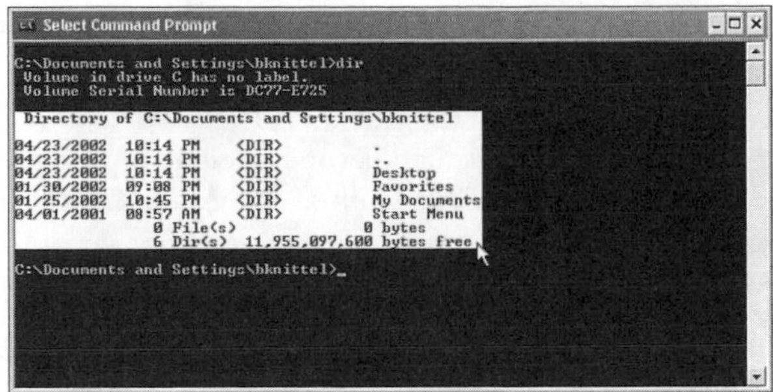

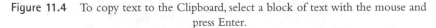

Figure 11.4 To copy text to the Clipboard, select a block of text with the mouse and press Enter.

> **Tip**
>
> The keyboard shortcut for Paste is worth learning: Alt+space, E, P.

By the way, "cut" isn't available—once something is typed in a Command Prompt window, it's typed and can't be removed.

If you need to run a mouse-aware MS-DOS program in a Command Prompt window, you'll want to disable the Select feature so that mouse movements will be sent to the program rather than being interpreted by the console program window. To disable the use of the mouse for copying text, select the window's Properties dialog box and uncheck Quick Edit, as shown earlier in Figure 11.2.

Command Editing and the History List

Command lines entries can be long, convoluted lists of program names and arguments, like this:

```
ibmfix -b -ic:\ibm\input\imports\filea.txt c:\ibm\output\impa.dat
```

Nobody expects you to be able to type something like this without making errors. CMD lets you edit a command before you press Enter so you can correct mistakes without having to retype the whole line. The additional editing functions that were provided by the optional program DOSKEY in DOS and Windows 9*x* are standard in CMD. Here are some ways that CMD lets you edit a command under construction:

- The left- and right-arrow keys let you move the cursor back and forth within the line. Ctrl+left arrow and Ctrl+right arrow move the cursor back and forth by whole words. Home and End move the cursor to the beginning and end of the line, respectively.

- By default, any characters you type are inserted at the cursor point, and the remaining text slides to the right. You can press the Ins key to toggle between insert and overwrite mode. (COMMAND.COM defaults to overwrite mode.)
- Command lines can extend in length beyond one line on the screen. If you type more characters than can fit on the width of the screen, CMD scrolls the line up. You can scroll to an earlier or later line with the left and right arrows. (COMMAND.COM doesn't let you scroll back to earlier lines.)
- If you press the F3 key, the command line is filled in with characters from the previously entered command, from the current cursor position to the end of the line.
- When you're finished editing, you can press Enter with the cursor at any place in the line.

Working with command-line programs can quickly get tedious if you have to type the same command over and over. Imagine typing in commands like this by hand, only to find that you should have typed `-a` instead of `-b` and need to do it all over again:

```
ibmfix -b -ic:\ibm\input\imports\filea.txt c:\ibm\output\impa.dat
ibmfix -b -ic:\ibm\input\imports\fileb.txt c:\ibm\output\impb.dat
ibmfix -b -ic:\ibm\input\imports\filec.txt c:\ibm\output\impc.dat
ibmfix -b -ic:\ibm\input\imports\filed.txt c:\ibm\output\impd.dat
```

Luckily, the CMD window keeps track of every line you type in, and it's easy to recall a previous command for editing or reuse. Here's how this works:

- You can press the up-arrow and down-arrow keys to scroll through the list of previously entered commands. If you find one you want to reuse, you can simply press Enter to run it again. Alternatively, you can edit the command using the keys described earlier.
- PgUp recalls the oldest command in CMD's list; PgDn recalls the most recent.
- If you press F7, CMD will display a list of recently entered commands. You can select one of these lines and press Enter to reuse it, or you can press Esc to dismiss the list of commands.

CMD has more editing features than I've listed here; these are just the most useful. To see the whole list, click Start, Help, and search for DOSKEY.

Tip

One feature you may want to read up on is the ability to define *macros*, which are whole command lines that you can call up by simply typing in a short abbreviation or keyword. Unix users know these as *aliases* and will be happy to know that they're available in Windows XP.

Name Completion

When you are typing command lines to CMD, you'll often need to type file and folder names. Name completion makes this easier—you can type just the first few letters of a file or folder name, strike a control key, and CMD will finish typing the name for you. This is a nifty but not widely known feature that, like most of the other fun new features in CMD, Microsoft has borrowed from the Unix operating system.

Here's how name completion works: If you press the filename-completion character (usually the Tab key), CMD will examine the characters to the left of the cursor and use this as the basis for a path and/or filename. The way to think of this is that when you type the completion character, CMD looks for any files whose names start with whatever you've typed so far. If there is a space or nothing at all to the left of the cursor, CMD looks for * (all files).

If CMD finds no matching file or folder name, it beeps and does nothing. (It should beep, anyway. It appears not to on Windows XP.) If it does find a matching name, CMD finishes typing the name for you. It looks like this:

```
c:\batch> edit b          ← I type edit and the letter b, then press Tab

c:\batch> edit bills.bat ← CMD finds a matching file and completes the name
```

If this is the correct name, you can just continue typing on the command line. This is a great timesaver! If the name that CMD types is not the one you were looking for, you can hit the completion key again to see the next matching name. Typing the key repeatedly cycles through all matching names. What's more, you can hold the Shift key down while typing the completion character to cycle backwards.

Tip

If you have to type a long pathname such as `\Documents and Settings\bknittel\My Documents`, you can use name completion for each part of the name. For this example, you could type the following:

`dir \d` (Tab) `\b` (Tab) `\m` (Tab)

Try this on your own computer (and use your own username instead of `bknittel`). It's pretty slick—CMD adds the required quotation marks and moves them into the correct positions automatically.

Directory name completion works in an identical fashion, except that it matches *only* folder names. Name completion is enabled by default, but not directory name completion. If you're content enough to use the Tab key to cycle through both file and folder names, just leave everything as it is. If you want to use a separate key to indicate that you want CMD to look only for directory names, I'll show you how later in the chapter under "Enabling Directory Name Completion" (it's not pretty).

Multiple Commands on One Line

CMD lets you type multiple separate commands on one command line, separated by an ampersand (&), as in this example:

```
dir & ping ftp.microsoft.com & ftp ftp.microsoft.com
```

CMD runs the three commands in turn, as if they had been entered on separate command lines:

```
dir
ping ftp.microsoft.com
ftp ftp.microsoft.com
```

This sounds trivial, but it can be very handy. First, when you're typing the same several commands over and over, you can simply hit the up-arrow key and use the history feature to recall all the commands at once.

Also, in batch files, which we'll cover in more detail in Chapter 12, "Batch Files for Fun and Profit," this feature can be used to put several commands on one `if` statement, as in this example:

```
if not exist list.dat dir c:\in >list.dat & dir c:\out >>list.dat
```

If the file `list.dat` does not exist, then CMD will run the two `dir` commands in turn. This can simplify the batch program.

There are two other ways to specify multiple commands on the same line. If you separate commands with two ampersands instead of one, for example,

```
ping ftp.microsoft.com && ftp ftp.microsoft.com
```

the second and subsequent commands are only run if the preceding command is successful (that is, if it exited with an error status value of 0). This lets you create lists of commands that won't plow on after encountering an error.

Another variation lets you use `||` to indicate that the second command is to be run *only* if the first command fails—that is, if the first command exits with a nonzero error status, as in this example:

```
firstcommand || echo The first command failed
```

Grouping Commands with Parentheses

With CMD's command extensions, you can group several command lines inside parentheses, and CMD will treat them as one command. This is useful with the `if` and `for` commands. For example, compound statements like the following are possible:

```
if exist c:\data\myfile.dat (
    echo Myfile.dat exists!
    copy myfile.dat d:\backups
```

```
    sort myfile.dat >myfile.out
    print myfile.out
)
```

Also, grouped commands can be used to collect the output of several programs into one file or pipe with redirection, as in this example:

```
(dir c:\data & dir c:\temp) >listings.txt
```

The commands must be separated by new lines or by the `&`, `&&`, or `||` separators I discussed earlier.

You can use grouped commands in batch files or at the command prompt. If you enter grouped commands at thc command prompt and haven't yet entered the closing parenthesis when you press Enter, CMD prompts you to continue entering the command line(s) by printing the following:

```
More?
```

This isn't really a question, so don't type "yes." Just continue typing command lines and end with a closing parenthesis and whatever goes after the parenthesis. Alternatively, you can press Enter by itself to stop the prompting.

Arguments, Commas, and Quotes

When a command-line program requires you to specify information such as the name of a file to process or an option to use, you usually type this information after the command name, with the items separated by spaces. For example, the `delete` command erases the file or files named on its command line:

```
delete somefile.txt anotherfile.txt
```

You can also separate command-line arguments with the semicolon (;) or comma (,), but this is not recommended; CMD accepts this only to be compatible with good old `COMMAND.COM`.

Unfortunately, because Windows filenames can contain spaces in the middle of the name, the command

```
delete C:\Documents and Settings\bknittel\My Documents\a.txt
```

will attempt to delete four files: `C:\Documents`, `and`, `Settings\bknittel\My`, and `Documents\a.txt`. To solve this problem, CMD interprets quotation marks (`"  "`) to mean that the text enclosed is to be treated as part of one single argument. For example, the command

```
delete "C:\Documents and Settings\bknittel\My Documents\a.txt"
```

deletes the one indicated file. The quotation marks are not seen as part of the filename; they just keep it all together.

Escaping Special Characters

As you've already seen, the following characters have special meaning to CMD:

```
< > ( ) & | , ; "
```

If you need to use any of these characters as part of a command-line argument to be given to a program (for example, to have the find command search for the character >), you need to *escape* the character by placing a caret (^) symbol before it. This indicates that the character is to be treated like any other character and removes its special meaning. To pass a ^ character as an argument, type ^^.

For example, the echo command types its arguments in the Command Prompt window. The command

```
echo <hello>
```

would cause a problem because CMD would think that you want to redirect input from a file named hello and that you want to redirect output to...well, there is no filename after >, so CMD would print an error message. However, the command

```
echo ^<hello^>
```

prints <hello>.

Configuring the CMD Program

The previous section described how CMD reads and interprets commands. In this section, I'll tell you a bit about how CMD may be adjusted to better meet your own needs.

AutoRun

Normally, when it first starts, CMD examines the Registry for values under the keys

```
HKLM\Software\Microsoft\Command Processor\AutoRun
```

and

```
HKCU\Software\Microsoft\Command Processor\AutoRun
```

(HKLM and HKCU are short for HKEY_LOCAL_MACHINE and HKEY_CURRENT_USER, respectively.) Any values with type REG_SZ (string) or REG_EXPAND_SZ (string with environment variables to be expanded) are taken as commands to be run when an instance of CMD first starts up.

AutoRun settings can be used to perform some of the functions that used to be provided by the AUTOEXEC.BAT file in DOS. In particular, you may want to run DOSKEY to set macros via an AutoRun command.

If necessary, you can disable AutoRun commands by starting CMD with `/D` on its command line, as I'll discuss later in the chapter.

Environment Variable Substitution

As it examines command lines that you've typed or that it has read from a batch file, CMD replaces strings of the form `%name%` with the value of the named environment variable. For example, the command

```
echo %path%
```

turns into

```
echo c:\windows\system32;C:\WINDOWS;C:\WINDOWS\System32\Wbem
```

which then types this text out. The command displays the value of the `path` variable. Environment variable substitution can be used anyplace on any command line, as long as the resulting text is a valid command.

Note

Environment variable names are not case sensitive. To CMD, `%path%`, `%Path%`, and `%PATH%` are all the same.

The Search Path

CMD has a mechanism that lets you store text information in named variables called *environment variables*. Environment variables are used to control the behavior of CMD and can also be used to store information in batch file programs. Environment variables can be defined in batch files, on the command line, or by Windows Script Host programs, and many are predefined by Windows.

One of the more important environment variables is `PATH`, which holds a list of directories that CMD searches to find programs. `PATH` is a list of folder names separated by semicolons. Its default value looks something like this:

```
c:\windows\system32;C:\WINDOWS;C:\WINDOWS\System32\Wbem
```

This path list tells CMD that when you type a command, it should look for the command's program file in these directories, in precisely this order:

- The current directory, which CMD always searches first
- `c:\windows\system32`
- `c:\windows`
- `c:\windows\system32\wbem`

If CMD finds the program file in one of these folders, it's run and no further folders are searched. This means that if there are command files or batch files with the same names in more than one search path folder, the one that will be run when you type its name is the one whose directory appears earliest in the path.

Tip

If the same program or batch file is in more than one folder in your search path, and the first one that CMD finds is not the one you want, then there is a workaround. You can type a full pathname before the command to eliminate any ambiguity about which copy of the program you want to use. For example,

```
c:\windows\system32\ping
```

tells CMD exactly where to find the PING program.

Windows sets the `PATH` variable when it starts CMD, and you should be careful when changing it; if you remove the important Windows directories, CMD won't be able to find many of the programs you'll want to use.

You can change the path to include your own directories using the `path` command. If you plan on writing your own batch files, Windows Script Host programs, or other application programs, it's a good idea to place them in a special folder of their own and then add that folder to the path. I'll show you how to do this in the next section.

Changing the Path

You can change the search path in two ways: First, you can set a new value for the `path` environment variable using the `set` command, as in this example:

```
set path=c:\batchfiles
```

Second, you can use the "shortcut" command, as shown here:

```
path c:\batchfiles
```

Both have the same effect: They set the environment variable `path` to `c:\batchfiles`, so CMD will only look for programs in this folder. This is probably not a good idea, though, because it removes the Windows folders from the path and makes all the standard command-line programs unavailable.

Note

The `path` and `set` commands only change environment variables for one instance of the CMD program.

If you want to make a change to `path` or any other environment variable so that the change appears in all future CMD prompt windows, you'll need to make the change on the System Properties dialog box, as I'll discuss later in the chapter, under "Setting Default Environmental Variables."

Most of the time, what you'll want to do is to add a new folder to the existing path list, usually at the beginning, so that any batch files you write or new programs you install can be run just by typing their name. This is a particularly handy time to use environment variable substitution and is such a common thing to do that it's a pattern.

Pattern

To add a directory to the beginning of the search path, use the following statement:

```
set path=directorypath;%path%
```

Here, *directorypath* should be the fully qualified folder name. Here's an example:

```
set path=c:\batchfiles;%path%
```

When CMD encounters this command—that is, if you type it at the command line or in a batch file—CMD first replaces the text `%path%` with the current value of PATH, so the command turns into this:

```
set path=c:\batchfiles;c:\windows\system32;C:\WINDOWS;C:\WINDOWS\System32\Wbem
```

Now, the new path starts with `c:\batchfiles` but still includes the standard Windows folders. If you place a batch file named `test.bat` in `c:\batchfiles` and then type `test` on the command line, your batch file will run.

You could also add a new folder to the *end* of the search path with a statement like this:

```
set path=%path%;c:\batchfiles
```

The ordering only matters if there are versions of the same command in more than one folder in the path; the version in the first folder to be searched will be the one that Windows runs.

Tip

If you mess up the path and CMD stops working, just close the Command Prompt window and open another. You'll be back in action.

Putting your own folders ahead of the Windows folders in the list can be a blessing or a curse. If you create a program or batch file with the same name as a standard Windows program, yours will run instead of the standard program. If this is what you want, great, but if not…the result can be very confusing.

The Adjustable Prompt

I mentioned earlier that the command prompt shows you the shell's current directory. For example, the prompt

```
C:\Documents and Settings\bknittel>
```

shows that my current drive is `C:` and the current directory is `C:\Documents and Settings\bknittel`. If you manage computers or use networking software to work with several computers at once, you may find yourself confused at times, wondering to which computer a Command Prompt window belongs! You can modify the command prompt to display more (or less) information using the hieroglyphics listed in Table 11.2. CMD examines the `PROMPT` environment variable for any of the character codes listed in the table and replaces them with the appropriate information.

Table 11.2 **Prompt Codes**

Code	Prints	Example
`$$`	`$`	`$`
`$_`	A new line.	
`$a`	`&`	`&`
`$b`	`|`	`|`
`$c`	`(`	`(`
`$d`	The current date.	Wed 04/24/2002
`$e`	ANSI escape (code 27).	
`$f`	`)`	`)`
`$g`	`>`	`>`
`$h`	A backspace.	
`$l`	`<`	`<`
`$n`	The current drive.	`C:`
`$p`	The current drive and path.	`C:\windows`
`$q`	`=`	`=`
`$s`	`(space)`	
`$t`	The current time.	`19:13:37.21`
`$v`	The Windows version number.	`Microsoft Windows XP [Version 5.1.2600]`
`$+`	Zero or more `+` signs to show depth of `pushd` commands.	`+++`
`$m`	The UNC name of the network drive plus a space, if the current drive is not local; otherwise, nothing.	`\\sumatra\cdrive`
Any other	Any other character is printed literally.	

To set the prompt, construct the desired series of codes and issue the command

```
set prompt=codes
```

or use the shortcut

```
prompt codes
```

For example,

```
prompt $t$h$h$h$h$h$h $m$p$g
```

prints the time, backspaces over the number of seconds, adds a space, and then prints the network path and current drive and directory. The resulting command prompt looks like this:

```
19:19 \\sumatra\cdrive K:\>
```

If you mess things up, `prompt $p$g` restores the prompt to its default value.

Tip

To make a permanent change to your prompt, right-click My Computer, choose Properties, Advanced, Environment Variables and then add a `PROMPT` definition under User Variables for....

Predefined and Virtual Environment Variables

Environment variables can be set in any of six places. If a given variable name is set in more than one place, the last definition is used. The sources are processed in the following order:

1. Predefined, built-in system variables (for example, `APPDATA`).
2. System-wide variables defined in the System Properties dialog box.
3. User-specific variables defined in the System Properties dialog box (as I mentioned in the previous section). However, a user-specific `PATH` definition does not replace the system-wide definition. Instead, it's added to the beginning ot the system definition.
4. Variables defined in logon scripts (batch or WSH-type).

   These first four sources are processed when a user logs on, and they form the user's default environment; the remaining sources are processed each time a new CMD process is started, and any changes are lost when CMD is closed.
5. Variables defined in `AUTOEXEC.NT`, if a DOS program is run.
6. Variables defined on the command line, in batch files, or in Windows Script Host scripts through `WshShell.Environment("Process")`.

The following variables are defined by default for all users (systemwide):

Variable Name	Usual Value
ALLUSERSPROFILE	C:\Documents and Settings\All Users
APPDATA	C:\Documents and Settings*username*\Application Data
CommonProgramFiles	C:\Program Files\Common Files
COMPUTERNAME	*computername*
ComSpec	C:\WINDOWS\system32\cmd.exe
HOMEDRIVE	C:
HOMEPATH	\Documents and Settings*username*
LOGONSERVER	(Varies)
NUMBER_OF_PROCESSORS	(Varies)
OS	Windows_NT
Path	C:\WINDOWS\system32;C:\WINDOWS ;C:\WINDOWS\System32\Wbem, but this varies depending on the location of Windows
PATHEXT	.COM;.EXE;.BAT;.CMD;.VBS;.VBE;.JS
PROCESSOR_ARCHITECTURE	(Varies)
PROCESSOR_IDENTIFIER	(Varies)
PROCESSOR_LEVEL	(Varies)
PROCESSOR_REVISION	(Varies)
ProgramFiles	C:\Program Files
PROMPT	PG
SESSIONNAME	(Varies)
SystemDrive	C:
SystemRoot	C:\WINDOWS
TEMP	C:\DOCUME~1*username*\LOCALS~1\Temp
TMP	C:\DOCUME~1\username\LOCALS~1\Temp
USERDOMAIN	*computername* or *domainname*
USERNAME	*username*
USERPROFILE	C:\Documents and Settings*username*
windir	C:\WINDOWS

In addition, when command extensions are enabled, several "virtual" environment variables are available. The following environment variable names are computed dynamically if used on a command line or in a batch file:

Name	Value
`CD`	The current directory drive and path
`DATE`	The current date, formatted as by the `DATE` command
`TIME`	The current time, formatted as by `TIME` command
`RANDOM`	A random number between 0 and 32,767
`ERRORLEVEL`	The exit status of the previous program
`CMDEXTVERSION`	The version number of command extensions
`CMDCMDLINE`	The command line used to start CMD itself

However, if you define a variable with one of these names, your defined value will always supercede the dynamic value.

The maximum size for an individual environment variable (name, equals sign, and value) is 8,192 bytes. The total size of all environment variables must be less than 65,536KB.

Setting Default Environment Variables

To define environment variables permanently so that they are defined whenever you log on, click Start, right-click My Computer, and select Properties. Next, view the Advanced tab and click Environment Variables. Windows will display the dialog box shown in Figure 11.5.

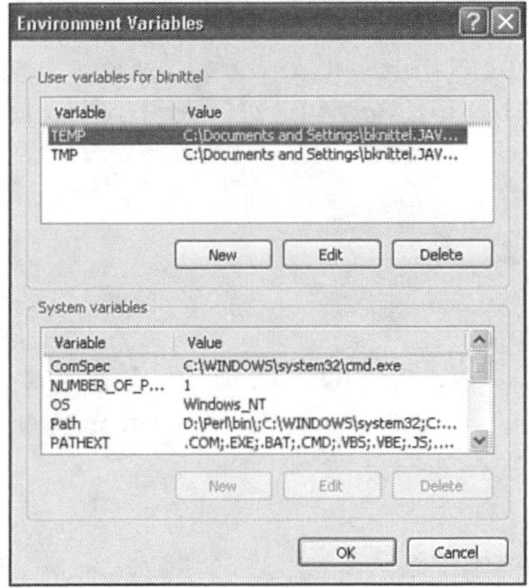

Figure 11.5 The Environment Variables dialog box lets you edit default environment variables for your account or for all users.

The top part of the dialog box lets you define the default variables for your account. You can click New to add a new variable, or you can click Edit or Delete to modify an existing entry.

The lower part of the dialog box edits the default variables provided to *all* user accounts. These settings can only be edited by an Administrator account, and the settings may be overridden by user-specific entries.

Note

You can also modify the default environment variables with WSH scripts by modifying the `Environment("system")` and `Environment("user")` collections, as discussed in Chapter 4, "File and Registry Access," under the section "Working with the Environment."

Built-In Commands

CMD recognizes and interprets several commands directly. Many of these commands are very helpful when writing batch files, as we'll discuss in the next chapter. In this section, Reference List 11.1 lists the built-in commands. I'll discuss some in more detail after the listing and will cover others in more detail in Chapter 12.

Many commands have features called *command extensions*. Command extensions are enabled by default in Windows XP, but they can be disabled if necessary.

REFERENCE LIST 11.1 CMD's Built-In Commands

`:`*`label`*

defines the target for a `goto` or call statement. Useful only in batch files.

`@command`

executes *`command`* without echoing it to the console, if echoing is enabled. This is mostly used at the very beginning of batch files to disable all command echoing: `@echo off`.

`a:`
`b:`
`c:`
`etc`

A command consisting solely of a letter and a colon changes the default or "current" drive to the indicated disk drive. Use the `cd` or `pushd` command to change the default or "current" directory.

`assoc` [`.`*`extension`*[=[*`filetype`*]]]

The `assoc` command displays or sets associations between file extensions such as `.DOC` and file types such as "Word.Document.8". (This is the information behind the associations that Explorer displays and edits in its Tools, Folder Options, File Types dialog box.) The `assoc` command can take several forms:

Command	Result
assoc	Lists all associations.
assoc *.xxx*	Lists the association for extension *.xxx*.
assoc *.xxx=*	Deletes the association for *.xxx*.
assoc *.xxx=type*	Sets the association for *.xxx* to *type*. *Type* must be a file type listed in the Registry under HKEY_CLASSES_ROOT.

The assoc command isn't too useful, but it can help you to quickly find the application associated with a given file extension. Use assoc to list the file type for the extension; then use the ftype command to find the linked application.

break
If CMD is being run under a debugger, this command causes a breakpoint. Under MS-DOS, this command was used to enable and disable Ctrl+C checking, but it has no such effect in Windows XP.

call *batchfile* [*arguments*...]
call :*label* [*arguments*...]
performs a "subroutine" call. Executes a secondary batch file or transfers control to a specified label within the current batch file. Control returns to the statement after the call when the subroutine reaches the end of file or an exit /B statement.

cd [/d] [[*drive*:]*directory*]
changes the current working directory to the specified path, which may be a relative or absolute path. If a drive letter is specified, the default directory for that drive is changed, but the working drive (the Command Prompt window's default drive) is not changed unless you add the /d option. With no arguments, cd prints the current directory.

As a convenience, you do not need to use quotes, even if the directory name contains spaces. For example,

```
cd \Documents and Settings
```

will work correctly. You can also use name completion to help fill in long pathnames if you are typing cd commands on the command line. For example, cd \Do followed by the Tab key should complete the path \Documents and Settings.

chdir
Chdir is identical to the cd command and takes the same arguments.

cls
Clears the screen (the Command Prompt window).

continues

REFERENCE LIST 11.1 Continued

`color` [*bf*]

allows you to change the background and text colors of the current Command Prompt window. The argument to `color` is a two-letter code. The first letter is the code for the screen background color, taken from the values listed in Table 11.5. The second letter is the code for the text color. For example, the command `color 1e` requests yellow text on a dark blue background. With no arguments, `color` restores the screen's colors to their initial settings.

You can also set a Command Prompt window's colors using its Properties dialog box.

`copy` `[/d][/v][/n][/y|/-y][/z][/a|/b]`
  `source``[/a|/b] [+`*`source`*`[/a|/b]]... [`*`destination`*`[/a|/b]]`

The `copy` command copies files from one location to another and can also make a copy of a file in the same directory but with a different name. The simplest version of the command just lists the name of the original (source) file and the name to give the copy:

```
copy mydata.dat e:\files\april2002data.dat
```

```
copy mydata.dat mydata.backup
```

The destination name can be a full filename or, if the copy is to have the same name as the original, just a folder pathname.

Wildcards may be used in the source filename to copy multiple files. If this is the case, the destination name must be a folder name.

If you list multiple source files on the command line separated by + signs, they are combined (concatenated) into one destination file. If you want to copy multiple files separately and can't write their names using a wildcard format, you'll need to issue multiple `copy` commands.

Other options may be specified on the command line, as listed here:

Option	Result
`/a`	Copies the file in ASCII (text) mode. A Ctrl+Z character in the file is taken to mean "end of file," and no more data is read.
`/b`	Copies the file in binary (data) mode.
	I have never needed the `/a` and `/b` options, but should you find them necessary, you can specify one or the other at the beginning of the `copy` command to apply to all files, or you can add them after individual file names.
`/d`	The destination file will be unencrypted, even if the original file is encrypted.
`/n`	Gives the destination copy a short "8.3" filename.

Option	Result
`/v`	Windows should read the copied file back and compare it to the original to be sure that the copy is correct. This option is especially useful when copying to floppy, Zip, or other removable disks.
`/y`	Lets `copy` overwrite any existing files without asking for confirmation.
`/-y`	Makes `copy` always ask for confirmation before overwriting an existing file.
`/z`	Lets copying resume after a temporary network disconnection and displays a percentage-complete indicator while copying. Used for copying across a network.

The `/y` argumentmakes `copy` silently overwrite any existing files of the same name as the destination file. If `/-y` is specified, `copy` always will prompt before overwriting.

The default behavior is to prompt if `copy` is entered from the command line, and not to prompt if `copy` is used in a batch file. You can change these defaults by assigning the value `/y` or `/-y` to the `COPYCMD` environment variable. In any case, if you specify `/y` or `/-y` on the command line, this overrides the default setting.

Any other `copy` options may be included in the `COPYCMD` environment variable to set the command's default behavior. The `COPYCMD` environment variable also affects the `move` command.

`date` [`/t` | *`newdate`*]
With no arguments, `date` displays the current date and requests that you type in a new date. You can press Enter to keep the current date. You can also set the date by specifying the new date on the command line. With `/t` on the command line, `date` displays the date without prompting for a replacement. The date must be formatted according to the localized date format. For example, in the U.S., the format is `mm-dd-yyyy` or `mm/dd/yyyy`. (Also see the `time` command.)

`del` [**`/P`**] [**`/F`**] [**`/S`**] [**`/Q`**] [**`/A`**[`:`]*`attributes`*]] *`filename ...`*
deletes files named on the command line. One or more filenames may be named, and wildcards may be used. The filenames may include a path. If no path is specified, they will be deleted from the current directory.

Caution

Files deleted by `del` are removed immediately and permanently. They do not go to the Recycle Bin.

continues

REFERENCE LIST 11.1 Continued

If a directory name is listed by itself, all the files in the directory are deleted, although the directory itself is not removed (for that, use the `rd` command). For example, the following two commands have the same effect:

```
del c:\temp\*.*
del c:\temp
```

Here are the command-line options:

Option	Effect
`/P`	Prompts to confirm deleting each file.
`/F`	Forces deletion of read-only files.
`/S`	Recurses subdirectories of the current or named directories, deleting any files with the specified name(s).
`/Q`	Quiet mode. Does not ask for confirmation if you enter `*.*` as the filename.
`/A`	Selects files to delete based on specified file attributes. After `/A` and an optional colon, enter one or more of the following attribute codes: `R`—Read-only files `S`—System files `H`—Hidden files `A`—Files with the archive bit set `-`—Before an attribute code, means *not* You can specify more than one attribute. For example, `/a:hr` indicates that only files that are both hidden *and* read-only will be deleted.

Here are some examples of `del` commands:

- `del myfile.doc`

  Deletes `myfile.doc` from the current directory
- `del /q c:\temp\*.*`

  Deletes all files in `C:\temp` without prompting
- `del /s c:\temp\*.tmp`

  Deletes `.TMP` files from `C:\temp` and all subfolders
- `del /a:h *.*`

  Deletes all files from the current directory, even hidden files

dir ***pathname*** **...** [/**p**][/**q**][/**w**|/**d**|/**b**|/**n**|/**x**][/**s**][/**l**][/**c**][/**4**]
[/**a**[**:**]*attributes*]][/**o**[**:**]*sortfields*]][/**t**[**:**]*timefield*]]

The `dir` command lists the names of files and/or subfolders found in specified folders. With no arguments the `dir` command lists all the files and folders in the current directory. The basic directory listing includes a title, a list of files with their sizes and last-modified dates, and a total count of files and bytes used. I'll discuss the `dir` command in more detail after this reference listing.

echo ON|OFF
echo *text*
echo.

The first version enables or disables echoing of batch file commands to the console during execution. The second version writes the specified ***text*** to the standard output, which will either appear in the console window or will be written to another file or program, if the standard output is redirected. The third version prints a completely blank line—that is, just a carriage return and line feed. Echo, by itself, prints its on/off status.

endlocal

(See `setlocal`.)

erase

`Erase` is identical to the `del` command and takes the same arguments.

exit [/**B**] [*exitcode*]

terminates the current Command Prompt console window or batch file. In a batch file, `exit /B` terminates the batch file (or the batch file subroutine) without terminating CMD as well. The optional numeric ***exitcode*** argument specifies an exit code. With `/B`, this command sets the `ERRORLEVEL` environment variable to the specified value; otherwise, it sets CMD's exit code.

for %*variable* **in (set) do** *command* [*arguments*]
for *modifier* %*variable* **in (set) do** *command* [***arguments***]

or in batch files

for %%*variable* **in (***set***) do** *command* [*arguments*]
for *modifier* %%*variable* **in (set) do** *command* [*arguments*]

executes ***command*** repeatedly, with ***variable*** taking on one of the values from a specified set of values at each iteration. The variable name is a single letter and is case-sensitive. In the usual usage, ***set*** is a list of strings or filenames (possibly specified with wildcards).

If the `for` command is used in a batch file, the percent signs must be doubled up to prevent them from being interpreted as argument or environment variable substitutions.

If an environment variable is used on the command line and their values change as the `for` command proceeds, the results may not be what you expect. See the section titled "Delayed Expansion" in Chapter 12 (page 509) for more information.

continues

REFERENCE LIST 11.1 Continued

The `for` command is discussed in more detail after the reference list.

`ftype` [*`.extension`*[=[*`filetype`*]]]
The `ftype` command is a partner to the `assoc` command and displays or sets the associations between file types such as "Word.Document.8" and the commands used to open the files for editing. The `ftype` command can take several forms:

Command	**Result**
`ftype`	Lists all associations
`ftype` *`FileType`*	Lists the association for the named *`FileType`*
`ftype` *`FileType=`*	Deletes an association
`ftype` *`FileType=command`*	Sets the `open` command for the named *`FileType`* to *`command`*

In the command string, symbols of the form `%1` and `%*` indicate how any other arguments from the original command line are to be passed to the `open` command. To get more information on the argument format for `ftype` commands, open a Command Prompt window and type **`ftype /?`**.

The `ftype` command isn't all that useful, but it can help you to find the application associated with a given file extension. Use the `assoc` command to list the file type for the extension; then use `ftype` to find the linked application. For example, I wanted to find out what program was used to run Perl programs on my computer. Here are the two commands I typed, shown in boldface, and the results printed by CMD:

```
C:\book\11>assoc .pl
.pl=Perl
C:\book\11>ftype Perl
Perl="D:\Perl\bin\perl.exe " "%1" %*
```

`goto` *`label`*
`goto :EOF`
directs CMD to jump to the line in the batch file starting with `:label` and to continue reading statements from that point. `Goto :EOF` jumps to the end of the file and, in effect, terminates the batch file. `Exit /B` does the same thing. This is used to terminate batch processing and to exit from a batch file subroutine started with the `call` statement.

```
if condition command1 [else command2]
```

or

```
if condition (
   commands...
) [else (
   commands...
)]
```

The `if` command is used mostly in batch files to perform commands based on conditions encountered as the batch program runs. `If`, `call`, and `goto` are what make the batch file language a real programming language.

`If` commands can execute one or more commands if *condition* test is true. An optional `else` clause lets you specify a command to run if *condition* is not true. The `if` command is discussed in detail on page 477, after the end of reference list.

md *foldername*

The `md` command creates a new directory (folder). The folder name can be a fully qualified path such as `c:\musicfiles`, or it can be specified relative to the current directory.

When command extensions are enabled, which is the default, `md` will create any intermediate directories in the path, if they do not already exist. This is another big improvement in CMD over `COMMAND.COM`. For example,

```
md "c:\musicfiles\folk\baguette quartette"
```

will work even if `c:\musicfiles` does not already exist.

Note

If the directory you are creating contains spaces in the name, you must enclose the *foldername* argument in quotes. If you omit the quotes, CMD will ignore anything on the command line after the first space.

mkdir *foldername*

`Mkdir` is identical to the `md` command and takes the same arguments.

move [/y|/-y] [*drive*:][*path*]*filename*[,...] *destination*

or

move [/y|/-y] [*drive*:][*path*]*foldername newname*

The `move` command moves files from one folder or drive to another, and it can also rename directories.

When moving files, `move` has the same effect as dragging the files to a new location with Windows Explorer. If the files are moving to a new directory on the same drive, they are not physically copied; Windows needs only to alter the directory entries. If the files are being moved from one drive to another, `move` copies the files to the new location and then deletes them from the original drive. The

continues

REFERENCE LIST 11.1 Continued

`filename` argument or arguments can include wildcards to move groups of files. The ***`destination`*** argument should be the path to the new folder or, if you are only copying one file, a path including a new filename.

The `/Y` argument makes `move` silently overwrite any existing files of the same name in the destination folder. If `/-Y` is specified, `move` will prompt before overwriting. The default behavior is to prompt if `move` is entered from the command line, and not to prompt if `move` is used in a batch file, unless the default is changed by the `COPYCMD` environment variable or overridden by `/Y` or `/-Y` on the command line. See the `copy` command earlier in this section for information about `COPYCMD`.

The second form of the command simply renames a directory, to maintain compatibility with older versions of Windows. You can rename directories with the `rename` command in Windows XP. Because CMD still implements the old meaning of `move`, you must use wildcards if you want to move all files in a folder. Here are two examples:

- The command `move c:\temp\*.* datafiles` moves all files in `c:\temp` into `datafiles`, which must be a subfolder of the current directory.
- The command `move c:\temp datafiles` renames `c:\temp` to `c:\datafiles`.

`path` ***`pathlist`***
sets the search path to ***`pathlist`***, a list of folder pathnames separated by semicolons. The `path` command with no arguments prints the current path. You can also set the path by assigning the ***`pathlist`*** value to the environment variable `PATH` in a `set` statement. If there are spaces in any of the names, the name should be enclosed in quotes, as in this example:

```
path "c:\program files\microsoft office";c:\windows\system32;c:\windows
```

The `PATH` value is used by DOS programs as well as Windows programs, so if you use DOS programs, you should use only the short 8.3 version of each name in the path. For example, the setting

```
path c:\progra~1\micros~1;c:\windows\system32;c:\windows
```

specifies the same list of folders but is compatible with both DOS and Windows programs.

`pause`
The `pause` command is used in batch files to let the user read some output before continuing. It prints the famous message "Press any key to continue" in the Command Prompt window and waits for the user to press…well, any key except Ctrl+C or Ctrl+Break, which terminate the batch file.

In new batch files, you may wish to use the `set /p` command to print a more friendly message. I'll discuss this in Chapter 12.

`popd`
(See `pushd`.)

prompt [*text*]
sets the prompt displayed in the Command Prompt window before each command line to *text*. If the prompt command is used without any arguments, the prompt is set back to the default setting, `$p$g`.

For more information about the prompt setting, see "The Adjustable Prompt," earlier in this chapter.

pushd *path*
popd
changes the current directory to the specified *path*. The previous current drive and directory are remembered, and popd restores the previous path. Pushd saves as many directory changes as you care to make, and each popd returns to the directory in effect before the corresponding pushd. Unlike with cd, if the path specified to pushd contains a drive letter, the current drive is changed as well.

When command extensions are enabled, you can specify a network path (for example, `\\server\sharename\path`) in a pushd command, and it will automatically map a drive letter to the network path, starting with the letter Z and working backwards. Popd automatically deletes the temporary drive mappings.

rd [**/s**] [**/q**] *path*
The rd command removes the directory named *path*.

You can delete a folder, including all of its files and subfolders, by specifying the /s option. This is very dangerous because the files are deleted immediately and are not moved into the Recycle Bin. Be careful when using /s. As a precaution, CMD will prompt you to confirm whether you really do want to delete the entire subdirectory tree. You can add /q on the command line to eliminate this prompt.

Without /s, the specified directory must be empty; otherwise, the command will print an error message and not delete the directory.

Tip

If you attempt to delete an apparently empty directory with rd but Windows complains that the directory is not empty, look for hidden files or folders by typing `dir /ah` *path*.

rem *text*
allows you to enter a remark (comment) in a batch file. The text is ignored. Special characters such as |, >, <, and & are also ignored after rem, so you can use these characters in the remark.

ren [*path*]*oldname newname*
Same as rename.

continues

REFERENCE LIST 11.1 Continued

`rename` [*`path`*]*`oldname newname`*

renames a file or folder from *`oldname`* to *`newname`*. If the file or folder is not in the current directory, you can specify its path. Note that *`newname`* must not include a path.

`rmdir`

`Rmdir` is the same as `rd` and takes the same arguments.

`set` [*`name`*[`=`[*`value`*]]]
`set /A` *`expression`*
`set /P` *`name=promptstring`*

sets and displays environment variables. The basic set command has several useful variations:

Command	**Result**
`set`	Displays the list of all environment variables.
`set` *`name`*	Displays any variable(s) starting with the letters *`name`*.
`set` *`name=`*	Deletes the variable *`name`*.
`set name=value`	Sets the variable *`name`* to the specified *`value`*. *`Value`* is taken literally—do not put spaces after the `=` sign, and do not use quotation marks unless you want those characters recorded in the variable.

You may use environment variable substitution in a `set` command. For example, to add `c:\batchfiles` to the beginning of the existing `PATH` value, you could use this command:

```
set path=c:\batchfiles;%path%
```

You may insert special characters, such as `>`, `<`, `&`, and `|`, into environment variables, but you must use `^` before them to prevent them from being interpreted as redirection commands or command separators. For example,

```
set envvar=some^|text
```

defines an environment variable named `envvar` with the value `some|text`.

With command extensions enabled, the `set` command lets you perform numerical calculations and prompt for input. For information on calculating with `set`, see "Performing Numerical Calculations in Batch Files," later in this chapter. For information on prompting, see "Prompting for Input" in Chapter 12 (page 512).

```
setlocal [ENABLEEXTENSIONS|DISABLEEXTENSIONS]
   [ENABLEDELAYEDEXPANSION|DISABLEDELAYEDEXPANSION]
commands
.
.
.
endlocal
```

`Setlocal` saves and restores the batch file environment state. `Setlocal` saves a record of all environment variables, the current drive letter, the current working directory of all drives, and the state of command extensions and delayed environment expansion. `Endlocal` restores these settings to their previous values. The optional arguments to `setlocal` let you enable or disable the command extensions and/or delayed expansion. (Delayed expansion is discussed in Chapter 12.)

The settings will revert to the previous state after `endlocal` or at the end of the batch file. This means that you cannot use `setlocal` in a batch file that is to change environment variables that will remain changed when the batch file ends and the command prompt returns.

`shift` [*/n*]

This command shifts the batch file arguments to the left. The optional argument */n* lets you start shifting at argument number *n*, leaving the lower-numbered arguments alone. The `shift` command is discussed in more detail in Chapter 12.

The `shift` command is used when you want to process a variable number of arguments given to a batch file; your batch file can process argument `%1`, shift, and repeat the process until the argument is blank.

```
start "title" [/Dpath] [/I] [/MIN | /MAX]
    [/SEPARATE | /SHARED]
    [/LOW  | /BELOWNORMAL | /NORMAL | /ABOVENORMAL |
     /HIGH | /REALTIME]
    [/WAIT] [/B] command [arguments]
```

Starts a *command* in a new window. The specified command can be a Windows program, a console program, or even the name of a document file, in which case CMD will start the associated application. If `start` is used in a batch file, the batch file will continue without waiting for the program to exit. Optional command-line parameters control how the program is run:

Parameter	Description
"*title*"	Sets the window title to the specified string. By default, the name of the program file is used.
/D*path*	Starts the program in the specified directory.
/I	Starts the program with the default initial environment variable settings, rather than with a copy of the current settings.
/MIN	Starts the window minimized.

continues

REFERENCE LIST 11.1 Continued

Parameter	Description
/MAX	Starts the window maximized.
/SEPARATE	If the program is a 16-bit Windows program, this parameter starts it in a separate memory space with its own copy of the Win16 environment.
/SHARED	If the program is a 16-bit Windows program, this parameter starts it in the shared memory space where it can interact with other 16-bit Windows programs.
/LOW /BELOWNORMAL /NORMAL /ABOVENORMAL /HIGH /REALTIME	Runs the program in the indicated priority class. Be cautious of using `/REALTIME`, which lets the program run to the exclusion of nearly anything else If the program is ill-behaved, you may have a very difficult time running the Task Manager to stop it.
/WAIT	Makes the `start` command wait until the program exits before continuing. This is useful in batch files to let you run a program with an altered priority.
/B	For command line (console) programs, this parameter runs the program in the current window. Ctrl+C handling is disabled by default, but Ctrl+Break should still work if you need to interrupt the program.

`time` [`/t` | *`newtime`*]

With no arguments, `time` displays the current time of day and requests that you type in a new time. You can press Enter to keep the current setting. With `/t` on the command line, `time` displays the time without prompting for a replacement. This is meant to be used in batch files. For example, to record the date and time that a batch file was run, you might use the following commands:

```
echo batch file run on >batchlog.txt
date /t >>batchlog.txt
time /t >>batchlog.txt
echo. >>batchlog.txt
other commands >>batchlog.exe
```

However, it might be neater to print both the date and the time on the same line with the statement `echo %date% %time% >>batchlog.txt`.

You can also set the time by specifying the new clock setting on the command line. The time must be formatted according to the localized time format. You enter times with or without seconds, in 24-hour format or in AM/PM format, as in these examples:

```
time 18:58
time 6:58:20 PM
```

title [*string*]
sets the title of the current Command Prompt window to the specified string. By default, the title is `Command Prompt`, and when a program is running, it's `Command Prompt - command line`.

type [*path*]*filename*
writes the specified file to the standard output. Normally this means that the file is displayed in the Command Prompt window. (For long files, the `more` command is a better choice, because it displays the file a page at a time.) You can also use `type` to append one file onto another. For example, the following commands run a `ping` command, display the result, and also add the result to a log file that accumulates new information every time the commands are run:

```
@echo off
cls
echo Testing connection to mycompany.com...
ping www.mycompany.com 2>&1 >ping.out
echo The results are:
type ping.out

echo.              >>ping.log
echo Test run at >>ping.log
date /t            >>ping.log
time /t            >>ping.log
type ping.out      >>ping.log
del ping.out
```

ver
displays the version of Windows XP on your computer.

verify [**on** | **off**]
`Verify on` instructs Windows to read back all data written to the hard disk by application programs immediately after writing, to ensure that the data can be read correctly. This is especially useful when writing to floppy or other removable disks. `Verify off` disables read-after-write checking. `Verify` with no arguments displays the current setting; the default is `off`. You can specify the `/V` option with the `copy` command to enable verification just for the copy operation.

vol [*drive*:]
Displays the label and volume serial number for a disk drive. By default, `vol` displays the information for the current drive. You can specify an alternate drive on the command line.

Extended Commands

CMD's built-in commands are a superset of the ones recognized by the old `COMMAND.COM` shell, and many have been extended with new features. The command extensions are enabled by default in Windows XP, although they can be disabled if necessary. Table 11.3 lists the extended commands and their added features.

If the extensions cause problems for you—for example, if you have to use old batch files that do not work with the new command versions and you cannot update them—you can start CMD with the extensions disabled. I'll discuss this in the section "Running CMD."

Table 11.3 **Commands Modified by Command Extensions**

Command	Features Added by Command Extensions
`assoc`	Only available with extensions enabled.
`call`	`call :label`
	Substitution modifiers (for example, `%~f1`)
`cd / chdir`	Option `/D` changes current drive.
	The current directory uses the directory's actual upper/lowercase.
`color`	Only available with extensions enabled.
`date`	Option `/T` prints the date without prompting for a new date.
`del / erase`	Option `/S` displays names of files being deleted.
`endlocal`	Restores `EXTENSIONS` and `DELAYEXPANSION` settings.
`for`	(Many options are available; see the description of `for`.)
`ftype`	Only available with extensions enabled.
`goto`	`goto :EOF`
`if...else`	`/I`, `IF CMDEXTVERSION`, `IF DEFINED`
	Comparisons such as `LEQ`.
`md / mkdir`	Creates intermediate directories if necessary.
`prompt`	`$+` and `$M` options.
`pushd / popd`	Accepts a network path and maps a drive letter.
`set`	`/A` and `/P` options.
	The `set` command with a partial name displays matching names.
`setlocal`	`ENABLE...` and `DISABLE...` arguments.
`shift`	`/n` option.
`start`	Starts nonexecutable files via file extensions. Uses `PATHEXT` expansion.
	Doesn't wait for Win32 commands to exit before prompting again.
	Uses the `COMSPEC` path when the command is CMD. Runs Explorer if the command is a folder name.
`time`	Option `/T` prints the time without prompting for a new time.

In the next few sections, I'll provide some additional detail on some of the more important commands.

Listing Files with the Dir Command

The `dir` command is one of the most helpful command-line programs. While it's often more efficient to use Explorer to view folder contents, `dir` has a few tricks up its sleeve that make it worth knowing about.

Without any command-line arguments, `dir` prints a listing of files and directories (folders) in the current directory. Here's a sample listing:

```
 Volume in drive C has no label.
 Volume Serial Number is DC77-E725

 Directory of C:\Documents and Settings\bknittel\My Documents

02/27/2002  01:12 PM    <DIR>          .
02/27/2002  01:12 PM    <DIR>          ..
02/27/2002  01:12 PM    <DIR>          Fax
02/19/2002  06:03 PM    <DIR>          herc360
08/16/2000  03:51 PM         2,665,373 iris1.mp3
08/16/2000  03:51 PM         2,461,696 iris2.mp3
02/04/2002  10:54 AM            34,205 Lcphx.022
03/23/2002  05:17 PM    <DIR>          My Music
04/05/2002  04:52 PM    <DIR>          My Pictures
02/19/2002  06:04 PM            75,776 os 360 gen.doc
02/25/2002  08:02 PM            15,872 paypal.xls
02/11/2002  07:08 PM           232,448 stnbyhour.xls
02/11/2002  07:27 PM            56,320 strita.xls
02/07/2002  09:07 PM                 0 todo.txt
               8 File(s)      5,541,690 bytes
               6 Dir(s)  11,918,438,400 bytes free
```

(If you've only ever used Macintosh or Windows-based computers, you may find it hard to believe that not too many years ago, this was the *only* way to view and locate files.)

So what are `.` and `..`? These two odd entries represent the current directory and its parent directory. They really serve no real purpose today; they're the software equivalent to your appendix, a remnant of MS-DOS's distant Unix ancestry, and you can ignore them.

The rest of the listing shows the names of the directory's files and subdirectories as well as their sizes and last-modified dates. The listing ends with a summary of file counts and sizes.

In Reference List 11.1, I showed all the command-line options you can use with `dir`. In this section, I'll go over a few of the ones that are particularly useful.

Paginating Long Listings

If `dir` prints more names than you can see on the screen at one time, you can scroll back through the listing using the Command Prompt window's scrollbar. You can also ask `dir` to print only 24 lines at a time, the amount that will fit in the default window size, by adding `/p` to any `dir` command. When you've caught up with the listing, press Enter to print the next screenful. For example, `dir %windir% /p` lists the contents of the Windows folder a page at a time.

Searching for Particular Files

You can specify individual filenames or folder names, using wildcards if desired, to limit the listing to specific files and locations. The command `dir *.exe` lists only files ending in `.exe`, and `dir m*.*` lists only files starting with the letter *m*.

You can add `/s` to any `dir` command to make the listing include all subdirectories of the folder in which `dir` starts its search. For example, `dir c:\*.mp3 /s /p` locates all MP3 files anywhere on drive C:, because it starts in the root directory `C:\` and examines all subdirectories. Of course, you can use the Windows Search window to perform this sort of task, but when you already have the Command Prompt window open, it can sometimes be quicker to type a command like this than to poke around with Windows. Of course, whether you use `dir` or the Search window, you'll only see files in folders for which you have read permission.

Making Columnar Listings

The options `/w` and `/d` print listings of filenames that are arranged in several columns; the exact number of columns is difficult to predict, because `dir` makes the columns wider or narrower depending on the length of the longest filename it finds. The difference between the two options is that `/w` lists the names by rows, whereas `/d` sorts them into columns. The `/w` listing looks like this:

```
 Volume in drive C has no label.
 Volume Serial Number is DC77-E725

 Directory of C:\simh\ibm1130\sw\dmsr2v12

[.]            [..]           ABOOTPT.asm    ABOOTPT.bin    ABOOTPT.lst
ASYSLDR1.asm   ASYSLDR1.bin   ASYSLDR1.lst   CSYSLDR2.asm   CSYSLDR2.bin
CSYSLDR2.lst   DBOOTCD.asm    DBOOTCD.bin    DBOOTCD.lst    DCILOADR.asm
DCILOADR.bin   DCILOADR.lst   dmsr2v12.zip   DSYSLDR1.asm   dsysldr1.bin
dsysldr1.lst   FSYSLDR2.asm   FSYSLDR2.bin   FSYSLDR2.lst   JADUPCO.asm
...
```

The `/w` and `/d` options are particularly useful to get printable listings of your files.

Printing Directory Listings

Don't you find it annoying that Windows Explorer has no "print" command? Ha! Here's an area where the command-line environment is much more capable. You can easily print a directory listing from the command line.

You can redirect the output of any `dir` command to your local printer, using commands such as the following:

```
cd \Documents and Settings\bknittel\My Documents\My Music
dir >lpt1
```

The first command selects the correct directory, and the `dir` command sends its output to the printer. This technique doesn't tell the printer to finish the last page of the listing, however, and you'll probably have to manually eject the last page.

You can redirect output to a network printer if you know its share name as in this example:

```
dir >//sumatra/okidata
```

Tip

You can gain a bit more control over the process by redirecting the listing to a file and then printing it with Notepad or a word processor. However, if you redirect the directory listing into a file in the same directory you're listing, the listing file will appear in the output. You can avoid this by directing the listing file into another directory, as with these commands:

```
cd \Documents and Settings\bknittel\My Documents\My Music
dir /s >..\list
notepad ..\list
del ..\list
```

Note that `..` represents the directory one level above the directory being listed. After printing the listing with Notepad, you can delete the scratch file.

Getting Lists of Filenames

The default directory listing format lists dates, sizes, times, header information, and a summary. The `/b` option asks `dir` to print a list of names only. The output of such a listing can be redirected to a file, where it can be used as input to programs, batch files, or Windows Script Host scripts that want, as input, a list of filenames.

When you use `/s` and `/b`, the `dir` command lists the full path for all files it displays. For example, from my Windows directory, `dir /b /s *.wav` prints a long list of files starting with these:

```
C:\WINDOWS\Help\Tours\WindowsMediaPlayer\Audio\Wav\wmpaud1.wav
C:\WINDOWS\Help\Tours\WindowsMediaPlayer\Audio\Wav\wmpaud2.wav
.
.
.
C:\WINDOWS\Help\Tours\WindowsMediaPlayer\Audio\Wav\wmpaud9.wav
C:\WINDOWS\Media\chimes.wav
C:\WINDOWS\Media\chord.wav
C:\WINDOWS\Media\ding.wav
C:\WINDOWS\Media\notify.wav
.
.
.
```

Sorting Listings

By default, `dir` sorts files by name. You can list files in some other order by using the `/o` option, followed by one or more letters indicating which parts of the file information to use for sorting. Reference List 11.1 shows the whole list of sort options. Some of the most useful combinations are listed here:

Option	Sorts
`/o-s`	By size. Largest first
`/odn`	By date. Oldest first, then by name
`/o-dn`	By date. Newest first, then by name
`/oen`	By type (extension), then by name

Listing Hidden Files

Normally, hidden files are omitted from `dir` listings. (What would be the point otherwise?) However, you can ask `dir` to list hidden files by adding `/ah` to the command line. The `/a` flag instructs `dir` to list files with specified attributes, and the `h` indicates that you want to see hidden files.

You can use the `/a` option to select files based on the other attributes listed in Reference List 11.1. For example, `/as` lists only system files, `/a-s` lists only files that are *not* marked as system files, and so on.

Setting Variables with the `Set` Command

From the days of MS-DOS version 1, Microsoft's batch file language had two striking deficiencies: the inability to perform string and numerical calculations, and the inability to prompt for input. With the command extensions enabled, alternate versions of the `set` command help remedy these problems to a great extent.

Performing Numerical Calculations in Batch Files

The command `set /A` ***`expression`*** evaluates a string as a mathematical expression. Any assignment statements in the expression cause CMD to format the result as a string and assign it to a named environment variable. ***`Expression`*** uses standard mathematical syntax. The operators allowed in the expression are listed here, in order of decreasing precedence:

Operators	Description
`( )`	Expression grouping.
`! ~ -`	Unary operators: boolean `NOT`, bitwise invert, and arithmetic negative.
`* / %`	Multiply, divide, remainder.

Operators	Description
`+ -`	Add, subtract.
`<< >>`	Bitwise shift left, shift right.
`&`	Bitwise AND.
`| ^`	Bitwise OR and exclusive OR.
`= *= /= %=` `+= -= &= ^=` `|= <<= >>=`	Assignment, and the combined operator/assignment operators borrowed from the C programming language. `A += 3` is the same as `A = A + 3`.
`,`	Separates multiple expressions.

Any alphanumeric words are taken to indicate environment variables. In an expression, if a named environment variable is undefined or does not contain a number, it is treated as the value `0`. Variables are treated as decimal numbers, except that numbers starting with `0x` are interpreted as hexadecimal (base 16), and numbers starting with `0` are treated as octal (base 8). Here are some examples:

```
set A=3
set /A B=A*2, C=2*(B+5)
```

These statements set environment variables `A` to `3`, `B` to `6`, and `C` to `22`.

If you use `set /A` in a batch file, it is silent, but if you type it on the command line, it displays the last value it calculates. For example, the command

```
set /A 3+3
```

types the result `6` without storing the result to any environment variable. It turns the command prompt into a nice, quick calculator.

String calculations—for example, to remove the extension from a filename—are not quite as cleanly implemented, but I'll show you what's available later in the section on environment variable substitution.

Conditional Processing with the `If` Command

The `if` command lets you run specific commands only if certain conditions are true. `If` is one of the central requirements of a true programming language, and the extended `if` command provided by CMD makes the batch file language much more useful than it was in the days of `COMMAND.COM`.

The basic formats of the `if` command are

`if` `condition` *`command`*

and

`if` *`condition`* **`(`***`command1`***`) else`** *`command2`*

The first version tests some condition and, if it's true, executes ***command***. If the condition is not true, the command is ignored.

The second version provides a second command that is run if the condition is false. In this version, one command or the other is run, depending on the condition.

You can group multiple commands in an `if` statement using parentheses. For example, the statements

```
if not exist input.dat (
    echo Attention: creating new input.dat file
    dir /b c:\inputs >input.dat
)
```

check to see whether file `input.dat` exists and, if it doesn't, run the `echo` and `dir` commands. Grouped commands make CMD batch files much easier to read and write than the DOS format, where you would have had to write this instead:

```
if exist input.dat goto haveinput
    echo Attention: creating new input.dat file
    dir /b c:\inputs >input.dat
:haveinput
```

You can use the `else` clause with grouped commands as well, in the following format:

```
if condition (
    commands
    ...
) else (
    commands
    ...
)
```

The indenting is optional; it just makes the commands easier to read.

There are several *`condition`* tests, as listed here:

- `[`**`not`**`]` *`strng1`* `==` *`strng2`*

  Compares *`strng1`* to *`strng2`* and is true if the strings are exactly equal, including case. The sense can be reversed by preceding the test with the word `not`.

- `[`**`not`**`]` **`errorlevel`** *`number`*

  Examines the exit status value of the last program that was run. The condition is true if the exit status is greater than or equal to *`number`*. `Not` reverses the sense; the test is true if the exit status is less than *`number`*.

- `[`**`not`**`]` **`exist`** *`filename`*

  The test is true if the named file exists. The sense can be reversed with `not`. To test for a directory, add `/nul` to the directory name; the null file will always appear to exist if the specified directory exists.

- `[/i] strng1 compareop strng2`

  compares two strings and returns the result of the comparison. If both the strings consist only of digits, the comparison is made numerically; otherwise, it's made alphabetically. If `/i` is used, the test is case-insensitive. *`Compareop`* is one of the following:

  `EQU`—Equal to
  `NEQ`—Not equal to
  `LSS`—Less than
  `LEQ`—Less than or equal to
  `GTR`—Greater than
  `GEQ`—Greater than or equal to

- **`cmdextversion`** *`number`*

  The test is true if the version number of the CMD extensions is greater than or equal to *number*. At the time of this writing, the command extension version number for Windows XP is 2. The test is always false if the command extensions are disabled.

- **`defined`** *`variable`*

  The test is true if the named environment variable is defined and is not empty.

The extended `if` statement is one of CMD's biggest improvements. Combined with environment variables, you have a decent programming language.

Scanning for Files with the `For` Command

You'll often want to perform some command repeatedly with each of several files. CMD provides a command named `for` that helps save typing: It repeats a command for each item in a specified list.

At its simplest, `for` runs a command for every item placed in its *set* (a list of items in parentheses). For example,

```
for %x in (a b c) do echo %x
```

prints out three lines:

```
a
b
c
```

The set consists of the strings `a`, `b`, and `c`. `For` creates a temporary variable named `x` and issues the command `echo %x` three times, with `x` taking on the values `a`, `b`, and `c` in turn. In the command, any occurrence of `%x` is replaced by the value of `x`, so this `for` command is the equivalent of issuing these three commands:

```
echo a
echo b
echo c
```

(By the way, the choice of which letter to use for the variable is completely arbitrary. I picked *x*, but you can use any of the lowercase letters *a* to *z* or the uppercase letters *A* to *Z*. Oddly enough, case matters here.)

If any of the items in the set contain the wildcard characters `*` or `?`, CMD replaces the items with the list of all matching filenames. Therefore, the command

```
for %x in (*.doc) do echo %x
```

runs the `echo` command once for each `.doc` file.

Note

One tricky thing about `for` is that the percent sign (`%`) is considered a special character in batch files. When you use a `for` command in a batch file, you have to double up all the `%` signs used with the `for` variable. The previous `for` statement would have to be written this way in a batch file:

```
for %%x in (*.doc) do echo %%x
```

If you write lots of batch files, you'll get used to this, but then you'll have to remember to use only one `%` sign if you type a `for` command directly at the command prompt.

I'll show you how to exploit the `for` command in batch files in the next chapter.

The `for` command in CMD is much more powerful than its `COMMAND.COM` equivalent. Several modifiers can be placed between the word `for` and the set to make `for` perform several useful tricks.

Using the `for` Command's Variable

As the `for` command runs through each of the files or words named in the *`set`* list, the variable you specify on the command line takes each of the set's values in turn. If the variable was specified as, say, `%x`, wherever `%x` appears after the keyword `do`, it will be replaced by the variable's value. CMD has added some additional ways to extract information from the variable, most of which treat the variable as a filename and let you extract just specific filename components. This makes it possible to construct for loops that could, for example, run through all the `.DOC` files in a folder and copy them to files named `.BACKUP`.

CMD edits the value of the variable based on extra characters you place after the `%` symbol and substitutes the edited version into the command line. The variable edits that CMD offers are listed in Table 11.4. (The same edits are available for the command line and subroutine arguments in batch files.)

Table 11.4 **Variable-Editing Functions**

Expression	Result
%*n*	Argument or variable *n* without editing.
%~*n*	Removes surrounding quotes (" ").
%~f*n*	Fully qualified pathname.
%~d*n*	Drive letter only.
%~p*n*	Path only.
%~n*n*	Filename only.
%~x*n*	File extension only.
%~s*n*	Short DOS 8.3 file and path.
%~a*n*	File attributes.
%~t*n*	Modification date/time of file.
%~z*n*	Length of file in bytes.
%~$PATH:*n*	Fully qualified name of first matching file when PATH is searched. If no file is found, the result is a zero-length string. The filename must include the proper extension; PATHEXT is not used.

The filename modifiers can be used in combination (for example, %~dp*n* returns the combined drive and path).

Tip

When using variable edits, it's best to use uppercase letters for your variable so that CMD can distinguish between the editing characters, which must always be in lowercase, and your variable. (You may notice that $PATH: is not in lowercase—the dollar sign and colon make it clear to CMD that this is an editing function and not the variable P.)

As an example, the following for loop copies only files under 1MB in size to a network folder:

```
for %X in (*.*) do if %~zX LSS 1000000 copy %X \\bali\myfiles
```

Processing Directories

The for command has several variations that change the way it interprets the contents of the listed set of names.

The variation **for /d** *%variable* **in (set) do** *command* works much like the standard for command, except that wildcards in set match only directory names. You can use this variation to perform a command or run a batch file in any or all of the subfolders of particular folders. For example,

```
for /d %d in (%homepath%\My Documents\My Music\*.*) do echo %d
```

lists the names of all the subfolders under the user's My Music folder.

Processing Files in Directories and Subdirectories

The variation **`for /r`** *`path`* **`%`***`variable`* **`in (`***`set`***`) do`** *`command`* runs the complete `for` command in the directory named by *`path`* and then in each of its subdirectories and their subdirectories, and so on. The wildcard matching operation on *`set`* is performed in each of these directories. For example, the command

```
for /r c:\data %x in (*.txt) do notepad %x
```

visits the folder `c:\data` and each of its subfolders, and in each one, it runs a copy of Notepad to display and edit every `.txt` file it finds. (This can open a lot of copies of Notepad.)

Numerical `for` Loop

The variation **`for /l %`***`variable`* **`in (`***`start#,step#,stop#`***`) do`** *`command`* makes the variable take on numeric values from *`start#`* to *`stop#`*, incrementing by `step#` at each turn. For example, the statement

```
for /l %v in (1,1,10) do echo %1
```

prints numbers from 1 to 10. The step value can be positive or negative. The set `(1,1,5)` generates the sequence `(1 2 3 4 5)`, whereas the set `(5,-1,1)` generates the sequence `(5 4 3 2 1)`.

Parsing Text

In its most unusual variation, the `for` command reads strings, the contents of a file, or the output of a command, and from this text extracts a series of values to use as the set.

This is the most complex of the `for` commands. In the simplest version, the command will extract just the first word from each line of text it reads. The definition of "word" is text delimited by one or more spaces or tabs. The command can be written to use any of three sources of data:

`for /f %`*`variable`* **`in (`***`filenames`***`) do`** *`command`*

`for /f "usebackq" %`*`variable`* **`in (``***`command1`***``) do`** *`command2`*

`for /f` `%variable` **`in ("`***`literal text`***`") do`** *`command`*

The first version examines all the files named in the filename set, which may use wildcards. The files are read as text files, and the first token (word) from each line is used as the source of values for the variable.

The second version runs *`command1`* as a CMD command line and then gathers its output. The first token on each output line is used as the source of values for the variable.

The third version looks at the literal text surrounded by quotes. This form would only make sense if used with environment variables within the quotes. The first token is used as the value for the variable.

If you use a set of one or more filenames and must use quotes to protect spaces in the filenames (to indicate you are specifying files and not literal text), use the `usebackq` modifier as in this version:

for /f "usebackq" *%variable* **in ("***filename***"...) do** *command*

Now, reading the first word from each line is not very interesting. The parsing system also lets you choose which tokens to extract, specify token delimiters, specify a line-terminating character, and pick up more than one token from each input line. You can specify any of the following items in quotes after `/f`:

Modifier	Description
eol=*c*	Indicates that all text after the character *c* is to be ignored.
skip=*n*	Skips the first *n* lines of the file before extracting tokens.
delims=*xyz...*	Specifies that the characters *x*, *y*, and *z* are the token delimiters, rather than a space and tab. For example, `delims=,` specifies the comma as the delimiter.
tokens=*x,y,m-n*	Selects which tokens on the input lines to return as variables. If more than one is listed, the `for` command assigns the values to additional variables in increasing alphabetical order after the one specified with `%`. Numbers separated by a dash indicate a range. For example, `tokens=1,4-7` would select input tokens 1, 4, 6, and 7 and would define four variables.
usebackq	Indicates that quotation marks in *set* indicate filenames, not literal text, and that single quotes indicate literal text.

The following `for` command runs the `arp` command to get a list of the computer's network adapter information. The `arp` command lists each of the computer's IP addresses and physical MAC addresses. The `for` command skips three headers lines and extracts two tokens from each remaining output line. The first is stored in the named variable `%a`, and the second in the next letter up, `%b`:

```
for /f "skip=3 tokens=1,2 usebackq" %a in (`arp -a`) do (
    echo IP address %a, MAC address %b
)
```

Note

One thing that `for /f` cannot do is parse the common CSV (comma-separated value) text format, because these files use quotes to surround text items and can have commas inside the items. The `for` statement is not smart enough to parse comma- and quote-delimited text.

Running CMD

When you open a Command Prompt window, Windows starts the `CMD.EXE` program. CMD prompts for commands and executes them, until you close the window or type the `exit` command. You can also run CMD using the Start, Run command, and you can open additional Command Prompt windows from the command line or from batch files, if there's a need. To open a new window from the command prompt, type **`start cmd`**. You can alter CMD's behavior by specifying additional command-line arguments, as I'll discuss shortly.

Tip

A good time to open an additional Command Prompt window is when you need to perform privileged administrative tasks. You can open a Command Prompt window that has Administrator privileges by typing

```
runas /user:Administrator cmd
```

on the command line or in the Start menu's Run dialog box. The new window will run under the Administrator logon name, and any programs you run from this command prompt will also have Administrator privileges. The only exception to this is that you can't run Explorer from this new window. Explorer is an odd program, and you can't have two copies running under two different accounts at the same time.

CMD has several command-line options. Although you won't often need to use these options, you may want to be familiar with them. The syntax of the CMD command line is as follows:

cmd [**/a** | **/u**] [**/q**] [**/d**] [**/t:***fg*] [**/e:on**|**off**] [**/f:on**|**off**] [**/v:on**|**off**] [[**/s**] [**/c** | **/k**] *command*]

You can give CMD a specific command line to execute, or you can start it without a command. In the latter case, it will repeatedly prompt for commands.

The options are described here. The features noted with an asterisk are discussed in the following sections:

Options	Description
/a	Causes standard output to use ANSI encoding.
/u	Causes standard output to use Unicode encoding.
/q	Turns the batch file echo default to off.
/d	Disables execution of AutoRun commands defined in the Registry.

Options	Description
`/t:bf`	Sets the background (window) and foreground (text) colors for the window. For example, `/t:80` specifies black text on a gray background. The color values are listed in Table 11.5.
`/e`	Enables or disables the command extensions.
`/f`	Enables or disables the file and directory name completion feature.
`/v`	Enables delayed environment variable expansion of `!varname!` items, as discussed in Chapter 12.
`/s`	Modifies the treatment of quotation marks on the command line, as discussed in Chapter 12.
`/c`	Executes the command(s) in *`command`* and then quits.
`/k`	Executes the command(s) in *`command`* and then reads further commands from the standard input until end of file or until the `exit` command is received.

If used, the `/c` or `/k` option must appear immediately before the *`command`* string. Anything after `/c` or `/k` is treated as part of the command to be run, rather than an argument to CMD.

Several nonstandard command-line arguments are also recognized, to maintain compatibility with batch files written for Windows NT 4.0:

Arguments	Description
`/x`	Same as `/e:on`. Enables command extensions.
`/y`	Same as `/e:off`. Disables command extensions.
`/r`	Same as `/c`. Executes *`command`* and quits.

The color codes used with `/t` are listed in Table 11.5.

Table 11.5 **Color Codes Used with** ***/t***

Value	Color
`0`	Black
`1`	Blue
`2`	Green
`3`	Aqua
`4`	Red
`5`	Purple
`6`	Yellow
`7`	White

continues

Table 11.5 **Continued**

Value	Color
8	Gray
9	Light Blue
A	Light Green
B	Light Aqua
C	Light Red
D	Light Purple
E	Light Yellow
F	Bright White

Disabling Command Extensions

To run an old batch file that will not function with the extended version of CMD's built-in commands, you can explicitly disable extensions with `/e:off` on the CMD command line. For example, to run an incompatible batch file, use the following:

```
cmd /e:off oldbatch.bat
```

If this needs to be the rule rather than the exception, you have my sympathies, and you can disable extensions by default through the Registry key `HKLM\Software\Microsoft\Command Processor\EnableExtensions`. If this `DWORD` value is present and set to `0`, command extensions are disabled. You can use `/e:on` on the command line to enable extensions for a particular instance of CMD.

Enabling Directory Name Completion

As mentioned earlier in the chapter, filename completion is enabled by default—the Tab key searches for a file *or* folder name matching the characters to the left of the cursor. A similar feature, called *directory name completion*, lets you use another key to match only directory names.

I'll show you how to enable directory name completion, but prepare yourself for some strangeness. First off, there's the matter of the odd default control key settings:

- By default, name completion is enabled and uses the Tab key, whereas directory name completion is disabled.
- If you run CMD with `/f:on` on the command line, name completion is enabled but now uses Ctrl+F. Directory name completion is enabled and uses Ctrl+D.
- If you run CMD with `/f:off` on the command line, both name and directory name completion are disabled.

If you want directory name completion to be enabled all the time, the best approach is to edit the Registry to change the default settings. The values `CompletionChar` and

`PathCompletionChar` set the key codes used for name completion and directory name completion, respectively. CMD looks for the values in the key

```
HKEY_CURRENT_USER\Software\Microsoft\Command Processor
```

which holds the settings for the current user. If they are not present there, CMD looks in

```
HKEY_LOCAL_MACHINE\Software\Microsoft\Command Processor
```

which sets the default for all users.

`CompletionChar` and `PathCompletionChar` are `DWORD` values that hold a number representing the associated control key. It's easiest to enter these values in decimal, where 1 = Ctrl+A, 2 = Ctrl+B, … 26 = Ctrl+Z. Some handy values to know are listed here:

Value	Key
4	Ctrl+D
6	Ctrl+F
9	Ctrl+I (Tab)
32	Disables completion

To use Ctrl+F for name completion and Ctrl+D for directory name completion, follow these steps:

1. Run the Registry editor with the command `regedit`.
2. Open `HKEY_CURRENT_USER` and find `Software\Microsoft\Command Processor`.
3. Double-click the already-present `CompletionChar` entry, click `Decimal`, and enter the number **`6`**. Click OK.
4. Select Edit, New, DWORD Value. Enter the name **`PathCompletionChar`**.
5. Double-click the new entry, click `Decimal`, enter the value **`4`**, and click OK.
6. Close the Registry editor and any Command Prompt windows.

From now on, when you start a Command Prompt window, Ctrl+F and Ctrl+D will work.

Just so you don't get surprised by CMD's behavior at some later date, when Registry settings have been made, CMD follows these rules for enabling name or directory name completion:

- If the Registry value is between `1` and `26`, completion is enabled unless you specify `/f:off` when you run CMD.
- If the Registry value is `32`, completion is disabled regardless of the `/f` option setting.
- If the `CompletionChar` value is defined as `9` (Tab) and the `PathCompletionChar` value is not defined, then CMD displays the default behavior described earlier.

This is all much more complex than it needs to be, which is why I suggest that unless you feel strongly about this feature, forget about directory name completion and use the Tab key when typing both file and folder names.

Getting More Information

There's quite a bit of information about the command line environment tucked away in Windows, but it's scattered far and wide. To read about the CMD program itself and the built-in commands, click Start, Help and Support and then search for the following strings:

- cmd
- command shell overview
- command-line reference
- command-line reference A-Z

You can also get information from the command-line `help` program. Type commands of the form

```
help cmd
help dir
help for
```

and so on, using any of the command or program names listed in this chapter. The `help` command automatically sends its output through `more` so you can view it a page at a time. Almost all command-line programs will display help information if you run them with `/?` as a command-line argument, so if help doesn't work, try running the program like this:

```
cmd /? | more
more /? | more
ping /? | more
```

12

Batch Files for Fun and Profit

ROAD MAP

- Batch files let you automate repetitive tasks and create nifty command shortcuts.
- The batch file language in Windows XP is greatly improved over the DOS/Win9x version.
- Like scripts, batch files can serve as documentation of critical business procedures.
- You should be familiar with the material in Chapter 11, "The CMD Command-Line Environment," before starting this chapter.

Why Batch Files?

While Windows Script Host is a powerful scripting and programming environment, the old-fashioned batch file can still be a useful, powerful tool in the Windows XP environment. Why? Whereas Windows Script Host programs use objects as tools to perform Windows management and data-processing tasks, batch files use *entire programs* as their tools. WSH scripts give you great control of the details of a task, whereas batch files let you work at a grosser, macro level. So, just as it's an advantage to have both small and large wrenches in your toolbox, it's an advantage to know how to write both scripts and batch files. Furthermore, like Windows Script programs, batch files serve as a form of documentation, because they capture critical business management information—procedures and configuration data—in written form.

In my work as both a software developer and writer, I've found that the batch files I write fall into three categories:

- Tiny files to manipulate the command-line environment. For example, I have several little batch files that change the working directory to the correct folder for specific projects, and perhaps add a directory to the search path. This way, I can open a Command Prompt window, type one word, and be ready to work with a particular project's files.

- Medium-sized files that perform a specific series of commands that I find myself typing over and over. For example, I frequently have to send updated versions of a particular set of files to a client. I use a batch file to update a ZIP file and e-mail the results so the whole job is taken care of with one command.
- Monster batch files that perform a long sequence of tasks and handle a variety of command-line options. In my work, these tend to involve custom-developed command-line programs for data-processing applications or Microsoft-provided utilities used to manage Windows—both the standard tools and those provided with the Windows Resource Kits. For example, I have a batch file that documents all the Internet domains managed by my Windows 2000 Server's DNS service. This batch file could reconstruct the entire set of domains if it is necessary to move to a new server. This kind of job is a snap for a batch file but would be a nightmare to reenter through the GUI.

In Chapter 11, I discussed all the commands built in to the CMD shell. In this chapter, I'll discuss the commands that are particularly useful in batch files and will give you some examples of the three categories of batch files I find useful.

Creating and Using Batch Files

Batch files are plain-text files. You can most easily create and edit them with Notepad. I suggest that you create a special folder just for your own batch files and add this folder to your search path (as discussed in Chapter 11) so that you can run them from any folder in any Command Prompt window.

You can place them in any folder you want. You can place them on your own hard drive, or you may wish to place your batch files on a shared network folder so they can be used from any computer. I place my personal batch files in a folder named `c:\bat`. To create this folder, open a Command Prompt window and type these commands at the prompt:

```
c:
mkdir \bat
cd \bat
```

To add this folder to the search path, follow these steps:

1. Click Start, right-click My Computer, and select Properties.
2. Select the Advanced tab and click Environment Variables.
3. Look in the list of variables defined under User variables for (*your-user-name*).
4. If there is already an entry named `PATH`, select it and click Edit. At the beginning of the Variable Value field, insert `C:\bat` and add a semicolon to separate this name from the names that are already there. The result should look something like what's shown in Figure 12.1.

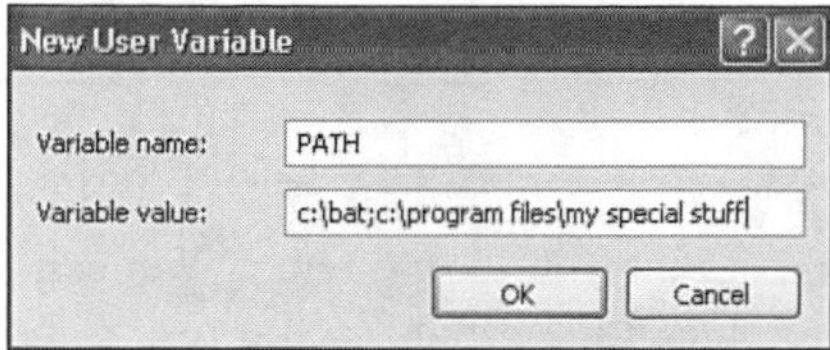

Figure 12.1 When adding a directory to the beginning of the path, be sure to place a semicolon after the new directory name.

If there is *not* already an entry named `PATH`, click New and enter `PATH` as the variable name. Enter `C:\bat` as the variable value.

5. Click OK three times to close the three dialog boxes. Close the Command Prompt window and open another one. Type `path` and press Enter. You should see `c:\bat` at the beginning of the path.

Note

If you want to make your batch files available to every user on your computer, log on as computer Administrator and follow this same procedure, except in step 3, edit the System Variables list instead of the User Variables list.

Once `c:\bat` has been added to your path, any batch files you create in this folder can be run just by typing their names at the command prompt.

Batch files should be given the extension `.cmd` or `.bat`. Either is fine. The `.bat` extension is more traditional, whereas `.cmd` makes it clear that the batch file is written for Windows NT/2000/XP, because DOS and Windows 9*x* will not recognize such files as batch files.

To create a sample batch file, open a Command Prompt window or use the one opened earlier in this section. Type the command

```
notepad test.bat
```

and then click Yes when Notepad asks, Do you want to create a new file? In the empty Notepad window, type the following lines:

```
@echo off
cls
echo The command line argument is %1
pause
```

Save the file and at the command line type this:

```
test xxx
```

The Command Prompt window should clear, and you should see the following:

```
The command line argument is xxx
Press any key to continue . . .
```

Press Enter, and the command prompt should return. You can use this procedure to create any number of batch files. One batch file you may want to create right now should be named `bat.bat`, with this one line inside:

```
pushd c:\bat
```

This falls into the "tiny handy" batch file category mentioned earlier. With this in place, if you type `bat` at any command prompt, your current directory will be changed to `c:\bat` so that you can edit or create batch files. Type `popd` to go back to whatever directory you were using beforehand.

Of course, you could just type `pushd c:\bat` directly. It may seem silly to create a batch file just to save nine keystrokes, but when you're actively developing batch files, you'll quickly find that this does make life easier.

I have about a dozen batch files like this that I use on a daily basis to move into directories for specific projects. For projects that use special command-line programs, the batch file has a second line that adds the program directory to the beginning of the search path, using a command such as this:

```
path c:\some\new\folder;%path%
```

If you find yourself frequently working with command-line programs, you will want to make "tiny handy" batch files for your projects as well.

Batch File Programming

In the following sections, I'll discuss programming techniques that take advantage of the extended commands provided by the CMD shell. The commands that are most useful in batch files are listed in Table 12.1.

Table 12.1 **Batch File Commands**

Command	Use
`call`	Calls batch file subroutine
`echo`	Displays text to the user
`setlocal/endlocal`	Saves/restores environment variables
`exit`	Terminates batch file
`for`	Iterates over files or folders
`goto`	Used for flow control
`if`	Executes commands conditionally
`pause`	Lets the user read a message

Command	Use
`pushd/popd`	Saves/restores the current directory
`rem`	Used for comments and documentation
`set`	Sets environment variables, performs calculations, and prompts for user input
`shift`	Scans through command-line arguments
`start`	Launches a program in a different window

The syntax and options for these commands were described in Chapter 11. If you've written batch files for DOS, Windows 9*x*, and Windows NT, you'll find that most of these commands have been significantly enhanced, so even if you are familiar with these commands, you should read their descriptions in Chapter 11.

Displaying Information in Batch Files

By default, batch files display or echo every line inside them to the Command Prompt window as they run. For complex batch files, this can be very distracting, as page after page of commands and messages scroll by. It's hard to read, and you may miss important error messages buried in the middle of the mess. Therefore, it's traditional to disable batch file echoing with the statement

```
@echo off
```

at the very beginning of the file. `Echo off` turns off the echoing feature, and the `@` at the beginning of the command prevents the `echo` command itself from being echoed before it can work its magic.

Tip

When you're debugging a batch file, it can be helpful to leave echoing turned on so that you can see what commands are being run. To turn echoing on temporarily, add `rem` so that the batch file's first line reads

```
rem @echo off
```

`Rem` turns this line into a comment. You can remove it later when the batch file is working correctly.

However, it's nice to have batch files tell you what's going on inside so that you'll know that something is actually happening. The `echo` command is great for this—it echoes whatever text follows the word `echo`, so you can throw helpful comments throughout the batch file like this:

```
@echo off
echo Starting to sort files...
.
.
.
```

```
echo Sending results to the printer...
.
.
.
echo Done.
```

Tip

Sometimes it's nice to see exactly how a program is going to be run by a batch file, especially when the program's command line is constructed on-the-fly with environment variables and arguments. To do this, put `@echo on` just before the program's command line and `@echo off` just after it. This way, CMD will display the actual command line as it runs the program.

You can also have `echo` commands display the environment variables and command-line arguments with which the program is working. For example,

```
echo Your user name is %username%
```

will print `Your user name is` followed by the contents of the `username` environment variable. I'll show examples of this kind of informational message throughout the chapter.

Argument Substitution

Many times you'll find that the repetitive tasks you encounter use the same programs but operate on different files each time. In this case, you can use command-line arguments to give information to the batch file when you run it. When you start a batch file from the command line with a command such as

```
batchname xxx yyy zzz
```

any items after the name of the batch file are made available to the batch program as arguments. The symbols `%1`, `%2`, `%3`, and so on are replaced with the corresponding arguments. In this example, anywhere that `%1` appears in the batch file, CMD replaces it with `xxx`. Then, `%2` is replaced with `yyy`, and so on.

Argument substitution lets you write batch files like this:

```
@echo off
notepad %1.vbs
cscript %1.vbs
```

This batch file lets you edit and then run a Windows Script Host program. If you name the batch file `ws.bat`, you can edit and test a script program named, say, `test.vbs` just by typing this:

```
ws test
```

In this case, CMD treats the batch file as if it continued the following:

```
@echo off
notepad test.vbs
cscript test.vbs
```

This kind of batch file can save you many keystrokes during the process of developing and debugging a script.

Besides the standard command-line arguments `%1`, `%2`, and so on, you should know about two special argument replacements: `%0` and `%*`. `%0` is replaced with the name of the batch file, as it was typed on the command line. `%*` is replaced with *all* the command-line arguments as they were typed, with quotes and everything left intact.

If I have a batch file named **test.bat** with the contents

```
@echo off
echo The command name is %0
echo The arguments are: %*
```

then the command **test a b c** will print the following:

```
The command name is test
The arguments are: a b c
```

`%0` is handy when a batch file has detected some problem with the command-line arguments the user has typed and you want it to display a "usage" message. Here's an example:

```
if "%1" == "" (
    rem - no arguments were specified. Print the usage information
    echo Usage: %0 [-v] [-a] filename ...
    exit /b
)
```

If the batch file is named `test.bat`, then typing **test** would print out the following message:

```
Usage: test [-v] [-a] filename ...
```

The advantage of using `%0` is that it will always be correct, even if you rename the batch file at a later date and forget to change the "usage" remarks inside.

Argument Editing

CMD lets you modify arguments as they're replaced on the command line. Most of the modifications assume that the argument is a filename and let you extract or fill in various parts of the name. When command extensions are enabled, CMD can insert edited versions of the arguments by placing a tilde (`~`) and some additional characters after the `%` sign. The editing functions let you manipulate filenames passed as arguments. Table 12.2 lists the edit options, using argument number 1 as an example.

Table 12.2 **Argument Editing Expressions**

Expression	Result
`%~1`	Removes surrounding quotes (").
`%~f1`	Fully qualified pathname.
`%~d1`	Drive letter only.
`%~p1`	Path only.
`%~n1`	Filename only.
`%~x1`	File extension only.
`%~s1`	Short DOS 8.3 file and path.
`%~a1`	File attributes.
`%~t1`	Modification date/time of file.
`%~z1`	Length of file in bytes.
`%~$PATH:1`	Fully qualified name of the first matching file when searching `PATH`. If no file is found, the result is a zero-length string. The filename must include the proper extension; `PATHEXT` is not used.

For example, if I ran a batch file with the argument `"under the hood.doc"`, the results would be as follows:

Expression	Result
`%~1`	`under the hood.doc`
`%~f1`	`C:\book\ch11\under the hood.doc`
`%~d1`	`C:`
`%~p1`	`\book\ch11`
`%~n1`	`under the hood`
`%~x1`	`.doc`
`%~s1`	`C:\book\ch11\UNDERT~1.DOC`
`%~a1`	`--a------`
`%~t1`	`04/20/2002 12:42 PM`
`%~z1`	`45323`
`%~$PATH:1`	

Here's how these features might be used: Suppose I have a series of files that I need to sort. The input files could come from any folder, but I want to store the sorted files in `C:\sorted` and give them the extension `.TAB` regardless of what the original extension was. I can write a batch file named `sortput.bat` to do this:

```
@echo off
sort <%1 >c:\sorted\%~n1.tab
```

The sort command will read the file as I've specified it on the command line, but the output file will use only the base part of the input file's name. If I run the command

```
sortput "c:\work files\input.txt"
```

the substituted command will be

```
sort <"c:\work files\input.txt" >c:\sorted\input.tab
```

Conditional Processing with If

One of the most important capabilities of any programming language is the ability to choose from among different instructions based on conditions the program finds as it runs. For this purpose, the batch file language has the if command.

The Basic If Command

In its most basic form, if compares two strings and executes a command if the strings are equivalent:

```
if string1 == string2 command
```

This is used in combination with command-line variable or environment variable substitution, as in this example:

```
if "%1" == "ERASE" delete somefile.dat
```

If and only if the batch file's first argument is the word ERASE, this command will delete the file somefile.dat.

The quotation marks in this command aren't absolutely required. If they are omitted and the command is written as

```
if %1 == ERASE delete somefile.dat
```

the command will still work as long as some command-line argument is given when the batch file is run. However, if the batch file is started with no arguments, then %1 would be replaced with nothing, and the command would turn into this:

```
if == ERASE delete somefile.dat
```

This is an invalid command. CMD expects to see something before the == part of the command and will bark if it doesn't. Therefore, it's a common practice to surround the items to be tested with some character—any character. Even $ will work, as shown here:

```
if $%0$ == $ERASE$ delete somefile.dat
```

If the items being tested are identical, they will still be identical when surrounded by the extra characters. If they are different or blank, you'll still have a valid command.

The `if` command also lets you reverse the sense of the test with the `not` option:

```
if not "%1" == "ERASE" then goto no_erase
```

Checking for Files and Folders

The `exist` option lets you determine whether a particular file exists in the current directory:

```
if exist input.dat goto process_it
    echo The file input.dat does not exist
    pause
    exit /b
:process_it
```

Of course, you can specify a full path for the filename if that's appropriate, and you can use environment variables and `%` arguments to construct the name. If the filename has spaces in it, you'll need to surround it with quotes.

The `not` modifier can be used with `exist` as well.

Tip

The `exist` test only checks for files, not folders. However, the special file `nul` appears to exist in every folder. You can perform the test

```
if exist c:\foldername\nul command
```

to see whether the folder *`c:\foldername`* exists.

Checking the Success of a Program

When a command line or even a Windows program exits, it leaves behind a number called its *exit status* or *error status* value. This is a number that the program uses to indicate whether it thinks it did its job successfully. An exit status of zero means no problems; larger numbers indicate trouble. There is no predetermined meaning for any specific values. The documentation for some programs may list specific error values and give their interpretations, which means that your batch files can use these values to take appropriate action. How? Through the `errorlevel` variation of the `if` command.

After running a command in a batch file, an `if` statement of the form

```
if errorlevel number command
```

will execute the command if the previous program's exit status value is the listed number or *higher*. For example, the `net use` command returns `0` if it is able to map a drive letter to a shared folder, and it will return a nonzero number if it can't. A batch file can take advantage of this as follows:

```
@echo off

net use f: \\bali\corpfiles
if errorlevel 1 goto failed
    echo Copying network data...
    if not exist c:\corpfiles\nul mkdir c:\corpfiles
    copy f:\*.xls c:\corpfiles
    exit /b
:failed
    echo Unable to access network share \\bali\corpfiles
    pause
```

Note

The `net use` command is discussed in Chapter 14, "Command-Line Programs." Its purpose is to map a drive letter to a network shared folder.

You can also use `not` with this version of the `if` command. In this case, the command is executed if the error status is *less* than the listed number. The error testing in the previous example can be rewritten this way:

```
if not errorlevel 1 goto success
    echo Unable to access network share \\bali\corpfiles
    pause
    exit /b
:success
    echo Copying network data...
    if not exist c:\corpfiles\nul mkdir c:\corpfiles
    copy f:\*.xls c:\corpfiles
```

In this version, the flow of the batch file is a bit easier to follow. However, even this can be improved upon, as you'll see next.

Performing Several Commands After `If`

Often, you'll want to execute several commands if some condition is true. In the old days, before the extended CMD shell came along, you would have to use a `goto` command to transfer control to another part of the batch file, as in the `if exist` example given in the previous section. With the extended version of `if`, this is no longer necessary.

The extended `if` command lets you put more than one statement after an `if` command, by grouping them with parentheses. For example, you can place multiple commands on one line, as shown here:

```
if not errorlevel 1 (echo The network share was not available & exit /b)
```

Or you can put them on multiple lines:

```
if not errorlevel 1 (
    echo The network share was not available
    pause
    exit /b
)
```

I recommend the second version, because it's easier to read. Look how much clearer the network file copying example becomes when parentheses are used instead of `goto`:

```
@echo off

net use f: \\bali\corpfiles
if errorlevel 1 (
    echo Unable to access network share \\bali\corpfiles
    pause
    exit /b
)
echo Copying network data...
if not exist c:\corpfiles\nul mkdir c:\corpfiles
copy f:\*.xls c:\corpfiles
```

You can also execute one set of commands if the `if` test is true and another if the test is false by using the `else` option, as in this example:

```
if exist input.dat echo input.dat exists else echo input.dat does not exist
```

You can use `else` with parentheses, but you must take care to place the `else` command on the same line as `if`, or on the same line as the closing parenthesis after `if`. You should write a multiple-line `if...else` command using the same format as this example:

```
if exist input.dat (
    echo Sorting input.txt...
    sort <input.txt >source.data
) else (
    echo Input.txt does not exist. Creating an empty data file...
    echo. >source.data
)
```

Extended Testing

The extended `if` command lets you perform a larger variety of tests when comparing strings, and it can also compare arguments and variables as numbers. The extended comparisons are listed in Table 12.3.

Table 12.3 **Comparison Operators Allowed by the *if* Command**

Variation	Comparison
`if string1 EQU string2`	Exactly equal
`if string1 NEQ string2`	Not equal
`if string1 LSS string2`	Less than
`if string1 LEQ string2`	Less than or equal to
`if string1 GTR string2`	Greater than
`if string1 GEQ string2`	Greater than or equal to
`if /i (comparison)`	Case-insensitive
`if defined name`	True if there is an environment variable *name*.
`if cmdextversion number`	True if the CMD extensions are version *number* or higher.

As an added bonus, if the strings being compared contain only digits, then CMD compares them numerically. For example, you could test for a specific exit status from a program with a statement like this:

```
some program
if %errorlevel% equ 3 (
    echo The program returned an exit status of 3 which
    echo means that the network printer is offline.
)
```

Processing Multiple Arguments

When you have many files to process, you may get tired of typing the same batch file commands over and over, like this:

```
somebatch file1.dat
somebatch file2.dat
somebatch file3.dat
...
```

It's possible to write batch files to handle any number of arguments on the command line. The tool to use is the `shift` command, which deletes a given command-line argument and slides the remaining ones down. Here's what I mean: Suppose I started a batch file with the command line

```
batchname xxx yyy zzz
```

Inside the batch file, the following argument replacements would be in effect before and after a `shift` command:

Before Shift	After Shift
%0 = batchname	%0 = xxx
%1 = xxx	%1 = yyy
%2 = yyy	%2 = zzz
%3 = zzz	%3 = (blank)
%4 = (blank)	%4 = (blank)

This lets a batch file repeatedly process the item named by `%1` and shift until `%1` is blank. This is a common process, so I'll list it as a pattern.

Pattern

To process a variable number of command-line arguments, use the `shift` command to delete arguments until they're all gone, as in this example:

```
@rem                                              Example File batch1201.bat
@echo off
if "%1" == "" (
    rem if %1 is blank there were no arguments. Show how to use this batch
    echo Usage: %0 filename ...
    exit /b
)

:again
rem if %1 is blank, we are finished
if not "%1" == "" (
    echo Processing file %1...

    rem ... do something with file %1

    rem - shift the arguments and examine %1 again
    shift
    goto again
)
```

You can also use the `for` command, which appears in a pattern later in this chapter.

If you want to have the program process a default file if none is specified on the command line, you can use this variation of the pattern:

```
@rem                                              Example File batch1202.bat
@echo off

if "%1" == "" (
    rem - no file was specified - process the default file "test.for"
    call :process test.for
) else (
    rem - process each of the named files
```

```
:again
    rem if %1 is blank, we are finished
    if not "%1" == "" (
        call :process %1
        rem - shift the arguments and examine %1 again
        shift
        goto again
    )
)
exit /b

:process
echo Processing file %1...
.
.
.
```

In this version, if no arguments are specified on the command line, the script will process a default file—in this case `test.for`. Otherwise, it will process all files named on the command line. This version of the pattern uses batch file subroutines, which are discussed later in the chapter under "Using Batch Files Subroutines."

The extended version of the `shift` command, `shift /n`, lets you start shifting at argument number *n*, leaving the lower-numbered arguments alone. The following illustrates what `shift /2` does in a batch file run with the command `"batchname xxx yyy zzz"`:

Before Shift	After Shift
`%0` = `batchname`	`%0` = `batchname`
`%1` = `xxx`	`%1` = `xxx`
`%2` = `yyy`	`%2` = `zzz`
`%3` = `zzz`	`%3` = (blank)
`%4` = (blank)	`%4` = (blank)

In actual use, you might want to use this feature if you need to have the batch file's name (`%0`) available throughout the batch file. In this case, you can use `shift /1` to shift all the remaining arguments, but keep `%0` intact. You may also want to write batch files that take a command line of the form

```
batchname outputfile inputfile inputfile ...
```

with an output filename followed by one or more input files. In this case, you could keep the output filename `%1` intact but loop through the input files with `shift /2`, using commands like this:

```
@rem                                         Example File sortmerge.bat
@echo off

rem be sure they gave at least two arguments
if "%2" == "" (
    echo Usage: %0 outfile infile ...
    exit /b
)

rem collect all input files into SORT.TMP

if exist sort.tmp del sort.tmp

:again
if not "%2" == "" (
    echo ...Collecting data from %2
    type %2 >>sort.tmp
    shift /2
    goto again
)

rem sort SORT.TMP into first file named on command line

echo ...Sorting to create %1
sort sort.tmp /O %1
del sort.tmp
```

Working with Environment Variables

Although environment variables were initially designed to hold system-configuration information such as the search path, they are also the "working" variables for batch files. You can use them to store filenames, option settings, user input from prompts, or any other information you need to store in a batch program. Environment variables were covered in Chapter 11. In the discussion of environment variable substitution, the `set` command was introduced as the way to set and modify environment variables.

However, you should know that, by default, changes to environment variables made in a batch file persist when the batch file finishes, because the variables "belong" to the copy of CMD that manages the Command Prompt window and any batch files in it. This is great when you want to use a batch file to modify the search path so that you can run programs from some nonstandard directory. However, it's a real problem if your batch file assumes that any variables it uses are undefined (empty) before the batch file starts. Here's a disaster waiting to happen:

```
@echo off
set /p answer=Do you want to erase the input files at the end (Y/N)?
if /i "%answer:~,1%" EQU "Y" set cleanup=YES
... more commands here
... then, at the end,
```

```
if "%cleanup%" == "YES" (
    rem they wanted the input files to be erased
    del c:\input\*.dat
)
```

If you respond to the prompt with `Y`, the environment variable `cleanup` will be set to `YES`, and the files will be erased. However, the next time you run the batch file, `cleanup` will *still* be set to `YES`, and the files will be erased no matter how you answer the question. Of course, the problem can be solved by adding the statement

```
set cleanup=
```

at the beginning of the batch file. In fact, good programming practice requires you to do so in any case (you should always initialize variables before using them), but the point is still important: Environment variables are "sticky."

In the old DOS days, a batch file program would usually add `set` statements to the end of batch files to delete any environment variables used by the program. However, CMD provides an easier method of "cleaning up."

If you plan on using environment variables as working variables for a batch file, you can use the `setlocal` command to make any changes to the variables "local" to the batch file. At the end of the batch file, or if you use an `endlocal` command, the environment will be restored to its original state at the time of the `setlocal` command. It would be prudent to put `setlocal` at the beginning of any batch file that does not require its environment changes to persist outside the batch file itself.

Environment Variable Editing

As with the old `COMMAND.COM`, in any command, strings of the form `%var%` are replaced with the value of the environment variable named `var`. One of CMD's extensions is to let you modify the environment variable content as it is being extracted. Whereas the edits for command-line arguments are focused around filename manipulation, the edits for environment variables are designed to let you extract substrings.

The following types of expressions can be used:

Expression	Result
`%name:~`*n*`%`	Skips the first *n* letters and returns the rest
`%name:~`*n*`,`*m*`%`	Skips *n* letters and returns the next *m*
`%name:,`*m*`%`	First (leftmost) *m* letters
`%name:~-m%`	Last (rightmost) *m* letters

Using the environment variable `var=ABCDEFG`, here are some examples:

Command	Prints
`echo %var%`	`ABCDEFG`
`echo %var:~2%`	`CDEFG`
`echo %var:~2,3%`	`CDE`
`echo %var:,~3%`	`ABC`
`echo %var:~-3%`	`EFG`

Expressions of the form `%name:`*`str1`*`=`*`str2`*`%` replace every occurrence of the string *`str1`* with *`str2`*. *`Str2`* can be blank to delete all occurrences of *`str1`*. You can start *`str1`* with an asterisk (*), which makes CMD replace all characters up to and including *`str1`*.

Using the environment variable `var=ABC;DEF;GHI`, here are some examples:

Command	Prints
`echo %var:;= %`	`ABC DEF GHI`
`echo %var:;=%`	`ABCDEFGHI`
`echo %var:*DEF=123%`	`123;GHI`

The first example listed is particularly useful if you want to use the `PATH` list in a `for` loop; `for` wants to see file or folder names separated by spaces, whereas `PATH` separates them with semicolons. I'll discuss this in more detail later on.

➔ For more details on working with environment variables, see "Setting Variables with the Set Command," **p. 476**.

Processing Multiple Items with the `For` Command

You'll often want to write batch files that process "all" of a certain type of file. Command-line programs can deal with filename wildcards: For example, you can type `delete *.dat` to delete all files whose name ends with `.dat`. In batch files, you can accomplish this sort of thing with the `for` loop.

Note

If you have a Unix background, the need for special statements to deal with wildcards may seem confusing at first. On Unix and Linux systems, the command shell expands all command line arguments with wildcards into a list of names before it starts up the command, so to the command it appears that the user typed out all of the names. This is called *globbing*. On DOS and Windows, the shell doesn't do this. When command-line arguments contain wildcard characters, it's up to the command or batch file to expand the name into a list of filenames.

The basic version of the `for` command scans through a set or list of names and runs a command once for each. The format for batch files is

```
for %%x in (set of names) do command
```

where *`set of names`* is a list of words separated by spaces. The `for` command executes *`command`* once for each item it finds in the set. At each iteration, variable `x` contains the current name, and any occurrences of `%%x` in the command are replaced by the current value of `x`. You can choose any alphabetic letter for the variable name. Also, upper- and lowercase matters, meaning *a* and *A* are different to the `for` command.

Note

When you type a `for` command directly at the command prompt, you only use single percent signs. In a batch file, you must double them up. Otherwise, they confuse CMD because they look sort of like command-line arguments. CMD could have been written to know the difference, but it wasn't, so we're stuck with this.

For example, the command

```
for %%x in (a b c d) do echo %%x
```

prints four lines: `a`, `b`, `c`, and `d`. What makes `for` especially useful is that if any item in the set contains the wildcard characters `?` or `*`, `for` will assume that the item is a filename and will replace the item with any matching filenames. The command

```
for %%x in (*.tmp *.out *.dbg) do delete %%x
```

will delete any occurrences of files ending with `.tmp`, `.out`, or `.dbg` in the current directory. If no such files exist, the command will turn into

```
for %%x in () do delete %%x
```

which is fine…it does nothing. To get the same "silent" result when specifying the wildcards directly in the `delete` command, you'd have to enter

```
if exist *.tmp delete *tmp
if exist *.out delete *.out
if exist *.dbg delete *.dbg
```

because `delete` complains if it can't find any files to erase.

As another example, the command

```
for %%F in ("%ALLUSERSPROFILE%\Documents\➥
    My Faxes\Received Faxes\*.tif") do echo %%~nF: received %%~tF
```

prints a list of all faxes received from the Windows Fax service and the time they were received.

Note

If you use variable substitution edits, choose as your `for` variable a letter that you don't need to use as one of the editing letters. `For` stops looking at the editing expression when it hits the `for` variable letter. For instance, in the example, if I had needed to use the `~f` editing function, I would have had to choose another variable letter for the `for` loop.

Several other forms of the `for` command are covered in Chapter 11, and you should make sure you are familiar with them. The extended `for` command lets you scan for directories, recurse into subdirectories, and several other useful things that you can't do any other way.

Using Multiple Commands in a `For` Loop

CMD lets you use multiple command lines after a `for` loop. This makes the Windows XP `for` command much more powerful than the old DOS version. In cases where you would have had to call a batch file subroutine in the past, you can now use parentheses to perform complex operations.

For example, this batch file examines a directory full of Windows bitmap (BMP) files and makes sure that there is a corresponding GIF file in another directory; if the GIF file doesn't exist, it uses an image-conversion utility to create one:

```
@echo off
setlocal
echo Searching for new .BMP files...

for %%F in (c:\incoming\*.bmp) do (
    rem output file is input file name with extension .GIF
    set outfile=c:\outgoing\%%~nF.gif
    if not exist %outfile% (
         echo ...Creating %outfile%
         imgcnv -gif %%F %outfile%
    )
)
```

Therefore, every time you run this batch file, it makes sure there is a converted GIF file in the `\outgoing` folder for every BMP file in the `\incoming` folder. This sample script uses several of the techniques we've discussed in this chapter:

- A `setlocal` statement keeps environment variable changes in the batch file from persisting after the batch is finished.
- The `for` loop and `if` command use parentheses to group several statements.
- The environment variable `outfile` is used as a "working" variable.
- The batch file uses `echo` statements to let you know what it's doing as it works.

A batch file like this can make short work of maintaining large sets of files. You might accidentally overlook a new file if you were trying to manage something like this manually, but the batch file won't.

As a final example, the following handy batch file tells you what file is actually used when you type a command by name. I call this program `which.bat`, and when I want to know what program is run by, say, the `ping` command, I type the following:

```
which ping
```

The batch file searches the current folder, then every folder in the `PATH` list. In each folder, it looks for a specific file, if you typed a specific extension with the command name, or it tries all the extensions in the `PATHEXT` list, which contains EXE, COM, BAT, and the other usual suspects:

```
@rem                                              Example file which.bat
@echo off

if "%1" == "" (
    echo Usage: which command
    echo Locates the file run when you type 'command'.
    exit /b
)

for %%d in (. %path%) do (
    if "%~x1" == "" (
        rem the user didn't type an extension so use the PATHEXT list
        for %%e in (%pathext%) do (
            if exist %%d\%1%%e (
                echo %%d\%1%%e
                exit /b
            )
        )
    ) else (
        rem the user typed a specific extension, so look only for that
        if exist %%d\%1 (
            echo %%d\%1
            exit /b
        )
    )
)
echo No file for %1 was found
```

As you can see, the `for` command lets you write powerful, useful programs that can save you time and prevent errors, and the syntax is cryptic enough to please even a Perl programmer.

Delayed Expansion

Environment variables and command-line arguments marked with `%` are replaced with their corresponding values when CMD reads each command line. However, when you're writing `for` loops and compound `if` statements, this can cause some unexpected results.

For example, you might want to run a secondary batch file repeatedly with several files, with the first file handled differently, like this:

```
call anotherbatch firstfile.txt FIRST
call anotherbatch secondfile.txt MORE
call anotherbatch xfiles.txt MORE
```

You might want to do this so that the first call will create a new output file, while each subsequent call will add on to the existing file.

You might be tempted to automate this process with the `for` command, using commands like this:

```
set isfirst=FIRST
for %%f in (*.txt) do (
    call anotherbatch %%f %isfirst%
    set isfirst=MORE
)
```

The idea here is that the second argument to `anotherbatch` will be `FIRST` for the first file and `MORE` for all subsequent files. However, this will not work. CMD will replace `%isfirst%` with its definition `MORE` when it first encounters the `for` statement. When CMD has finished processing `%` signs, the command will look like this:

```
set isfirst=FIRST
for %%f in (*.txt) do (
    call anotherbatch %%f FIRST
    set isfirst=MORE
)
```

Because `FIRST` is substituted before the `for` loop starts running, `anotherbatch` will not see the value of `isfirst` change, and the result will be

```
call anotherbatch firstfile.txt FIRST
call anotherbatch secondfile.txt FIRST
call anotherbatch xfiles.txt FIRST
```

which is not at all what you wanted.

There is a way to fix this: Delayed expansion lets you specify environment variables with exclamation points rather than percent signs, as an indication that they are to be expanded only when CMD actually intends to really execute the command. Because `!` has not traditionally been a special character, this feature is disabled by default. To enable delayed expansion, specify `/V:ON` on the CMD command line or use `SETLOCAL` to enable this feature inside the batch file. The statements

```
setlocal enabledelayedexpansion
set isfirst=FIRST
for %%f in (*.txt) do (
    call anotherbatch %%f !isfirst!
    set isfirst=MORE
)
```

will work correctly.

Although delayed expansion is disabled by default in Windows XP, you can change the default setting through the Registry key `HKLM\Software\Microsoft\Command Processor\EnableExtensions`. If this `DWORD` value is present and set to `0`, command extensions are disabled by default. Any nonzero value for `EnableExtensions` enables them.

Another place delayed expansion is useful is to collect information into an environment variable in a `for` list. The following batch file adds `c:\mystuff` and every folder under it to an environment variable named `dirs`:

```
setlocal ENABLEDELAYEDEXPANSION
set dirs=
for /R c:\mystuff %%d in (.) do set dirs=!dirs!;%%d
```

The `for` statement recursively visits every folder, starting in `c:\mystuff`, and `%%d` takes on the name of each folder in turn. The `set` statement adds each directory name to the end of the `dirs` variable.

Using Batch File Subroutines

The CMD shell lets you write batch file subroutines using the `call` command. Although the new ability to group statements with parentheses makes batch file subroutines somewhat less necessary than they were in the past, the subroutine is still an important tool in batch file programming.

For example, in a task that involves processing a whole list of files, you might write a batch file subroutine to perform all the steps necessary to process one file. Then, you can call this subroutine once for each file you need to process.

In the old days of `COMMAND.COM`, batch file subroutines had to be placed in separate BAT files. You can still do this, but with CMD, you can also place subroutines in the same file as the main batch file program. The structure looks like this:

```
@rem                                        Example File batch1203.bat
@echo off

rem MAIN BATCH FILE PROGRAM -----------------------

rem call subroutine "onefile" for each file to be processed:
cd \input
for %%f in (*.dat) do call :onefile %%f    ← subroutine called here

rem main program must end with exit /b or goto :EOF
exit /b

rem SUBROUTINE "ONEFILE" -------------------------
:onefile
echo Processing file %1...
echo ... commands go here ...
exit /b
```

The `call` command followed by a colon and a label name tells CMD to continue processing at the label. Any items placed on the `call` command after the label are arguments passed to the subroutine, which can access them with `%1`, `%2`, and so on. The original command-line arguments to the batch file are hidden while the call is in effect.

Processing returns to the command after the call when the subroutine encounters any of these conditions:

- The end of the file is reached.
- The subroutine deliberately jumps to the end of the file with the command `goto :EOF`.
- The subroutine executes the command `exit /b`.

Normally, any of these conditions would indicate the end of the batch file, and CMD would return to the command prompt. After `call`, however, these conditions just end the subroutine, and the batch file continues.

Caution

You must be sure to make the main part of the batch file stop before it runs into the first subroutine. In other scripting languages such as VBScript, the end of the "main program" is unmistakable, but in the batch file language it is not. You must use `goto :EOF` or `exit /B` before the first subroutine's label; otherwise, CMD will plow through and run the subroutine's commands again.

Prompting for Input

If your batch file has to print a message you definitely don't want the users to miss, use the `pause` statement to make the batch file sit and wait until they've read the message and acknowledged it. Here's an example:

```
echo The blatfizz command failed. This means that the world as
echo we know it is about to end, or, that the input file needs to
echo be corrected.
pause
exit /b
```

If you want to ask a user whether to proceed after a mishap, or if you want the batch file to prompt for input filenames or other data, you can use the new extended `set /p` command. `Set /p` reads a user's response into an environment variable, where it can be tested or used as a command argument. Here's an example:

```
:again
   echo The input file INPUT.DAT does not exist
   set /p answer=Do you want to create it now (Y/N)?
   if /i "%answer:~,1%" EQU "Y" goto editit
```

```
if /i "%answer:~,1%" EQU "N" exit /b
echo Please type Y for Yes or N for No
goto again
```

These commands ask the user to type a response, examine the leftmost letter with `%answer:,1%`, and take the appropriate action only if the user types a valid response. In fact, this is a good pattern to remember.

Pattern

To prompt a user for a yes/no answer, use a series of commands following this pattern:

```
:again
   echo If the question is long or requires an explanation,
   echo use echo commands to display text before the question.
   set /p answer=Ask the question here (Y/N)?
   if /i "%answer:~,1%" EQU "Y" command to execute for Yes
   if /i "%answer:~,1%" EQU "N" command to execute for No
   echo Please type Y for Yes or N for No
   goto again
```

Put a single space after the question mark on the `set /p` command. If you use this pattern more than once in the same batch file, be sure to use a different label for each one. I used `again` in this version, but you can use any word as the label.

You can modify this pattern to create a menu. You can write a prompt like this:

```
echo Options: [A]dd, [D]elete, [P]rint, [Q]uit, [H]elp"
set /p answer=Enter selection:
```

In this example, instead of comparing the response to the letters Y and N, you would compare it to A, D, P, Q, and H.

Useful Batch File Techniques

As mentioned in Chapter 10, "Deploying Scripts for Computer and Network Management," I like to make scripts and batch files "user friendly," not only so that they can be used more easily by other people, but also because I know that three weeks after I write a program, I'll have forgotten how to use it, what it does, and how it works. I sometimes find myself standing in front of the refrigerator wondering what I was after when I opened it, so this isn't surprising.

With this in mind, in this section I'll cover a few techniques and tricks that I use to make batch files more helpful, useful, and reliable.

Processing Command-Line Options

You may want your batch files to act like the Windows built-in commands and have them recognize options that begin with `/` or `-`. It's very helpful to have a batch file recognize `/?` as a request to display information about the program itself.

The `shift` command is useful here. At the beginning of the batch file, you can examine the first argument (`%1`) and see whether it starts with `/`. If it does, it's an option. You can set an environment variable, delete the argument with `shift`, and then repeat the process until all options have been removed.

The following three command options can be useful to implement:

Option	Meaning
`/?`	Help. Prints help info and quits.
`/v`	Verbose. Turns on debugging printouts.
`/q`	Quiet. Disables normal printouts.

Here's how I process these options at the beginning of a batch file:

```
@rem                                           Example File batch1204.bat
@echo off
setlocal
rem - initialize options to their default values
set verbose=NO
set quiet=NO
:again
    set arg=%1
    if "%arg:,1%" == "/" (
        if "/i" %arg% EQU "/v" (
            set verbose=YES
        ) else if "/i" %arg% EQU "/q" (
            set quiet=YES
        ) else (
            :usage
            echo Usage: %0 [/v ^| /q] filename...
            echo.
            echo This batch file copies each of the files to the
            echo network folder. Other helpful information goes here.
            exit /b
        )
        shift /1
        goto again
    )
```

Here are some notes about the programming in this example:

- To examine the leftmost character of each argument, the program copies it to the environment variable `arg` and then examines the first character with `%arg:,1%`. Because the argument could be empty, the first `if` statement has to use quotes around the strings being compared.
- Because the remaining `if` commands are only reached if `arg` starts with `/`, it definitely is not empty, so there is no need to use quotes around the other tests. However, it's a good habit to use them anyway.

- The final `else` prints the usage information if the user types `/?` or any invalid option.
- The `shift` command uses `/1` so that `%0` will be left alone and will always contain the name of the batch file.

Later in the batch file, you can use the values of the environment variables `verbose` and `quiet` to determine whether to print messages. Extra debugging information can be printed like this:

```
if "%verbose%" == "YES" echo Got to the part where we'll clean out the folder
```

Similarly, normal messages such as `Processing file %1` and `pause` commands that stop the batch file can be disabled if the `/Q` option is given:

```
if not "%quiet%" == "YES" echo Processing file %1...
```

I use the strange `if not` test in this case as a failsafe measure: If the variable `quiet` is not defined, I'd rather have the output appear. (This is an important part of making reliable programs: To the extent possible, have programs anticipate things that should never happen and try to make the best of the situation should they occur.)

Tip

The quiet option is a good one to provide if you want to run the batch file with the Command Scheduler. If the quiet option is enabled, the batch file should never "pause."

Once the batch file has read and eliminated any command-line options, `%1` indicates the first filename, or whatever the command-line argument means in your application. If you expect at least one argument, you can print out the usage information and quit if it's missing:

```
if "%1" == "" goto usage
```

This sends the batch program back to the label `:usage`, which you'll find back in the part of the batch file that processes the command-line options.

Then, if your batch file processes an arbitrary number of input items, you can process each of them in turn using a batch file subroutine:

```
for each %%x in (%*) do call :process %%x
exit /b
```

In this example, `%*` will be replaced with all the remaining command-line arguments. Any wildcards in the names will be expanded into matching filenames, and the `for` command will call the batch file subroutine `process` with each item in turn.

The batch file subroutine `process` will receive the item as argument number 1, so it will usually start like this:

```
:process
if not "%quiet%" == "YES" echo Processing %1...
```

Managing Network Mappings

If your batch file uses network folders, you may want to map one or more drive letters to shared folders. The problem is that the drive letter you want to use may already be in use. You have to use a creative strategy to deal with this. I have three suggestions.

Use UNC Pathnames

In many cases, you can avoid mapping a drive letter entirely. Most Windows command-line programs will accept UNC pathnames, so you can use the `\\server\sharename\...` format directly. For example, I used a batch file while I was writing this book to save backup copies of the content on another computer:

```
@echo off
echo Backing up chapter files
xcopy c:\book\*.* \\bali\brian\bookbackup /S/Z/Y/M
```

This copied the files to the server `\\bali`, to subfolder `bookbackup` of the shared folder `brian`.

Use `Pushd` to Assign a Random Drive Letter

The `pushd` command will assign a random drive letter if you specify a network path. If you can write your batch file commands to use the current directory so that you don't need to know the drive letter, so much the better. My backup batch file could have been written this way:

```
pushd \\bali\brian\bookbackup
xcopy c:\book\*.* . /S/Z/Y/M
popd
```

You can also determine the drive letter that `pushd` creates using the `%cd%` environment variable. This "virtual" variable always returns the current drive letter and path. After the `pushd` command, it might have the value `Y:\`.

Be sure to end the batch file with `popd` to release the temporary drive letter.

Delete Previous Mappings Before Starting

If you want or need to use fixed, mapped network drive letters, you should take a heavy-handed approach to mapping: Delete any preexisting mapping of your desired drive letter first and then map it to the desired network folder.

Because the network drive may or may not be mapped when the batch file starts, I like to use `net use` to delete any existing mapping. If you redirect its output to the `nul` file, any error messages simply disappear. This prevents the batch file from displaying an error message if the drive letter is not mapped when it starts. Here's an example:

```
rem - map drive G to the network folder

net use g: /del >nul 2>nul        & rem - delete previous mapping if any

net use g: \\server\sharename     & rem - make new mapping
if errorlevel 1 (
    echo The network folder is not available
    if not "%quiet%" == "YES" pause
    exit /b
)
```

Checking for Correct Arguments

If your batch file accepts filenames as input, it's possible that the batch file's user will type a name incorrectly. It's best to detect this as quickly as possible, rather than letting whatever programs the batch file runs encounter invalid filenames. Before taking any other action with the files, you can perform a quick check of the names the user entered with a loop like this:

```
for %%f in (%*) do (
    if not exist %%f echo Error: file %%f does not exist & exit /b
)
```

Of course, this assumes that all the command-line arguments are filenames—you will have to write a checking procedure that's appropriate to your own needs. The idea is that whenever possible, you should validate all input before starting to work with it.

Keeping Log Files

If you write batch files to use with the Command Scheduler, you won't be able to see any error messages your batch program prints if it runs into trouble. As mentioned in Chapter 10, it's important to have unattended programs keep a record of their activity so that you can confirm whether they're working correctly; if they're not, you can find out what is going wrong.

When I write a batch file for unattended use, I usually have it create a log file as its first step and store the current time and date in the file. Then, I sprinkle `echo` commands throughout the program to add a running commentary to the log file. The structure looks like this:

```
@echo off
set logfile=MYBATCH.LOG
echo Batch command: %0 %* >%logfile%
echo Started at %date% %time% >>%logfile%
echo ----------------------- >>%logfile%
```

I use an environment variable for the name of the log file so that if it's necessary to change its name, I only need to edit the `set` command at the beginning of the file.

Adding the time and date lets you quickly determine whether the scheduled batch process is actually being run.

Then, throughout the batch file you can use `echo` commands similar to the ones used at startup to add to the log file. Record the names of files processed, add a note at the beginning of each major group of commands, and definitely record any problems encountered. It's best to display messages to the standard output as well as to the log file:

```
@rem                                       Example File batch1205.bat
set logfile = mappit.log

echo Mapping network drive...
echo Mapping network drive... >>%logfile%

net use m: \\server\sharename
if errorlevel 1 (
    echo Unable to use shared folder \\server\sharename
    echo Unable to use shared folder \\server\sharename >>%logfile%
    echo Quitting prematurely! >>%logfile%
    exit /b
)
```

This way, you can see the output yourself if you run the batch file manually.

Finally, it's a good idea to record a final entry just before the batch file exits so that you know it didn't get stuck just before the last command. The final commands in the batch file's main program section might look like this:

```
echo ---------------------- >>%logfile%
echo Ended at %date% %time% >>%logfile%
```

In fact, you might want to have the program jump down to these final statements even after encountering a fatal error. Instead of using `exit /b` after encountering the network error, I could have written `goto done` and put this at the end of the batch file:

```
:done
echo ---------------------- >>%logfile%
echo Ended at %date% %time% >>%logfile%
```

This way, the log file should *always* end like this:

```
-----------------------
Ended at Thu 05/02/2002 23:54:12.90
```

If it doesn't, I'll know that something quite unexpected must have happened.

Tip

If you use many scheduled batch files, you might want to use the techniques described in Chapter 10 to create a "management summary" showing the results of each of them.

13

The MS-DOS Environment Under Windows XP

ROAD MAP

- Windows XP simulates the MS-DOS environment for old programs.
- You can give old DOS programs as much memory as they want.
- AUTOEXEC.BAT and CONFIG.SYS are alive and well...sort of.
- DOS compatibility is good but not perfect; you may have problems with some games and old modem and networking software.

MS-DOS Programs on Windows XP

OLD PROGRAMS NEVER DIE, THEY JUST GET harder to maintain. That's an old programmer's proverb—well, no, it's not really. But you'll quickly find that it's true if you have to use or support MS-DOS programs on Windows XP. Some programs that are based on this original 16-bit, character-based PC operating system are still in use today, and whereas Windows 95 and 98 had MS-DOS running underneath, MS-DOS is nowhere to be found on a computer running Windows XP, 2000, or NT.

Instead, these Windows NT–based operating systems *emulate* DOS for the old programs. That is, Windows provides a software environment that simulates the same disk, keyboard, printer, and screen functions that MS-DOS provided. It's called the Windows NT Virtual DOS Machine.

The Virtual DOS Machine

MS-DOS programs interacted directly with the computer's hardware: They could directly manipulate the display adapter to change the screen resolution, they could directly address the computer's serial and parallel ports to control modems and printers, and they interacted with the operating system through special processor instructions called *software interrupts*. None of these are allowed of a Windows program today. All hardware is strictly controlled by the operating system kernel and its device drivers so that errant user programs can't bring down the operating system. (Of course, errant device drivers can and do.)

When you attempt to run any program, Windows examines the program file to determine what operating system environment it requires. Program files ending with `.COM` are always MS-DOS programs. Files ending with `.EXE` could be Win32, Windows 3.1, or MS-DOS programs. In this case, Windows examines the first few bytes of the program file, which indicate the difference.

When it finds that it has been asked to run an MS-DOS program, Windows starts a program called `ntvdm.exe`, which in turn reads and interprets the DOS program. NTVDM acts as the mediator between the DOS program and Windows XP and performs the following functions:

- It allocates memory organized in the fashion of the old PC architecture: 640KB of memory is available for the simulated DOS environment and the application program, and the expanded and extended memory interfaces that let MS-DOS reach beyond the 1MB point are simulated as well.
- NTVDM handles any software interrupts that the program issues, and it translates the MS-DOS system requests into Windows XP equivalents.
- NTVDM sets aside memory that appears to the MS-DOS program to be the display adapter's memory. NTVDM monitors this memory, and when changes occur, draws corresponding changes in the Command Prompt window.
- If the program issues instructions to put the display adapter into a graphics mode, NTVDM changes the Command Prompt window to full-screen mode. Windows then switches the display adapter to the requested graphics mode and relays any "safe" hardware instructions from the MS-DOS program to the display adapter. All the modifications are monitored, however, and control can be taken back at any time.
- Printing and serial port access is monitored in a similar way. NTVDM intercepts any processor instructions that attempt to manipulate the printer or serial ports, determines the program's intent, and uses Windows functions to produce the same effect.
- NTVDM provides mouse support through the DOS standard mouse device driver. This driver is built in to NTVDM and does not have to be loaded separately.

This sounds like a lot of work, and it is. NTVDM is nearly 400KB in length, larger than the entire memory available in early PCs. Happily, only 32KB of this appears in the 640KB memory space seen by the MS-DOS program. The simulated device drivers are tiny, because most of the real work is done elsewhere in the NTVDM program.

Note

One side effect of the emulation scheme is that when you run an MS-DOS program, the program appears in the Task Manager's Processes list as `ntvdm.exe`. If you run WordPerfect, you won't see `wp.exe` listed. I'll talk more about this at the end of the chapter.

By the way, if asked by an application program, NTVDM advertises itself as running MS-DOS version 5.0. I have no idea why Microsoft chose DOS 5 over DOS 6.

In most cases, DOS programs work well. NTVDM is not perfect, however. For example, NTVDM's emulation of some hardware is not quite perfect. Also, NTVDM doesn't mimic old MS-DOS-type networking functions quite precisely enough to fool all programs. I've run into these sorts of problems:

- DOS programs that use network printers, such as the old DOS FoxPro database program, don't always eject a page after printing, or sometimes eject too many pages.
- Modem software like Norton-Lambert's Close-Up remote-control software doesn't work perfectly. Data is lost between the software and the modem, resulting in slow communications and even modem hang-ups.
- Games that attempt to use NTVDM's Sound Blaster emulation may generate hideous screeching sounds or may crash entirely.

Unfortunately, when problems like these do occur, there is little or nothing you can do about it.

Besides `NTVDM.EXE` and `COMMAND.COM`, in the name of compatibility (but probably just for sentimental reasons), Windows XP comes with some old DOS 5.0 utility programs. These are the original MS-DOS 16-bit programs. They work just as they always did—no improvements have been made. These old-timers include the following:

`append`	`fastopen`*	`mem`
`debug`	`graftablnlsfunc`	`setver`
`edit`	`graphics`	`share`*
`edlin`	`loadfix`	
`exe2bin`	`loadhigh`	

The programs marked with an asterisk (*) do nothing, because Windows performs these functions automatically. They are provided for compatibility. (Presumably, they're there to fool any old applications, batch files, or installation programs that require these now-unnecessary commands.) One additional compatibility program deserves special mention: `forcedos`.

`forcedos`

When you attempt to run any program, Windows XP examines the program's executable file to determine what sort of program it is: 32-bit Windows, 16-bit Windows, OS/2, DOS, and so on. Usually, Windows does a good job of determining the environment required by a program, but it sometimes fails. If you find that it fails to correctly identify a program as a DOS program, you can force Windows to run the program in the MS-DOS environment by adding `forcedos` to the beginning of the command line. Here is the syntax:

```
forcedos [/d folder] program arguments...]
```

MS-DOS and `COMMAND.COM`

As mentioned in Chapter 11, "The CMD Command-Line Environment," and Chapter 12, "Batch Files for Fun and Profit," Windows XP uses a new command prompt shell program named `CMD.EXE`. As it turns out, to maintain maximum compatibility with old MS-DOS programs and old batch files, `COMMAND.COM` is actually still available. The clunky old batch file language we all knew and "loved" is still there.

Here's how it works: If you run an MS-DOS program in a Command Prompt window, CMD assumes that you're going to work in the 16-bit world for a while. So, when the DOS program finishes, the window switches to the `COMMAND.COM` shell. You'll notice several differences:

- The current directory name is changed to its old-style 8.3 equivalent. For example, if your current directory had been `C:\Documents and Settings\naleks`, when the DOS program exits, the directory will be displayed as `C:\DOCUME~1\NALEKS`.
- Environment variable names change to all uppercase letters.
- The extended versions of the built-in commands will be unavailable. Table 11.4 lists the affected commands.
- If you've run `COMMAND.COM` explicitly, you cannot close the window by clicking its close button—`COMMAND.COM` doesn't get the message to quit. You'll have to type **`exit`** to close the window.

These changes make it more likely that old programs and batch files will be able to run. However, if you want, you can keep `CMD.EXE` as your command shell even when using MS-DOS programs, by configuring the MS-DOS environment. I'll discuss this in the following sections.

Configuring the MS-DOS Environment

To maintain compatibility with as many old DOS programs as possible, NTVDM can be configured in several ways to mimic an older environment. You can configure

NTVDM's memory and window options through a properties dialog box, and you can configure the virtual DOS environment itself through configuration files that mimic the old `CONFIG.SYS` and `AUTOEXEC.BAT` files. Here is how the default configuration works:

- By default, NTVDM gives the MS-DOS program as much regular and DMPI (DOS Protected Mode Interface) memory as it asks for. No Extended (XMS) or Expanded (EMS) memory is available.
- NTVDM reads configuration options from `\windows\system32\config.nt` and executes the batch file `\windows\system32\autoexec.nt` before running the program. These files are installed along with Windows and contain important default settings that permit the use of high memory, networking, and emulated Sound Blaster sound hardware.

These settings should work for most MS-DOS programs. However, if you need specially tuned DOS environments for special applications, you may want to configure Windows shortcuts for these applications, or at least create shortcuts that open custom-configured Command Prompt windows.

To create a customized MS-DOS environment, right-click the name of the MS-DOS program you want to run and select Properties. If you change any of the default properties and save the settings, Windows will create a file with the same name as the program file, but with extension `.PIF`. This PIF file holds the customized settings. It is listed in Explorer as a "Shortcut to MS-DOS Program." Use this shortcut to run the program. If you need to run a batch file before running the program, follow this same procedure.

Note

You must use the shortcut to start the MS-DOS program in order to take advantage of any configuration changes you've made. If you run the EXE file directly, Windows will not know to look at the PIF (shortcut) file.

Window and Memory Options

The Properties dialog box for a MS-DOS application shortcut (PIF file) lets you set the virtual MS-DOS environment's memory display and mouse properties. To customize these properties, right-click the MS-DOS application file itself, or if you've already created customized properties, you can right-click the MS-DOS Application Shortcut icon, and then select Properties.

Here are the most common settings to change:

- The working folder on the Program page
- The Extended Memory and Initial Environment options on the Memory page
- The Always Suspend option on the Misc page

In the next sections, I'll describe all the property pages in more detail so you can see what configuration options are available. The General, Security, Summary, and Backup pages (if they appear on your system) are the same as for any other Windows file, so I won't describe them here.

Program Settings

The Program tab displays a typical Shortcut property page and has the following settings (see Figure 13.1):

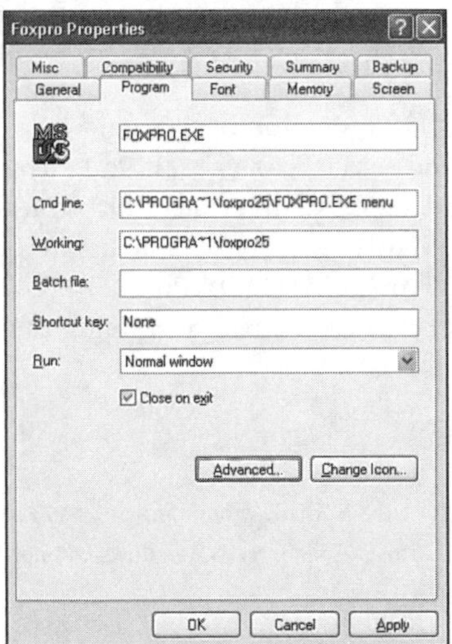

Figure 13.1 The MS-DOS Shortcut Program tab. The Advanced button lets you specify a custom `config.nt` or `autoexec.nt` file.

- **Cmd Line**. The path to the MS-DOS program file, or batch file, and any additional command-line arguments you need. If you enter **?** on the command line, Windows will prompt you for command-line arguments when you run the shortcut. Whatever you type will be used in place of `?`.
- **Working**. The drive and folder to use as the initial working directory for the program. If you leave this field blank, the initial directory will be the one containing the MS-DOS program. If the shortcut will be used by several people,

you may want to use environment variables in this path. For example, `"%userprofile%\My Documents"` will specify the user's own My Documents folder.

- **Batch File**. Ostensibly, the name of a batch file to run before starting the program. As far as I can tell, however, this feature does work.
- **Shortcut Key**. Optional. Specifies a hotkey that is supposed to start the program. However, this feature does not appear to work either.
- **Run**. Selects the initial window size: Normal, Maximized, or Minimized (icon). Full Screen is different; see the screen settings.
- **Close on Exit**. If this option is checked, the window will close when the program exits. If this option is unchecked, the window will remain open but inactive, and the title will include the word "Inactive." You will want to leave this checked in most cases.

Tip

If a DOS program fails to run, uncheck this box and try to run the program again. You'll then have time to read any error messages that appear.

The Program tab also lets you specify alternate configuration and startup batch files to use instead of `CONFIG.NT` and `AUTOEXEC.NT`. To change the configuration files associated with a shortcut, click the Advanced button and enter the paths and names of the desired files. The default values are `%SystemRoot%\SYSTEM32\CONFIG.NT` and `%SystemRoot%\SYSTEM32\AUTOEXEC.NT`. I will describe the settings in these files shortly.

Tip

If your MS-DOS program has timing or speed problems, it may be that it expects to be able to change the settings of the PC's timer chips. If you click the Advanced button and check the Compatible Timer Hardware Emulation option, the problem may go away.

Font Settings

The Font tab lets you select the font used when the program is running in a window. The default setting, Auto, lets Windows resize the font as you resize the window, but you can specify a fixed size. If you do, the window will not be resizable.

Tip

If you want to switch to a fixed font size, you can do it while the program is running. Right-click the upper-left corner of the program's window, select Properties, and view the Font tab. Make any desired changes and then choose Save Properties for Future Windows with the Same Title when Windows offers you this option.

Memory Settings

The Memory tab, shown in Figure 13.2, lets you specify the type and amount of memory to make available to the MS-DOS program. The plethora of memory types came about as different ways of coping with the original PC's limited memory hardware options. Some programs can use any type of memory, but others specifically require access to XMS or EMS memory. Here's a list of the settings:

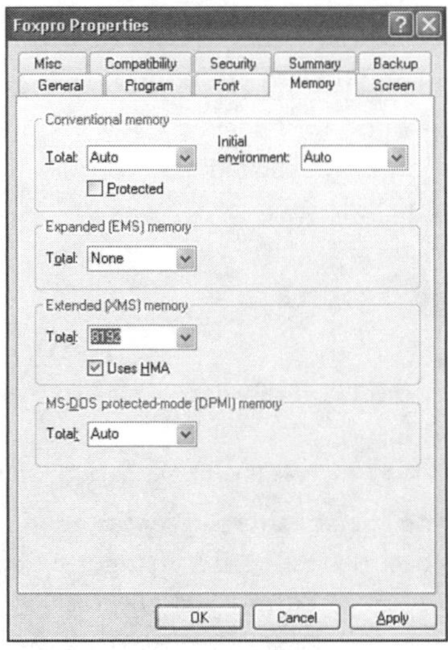

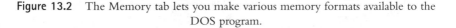

Figure 13.2 The Memory tab lets you make various memory formats available to the DOS program.

- **Conventional Memory, Total.** The amount of memory between 0 and 640KB. The Auto setting provides up to 640KB. You will probably never need to alter this setting.
- **Initial Environment.** The number of bytes to set aside for environment variables. Auto directs NTVDM to use the amount specified in the `SHELL` setting in `CONFIG.NT`. If you use complex batch files, you may want to increase this setting to 2000 bytes or more.
- **Protected.** If checked, this option prevents the program from altering memory in the range occupied by the simulated MS-DOS system components. Check this box only if you experience unexplained crashes.
- **Expanded (EMS) Memory.** If your program requires EMS (paged) memory, set this to Auto or a fixed number.
- **Extended (XMS) Memory.** If your program can use XMS expanded memory, set this to Auto or a fixed number.

- **Uses HMA**. This option normally has no effect because the High Memory Area is used by the simulated MS-DOS program.
- **MS-DOS Protected-Mode (DPMI) Memory**. By default, this option is set to Auto. You can disable or permit a fixed amount of DPMI memory, if necessary.

Screen Settings

The screen settings let you determine whether the program has "direct" access to the whole screen at startup. These settings include the following:

- **Usage**. Lets you select between full-screen and window as the initial display mode. In full-screen mode, the MS-DOS program takes over the primary display and can display graphics.
- **Restore Settings at Startup**. If this option is checked, the last-used window size and font will be reused the next time you start the program. If you want to provide a consistent environment for multiple users, uncheck this box, make the appropriate initial settings, and then make the PIF file nonwritable by other users using file security settings.
- **Fast ROM Emulation**. When this option is checked, the Virtual DOS Machine emulates the graphics functions normally provided by the display adapter's built-in (read-only memory) BIOS program.
- **Dynamic Memory Allocation**. When this option is checked, Windows releases memory assigned to the virtual graphics display when the program switches from graphics to text display. If you get a blank screen when the program switches back, try unchecking this box.

When the MS-DOS program is running and attempts to change the display from text-based to graphical, Windows will automatically switch to full-screen mode. You can manually switch back and forth between full-screen and window mode by pressing Alt+Enter. If the program is using a text display, you can continue using it in window mode. If it is displaying graphics, however, the program will be suspended (frozen) and minimized unless it's in full-screen mode. Windows, unfortunately, can't display a little windowed version of the DOS graphical display.

Miscellaneous Settings

The Miscellaneous Settings tab determines how the program behaves when it's running in a window. Most of the settings are self-explanatory. The tab is shown in Figure 13.3. Here are the less obvious settings:

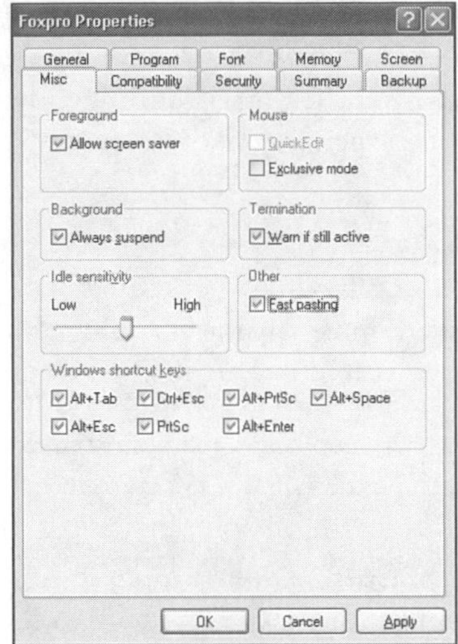

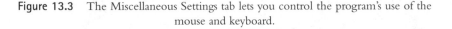

Figure 13.3 The Miscellaneous Settings tab lets you control the program's use of the mouse and keyboard.

- **Always Suspend**. If this option is checked, the MS-DOS program will be frozen when it's not the active window. Because MS-DOS programs didn't anticipate multitasking, they tend to burn lots of CPU time even when idle. Suspending the program when you're not using it makes your system more responsive. However, if you are running a communications or database program that needs to run while you do other things, uncheck this box.
- **Idle Sensitivity**. This is also related to the idle CPU issue. Windows tries to guess when the DOS program is just spinning its gears doing nothing and gives it a lower priority when it thinks this is the case. A high Idle Sensitivity setting means that Windows will lean toward thinking the program is idle, resulting in snappier performance for other applications. A lower Idle Sensitivity setting will make Windows give the DOS application more time. The DOS application will be better able to perform background (noninteractive) processing, while making your Windows applications more sluggish. Raise this setting if your DOS program makes everything else too slow, or lower it if your DOS program can't get its job done. In the latter case, also uncheck Always Suspend.
- **Exclusive Mode**. Dedicates the mouse to the DOS program.
- **Fast Pasting**. Determines how quickly Windows will stuff simulated keystrokes into the MS-DOS programs when you paste in text from the Windows clipboard using Alt+space, Edit, Paste. If characters are lost when pasting, uncheck this option.

- **Windows Short Keys.** These check boxes let you determine which special keystrokes should be passed to Windows rather than to the MS-DOS programs. If your MS-DOS program needs key combinations such as Alt+Tab and Alt+Enter, you will need to uncheck the relevant boxes on this page. The DOS program will get these keystrokes in full-screen mode or when its window is active, so be prepared to lose the corresponding Windows shortcut.

  It's especially tricky if you uncheck Alt+Enter and the program switches to full-screen mode. You will have to type Ctrl+Alt+Del to bring up the Task Manager if you want to switch back to the Windows desktop before the program exits.

Compatibility Settings

Windows XP compatibility settings let you limit the abilities of the virtual display adapter seen by the MS-DOS program. The relevant settings are Run in 256 Colors and Run in 640×480 Screen Resolution. If your MS-DOS program has problems displaying graphics screen, try checking these boxes.

CONFIG.NT

Just as MS-DOS used `CONFIG.SYS` to make initial memory allocations and to load device drivers, NTVDM uses `CONFIG.NT` to configure the virtual DOS environment.

The default `CONFIG.NT` file as installed by Windows is located in `\windows\system32` and contains several pages of comment text, which you may wish to read. Here are the default settings in this file:

```
dos=high,umbdevice=%systemroot%\system32\himem.sys
files=40
```

You can edit `CONFIG.NT` to modify the defaults for all MS-DOS applications, or you can create alternate files using a different name for use with specific applications. In the latter case, use the Advanced button on the Program Settings properties page for the program's shortcut to enter the alternate filename. I'll use the name `CONFIG.NT` in the discussion that follows to refer to any config file.

> **Note**
>
> If you use MS-DOS database applications, you will probably want to increase the `FILES=` setting in `CONFIG.NT` to `100` or more. You may also want to add the ANSI cursor control module with the line
>
> `device=%systemroot%\system32\ansi.sys`
>
> Otherwise, you'll rarely need to change these settings.

The full set of options for `CONFIG.NT` is provided in Reference Listing 13.1.

REFERENCE LIST 13.1 `Config.NT` Settings

`COUNTRY=`*`xxx`*`[,`*`[yyy]`*`[,[` *`[path]`*`]`*`filename`*`]]`

tells MS-DOS to use an alternate character set and date/time format. *`xxx`* is a country/region code, *`yyy`* is an optional code page designator, and *`filename`* designates an optional driver containing country code information. If you use the virtual MS-DOS environment outside the U.S., view the Help and Support Center and search for "country."

`DEVICE=`*`[path\]filename [parameters]`*

loads a device driver. Hardware device drivers will almost certainly *not* work in Windows XP, but certain software services implemented as drivers will. Examples include `himem.sys`, which is required to let MS-DOS programs access memory above 640KB, and `ansi.sys`, which interprets character sequences that some DOS programs use to control the cursor. These drivers are located in folder `%systemroot%\system32`.

`DEVICEHIGH=`*`[path\]filename [parameters]`*
`or`
`DEVICEHIGH [SIZE=`*`xx`***`]`** *`[path\]filename [parameters]`*

similar to *`device`* but attempts to load the device driver into upper memory blocks, leaving more conventional memory for MS-DOS applications. If there is insufficient room in upper memory or if the device `himem.sys` has not been loaded, the driver will be loaded into conventional memory. The alternate `size=`*`xx`* format lets you specify the number of bytes of high memory that must be free; *`xx`* must be specified in hexadecimal.

`DOS=[HIGH|LOW][, UMB|NOUMB]`

`DOS=HIGH` specifies that MS-DOS should move parts of itself into the high memory area (the first 64KB past 1MB). The default is `LOW`, where DOS resides entirely in conventional memory. The optional keyword `UMB` indicates that DOS should make upper memory area blocks (the memory beyond 1MB+64KB) available for DOS, devices, and programs.

`DOSONLY`

If this keyword is present in `CONFIG.NT`, `COMMAND.COM` will only be permitted to run MS-DOS programs. Normally, if you typed the name of a Windows program at its command prompt or in a batch file, it would run the Windows program in a separate environment. This may disrupt some DOS terminate-and-stay-resident (TSR) programs, so the `DOSONLY` option lets you prevent this from happening.

`ECHOCONFIG`

If the command `ECHOCONFIG` appears, `CONFIG.NT` commands are echoed to the Command Prompt window while NTVDM is initializing. The default is for the commands not to be displayed.

`FCBS=`*`n`*

File Control Blocks (FCBs) is an archaic structure used by DOS version 1.0 programs to manage files. Few, if any, surviving MS-DOS programs require FCBs, but if you have one, you can use the `FCBS` statement to instruct NTVDM to allocate space for *n* of them. (At this late date, if you do need them, you'll already know it, as you'll have had to deal with this on every prior version of DOS and Windows.)

FILES=*n*
sets the maximum number of concurrently open files available to MS-DOS applications. The default value is `20`. You may want to increase this number to `100` or more if you use database applications such as MS-DOS FoxPro.

INSTALL=[**path**]*filename* [*parameters*]
loads a TSR into memory prior to running `AUTOEXEC.NT`.

One program that you may need to install in `AUTOEXEC.NT` is `setver.exe`. Setver intercepts programs' requests to find out what version of DOS is running, and it lies to them. Its purpose is to let you run programs that would otherwise be unhappy to find that they're running on DOS version 5.0, which is what NTVDM would tell them. If your MS-DOS application complains about the DOS version number, open the Help and Support Center and search for "setver."

NTCMDPROMPT
By default, when an MS-DOS program is run from the command line or a batch file and exits, CMD runs `COMMAND.COM` to handle all further commands. This makes it possible to run old MS-DOS batch files. If you specify `NTCMDPROMPT` in `CONFIG.NT`, CMD will not run `COMMAND.COM`, but will remain in control between MS-DOS programs. This lets you write modern batch files to use with MS-DOS programs.

SHELL=[*path*]*filename* [*parameters*]
specifies an alternate shell program to use if you do not want to use `COMMAND.COM` as the MS-DOS shell. You can also use this command to specify `COMMAND.COM` with startup options. For example, the entry

```
shell=%systemroot%\system32\command.com /E:2048/P
```

requests 2048 bytes for environment variables. The `/P` option is required to prevent `COMMAND.COM` from exiting after processing one command.

STACKS=*n,s*
When a hardware interrupt occurs, NTVDM needs "memory stack" space to temporarily store information for the interrupt handler. The `stacks` option lets you instruct NTVDM to allocate separate stack space for interrupt handlers. The numbers *n* and `s` instruct NTVDM to allocate *n* blocks of `s` bytes each. *N* can be `0` or `8` through `64`. *S* can be `0` or `32` to `512`. The default values are `9` and `128`, respectively. If necessary, you can save memory for program use by specifying `stacks=0,0`; this may or may not cause a program crash. You can specify `stacks=8,512` to allocate plenty of stack space if you suspect that interrupt handlers are causing DOS crashes.

continues

REFERENCE LIST 13.1 Continued

SWITCHES=/K

Makes MS-DOS programs treat the keyboard as a "conventional" 96-key keyboard even if it uses the extended 102+ key layout. If you use this switch and also load `ansi.sys`, specify `/k` after `ansi.sys` as well.

The following items are permitted in `CONFIG.NT` for compatibility with historical `CONFIG.SYS` settings but have no effect in Windows XP:

- `buffers`
- `driveparm`
- `lastdrive` (`lastdrive` is always `Z`)

AUTOEXEC.NT

`AUTOEXEC.NT` serves the same purpose `AUTOEXEC.BAT` did on MS-DOS systems: It is a batch file that lets you run programs that set up the command environment before you begin working. The default version of `AUTOEXEC.NT` installed with Windows is located in `\windows\system32` and contains the following commands:

```
lh %SystemRoot%\system32\mscdexnt.exe
lh %SystemRoot%\system32\redir
lh %SystemRoot%\system32\dosx
SET BLASTER=A220 I5 D1 P330 T3
```

MSCDEXNT provides support for CD-ROM drives, REDIR is the network interface, DOSX provides upper-memory support (it serves the same purpose `EMM386.EXE` did on MS-DOS), and the `SET` command provides DOS programs with information about the simulated Sound Blaster sound hardware. No matter what kind of sound system your computer has, MS-DOS programs "see" a Sound Blaster–compatible card (although the emulation is less than perfect).

In addition, if you've installed the Client for Novell Networks, `AUTOEXEC.NT` will also run `nw16.exe` and `vwipxspx.exe`, which give DOS applications access to the Novell application programming interface (API).

You can load other programs and set environment variables in `AUTOEXEC.NT`, but remember that they will be loaded every time you run an MS-DOS program. If you need particular terminate-and-stay-resident programs only for some MS-DOS applications, set up a customized AUTOEXEC file just for those applications.

Tip

One program that's handy to add to `AUTOEXEC.NT` is `doskey`, which gives `COMMAND.COM` the same editing commands as those provided by `CMD.EXE`, and in addition, it lets you define abbreviated commands called *aliases*. To read about this program, start the Help and Support Center and search for "doskey."

You can map drive letters with Windows Explorer using the Tools, Map Network Drive menu, or you can map drive letters from the command prompt using the `net use` command. I'll talk about `net use` in Chapter 14, "Command-Line Programs."

Note

DOS applications do not expect to see computer names or folder and printer share names longer than eight letters. You will have to be careful to use short names when you configure your network if you want any network-aware MS-DOS applications to be able to see the shared resources.

MS-DOS and Novell Networking

Novell Corporation's NetWare networking software used a similar series of software layers, although the details and protocols were different than Microsoft's. If you install support for Novell Networking on Windows XP, the network setup program will add additional Novell IPX/SPX interface programs to `AUTOEXEC.NT`. This will let NTVDM provide Novell look-alike services to your MS-DOS programs.

Note

If you need access to the Novell network in programs that use custom AUTOEXEC batch files, you'll need to manually copy the commands into the custom files. Use the same sequences of commands that you find in `AUTOEXEC.NT`.

Microsoft's implementation of Novell's IPX/SPX protocols is not complete, however, so the MS-DOS environment will not support many of the old MS-DOS configuration utilities that were used to manage Novell file servers. Printing is also not well supported. The Novell client software, which you can download from `www.novell.com`, does a much better job. However, you should only install the Novell client software if you are sure you need it. As hard as it is to believe, the Novell client tends not to do as good a job as Microsoft's client at file server access.

Printing from MS-DOS

MS-DOS applications ran in an environment where there was no competition for computer hardware. Only one program ran at a time, so it was acceptable for a program to send data directly to printer hardware. On Windows, because many programs can run at once, the operating system must mediate between programs and resources.

NTVDM takes care of this discrepancy by providing "virtual" LPT ports to MS-DOS applications. When an MS-DOS application issues instructions that would send data to a printer, NTVDM intercepts the instructions and instead sends the data to the Windows spooler so that output from the MS-DOS program and other concurrent

MS-DOS Environment Variables

In MS-DOS, memory is a limited resource, and MS-DOS is particularly stingy with environment variable space. If you need to define more than a dozen or so environment variables in any MS-DOS–style batch files, you'll probably need to extend the amount of space allocated to environment variables either on the Properties dialog box of an associated shortcut or in a `shell=` command in a `CONFIG.NT` file. These techniques were described earlier in the chapter.

When you first start an MS-DOS program or `COMMAND.COM`, NTVDM inherits the default Windows environment, but with the following changes:

- All variable names are changed to uppercase. MS-DOS programs do not expect to find lowercase letters in environment variable names.
- The `COMSPEC` variable is added, which contains the path and filename of the command shell (usually `COMMAND.COM`).
- The `TEMP` and `TMP` variables are reset to the system default, rather than the user-specific setting.
- Path names in all environment variables are changed to use DOS-compatible 8.3-character names.

MS-DOS and Networking

In the days of MS-DOS, networking was an expensive and fairly uncommon option. Networking software for DOS was bulky, balky, and an afterthought to boot. Microsoft's networking product required you to load hardware-specific device drivers, followed by programs that managed network protocols, followed finally by a software layer that provided file services to DOS.

One lucky result of this was that MS-DOS application programs never dealt with network hardware directly; they let DOS and its underlying network layers take care of the details. The NTVDM environment supplies the same services through the `redir.exe` program that is loaded in `AUTOEXEC.NT`, so MS-DOS programs can use today's fast, inexpensive networks.

Note

If you create custom AUTOEXEC files and want your DOS applications to be able to use networking, you must load `redire.exe` in your custom files just as it's loaded in `AUTOEXEC.NT`.

DOS programs, however, usually were not designed to handle UNC format filenames—that is, filenames such as `\\myserver\officefiles\march\plans.doc`. If you want to access network files from MS-DOS applications, you'll have to map a drive letter to connect to the network folder and then have the MS-DOS program use that drive letter for file access.

Windows applications aren't mixed together. If you look at the printer queue while a DOS application is printing, you'll see these print jobs labeled as "Remote Downlevel Document."

Because DOS programs were completely responsible for managing the attached printers, Windows spools output from MS-DOS in "raw" mode, meaning the output is sent to the printer verbatim. This may include text, control sequences, and graphics commands. If the MS-DOS printer uses control sequences for the wrong printer model, you'll get some very strange printouts. But, it was this way back in the old days as well.

For local printers that are connected to hardware port LPT1, LPT2, or LPT3, you may instruct your MS-DOS programs to use the port directly.

Print Redirection

If you need to use network printers or printers connected to USB ports, it's another matter. MS-DOS programs have no idea what USB is, and with few exceptions (WordPerfect being one of them), DOS programs didn't provide for explicit connections to remote printers either.

However, you can work around this by mapping LPT ports to shared printers using the `net use` command. Just as you can map drive letters to shared folders, you can map printer ports to shared printers. I'll discuss the `net use` command in more detail in Chapter 14, but here are some specific tips for using this command to set up printing for MS-DOS applications:

- There is no law that says that you can only use printers shared by *other* computers. If you want to use a USB-based printer on your own computer, you can share it and use a `net use` command to map it to a virtual LPT port. Your MS-DOS applications will then be able to send information to the printer.
- You must map shared printers to LPT ports that are *not* actually in use on your computer. For example, if you have a printer connected to LPT1, you cannot map a network printer to LPT1.
- You are not necessarily limited to LPT1, LPT2, and LPT3. You can map shared printers to devices LPT1 up to LPT9. Some MS-DOS programs will accept these larger numbers, and some won't. You'll have to experiment.

The basic `net use` command to map a printer looks like this:

```
net use lpt3: \\server\printname
```

Here's the command to undo a mapping:

```
net use lpt3: /d
```

For more details, see Chapter 14.

Print Screen

On Windows XP, the Print Screen function does not work as it did in the real MS-DOS. When an MS-DOS program is running in window mode, the Prt Scr key works just as it normally does in Windows: It copies a bitmap picture of the screen or current window to the Clipboard. In full-screen mode, the Prt Scr key doesn't send the screen to the printer. Instead, it copies the screen's *text* to the Clipboard. To print it, you'll need to paste the text or bitmap into a document and print it as a separate step.

Configuring Serial Communications with MS-DOS

The NTVDM environment tries to make the computer's COM ports available to MS-DOS programs through a bag of virtual hardware tricks. NTVDM captures attempts by the DOS program to issue instructions to the serial port's hardware and, from the pattern of commands, determines what the program is trying to do. It then performs these actions through the Windows programming interface.

DOS-based serial communication software used direct hardware control and interrupt drivers that received information directly from the hardware when information was arrived from the modem or other remote serial device. NTVDM simulates these hardware interrupts *fairly* successfully. Most DOS-based serial communications programs will work under Windows XP, although some won't.

This can be a point of difficulty for businesses upgrading communications, remote access, and remote support systems from DOS and older versions of Windows. If your software doesn't work under Windows XP, there is unfortunately nothing you can do to improve the situation. If your old application does not function correctly, you'll either have to dual-boot your computer between Windows XP and DOS, revert to an older version of Windows or develop new software.

Using Special-Purpose Devices for MS-DOS

NTVDM provides limited hardware support for MS-DOS applications. As mentioned, it intercepts and simulates interaction with LPT parallel ports, COM serial ports, the keyboard, and the video display. It provides DOS-mediated network and file access; it provides a mouse driver and fools MS-DOS programs into thinking that there is Sound Blaster–compatible hardware, if your system has any sort of sound support. But that's the end of the virtual hardware support.

If you depend on access to special-purpose hardware, either through direct control or through device drives, you are probably out of luck. If your program attempts to access any other hardware devices, NTVDM will either stop the program dead in its tracks or, at best, will prevent the hardware access from occurring.

If you really depend on custom hardware and can't afford to develop a proper Windows-based device driver for it, there *is* one thing you can try. I can't vouch for it, and I must warn you that it could severely compromise the integrity of your Windows XP system. My attorneys insist that I tell you this is completely *at your own risk*, but here it is: There is a way to open a "window" in the Windows barrier between user programs and the system hardware. It will let you issue `INP` and `OUT` instructions to a range of physical I/O ports. You can find software to do this at `www.beyondlogic.org/porttalk/porttalk.htm`. With the device's physical ports made available, you can communicate with the device. However, interrupts and DMA will not work. Again, this is a last-resort option. It would be better to invest in developing a proper Windows device driver.

Managing MS-DOS Programs

You can use MS-DOS applications as you always did. However, whereas the old programs think they're back in 1985, you're not, and there are a few points to remember:

- MS-DOS programs can't deal with long file or folder names. You'll have to use the so-called "8.3" filenames that Windows provides just for this purpose. You may have seen these mangled names before. They look like `C:\PROGRA~1\MICROS~1`.

  For files that you will use *only* with DOS applications, it's best to use only short file and folder names that don't need to be mangled. For example, you can create folders such as `C:\offdocs`, instead of `c:\office documents`, and filenames such as `feblist.doc` instead of `february resource lists.doc`.
- If you need to find the mangled name of an existing file or folder, use the `dir` command-line command with the `/x` option. This displays the short version along with the full name.
- The mouse should work if the program is mouse-aware. If your mouse simply highlights blocks of text on the screen instead of controlling the application, right-click the window's title bar, select Properties, view the Options tab, and uncheck Quick Edit.
- For programs that were not designed for use with the mouse, you can use the Quick Edit feature to copy text from the screen, and you can paste text to the DOS application with the shortcut Alt+space, E, P.

When Things Go Awry

As mentioned earlier, when you run MS-DOS programs under Windows XP, as far as Windows is concerned, the actual application in use is called `ntvdm.exe`. Even though the application is running in a simulated MS-DOS world, NTVDM intercepts the usual Windows key combinations that control window behavior: Alt+space opens the system menu, and so on. In addition, Ctrl+C or Ctrl+Break usually terminate a DOS application, although some programs have special exit key sequences.

As mentioned earlier, you can disable the Windows keyboard functions if these keystrokes are needed by the DOS application. This will make you rely more on the mouse to manage the application window, but it's a small price to pay.

If you need to terminate an MS-DOS application that's run amok, you'll be pleasantly surprised that the Reset button will probably not have to be used. In most cases, you can click the Close button on the application's window. After a few seconds, Windows will ask if you want to terminate the application. If you click Yes, it's summarily dispatched and the problem is solved. (Of course, if you haven't saved your data, you'll lose it, and there's a chance that the application will have corrupted one or more of its data files, but this was the case under MS-DOS as well.)

You can also use the Windows Task Manager to remove unruly DOS applications. This may be necessary if you are running a DOS application in full-screen mode and cannot return to the Windows desktop with Alt+Enter. In this case, you should do what you would have done under MS-DOS: press Ctrl+Alt+Del. Instead of rebooting the computer, however, this will switch you out of full-screen mode and will display the Windows Task Manager.

If you're happy enough to let the DOS program keep running, you can just press Esc to dismiss the Task Manager.

If you need to kill the DOS application, you have two choices: If the task is clearly identifiable on the Applications tab, you can select the task name and click End Task. After a few seconds, you'll be able to terminate the program.

However, the window title may not reflect the name of the current DOS application. It's more likely to say "Command Prompt - command" or just "Command Prompt." If you have several MS-DOS applications open, you may have a hard time finding the right one to terminate. I suggest closing the applications that are still responding to narrow down the choices. You can also use the Processes tab; look for `ntvdm.exe` and terminate this task.

14

Command-Line Programs

ROAD MAP

- More than 140 command-line programs are provided with Windows XP.
- You can get some jobs done faster with a command-line utility than with a GUI program.
- This chapter covers the most important command-line programs—the ones you really need to know how to use.
- Windows XP has a tool that lets you create simple installation programs to distribute your own programs and scripts—if you know where to find it.

Windows Command-Line Programs

NEARLY 400 EXECUTABLE PROGRAMS ARE INSTALLED along with Windows XP. Some of these are familiar, standard Windows programs such as Notebook, Windows Media Player, Solitaire, and Internet Explorer. Many are system service programs that we never interact with directly. However, it may surprise you as much as it did me to find that over 140 of them, or about 35%, are command-line programs. The operating system is called *Windows*, after all, not *Prompts*, so what's with all these command-line programs?

It turns out that the command-line programs fall into three general categories:

- Maintenance and administrative programs that have graphical equivalents. The command-line versions make it possible to perform maintenance operations with batch files and scripts. Also, it's sometimes easier to type a command line with filenames and wildcards than it is to poke at individual files with Explorer.
- Batch file and command-line tools such as `cmd`, `more`, and `findstr`. These programs are useful when creating and using batch files, when working with text files, and when navigating through the command-line environment.

- TCP/IP networking tools and utilities inherited from the Unix operating system, where today's Internet grew up. These utilities are used to manage Windows networking as well as to interoperate with Unix systems.

All the command-line programs are listed in Appendix E, "Windows XP Program Reference," which starts on page 657. You may want to take a look at that listing to get a feel for the type of programs available.

So how do you use these programs? As I've mentioned before, many command-line programs are self-documenting: You can type the command name followed by `/?` or type `help` *`commandname`* at the command prompt to see the program's description, syntax, and sample uses. Many are also written up in the Windows Help and Support Center. Therefore, it doesn't make a lot of sense for me to reproduce all that information in this book.

Instead, I'm going to focus on describing what I consider the essential command-line programs—the ones that will give you the biggest boost in productivity and power as you use and manage Windows XP.

The Essential Command Line

Besides the built-in commands that are part of the CMD shell (discussed in Chapter 11, "The CMD Command-Line Environment"), about 20 other command-line programs come in handy on a day-to-day basis. They fall into five categories:

- **GUI shortcuts**. Standard Windows programs that you can activate just by typing their name: `calc`, `control`, `mmc`, `notepad`, and `regedit`. The `start` command is also handy.
- **General-purpose shell programs**. Utilities to simplify life on the command line: `findstr`, `more`, `tree`, and `xcopy`.
- **File-management tools**. Programs that manage file permissions and access controls: `attrib` and `cacls`. (`Cacls`, by the way, is the only tool available that lets you manage file permissions on NTFS-formatted disks under Windows XP Home Edition without booting up in safe mode.)
- **Management power tools**. Programs that control Windows XP as well as its services and applications: `driverquery`, `runas`, `sc`, `tasklist`, and `taskkill`.
- **Networking utilities**. Tools for using and managing Windows Networking in general and TCP/IP networks in particular: `ipconfig`, `net`, `netstat`, `nslookup`, `ping`, and `tracert`.

I'll describe these programs in this chapter.

GUI Shortcuts

The first set of essential command-line programs aren't actually command-line programs at all—they're standard Windows Graphical User Interface (GUI) programs. However, I've added them here to illustrate an important point: If you enter the name of a GUI program file on the command line, Windows runs the program in the normal way. So, when you're working at the command prompt, if you know a GUI program by name, you can spare yourself a lot of poking around on the Start menu. Six commands that you'll find handy to know are listed here:

- `calc`. Runs the Windows Calculator accessory.
- `control`. Opens the Control Panel. I'll discuss this command in more detail in moment.
- `mmc`. Opens the Microsoft Management Console. From the MMC menu, you can click File, Add/Remove Snap-In to add any MMC tool that you'd like to use.
- `notepad`. Runs Windows Notepad. To edit a particular file, type the file's name after `notepad`.
- `regedit`. Runs the Registry Editor, which is not normally found on the Start menu.
- `start`. Followed by the name of a file, this command launches the associated application and opens the file. For example, `start somefile.xls` will launch Microsoft Excel and open `somefile.xls`. For many registered programs, `start` *`programname`* will run the program even if the program file isn't in the search path. For example, `start excel` and `start winword` open Excel and Word, respectively.

You may find that you often want to run other GUI programs while you're working at the command prompt. If you hate taking your hands off the keyboard to use the mouse, just find the program's name and you can run it directly.

Tip

To find the name of a Windows program file, right-click the program's menu entry or shortcut. Select Properties and then look at the Target field on the Shortcut properties page.

The Control Panel is actually a "shell" program, much like MMC. The actual work is done by plug-in programs or "applets" called CPL files. If you know the name of a plug-in, you can enter its name on the command line after the `control` command and jump directly to the desired Control Panel applet. If you want to access the Control Panel from the command line, it's enough just to type `control` and use the GUI from there. However, if you want to run a particular control applet from a batch file, WSH script, or shortcut, this is a great way to make the user's job easier.

The standard Control Panel applets are listed in Table 14.1. Some CPL files contain more than one applet. In these cases, you can specify which to run by adding additional words after the name of the CPL file.

Table 14.1 **Control Panel Applets**

Command Arguments	**Control Panel Applet Displayed**
`access.cpl`	Accessibility Options
`appwiz.cpl`	Add/Remove Programs
`desk.cpl`	Display Properties
`fonts`	Fonts Folder
`hdwwiz.cpl`	Add Hardware Wizard
`inetcpl.cpl`	Internet Properties (used by Internet Explorer and Outlook Express)
`intl.cpl`	Regional and Language Options
`joy.cpl`	Game Controllers
`main.cpl`	Mouse Properties
`main.cpl keyboard`	Keyboard Properties
`main.cpl pc card`	PCMCIA Card Properties
`mmsys.cpl`	Sounds and Audio Devices
`ncpa.cpl`	Network Connections
`nusrmgr.cpl`	User Accounts (new Windows XP version)
`nwc.cpl`	Client Services for NetWare
`odbccp32.cpl`	ODBC Data Source Administrator
`powercfg.cpl`	Power Options
`sysdm.cpl`	System Properties
`telephon.cpl`	Phone and Modem Options
`timedate.cpl`	Date and Time Properties

For example, you can open the Network Connections Control Panel directly by typing

```
control ncpa.cpl
```

on the command line, in a shortcut, in the Start menu's Run dialog, or in a batch file.

Tip

You don't have to open a Command Prompt window to run a command-line program. Just type [window key]+R and the Run dialog box will pop up. Then type in your command line and press Enter.

Tip

You can run a Control Panel applet as the system administrator using the runas command, which I'll discuss later in the chapter. The command line to use is

```
runas /user:Administrator "control applet.cpl"
```

Runas will prompt you for the Administrator password and then open the Control Panel window.

General-Purpose Shell Programs

At the command prompt, you'll find yourself using the built-in commands, such as `pushd`, `cd`, and `dir`, quite frequently. There are four other programs you should know about: `findstr`, `more`, `tree`, and `xcopy`. These come in handy in many situations—to examine the contents of text, script, and batch files, to examine directories, and to copy files.

findstr

`Findstr` is an enhanced version of the old text-searching program `find`. In its basic form, `findstr` scans one or more files, or the standard input, for text strings and prints those lines that contain the desired string. This is handy when you know what you're looking for but can't remember what file contains it, or to extract and condense specific information from files. It's especially helpful in batch files that gather information from programs that generate more text than you need; `findstr` can help you automatically cull the information.

In its most basic usage, `findstr` prints out any lines that contain the string or strings specified on its command line. For example, suppose I have a file named `afile` with this text inside:

```
Now is the time for
all good men to
come to the aid of their party.
The rain in Spain falls
mainly in the plain.
```

The command `findstr "to all" afile` prints the following text:

```
all good men to
come to the aid of their party.
```

It found both `"to"` and `"all"` on the first line as well as `"to"` on the second. The words on the command line can be specified in any order, and they don't have to be complete words: `findstr "a"` will extract any input lines that contain the letter *a*.

You can search multiple files by specifying them at the end of the command line. Here's an example:

```
findstr "to all" afile *.txt d:\input\*.txt
```

`Findstr` is a filter, which means that if you don't name any files on its command line, it will read from the standard input, and it always writes its results to the standard output. You can use `findstr` to find any files with the uppercase letters "FOR" in their name by using a command such as this:

```
dir | findstr "FOR"
```

Also, you can direct the output of the `findstr` command to a file or another program by using the > or | symbol.

Tip

In batch files, `findstr` can be especially useful with the extended `for /f` command, which can parse the output of a command, as discussed in Chapter 11. For example, you can write a command such as this:

```
for /f "usebackq" %%n in (`someprogram | findstr "text"`) do (
    somecommand %%n
)
```

This command runs a program named `someprogram` and filters the output through `findstr`. The first token on each output line is passed to `somecommand`.

`Findstr` has many options, which you can view by typing `findstr /?` on the command line. I won't list them all here, but I will discuss several of the most useful ones.

Case-Insensitive Searching

You can specify `/I` before the search pattern to have `findstr` ignore uppercase/lowercase when matching strings. You'll find that you need `/I` more often than not. For example,

```
dir | findstr /i "for"
```

will print the name of any file containing "for," "FOR," or "foR," or any other combination of upper- or lowercase.

Literal String Matching

As mentioned earlier, if you specify several words on the `findstr` command line, it searches for any of the words. You can instruct `findstr` to search for an exact string, including spaces, with the `/C` option. Using the sample input `afile` listed earlier, the command

```
find str /i /C:"the rain" afile
```

prints just the line, "The rain in Spain falls."

Positional Searching

The options /B and /E instruct findstr to look for the desired search text only at the very beginning or end of each text line, respectively.

Searching Multiple Files

To search more than one file, you can specify more than one filename on findstr's command line. In this case, when findstr finds a matching text line, it precedes each output line with the name of the file in which it found the text. When it's displaying this directly to the Command Prompt window, it highlights the filename in a brighter color. The output might look like this:

```
C:\book\14>findstr "text" *.txt
a.txt:this is more text
b.txt:this is a text file
c.txt:when entering text
```

You can instruct findstr to search the specified files and any subdirectories of the paths you specify by adding the /S option. Here's an example:

```
findstr /s "text" c:\book\*.txt
```

You can also tell findstr to look in a file for a list of files to search by using /G:*filename*. For example, the command findstr /I /F:filelist "computer" opens the file named filelist. It's assumed that each line of this file is the name of a file to be searched. Findstr looks into each of these files for the word *computer*. Also, /F:/ instructs filelist to read the list of files from the standard input. For example, the command

```
dir /od /b *.log | findstr /F:/ "Administrator"
```

uses dir to create a list of .log filenames in date order. Findstr then searches these files for the word *Administrator*.

Getting Extra Information

Several findstr options add or remove information from the output line. These options are listed here:

Option	Output
/V	Prints lines that do *not* match
/N	Prints line numbers before each line
/M	Prints only names of files that contain a match
/O	Prints the character offset to each matching line
/P	Skips files with nonprinting (binary) characters

Matching Text with Wildcards

The most powerful feature of `findstr` is its ability to match text using wildcards, or more precisely *regular expressions*, which let you specify how to match strings with variable information.

Regular expressions are composed of characters to be matched, plus special items that describe how the matching string may vary. The special regular expression items are listed in Table 14.2.

Table 14.2 **Special Items for Regular Expressions**

Item	Matches
`.`	Any one character.
`*`	Zero or more occurrences of the previous item.
`^`	The beginning of the line.
`$`	The end of the line.
`[xyz]`	Any of the characters listed inside the brackets. The list may contain individual letters and/or ranges of letters. For example, `[A-Za-z]` matches the letters *A* through *Z* and *a* through *z*.
`[^xyz]`	Anything *but* the characters in set `xyz`.
`\<`	The beginning of a word.
`\>`	The end of a word.
`\x`	Literal character `x`, usually used with `*`, `.`, and so on.

If you haven't encountered these before, regular expressions take some getting used to. To start with, forget about the asterisk (`*`) as you remember it from its use with DOS wildcards, as in `del *.txt`. In regular expressions, `*` indicates that the search character or expression that comes *before* it is both optional and repeatable. For example, `ab*c` matches `ac`, `abc`, `abbc`, `abbbc`, and so on, but not `abxyzc`, because this search pattern looks for `a`, followed by zero or more `b`'s, followed by `c`.

In regular expressions, the period (`.`) is the wildcard character. A single period matches exactly one character, any character. For example, `a.c` matches `axc`, `a-c`, and `a c`—even a space counts as a character. Join `.` with `*`, and you now have the DOS-type wildcard: `a.*c` matches `ac`, `axc`, `a123c`, and so on. In other words, it matches anything starting with *a* and ending with *c*.

Note

`Findstr` interprets the following special characters as regular expression operators by default:

```
. * ^ $ [ ] \
```

If you want to search for a string with these characters but don't want to use regular expressions, you can either precede the special characters with a backslash (`\*`, `\^`, `\\`, and so on), or you can use the `/L` option to tell `findstr` to be "literal."

As an example of how powerful regular expressions can be, suppose we wanted to extract from a file (or a program's output) all lines that begin with a date. We could use this search:

```
findstr "^[0-9][0-9]/[0-9][0-9]/[0-9][0-9]*" filename
```

The first character, `^`, "anchors" the search to the beginning of each input line; dates that don't start in column 1 won't be matched. Then, the pattern matches lines starting with dates such as 12/03/02 as well as 12/03/2002.

As another example, suppose you are stuck on the morning's crossword puzzle and want to find all five-letter words starting with the letter *A* and ending with the letter *E*. You could use this:

```
findstr /i "\<a[a-z][a-z][a-z]e\>" dictionary.txt
```

If you were sure that the file contained no spaces, you could also write the following:

```
findstr /i "a...e" dictionary.txt
```

With spaces in the input file, however, this pattern might match something such as "`the area I entered`," which is not what you are after.

> **Note**
>
> Regular expressions are very powerful pattern-matching tools. If you haven't run into them before, search `www.google.com` for "regular expressions" to read more about them. Beware, though: They come in many flavors. `Findstr`'s version is fairly limited and is missing ?, +, ( ), and other operators to which Unix users are accustomed.

more

I briefly mentioned `more` in Chapter 11, but it has some extra options and functions that I wanted to describe in more detail. Here's its full set of command line options:

```
more [/E [/C] [/P] [/S] [/Tn] [+n]] [filename...]
```

With no extra arguments, `more` displays the standard input or the named files a page at a time. If you use the `/E` option, `more` gains some extra capabilities that can be handy. After `/E`, you can add any of the following options:

Option	Description
`/C`	Clears the screen before displaying text.
`/P`	Expands formfeed characters into blank lines.
`/S`	Squeeze. Displays multiple blank lines as a single blank line.
`/Tn`	Sets tab stops at every *n* spaces. The default is 8.
`+n`	Starts displaying the file at line number *n*, skipping lines 1 through *n*–1.

If you find that you use any of these all the time, you can put them into an environment variable named MORE to make them the default settings. For example,

```
set MORE=/E /C /P /S
```

in your logon script, or similar settings made in the System Properties' Environment Variables dialog box, will make the /E, /C, /P, and /S options active by default.

As cool as more is, it can't scroll backward through the file. For this reason, I sometimes find that the Notepad accessory makes a better text viewer. To turn Notepad into a command-line filter, I wrote the following batch file, named view.bat, which is in a folder that's in my standard search path:

Example File view.bat

```
@rem
@echo off
if "%1" == "" (
    rem --- save standard input to temp file and display it
    more >C:\temp\view.tmp
    notepad C:\temp\view.tmp
    del C:\temp\view.tmp
) else (
    rem --- open file(s) with notepad
    for %%f in (%*) do start notepad %%f
)
```

➔ To learn more about the search path, see "Creating and Using Batch Files," p. 490.

If this batch file is given the name of one or more files on its command line, it displays the files with Notepad. Otherwise, it acts as a filter—it uses more to save the standard input to a temporary file and then displays the temporary file with Notepad. Therefore, you can enter a command like this:

```
dir c:\windows\system32 | view
```

It's a nice marriage of the GUI and command-line worlds.

(It may seem odd to use more this way. When its output is directed to a file rather than the console window, it doesn't perform its paging duties but rather just copies the standard input through to the output. It's the only standard Windows utility that can do this, so it's the only way to create a batch file filter.)

tree

Tree is a nifty, simple command-line tool that answers the question, What subdirectories are there inside this folder? You'll often wonder this as you poke around in the command-line environment.

If I type tree at the command prompt, the output looks like this:

```
C:.
????batch files
????figures
```

```
?   ????line
?   ????screen
????review
????scripts
```

Using text-based graphics, this shows that the current directory has four subdirectories: `batch files`, `figures`, `review`, and `scripts`. Also, `figures` has two subdirectories of its own (`line` and `screen`).

You can specify a starting drive and path on the command line, if you want to view another directory, and you can add the `/F` option, which makes `tree` list filenames as well as folders.

> **Tip**
>
> In directories with many subdirectories, the output of `tree` can be confusing and may scroll off the screen. If this happens, I have another handy batch file for you. It's called `e.bat`, and it has only two lines:
>
> ```
> @rem    Example file e.bat
> @echo off
> if "%1" == "" (explorer /e,.) else explorer /e,"%1"
> ```
>
> This batch file fires up Windows Explorer with the current directory selected in the Folder view. If you get lost at the command prompt, just type `e` and press Enter to get the GUI view. Problem solved in two keystrokes! (As you might have guessed by now, I'm somewhat impatient.)

xcopy

If you need to copy a large group of files, `xcopy` is the tool of choice. Granted, you can click on files and folders with Windows Explorer and drag them around on the screen, and that's fine when you only want to do it once, but sometimes the command-line method is much more sensible. Here are some examples:

- If you want to copy the same set of files repeatedly, or on a scheduled basis, creating a batch file that uses `xcopy` lets you set the process up once and use it as many times as necessary.
- If you want to maintain a backup copy of files and folders in the most efficient way possible, `xcopy` can automatically copy only changed files, to minimize the amount of time required and the amount of data moved.

`Xcopy` is similar to its simpler cousin `copy`. In the most basic usage, you type `xcopy` *`from to`*, where *`from`* is the name of the file or folder you want to copy and *`to`* is the location in which you want to make the copy. However, `xcopy` has a staggering number of command-line options—27 in all—that can make it do several more interesting things. I'd describe them all here, but several "save the forest" groups are already staging protests outside my office as it is (notwithstanding the fact that I'm a member). So,

I'll just describe some useful `xcopy` applications. You can see the full list by typing `xcopy /? | more` at the command prompt, or you can open the Help and Support Center and search for `xcopy`.

Copying Subdirectories

If you add the `/S` option, `xcopy` will copy all subfolders as well, recursively, except for empty subfolders. The `/E` option copies even empty folders, thus retaining the exact directory structure of the original. If you use either of these options, you should also use the `/I` option to indicate the destination name is a folder, not a filename. For example,

```
xcopy c:\book e:\book /E /I
```

copies the directory `C:\book` and all files and folders within it to drive E:.

Making Backups

You can use `xcopy` to make backup copies of files and folders into another folder, onto another disk drive or a CD-RW drive, or to a network shared folder. When making backup copies, add the `/K` option so that `xcopy` preserves file attributes such as System and Read-Only in the copies. In addition, when copying to a network folder, add `/Z` so that `xcopy` can continue copying after brief network interruptions. Here's an example:

```
xcopy c:\book \\bali\bookfiles /K /E /I /Z
```

You can easily make a backup of your own personal My Documents folder. It's easiest to use the `userprofile` environment variable to specify the path, as in this example:

```
xcopy "%userprofile%\My Documents" e:\backup /K /E /I
```

This doesn't copy hidden files, however, and doesn't back up your personal settings and Registry entry files. You can't do this with `xcopy` while you're logged in, because the hidden Registry file `NTUSER.DAT` cannot be opened for copying while the account is logged on. If you have Administrator privileges, though, you can copy another user's entire profile by specifying the `/H` option to copy even hidden files, with a command like this:

```
xcopy "C:\documents and settings\username" e:\backup /H /K /E /I
```

Here, *`username`* is the name of one of the computer's user accounts. (You can't use the `userprofile` environment variable in this case because it points to the Administrator account's folder, not the desired user's.)

To back up *all* the profiles on the computer, you could use the command

```
xcopy "C:\documents and settings" e:\backup /H /K /E /I
```

although you would need Administrator privileges to do this, because it requires `xcopy` to read other users' files.

Copying Only Updated Files

If you do use xcopy to create backups of a set of files and folders, you'll want to run the xcopy command periodically to keep the backup up-to-date. In this case, you don't want to have to copy files that haven't been changed. Use the /D option to instruct xcopy only to copy files that are newer than any copy in the backup set. This saves time and reduces network traffic. You'll also need to add the /R option so that xcopy can write over old copies of read-only files. Now you can see xcopy in its full alphabet-soup glory. The command

```
xcopy "%userprofile%\My Documents" e:\backup /H /K /R /E /D /I
```

copies your My Documents folder and all subfolders, but it only copies files that are newer than any already copied to e:\backup. Also, all file attributes are preserved.

The /D option serves double duty—you can also use it to specify a date, and xcopy will only copy files changed or created on or after the specified date. See the online help for more information on this usage.

Unattended Backups

Xcopy can't copy files that are in use by application programs, nor can it copy the personal Registry information of a user who is logged on. So, for backup purposes, it's helpful to put xcopy commands into a batch file and use the Task Scheduler to run the batch when users are not likely to be logged on. If you do this, you should add the /C option to tell xcopy to continue even if it encounters errors. If someone is up late and has a document file open, for example, /C lets xcopy continue to copy other files and folders.

For instance, you could write a batch file to copy all users' My Documents folders onto a network folder using this command:

```
pushd "c:Documents and Settings" for /D %%d in (*.*) do (
    xcopy "%%d\My Documents" "\\server\backups\%%d" /H/K/R/E/C/D/I/Z
)
```

You'd have to be sure to set up a network shared folder for this purpose before running the batch file and to use the correct server and share name in the xcopy command.

Note

Some other handy general-purpose programs you might want to look into on your own are sort and find. Find is a simplified version of findstr. Sort lets you sort text files alphabetically.

File-Management Tools

Windows XP gives users the choice of formatting their hard disks with either of two file system structures: File Allocation Table (FAT) or NT File System (NTFS). Both systems provide ways to make files invisible (hidden) and unalterable (read-only). In addition, NTFS provides a user and group security scheme that lets the user determine exactly who can view, create, modify, and delete files on a file-by-file and folder-by-folder basis. Although you can control these file attributes from the Windows Explorer GUI, Microsoft has also provided command-line tools to manage file attributes.

These utilities can be used in batch files to set up and maintain user folders. For example, you can make a batch file that creates a folder on a file server for each newly added user and then adds the appropriate NTFS permissions to secure the folder.

In addition, Windows XP Home Edition does its best to entirely conceal the existence of NTFS file permissions. The Explorer GUI has no means of viewing or modifying permissions, yet they still exist and still affect users' access rights to the file system. The `cacls` command lets you view and modify NTFS permissions on Windows XP Home Edition, either to create restricted folders outside the users' normal profile folders or to repair problems.

Note

XP Home Edition users can gain access to the NTFS Security Properties GUI by booting up in Safe Mode and logging on as Administrator.

attrib

Microsoft's FAT and NTFS file systems support a set of primitive file "attributes" that can be used to indicate that a file is to receive special treatment. For example, the read-only attribute prevents Windows or DOS from writing data to the file or deleting it. These attributes don't offer as much protection as the user-level security system used on NTFS formatted disks, but they do help prevent accidents.

The `attrib` command displays and changes the basic file attributes, which are listed here:

Code	Attribute	Description
R	Read-Only	The file can be read but not written.
A	Archive	The file has been modified since the last backup. The Archive attribute is rarely used.
S	System	The file is an operating system file.
H	Hidden	The file is not visible to `dir` and most other commands.

These attributes can be viewed and changed in Windows Explorer, but it can be helpful to monitor them from the command line as well. The syntax of the `attrib` command is

attrib [+|-*x* ...] *filename* [**/S** [**/D**]]

where *x* is one of the attribute code letters R, A, S, or H. *Filename* can contain wildcards. Specifying +*x* sets the attribute, and -*x* clears the attribute. If you do not specify any + or - options, attrib lists the current attribute settings of the named file.

The /S option makes attrib apply itself to files in all subfolders of the specified or current folder, and /D makes attrib apply attributes to folders as well as files.

Finding Hidden Files

The command attrib with no arguments lists all files in the current directory, including hidden files. This makes it easy to find hidden files. Here's a sample listing:

```
A           C:\Documents and Settings\bknittel\book.txt
A   H       C:\Documents and Settings\bknittel\NTUSER.DAT
A   H       C:\Documents and Settings\bknittel\ntuser.dat.LOG
A  SH       C:\Documents and Settings\bknittel\ntuser.ini
A           C:\Documents and Settings\bknittel\test.bat
```

All these files have their Archive attribute set. Three are hidden, and NTUSER.INI is marked as System and Hidden. SH files are also called *super hidden*, because no program will touch them unless you remove the S and H attributes.

The command dir /ah also lists hidden files but doesn't show you which files are hidden and which are not.

Setting and Clearing Attributes

Attrib lets you set and clear attributes. To remove the Read-Only attribute from all files in the current folder, type this:

```
attrib -r *.*
```

Alternatively, to make all files read-only, type

```
attrib +r *.*
```

To edit a "super hidden read-only" file such as the Windows XP boot configuration file C:\BOOT.INI, you could use the System Properties dialog box, or you could remove the S, R and H attributes manually, as in this example:

```
attrib -s -h -r boot.ini
notepad boot.ini
attrib +s +h +r boot.ini
```

After editing a file such as boot.ini, it's good practice to restore the file attributes to their original settings, as shown in the example.

The recursive option /S lets you modify attributes in subdirectories. For example, if you've copied a set of MP3 files from a CD-ROM drive onto your hard disk, you'll find that all the files are marked Read-Only. The following commands show how to fix this:

```
cd \music
attrib -r *.mp3 /s
```

For fun, compare this to sample script `script 0407.vbs` in Chapter 4, "File and Registry Access."

`cacls`

Windows XP can use disks formatted with the NTFS file system. In addition to the Read-Only, Hidden, System, and Archive attributes, files and folders can have user-level security attributes as well. User-level security allows users and administrators to control who has access to files and folders and to determine exactly what these users can do. Separate attributes determine whether one can create, delete, read, write, execute, or manage each file and folder.

In most cases, you can manage these properties most effectively with the Properties dialog box in Windows Explorer. However, there are three situations in which the command line is an important alternative:

- When Simple File Sharing is enabled, Windows hides the GUI for file permissions and instead manages all file permission settings automatically.
- On Windows XP Home Edition, Simple File Sharing cannot be disabled. There is no easy way to gain GUI access to file and folder permissions, even though they are active on NTFS-formatted disks.
- Network and system managers may want to modify file permissions with batch files so that the task can be automated and documented.

The Problem with Simple File Sharing

I'd like to take a moment to explain a big potential problem with Simple File Sharing. The problem has to do with moving files between private and shared document folders.

If a file is created in a user's private directory, it will have all access rights enabled for the owner, but no permissions enabled for any other user. This is how Windows makes the files "private." Normally, when files are moved from one folder to another, either with the `move` command or with Windows Explorer, the files' permission settings are not changed. Therefore, if the owner were to drag a private file to a public, shared folder such as Shared Documents (`c:\Documents and Settings\All Users\My Documents`), the file would not be readable by others unless the owner manually opens the file's Properties dialog box and added rights for other users.

This is fairly complex and unintuitive for most users, and it's impossible on Windows XP Home Edition. So, when Simple File Sharing is enabled, Explorer changes its behavior: When it moves files, it changes each file's permission settings to match the default settings of the target directory. Therefore, if you drag a file from a private folder to a shared folder, the file's security settings will be modified to allow reading and writing by others. Likewise, dragging a file from a public folder to a private folder removes the public access permissions.

However, if something goes wrong with this process, or if users move files with Simple File Sharing turned off or with the `move` command-line program, file permissions are not updated, and this can lead to confusion. On Windows XP Home Edition, this can leave files inaccessible.

> Enter `cacls`, which can alter file permissions from the command line. If you're a system manager or a Windows XP power user, you'll want to remember this command in case you ever end up with files stranded by inappropriate file permissions.
>
> Home Edition users can also boot up in Safe Mode and log on as Administrator to gain access to the file Security Properties page in the Explorer GUI. By the way, another problem with Simple File Sharing is the weird place that Microsoft has put the check box that turns it on and off. It's in Windows Explorer, under Tools, Folder Options on the View tab, at the end of the list of advanced options. I recommend that you use a Computer Administrator account to check or uncheck it.

`Cacls` modifies the Access Control List (ACL) that's attached to each file on an NTFS disk. ACLs list users and user groups, along with the associated permissions to read, write, execute, and change files. Files and folders can also inherit permissions from the folder that contains them.

The syntax for the `cacls` command is

```
cacls filename [/T] [/E] [/C] [/G user:perm ...]
    [/R user ...] [/P user:perm ...] [/D user ...]
```

where *`filename`* is the name of the file or folder whose permission you want to modify. You can specify wildcards in the name.

With no other options, `cacls` lists the file or folder's current permission settings. The listing includes the names of users and groups with permissions to the file or folder, followed by code letters that indicate what rights the user or group has. The permission codes may be one of the following:

Code	Meaning
`R`	Read an existing file or folder's contents
`W`	Write (create a new file)
`C`	Read, write, and change an existing file
`F`	All of the above, plus modify permissions

In some cases, when unusual combinations of permissions are applied to a file (for example, Read and Write but not Change), `cacls` may print a more detailed list of specific permissions. `Cacls` can list but not modify these custom permission combinations.

When listing the permissions for a folder, `cacls` may also print the additional codes `(OI)`, `(CI)`, and `(IO)`, which have the following meanings:

Code	Meaning
`CI`	Container Inherit. The entry applies to subfolders of this folder.
`OI`	Object Inherit. The entry applies to files in this folder.
`IO`	Inherit Only. The access entry applies to subfolders and files but not to the folder itself.

For a typical private file, the `cacls` listing might look like this:

```
C:\plans\strita.xls JAVA\bknittel:F
                    NT AUTHORITY\SYSTEM:F
                    BUILTIN\Administrators:F
```

This indicates that three entities have Full permissions to this file. The entities are as follows:

- `JAVA\bknittel`, a standard local user account. Local user account names begin with the name of the computer.
- `NT AUTHORITY\SYSTEM`, the Windows operating system itself. `SYSTEM` is usually granted rights to all files.
- `BUILTIN\Administrators`, the local "Administrators" group. The Administrator account and any other Computer Administrator users are members of this group.

These are the normal settings for a private file. For public files, an additional entry, either `Everyone:R` or `Everyone:RWC`, gives all other users the ability to read or to read and change the file.

With command-line arguments, `cacls` modifies file permissions. The arguments are described in Table 14.3.

Table 14.3 **Options for the *cacls* Command**

Option	Description
`/T`	Recursively processes all subfolders, seeking the specified name or names. With filename `*.*`, this option processes all files in all subfolders.
`/E`	Edits the file or folder's ACL. Permissions on the command line are added to any existing permissions. Without `/E`, the file's ACL is deleted and then replaced with the permissions specified on the command line.
`/C`	When the filename is specified with wildcards, `/C` makes `cacls` continue with other files if it encounters an error. An error may occur if you do not have permission to modify the settings of a file or if the file is in use.
`/G` *`user:perm`*	Grants (adds) the listed permissions for the specified user or user group. *`Perm`* can be any or all of the letters `R` (Read), `W` (Write), `C` (Change) and `F` (Full Control). You can list more than one *`user:perm`* item to add permissions for multiple users or groups.
`/R` *`user`*	Removes all permissions for the specified user or group. This option is only applicable when used with `/E`.
`/P` *`user:perm`*	Replaces the permissions for the specified user or group with the listed codes. In addition to the four codes listed under `/G`, you can specify `/P` *`user`*`:N`, which means *no permissions*. This is the same as specifying `/R`.
`/D` *`user`*	Denies access by the specified user. Be careful with `/D`, because it "trumps" any permissions to access the file.

Checking Permissions

If users have difficulty accessing a file, the easiest way to identify the problem is to view the file's properties in Windows Explorer. Select the Security tab and view the settings for each entry. If the Security tab doesn't appear on Windows XP Professional, you can temporarily disable Simple File Sharing to make it appear. Click Tools, Folder Options,View and uncheck Simple File Sharing at the bottom of the Advanced Settings list.

If you don't want to do this or if you have Windows XP Home Edition, log on as a Computer Administrator, open a Command Prompt window, change to the directory containing the file in question, and then type `cacls` *`filename`*. The listing should show you whether the user has access to the file.

Granting Permissions to Everyone

If a file has been moved to a public, shared folder but isn't accessible by other users, you can fix the problem with `cacls`. Log on as a Computer Administrator or as the owner of the file, open a Command Prompt window, change to the folder containing the file, and type the command

```
cacls filename /E /G everyone:RWC
```

where *`filename`* is the name of the file you'd like to make available. You can use wildcards (for example, `*.*`) to fix multiple files with one command. You can also name specific users. For example,

```
cacls filename /E /G norm:RWC bob:RWC
```

grants permissions to the user accounts Norm and Bob, without making the file available to Everyone. (However, if Simple File Sharing is enabled, Norm and Bob won't be able to access the file over the network. You have to grant access to Everyone for network users to be able to use a file when Simple File Sharing is in effect.)

Making a File or Folder Private

To make a file private, it's best to remove specific users and groups using the `/R` command. For example, to remove access by Everyone, use the following command:

```
cacls filename /E /R everyone
```

To modify a folder and all the folder's contents, you can modify the folder's properties and then use the recursive option to modify all files and subfolders, as in this example:

```
cd \foldername
cacls . /E /R everyone
calcs *.* /T /E /R everyone
```

Caution

Be *very* careful when using `cacls` with folders. If you remove essential permissions from a system folder such as `\Windows`, the operating system may stop working. Use the GUI to make changes in file permissions whenever you can.

Management Power Tools

Quite a few command-line utilities are available that make short work of some tedious Windows management tasks. This section shows you some handy tools to help you manage Windows XP computers from the command line.

driverquery

`Driverquery` lists the names of all device drivers installed on a computer. You can list the drivers for the local computer or another computer on your network. The default listing format looks like this:

```
Module Name  Display Name           Driver Type   Link Date
============ ====================== ============= ======================
ACPI         Microsoft ACPI Driver  Kernel        8/17/2001 1:57:52 PM
ACPIEC       ACPIEC                 Kernel        8/17/2001 1:57:55 PM
aec          Microsoft Kernel Acous Kernel        10/12/2001 1:45:40 PM
AFD          AFD Networking Support Kernel        8/17/2001 6:30:36 PM
AsyncMac     RAS Asynchronous Media Kernel        8/17/2001 1:55:29 PM
atapi        Standard IDE/ESDI Hard Kernel        8/17/2001 1:51:49 PM
.
.
.
```

You can run `driverquery` with no arguments to display the list for the local computer, or you can add `/S` ***`computername`*** to list the drivers on another computer. If you are denied access to the remote computer, you can add the additional options `/u` ***`username`*** `/p` to use an alternate account, such as Administrator. `Driverquery` will prompt you for the account's password.

Note

If you have a network drive mapped to the remote computer using your own user account, you will not be able to specify an alternate account name to `driverquery`, because Windows only permits you to attach to a given remote computer with one account at a time.

By default, `driverquery` prints a table formatted as shown in the earlier example. If you want to import the information into a spreadsheet, you can add the option line break `/FO CSV` to format the results with quotes and commas between the columns.

`Driverquery` has a few other options that you can try. The most interesting are `/V`, which adds additional columns such as the device driver's filename and its running/not running status, and `/SI`, which adds information about the driver's installation file and manufacturer. Despite what the online help says, `/SI` displays information about unsigned drivers as well as signed drivers.

To see the whole list of options, type `driverquery /?`.

runas

Windows XP limits the ability of most user accounts to modify the operating system and to view other users' files. When you need to perform a management operation, though, it can be inconvenient to log off and back on as Administrator.

The `runas` command lets you run some applications as another (usually privileged) user while remaining simultaneously logged on with your own user account. `Runas` is great when you want to run a setup program or examine files you don't normally have access to. If you used `runas` with Windows 2000, you'll be pleased to find that there is no longer a long delay when it starts up the requested program.

Here's the syntax of `runas`:

runas [(**/noprofile** | **/profile**)] [**/env**] [**/netonly**] [**/smartcard**]
  /user:*username command*

If *command* contains spaces or command-line arguments, you must surround it with quotes.

After you type the command, `runas` prompts for the alternate account's password. The command options are shown in Table 14.4.

Table 14.4 **Options for the *runas* Command**

Option	Description
`/noprofile`	Tells `runas` not to load the user's Registry settings. This may cause some programs to malfunction.
`/profile`	Loads the user's Registry settings. This is the default.
`/env`	Uses the current environment variables rather than the user's default variables.
`/netonly`	The command will only be used to access the network, not local files.
`/smartcard`	Obtains the user credentials from a smartcard.
`/user:`*username*	Runs the command using the specified user account.
`command line`	The command to run and its arguments.

There are two common uses for `runas`. The first is to install a program from a CD, as in this example:

```
runas /user:Administrator d:setup
```

The second is to open a Command Prompt window with Administrator privileges:

```
runas /user:Administrator cmd
```

You cannot run Windows Explorer or any of its derivative programs—Control Panel, My Computer, My Documents, and so on—due to the fact that Explorer is not a normal program but rather is tied in peculiar ways into the Windows operating system itself. (This could conceivably change as a result of pending antitrust remedies, but for now, it's a limitation.) However, you can run individual Control Panel applets if you know the associated CPL filename (refer to Table 14.1). For example, you can run the System Properties applet with this command:

```
runas /user:Administrator "control sysdm.cpl"
```

tasklist

`Tasklist` displays a list of all running processes on the system. This information is helpful when you want to see whether a program is running inappropriately or if you suspect that some essential program or system service is no longer running. It can also display information about the DLL program files in use by each process.

`Tasklist` has several options that you can see by typing `tasklist /?`. Here, I'll just discuss the most interesting options. With no option, `tasklist`'s default output looks something like this:

```
Image Name                   PID Session Name     Session#    Mem Usage
========================= ====== ================ ======== ============
System Idle Process            0 Console                 0         20 K
System                         4 Console                 0        216 K
smss.exe                     484 Console                 0        348 K
csrss.exe                    540 Console                 0      2,756 K
winlogon.exe                 568 Console                 0      2,896 K
.
.
.
setiathome.exe              1516 Console                 0     16,324 K
cmd.exe                     2604 Console                 0        900 K
tasklist.exe                2112 Console                 0      2,824 K
```

The columns are explained in Table 14.5.

Table 14.5 **Columns Headings in the *tasklist* Printout**

Heading	**Description**
Image Name	The name of the program file.
PID	Process Identifier. A number that uniquely identifies each running program.
Session Name	This field is blank for programs started as Windows services and displays Console for programs started by users physically at the computer. The session name will be different for users attached via Remote Desktop or Windows Terminal Services.
Session#	When you use Fast User Switching, the first logged-on user's tasks are listed under session #0, the second user's tasks under session #1, and so on.
Mem Usage	The amount of memory in use by the program. This may total more than the amount of physical memory because some programs may be paged out.

The listing shows both system service processes and user programs. The `/V` option adds additional columns: the program status (running/not responding), the program's username, total CPU time, and window title, if any.

You can export `tasklist`'s output to a spreadsheet by adding the `/FO CSV` option. For example, the command

```
tasklist /fo csv >tasks.txt
```

saves the current task list into a text file that you can then import into an Excel spreadsheet as a comma-delimited file.

System service tasks may actually provide several distinct services. The `/SVC` option lists the services provided by each task, as in this example:

```
Image Name                   PID Services
==================== ====== ========================================
services.exe                 612 Eventlog, PlugPlay
lsass.exe                    628 PolicyAgent, ProtectedStorage, SamSs
svchost.exe                  796 RpcSs
svchost.exe                  940 Dnscache
svchost.exe                  968 LmHosts, RemoteRegistry, SSDPSRV, WebClient
spoolsv.exe                 1036 Spooler
.
.
.
```

Software developers may be interested in seeing which DLL files are loaded by each task. The `/M` option prints this information, as in this example:

```
Image Name                       PID Modules
========================= ====== ======================================
cmd.exe                         2876 ntdll.dll, kernel32.dll, msvcrt.dll,
                                     USER32.dll, GDI32.dll, ADVAPI32.dll,
                                     RPCRT4.dll, Apphelp.dll
```

You can also view the task list information for another computer by adding the `/S` *`computername`* option. As with `driverquery`, you may need to use a privileged account name by additionally adding `/U` *`username`* `/P`.

`Tasklist` is most helpful when a program has crashed but left "pieces" of itself running. Microsoft Word is notorious for this; sometimes Word crashes and disappears from the normal Task Manager Applications display, but `tasklist` will show that a process named `winword.exe` is still running. You can't start Word again until this rogue process has been terminated with `taskkill`.

taskkill

`Taskkill` lets you terminate programs running on your computer or another networked computer based on the program's username, session number, Process ID (PID) number, or program name. `Taskkill` is especially useful because it can sometimes terminate tasks that refuse to disappear when you try to kill them with the Task Manager dialog box.

`Taskkill` has many options, more than you'll ever need. In fact, it should have been named `overkill`. (Sorry, I had to.) You can see the whole list by typing `taskkill /?`. Here, I'll discuss just a few of the most useful options.

Killing a Process by PID Number

If you can find the PID number of an errant program either in the output of `tasklist` or in the Task Manager dialog box, then you can type

```
taskkill /pid pidnumber /f /t
```

entering the actual process ID number in place of *`pidnumber`*.

The `/F` option tells Windows to terminate the task "forcefully," and `/T` terminates any child tasks or subprograms started by the program in question. In most cases, this solves the problem. If this doesn't work, you might try running the `taskkill` program as Administrator:

```
runas /user:Administrator taskkill /pid pidnumber /f /t
```

`Taskkill` can also terminate processes on a remote computer using the `/S` *`computername`* option, following the same format described earlier for `tasklist`.

Killing the Processes of Another User

If you have to kill tasks belonging to another user (for example, one who has logged off using Fast User Switching), you must use an Administrator account. It's probably best to log on as Administrator and use the Task Manager dialog box to fix this, but you can use `taskkill` as well. The command would be

```
taskkill /FI "USERNAME eq username"
```

where *`username`* is the account's name; it can be a plain name for a local account, or it can be `username@domain` or `domain\username` for a domain account. You can run this from a nonprivileged account using the `runas` command, as shown in a previous example.

Use this form of the command first to let any programs that are willing to exit gracefully do so. Then, repeat the command with `/F /T` at the end to dispatch any stragglers.

Killing Processes by Program Name

You can terminate a task based on its program name using this form of the `taskkill` command:

```
taskkill /IM programfile
```

Here, *`programfile`* is the name of the program's EXE file (for example, `winword.exe`). You can use wildcards with this name; for example, `note*` kills `notepad.exe` as well as note-anything-else. Be *very* careful when using wildcards, because you don't want to terminate any essential Windows services by accident.

sc

`Sc` is called the Service Controller program, and for good reason. `Sc` can manage just about every aspect of installing, maintaining, and modifying system services and device drivers on local and networked Windows XP computers. It's another command with a huge number of options, which you can list by typing `sc /?`. It has so many options that after printing the `/?` help information, it prompts you to see whether you want to view additional information about its `query` and `queryex` subcommands.

The basic format of an `sc` command is as follows:

`sc` [*`servername`*] *`command`* [*`servicename`* [*`option`* ...]]

If the *`servername`* argument is omitted, `sc` operates on the local computer. There is no provision for entering an alternate username or password, so you'll need to be logged on as Administrator or use the `runas` command if you want to do more than view the installed services.

In the next sections, I list some of the more useful sc commands. If you maintain Windows XP computers, you should carefully examine the complete list of commands yourself, though, because you may have different ideas about what makes a command interesting.

Listing Installed Services

The command sc queryex prints a long list of installed services along with their current run states. A typical service listing looks like this:

```
SERVICE_NAME: Dhcp
DISPLAY_NAME: DHCP Client
       TYPE               : 20  WIN32_SHARE_PROCESS
       STATE              : 4  RUNNING
                               (STOPPABLE,NOT_PAUSABLE,ACCEPTS_SHUTDOWN)
       WIN32_EXIT_CODE    : 0  (0x0)
       SERVICE_EXIT_CODE  : 0  (0x0)
       CHECKPOINT         : 0x0
       WAIT_HINT          : 0x0
       PID                : 844
       FLAGS              :
```

The most useful parts of this listing are detailed in Table 14.6.

Table 14.6 **Useful Fields in *sc queryex* Printout**

Field	Description
SERVICE_NAME	The "short" name for the service. This name can be used with the net command to start and stop the service.
DISPLAY_NAME	The "long" name for the service. This name is displayed in the Services panel in Windows Management.
STATE	The service's current activity state.
PID	The service's process identifier.

You can add type= driver or type= service (with a space after the equals sign) to the sc queryex command to limit the listing to just drivers or just services.

Starting and Stopping Services

System managers occasionally need to start and stop services for several reasons: to reset a malfunctioning service, to force a service to reinitialize itself with new startup data, or to temporarily stop a service while other services are being maintained. You can manage services using the GUI Windows Management tool, but when you have to perform this sort of task frequently, it's more convenient to use a batch file. For instance, I use a batch file to stop and restart my company's mail server after I make changes to its configuration file. Typing the batch file's name (downup, in case you're curious) is much easier than navigating through Computer Management.

To use `sc` to start and stop services on a local or remote computer, you must know the service's "short" name. The easiest way to find a service's short name is to use `sc queryex` to get the listing of all service names. Then, you can use the commands

```
sc stop servicename
sc \\computername stop servicename
```

to stop a service on the local computer or on a remote computer specified by *`computername`*, respectively. Likewise, you can use the commands

```
sc start servicename
sc \\computername start servicename
```

to start services.

Note

Sc has many other commands that let you install and configure services as well as interrogate their operational status and dependency lists. The installation commands can be especially useful if you need to deploy services in an enterprise environment.

Networking Utilities

Networking is one the strongest features of Windows, and this shows in the breadth of command-line utilities provided for network management and debugging. Besides the tools provided to manage Windows networking for file and printer sharing, Windows comes with a whole set of standard TCP/IP programs that any Unix user will find instantly familiar. The Berkeley Unix "r" programs and the Unix printer programs `lpq` and `lpr` are here, as are standard TCP/IP tools such as `ping`, `ftp`, and `nslookup`. I don't have room to describe all the networking tools provided with Windows, but I've chosen six that I've found to be extremely useful. You can find the others listed in Appendix E.

ipconfig

`Ipconfig` is a handy utility that shows you the status of your computer's TCP/IP networking configuration. It's especially useful when you use dial-up networking, Virtual Private Networking (VPN), or LAN adapters with automatic IP address assignment, because `ipconfig` can tell you what IP address information has been assigned to these dynamically configured connections. `Ipconfig` can also release and re-request automatically assigned IP addresses for your LAN adapters.

Listing IP Address Information

In its simplest form, the command `ipconfig` displays the current IP address, subnet mask, and gateway address for any active LAN adapters and dial-up networking connections, including dial-up Internet connections. The output looks like this:

```
Windows IP Configuration

Ethernet adapter Local Area Connection:

        Connection-specific DNS Suffix  . : mycompany.com
        IP Address. . . . . . . . . . . . : 192.168.0.3
        Subnet Mask . . . . . . . . . . . : 255.255.255.0
        Default Gateway . . . . . . . . . : 192.168.0.1
```

With the `/all` option, `ipconfig` displays additional information about each connection. The output looks like this:

```
Windows IP Configuration

        Host Name . . . . . . . . . . . . : java
        Primary Dns Suffix  . . . . . . . :
        Node Type . . . . . . . . . . . . : Unknown
        IP Routing Enabled. . . . . . . . : No
        WINS Proxy Enabled. . . . . . . . : No
        DNS Suffix Search List. . . . . . : mycompany.com

Ethernet adapter Local Area Connection:

        Connection-specific DNS Suffix  . : mycompany.com
        Description . . . . . . . . . . . : SMC EZ Card 10/100 PCI
        Physical Address. . . . . . . . . : 00-E2-4F-11-39-47
        Dhcp Enabled. . . . . . . . . . . : No
        IP Address. . . . . . . . . . . . : 192.168.0.3
        Subnet Mask . . . . . . . . . . . : 255.255.255.0
        Default Gateway . . . . . . . . . : 192.168.0.1
        DNS Servers . . . . . . . . . . . : 192.168.0.2
```

This is very helpful information to have when you're diagnosing network and Internet problems. What's more, if you're using a dial-up connection or a DHCP-configured LAN connection, this is the only way to get this information. The most important items are listed in Table 14.7.

Table 14.7 **Information Displayed by *ipconfig /all***

Heading	Description
Host Name	This computer's name for TCP/IP purposes; does not necessarily match the Windows Networking computer name.
Primary DNS Suffix	The primary DNS domain name for the computer. This is set in the System Properties dialog box by clicking Change, More.

Heading	Description
Node Type	The NetBIOS node type. This is usually Hybrid on systems that use NetBIOS networking.
Connection-specific DNS Suffix	The DNS domain name for a specific connection.
Description	The name of the network adapter or dial-up networking adapter for this connection.
Dhcp Enabled	Yes, if the connection is set for automatic configuration.
IP Address	The IP address assigned to this connection.
Subnet Mask	The subnet mask for this connection.
Default Gateway	The default gateway (router) for this connection.
DNS Servers	DNS servers.

`Ipconfig` information can be especially helpful in debugging certain networking problems:

- If the IP address is listed as Autoconfiguration IP Address, then Windows was unable to locate a DHCP server for this LAN adapter. Unless you have built a small network without a DHCP server, a connection-sharing router, or Windows Internet Connection Sharing, this usually indicates a failure of the network wiring or of the DHCP server.
- If the IP address is listed as 0.0.0.0, the indicated adapter is disconnected.
- If the IP address is inappropriate for the network to which you are connected, you have probably relocated your computer from one network to another and need to reset and renew your IP address. I'll show how in a moment.

Resetting Automatically Assigned Addresses

If your network uses DHCP to automatically assign IP addresses to computers, you may occasionally run into problems where an address is not assigned to your computer or is not reassigned when you unplug from one network and connect to another. You can quickly fix this problem with `ipconfig` by typing the commands

```
ipconfig /release
ipconfig /renew
```

Tip

These commands will often restore a disabled cable modem or DSL connection.

Examining and Clearing the DNS Cache

When Windows has to find the IP address for a given hostname, it remembers the results for a short time in order to save time when making subsequent connections to the same site. If Windows fails to find an address for a given name, this fact is also remembered for a short time—again, to save time and trouble for future lookups. The information is stored in what's called the DNS Resolver Cache.

You can display the contents of this cache with the command `ipconfig /displaydns`. You can erase all the cached information with `ipconfig /flushdns`. This can be helpful if, for example, your organization changes IP addresses or if a site was temporarily offline but has been restored. Clearing the DNS cache removes all obsolete information.

Other variations of the `ipconfig` command let you reset the DHCP information for individual adapters and let you assign a DHCP "class" name. Type `ipconfig /?` for more information.

net

The `net` command provides several tools for configuring network mappings and shares, and it can even add user accounts. It's a strange command that dates back to the earliest days of networking with PCs. The `net` command has 22 subcommands. You can view the list of commands online by typing `net help`, and you can get additional help for any individual command by typing `net help` ***`command`***, where ***`command`*** is one of the names listed in the following sections. If you type `net /?` or `net command /?`, you still get online help, although the text is less detailed.

I'll won't describe all 22 of the `net` commands in the following sections. The three most useful, important commands are `net help`, `net use`, and `net view`. These are useful on a day-to-day basis. Several others can be used to manage Windows and user accounts.

net continue

The command `net continue` resumes a system service that was suspended by `net pause`. The `net` command, like `sc`, can be used to control system services. The syntax is `net continue "`*`servicename`*`"`, where *`servicename`* is the "display" name for the service. If the name contains spaces, you must surround it in quotes.

`Net continue`, `net pause`, `net start`, and `net stop` work only with the local computer. The `sc` command, discussed earlier in the chapter, can work with the local computer or with any networked computer, so for service management, I recommend that you use `sc` instead of the `net` commands.

net file

The command `net file` displays the names of all the local computer's shared files that are currently opened by remote network users. The output looks like this:

```
ID        Path                              User name          # Locks
----------------------------------------------------------------------
17        c:\book\test1.bat                 ADMINISTRATOR      0
```

The listing shows the local names of the files and the user account that is using each file, but not the computer from which the remote user has connected. If necessary, you can close a file opened by a remote user by typing `net file` *`id`* `/close`, where *`id`* is one of the ID numbers displayed in the `net file` listing. You would only want to do this if you were sure that the remote user had gone away or that his or her computer had crashed.

net group

The command `net group` adds domain global groups to Windows NT 4 and Windows 2000 Domain Controller computers. Groups are used to simplify file security on disks formatted with the NTFS file system: You can add users to a group and then assign file permissions to the group, rather than to the individuals. Here's the syntax for creating and deleting global groups:

```
net group groupname [/comment:"text"] /add [/domain]
net group groupname [/comment:"text"] /delete [/domain]
```

The optional `/comment` option adds a text description of the group. The `/domain` option must be used if the `net group` command is issued from a domain member computer rather than from the domain controller. You must have Domain Administrator privileges to use this command.

You can add users to and delete users from the group with the following commands:

```
net group groupname username... /add
net group groupname username... /delete
```

However, usernames may not contain `@`, `/`, or `\` characters, so in an Active Directory environment, this command may not be terribly useful.

net help

The command `net help` displays online help for any of the `net` commands. Type `net help` for a complete listing of the documented commands.

net helpmsg

The command `net helpmsg` *`number`* displays the error message text for a numerical Windows error code. These numerical codes are displayed by some programs.

net localgroup

The command `net localgroup` creates local security groups on the local computer. `Net localgroup` works on any version of Windows NT, 2000, and XP, including Home Edition.

The syntax for creating and deleting local groups is as follows:

```
net localgroup groupname [/comment:"text"] /add [/domain]
net localgroup groupname [/comment:"text"] /delete [/domain]
```

The optional `/comment` option adds a text description of the group. The `/domain` option adds the group as a Domain Local group on the current domain controller, rather than on the local workstation.

You can add users to and delete users from the group with the following commands:

```
net localgroup groupname username... /add
net localgroup groupname username... /delete
```

net pause

The command `net pause` temporarily suspends a system service. The syntax of the command is

```
net pause "servicename"
```

See the `net continue` command discussion for more information about the service control. You can get a list of currently running services by typing `net start`.

net print

The command `net print` lets you view and manage the print queues of the local computer.

Here's the syntax to view a remote printer queue:

```
net print \\computername\sharename
```

This lists any pending print jobs. For example, on my network, the command `net print \\sumatra\okidata` printed this listing:

```
Name                          Job #      Size             Status
-------------------------------------------------------------------------
okidata Queue               1 jobs
     bknittel                 109      12380            Waiting
```

The listing shows that one print job is pending, which `bknittel` submitted. The job identification number 109.

You can suspend, release, or delete a print job with the following command:

```
net print \\computername jobnumber {/hold | /release | /delete}
```

For example, `net print \\sumatra 109 /delete` deletes the job pending in my printer's queue.

`Net print` is not as useful as the Printers & Faxes Control Panel display, but it might be useful if you are connecting to a Windows computer using text-based `telnet`. If you want to automate print job management, though, Windows Script Host with WMI is probably a better approach.

net send

The command `net send` sends a message to other users on your network. The syntax is

```
net send {name | * | /domain[:dname] | /users} "message text"
```

The message text is sent to one or more users, depending on the format of the name:

Format	Sends the Message To
name	A specific user or computer
*	All users on the local network
/domain	All users in the current domain
/domain:name	All users in the specified domain
/users	All users attached to files or printers shared by this computer

Messages are only received by currently logged-on users. You can use `net send` to announce imminent system shutdowns and maintenance concerns, but it's not very useful beyond this.

Caution

Net messaging is neither secure nor reliable. The messaging service doesn't always work. Also, if someone registers your logon name before you log on, when you do log on your computer will not be able to register your name. You'll receive no warning, and the other user will receive messages addressed to you.

Don't rely on `net send` for any important messaging, and if you do use it for maintenance announcements, you should use it in addition to, not instead of, normal communication methods, such as e-mail, corporate memos, and so on.

net session

The command `net session` displays all the connections from other computers to your computer's shared files and printers. A session represents the connection itself, and there is only one per remote computer, regardless how many files the other computer is using. (There may be an additional session listed for a given remote computer if that computer is using your computer's shared Internet connection.) The output of the `net session` looks like this:

```
Computer            User name         Client Type        Opens Idle time
-------------------------------------------------------------------------
\\BALI              ADMINISTRATOR     Windows 2000 2195      1 00:00:00
\\SUMATRA                             Windows 2000 2195      3 00:00:17
```

The listing shows the names of the remote computers connected to yours, the remote user's name (if known), the remote computer's operating system, the number of files or folders that the remote user has open, and the amount of time since the last activity.

You can find out more about the activities of an individual connection with the command

```
net session \\computername
```

which lists the shared folders and printers that the remote user is currently using.

In case of an emergency, you can forcibly disconnect a remote user with the following command:

```
net session \\computername /delete
```

net share

The command `net share` displays and manages shared folders offered by your computer. The basic command `net share` displays a list of all folders currently shared by your computer. On my computer, for instance, the listing looks like this:

```
Share name   Resource                        Remark
-------------------------------------------------------------------------------
IPC$                                         Remote IPC
C$           C:\                             Default share
ADMIN$       C:\WINDOWS                      Remote Admin
CDROM        E:\
SharedDocs   C:\DOCUMENTS AND SETTINGS\ALL USERS.WINDOWS\DOCUMENTS
```

The `IPC$`, `C$`, and `ADMIN$` shares are set up by Windows for administrative use. Windows XP automatically shares the All Users "My Documents" folder as "SharedDocs." I added the `CDROM` share myself.

You can also use `net share` to add and delete shared folders from the command line. There are three versions of the command. Here's the first version:

```
net share sharename=drive:path [/users:number | /unlimited]
    [/remark:text] [/cache:{Manual | Documents | Programs | None}]
```

This shares the folder specified by *`drive:path`* as shared folder *`sharename`*. You can optionally limit the number of connections to the share with the `/users` option. You can record descriptive text with the `/remark` option, and on Windows XP Professional, you can specify how the files in this folder are to be treated if the remote user requests them to be made available while offline.

```
net share sharename [/users:number | /unlimited]
    [/remark:text] [/cache:{Manual | Documents | Programs | None}]
```

This version of the command changes the user restrictions, remark text, and offline usage hints for an existing share.

```
net share {sharename | devicename | drive:path} /delete
```

This final version of the command cancels sharing of a folder or printer. You can specify the share name or drive and path to cancel folder sharing, or you can specify the name of a printer queue to cancel printer sharing.

`Net share` is a convenient way to share and "unshare" folders, and it can be faster to use than the Windows Explorer GUI.

net start

The command `net start` lists active services. The names listed by this command are the long "display" names that you can also view with the `sc queryex` command, described earlier in the chapter. `Net start`, however, lists only running services.

You can start an inactive service with the command `net start "servicename"`. However, `net start` can only start services on the local computer. The `sc` command is more useful because it can also start services on remote computers.

net statistics

The command `net statistics workstation` displays information about your computer's use of remote network resources. It lists the number of bytes sent and received, the total read and write operations, and error statistics.

The command `net statistics server` displays information about other computers' use of files and printers shared by your computer, including bytes sent and received, password errors, and the number of files opened.

net stop

The command `net stop "servicename"` stops a system service on your computer. You must specify the long "display" name of the service, as listed by `sc queryex` or `net start`.

Tip

If you suspect that someone is inappropriately accessing shared files on your computer, you can instantly stop file sharing by typing `net stop server`. If you are not a computer administrator, you must type `runas /user:Administrator "net stop server"`.

net time

Keeping a group of computers' clocks accurate and in sync is an important but tedious task. Windows can be configured to automatically set the computer's clock to match that of another computer. This way, you only need to worry about keeping one clock set correctly, and the others will match it.

Windows XP computers that are members of a domain network usually are configured to automatically sync clocks to the domain controller or another master computer. Standalone or workgroup computers are usually set up to synchronize over the Internet to `time.windows.com` or a national time server. You can also use the `net time` command to manage clock settings and to verify correct configuration. `Net time` allows you to synchronize your computer's clock to a master clock on your network, or to display or modify a domain member computer's automatic synchronization settings. There are several versions of the command. Here's the first:

```
net time [/set]
```

This version displays the date and time on the computer designated as your domain's master time server. This variation is valid only on domain member computers. With the `/set` option, this command sets your computer's clock to match the master computer's.

```
net time {\\computername | /domain[:domainname] | /rtsserver[:domainname]} [/set]
```

This version of the command displays the time on a specified computer, on the primary domain controller of the current or specified domain, or on the Reliable Time Server of the current or specified domain. With the `/set` option, this command sets your computer's clock to match this time. This command can be used on workgroup or domain member computers to synchronize clocks to a central computer.

```
net time [\\computername] /querysntp
```

This version of the command displays the current or specified computer's designated master Network Time Protocol (NTP) server. This command lets you verify that domain member computers are correctly configured.

```
net time [\\computername] /setsntp:"server list"
```

This final version of the command designates one or more NTP servers as the time server for the local or specified computer. The server list can be one or more DNS names or IP addresses separated by spaces. When the computer synchronizes its clock, it will try each NTP server in turn until it finds one that responds.

Tip

If network Internet access isn't available on your small workgroup network, you can still get the benefits of a central clock. Choose one computer to be the master time keeper. Suppose its name is "homer." On your other computers, put the command `net time \\homer /set` in each user's logon script or in the Local Computer Policy Logon or Startup script. This will sync up each computer's clock to the timekeeper whenever someone logs on.

net use

The command `net use` is the most important and useful of the `net` commands because it lets you map network drives and network printers from the command line.

It's useful not only while working directly at the command prompt, but especially in batch files, where it can automatically configure the necessary network environment before the batch file starts copying or printing files.

Here are the most useful variations of the command:

```
net use
```

This version of the command displays a list of all network drive and printer mappings currently in effect. This is a *very* useful command because it instantly shows you what network drives are available and where they point.

```
net use drive: \\computer\sharename
```

This version of the command maps drive letter `drive` to a network shared folder named `\\computer\sharename`. This is the plain-vanilla version of the command. The next variation shows all the available options.

```
net use drive: \\computer\sharename[\subfolder...]
   [[password] {/user:username | /smartcard} [/savecred]]
   [/persistent:{yes|no}]
```

If you specify one or more subfolder names after the share name, the mapped drive will consider that subfolder to be the root directory of the drive, and it will not be able to "see" upper-level directories. Novell NetWare users are familiar with this as the "map root" function.

The `/persistent` option lets you specify whether the mapping will be automatically reinstated when you log off and back on. The default setting is `yes`, although you can change the default.

By default, the connection to the remote computer is made using your username and password. If you wish to use an alternate account, you can add the `/user` option or the `/smartcard` option. If you specify a username, you can enter it in any of the standard formats: *`username`*, *`domain\username`*, or *`username@domain`*.

Note

You can only connect to a given remote computer with one user account at a time. It's not possible to map one drive letter using your own account and a different drive letter with an alternate account.

You can specify the alternate account's password on the command line just before the `/user` option. It's a security risk to store passwords in batch files, however. Fortunately, two better alternatives are available. If you omit the password or specify `*` in its place, `net use` will prompt you for the password. You can also instruct `net use` to prompt once and then remember the password by adding the `/savecred` option.

```
net use lptN: \\computer\sharename [user and persistence options]
```

This version of the command maps a remote network printer to an LPT port for use by DOS programs. You can map ports LPT1 through LPT9, if desired; however, you cannot map an LPT port name that is used by a locally attached printer. This version of the command supports the same alternate user and `/persistent` options as the drive-mapping command described previously.

net use *device*: **/del**[**ete**]

This version of the command deletes a drive or printer mapping. *Device* is the drive letter or LPT port to delete.

net use *drive*: **/home**

This version of the command maps a drive letter to your account's designated "home" directory. This command works only when you are logged on to a domain user account and when the system administrator has specified a home directory for your account. This command can be helpful in batch files and logon scripts.

As mentioned earlier, `net use` by itself displays all network mappings. The listing looks like this:

```
Status       Local      Remote                   Network
-------------------------------------------------------------------------------
OK           K:         \\sumatra\cdrive         Microsoft Windows Network
OK           LPT1       \\sumatra\okidata        Microsoft Windows Network
```

This shows that drive K: is mapped to shared folder `\\sumatra\cdrive`, and that DOS printer LPT1 is mapped to `\\sumatra\okidata`.

The Status column shows that the connections to `\\sumatra` are currently active. You may see the status change to Disconnected when you first log on or after 20 minutes or so of inactivity, but this usually is not an indication of a problem. Windows reestablishes the connection automatically when you attempt to use the drive or printer.

I have found `net use` to be of most use in making batch files that I use for automatic backups and to use networked applications. Here's one automatic backup batch file I use:

```
@rem                                          Example File batch1401.bat
@echo off
net use z: /del >nul 2>nul
net use z: \\bali\backups
if errorlevel 1 (
    echo The network drive is not available
    exit /b 1
)
xcopy "%userprofile%\My Documents" "z:\%username%" /H/K/R/E/D/I/Z/C
if errorlevel 1 (
    echo The backup copy encountered errors
    exit /b 1
)
net use z: /del
```

The first net use command in this program deletes any existing mapping for drive Z. Because there may not be a current mapping and I don't want to see the error message if there isn't, the standard output and standard error streams are redirected to the "null" file—the output just disappears.

The second net use command maps drive Z: to a backup folder on my file server. Then, xcopy copies my My Documents folder to my own personal subdirectory on the file server. The environment variables %userprofile% and %username% let any user on my network use the same batch file. The script ends by removing the drive mapping as part of a general good-housekeeping practice.

There are three additional variations of net use that I've found to be of little or no practical use. Here's the first variation:

```
net use \\computer\sharename[\subfolder...]
   [[{password | *}] {/user:username | /smartcard} [/savecred]]
   [/persistent:{yes|no}]
```

This version of the command establishes a connection to a shared folder without mapping a drive letter. This allows quicker access if you later connect to the shared folder using its UNC name (*computer**sharename*) in Windows Explorer or other applications.

```
net use \\computer\sharename /delete
```

This version of the command disconnects a shared folder that was attached without a drive letter.

```
net use /persistent:(yes | no)
```

This version of the command sets the default persistence setting to yes or no. This default will apply when you issue future net use commands without specifying the /persistent option.

Most of the time, you'll use just the basic versions of net use.

net user

The command net user without options lists all local user accounts on the computer. Net user *username* lists information for the specified user account, including the last logon date, the user's full name, time and station restrictions, profile and home directories, the logon script setting, and group memberships.

You can also use net user to create and manage accounts. There are several variations. Here's the first:

```
net user username [password] /add options [/domain]
```

This version of the command creates a user account with the specified username. If you omit the password, the account will be created with no password. You can set the account's password on the command line, or you can specify `*`, which will make `net user` prompt you to enter the new account's password. The `/domain` option adds the account as a domain account rather than as a local account. The options are listed in Table 14.8.

net user *username* [*password*] *options* [**/domain**]

This version of the command modifies the password and/or options of an existing local or domain account. For example, `net user` *`username`* `/active:no` disables an account without deleting it. The options are listed in Table 14.8.

net user *username* **/delete** [**/domain**

This final version of the command deletes the specified user account from the local computer or from the domain controller.

Table 14.8 lists the account options that `net user` can set or modify.

Table 14.8 **Options for the *net user* Command**

Option	**Description**
/active:{**yes** | **no**}	Activates or deactivates the account; inactive accounts cannot access the server or log on.
/comment:"*text*"	Adds a descriptive label for the account.
/countrycode:*n*	Sets the account's primary language code number to *n*.
/expires:{*date* | **never**}	Sets the expiration date for the account. If specified, *date* uses the local date format.
/fullname:"*name*"	Sets the user's full name.
/homedir:"*path*"	Sets the account's home directory. This can be a network path. Quotes are required if the path contains spaces.
/passwordchg:{**yes** | **no**}	Determines whether the user is allowed to change the account's password. The default is `yes`.
/passwordreq:{**yes** | **no**}	Determines whether the account requires a nonblank password. The default is `yes`.
/scriptpath:"*path*"	The path to the logon script relative to the server's script directory.
/times:{*times* | **all**}	Determines the times of day that the account may log on. Type `net help user` for the syntax.
/usercomment:"*text*"	Sets an administrator-only comment.
/workstations:{*list* | *****}	Determines the workstations that the account may use. Type `net help user` for the syntax.

`Net user` can be very helpful if you need to frequently create large groups of user accounts. For example, you can write a batch file to create user accounts for a college class using a program similar to this:

```
@rem                              Example File mkaccount.bat
@echo off

rem ------------------------------------------
rem Create a student account
rem Be sure the command line contains a classname, username and password
rem ------------------------------------------

if "%3" == "" (
    echo Usage: mkaccount classname username password
    exit /b
)

rem ------------------------------------------
rem Attempt to create the account. Throughout this
rem batch file %1 is the class name (e.g. CS101),
rem %2 is the new logon name (e.g. asmith), and
rem %3 is the initial password (e.g. xyz123)
rem ------------------------------------------

net user "%2" "%3" /add /passwordreq:yes /domain

if errorlevel 1 (
    echo Unable to create account %2
    pause
    exit /b
)

rem ------------------------------------------
rem Add the new user to the class group and the
rem students group
rem ------------------------------------------

net group "%1" "%2" /add
net group students "%2" /add

rem ------------------------------------------
rem Create the user's profile folder and grant
rem Full access rights to the new student account. The
rem teacher already has full rights to
rem \classes\classname so she or he will inherit rights
rem to the student's directory.
rem For the roaming profile to work, the "students" group
rem must have read permissions on the class folder but
rem but this permission must not apply to subfolders.
rem ------------------------------------------

mkdir "d:\home\classes\%1\%2"
cacls "d:\home\classes\%1\%2" /E /G "%2:F"

rem ------------------------------------------
rem Assign the profile folder using the network path
```

```
rem \\server\classes to the folder d:\home\classes
rem ----------------------------------------

net user "%2" /profilepath:"\\server\classes\%1\%2" /domain
```

This batch file uses `net user` to create a student account, adds the account to the domain groups for the class and for all students, creates the account's profile folder, grants the new account full rights to its profile, and then assigns the profile folder to the account. This batch file can be called from a batch file containing the class roster. Here's an example:

```
@echo off
call mkaccount CS101 abaker DK@$g931xC
call mkaccount CS101 bsmith OXD2ba-12#
call mkaccount CS101 cfong  PXc43L$*Qf
.
.
.
```

net view

The command `net view` displays the networked computers that your computer has seen (that is, it can display the "Network Neighborhood"), and it can also list the shared folders and printers available on a remote computer. For this reason, `net view` is quite useful in debugging Windows networking problems.

The plain command `net view` displays the list of known active computers in the current workgroup or domain. The list looks like this:

```
Server Name            Remark
-------------------------------------------------------------------
\\BALI                 Our Humble File Server
\\JAVA                 Brian's Workstation
```

You can add the option `/domain` to display a list of all known domains and workgroups on the current network, or you can add `/domain:`*`domainname`* to display a list of computers in the specified domain or workgroup.

The command `net view \\`*`computername`* displays a list of folders and printers shared by the specified computer. The list looks like this:

```
Shared resources at \\bali

Share name  Type   Used as  Comment
-----------------------------------------------------------
cdrive      Disk
faxes       Disk   F:
Laserjet    Print           Two bins
temp        Disk   X:
```

This is a good way to get a quick list of network resources that you can then use with `net use`. Items with drive letters listed under the Used as column are already mapped.

You can view the offline file-caching settings for a set of shared folders by adding the option `/cache` after *`computername`* (for example, `net view \\bali /cache`). In this case, the Comments column is replaced with the file-caching settings for each shared folder. This applies to shares provided by Windows XP Professional, Windows 2000 Pro and Server, and Windows .NET server only.

Finally, if your network includes Novell NetWare file servers, two additional forms of `net use` let you view a list of available NetWare servers and a server's shared resources:

```
net view /network:nw
net view /network:nw \\servername
```

netstat

`Netstat` lists the status of your computer's TCP/IP protocol subsystem. Its main use is to list the names of remote computers to which your computer is attached; the listed connections indicate either that your computer is using a resource offered by another computer or that another computer is connected to yours. `Netstat` can list TCP and UDP ports that your computer has open for listening. These indicate services that your computer is offering to the network or the Internet. `Netstat` can also print statistics about TCP/IP networking traffic and errors.

You can view the full syntax by typing `netstat /?`. In the following section, I'll describe the most useful options.

Listing Active Connections

The `netstat` command with no options lists all current TCP connections between your computer and others. By default, `netstat` attempts to convert the remote computers' IP addresses into names. This can take a long time, so you can print a faster all-numeric listing by adding the `-n` option. The connection table looks like this:

```
Proto  Local Address     Foreign Address                      State
TCP    java:4273         sumatra.mycompany.com:microsoft-ds  ESTABLISHED
TCP    java:4319         bali.mycompany.com:netbios-ssn      ESTABLISHED
TCP    java:netbios-ssn  sumatra.mycompany.com:2430          ESTABLISHED
TCP    java:4564         msgr-cs122.msgr.hotmail.com:1863    ESTABLISHED
```

Each line represents one connection. The Local and Foreign Address columns indicate the names of the computers involved in the connections and the port number or name for the connection. The port indicates the type of network service: `http` or `80` indicates a Web server connection, `137` through `139` or `netbios-x` indicate Windows File Sharing, and so on.

It's sometimes possible to tell from the port numbers which computer—yours or the remote computer—is offering the service and which is the client or consumer of the service. In *most* cases, the server side of a TCP connection uses a port number below 1024, whereas the client side uses a port number above 1024. This is not always the case, because some services use large port numbers on the server side. For example, TCP port 3389 is used by Microsoft's Remote Terminal Services and Remote Desktop, port 5190 is used by the AOL Instant Messenger service, and port 1863 is used by Microsoft Messenger. In these cases, the end of the connection that is using the "standard" port number is the server side.

The preceding sample listing shows that the local computer, Java, is using shared files on both Sumatra and Bali, because it has a connection to these computers' NetBIOS session (`netbios-ssn`) ports. Bali, in turn, is using shared files on Java, because it has made a connection to Java's NetBIOS port. Finally, Java has a connection to Microsoft's Messenger service.

Tip

The list of "well known" ports is in the file `\windows\system32\drivers\etc\services`. You can add to this file if you want `netstat` to be able to print the names of additional network services. For starters, you could add the following entries to the end of your computer's `services` file:

```
msmsgs      1863/tcp    #Microsoft Messenger
tsc         3389/tcp    #Microsoft Remote Terminal Services
aim         5190/tcp    #AOL Instant Messenger
pcaw-ssn    5631/tcp    #PC Anywhere session
pcaw-scan   5632/udp    #PC Anywhere server discovery
```

The State column indicates the status of the connection and will usually be one of the following values:

State	Meaning
`LISTEN`	Your computer will accept incoming connections on this port.
`SYN_SEND`	Your computer is attempting to open this connection. The other computer has not yet replied.
`ESTABLISHED`	There is an active connection.
`FIN_WAIT_1` or `2`	The connection is being shut down
`CLOSE_WAIT`	The connection has been closed. This entry will remain for a while.

Listing Open Ports (Servers)

You can see the full list of ports to which your computer answers with the command `netstat -a`. This adds to the listing all ports that have no current connection but for which your computer is listening. Each one of these potentially indicates a service that your computer is offering to other networked computers, or to the Internet at large if you have no firewall in place. The list of ports printed by a Windows XP computer is alarmingly long, and most of the port numbers are not standard numbers associated with well-known services.

If you add the `-o` option, `netstat` additionally prints the Process Identification (PID) number of the program that has opened each port. You can combine this information with the output of `tasklist` to determine which program is associated with each connected or waiting port.

Listing Statistics

The `-e`, `-s`, and `-p` options display Ethernet and per-protocol summary statistics. See the online help for descriptions of these options.

Constant Monitoring

You can add a number (*n*) to the end of the `netstat` command line to make it repeat its printout every *n* seconds. This makes it possible to watch connections come and go during debugging, or to watch statistics change over time.

nslookup

`Nslookup` is a tool that interactively queries Domain Name Service (DNS) servers. `Nslookup` lets you find IP addresses given hostnames, and vice versa, and can also help you identify Internet miscreants—spammers and hackers.

Note

`Nslookup` is a complex program and could easily take up an entire chapter itself. The Help and Support Center has fairly detailed information about each of its commands but does not provide much in the way of a tutorial. For a thorough introduction to DNS and `nslookup`, the acknowledged "bible" is *DNS and Bind*, by Paul Albitz and Cricket Liu, published by O'Reilly.

In this chapter, there isn't room to document all of `nslookup`'s commands, but I'll describe a few practical applications to show you what it can do.

Finding an IP Address Given a Hostname

To look up the IP address for a given DNS hostname, just type `nslookup` *`hostname`*. If the host is in your default domain, you can omit the domain name from the command. Otherwise, it's best to spell out the full domain name and add a period at the end. For example,

```
nslookup www.microsoft.com.
```

prints the following text:

```
Server:  sumatra.mycompany.com
Address:  192.168.0.2

Non-authoritative answer:
Name:    www.microsoft.akadns.net
Addresses:  207.46.230.218, 207.46.197.100, 207.46.197.113, 207.46.230.219
Aliases:  www.microsoft.com
```

The "Server" lines tell which DNS server provided the answer; in this case, the one on my network. The "Non-authoritative answer" heading indicates that my DNS server already had the requested information on hand from an earlier lookup, so it did not need to contact Microsoft's primary, or *authoritative*, DNS server directly. Finally, `nslookup` prints out a choice of several IP addresses for this Web site. Take your pick.

Finding the Hostname for an IP Address

The Internet's DNS system provides a reverse-lookup mechanism that lets you find the name associated with an IP address. You can type `nslookup 207.46.230.218` and `nslookup` will print the following:

```
Server:  sumatra.mycompany.com
Address:  192.168.0.2

Name:    microsoft.com
Address:  207.46.230.218
```

This indicates that the standard or *canonical* name for this IP address is `microsoft.com`. Other hostnames may also return this IP address (you saw earlier that `www.microsoft.com` is one), but this is the main name. It's not uncommon for companies to set up several names, such as `mycompany.com`, `ftp.mycompany.com`, `www.mycompany.com`, and `mail.mycompany.com`, all pointing to the same IP address.

One good use of this reverse-lookup capability is to help identify the source of spam e-mails. If you can identify the name of the computer from which the spam originated, you may be able to report the miscreant to the responsible ISP and get the account shut down. Although spammers always use a fake computer name and return address in their mailings, the IP addresses in the "Received by:" lines don't lie and indicate the mail's origin.

However, many ISPs and companies do not maintain reverse name lookup information, so the `nslookup` command cannot tell you the domain name of some IP addresses. `Nslookup` can still help, if you look up Start of Authority information.

Examining Start of Authority Information

When you cannot determine the hostname and domain of a specific IP address, you *may* still be able to determine the name of the company that owns the IP address through additional `nslookup` queries. For this we can't use the simple command-line

Testing a DNS Server

You can use `nslookup`'s prompt mode to test a specific DNS server. You may want to do this after setting up a server in your organization. To do this, type the following commands:

```
nslookup
server hostname or ipaddress
```

Here, *`hostname`* or *`ipaddress`* is the name or address of the server you wish to test. Then, as `nslookup` continues to prompt you for input, enter hostnames or IP addresses. `Nslookup` will send the requests to the specified server for resolution. Type `exit` when you're done.

ping

This venerable tool sends small data packets to a designated target computer or network router, which is supposed to send them right back. `Ping` tallies up the percentage of data packets that make a successful roundtrip. `Ping` therefore lets you know whether the target computer and all Internet connections between you and that computer are working. For example, when I typed `ping www.berkeley.edu`, I received the following printout:

```
Pinging arachne.berkeley.edu [169.229.131.109] with 32 bytes of data:

Reply from 169.229.131.109: bytes=32 time=22ms TTL=242
Reply from 169.229.131.109: bytes=32 time=21ms TTL=242
Reply from 169.229.131.109: bytes=32 time=22ms TTL=242
Reply from 169.229.131.109: bytes=32 time=20ms TTL=242

Ping statistics for 169.229.131.109:
    Packets: Sent = 4, Received = 4, Lost = 0 (0% loss),
Approximate round trip times in milli-seconds:
    Minimum = 20ms, Maximum = 22ms, Average = 21ms
```

(There's that canonical name business again: `ping` looked up the IP address for the name I typed and then looked up that address's canonical name. That's why the listing says `arachne.berkeley.edu` instead of `www.berkeley.edu`.) You can see that all four of the test probes that `ping` sent were returned. Each roundtrip took about 20 milliseconds.

If you're testing a network wiring problem, you might find `ping`'s `-t` option useful. `Ping -t` tests the network connection constantly, instead of just four times, so you can poke around with your network's wiring and hubs. Look for the telltale flashing lights that show `ping`'s data packets traveling by.

interface but rather must start `nslookup` without options. In this mode, it prompts for commands in its own query language.

Here's how this authority search works: IP addresses have the familiar format *aaa.bbb.ccc.ddd* (four groups of numbers between 1 and 255—for example, 63.194.114.254). If `nslookup` can't find the name of address *aaa.bbb.ccc.ddd*, it may at least be able to determine what company is responsible for the block of all addresses starting with *aaa.bbb.ccc*. To check, type the following commands:

```
nslookup
set type=any
ccc.bbb.aaa.in-addr.arpa.
```

That is, enter the three sets of numbers in reverse order, from last to first, followed by `in-addr.arpa`. (To investigate the block containing address 63.194.114.254 we'd type 114.194.63.in-addr.arpa. With any luck, `nslookup` will print something like this:

```
114.194.63.in-addr.arpa nameserver = ns1.pbi.net
114.194.63.in-addr.arpa nameserver = ns2.pbi.net
114.194.63.in-addr.arpa
        primary name server = ns1.pbi.net
        responsible mail addr = postmaster.pbi.net
        serial  = 200203060
        refresh = 3600 (1 hour)
        retry   = 900 (15 mins)
        expire  = 604800 (7 days)
        default TTL = 3600 (1 hour)

ns1.pbi.net     internet address = 206.13.28.11
ns2.pbi.net     internet address = 206.13.29.11
```

This shows the name of the DNS server that is responsible for this block of IP addresses, and the attached domain name should tell you the name of the company that owns the IP addresses, or the ISP that manages them.

If you're pursing a spammer or hacker, this information should point you in the right direction for reporting the problem or obtaining further information. You might try contacting the "responsible mail address" contact listed by `nslookup`. Turn the first period into an at sign (@) to get the mail address; `postmaster@pbi.net` in this example. For big companies, however, this e-mail address is probably not monitored. You may have better luck with abuse@*domainname*.

If `nslookup` can't find information about the IP addresses, you can try typing the following:

```
bbb.aaa.in-addr.arpa.
```

However, even if this does result in information, the responsible party is probably a top-level national Internet Service Provider, and it's unlikely that they will be interested in assisting you with whatever project you're on.

To get out of `nslookup`'s prompt mode, type `exit`.

Tip

When you're trying to diagnose a flaky Internet connection, start out by pinging your computer's gateway IP address and its DHCP server IP address first. The `ipconfig` program can give you these numbers. This test will tell you whether your computer is able to communicate with its nearest neighbor. If the `ping` test fails, then you have a problem with your network or modem connection itself, and the Internet is not to blame.

`Ping` lets you specify the size of the data packets it sends. I have found that a flaky DSL Internet connection can sometimes transmit short packets without any problems but can't send large packets at all. Because `ping` sends small 32-byte packets by default, this can make it appear that the DSL connection is working. It's very confusing when you can ping Internet sites but not connect to them with Internet Explorer. Adding the option `-s 800` tells `ping` to send 800-byte packets. If you consistently find that small packets get through your Internet connection whereas large ones don't, you may have a problem with the wiring between your DSL modem and the telephone company's central office.

Note

Many Internet hosts do not return `ping` packets. Don't even bother trying to ping `www.microsoft.com` or `www.intel.com`. They won't respond. If you're trying to determine whether your Internet connection is working, try pinging one of your ISP's mail or DNS servers; they're more likely to respond.

tracert

The Internet consists of hundreds of thousands of computers and network routers connected to one another through various types of data connections: fiber optic, ATM, Ethernet, telephone line, microwave, and others. To get from your computer to an Internet host, your data has to "hop" across anywhere from 4 to 20 such connections as it zigzags its way around the globe. (If you've ever flown Southwest Airlines cross-country, you know what this is like.) If there's a failure anywhere along the way, your data won't reach its destination. The problem is, when you can't reach an Internet host, you don't know whether the desired computer is down or there's just an Internet outage somewhere in between.

`Tracert` can tell the difference. Here's how it works: The command `tracert` *`hostname`* sends a small data packet to the specified computer, just like `ping`. However, the packet carries a marker that says it's allowed to make only one hop towards its goal. After it makes one hop, it's considered undeliverable and is sent back by the first router. This is a good thing—if this packet makes it back to you, you know that the connection from your computer to at least one Internet router is working. `Tracert` then sends another packet with only enough "postage" to make *two* router hops. If this one makes it back, you know that the connection from the first router to the second is working. `Tracert` repeats this over and over until the packet either reaches the desired destination, as illustrated in Figure 14.1, or stops coming back. In the former case, you know that the entire network path is working. In the latter, you have found out how far your data goes before it stops, and this tells you where the outage is.

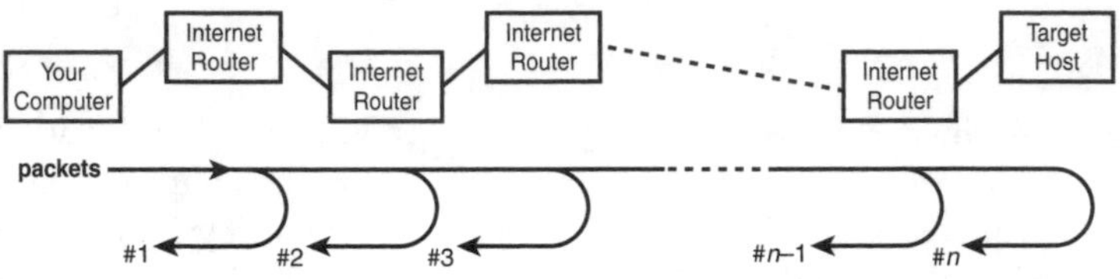

Figure 14.1 `Tracert` maps out the path from your computer to a remote Internet host.

Here's an example: Suppose my mail program says it can't connect to my mail server, `mail.pacbell.net`. If I type `tracert mail.pacbell.net` and see the message

```
Tracing route to mail.pacbell.net [64.164.98.8]
over a maximum of 30 hops:

  1     3 ms     2 ms     2 ms  11.22.33.1
64.220.177.1 reports: network unreachable
```

then I know that the data made one successful hop to `11.22.33.1`, which is my DSL router. However, that router said it could not pass the data any further. This means that the problem is close to me; my network connection is down, and I should call my ISP for assistance.

On the other hand, if the report looked like the following, then the entire network path is working:

```
Tracing route to mail.pacbell.net [64.164.98.8]
over a maximum of 30 hops:

  1     3 ms     2 ms     2 ms  64.220.177.1
  2    25 ms    15 ms    16 ms  65.104.11.1
  3    17 ms    15 ms    20 ms  205.158.11.61
  4    16 ms    19 ms    20 ms  64.0.0.129
  5    22 ms    19 ms    17 ms  64.220.0.62
  6    18 ms    19 ms    24 ms  64.220.0.21
  7    23 ms    21 ms    19 ms  bb1-p3-2.pxpaca.sbcglobal.net [151.164.8
  8    18 ms    23 ms    19 ms  bb2-p9-0.sntc01.pbi.net [64.161.1.21]
  9    27 ms    19 ms    27 ms  64.161.1.26
 10    18 ms    19 ms    19 ms  bb1-p15-0.pltn13.pbi.net [64.161.124.253
 11    22 ms    18 ms    19 ms  srvr1-vlan40.pltn13.pbi.net [64.164.97.2
 12    19 ms    22 ms    23 ms  mta7.pltn13.pbi.net [64.164.98.8]
Trace complete.
```

If the mail server is not responding, it's not due to a connection problem. The mail server itself is probably not working.

If `tracert`'s test showed that data made three or more hops but failed to reach the destination, then we would conclude that that the problem is with routers that belong to the Internet's "backbone," and there is not much we mere mortals can do about that.

Tip

`Tracert` is a great tool for diagnosing problems, and it's even more valuable when you know what its output should look like when your Internet connection is working properly. It's a good idea to point `tracert` at a few distant locations and record the result—direct the output into a file and save or print it. This way, you'll have something to compare it to if things break down.

Some other handy networking programs you might want to look into on your own are `arp`, `ftp`, `nbtstat`, `netsh`, `pathping`, and `route`. `Netsh` lets you configure network adapters, routing tables, and filters, and it has a complex command-line environment of its own. Most of its commands, however, work only on Windows 2000/.NET Server.

III

Appendixes

VBScript Reference

VBScript 5.6 Language Features

THIS APPENDIX PROVIDES A QUICK REFERENCE for VBScript version 5.6. This reference covers only the features of VBScript used with Windows Script Host. Language features that apply only to its use in Internet Explorer and ASP server scripting have been omitted.

For more detailed documentation of VBScript language features, you can download the most recent Microsoft VBScript reference manual from the Downloads section of `msdn.microsoft.com/scripting`. Check the Microsoft site in any case to see whether a more recent version has been released.

If you are familiar with Visual Basic or Visual Basic for Applications, you will note that some VB and VBA language features are not provided in VBScript. The specific differences between these versions are described in the Microsoft VBScript Reference manual at the end of this appendix.

Syntax

In this reference, the following conventions are used:

- Parts of program statements that must be typed literally are shown in **`boldface`**.
- Items that represent something that must be replaced with your own choice of variable names or expressions are shown in *`italics`*.

- Optional parts are placed in square brackets ([ ]).
- Items that may be repeated arbitrarily are followed with ellipses (...).
- Items from which you must choose one are listed in curly brackets ({ }), separated by vertical lines (|), as in {**this** | **that**}.

General Structure of a VBScript Program

A VBScript program consists of ASCII text. Whitespace (spaces, tabs, and blank lines) is permitted to improve readability. Case is not significant.

There is no limit to the length of source code lines. However, to improve readability, you may break long program lines into two or more shorter lines. You must end broken-up lines with the underscore (_) character and continue them on the subsequent line (or lines). Here's an example:

```
wscript.echo "This is a long " & _
    "input line, isn't it?"
```

The main program body consists of all input lines outside of `Class`, `Sub`, or `Function` groups. Generally, global variable definitions should be entered first, followed by the main script program, followed by class, subroutine, and function definitions.

VBScript ignores anything after a single quote (') character, treating it as a comment.

Data Types and Variables

VBScript variable names may have up to 255 characters, must begin with a letter, must not contain blanks, periods, or punctuation characters, and must not be one of the reserved language keywords, such as `public` or `while`.

In VBScript, all variables are of type Variant. A Variant may hold integers, floating-point numbers, dates, times, date-times, strings, Boolean values, and object references. When Variants are combined in expressions, VBScript attempts to interpret them in such a way as to make the expression sensible. For example, when you combine a numeric Variant and a string Variant with the string concatenation operator (`&`), VBScript automatically converts the number to a string. When combining numeric and string Variants with the numeric operators, VBScript attempts to convert the string to a number.

To force VBScript to use a particular conversion or interpretation in expressions, use the conversion functions `CStr()`, `CInt()`, `CDbl()`, and so on.

Table A.1 lists the Variant types and examples of constant expressions that may be used in programs.

Table A.1 **VBScript Variant Types and Constants**

Variant Type	Constant Example	Remarks
Integer, Short	`123` `&H12AB` (hex) `&O177777` (octal)	Range: –32768 to 32767

Integer, Long	`1234567`
	`&H47DFE123`
	`&O123456712`
		Range: –2147483648 to 2147483647

Floating Point, single precision	`3.1416`	Range: $\pm 3.4\times 10^{\pm 38}$, seven digits accuracy
Floating Point, double precision	`3.14159265359`	Range: $\pm 1.8\times 10^{\pm 308}$, 15 digits accuracy
Currency	`100.47`	Range: ±922,337,203,685,477.5808. Currency values retain only four decimal places.
String	`"abc"`	A quotation mark may be embedded in the string by doubling it (for example, `"a "" quote"` represents *`a " quote`*
Date	`#03/02/2002#` `#March 2, 2002#`	The short date form is interpreted according to the Windows Locale setting.
Time	`#14:30:15#` `#2:30:15 PM #`	
Date-Time	`#03/02/2002 14:30:15#` `#March 2, 2002 2:30:15 PM #`	You may force a specific output conversion format with `FormatDateTime`. Date-times are stored as floating-point numbers.
Boolean	`True` `False`	
Object	`Nothing`	`Nothing` is a predefined null object reference.
Empty	`Empty`	Uninitialized.
Null	`Null`	Defined as invalid. Using a Null value has various results: In Boolean expressions it's treated as `False`. In numeric expressions, the result is always `Null`. In most other cases, an error is generated.

Note on Dates and Times

Variants of type Date, Time, and Date-Time (combinations of a date and a time of day) are encoded as floating-point numbers. Dates are stored as the number of days since January 1, 1900. Dates prior to that epoch are allowed and are stored as negative numbers. Times are stored as fractions of a day, with one second equaling 0.0000115741. A Date, then, is an integer number of days. A Time is a number between 0 and 0.9998842593, and a Date-Time is a floating-point number combining both of these. For example, the representation of `#March 2, 2002 2:30:15 PM#` is `37317.6043402778`.

This is important to know if you wish to use date, time, or date-time values in mathematical operations. Care must be taken in the interpretation of the sums and differences of dates and times with numeric or other date-time values. It's best to use the functions `DateAdd` and `DateDiff` to perform computations on dates and times.

Variable Scope

By default, when a variable is declared or created in the main body of a script file, it has public (global) scope and is accessible in the main script and in all procedures (subs and functions) called in the script. Variables defined within procedures, by default, have private (local) scope and are accessible only within the procedure in which they're declared. When the defining procedure terminates, the variable is destroyed.

The keywords `Public` and `Private` may be used to override the default behavior. In the main script program, `Private` variables will not be visible to called procedures. In procedure, a variable declared `Public` will be visible to any other procedures it calls. (However, the variable will still be destroyed when the defining procedure ends.)

A variable may also be set without having first been declared with `Dim`, `Private`, or `Public`. In the main script program, this creates a public variable. If a procedure references a variable name previously defined as `Public`, the public copy is used. Otherwise, a private variable is created.

Procedures may define private variables with the same names as public variables defined elsewhere. In this case, the procedure creates a local, private variable and cannot see the public version.

Expressions and Operators

The following precedence order is used when evaluating expressions:

1. Subexpressions in parentheses
2. Arithmetic operators

3. Comparison operators
4. Logical operators

Note

VBScript always evaluates the entire expression, even when it's not necessary. Therefore, the following type of test will not protect a program from an argument value error:

```
a = -3
if a > 0 and sqr(a) > 2 then ...
```

Arithmetic Operators

Listed in order of precedence from highest to lowest, the arithmetic operators are as follows:

Operator	Meaning
`^`	Exponentiation
`-`	Unary negation
`*`	Multiplication
`/`	Division
`\`	Integer division
`mod`	Modulus (integer remainder)
`+`	Addition
`-`	Subtraction
`&`	String concatenation

Comparison Operators

Comparison operators have equal precedence and are evaluated in left-to-right order, as shown here:

Operator	Meaning
`=`	Equal to
`<>`	Not equal to
`<`	Less than
`>`	Greater than
`<=`	Less than or equal to
`>=`	Greater than or equal to
`is`	Object equivalence

Logical Operators

Logical operators perform logical operations on Boolean values and bitwise operations on numeric values. Listed in order of precedence from highest to lowest, the logical operators are as follows:

Operator	Meaning
`not`	Negation
`and`	Conjunction
`or`	Disjunction
`xor`	Exclusion (different)
`eqv`	Equivalence (same)
`imp`	Implication (same, or second value true)

Results of Mathematical Operations

The Variant subtype resulting from a mathematical operation (addition, multiplication, and so on) depends on the types of the two values being operated upon. In Table A.2, locate the row corresponding to one value's type and then the column corresponding to the other value's type. Look in the intersection of the row and column to find the type of result. Some combinations may produce unexpected results (see the indicated footnotes for details).

In addition to the Variant types listed in Table A.2, variables may be `Empty` (defined but not initialized) or `Null` (defined as invalid). In mathematical operations, an `Empty` variable is treated as `0` or the empty string. If a `Null` value is used in an expression, an error occurs.

Table A.2 ***Results of Mathematical Options***

Types		**I**	**L**	**S**	**D**	**C**	**G**	**Da**	**T**	**DT**	**B**
Int	**I**	I[1]	L[1]	S[1]	D	C	?[6]	Da[4]	DT[3]	DT[4]	I
Long	**L**	L[1]	L[1]	S[1]	D	C	?[6]	Da[4]	DT[3]	DT[4]	L
Single	**S**	S[1]	S[1]	S[1]	D	C	?[6]	DT[4]	DT[3]	DT[4]	S
Double	**D**	D	D	D	D	C	?[6]	DT[4]	DT[3]	DT[4]	D
Currency	**C**	C	C	C	C	C	?[6]	DT[4]	DT[3]	DT[4]	C
String	**G**	?[6]	?[6]	?[6]	?[6]	?[6]	G[5]	?[6]	?[6]	?[6]	?[6]
Date	**Da**	Da[4]	Da[4]	DT[4]	DT[4]	DT[4]	?[6]	Da[2]	DT[4]	DT[2]	Da[4]
Time	**T**	DT[3]	DT[3]	DT[3]	DT[3]	DT[4]	?[6]	DT[4]	T[3]	DT[2]	DT[4]

Types		I	L	S	D	C	G	Da	T	DT	B
Date-Time	**DT**	DT[4]	DT[4]	DT[4]	DT[4]	DT[4]	?[6]	DT[2]	DT[2]	DT[2]	DT[4]
Boolean[7]	**B**	I	L	S	D	C	?[6]	Da[4]	DT[4]	DT[4]	I

1. If the magnitude of the result exceeds the range of the expected type, VBScript automatically uses a more capacious type. When necessary, Integer is promoted to Long, and Long and Single to Double.

2. For subtraction, the result should be interpreted as the number of days (and/or fractional days) difference. For other operators, the result is meaningless.

3. If the result is 24 hours or greater, the answer is a meaningless date-time.

4. The result is only sensible with addition and subtraction.

5. The + operator performs concatenation. It is better to use the `&` operator for this. Other operations are not permitted.

6. If the string value can be interpreted as a number, date, time, or date-time, the result will be what it would have been had the value been that other type. If the string cannot be interpreted, VBScript will halt with an error message.

7. The Boolean values `True` and `False` are treated as the integer values `-1` and `0`, respectively, in mathematical operations.

Program Statements

The general structure of a VBScript program is as follows:

```
[global variable declarations]

main procedure VBScript Statements

[subs and functions]
```

Program statements may be split onto multiple lines to improve readability. When a line ends with the underscore character (_), the next line is considered to be part of the same statement.

VBScript program statements are listed in Table A.3.

Note

In Table A.3, *`condition`* refers primarily to an expression or variable with a Boolean (`True` or `False`) value. However, VBScript also accepts a string or numeric value where a Boolean value is expected. For numeric values, zero is treated as `False` and any nonzero value as `True`. The string values `"True"` and `"False"` are accepted, as are strings that can be interpreted as numbers.

Table A.3 **VBScript Statements**

Statement	Remarks
[**Call**] *name* [(*argumentlist*)]	Transfers control to a subroutine or function. The keyword `Call` is optional. If you use the `Call` keyword, surround any arguments passed with parentheses. If you omit the `Call`, omit the parentheses. If you use `Call` to execute a function, its return value is ignored.
Class *name* *statements...* **End Class**	Defines a new object type. The VBScript `Class` statement is not discussed in this book. Instead, use the more powerful WSC file format described in Chapter 9, "Creating Your Own Scriptable Objects."
[{**public**|**private**}] **Const** *name*_ = *expression* [, ...]	Defines a constant that can be used in the script.
Dim *name*[([*subscripts*])]_ [,...]	Declares an array variable. Use parentheses without *subscripts* inside to create a dynamic array resizable with `ReDim`. Up to 60 dimensions may be specified. Indexes always start at 0. Without parentheses, `Dim` declares a scalar variable. This is used when you use Option Explicit to force the declaration of all variables.

Do [{**While** | **Until**}]_
  condition]
    [*statements...*]
    [**Exit Do**]
    [*statements...*]
Loop
    or
	Executes statements inside the `Do...Loop` construct under control of a Boolean *condition* statement. The optional `Exit Do` statement can be used to break out of the loop.

Do
    [*statements...*]
    [**Exit Do**]
    [*statements...*]
Loop [{**While** | **Until**}]_
  condition]
	`Do...Loop` can also be used with no condition statement, in which case `Exit Do` (or `Exit Sub`, and so on) must be used.

Erase *arrayname*	With a fixed-size array, this statement reinitializes all of its elements to the "uninitialized" state. With a dynamically sized array, it deletes the array's contents so that `ReDim` must be called before the array can be used again.

Statement	Remarks
`Execute string`	Executes the VBScript statement in the string argument. This can be used to execute arbitrary VBScript commands determined at runtime. The command runs in the script's global namespace context, but any variables/functions/classes defined are not visible outside the calling procedure.
`ExecuteGlobal string`	This statement is like `Execute`, but any variables, classes, or functions defined in the statement are created in the global namespace and persist. Useful to define a global procedure or class at runtime.

`Exit Do`
`Exit For`
`Exit Function`
`Exit Property`
`Exit Sub`
	The `Exit` statement provides a quick exit to a loop or procedure. `Exit Do` and `Exit For` cause execution to continue with the next statement after a `Do` or `For` loop, respectively. `Exit Function`, `Exit Property`, and `Exit Sub` terminate procedures.

`For Each element in group`
`[statements...]`
`[Exit For]`
`[statements...]`
`Next [element]`
	Executes statements once for each member of the array or collection object named ***group***.
	On each turn, variable ***element*** takes the next sequential value from ***group***.
	The `Exit For` statement is optional and can be used in as many places as necessary.
	The ***element*** variable may be named again on the `Next` line to improve program readability.

`For counter = startval to_`
`endval [, increment]`
`[statements...]`
`[Exit For]`
`[statements...]`
`Next [counter]`
	Executes a group of statements a number of times. Variable ***counter*** takes values from ***startval*** to ***endval***. ***Counter*** is incremented by the ***increment*** value at the end of every iteration. ***Increment*** may be negative. The default increment is 1.
	The `Exit For` statement is optional and can be used in as many places as necessary.
	The ***counter*** variable may be named again on the `Next` line to improve program readability.

`[{Public [Default] | Private}]_`
`Function name [(arguments)]`
`[statements...]`
`[name = expression]`
`[Exit Function]`
`[statements...]`
`End Function`
	Declares a function—a procedure that returns a result value—named ***name***. A list of ***arguments*** may be specified by listing one or more names separated by commas.

continues

Table A.3 **Continued**

Statement	Remarks
arguments: [{**ByVal**|**ByRef**}] *argname* [, ...]	The return value is specified by assigning a value to the name of the function as if it were a variable. Argument names may be preceded with the optional keyword `ByRef` or `ByVal` to indicate pass-by-reference or pass-by-value. The default is `ByRef`, in which the variable in the calling procedure is modified if the function modifies the argument. If a variable is passed using `ByVal`, the function receives a copy of the variable and the original is never modified. The `Exit Function` statement is optional and can be used in as many places as necessary. The `Public` and `Private` keywords determine whether the function is visible outside the script. (This matters in WSF files where there may be multiple scripts in one file). In a class definition, the `Default` keyword indicates that the function is the default method for the class.
If *condition* **Then** *statement_* [**Else** *statement*]	Executes a statement or group of statements depending on a Boolean *`condition`* expression.

If *condition* **Then**
    statements...
[**ElseIf** *condition* **Then**
    statements...]
[**Else**
    statements...]
End If
	If the one-line version is used, multiple statements may be used after `Then` or `Else` by separating them with colons (`:`). However, all must still fit on one line. When multiple statements are needed the full `If...End If` version is preferred.

On Error Resume Next **On Error Goto 0**	`On Error Resume Next` indicates that if a program error is detected, VBScript should continue executing the script at the statement after the error. `On Error Goto 0` restores the default "stop on error" behavior. `On error` statements clear the `err` object.
Option Explicit	Requires that all variables be declared in `Dim`, `Private`, `Public`, or `ReDim` statements before being used; otherwise, an error is generated. Can help you detect typos and scoping problems in scripts. Must be the first statement in the script.

Statement	Remarks
Private *name*[**(***subscripts***)**][, ...]	Declares variables visible only in the script in which they appear. Like `Dim`, arrays may be defined.
Public *name*[**(***subscripts***)**][, ...]	Defines variables (or arrays) visible to all procedures in all scripts. `Public` statements cannot be placed inside subprograms such as `Sub`, `Function`, and so on.
Randomize [*number*]	Initializes the random number generator used by function `rand()`. If *`number`* is specified, this is used as the seed value. If *`number`* is omitted, a seed value is derived from the current time. With a given seed number (or, with no `Randomize` statement), `rand()` will always generate the same sequence of random numbers.
Redim [**Preserve**]_ *name*(*subcripts*)[, ...]	Changes the size of array *`name`* to use new subscript values. It's used with arrays declared with `Dim` *`name`*`()`. The keyword `Preserve` resizes the array without deleting all existing values.
Rem *text*	Comment text that is ignored by VBScript.

Select Case *expression*
    Case *expression* [, ...]
        statements...
  [**Case** *expression* [, ...]
        statements...]
  [**Case Else**
        statements...]
End Select
	Executes a set of expressions based on the value of *`expression`*. If the value of the expression is listed in one of the `Case` entries, the statements below the `Case` are executed. The optional `Case Else` group serves as a catchall.
	If the *`expression`* value is not listed and there is no `Case Else`, no statements are executed.

Set *var* = *objectexpr* **Set** *var* = **New** *classname* **Set** *var* = **Nothing**	Sets a variable named *`var`* to refer to an object. The `Set` keyword is required for *all* assignments that refer to an object. The value assigned to the object variable may be another object variable or an object expression (for example, `fso.Folders`), a new instance of an object class, or `Nothing`, which releases the former object held by *`var`*.
Stop	Stops the execution of the script at this statement if the script is running in a debugger; otherwise, it has no effect. The `Stop` statement is helpful when you're debugging WSC object scripts, as discussed in Chapter 9.

continues

Table A.3 **Continued**

Statement	Remarks
[{**Public** [**Default**] | **Private**}]_ **Sub** *name* [(*arguments*)] [*statements*...] [**Exit Sub**] [*statements*...] **End Sub** *arguments*: [{**ByVal**|**ByRef**}] *argname* [,_ ...]	Declares a subroutine—a procedure that does not return a result value—named *name*. A list of *arguments* may be specified by listing one or more names separated by commas. See the remarks for function for a description of the argument list. The Exit Sub statement is optional and can be used in as many places as necessary. The Public and Private keywords determine whether the subroutine is visible outside the script. In a class definition, the Default keyword indicates that the subroutine is the default method for the class.
While *condition* *statements...* **Wend**	Like Do While...Loop. Use Do While instead.

With *object*
statements...
End With
	Allows you to work with a given object without typing the object's full name each time it's used. Speeds program operation and spares your fingers. With statements may be nested. Within a With block, references to the selected object's properties and methods start with a period rather than the object name. Here's an example:
	`set fso = new Scripting.FileSystemObject`
	`with fso`
	`for f in .Folders`
	`...`

Functions

The built-in functions provided with VBScript are shown in Table A.4.

Table A.4 **VBScript Functions**

Function	Remarks
Abs(*value***)**	Returns the absolute value of a numeric argument.
Array(*arglist***)**	Creates an array and assigns its elements the values passed as arguments.

Function	Remarks
Asc(*string*)	Returns the ANSI value of the first character in a string argument. (ANSI values are the same as ASCII for letters, numbers, and the standard punctuation characters.)
Ascb(*string*)	Returns the first byte of a string argument.
Ascw(*string*)	Returns the first character code of a Unicode string.
Atn(*number*)	Returns the arctangent of a number (uses radians).
CBool(*expr*)	Converts any numeric expression or string to Boolean. Numeric 0 returns `False`; nonzero returns `True`. The strings `"true"` and `"false"` in any case are also accepted.
CByte(*expr*)	Converts any numeric expression or string to a byte (8-bit) value.
CCur(*expr*)	Converts any numeric expression or string to a Currency value. At most four decimal places are retained.
CDate(*expr*)	Converts a string date or numeric expression to a Date value. String arguments must match the locale specific format. Numeric values are interpreted with the integer part equaling date and the fraction part equaling the time. (You can use the `IsDate` function to validate a string representation before attempting to convert it.)
CDbl(*expr*)	Converts any numeric expression or string to a double-precision floating-point value. (Not useful in WSH.)
Chr(*value*)	Returns a single-character string corresponding to the ANSI value.
CInt(*value*)	Converts any numeric expression or string to a short (16-bit) integer value. Input numbers outside the range –32768 to 32767 will cause an error.
CLng(*value*)	Converts any numeric expression or string to a long (32-bit) integer value. Numbers are rounded to the nearest integer.
Cos(*number*)	Returns the trigonometric cosine of *number*, specified in radians. If given degrees, use `cos(`*number*`*atn(1)/45)`.
CreateObject(*servername.typename*_ [, *location*])	Creates an object of type *servername.typename*. The optional *location* specifies a network node.

continues

Table A.4 **Continued**

Function	Remarks
CSng(*value***)**	Converts any expression to a single-precision floating-point value. (Not useful in WSH.)
CStr(*value***)**	Converts any expression to a string representation. Works with Boolean, Date, and all numeric types.
Date	Returns the current date.
DateAdd(*interval, number, date***)**	Adds a number of specified interval units to a date. *Interval* is a string with one of the values listed in "Date Function Intervals," later in this appendix.
DateDiff(*interval, date1,*_ *date2* [, *firstdayofweek* [,_ *firstweekofyear*]]**)**	Returns the number of intervals between two dates, where *interval* is a string with one of the values listed in "Date Function Intervals," later in this appendix. When asking for the result in periods of a week or more, you may wish to specify the day that the week is considered to start on (the default is Sunday) as well as the week that the year is considered to start on (the default is January 1). For further information, see the section "Date and Time Constants," later in this appendix.
DatePart(*interval, date* [,_ *firstdayofweek* [,_ *firstweekofyear*]]**)**	Returns the specified part of the given date, where *interval* is one of the string values listed under "Date Function Intervals," later in this appendix. When asking for the day of the week or the week of the year, you may wish to specify the starting day or week. For further information, see the section "Date and Time Constants," later in this appendix.
DateSerial(*year, month, day***)**	Returns a Date value given a year, month, and day. *Month* is a number from 1 to 12.
DateValue(*date***)**	Returns a Date value, given a string representation of a date or date and time. If the string specifies a date and a time, the time portion is ignored. Can also be passed Date values.
Day(*date***)**	Returns the day number (1–31) of a date.
Eval(*expression***)**	Evaluates a string containing a valid VBScript expression as text and returns the result.
Exp(*value***)**	Returns e^{value}, where e is the base of natural logarithms.

Function	Remarks
`Filter(InputStrings, Value [,_ Include [, Compare]])`	Returns an array containing those elements of string array `inputstrings` that match `value`. Here are the other arguments: `value`—The substring to search for. The filter looks for elements of `inputstrings` that equal or contain `value`. `include`—If passed and `False`, this argument returns those strings that do *not* contain a value. `compare`—Specifies the type of comparison to make: `vbBinaryCompare` or `vbTextCompare`. The default is text. See "String Constants," later in this appendix.
`Fix(value)`	Truncates the fractional part of a numeric `value` and returns the integer portion only. In contrast to `Int()`, with a negative value `Fix()`, this function returns the negative integer value with the smallest magnitude (for example, `Fix(-3.3) = -3`).
`FormatCurrency(value [,_ NumDigitsAfterDecimal [,_ IncludeLeadingDigit [,_ UseParensForNegativeNumbers [,_ GroupDigits]]]])`	Returns the value of `expression` formatted as a string using the currency symbol defined in the Windows Locale settings. Optional arguments include the following: `NumDigitsAfterDecimal`—The number of decimal places to display. The default is locale specific. `IncludeLeadingDigit`—A tristate constant specifying whether a leading zero is to be displayed with fractional values. See "Tristate Settings," later in this appendix, for the values permitted. `UseParensForNegativeNumbers`—A tristate constant specifying whether to indicate negative numbers with `-` or `( )`. `GroupDigits`—A tristate constant specifying whether to group digits in large numbers with commas (or another local-specific character).
`FormatDateTime(DateVal[, Format])`	Formats a Date or Date-Time as a string. One of the constants listed in "Date Formatting Constants," later in this appendix, may be specified to ensure a particular output format.

continues

Table A.4 **Continued**

Function	Remarks
FormatNumber(*value* [,_ *NumDigitsAfterDecimal* [,_ *IncludeLeadingDigit* [,_ *UseParensForNegativeNumbers* [,_ *GroupDigits*]]]])	Returns a numeric value formatted as a string. The optional arguments are the same as those listed under `FormatCurrency`.
FormatPercent(*value* [,_ *NumDigitsAfterDecimal* [,_ *IncludeLeadingDigit* [,_ *UseParensForNegativeNumbers* [,_ *GroupDigits*]]]])	Returns a numeric value multiplied by 100, formatted as a string and followed with the `%` character. The optional arguments are the same as those listed under `FormatCurrency`.
GetLocale()	Returns the current locale identifier value. The locale ID values are listed in the Microsoft Windows Scripting documentation file under "Locale ID (LCID) Chart."
GetObject([*filename*] [, *class*])	Like `New` but this function obtains an object using either the application's data file *filename*, implying the application and object type, or an object moniker. If *filename* is specified, the application is instructed to open the file. The name may be followed with !*subpart* when only a part of the original file is desired (for example, in Excel workbooks).
	If the filename is omitted, the class name must be specified.
GetRef(*procname*)	Used in HTML scripts (not applicable to WSH).
Hex(*value*)	Formats the integer part of *value* to a hexadecimal string. Uppercase letters are used.
Hour(*time*)	Returns the hour of the *time* value—an integer from 0–23.
InputBox(*prompt* [, *title* [,_ *default*][, *xpos*, *ypos*] [,_ *helpfile*, *context*])	Displays a dialog box with an input field into which the user may type a string. Returns the string entered by the user. The only required argument is *prompt*, which specifies text to display to the user, up to about 1,024 characters. The text is word-wrapped if necessary. Line breaks can be forced by inserting `vbCr`, `vbLf`, or `vbCrLf` in the string. Here are the optional parameters: *title*—Text to display in the title bar of the dialog box. The default is "VBScript."

Function	Remarks
	default—The default text to put in the input field when the box is first displayed. *xpos*, *ypos*—The location to display the dialog box, in 1/1440-inch units from the left and top edges of the screen. The default is centered. *helpfile*, *context*—If you have created a Windows help file for your application, this is the full path and numeric context identifier for the associated help text.
InStr([*start*,] *string1*,_ *string2* [, *compare*]**)**	Returns the starting position of *string2* if found in *string1*, or `0` if *string2* cannot be found. The optional argument *start* indicates the starting position in *string1* to begin the search. *Compare* indicates the type of string search to perform; the default is text. See "String Constants," later in this appendix.
InStrRev([*start*,] *string1*,_ *string2* [, *compare*]**)**	Like `InStr` but searches starting at the right end of the string. For example, `InStrRev("ABCAB","AB") = 4`.
Int(*value***)**	Truncates the fractional part of a numeric *value* and returns the integer portion only. Negative fractional values are reduced to the next lower negative number. For example, `Int(-3.3) = -4`.
IsArray(*varname***)**	Returns `True` if the variable *varname* is an array. Otherwise, it returns `False`.
IsDate(*expr***)**	Returns `True` if the value *expr* is a Date or Date-Time value or can be interpreted as a Date. Otherwise, it returns `False`.
IsEmpty(*expr***)**	Returns `True` if the variable or expression is the `Empty` (uninitialized) value. Otherwise, it returns `False`. The test `If` *variable* `= Empty` also works.
IsNull(*expr***)**	Returns `True` if the variable or expression is the `Null` value. The test `if variable = Null` causes an error.
IsNumeric(*expr***)**	Returns `True` if the expression is a numeric value or can be interpreted as a numeric value. Otherwise, it returns `False`.
IsObject(*varname***)**	Returns `True` if the variable is an object reference. Otherwise, it returns `False`.

continues

Table A.4 **Continued**

Function	Remarks
Join(*array* [, *delimiter*]**)**	Returns a string consisting of all the elements of the *array*, joined with the *delimiter* string, which defaults to " ". The entries are converted to strings if necessary.
LBound(*arrayname* [, *dimension*]**)**	Returns the array index lower bound of the specified dimension. Always returns 0 in VBScript.
LCase(*string***)**	Returns the string expression with all the characters in lowercase.
Left(*string*, *length***)**	Returns the leftmost *length* characters of the string expression. If the string has fewer than *length* characters, the return value is the entire string.
Len(*string***)**	Returns the length of the string expression in characters.
LoadPicture(*picturename***)**	Used in HTML scripts (not applicable to WSH).
Log(*value***)**	Returns the natural logarithm of the numeric *value*. *Value* must greater than 0. To get log base *n*, use log(*value*)/log(*n*).
LTrim(*string***)**	Returns the string expression less any leading spaces.
Mid(*string*, *start*[, *length*]**)**	Returns *length* characters from the string expression, starting at position *start*. If the string has fewer than *start* characters, the zero-length ("") string is returned. If the string has fewer than *length* characters after the starting position, the return value is whatever's available.
Minute(*time***)**	Returns the minute of the hour of the *time* or Date-Time value (an integer between 0 and 59).
Month(*date***)**	Returns the number of the month of the *date* value (an integer from 1 to 12).
Monthname(*month*, [*abbrev*]**)**	Returns the text name of the *month* (a number from 1 to 12). If *abbrev* is passed and is True, the returned month name is abbreviated, for example, "Oct").

Function	Remarks
MsgBox(*prompt* [, *buttons* [,_ *title* [, *helpfile*, *context*]]]**)**	Displays a pop-up message box with at least one button the user must select before the script proceeds. The return value indicates which button the user selected; see "MsgBox Constants," later in this appendix. The only required argument is *prompt*, which specifies the text to display to the user, up to about 1,024 characters. The text is word-wrapped if necessary. Line breaks can be forced by inserting vbCr, vbLf, or vbCrLf in the string. Here are the optional parameters: *buttons*—A number indicating what types of buttons and possibly which icon to display. The value is the sum of one or more of the values listed in "MsgBox Constants," later in this appendix. *title*—The text to display in the title bar of the dialog box. The default is "VBScript." *helpfile*, *context*—If you have created a Windows help file for your application, this parameter specifies the full path and numeric context identifier for the associated help text.
Now	Returns the current date and time.
Oct(*value***)**	Formats the integer part of *value* to an octal string.
Replace(*expr*, *find*,_ *replacewith* [, *start*_ [, *count* [, *compare*]]]**)**	Returns the string *expr* with occurrences of the string *find* replaced by the string *replacewith*. Here are the optional arguments: *start*—The starting position in *expr* to begin replacing occurrences of *find*. *count*—The maximum number of occurrences to replace. The default is -1, which means make all possible replacements. *compare*—The type of comparison to make: vbBinaryCompare or vbTextCompare. The default is text. See "String Constants," later in this appendix.
RGB(*red*, *green*, *blue***)**	Returns a long integer representing an RGB color value: *red*, *green*, and *blue* are numbers from 0 to 255.

continues

Table A.4 **Continued**

Function	Remarks
Right(*string*, *length***)**	Returns the rightmost *length* characters of the string expression. If the string has fewer than *length* characters, the return value is the entire string.
Rnd[(*value*)]	Returns a random number in the range `0 <= Rnd < 1`. The optional *value* argument indicates how to select the number. If *value* is less than `0`, the name number is returned every time using *value* as the seed. If *value* is equal to `0`, the most recently generated number is returned again. If *value* is greater than `0` or not supplied, the next number in the sequence is returned. Each returned value is kept as the seed for the next call. See `Randomize`. To get a random integer between A and B, inclusive, use `int(A+Rnd*(B-A+1))`
Round(*value* [, *nplaces*]**)**	Rounds the numeric *value* to *nplaces* decimal places. The default for *nplaces* is `0`. This is helpful for financial calculations.
RTrim(*string***)**	Returns the string expression less any trailing spaces.
ScriptEngine	Returns "VBScript."
ScriptEngineBuildVersion	Returns the VBScript build number (for example, `6626`).
ScriptEngineMajorVersion	Returns the major version number of the current version of VBScript (for example, `5`).
ScriptEngineMinorVersion	Returns the minor version number of the current version of VBScript (for example, `6`).
Second(*time***)**	Returns the second of the minute of the time or date-time value (a number between `0` and `59`).
SetLocale(*localeid***)**	Sets the VBScript locale to the specified identifier value and returns the previous value. For a list of values, see the Microsoft Windows Scripting documentation file under "Locale ID (LCID) Chart."
Sgn(*value***)**	Returns an integer indicating the sign of the numeric *value*. The return value is `-1` if *value* is less than `0`, `0` if *value* is equal to `0`, or `1` if *value* is greater than `0`.

Function	Remarks
`Sin(value)`	Returns the trigonometric sine of `number`, specified in radians. If given degrees, use `sin(number*atn(1)/45)`.
`Space(number)`	Returns a string consisting of `number` blanks.
`Split(string [, delimiter [,_ count [, compare]]])`	Returns an array consisting of substrings of the `string` argument, divided at occurrences of the `delimiter` string. The default for `delimiter` is `" "`. Here are the optional arguments: `count`—The maximum number of substrings to return. The default is `-1`, which means as many as can be found. `compare`—The type of comparison to make when searching for `delimiter`: `vbBinaryCompare` or `vbTextCompare`. The default is text. See "String Constants," later in this appendix.
`Sqr(value)`	Returns the square root of the numeric `value`, which must be greater than or equal to `0`.
`StrComp(string1 [, string2 [,_ compare]])`	Compares `string1` and `string2` in a case-sensitive, lexicographic sense and returns `-1` if `string1` is less than (before) `string2`, `0` if `string1` is equal to `string2`, or `1` if `string1` is greater than `string2`. The optional argument is `compare`, which specifies the type of comparison to make when searching for `delimiter`: `vbBinaryCompare` or `vbTextCompare`. The default is text. See "String Constants," later in this appendix.
`String(number, char)`	Returns a string consisting of `number` repetitions of the specified character. `Char` can be a numeric character code or a string. If `char` is a string, only its first character is used.
`StrReverse(string)`	Returns the `string` argument with its characters reversed, left to right.
`Tan(value)`	Returns the trigonometric tangent of `number`, specified in radians. If given degrees, use `tan(number*atn(1)/45)`.
`Time`	Returns the current time of day as a Time value.
`Timer`	Returns the number of seconds since midnight.
`TimeSerial(hour, minute, second)`	Returns a Time value given an hour (`0–23`), minute (`0–59`) and second (`0–59`).

continues

Table A.4 **Continued**

Function	Remarks
`TimeValue(expr)`	Returns a Time value given a date-time or string representation of a time. (Should have been named `CTime`, because it acts like the other conversion functions.)
`Trim(string)`	Returns the string expression less any leading or trailing spaces.
`TypeName(varname)`	Returns a string description of the variant subtype of the specified variable. Like `VarType` but returns, for example, `"String"` instead of `8`.
`UBound(arrayname [, dimension])`	Returns the upper bound of the specified *`dimension`* of an array.
`UCase(string)`	Returns the string expression with all the characters in uppercase.
`VarType(varname)`	Returns a value indicating the Variant subtype of a variable. The return value is one of those listed under "Variable Type Constants," later in this appendix.
`Weekday(date [, firstday])`	Returns a number (1–7) indicating the day of the week of the *`date`* value. You may specify which day is the first (1) day with *`firstday`*, which must be one of the values listed in "Date and Time Constants," later in this appendix. The default is `vbSunday`.
`WeekdayName(number, abbrev,_ firstday)`	Returns a string containing the name of the day specified by the day *`number`* (1–7). If *`abbrev`* is passed and is `True`, the returned name is an abbreviated form (for example, "Wed"). See `Weekday` for a description of *`firstday`*.
`Year(date)`	Returns the year of the *`date`* value as an integer (for example, `2002`).

Date Function Intervals

Date functions such as `DateAdd`, `DateDiff`, and `DatePart` take an interval argument, which is a string with one of the values listed in Table A.5.

Table A.5 **Intervals Used with *DateAdd*, *DateDiff*, and *DatePart***

Value	Meaning
`"YYYY"`	Year
`"q"`	Quarter
`"m"`	Month
`"y"`	Day of year (for example, 1...365)
`"d"`	Day
`"w"`	Weekday
`"ww"`	Week of year (for example, 1...52)
`"h"`	Hour
`"n"`	Minute
`"s"`	Second

Predefined Constants

VBScript predefines the constants discussed in the following subsections. When possible, use the constant names rather than their numeric values to help improve program readability.

Special Values

The constants listed in Table A.6 define the Boolean values `True` and `False` as well as special variable values that can't otherwise be assigned.

Table A.6 **Special Constants**

Constant	Description
`Empty`	The value of a declared but uninitialized variable.
`False`	The Boolean `False` value. Numerically equivalent to `0`.
`Nothing`	Assigning `Nothing` to a variable disconnects the variable from an object, and if no other references exist, the object is released (destroyed).
`Null`	The `Null` value is used to indicate invalid data. `Null` is not the same as `Empty`.
`True`	The Boolean `True` value. Numerically equivalent to `-1` (all bits set).

You can test for the values `Empty` and `Null` with the functions `IsEmpty()` and `IsNull()`. Attempting to use a `Null` value in any other expression results in an error.

Color Constants

Some objects have color properties (for example, window backgrounds and text). For these properties, you may use one of the predefined constants listed in Table A.7 or the `RGB` function.

Table A.7 **Color Constants**

Constant	Value	Description
vbBlack	&h00	Black
vbRed	&hFF	Red
vbGreen	&hFF00	Green
vbYellow	&hFFFF	Yellow
vbBlue	&hFF0000	Blue
vbMagenta	&hFF00FF	Magenta
vbCyan	&hFFFF00	Cyan
vbWhite	&hFFFFFF	White

Comparison Constants

Some string-comparison functions permit you to specify whether to perform a text or binary string comparison. Binary comparisons are useful when your system uses Unicode (wide) characters and you wish to search for a specific list of binary values. In the default search mode, the search string would be converted to Unicode values before searching. If you're using plain ASCII text, the default text comparison mode is fine. Table A.8 lists the comparison constant values.

Table A.8 **Comparison Constants**

Constant	Value	Description
VbBinaryCompare	0	Performs a binary comparison
VbTextCompare	1	Performs a textual comparison

Date and Time Constants

Date and Time constants, as listed in Table A.9, are used by the functions `DateDiff()`, `DatePart()`, `Weekday()`, and `WeekdayName()` to let you specify the day and week considered to start the week and year. This is especially useful when you are computing the difference between two dates in intervals of a week or more.

Table A.9 **Date and Time Constants**

Constant	Value	Description
VbSunday	1	Sunday
VbMonday	2	Monday
VbTuesday	3	Tuesday
VbWednesday	4	Wednesday
VbThursday	5	Thursday
VbFriday	6	Friday
VbSaturday	7	Saturday
VbUseSystemDayOfWeek	0	The first day of the week, as specified by system locale settings
vbFirstJan1	1	The week in which January 1 occurs
VbFirstFourDays	2	The first week that has at least four days in the new year
VbFirstFullWeek	3	The first full week of the year

Date Formatting Constants

`FormatDateTime()` uses the Date formatting constants listed in Table A.10 to generate a specific desired output format.

Table A.10 **Date Formatting Constants**

Constant	Value	Description
VbGeneralDate	0	Displays a date and/or time in the format specified by locale settings. Given a real number, this constant displays the date plus the time; integer only displays date only; fraction only displays time only. For real numbers, it displays a date and time.
VbLongDate	1	Displays a date using the long date format specified by the locale settings.
VbShortDate	2	Displays a date using the short date format specified by the locale settings.
VbLongTime	3	Displays a time using the long time format specified by the locale settings.
VbShortTime	4	Displays a time using the short time format specified by the locale settings.

`MsgBox` Constants

The constants listed in Table A.11 are used in the *`button`* (second) argument to `MsgBox`. Multiple values may be added together, at most one each of the button type, icon, default, and modality values.

Table A.11 **Message Box Constants**

Constant	Value	Description
`vbOKOnly`	0	Displays the OK button only.
`vbOKCancel`	1	Displays the OK and Cancel buttons.
`vbAbortRetryIgnore`	2	Displays the Abort, Retry, and Ignore buttons.
`vbYesNoCancel`	3	Displays the Yes, No, and Cancel buttons.
`vbYesNo`	4	Displays the Yes and No buttons.
`vbRetryCancel`	5	Displays the Retry and Cancel buttons.
`vbCritical`	16	Displays the Critical Message icon.
`vbQuestion`	32	Displays the Warning Query icon.
`vbExclamation`	48	Displays the Warning Message icon.
`vbInformation`	64	Displays the Information Message icon.
`vbDefaultButton1`	0	The first button is the default.
`vbDefaultButton2`	256	The second button is the default.
`vbDefaultButton3`	512	The third button is the default.
`vbDefaultButton4`	768	The fourth button is the default.
`vbApplicationModal`	0	Application modal. The user must respond to the message box before continuing work in the current application.
`VbSystemModal`	4096	System modal. On Win32 systems, this constant provides an application modal message box that always remains on top of any other programs you may have running.

The return value from `MsgBox` is one of the values listed in Table A.12.

Table A.12 ***MsgBox* Return Values**

Constant	Value	Description
`VbOK`	1	The OK button was clicked.
`vbCancel`	2	The Cancel button was clicked.
`vbAbort`	3	The Abort button was clicked.
`vbRetry`	4	The Retry button was clicked.
`vbIgnore`	5	The Ignore button was clicked.
`vbYes`	6	The Yes button was clicked.
`vbNo`	7	The No button was clicked.

String Constants

The string constants listed in Table A.13 offer a convenient way to add line termination to your strings; generally these are added (concatenated) to other strings.

Table A.13 **String Constants**

Constant	Value	Description
`VbCr`	`Chr(13)`	Carriage return.
`VbCrLf`	`Chr(13) & Chr(10)`	Carriage return and line feed.
`VbFormFeed`	`Chr(12)`	ASCII form feed.
`VbLf`	`Chr(10)`	Line feed.
`VbNewLine`	`Chr(13) & Chr(10)`, or `Chr(10)`	Platform-specific newline character (whatever is appropriate for the platform).
`vbNullChar`	`Chr(0)`	Character having the value `0`.
`vbNullString`	String pointer with the value `0`	Not the same as a zero-length string (`""`). Used for calling external procedures.
`vbTab`	`Chr(9)`	ASCII horizontal tab.
`vbVerticalTab`	`Chr(11)`	ASCII vertical tab.

Tristate Settings

Tristate constants, as listed in Table A.14, allow you to use default settings or override them in calls to `FormatCurrency()`, `FormatNumber()`, and `FormatPercent()`.

Table A.14 **Tristate Constants**

Constant	Value	Description
`VbUseDefault`	`-2`	The default taken from the locale settings
`VbTrue`	`-1`	`True`
`VbFalse`	`0`	`False`

Variable Type Constants

The `VarType()` function returns one of the values listed in Table A.15 to indicate the Variant subtype of the variable or expression it is passed.

Table A.15 **VarType Constants**

Constant	Value	Description
`VbEmpty`	`0`	Uninitialized (default).
`VbNull`	`1`	Contains no valid data.
`VbInteger`	`2`	Integer (16-bit) subtype.
`VbLong`	`3`	Long (32-bit) integer subtype.
`VbSingle`	`4`	Single (32-bit) floating-point subtype.
`VbDouble`	`5`	Double (64-bit) floating-point subtype.
`VbCurrency`	`6`	Currency subtype.
`VbDate`	`7`	Date subtype.
`VbString`	`8`	String subtype.
`VbObject`	`9`	Object.
`VbError`	`10`	Error subtype.
`vbBoolean`	`11`	Boolean subtype.
`vbVariant`	`12`	Variant (used only for arrays of variants).
`vbDataObject`	`13`	Data-access object.
`vbDecimal`	`14`	Decimal subtype.
`vbByte`	`17`	Byte (8-bit) subtype.
`VbArray`	`8192`	Array. This value is always added to one of the basic data type values (for example, `9004 = 8192+12`, which equals an array of variants).

Miscellaneous Constant

The `vbObjectError` constant, shown in Table A.16, is used with the `Err` object.

Table A.16 **Object Error Base Constant**

Constant	Value	Description
`VbObjectError`	`-2147221504`	The base value for user-defined error numbers used with the `Err` object.

VBA Features Omitted from VBScript

VBScript is a scaled-down version of Visual Basic for Applications (VBA), which is itself a scaled-down version of Microsoft Visual Basic (VB). Programmers familiar with VBA through its use as the Word/Excel macro language should be aware that some familiar language features are not available in VBScript.

Table A.17 summarizes the features omitted from and added to VBScript.

Table A.17 **Differences Between VBScript and Visual Basic**

Statement or Function	Remarks
`!`	*`object!keyname`* cannot be used to access an item in a collection. Use *`object`*`.item(`*`keyname`*`)` instead.
`#Const`	Compile-time constants are not supported. Use `Const` instead.
`#If...Then, #Else`	Conditional compilation is not supported.
`Clipboard`	The `Clipboard` object is not provided.
`Collection`	Ad hoc `Collection` objects cannot be created. Some predefined objects return collections, however.
`CVar` `CVDate`	Unnecessary. All variables are of type Variant already.
`Date`	All variables are of type Variant.
`Debug.Print`	Use `Wscript.Echo` instead.
`Declare`	External DLLs are not accessible.
`DefBool` and so on	All variables are of type Variant.
`DoEvents`	Use `Wscript.Sleep` instead.

`End`	Not supported. You may, however, place your script's main code in a `Sub` and use `Exit Sub`. Here's an example:
	`myscript`
	`sub myscript`
	`    ...`
	`    exit sub`
	`    ...`
	`end sub`

`Erl`	The `Erl` function (which indicates the line number of the last error) is not available.
`Error`	Not available. Use `err.raise` instead..
`FV, IRR, PV`, and so on	Financial functions are not provided.
`Gosub...Return`	`Gosub` and labels are not supported.
`GoTo`	`Goto` and labels are not supported.
`Integer`	All variables are of type Variant.
`Is` (in `Select Case`)	Object typing with `Is` isn't supported in `Select Case`.
`Like`	Pattern matching is not directly supported. Use the `RegExp` object.
`Link`*`xxx`*	DDE is not supported.
`Long`	All variables are of type Variant.
`LSet` and `Rset`	Not supported.
`Mid` statement	The `Mid` assignment statement (`mid` on the left side of `=`) is not supported.
`On...GoSub` `On...GoTo`	Event and error handling are not supported.

continues

Table A.17 **Continued**

Statement or Function	**Remarks**
`Open`, `Read`, `Write`, `Close`, and so on	Basic file I/O is not supported. Use `FileSystemObject` instead.
`Option Base`	In VBScript, all array indexing starts at 0.
`Option Compare` `Option Private Module`	These option settings are not applicable.
`Optional`	Arguments may not be specified as optional. You may indicate unspecified arguments by passing the value `Null` and testing with `IsNull()` in the procedure.
`ParamArray`	`ParamArray` arguments are not supported.
`Resume` `Resume Next`	Error trapping is not supported.
`SendKeys`	Not a built-in statement. Use `Wscript.Sendkeys` instead.
`Static`	Static (persistent) variables are not supported.
`Str`	Use `CStr()`.
`StrConv`	The `StrConv()` function is not supplied. Use `UCase()` or `LCase()` if possible.
`Time`	All variables are of type Variant.
`To` (in Select Case)	Expression ranges with `To` are not supported in `Select Case`.
`TypeOf`	`If TypeOf` and `Select Case TypeOf` are not supported. Use `VarType()` or `TypeName()` instead.
`Val`	Use `CDbl()`, `CInt()`, or possibly `Eval()`.

B
Object Reference

THIS APPENDIX LISTS THE PROPERTIES and methods of the Automation objects described in this book. For descriptions of the purpose and use of these properties and methods, follow the cross reference to the indicated reference list or table.

Collection and Dictionary Objects

JScript Enumerator allows JScript programs to scan collection objects. See Reference List 3.1 on page 95.

Properties

item

AtEnd

MoveFirst

MoveNext

Object REXX COM Extensions permit Object REXX programs to access constants and prototypes in COM type libraries. See Reference List 3.2 on page 101.

Methods

GETCONSTANT

GETKNOWNEVENTS

GETKNOWNMETHODS

GETOUTPARAMETERS

Scripting.Dictionary stores and retrieves information in an associative array or symbol table. See the Windows Script Host documentation.

Properties	Methods
Count	Add
CompareMode	Exists
Item	Items
Key	Keys
	Remove
	RemoveAll

Script Management and Utility Objects

Wscript provides information about the WSH runtime environment. See Reference List 3.3 on page 103.

Properties	Methods
Arguments	CreateObject
FullName	DisconnectObject
Interactive	Echo
Name	GetObject
Path	Sleep
ScriptFullName	Quit
ScriptName	
StdErr	
StdIn	
StdOut	
Version	

Err describes the last error that occurred during the execution of a script. See the Windows Script Host documentation.

Properties	**Methods**
`Description`	`Clear`
`HelpContext`	`Raise`
`HelpFile`	
`Number`	
`Source`	

`Named` describes the set of named arguments (options) passed on the script's command line. See Reference List 10.2 on page 391.

Properties	**Methods**
`Item`	`Count`
`Length`	`Exists`

`Unnamed` describes the set of unnamed arguments passed on the script's command line. See Reference List 10.3 on page 394.

Properties	**Method**
`Item`	`Count`
`Length`	

`WSHRemote` represents the connection to a script executing on a remote computer. See Reference List 10.4 on page 406.

Properties	**Methods**
`Status`	`Execute`
`Error`	`Terminate`

`RegExp` searches and parses strings with regular expression patterns. See the Windows Script Host documentation.

Properties	**Methods**
`Global`	`Execute`
`IgnoreCase`	`Replace`
`Pattern`	`Test`

`Match` describes the results of a `RegExp` search. See the Windows Script Host documentation.

Properties
`FirstIndex`
`Length`
`Value`

File Access Objects

`Scripting.FileSystemObject` provides access to drives, files, and folders. See Reference List 4.1 on page 115.

Property	**Methods**
`Drives`	`BuildPath`
	`CopyFile`
	`CopyFolder`
	`CreateFolder`
	`CreateTextFile`
	`DeleteFile`
	`DeleteFolder`
	`DriveExists`
	`FileExists`
	`FolderExists`
	`GetAbsolutePathName`
	`GetBaseName`
	`GetDrive`
	`GetDriveName`
	`GetExtensionName`
	`GetFile`
	`GetFileName`
	`GetFolder`
	`GetParentFolderName`
	`GetSpecialFolder`
	`GetTempName()`
	`MoveFile`
	`MoveFolder`
	`OpenTextFile`

`Drive` describes a single hard drive or drive partition. See Reference List 4.2 on page 125.

Properties

`AvailableSpace`

`DriveLetter`

`DriveType`

`FileSystem`

`FreeSpace`

`IsReady`

`Path`

`RootFolder`

`SerialNumber`

`ShareName`

`TotalSize`

`VolumeName`

`Folder` describes a single folder or directory. See Reference List 4.3 on page 129.

Properties	Methods
`Attributes`	`Copy`
`DateCreated`	`Delete`
`DateLastAccessed`	`Move`
`DateLastModified`	
`Drive`	
`Files`	
`IsRootFolder`	
`Name`	
`ParentFolder`	
`Path`	
`ShortName`	
`ShortPath`	
`Size`	
`SubFolders`	
`Type`	

`File` describes a single file. See Reference List 4.4 on page 134.

Properties	Methods
Attributes	Copy
DateCreated	Delete
DateLastAccessed	Move
DateLastModified	OpenAsTextStream
Drive	
Name	
ParentFolder	
Path	
ShortName	
ShortPath	
Size	
Type	

TextStream reads from or writes to a text file. See Reference List 4.5 on page 140.

Properties	Methods
AtEndOfLine	Close
AtEndOfStream	Read
Column	ReadAll
Line	ReadLine
	Skip
	SkipLine
	Write
	WriteBlankLines
	WriteLine

XML/HTML Processing Objects

DOMDocument provides structured access to an XML or HTML file. This is a partial listing. See Reference List 4.6 on page 159.

Properties	Methods
async	createCDataSection
childNodes	createComment
documentElement	createDocumentType
parseError	createElement

Properties	Methods
xml	createProcessingInstruction
	createTextNode
	getElementsByTagName
	load
	loadXML
	Save
	selectNodes
	selectSingleNode

IXMLDOMNode represents a single element in an XML or HTML file. This is a partial listing. See Reference List 4.7 on page 161.

Properties	Methods
attributes	appendChild
childNodes	hasChildNodes
firstChild	insertBefore
lastChild	removeChild
nextSibling	replaceChild
nodeName	selectNodes
nodeType	selectSingleNode
nodeTypeString	setAttribute
nodeValue	
ownerDocument	
previousSibling	
xml	

IXMLDOMNamedNodeMap hosts a list of element attributes. This is a partial listing. See Reference List 4.8 on page 164.

Property	Methods
length	getNamedItem
	item

IXMLDOCNode describes a single element attribute. See Table 4.4 on page 164.

Properties

nodeName

nodeValue

specified

Program Environment Objects

WScript.Shell provides an interface to the desktop and the current Windows programming environment. See Reference List 4.9 on page 171.

Properties	Methods
CurrentDirectory	AppActivate
Environment	CreateShortcut
SpecialFolders	Exec
	ExpandEnvironmentStrings
	LogEvent
	Popup
	RegDelete
	RegRead
	RegWrite
	Run
	SendKeys

WshScriptExec interacts with a program started with the WScript.Shell object's Exec method. See Reference List 4.10 on page 176.

Properties	Method
ExitCode	Terminate
ProcessID	
Status	
StdErr	
StdIn	
StdOut	

WSHShortcut describes and manages a desktop shortcut. See Reference List 4.11 on page 179.

Properties	Method
`Arguments`	`Save`
`Description`	
`FullName`	
`Hotkey`	
`IconLocation`	
`TargetPath`	
`WindowStyle`	
`WorkingDirectory`	

`WSHEnvironment` describes the current environment variables and manages the initial logon environment definitions. See Reference List 4.12 on page 183.

Properties	Methods
`Item`	`Count`
`Length`	`Remove`

Network and Printer Objects

`WSHNetwork` manages a computer's network mappings. See Reference List 5.1 on page 192.

Properties	Methods
`ComputerName`	`AddPrinterConnection`
`UserDomain`	`AddWindowsPrinterConnection`
`UserName`	`EnumNetworkDrives`
	`EnumPrinterConnections`
	`MapNetworkDrive`
	`RemoveNetworkDrive`
	`RemovePrinterConnection`
	`SetDefaultPrinter`

Messaging Objects

`CDO.Message` represents an outgoing e-mail message. See Reference List 6.1 on page 220.

Properties	Methods
Attachments	AddAttachment
AutoGenerateTextBody	AddRelatedBodyPart
BCC	CreateMHTMLBody
BodyPart	Forward
CC	GetInterface
Configuration	GetStream
DataSource	Post
DSNOptions	PostReply
EnvelopeFields	Reply
Fields	ReplyAll
FollowUpTo	Send
From	
HTMLBody	
HTMLBodyPart	
Keywords	
MDNRequested	
MIMEFormatted	
Newsgroups	
Organization	
ReceivedTime	
ReplyTo	
Sender	
SentOn	
Subject	
TextBody	
TextBodyPart	
To	

Fields holds a set of named parameters for a message or message body part. See Reference List 6.2 on page 228.

Properties	Method
Count	Update
Item	

`BodyParts` contains a list of message subcomponents. See Reference List 6.3 on page 232.

Properties	Methods
`Count`	`Add`
`Item`	`Delete`
	`DeleteAll`

`CDO.BodyPart` contains one message subcomponent, such as an attachment. See Reference List 6.4 on page 232.

Properties	Methods
`BodyParts`	`AddBodyPart`
`Charset`	`GetDecodedContentStream`
`ContentMediaType`	`GetEncodedContentStream`
`ContentTransferEncoding`	`GetFieldParameter`
`Fields`	`GetInterface`
`Filename`	`GetStream`
`Parent`	`SaveToFile`

`Stream` reads data from or writes data to a message subcomponent. See Reference List 6.5 on page 236.

Property	Methods
`EOS`	`Read`
	`ReadText`
	`SaveToFile`

`CDO.Configuration` configures the delivery method for a message. See Reference List 6.6 on page 237.

Property	Method
`Fields`	`Load`

Windows Management Interface (WMI) Objects

`SWbemLocator` mediates the connections between a client script and WMI service providers on local and remote computers. See "Connecting with the `WbemScripting.SWbemLocator` Object," page 271.

Method

`ConnectServer`

`SWbemServices` represents the connection to a namespace on a managed computer. Partial listing follows. See Reference List 7.1 on page 282.

Property	Methods
`Security`	`Delete`
	`ExecMethod`
	`ExecQuery`
	`InstancesOf`

`SWbemObject` provides basic properties for dynamic management objects that are derived from `SWbemObject`. See Reference List 7.2 on page 286.

Properties	Methods
`Methods`	`Delete`
`Path`	`Instances`
`Properties`	`Put`

`Win32_Service` describes a system service process. See Reference List 7.3 on page 292.

Properties	Methods
`DesktopInteract`	`StartService`
`DisplayName`	`StopService`
`Name`	`PauseService`
`PathName`	`ContinueService`
`Started`	`InterrogateService`
`StartMode`	`ChangeStartMode`
`StartName`	
`State`	
`Status`	

(There are more than 100 other WMI objects.)

Active Directory Scripting Interface (ADSI) Objects

`IADs` provide basic properties for dynamic management objects that are derived from `IADs`. See Reference List 8.1 on page 311.

Properties	Methods
`AdsPath`	`Get`
`Class`	`GetEx`
`GUID`	`GetInfo`
`Name`	`GetInfoEx`
`Parent`	`Put`
`Schema`	`PutEx`
	`SetInfo`

`IADsContainer` and **`IADsCollection`** describe organizational structures and groups. See Reference List 8.2 on page 313.

Properties	Methods
`Count`	`CopyHere`
`Filter`	`Create`
`Hints`	`Delete`
	`GetObject`
	`MoveHere`

`IADsComputer` describes one domain member computer. See Reference List 8.3 on page 317.

Properties

`Division`

`OperatingSystem`

`OperatingSystemVersion`

`Owner`

`Processor`

`ProcessorCount`

`IADsComputerOperations` manages a computer. See Reference List 8.4 on page 317.

Property	Method
`Status`	`Shutdown`

`IADsDomain` represents a security domain. See Reference List 8.5 on page 318.

Properties	Method
`AutoUnlockInterval`	`SetInfo`
`Filter`	
`IsWorkgroup`	
`LockoutObservationInterval`	
`MinPasswordAge`	
`MinPasswordLength`	
`MaxBadPasswordsAllowed`	
`MaxPasswordAge`	
`PasswordAttributes`	
`PasswordHistoryLength`	

`IADsFileService` and **`IADsFileServiceOperations`** describe and manage the file and printer sharing service on a computer. See Reference List 8.6 on page 321.

Properties

`Description`

`MaxUserCount`

`Resources`

`Sessions`

`IADsResource` describes a single shared resource. See Reference List 8.7 on page 322.

Properties

`Name`

`User`

`UserPath`

`Path`

`LockCount`

`IAdsFileShare` describes a single shared folder. See Reference List 8.8 on page 323.

Properties

`CurrentUserCount`

`Description`

`HostComputer`

`MaxUserCount`

`Name`

`Path`

IADsGroup represents a local or domain security group. See Reference List 8.9 on page 325.

Properties	**Methods**
Description	Add
Name	IsMember
	Members
	Remove

IADsNameSpaces lists the ADSI service providers available to the computer running the script. See "IADsNameSpaces," page 326.

Property

DefaultContainer

IADsPrintJob describes a queued print job. See Reference List 8.10 on page 327.

Properties

Description

HostPrintQueue

Notify

NotifyPath

Priority

Size

StartTime

TimeSubmitted

TotalPages

UntilTime

User

UserPath

IADsPrintJobOperations manages a print job. See Reference List 8.11 on page 329.

Properties	**Methods**
Status	Pause
TimeElapsed	Resume
PagesPrinted	
Position	

`IADsPrintQueue` describes the queue for a shared network printer. See Reference List 8.12 on page 330.

Properties

`BannerPage`

`Datatype`

`DefaultJobPriority`

`Description`

`HostComputer`

`Location`

`Model`

`Name`

`PrintDevices`

`PrinterPath`

`PrintProcessor`

`Priority`

`Starttime`

`UntilTime`

`IAdsPrintQueueOperations` manages a print queue. See Reference List 8.13 on page 332.

Properties	**Methods**
`PrintJobs`	`Pause`
`Status`	`Purge`
	`Resume`

`IADsService` describes a system service process. See Reference List 8.14 on page 334.

Properties	**Method**
`Dependencies`	`SetInfo`
`DisplayName`	
`ErrorControl`	
`HostComputer`	
`LoadOrderGroup`	
`Name`	
`Path`	
`ServiceAccountName`	
`ServiceAccountPath`	

Properties	Method
ServiceType	
StartType	
StartupParameters	
Version	

IADsServiceOperations manages a system service process. See Reference List 8.15 on page 336.

Property	Methods
Status	Continue
	Pause
	SetPassword
	Start
	Stop

IADsSession describes the connection between a network client and computer sharing its resources. See Reference List 8.16 on page 337.

Properties
Computer
ComputerPath
ConnectTime
IdleTime
User
UserPath

IADsUser describes a domain or local computer user account. See Reference List 8.17 on page 338.

Properties	Methods
AccountDisabled	ChangePassword
Description	SetInfo
FullName	SetPassword
Groups	
HomeDirectory	
IsAccountLocked	
LastLogin	
LastLogoff	
Profile	

RootDSE describes the properties of the local LDAP server. See Reference List 8.18 on page 344.

Properties

`currentTime`

`defaultNamingContext`

`dnsHostName`

`namingContexts`

`rootDomainNamingContext`

`serverName`

`supportedLDAPVersion`

IADsO and **IADsOU** describe organizational units in an enterprise's business structure. See Reference List 8.19 on page 345.

Properties

`BusinessCategory` (`IADsOU` only)

`Count`

`Description`

`FaxNumber`

`Filter`

`LocalityName`

`Name`

`Parent`

`PostalAddress`

`SeeAlso`

`TelephoneNumber`

C

WSF and WSC File Format Reference

XML Conformance

WSF FILES ENCAPSULATE ONE OR more script programs that can be run with the `wscript` or `cscript` programs. WSC files define scriptable automation (COM) objects written in a WSH-supported language. Both file types are formatted with Extensible Markup Language (XML) tags that define the structure of the program or component.

By default,

- tag and attribute names are case insensitive,
- attribute values need not be enclosed in quotes, if the value contains no spaces, and
- the `<script>` element is "opaque" to the parser, so script code inside the `<script>` element can use XML's special characters (`<`, `>`, and `&`) without special consideration.

If the WSF or WSC file begins with the line

```
<?XML version="1.0" ?>
```

then strict XML syntax compliance is required of the file. When strict compliance is in effect

- tag and attribute names are case sensitive,
- all attribute values must be enclosed in quotes, and
- `<script>` elements are not opaque, so script code must be enclosed in `<![CDATA[ ... ]]>` tags. Without the `CDATA` markup, XML special characters in scripts, such as < and >, would have to be entered as entities `<` and `>`, respectively.

XML elements with no end tag use this format:

```
<tagname [attributes] />
```

The special tag indicator `/>` is *required* to show that the element contains no content and no end tag will follow. (This applies only to element tags and not to the special `<!>` and `<?>` directive formats.)

Structure of a WSF Script File

The following listing shows the general order of elements in a WSF script file; however, not all the elements need to be used. Parameters and most end tags are not shown; see the tag syntax listing for each tag's syntax definition. Ellipses (...) indicate elements that may be repeated.

```
<?xml?>
<package>
    <comment>
    <job>...
        <?job?>
        <runtime>
            <description>
            <named>...
            <unnamed>...
            <example>
            <usage>
        </runtime>
        <object>
        <reference>
        <resource>
        <script>...
    </job>...
</package>
```

Structure of a WSC Component File

The following listing shows the general order of elements in a WSC component script file; however, not all the elements need to be used. Parameters and most end tags are not shown; see the tag syntax listing for each tag's syntax definition. Ellipses (...) indicate elements that may be repeated.

```
<?xml?>
<package>
    <comment>
    <component>...
        <?component?>
        <public>
            <property><get><put></property>
            <method><parameter>...</method>
            <event>
        </public>
        <registration>
        <object>
        <reference>
        <resource>
        <script>...
    </component>...
</package>
```

Tag Syntax

This section briefly describes the syntax for each tag. For more detailed information, see the reference lists in Chapter 9, "Creating Your Own Scriptable Objects," and Chapter 10, "Deploying Scripts for Network Management," or the downloadable Microsoft Windows Script Technologies help file mentioned in Chapter 1, "Introduction to Windows Script Host."

`<?XML Version="1.0" [standalone="yes"]?>`

Requests strict XML conformance. Must be the first line of the file.

`<?component error="value" debug="value" ?>`

Enables error messages and debugging of a component (WSC only).

`<?job error="value" debug="value" ?>`

Enables error messages and debugging of a script job (WSF only).

```
<! [CDATA[
    protected text
    .
    .
    .
]]>
```

Used to enclose the contents of the `<script>` tag when using strict XML conformance. Must not be used when strict XML conformance is not specified.

```
<!-- any text
    .
    .
    .
-->
```

Indicates comment text that is to be ignored by the parser.

```
<comment>
    any text
    .
    .
    .
</comment>
```

Indicates comment text that is to be ignored by the parser.

```
<component [id="componentID"]>
    component markup: registration, public,
    implements and script elements
    .
    .
    .
</component>
```

Encloses the definition of an object (WSC only).

```
<description>any text</description>
```

Describes the purpose of the script for `ShowUsage` (WSC only).

```
<event name="name" [dispid="id"]/>
```

Declares an event that the component may fire.

```
<example>example text</example>
```

Lists a sample command line (WSF only).

```
<get [name="functionname"]/>
```

Indicates that a property is readable and the name of the function that returns the property value.

```
<job [id="jobid"]>
    job content: <?job?>, <script>, other elements
    .
    .
    .
</job>
```

Encapsulates one self-contained script program (WSF only). A WSF file may contain a single job or multiple jobs enclosed in a `<package>` element. The job or jobs to be executed can be specified on the command line when the WSF file is run using a command line of the form `cscript somescript.wsf //job:`*`jobid`*.

```
<method name="methodname" [internalName="functionname"]
      [dispid="dispID"]>
   [<parameter name="paramname"/>...]
</method>
```

Declares a method and associated function (WSC only). If no parameters are defined, the `method` tag can be closed with `/>` and the `</method>` end tag omitted.

```
<named name="argname" helpstring="description" type="argtype" required="boolean"/>
```

Defines a named argument's name and type (WSF only).

```
<object id="name" {classid="clsid:GUID" | progid="progid"}
[events="{true|false}"]/>
```

Creates an object variable with global scope.

```
<package>
    one or more job or component elements
    .
    .
    .
</package>
```

Encloses one or more jobs or components in a WSF or WSC file, respectively.

```
<property name="propertyname" [internalname="varname"]/>
```

or

```
<property name="propertyname" [get][put]>
    [<get [internalname="functionname"]/>]
    [<put [internalname="functionname"]/>]
</property>
```

The first form declares a read/write property and an associated variable. The second form declares a property and an associated function or functions (WSC only).

```
<public>
    Interface definition: property, method, event elements
</public>
```

Encloses the definition of an object's interface (WSC only).

```
<put [name="subroutinename"]/>
```

Indicates that a property is writeable (WSC only).

```
<reference {object="progid" | guid="GUID"}
    [version="version"]/>
```

Imports a type library and imports the library's constants.

```
<registration progid="progid" [classid="GUID"]
     [description="text"] [version="number"]
     [remotable="boolean"]>
  [<script>
      optional registration and unregistration script
  </script>]
</registration>
```

Sets object registration information and procedure (WSC only). If no associated `script` is required, the `registration` tag can be closed with `/>` and the end tag omitted.

```
<resource id="resourceid">
    text or number
</resource>
```

Defines a named resource value.

```
<runtime>
    argument definitions: named, unnamed, example elements
    .
    .
    .
</runtime>
```

Encloses argument syntax declarations (WSF only).

```
<script [language="name"]>
<![CDATA[
    script code
    .
    .
    .
]]>
</script>
```

Encloses script code in the named language (for example,VBScript or JScript). The `<![CDATA[` and `]]>` tags are used if and only if strict XML conformance is in effect.

```
<script language="name" src="location">
```

Imports an external file containing script procedures. The file's *location* can be specified as filename with a drive and full path, a UNC-formatted shared filename, or a URL. The file must not contain any XML markup.

```
<unnamed name="argname" helpstring="description"
    many="boolean" required="{boolean|number}"/>
```

Defines an unnamed command-line parameter (WSF only). The named and unnamed specifications are used by the `ShowUsage` method to construct a syntax-definition string.

```
<usage>
    descriptive text
</usage>
```

Provides syntax description for the `ShowUsage` method and overrides the default self-generated text.

D

CMD and Batch File Language Reference

The CMD Command Line

THE FORMAT OF THE CMD command line is

cmd [**/a** | **/u**] [**/q**] [**/d**] [/t:*bf*] [**/e:on**|**off**] [**/f:on**|**off**] [**/v:on**|**off**] [[**/s**] [**/c** | **/k**] *command*]

The options are listed in Table D.1.

Table D.1 **CMD Command-Line Options**

Option	Description
/a	Causes standard output to use ANSI encoding.
/u	Causes standard output to use Unicode encoding.
/q	Turns batch file echo default to off.
/d	Disables execution of AutoRun commands defined in the Registry.
/t:*bf*	Two digits set the background (window) and foreground (text) colors for the window. For example, **/t:1e** specifies yellow text on a blue background. The color values are listed in Table 11.5 on page 485.
/e	Enables or disables the command extensions.
/f	Enables or disables the file and directory name completion feature.

continues

Table D.1 **Continued**

Option	Description
`/v`	Enables or disables delayed environment variable expansion of `!varname!` items, as discussed in Chapter 12, "Batch Files for Fun and Profit."
`/x`	Same as `/e:on`.
`/y`	Same as `/e:off`.
`/s`	Modifies the treatment of quotation marks on the command line, as discussed in Chapter 12.
`/c`	Executes the command(s) in *`command`* and then quits.
`/r`	Same as `/c`.
`/k`	Executes the command(s) in *`command`* and then reads further commands from the standard input until end of file or until the `exit` command is received.

Batch File Argument and `for` Variable Replacement

The expressions listed in Table D.2 expand into batch file command-line arguments and `for` command variables. In the expressions, *n* is an argument number or the letter corresponding to a `for` command variable.

Table D.2 **Argument and *for* Variable Replacement and Editing**

Expression	Result
%*n*	Argument or variable *n*.
%~*n*	Removes surrounding quotes (").
%~f*n*	Fully qualified path name.
%~d*n*	Drive letter only.
%~p*n*	Path only.
%~n*n*	File name only.
%~x*n*	File extension only.
%~s*n*	Short DOS 8.3 file and path.
%~a*n*	File attributes.
%~t*n*	Modification date/time of file.
%~z*n*	Length of file in bytes.
%~$PATH:*n*	Fully qualified name of first matching file when searching the `PATH`. If no file is found, the result is a zero-length string. The filename must include the proper extension; `PATHEXT` is not used.

The filename modifiers can be used in combination—for example, %~dp*n* returns the combined drive and path. For more examples, view the Windows Help and Support Center and search for "for".

Environment Variable Expansion

The expressions listed in Table D.3 expand into environment variable values. In the expressions, *name* is the name of an environment variable.

Table D.3 **Environment Variable Replacement and Editing**

Expression	Result
%*name*%	Value of environment variable *name*.
%*name*:~*n*%	Skips the first *n* letters and returns the rest.
%*name*:~*n*,*m*%	Skips the first *n* letters and returns the next *m*.
%*name*:~,*m*%	First (leftmost) *m* letters.
%*name*:~-m%	Last (rightmost) *m* letters.
%*name*:*str1*=*str2*%	Replaces every occurrence of *str1* with *str2*. *Str2* can be blank to delete all occurrences of *str1*. *Str1* can start with * to match any string characters ending with *str1*.
!*name*!	When Delayed Expansion is enabled with /v:on or setlocal ENABLEDELAYEDEXPANSION, this expression is replaced with the value of variable *name* just before the command is executed.

Predefined Environment Variables

Table D.4 lists the default environment variables defined automatically or by the System Properties dialog box. Table D.5 lists "dynamic" variables that automatically reflect system properties.

Table D.4 **Predefined Environment Variables**

Variable Name	Usual Value
ALLUSERSPROFILE	C:\Documents and Settings\All Users
APPDATA	C:\Documents and Settings*username*\Application Data
CommonProgramFiles	C:\Program Files\Common Files
COMPUTERNAME	*computername*
ComSpec	C:\WINDOWS\system32\cmd.exe
HOMEDRIVE	C:
HOMEPATH	\Documents and Settings*username*
LOGONSERVER	(Varies)
NUMBER_OF_PROCESSORS	(Varies)
OS	Windows_NT

continues

Table D.4 **Continued**

Variable Name	Usual Value
`Path`	`C:\WINDOWS\system32;C:\WINDOWS;C:\WINDOWS\System32\Wbem`, but this varies depending on the location of Windows
`PATHEXT`	`.COM;.EXE;.BAT;.CMD;.VBS;.VBE;.JS`
`PROCESSOR_ARCHITECTURE`	(Varies)
`PROCESSOR_IDENTIFIER`	(Varies)
`PROCESSOR_LEVEL`	(Varies)
`PROCESSOR_REVISION`	(Varies)
`ProgramFiles`	`C:\Program Files`
`PROMPT`	`$P$G`
`SESSIONNAME`	(Varies)
`SystemDrive`	`C:`
`SystemRoot`	`C:\WINDOWS`
`TEMP`	`C:\DOCUME~1\`*`username`*`\LOCALS~1\Temp`
`TMP`	`C:\DOCUME~1\username\LOCALS~1\Temp`
`USERDOMAIN`	*`computername`* or *`domainname`*
`USERNAME`	*`username`*
`USERPROFILE`	`C:\Documents and Settings\`*`username`*
`windir`	`C:\WINDOWS`

Table D.5 lists additional dynamic environment variables that are available when command extensions are enabled. If variables with these names are defined using the `SET` command or in the System Properties dialog box, these fixed definitions will take precedence, and the dynamic values will not be available.

Table D.5 **Dynamic Environment Variables**

Variable Name	Dynamic Value
`CD`	Current directory drive and path
`DATE`	Current date, formatted as by the `DATE` command
`TIME`	Current time, formatted as by the `TIME` command
`RANDOM`	Random number between 0 and 32767
`ERRORLEVEL`	Exit status of previous program
`CMDEXTVERSION`	Version number of command extensions
`CMDCMDLINE`	Command line used to start CMD itself

Command Formatting

Table D.6 lists the input/output redirection options. Multiple redirection options may be used on one command.

Table D.6 **Redirection and Multiple Command Formats**

<table>
<tr><th>Format</th><th>Result</th></tr>
<tr><td>command >filename</td><td>Directs output to file filename.</td></tr>
<tr><td>command >>filename</td><td>Appends output to filename.</td></tr>
<tr><td><i>command</i> <<i>filename</i></td><td>Command reads input from <i>filename</i>.</td></tr>
<tr><td>command 1>filename</td><td>Redirects standard output (same as >).</td></tr>
<tr><td>command 1>>filename</td><td>Appends standard output.</td></tr>
<tr><td>command 2>filename</td><td>Redirects standard error.</td></tr>
<tr><td>command 2>>filename</td><td>Appends standard error.</td></tr>
<tr><td>command 2>&1</td><td>Sends standard error to the same destination as standard output. Then, standard output can be redirected or piped.</td></tr>
<tr><td>command1 | command2</td><td>Standard output of command1 is piped to the standard input of command2.</td></tr>
<tr><td>command1 & command2</td><td>Multiple command run sequentially.</td></tr>
<tr><td>command1 && command2</td><td>Like &, but command2 is run only if command1 is successful (exits with error status 0).</td></tr>
<tr><td>command1 || command2</td><td>Opposite of &&; command2 is run only if command1 fails.</td></tr>
<tr><td>(command(s))</td><td>Nests commands for if and for.</td></tr>
<tr><td>^x</td><td>Escapes special character x.</td></tr>
</table>

Built-In Commands

Table D.7 lists the built-in commands implemented by CMD.

Table D.7 **Built-in Commands**

Command	Purpose
@*command*	Executes *command* without echoing it to the console.
:*label*	Identifies the target of goto *label* or call :*label*.
assoc	Associates file extensions with file types.
break	Causes a breakpoint in debugger; otherwise, it has no effect.
call *batchfile* [*arguments...*]	Performs a "subroutine" call.
call :*label* [*arguments...*]	
cd [[*drive*:]*directory*]	Changes the current working directory.
chdir [[*drive*:]*directory*]	Same as cd.
cls	Clears the screen (window).
color *bf*	Changes the screen color to b and the text color to f, using the codes listed in Table 11.5.

continues

Table D.7 **Continued**

Command	Purpose
copy [**/d**][**/v**][**/n**][**/y** | **/-y**] [**/z**][**/a** | **/b**] *source* [**/a** | **/b**] [+*source* [**/a** | **/b**]]... [*destination* [**/a** | **/b**]]	Copies files or folders from *source* to *destination*. The options are: /d—Decrypt files /v—Verify file integrity /y—Don't confirm overwrite /z—Network file copy /a—Use eASCII interpretation /b—Use binary interpretation
date [**/t** | *mm-dd-yyyy*]	Displays or sets the date. /t means don't prompt for a new date.
del *filename* ...[**/p** | **/q**][**/f**][**/s**] [**/a**[**:***attributes*]]	Deletes files, bypassing the Recycle Bin. The options are: /p—Prompt to confirm /f—Delete read-only files /s—Delete files in all subdirectories /q—Do not confirm /a—Delete files with specified attributes The attribute codes are: R—Read-Only S—System H—Hidden A—Archive Note that - before S, H, R, or A means to "select the file if the attribute is not set."
dir *pathname* ... [**/p**][**/q**][**/w** | **/d** | **/b** | **/n** | **/x**][**/s**] [**/l**][**/c**][**/4**] [**/a**[[**:**]*attributes*]] [**/o**[[**:**]*sortfields*]] [**/t**[[**:**]*timefield*]]	Displays lists of files and/or folders in directories. The options are: /p—Pause every screen full /q—Display file owners' names /w—Multicolumn wide listing /d—Like /w but sorts columns /n—Long list format /x—Display 8.3 names /b—Brief listing: names only /s—Recurse into subfolders /l—Display names in lowercase /c—Use 1000's separators /4—Use four-digit year format /a—Select by attributes /o—Set sort order /t—Choose time field for sort or time to display
echo on | **off**	Enables or disables echo.
echo *text*	Types *text*.

Command	Purpose
echo.	Types a blank line.
endlocal	Restores variables and settings to pre-setlocal values.
erase	Same as del.
exit [/b] [*exitcode*]	Terminates the command or batch file. /b means terminate batch, not CMD.
for [*modifier*] %*variable* **in** (*list*) **do** *command*	Executes *command* for each item in *list*. *List* can contain wildcards to match filenames. *Variable* is a single, case-sensitive letter that may be substituted anywhere in *command* or *arguments* using the replacement options listed in Table D.3. See Table D.7 for the *modifier* options. Use %% in batch files.
ftype *filetype* [=[*OpenCommand*]]]	Displays or sets associations from file types to the "file open" command.
goto *label*	Jumps to *label*.
goto :EOF	Jumps to end of file.
if *condition command* **if** *condition* (*command*) **else** *command* **if** *condition* (*commands*) **else** (*commands*) Conditions: [**not**] *strng1* == *strng2* [**not**] **errorlevel** *number* [**not**] **exist** *filename* [/**i**] *strng1 compareop strng2* **cmdextversion** *number* **defined** *variable*	Executes *command* if the condition is true. The optional *else* command is executed if the condition is not true. *Commands* can span more than one line if enclosed in parentheses. *Compareops* are as follows: EQU—Equal to NEQ—Not equal to LSS—Less than LEQ—Less than or equal to GTR—Greater than GEQ—Greater than or equal to /i means ignore case in comparison.
md *pathname*	Creates directory path.
mkdir *pathname*	Same as md.
move [/**y**|/**-y**] *frompath topath*	Moves files or folders. Here's the one option: /y—Don't confirm overwrite
path [*folder*[;*folder*...]	Sets the search path and path environment variable.
pause	Prints "Press any key to continue" and waits.
popd	Restores the previous current directory saved by pushd.

continues

Table D.7 **Continued**

Command	Purpose
prompt *TextAndCodes*	Sets the command prompt string and the `prompt` environment variable.
pushd *path*	Changes the directory and can also map a network drive.
rd [**/s**] [**/q**] *path*	Removes the directory named by *path*. With `/s`, it recursively deletes all subdirectories. Option `/q` suppresses the confirmation prompt.
rem *text*	Remark text.
rename *oldname newname*	Renames files or folders.
rmdir [**/s**] [**/q**] *path*	Same as `rd`.
set [*name*[=[*value*]]]	Sets or displays an environment variable.
set /a *expression*	Calculates an arithmetic expression. See Table D.2.
set /p *name=promptstring*	Prompts for input.
setlocal [**enableextensions** | **disableextensions**] [**enabledelayedexpansion** | **disabledelayedexpansion**]	Saves environment variables, the working directory, and option settings.
shift [**/***n*]	Shifts batch arguments. /*n* means shift from argument *n*.
start "*title*" [**/d***path*] [**/i**] [**/min** | **/max**] [**/separate** | **/shared**] [**/low** | **/belownormal** | **/normal** | **/abovenormal** | **/high** | **/realtime**] [**/wait**] [**/b**] *command* [*arguments*]	Starts a command in a new window. The options are: `/d`—Set default directory `/i`—Use initial environment `/min`—Start minimized `/max`—Start maximized `/separate`—Separate Win16 process `/shared`—Common Win16 process `/low.../realtime`—priority `/wait`—Wait for exit `/b`—Use same window
time [**/t** | *hh***:***mm***:***ss*]	Displays or sets the time. `/t` means don't prompt for new time.
title [*string*]	Sets the window title.
type *filename*	Writes a file's contents to the standard output.
ver	Displays the Windows version.
vol [*drive***:**]	Displays the disk volume label.

For Command Modifiers

Table D.8 lists the modifiers that may precede the (*list*) entry in a for command when command extensions are enabled.

Table D.8 **The *for* Command Modifiers**

Modifier	Effect
/D	Wildcards in *set* match directories only.
/R [*path*]	Executes the for statement in the specified directory and all of its subdirectories.
/L	Steps *variable* through a range of numeric values. *Set* must be in the form *start#,step#,end#*.
/F["keywords"]	Reads the contents of the file(s) named in *list* and parses them for text strings. The results are used as the set of values for the for variable. The output of a command can be used as the text source by specifying (`*command*`) as the (*list*) entry. The hideous syntax for this option is discussed in the Help and Support Center; search for "for".

Set /A Expression Operators

The operators listed in Table D.9 may be used in arithmetic expressions in the set /a command. The operators are listed in decreasing order of precedence.

Table D.9 **The *set /a* Expression Operators**

Operators	Functions
( )	Expression grouping
! ~ -	Unary operators: boolean NOT, bitwise invert, arithmetic negative
* / %	Multiply, divide, remainder
+ -	Add, subtract
<< >>	Bitwise shift left, shift right
&	Bitwise AND
| ^	Bitwise OR and exclusive OR
= *= /= %=	Assignment. Also the combined operator/assignment operators
+= -= &= ^=	borrowed from the C programming language: A += 3 is the same
|= <<= >>=	as A = A + 3.
,	Separates multiple expressions.

Any alphanumeric tokens are taken to indicate environment variables. In an expression, if a named environment variable is undefined or does not contain a number, it is treated as the value `0`. Variables are treated as decimal numbers, except that numbers starting with `0x` are interpreted as hexadecimal (base 16), and numbers starting with `0` are treated as octal (base 8).

Windows XP Program Reference

THIS APPENDIX LISTS ALL THE EXECUTABLE programs provided with Windows XP that can be used from the command line or as windowed programs. Executable programs that operate only as system services or which are otherwise not directly usable are not listed. Some XP installations include extra programs not listed here, and some do not include all of these standard programs. Variations occur due to differing hardware configurations—Windows tends not to install software when there is no installed hardware that can use it—and due to corporate licensing and policy decisions.

Accessibility Aids

Accessibility aids adapt Windows for vision- or hearing-impaired users.

Program	Purpose
`accwiz`	Accessibility Wizard
`magnify`	Magnifies the current screen
`narrator`	Onscreen narrator
`utilman`	Configures Accessibility features

Administrative Tools

The following programs can be used to configure and manage Windows.

Program	Purpose
`asr_fmt`	Automated System Recovery backup and restore
`asr_ldm`	Automated System Recovery Logical Disk manager
`bootcfg`	Modifies the `BOOT.INI` configuration file
`cscript`	Windows Scripts Host (command-line version)
`diskperf`	Starts the physical disk performance counters
`driverquery`	Lists the installed device drivers
`esentutl`	MS database utility
`eventcreate`	Adds an event to the event log
`eventquery`	Lists events from the event log*
`eventtriggers`	Displays and configures event triggers
`fsutil`	Manages the Windows file system
`gpresult`	Computes and displays Group Policy Resultant Set of Policy
`gpupdate`	Forces the update of Local and Group Policy settings
`grpconv`	Program Manager Group converter
`iexpress`	Creates simple Installer applications
`lodctr`	Installs, backs up, or restores performance-counter definitions
`logman`	Schedules the automatic collection of performance information
`msg`	Sends a message to another user
`odbcconf`	Configures ODBC drivers and data sources
`openfiles`	Displays files in use by local processes or network users
`pagefileconfig`	Manages the virtual memory page file*
`prncnfg`	Configures printers*
`prndrvr`	Installs and lists print drivers*
`prnjobs`	Manages print jobs*
`prnmngr`	Manages local and network printer connections*
`prnqctl`	Prints test pages as well as starts and stops the printer queue*
`qprocess`	Displays information about processes (local or remote)
`qwinsta`	Displays information about Terminal Services sessions
`reg`	Edits or displays Registry data
`regedit`	Edits the Registry
`regini`	Creates Registry entries and sets permissions
`relog`	Changes the format or rate for performance log files
`reset`	Deletes a Terminal Services session
`rsm`	Manages removable storage media pools
`runas`	Runs a program with another user's credentials
`rundll32`	Launches a 32-bit DLL program
`rwinsta`	Resets the session subsystem hardware and software to their known initial values
`sc`	Displays and manages installed services
`schtasks`	Displays and manages scheduled tasks

Program	Purpose
sdbinst	Application compatibility database installer
sfc	Verifies system file integrity
shadow	Monitors or controls a Terminal Services session
shutdown	Shuts down, logs off, or restarts a computer
syskey	Encrypts and secures the system database
systeminfo	Displays a system hardware and software summary
taskkill	Terminates a process
tasklist	Lists active processes
tracerpt	Gathers or summarizes event trace information
tsdiscon	Disconnects a Windows/Terminal Services session
tskill	Terminates a process in a Terminal Services session
tsprof	Copies and manages Terminal Services user profiles
tsshutdn	Shuts down or restarts a Terminal Services server
typeperf	Displays performance data
unlodctr	Removes performance-counter definitions
vssadmin	Displays shadow copy backups and providers
winmsd	Displays system-configuration information
wmic	Queries and manages Windows XP via Windows Management Instrumentation
wscript	Windows Script Host (windowed version)

**VBScript program*

Built-In and Batch File Commands

The following commands are implemented by `CMD.EXE` and perform basic file and console window management functions as well as provide the basis for the batch file programming language.

Program	Purpose
assoc	Associates filename extensions with file types
break	Causes breakpoint if `cmd` is run in a debugger
call	Calls subroutines (batch files)
cd	Challenges the current working directory (same as `chdir`)
chcp	Changes the console code page
chdir	Changes the current working directory
cls	Clears the command prompt window
cmd	Command shell
color	Changes the Command Prompt window color
copy	Copies files and/or folders
date	Displays or sets the date
del	Deletes files (same as `erase`)
dir	Displays a file directory

continues

Program	Purpose
`echo`	Displays text
`endlocal`	Restores environment variables
`erase`	Deletes files (same as `del`)
`exit`	Ends a program or subroutine
`for`	Repeat command (many options)
`ftype`	Associates file types to "open" commands
`goto`	Goes to the label in a batch file
`help`	Displays command-line program usage information
`if`	Executes a command conditionally
`md`	Creates a directory (same as `mkdir`)
`mkdir`	Creates a directory (same as `md`)
`move`	Moves files or folders
`path`	Sets the command search path
`pause`	Stops a batch file until the user presses Enter
`popd`	Restores the current directory
`prompt`	Sets the command-line prompt
`pushd`	Saves the current directory
`rd`	Removes a directory (same as `rmdir`)
`rem`	Remarks or comments text
`ren`	Renames files or folders (same as `rename`)
`rename`	Renames files or folders (same as `ren`)
`rmdir`	Removes a directory (same as `rd`)
`set`	Sets environment variables
`setlocal`	Saves the current environment
`shift`	Deletes and moves command-line arguments
`start`	Runs a command or opens a document in a new window
`time`	Displays and sets the time of day
`title`	Sets the window title
`type`	Copies a text file to the console window
`ver`	Displays the operating system version
`verify`	Controls automatic verify-after-write
`vol`	Displays disk volume label

DOS Commands

The following programs are provided for compatibility with DOS programs and legacy DOS batch files.

Program	Purpose
`append`	Makes directories appear "local" (archaic)
`command`	MS-DOS command shell
`debug`	Debugs programs (archaic)
`diskcomp`	Compares two floppy disks

Program	Purpose
`diskcopy`	Copies a floppy disk
`doskey`	Command-line aliases and editing extensions
`dosx`	DOS Extender, loaded in `AUTOEXEC.NT`
`edit`	Edits text files
`edlin`	Edits text files (primeval)
`exe2bin`	Converts EXE files to COM files (archaic)
`fastopen`	Does nothing on Windows XP
`forcedos`	Runs a program in the MS-DOS environment
`graftabl`	Enables the display of graphics characters in the MS-DOS environment
`graphics`	Loads the graphics printer driver (obsolete)
`loadfix`	Runs a program above the first 64KB of memory
`loadhigh`	Loads an MS-DOS TSR program into high memory
`mem`	Displays free memory in the MS-DOS subsystem
`mode`	Configures port, display, and keyboard settings
`mscdexnt`	MS CD Extensions, loaded in `AUTOEXEC.NT`
`nlsfunc`	Loads country/region information
`ntvdm`	MS-DOS virtual machine environment
`nw16`	NetWare 16-bit redirector, loaded in `AUTOEXEC.NT`
`print`	Copies a file to a local LPT-port printer
`redir`	Networking redirector, loaded in `AUTOEXEC.NT`
`setver`	Lies about the MS-DOS version to old applications
`share`	Does nothing on Windows XP
`subst`	Maps a drive letter to a local folder
`vwipxspx`	NetWare protocol stack, loaded in `AUTOEXEC.NT`

File-Management Commands

The following commands manage files, disks, and directories.

Most GUI disk-management programs and tools have command-line counterparts.

Program	Purpose
`attrib`	Displays and sets file/folder attributes
`cacls`	Displays and modifies NTFS permissions
`chkdsk`	Checks and repairs file system integrity
`chkntfs`	Schedules automatic `chkdsk` at boot time
`cipher`	Encrypts and decrypts files and folders
`comp`	Compares files
`compact`	Enables and disables file and folder compression
`convert`	Schedules the conversion of a volume from FAT to NTFS
`defrag`	Defragments a disk volume

continues

Program	Purpose
`diantz`	Compress files into a CAB file (same as `makecab`)
`diskpart`	Manages disk partitions
`expand`	Expands a file from a CAB file
`fc`	Compares files
`find`	Finds text in files
`findstr`	Finds text in files using regular expressions
`format`	Formats a fixed or removable disk
`label`	Sets the volume label on a disk or mount point
`makecab`	Compresses files into a CAB file
`mountvol`	Creates, deletes, and lists volume mount points
`recover`	Extracts data from a damaged disk
`replace`	Replaces files
`tree`	Displays the directory structure
`xcopy`	Copies multiple files

Handy Programs

A few programs are useful but difficult to categorize, including the following three.

Program	Purpose
`logoff`	Logs off from Windows
`more`	Displays text a page at a time
`sort`	Sorts text files alphabetically (filter)

Networking Tools

Windows comes with a large set of programs that let you manage, configure and use Windows networking functions.

Program	Purpose
`atmadm`	Manages ATM network connections
`getmac`	Displays network adapter MAC addresses
`ipsec6`	Configures IPSec over IPv6 security
`ipv6`	Installs and configures IPv6
`ipxroute`	Displays and edits the TCP/IP routing table
`mrinfo`	Multicasts routing using SNMP
`nbtstat`	Displays NetBIOS-over-TCP/IP statistics and name tables
`net`	Networking management utility
`netsh`	Network-configuration utility
`pubprn`	Publishes printers to Active Directory*

Program	Purpose
qappsrv	Displays the available application terminal servers on the network
rasautou	Creates a RAS connection
rasdial	Starts and ends Dial-up Networking connections
rasphone	Pop-up Dial-up Networking manager

**VBScript program*

Server Management Tools

The following management programs are available only on Windows 2000 Server and will likely be made available on Windows .NET server as well.

Program	Purpose
change	Manages Terminal Services
cprofile	Compacts and scavenges user profile folders
eventwin	Configures event-to–SNMP trap mapping
evntcmd	Translates events into SNMP traps
flattemp	Enables or disables flat temporary folders
ipseccmd	Configures and displays IPSec Security policies
macfile	Manages File Services for Macintosh
pbadmin	Administers phonebooks
proquota	Manages profile quotas
register	Registers system resource programs in Terminal Services
tscon	Connects to a Terminal Services session

Software Development Aids

Several programs are used to configure Windows program exception handling and to configure system services used in the development of advanced Java and Windows applications.

Program	Purpose
clspack	Lists Java system packages
drwatson	Dr. Watson for Win16 programs
drwtsn32	Configures Dr. Watson for Win32 programs
iexpress	Creates simple Installer applications
jdbgmgr	Microsoft debugger for Java
jview	Command-line loader for Java
mqbkup	MS Message Queue backup and restore utility
ntsd	System-level debugger
regsvr32	Registers a DLL file as a COM component
setdebug	Enables and disables ActiveX debugging for Java
wjview	Command-line loader for Java

TCP/IP Utilities

Windows includes a complement of TCP/IP utilities that provides cross-platform compatibility with Unix systems as well as general-purpose TCP/IP diagnostic and configuration tools.

Program	Purpose
`arp`	Displays and edits the ARP cache
`finger`	Displays information about a user (Unix)
`ftp`	File Transfer Protocol
`hostname`	Displays the local computer's TCP/IP hostname
`ipconfig`	Displays the TCP/IP configuration and manages DHCP leases
`lpq`	Displays the printer queue (Unix)
`lpr`	Prints a file (Unix)
`netstat`	Displays the current TCP/IP connections and open sockets
`nslookup`	Queries DNS servers
`pathping`	Tests TCP/IP connectivity
`ping`	Tests TCP/IP connectivity
`ping6`	IPv6 Ping
`prnport`	Manages TCP/IP printers*
`proxycfg`	Sets the HTTP Proxy server
`rcp`	Copies files to another computer (Unix)
`rexec`	Unix remote execute
`route`	Displays or edits the current routing tables
`rsh`	Remote shell (Unix)
`telnet`	Establishes a command-line session on another computer
`tftp`	Trivial File Transfer Protocol
`tlntadmn`	Telnet Server Administrator
`tlntsess`	Displays the current Telnet sessions
`tracert`	Checks TCP/IP connectivity
`tracert6`	IPv6 trace route

**VBScript program*

Windows GUI Programs

The following programs comprise the standard set of Windows application programs provided with Windows XP. They are usually run from the start menu, but they can be run from the command line, scripts, or batch files as well.

Program	Purpose
`calc`	Windows calculator
`cleanmgr`	Disk-cleanup program
`cliconfg`	SQL Server client network utility
`clipbrd`	Clipboard viewer (multiuser)

Program	Purpose
control	Opens the Control Panel
dcomcnfg	Displays and manages DCOM configuration
ddeshare	Displays DDE shares on a local or remote computer
dvdplay	Windows DVD player
dxdiag	Direct-X diagnostics
eudcedit	Private character editor
eventvwr	Event Viewer
explorer	Windows Explorer
fontview	Displays fonts in a font file
freecell	A popular Windows game
fxsclnt	Fax console
fxscover	Fax cover page editor
fxssend	Send Fax Wizard
hh	HTML Help
mixer	Sound control
mmc	Microsoft Management Console
mobsync	Synchronization Manager/Wizard
mplay32	MS Media Player
mshearts	Hearts card game
mspaint	Microsoft Paint
mstsc	Terminal Services client (remote desktop)
netsetup	Network Setup Wizard
notepad	Notepad accessory
ntbackup	Backs up and restores files
osk	Onscreen keyboard
osuninst	Uninstalls Windows XP
packager	Embeds objects into files (Object Packager)
perfmon	Performance console with a Windows NT 4 settings file
progman	Windows 3.1/NT 4–style Program Manager
regedt32	Registry editor (old version)
rtcshare	NetMeeting Desktop Sharing
secedit	Manages and analyzes system security policies
shrpubw	Create and Share Folders Wizard
sigverif	Signature verifier for system files
sndrec32	Sound Recorder
sndvol32	Volume control
sol	Windows Solitaire game
spider	Spider Solitaire game
sysedit	Edits obsolete Windows configuration files
taskmgr	Starts the Task Manager (same as Ctrl+Alt+Del)
tcmsetup	Manages the TAPI Telephony client

continues

Program	Purpose
tourstart	Runs the "Welcome to Windows" program
verifier	Driver Verifier Manager
wiaacmgr	Scanner and Camera Wizard
winchat	Windows Chat
winhelp	Windows Help (HLP file) viewer
winhlp32	Windows Help file viewer
winmine	Minesweeper game
winver	Displays the current version of Windows
write	WordPad accessory
wupdmgr	Windows Update (launches Internet Explorer)

F

Index of Patterns and Sample Programs

Index of Patterns

continues

Index of Sample Scripts and Batch Files

continues

Chapter	Filename	Description	Page
	`script0603.vbs`	Sends a simple message.	252
	`mailfiles.vbs`	Mails files named on the command line to a specific user.	253
	`scanmail.vbs`	Automatically mails files found in a drop folder.	254
7	`script0701.vbs`	Shows how to manage a list of computers.	273
	`script0702.vbs`	Schedules a computer's drives to be checked upon reboot.	283
	`script0703.vbs`	Terminates Windows applications by name.	284
	`listprops.vbs`	Lists all properties and methods for a WMI object.	288
	`script0704.vbs`	Lists network adapter information for a set of computers.	290
	`script0705.vbs`	Lists hotfixes applied to a set of computers.	291
	`script0706.vbs`	Lists the status of installed services on a set of computers.	294
8	`script0801.vbs`	Lists all services, users, and groups on a computer.	309
	`script0802.vbs`	Deletes a domain or local user account.	315
	`script0803.vbs`	Lists all groups in a domain or computer using the object class.	316
	`script0804.vbs`	Lists all groups in a domain or computer using filtering.	316
	`script0805.vbs`	Lists all users in a domain or computer.	320
	`script0806.vbs`	Lists all network users connected to a server.	322
	`script0807.vbs`	Lists all shared files in use by network users.	322
	`script0808.vbs`	Lists all shared files in use, ordered by username.	323
	`script0809.vbs`	Lists all folders shared by a computer.	324
	`script0810.vbs`	Shares a folder.	324
	`script0811.vbs`	Creates a security group and adds users.	326
	`script0812.vbs`	Lists users in a security group.	326
	`script0813.vbs`	Lists all print jobs queued for a shared printer.	328
	`script0814.vbs`	Lists all printers shared by a computer.	331
	`script0815.vbs`	Lists the status of installed services on a computer.	336
	`script0816.vbs`	Lists all network users connected to a server.	337
	`script0817.vbs`	Lists Active Directory containers using LDAP.	343
	`allpass.vbs`	Changes a user's password on all computers in a workgroup.	346
9	`simple.wsc`	Simple object.	354
	`script0901.vbs`	Tests the simple object.	357
	`script0902.vbs`	Tests two instances of the simple object.	357
	`scriptmail.wsc`	`Scriptmail.Message` object. Sends basic e-mail messages.	375
	`script0903.vbs`	Demonstrates the `Scriptmail.Message` object.	378
10	`deploy.vbs`	Deploys network printer updates to a large list of computers.	403

Index

SYMBOLS

A

B

C

D

E

H

I

J – L

M

N

O

P

Q – R

S

T

U

V

W

X – Z